The SAGE Sourcebook of
Advanced Data Analysis Methods for Communication Research

The SAGE Sourcebook of
Advanced Data Analysis Methods for Communication Research

EDITED BY

Andrew F. Hayes
The Ohio State University

Michael D. Slater
The Ohio State University

Leslie B. Snyder
University of Connecticut

SAGE Publications
Los Angeles • London • New Delhi • Singapore

Copyright © 2008 by Sage Publications, Inc.

All rights reserved. No part of this book may be reproduced or utilized in any form or by any means, electronic or mechanical, including photocopying, recording, or by any information storage and retrieval system, without permission in writing from the publisher.

For information:

Sage Publications, Inc.
2455 Teller Road
Thousand Oaks, California 91320
E-mail: order@sagepub.com

Sage Publications India Pvt. Ltd.
B 1/I 1 Mohan Cooperative Industrial Area
Mathura Road, New Delhi 110 044
India

Sage Publications Ltd.
1 Oliver's Yard
55 City Road
London EC1Y 1SP
United Kingdom

Sage Publications Asia-Pacific Pte. Ltd.
33 Pekin Street #02–01
Far East Square
Singapore 048763

Printed in the United States of America

Library of Congress Cataloging-in-Publication Data

Hayes, Andrew F.
  The SAGE sourcebook of advanced data analysis methods for communication research/Andrew F. Hayes, Michael D. Slater, Leslie B. Snyder.
    p. cm.
  Includes bibliographical references and index.
  ISBN 978-1-4129-2790-1 (cloth)
  1. Communication—Research—Statistical methods. I. Slater, Michael D. II. Snyder, Leslie B. III. Title.

P93.7.H388 2008
302.2072′7—dc22   2007020635

Printed on acid-free paper.

07   08   09   10   11   10   9   8   7   6   5   4   3   2   1

Acquiring Editor:	Todd R. Armstrong
Editorial Assistant:	Katie Grim
Production Editor:	Sarah K. Quesenberry
Copy Editor:	Cheryl Rivard
Typesetter:	C&M Digitals (P) Ltd.
Proofreader:	Dorothy Hoffman
Indexer:	Kathy Paparchontis
Marketing Manager:	Carmel Withers
Cover Designer:	Janet Foulger

Contents

Chapter 1. Overview   1
    *Michael D. Slater, Andrew F. Hayes,
and Leslie B. Snyder*

**Chapter 2. Contemporary Approaches to
Assessing Mediation in Communication Research**   13
    Kristopher J. Preacher and Andrew F. Hayes

**Chapter 3. Assessing Change and Intraindividual Variation:
Longitudinal Multilevel and Structural Equation Modeling**   55
    Kimberly L. Henry and Michael D. Slater

**Chapter 4. Time Series Analysis: Traditional
and Contemporary Approaches**   89
    Itzhak Yanovitzky and Arthur VanLear

Chapter 5. Event History Analysis for Communication Research   125
    Leslie B. Snyder and Ann A. O'Connell

**Chapter 6. Estimating Causal Effects in
Observational Studies: The Propensity Score Approach**   159
    Itzhak Yanovitzky, Robert Hornik, and Elaine Zanutto

**Chapter 7. Commentary on the Uses and Misuses of
Structural Equation Modeling in Communication Research**   185
    R. Lance Holbert and Michael T. Stephenson

Chapter 8. Multilevel Modeling: Studying People in Contexts   219
    *Hee Sun Park, William P. Eveland, Jr.,
and Robert Cudeck*

Chapter 9. Communication Network Analysis   247
    Thomas W. Valente

Chapter 10. Scaling and Cluster Analysis   275
    David R. Roskos-Ewoldsen and Beverly Roskos-Ewoldsen

**Chapter 11. Contemporary Approaches to
Meta-Analysis in Communication Research**   311
*Blair T. Johnson, Lori A. J. Scott-Sheldon,
Leslie B. Snyder, Seth M. Noar,
and Tania B. Huedo-Medina*

**Chapter 12. Approaches to the Handling of
Missing Data in Communication Research**   349
Ofer Harel, Rick Zimmerman, and Olga Dekhtyar

Index   373

About the Editors   383

About the Contributors   385

Acknowledgments

Our first undertaking as editors was the production of a special issue of *Human Communication Research* on multilevel modeling published in 2006. We learned a lot about the editing process from that project, lessons that were valuable and that we applied to the production of this book. Whether editing a special issue of a journal or an entire book, the production of a quality product depends on the assistance and cooperation of many people working with a common goal. Of course, the quality of an edited book is most dependent on the authors, and we thank each and every one of them for the time and effort they spent writing for us in exchange for very little compensation. Their willingness to do so attests to their dedication to the field of communication.

As every author knows, even the best writer can benefit and improve from the feedback of his or her peers, so the chapters in this book were reviewed by one or more scholars in the field with familiarity on the topic before we requested revisions. Those reviewers included Dale Brashers (Department of Speech Communication, University of Illinois at Urbana-Champaign), J. Alison Bryant (Nickelodeon/MTV Networks), Mai Do (Department of International Health and Development, Tulane University School of Public Health and Tropical Medicine), David Fan (Department of Genetics, Cell Biology, and Development, University of Minnesota), Li Gong (SAP), Al Gunther (Department of Life Sciences Communication, University of Wisconsin-Madison), Betty LaFrance (Department of Communication, Northern Illinois University), Hye-jin Paek (Department of Advertising and Public Relations, Grady College of Journalism and Mass Communication, University of Georgia), Jochen Peter (Amsterdam School of Communication Research, University of Amsterdam), and Jim Schrieber(School of Education, Duquesne University). We thank them for their contribution to this project and hope they enjoy the result. We also want to express our appreciation to Todd Armstrong and the staff at SAGE Publications, for their enthusiasm and open-mindedness, and to the reviewers of the project's initial proposal: Joseph N. Cappella (Annenberg School for Communication, University of Pennsylvania), R. Lance Holbert (School of Communication, The Ohio State University), Peter Monge (Annenberg School for Communication and The Marshall School of

Business, University of Southern California), David R. Roskos-Ewoldsen (Department of Communication Studies, College of Communication and Information Sciences, The University of Alabama), Dietram A. Scheufele (School of Journalism and Mass Communication, University of Wisconsin, Madison), and James E. Shanahan (Department of Communication, Cornell University).

Finally, we want to acknowledge our families for their never-ending patience and encouragement, a priceless resource we truly treasure.

Overview 1

Michael D. Slater

Andrew F. Hayes

Leslie B. Snyder

A few years ago, one of us (Slater) gave a public research presentation on the role of televised violence in enhancing or prompting adolescent aggression. The analysis described during the presentation was based on a technique called *multilevel modeling*, a method that is by no means new but that has only recently begun to be used by communication researchers. The talk prompted a question by one of the editors of this book (Hayes) during the Q&A period. What responsibilities do we have as educators of the next generation of communication scholars to help students in the field acquire state-of-the-art analytical methods, methods that are sometimes mathematically complicated and require a solid prerequisite understanding of techniques that students may have only limited exposure to? And if the responsibility is ours, how can we satisfy this responsibility given that (a) most students of communication would much rather spend their time learning communication theory and conducting research rather than sitting through coursework in statistics, and (b) the four to five years that students spend in graduate study is simply not sufficient time given that one could spend years, indeed a lifetime, developing expertise in any single statistical method?

The response to this question, realistic but albeit somewhat disappointing to a statistics educator, was that about all we can do in the short time that students in communication spend with us is to expose them to what is possible, give them a feel for how a technique might be used, and point them in the right direction so that they can acquire whatever skills their time and interests allow. Most communication departments do not employ statisticians, and if they did, the bulk of their instructional time would be spent teaching core methodological coursework rather than advanced seminars on cutting-edge statistical topics. A shame this might be, but most communication departments will probably always have to rely for the most part on other departments to teach statistical methods or on the wherewithal of students to teach themselves.

To be sure, we can teach the basics ourselves, and that we often do. But the basics—least-squares regression, analysis of variance, and other commonly used statistical methods—can get us only so far. With just a handful of statistical tools hanging around our work belts, the discipline either ends up looking the other way when we try to sink a screw with a hammer or we make excuses by arguing that even though we may have done something less than ideal if not outright inappropriate, everyone else does it so what harm is done?

In the months following this talk, we had several face-to-face and e-mail interchanges, exchanging perspectives about statistics education and how we could at least in part fulfill our perceived obligation to students by giving them a resource to which they could turn to begin to acquire some of the advanced skills that they will one day find useful in either their own research or understanding someone else's. Eventually we joined with Leslie B. Snyder when she raised a similar concern about the difficulty of established scholars keeping up with statistical advances, and the result is the book you are now holding in your hands.

To us, data analysis means much more than merely finding an optimal way to handle a given data structure and hypothesis test, important though that is. Data analysis is far more than following a flow chart in a statistical methods text to figure out what method you should use given your problem at hand. Just as our research method might influence the kinds of analyses we conduct (i.e., the endpoint in the flow chart), the analyses that we are capable of conducting can also guide the kinds of questions that we ask. If you don't know what is possible analytically, this can constrain the kinds of research questions and hypotheses that you test. So statistical methods direct our attention to questions and hypotheses to which our intuition might fail to lead us. Our reliance on available statistical algorithms for structuring our thinking limits the sophistication and utility of the questions we are able to ask in our research efforts. This is why it is so exciting when the emergence of new statistical methods makes it possible to ask new kinds of research questions, to develop and test more sophisticated theories about social experience.

In practical terms, the existence of new software packages and greater processing abilities of personal computers is an important enabler to using the methods in this book. Some techniques have been around for a long time but were impractical for most nonstatisticians. Often researchers learned to live with unrealistic statistical assumptions from the days of limited computer capacity and lack of appropriate software. However, there is no longer any reason to make many of the compromises that are still made regularly. New versions of older statistical packages have incorporated some of the techniques in this book, making them easily accessible to a large number of scholars. Specialized user-friendly packages deal with other techniques. We expect that as researchers test some of the unrealistic statistical assumptions made in the past, there will be cases where contradictory findings in prior research will be explained.

The main objective of this book is to introduce many of these newer methods as well as those that have been around a while but are underutilized or misused to communication researchers and researchers in training. Our hope is that familiarity with the methods discussed in this book will encourage the development of the field in a number of ways. For instance, some of the methods discussed in this book—notably multilevel modeling—can be fruitfully used to help develop and test theory that explores the relationships between the individual and the larger community. We hope that after exposure to some of these methods we will see increasingly sophisticated tests of communication processes over time, including research that explores the ways in which variability in individual experience matters in understanding communication phenomena. We would like to see more longitudinal research in which the lags or time points are matched in frequency to the processes under study using time series designs, rather than depending solely on panels measured once or twice a year when relevant causal processes in fact move much more quickly. Such research would move theory and understanding in this field significantly ahead. We also include several chapters that discuss some of the modern developments in topics that many communication researchers may already have been aware of or that are on the horizon and are likely to be more widely used. For example, we include a chapter on modern methods of statistically assessing mediation, as well as approaches to handling missing data.

This is an ambitious agenda for a single collection. Clearly, it would be impossible to provide enough information to train researchers to execute all these different methods in a book of this length. Each chapter, if given such treatment, would require sections of bookshelves to house. Our intention is to explain what these methods are and much of what they can do, not to formally teach all the subtle (and often complicated) nuances of the mathematics or implementation in available computing software. Our objectives are to encourage communication researchers to see how these analytical techniques can be used. We want readers to be able to see how such methods might apply to the research questions about which they care, to be able to think in new ways about hypotheses they might be able to test, and to identify the methods that are most likely to move their research programs forward. We want to provide enough information about the methods so readers have an idea of what is involved from a statistical perspective and can begin further exploration of the method clearly oriented with respect to the task ahead. To support this, each chapter recommends several sources for learning the details of the method and includes cautions, suggestions, and other "words to the wise" regarding exploration and use of the method. For those readers who have the opportunity to collaborate with trained statisticians, these chapters should provide enough background to permit intelligent questions and discussion regarding methods that these statisticians are increasingly likely to recommend.

We hope that this book will be looked over by communication researchers unfamiliar with these methods, to ascertain whether the approaches are of interest and to gain enough familiarity to understand relevant literature using the methods. We hope it will be read by doctoral students who want to be aware of methods that might be best suited for their own intended areas of research. In fact, we especially hope that it will be read by such students and their advisors. Current and upcoming generations of doctoral students are more likely than their time-pressed mentors to be able to take additional statistical coursework and delve more deeply into methods of interest. Such doctoral students will play a key role in moving our field (and their advisors) forward.

To support achieving these objectives, we have asked authors to write overview chapters without dependence on mathematical derivations and heavy dependence on formal statements regarding statistical models. We want readers to take away understanding and insights about the methods and their use. More often than not, of course, it is necessary to present equations to clearly articulate what a method is and does, so we have not constrained the authors when such detail is truly necessary. But at the same time, we have encouraged them to produce writing in which the forest is evident, given the trees. We want readers to be able to scan the chapter for a conceptual overview regarding the method's uses and capabilities without losing the logical flow while trying to keep track of which Greek letter refers to what and the interpretation of various subscripts.

In sum, we have tried to assemble the book that we've been wishing we had on our bookshelves, for our own reference and to share with collaborators, students, and colleagues. We hope you, the reader, find these chapters provocative and useful. We hope that they will point you in the direction of methods that will allow you to pose better questions, design better studies, increase the sophistication of theories about communication phenomena and processes, and increase insight into the peculiarities and patterns of human interaction, exchange, and behavior.

Chapter Overviews

In the remainder of this introductory chapter, we describe each chapter in this volume in a couple of paragraphs to give you a flavor of what to expect in the pages that follow. Although we believe that each chapter should be read eventually, we have designed the book so that each chapter stands by itself. No chapter serves as a necessary prerequisite to others, so you may progress through the book buffet style if you choose, selecting only those chapters that appeal to your immediate interests and research goals.

MEDIATION

Most theories and hypotheses about communication processes involve multivariate relationships in which a variable transmits its effect indirectly through one or more intervening variables. Such effects are called *mediated* effects. In the mid-1980s, Baron and Kenny (1986) described a set of conditions for establishing mediation that is widely used in the social sciences, including communication. This approach is only one of many available, and recent research suggests that its disadvantages (relatively lower statistical power and in some cases irrelevance to the primary question of interest) may outweigh its primary advantage (ease of implementation). In the lead chapter by Preacher and Hayes, you will find a discussion of mediation and an overview of some of the modern statistical developments in the assessment of mediated effects and the estimation and testing of the size of indirect effects.

LATENT GROWTH MODELING

The study of communication processes is greatly facilitated by the use of longitudinal data. Over recent years, considerable progress has been made in studying processes of over-time change using *latent growth models,* introduced in Chapter 3. The chapter also introduces another concept rarely explored in communication research, but that is worthy of attention given its potential for developing and testing theory: the study of *intrapersonal* variability in longitudinal data. When conceptualized as a between-person phenomenon, cause implies that people who differ from each other on the causal agent are also expected to differ from each other on the presumed outcome (i.e., the variable the causal agent putatively affects). Causation can also be conceptualized as a within-person phenomenon. If some variable X causally affects Y, then when a person is relatively high on X compared to his or her "normative" state on X, then we would also expect him or her to be relatively high (or low) on Y relative to his or her normative state on Y. To think about causal effects only in terms of how people differ from each other overlooks that people also vary within themselves over time, and by modeling *intraindividual* variation in the variables in a causal system, we are in a position to better understand the process at work. To approach the implications of this intuitively: As individuals, our mental and emotional energy is primarily focused on our own "ups and downs," not on the ways we are different from other people. Those of us who are parents of teens know how worrisome a particularly difficult stretch of days or weeks is in terms of implications for a youth's behavior. For instance, if one is trying to assess the impact of a communication stimulus such as a type of media exposure on a child's behavior, it is possible to tie deviation from a child's *own mean exposure* over time to that behavior while simultaneously modeling how people differ from *each oth*er on average in their behavior as a function of variations in exposure. Very little empirical research attempts to account for intraindividual variability. Henry and Slater introduce methods that can allow us to tease out which communication phenomena change a person away from his or her normal state and which change the norm for the person. Such analyses are likely to become an essential part of research on topics including media effects on teens and children, political socialization, training in organizational settings, and couples and parent/child communication.

TIME SERIES ANALYSES

An important take-away message of Chapter 3 is the cost to theory development of excessive dependence on single-occasion cross-sectional research, and the importance of explicitly studying over-time social processes. When variables are measured on multiple occasions, repeated measures of analysis of variance has typically been the method of choice for communication researchers. Latent growth modeling does represent an alternative and better approach. But not all data obtained over time take a form suitable for latent growth modeling because it requires disaggregated data, meaning data for variables measured at the individual level. Researchers often have only aggregated data available, meaning some kind of summary statistic calculated over many individuals or other units of analysis at a given period of time. Furthermore, latent growth modeling isn't well suited to the analysis of long sequences of measurements, such as data collected over many months, years, or even decades.

In Chapter 4, Yanovitzky and VanLear introduce *time series analysis*, a method widely used in such fields as economics but that can be exploited to study communication processes as well. Time series analysis would typically be used when some kind of aggregate statistic is available at regular time intervals. An aggregate statistic might be the total number of dollars spent in a month on advertising in the magazine industry, or the percent of people who approve of the president's job performance, or the number of viewers of the top-rated television show. The goal of time series analysis is not only to model the trend or cyclical nature of the series but also to predict its values from key events or the values of another series for which data are available at the same interval. For instance, time series analysis might be used to examine how public opinion about the importance of regulating emissions to combat global warming fluctuates as a function of the frequency of attention the topic receives in major newspapers. Alternatively, it could be used to assess how public opinion about global warming policy shifts up or down as a function of key events in the media environment, such as the release of a movie such as *The Day After Tomorrow* or mentions of environmental degradation in presidential State of the Union speeches. In addition to a description of "classical" time series analysis such as ARIMA modeling, the authors introduce *spectral analysis* to the communication field. Even veteran time series analysts will find something for them in this chapter.

EVENT HISTORY ANALYSIS

Sometimes in communication research we deal with categorical outcomes, such as whether or not people perform a behavior or what group people identify with. It is often possible to conceptualize these outcomes as "states"—being in a state of doing the behavior or identifying with the group—that people move in and out of. By situating changes in state in time ("events"), we can analyze which independent variables are more likely to lead to changes in state. For example, studies can examine which factors affect the likelihood of compliance with a communication campaign or other persuasive message. It is also possible to examine movement between more than two states, such as might be desirable in relational studies of single, married, and divorced status. Conceptually, the approach can provide a framework for thinking about communication status in time or the impact of communication on changes in status or membership over time.

The tools of *event history analysis* (also called *survival analysis* in the biomedical fields), the topic of Chapter 5 by Snyder and O'Connell, provide an easy way to analyze data in this way. As a regression-based procedure, event history analysis is not difficult to learn. Another advantage is the retention of data on cases that drop out of a study. Although the technique has been used in sociology in other fields since the mid-1980s, there have been limited communication applications to date. However, it is now available in major statistical packages, making it more accessible to researchers. The approach also opens up possibilities for collecting and analyzing retrospective data on when change happened in the past to supplement or replace expensive panel data.

PROPENSITY SCORING

Much communication research is associational, depending on relationships tested in nonexperimental designs. In such cases, one's confidence in the associations reported depends on effective use of statistical controls. Unfortunately, even if dozens or hundreds of control variables can be measured, it is normally not feasible to incorporate them all in a single model without introducing impossible problems of collinearity and using up sample degrees of freedom. Yanovitzky, Hornik, and Zanutto describe *propensity scoring* in Chapter 6. Using propensity scoring, a virtually unlimited number of covariates can be modeled into a single vector that becomes the control variable in analyses. This chapter not only describes the method and its uses but also notes ways in which claims about it can be oversold. For example, it is sometimes described as creating the equivalent to random sampling in terms of the quality of the adjustment it provides, but that would be true only in the impossible case of a study in which all relevant covariates had been identified and measured without error, and in which no mediators were inadvertently included as covariates. Nonetheless, propensity scoring provides a very powerful means to adjust for third-variable effects in data analyses.

STRUCTURAL EQUATION MODELING

The use of *covariance structure modeling*, which includes such techniques as confirmatory factor analysis and structural equation modeling, has exploded in the field over the past decade or so. However, this widespread adoption has brought with it a variety of misuses and misinterpretations of the method as well as underutilization of some of its potential capabilities. For example, it is well known that causal claims are hard to justify using cross-sectional data. However, one still often sees claims of support for a theoretical casual model in which a group of manifest variables measured cross-sectionally are tied together such that most possible paths are included. Such nearly saturated models have almost perfect fit, and so fit is an almost meaningless concept in such contexts. Researchers often fail to acknowledge that near-perfect fit is expected for a nearly saturated model. Even in models with many degrees of freedom available for model testing, good fit certainly cannot be used to support a claim that the causal model is supported or a causal claim is justified. Furthermore, investigators rarely acknowledge the *equivalent models problem*—that any model has corresponding models that produce equally good fit merely by, for example, reversing the path of a putatively causal link. Conversely, one too seldom sees rigorous tests of theoretically specified alternative models, hierarchically nested models, mediation, or moderation, typically using inferential statistics or the kinds of methods introduced in Chapter 2 of this book.

In Chapter 7, Holbert and Stephenson provide a commentary on the uses and misuses of structural equation modeling. This chapter is somewhat unlike others in this book, in that it is written under the assumption that the reader will have some familiarity with structural equation modeling, at least with respect to common practice in the field. Furthermore, whereas other chapters provide specific data-driven examples of the use of the method, interpretation of statistics, and the like, Holbert and Stephenson instead restrict their discussion to ways in which the method can be better used and comment on some of its misuses. Thus, the reader is not going to learn how to estimate a structural equation model by reading this chapter. However, he or she will come away more informed about how it can be used and will be in a position to more critically evaluate its implementation in the communication literature.

MULTILEVEL MODELING

Multilevel modeling, also known as hierarchical linear modeling or random coefficients regression, is widely used in organizational settings such as schools for evaluation and policy research. It has enormous potential for theory development and testing in communication, a point made in Chapter 8 by Park, Eveland, and Cudeck, because communication phenomena typically cross levels of analysis. Interpersonal communication involves not just individual data but data clustered by dyad or small group. Of course, organizational communication has as its major concern communication of individuals within and between groups within organizational hierarchies. Political communication is increasingly concerned with the relationship between community characteristics such as heterogeneity and the existence of political institutions with patterns of political discussion and individual action. Research in mediated communication acknowledges but rarely systematically studies how variability in media type or content at the community or regional level accounts for variation in individual-level outcomes. This is especially important in field research and program evaluations, in which objective measures of market-level variation are often available but prior research has tended to rely on self-reported exposure at the individual level, which is confounded with many other individual differences.

The statistical problems with analyzing multilevel data as if they were from one level, and how conflating levels interferes with theory development, have long been recognized and bemoaned in the communication discipline. Analyses that simply enter group-, organizational-, or community-level variables on the individual level are typically incorrect statistically; intraclass correlation is ignored, standard errors are wrong, and inferences become problematic. Multilevel models address this statistical problem. And they do much more—they make possible ways of looking at data and framing hypotheses that otherwise would probably not occur to a researcher.

Using multilevel analysis, one can look directly at cross-level interactions—how the effects of individual-level variables are contingent on couple, group, organizational, or community factors. One can not only identify effects of variables conventionally in terms of regression coefficients, but one can simultaneously test effects of variability (the random effects). In a political context, one can not only ask about the effects of a community being on a liberal to conservative continuum but can also look in the same model at the effects of amount of variability in ideological orientation within that community. One can also control for the average of individual-level variables at the group or community level, if the within-group sample is adequately large, and look at individual-level effects of deviation from group norms—with obvious implications for study of theories of conformity such as spiral of silence, as well as for study of activism or extremism.

SOCIAL NETWORK ANALYSIS

Multilevel modeling provides a powerful way to explore the relationships between individuals in social systems and social entities within larger social entities. However, one of the most effective ways to characterize interpersonal connectedness within a social group is *network analysis*. In Chapter 9, Valente gives an overview of this versatile but underutilized method, describing the various indices one can compute to quantify aspects of a social network as well as individuals within that network. Social networks analysis has a number of uses in the communication field, such as the study of information diffusion, group cohesion, and leadership and influence, to name just a few. This chapter gives a brief but thorough introduction to network analysis and provides examples of how it has been and can be used in the field.

CLUSTER ANALYSIS AND MULTIDIMENSIONAL SCALING

Most communication researchers have some familiarity with factor analysis, a statistical method for discovering and quantifying the latent variables that underlie the associations between variables. Factor analysis is generally undertaken when the investigator has a set of quantitative measurements on variables presumed to be correlated through the latent variable or variables they have in common. But we often are interested in understanding the latent dimensions that underlie our perceptions of *categories* or *sets of objects*. Such dimensions can be revealed by asking people to evaluate how similar or dissimilar objects are to each other and then mathematically analyzing these similarity judgments to see what dimensions separate the objects in some kind of conceptual, quantitative space. They can also be revealed by having people evaluate each object on a variety of variables and then quantify similarity in the patterns of evaluations between and within objects. For instance, we might seek to understand how people represent and distinguish between different kinds of television shows, such as dramas, situation comedies, and reality shows. Methods such as *cluster analysis* and *multidimensional scaling*, the topic of Chapter 10 by David and Beverly Roskos-Ewoldsen, can be used to ascertain the similarities and dissimilarities people perceive between shows as well as the dimensions that people might be using when making those judgments. Such analyses can reveal how people organize and classify objects and the processes that produce categorical representations of messages, messages sources, and other aspects of communication.

META-ANALYSIS

Experts in a research area and even casual followers of research on a given topic cannot help but notice that the corpus of literature is anything but consistent. It seems that frequently there are as many studies supporting a particular theoretical proposition or hypothesis as are there studies contradicting it. The interpretation of a collection of studies is a subjective process, which means that the conclusion one is likely to reach when reviewing the literature is, to some extent, in the eyes of the beholder. Meta-analysis has brought a modicum of objectivity to the process of a literature review by making the results of any given study a single data point that contributes to an empirical analysis of research findings on a common topic. Thus, meta-analysis is quite literally the analysis of analyses. A study outcome, when converted to a standard metric of effect size, becomes the outcome variable in an analysis focused on ascertaining the average effect size in the literature, whether there is more heterogeneity in the effects across studies than can be explained by chance alone, and what systematic variations between studies (whether population sampled, method, published or unpublished, or other potential moderators) account for variation in effect size across studies. Meta-analysis has taken the social sciences by storm, and it seems not a year goes by in which no meta-analysis of some topic of relevance to the field of communication is published. In Chapter 11, Johnson and colleagues describe what all the fuss is about and give readers a broad overview of not only the value of meta-analysis to the field but also how to conduct a meta-analysis of your own.

MISSING DATA

We close the book with what arguably is one of the most important chapters of all. Most of us have been taught that the best way to deal with missing data is not to have them. But missing data are inevitable, especially in field-based or longitudinal studies. When they do occur (and we promise they will), you must deal with them properly at the data analysis stage. In Chapter 12, Harel, Zimmerman, and Dekhtyar advise us to forget what we may have been told about missing data—that the elimination of any case with even a single missing value is the best and safest approach to handling missing values because it is the most conservative approach. Although listwise deletion can in some ways be conservative, it is neither best nor safest. Listwise deletion distorts means and variability and ignores an enormous amount of information available in a data set that can be used to provide statistically valid estimates of those missing values. Under appropriate conditions (which can be reasonably assessed), one can use methods such as full information maximum likelihood and, even better, multiple imputation to statistically model missingness, and maintain the variability, standard errors, and mean estimates that are best justified by the data. If we are to move to more sophisticated kinds of data collection, we as a field need to learn how to handle missing data in more sophisticated ways.

On to the Fun

We encourage you to try some of the techniques in this book not because it's fun to try them (though it often is) or because it is a way to impress other researchers with your savvy (which it might), but because they will help you to better understand what your data have to say and how to frame new and interesting theory-building questions. Before deciding to make a time investment in learning the nitty-gritty details of a particular technique, use the following chapters to assess which methods may help you reframe your work or help you solve a thorny analysis problem. The editors have found tremendous methodological and theoretical value in using some of the techniques ourselves, and we are eager to share them with our colleagues in the field. We are also excited about what we have learned from each of the chapters and how they have helped reshape the way we think about some of our own research questions and ways to answer them. We hope you find much to think about, and much to use, in the chapters that follow.

As one of us commented in the preface to an earlier book, a book is never done—you simply run out of time. Run out of time we did. There are many other chapters we would have loved to have included in this book, and each chapter we did publish could have easily consumed twice as many pages. Nevertheless, we believe that each chapter strikes a nice balance between readability, breadth of coverage, and usefulness to the typical communication scholar. We want to take a moment here to thank each of the authors for the time they invested in writing their chapter. Writing for an edited book carries little glory in these days of citation counting and other techniques university administrators use to quantify the productivity of a scholar. The fact that these very busy people were willing to write for us attests to their dedication to the field and their passion for the topic of their chapter. We also want to thank the numerous reviewers whom we consulted for advice on how to best improve earlier drafts. Reviewing also comes with few thanks, and we appreciate their willingness to improve the product you hold in your hands before it went to print. Finally, the production and editorial staff of Sage Publications deserves credit for their hard work behind the scenes producing a book we believe you will be proud to display on your bookshelf and recommend to your students and colleagues. Now on to the fun!

Contemporary Approaches to Assessing Mediation in Communication Research

2

Kristopher J. Preacher

Andrew F. Hayes

Communication scientists routinely ask questions about causal relationships. Whether it is examining the persuasive impact of public service announcements on attitudes and behavior, determining the impact of viewing political debates on political knowledge or voter turnout, or assessing whether success in achieving one's Internet browsing goals prompts greater interest in e-commerce, communication scholars frequently conduct research to answer questions about cause. Data analysis usually focuses on examining if the putative causal variable, whether manipulated or measured, is related to the outcome using a linear model such as analysis of variance or linear regression. In many arenas of research, such analyses, when accompanied by good research design, are sufficient to answer the question as to whether variation in X causes variation in Y. But deeper

Authors' Note: This work was funded in part by National Institute on Drug Abuse Grant DA16883 awarded to the first author. We thank several reviewers for providing useful feedback, Sri Kalyanaraman for his generosity in providing the data for use in this chapter, and Jason Reineke for assistance in the content analysis.

understanding accrues when researchers investigate the *process* by which a given effect is produced. Although it might be interesting and even important to discover, for instance, that learning about political news is affected by whether exposure occurs through print or online formats, we usually want to understand more about how these effects or relationships arise—the *mechanisms* that produce and explain the associations.

When we ask questions about mechanism rather than simply whether or not an effect exists, we are asking about *mediation*—the process through which X exerts its effect on Y through one or more *mediator* variables. If a variable M is causally situated between X and Y and accounts for their association (at least in part), we say that M *mediates* the relationship, a term first used in this context by Rozeboom (1956). It is also said that X has an *indirect effect* on Y through M.[1] The mediator, M, sometimes called an *intervening variable* or a *mechanism* (Hoyle & Robinson, 2004), can be said to explain how a given effect occurs.

Before the cognitive revolution of the 1950s, there was little interest in mediation effects among scientists steeped in the behaviorist tradition. A notable exception was a paper by MacCorquodale and Meehl (1948) distinguishing between *intervening variables* (determinate functions of variables used for convenience) and *hypothetical constructs* (what we today call mediators). The first formal term for what is now called mediation was *interpretation* (Hyman, 1955). Hyman notes, "When the analyst interprets a relationship, he determines the process through which the assumed cause is related to what we take to be its effect" (p. 276). Hyman referred to mediators as *test factors* or *intervening variables* and laid out statistical criteria for establishing mediation that are identical to those popularized decades later by Judd and Kenny (1981) and Baron and Kenny (1986). Much methodological research has been conducted since these landmark contributions. In particular, David MacKinnon and colleagues (e.g., MacKinnon & Dwyer, 1993; MacKinnon, Warsi, & Dwyer, 1995; MacKinnon, Lockwood, Hoffman, West, & Sheets, 2002) have done much in recent years to promote the rigorous assessment of mediation using a variety of sophisticated methods.

McLeod and Reeves (1980) highlighted the importance of studying the mechanisms of media effects, and media researchers have increasingly focused their attention on examining and explaining the mechanisms that produce media effects rather than simply asking whether and to what extent those effects exist (also see McLeod, Kosicki, & Pan, 1996). Indeed, there are numerous examples in the media effects literature of studies testing the extent to which media's effect is mediated, or media itself functions as a mediator, in the relationship between two other variables. For example, Eveland (2001) and Eveland, Shah, and Kwak (2003) found that attention to news media and elaborative processing mediate the effect of surveillance gratification seeking on public affairs knowledge. Scheufele (2002) tested whether the influence of newspaper news use and interpersonal discussion on political participation is mediated by political knowledge. Holbert, Shah, and Kwak (2003) identified viewing of traditional drama, progressive drama, and situation comedy as three mediators of the effect of ideology on opinions concerning women's rights. And Chang (2001) identified advertisement-evoked emotion as a mediator of the effect of advertisement valence on political candidate evaluation and attitude toward the advertisement.

But media effects researchers are certainly not the only scholars in communication interested in studying mechanisms and empirically testing hypotheses about mediation. Lee and Nass (2004) found evidence that the effect of synthetic voices on persuasion is mediated by listeners' sense of social presence. Millar (2002) identified feelings of guilt as one of the mechanisms through which the door-in-the-face technique leads to increased compliance to requests. Knobloch and Carpenter-Thune (2004) examined the extent to which relational uncertainty functions as a mediator of the relationship between feelings of intimacy and the avoidance of certain conversational topics in interpersonal discussion. Hart and Miller (2005) reported evidence that the effect of experiencing certain organizational socialization tactics on feelings of role ambiguity in newly hired managers was mediated by the degree to which the manager received performance appraisals. Other examples can be found in abundance in the organizational, interpersonal, new technology, health, and political communication literature.

An informal content analysis of the major communication journals further reveals that considerable journal space is devoted to testing hypotheses about the extent to which the relationships between constructs of interest to the field are mediated, as well as whether communication variables themselves serve as mediators of interesting and important relationships. We examined the 2002 through 2005 volumes of *Communication Research, Human Communication Research, Journal of Communication, Journalism and Mass Communication Quarterly,* and *Media Psychology,* counting the number of empirical articles (defined as articles that reported the conceptualization, analysis, and results of a research study of some kind) as well as those that reported some kind of formal or informal test of mediation. The results of this perusal through the pages of the communication journals revealed that roughly 1 in 8 included an empirical test of mediation. Indeed, it is difficult to open a volume of these journals and not find such a test somewhere in its pages.

Yet despite the clear importance of understanding mechanisms that drive communication effects and the role of communication as a mediator in social, cognitive, and behavioral phenomena, mediation is a topic that is largely absent from most introductory methods and statistics texts (Pituch, 2004). Even statistical methods books that explicitly target communication scholars (e.g., Hayes, 2005) dedicate only a few pages to the topic. In part to address this lack of coverage, we dedicate the bulk of this chapter to discussing strategies by which mediation hypotheses may be formally tested statistically. We also discuss useful extensions of these strategies, such as how to address hypotheses that involve both mediation and moderation effects.

We suggest ways to proceed when theory implies that multiple mediators may intervene between two variables, and we explain how to address mediation hypotheses in modeling paradigms other than least squares multiple regression, such as structural equation modeling (SEM) and multilevel modeling. We describe how a priori consideration of study design, causality, and statistical power contribute to hypothesis tests with sound scientific bases, and we suggest ways to quantify effect size to facilitate communication of research findings. Finally, we address some practical software concerns for scientists who wish to undertake the rigorous investigation of hypotheses involving indirect effects. Throughout, we concentrate on communicating a conceptual and practical understanding of mediation without getting too deeply involved in the underlying mathematics. For the interested reader, we provide many references to sources with more thorough information. Finally, most of what we discuss may be accomplished using ordinary multiple regression, although SEM may also be used.

Statistical Approaches to Assessing Mediation

In this section, we survey several methods that have been used to quantify and test the statistical significance of mediation effects. The *simple mediation* model is depicted graphically in Figure 2.1. We refer to this as a simple mediation model because it involves only a single proposed mediating variable. Later in the chapter we describe more complicated mediation models such as models with more than one mediator.

The top panel of Figure 2.1 represents a causal process in which X, the independent variable, affects Y, the dependent variable. Path c quantifies this effect, called the *total effect* of X on Y. Although it is common in communication research to index relationships using standardized paths (i.e., derived using standardized variables), most methods for assessing mediation rely on unstandardized paths, and we encourage researchers to follow this tradition. The bottom panel illustrates the components of the total effect. Path a represents the causal effect of the independent variable on the proposed mediator, M. Path b represents the causal effect of the mediator on the dependent variable, controlling for the independent variable, whereas path c' represents the causal effect of the independent variable on the dependent variable controlling for the mediator. In the language of causal analysis, c' is the *direct effect* of X on Y and is distinguishable from the total effect, c, in that the direct effect partials out from the total effect that part of the causal effect that is shared with M. That is, it represents the part of the effect of X on Y in the model that is unique to X. Path b can also be considered a direct effect, in this case the direct effect of the mediator on the outcome variable. The *indirect effect* of X on Y is represented as the two paths linking X to Y through M, which in Figure 2.1 are the

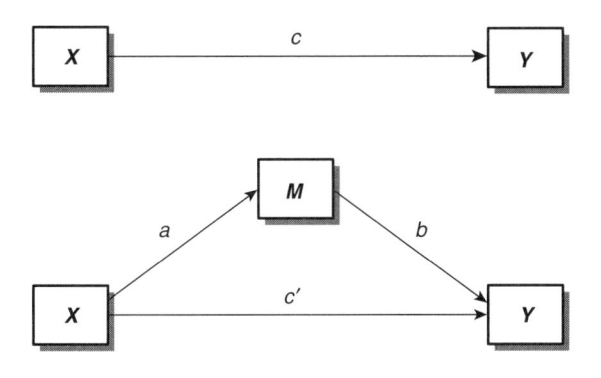

Figure 2.1 A Simple Mediation Model

a and b paths. As will be discussed, in causal analysis it is common to quantify the indirect effect of X on Y through M as the product of the a and b paths. In simple mediation models of this sort, it can be shown that the total effect of X on Y is equal to the sum of the direct and indirect effects. That is, $c = c' + ab$. Simple algebraic manipulation shows that the indirect effect is the difference between the total and the direct effects of X on Y: $ab = c - c'$.

CAUSAL STEPS STRATEGY

By far the most popular approach to testing a hypothesis of mediation is the *causal steps* strategy (or *serial approach;* Hoyle & Robinson, 2004), in which the researcher must satisfy a series of criteria before a pattern of effects can be termed mediation. Popularized by Judd and Kenny (1981) and Baron and Kenny (1986), the causal steps approach is most directly attributable to Hyman (1955, p. 280), although his text is cited very rarely. His criteria for establishing that an effect is mediated are as follows:

1. The presumed mediator (M) should be related to the assumed causal variable (X).

2. The mediator should be related to the assumed effect, Y.

3. When the sample is stratified according to the presumed mediator, the (partial) relationship between X and Y should be smaller than the relationship prior to stratification.

Hyman's second criterion is an example of what he termed a *marginal effect*, a term he applied to both the $X \rightarrow M$ and $M \rightarrow Y$ relationships. M is said to *interpret* the original relationship if these criteria are met. Hyman also emphasized the necessity that *X* temporally precede *M,* an important consideration for a purportedly causal model. Implicit in the third criterion is the requirement that *X* is related to *Y*—that there exists a relationship between the presumed cause and the presumed effect to be explained.

Readers familiar with the Judd and Kenny (1981) and Baron and Kenny (1986) criteria for establishing mediation will find Hyman's criteria familiar. According to Judd and Kenny (1981, p. 605), the criteria for concluding that mediation exists are the following:

1. The treatment, *X,* affects the outcome variable, *Y.*

2. Each variable in the causal chain affects the variable that follows it in the chain, when all variables prior to it, including the treatment, are controlled.

3. The treatment exerts no effect upon the outcome when the mediating variable is controlled.

Kenny, Kashy, and Bolger (1998) note that only the last two of these steps are actually required, since a reduction in the strength of *c* implies that *c* was nontrivial before the mediator was introduced into the model. Baron and Kenny's criteria are similar to Hyman's but are stated in terms more explicitly related to statistical significance (p. 1176):

1. Variations in levels of the independent variable significantly account for variations in the presumed mediator.

2. Variations in the mediator significantly account for variations in the dependent variable.

3. A previously significant relationship between the independent and dependent variables is no longer significant after controlling for the mediator.

To illustrate the causal steps strategy as well as other procedures we describe later, we will use data from Kalyanaraman and Sundar (2006), who examined the mechanisms linking Web portal customization to user attitudes. In this study, 60 participants were randomly assigned into one of several experimental conditions in which they were directed to a *MyYahoo* Web portal that had been customized to varying degrees (low, moderate, or high) across participants based on a pretest questionnaire each participant completed prior to coming to the laboratory. During the study, participants were asked to surf the Web using the portal for eight minutes, after which they completed a questionnaire. The independent variable in this example is *perceived customization,* which reflects how customized the participants felt the portal was to their own interests and how "unique" it was to them (higher = greater perceived customization). The dependent variable is *attitude toward the portal* (higher = more positive attitude). Three additional variables were proposed as potential mediators of any relationship found between perceived customization and attitude: (1) perceived interactivity, (2) perceived novelty, and (3) perceived community. Perceived interactivity gauges the extent to which a user feels the experience with a Web page is an interactive exchange of information and feedback that the user controls. Perceived novelty quantifies the extent to which the user feels that the Web page is providing a unique service compared to other sites and somehow stands out as different. Perceived community measures a person's sense of "belongingness" and the extent to which the Web portal was perceived to welcome and want the user. These variables are scaled positively, such that a higher score reflects more of the construct. Greater detail on the measurement and study procedures can be found in Kalyanaraman and Sundar (2006).[2]

Drawing on this example, it may be of interest to determine whether perceived interactivity (M) mediates the effect of perceived customization (X) on attitudes toward the Web portal (Y). Baron and Kenny's (1986) criteria oblige us to estimate the paths in Figure 2.1, most easily using ordinary least squares (OLS) regression, although other estimation methods could be used. More specifically, we estimate the coefficients of the following models:

$$\hat{Y} = i_1 + cX$$
$$\hat{M} = i_2 + aX$$
$$\hat{Y} = i_3 + c'X + bM$$

where the i's are intercept terms and the carets over Y and M represent that these are estimated values. Using the Kalyanaraman and Sundar (2006) data, individual OLS regressions (or using the SPSS macro provided by Preacher and Hayes, 2004) reveal that the total effect is positive and different from zero, $c = 0.5119$, $SE = 0.0588$, $t(58) = 8.7183$, $p < .001$. Thus, greater perceived customization is associated with more positive attitudes toward the portal. Second, perceived customization does predict perceived interactivity, the putative mediator, $a = 0.4013$, $SE = 0.0778$, $t(58) = 5.1592$, $p < .001$. The greater the perceived customization, the more interactive the user perceives the Web portal to be. Third, perceived interactivity is significantly and positively related to attitude when controlling for perceived customization, $b = 0.3011$, $SE = 0.0917$, $t(57) = 3.2826$, $p < .002$. This suggests that the relationship between the mediator and the outcome is not spurious (due to both being caused by perceived customization) or epiphenomenal (which occurs when a predictor is correlated with an outcome only because the predictor is correlated with another variable that is causally related to the outcome). Finally, the direct effect of perceived customization on attitude is smaller than the total effect, $c' = 0.3911$, $SE = 0.0656$, $t(57) = 5.9575$, $p < .001$. According to Baron and Kenny's criteria, this pattern is consistent with a claim that *partial mediation* is occurring, as the direct effect of customization on attitude is statistically different from zero even after controlling for the mediator (we elaborate on the distinction between partial and complete mediation later). That is, part of the mechanism producing the effect of customization on attitudes is the tendency for more customized Web portals to be perceived as more interactive, which in turn leads to more positive attitudes.

The causal steps approach is by far the most commonly used method for assessing mediation. The criteria have recently been extended for use in within-subject designs as well (Judd, Kenny, & McClelland, 2001). But despite its simplicity and intuitive appeal, the causal steps strategy suffers from serious limitations relative to other methods we discuss soon. First, it is possible to observe seemingly paradoxical effects using this approach. For example, a significant c and nonsignificant c' may differ by a trivial amount in absolute terms, yet the causal steps criteria would indicate that mediation is occurring (a possible Type I error; Holmbeck, 2002). Particularly in large samples, it is possible to observe significant yet widely differing c and c' estimates, which might lead to the conclusion that mediation is of trivial magnitude (a possible Type II error).[3] Furthermore, the causal steps strategy has been found to exhibit below-expected Type I error rates as well as to suffer from very low power (MacKinnon et al., 2002; Pituch, Whittaker, & Stapleton, 2005), perhaps because significance requirements are placed on several regression coefficients. According to this approach, mediation cannot be claimed unless all relevant paths are statistically significant. Other approaches described below do not impose statistical significance requirements on all paths. Importantly, the causal steps strategy obliges the researcher to infer the presence and extent of mediation from a pattern of hypothesis tests, none of which directly addresses the hypothesis of interest—whether the causal path linking X to Y through M is nonzero and in the direction expected. Finally, because it does not directly estimate the size of the indirect effect, there is consequently no way to obtain a confidence interval for the population indirect effect (Pituch et al., 2005). Although the causal steps strategy is important to understand because of its widespread use, we believe its disadvantages relative to alternatives described later are large enough to warrant a recommendation that it not be used.

PARTIAL CORRELATION STRATEGIES

Olkin and Finn (1995, p. 160) describe a method of assessing mediation using correlations. Their point estimate of the mediation effect is $r_{YX} - r_{YX.M}$, where r_{YX} is the simple correlation between X and Y and $r_{YX.M}$ is the partial correlation between X and Y controlling for M. Mediation is assessed by calculating the ratio of $r_{YX} - r_{YX.M}$ to its standard error and deriving the *p*-value using the standard normal distribution or by constructing a confidence interval for the population value $\rho_{YX} - \rho_{YX.M}$. A few cautions are relevant to this method. First, Olkin and Finn's (1995) standard error contains a mistake; a corrected standard error is provided by Lockwood and MacKinnon (2000) and MacKinnon et al. (2002). Second, the test is cumbersome to conduct by hand, and we know of no software that implements it. Furthermore, Kenny (personal communication) and MacKinnon et al. (2002) note that even in the absence of mediation, the partial correlation method can lead to a spurious conclusion of mediation—a Type I error. We do not recommend that the partial correlation strategy be used.

DIFFERENCES IN COEFFICIENTS STRATEGIES

Noting that a nontrivial drop in the X→Y effect after partialing out the mediator constitutes positive evidence for mediation, several authors have examined the distributional properties of $c - c'$. MacKinnon et al. (2002) examine three such methods, proposed by Clogg, Petkova, and Shihadeh (1992), Freedman and Schatzkin (1992), and McGuigan and Langholtz (1988). All three methods suffer from statistical limitations, as detailed by MacKinnon et al. (2002). In addition, note that $c - c'$ is not a particularly useful way to quantify an indirect effect in models with multiple mediators or those involving both moderation and mediation, to be discussed later. We do not recommend that differences in coefficients strategies be used.

NESTED MODEL STRATEGY

Judd and Kenny (1981) and Holmbeck (1997) suggest a method of testing mediation hypotheses that takes advantage of a key feature of structural equation modeling—the ability to constrain model parameters to fixed values. This strategy makes use of the chi-square model fit index (χ^2) given as standard output by SEM software. Keeping sample size constant, the better a model fits data, the smaller the value of χ^2 will be. Tests of nested models[4] may be conducted by comparing values of χ^2 derived from the constrained and full models. When using path analysis, a completely saturated model will yield a χ^2 of zero. Thus, any constraints placed on such a model will necessarily increase χ^2 to a degree reflecting the unreasonableness of the constraint given the data. A test of the difference in fit between two nested models may be conducted by computing the difference in χ^2 values and comparing the result to a χ^2 distribution with degrees of freedom (*df*) equal to the difference in *df* between the two models (*df* = 1 in the case of simple mediation). If the value of χ^2 exceeds the critical value established by df and the desired α level for the test, then the models are said to have significantly different fit.

If the hypothesis is one of simple mediation, then using the nested model strategy would entail estimating two models—one estimating the direct effect of X on Y (c') and one in which c' has been constrained to zero. If complete mediation is occurring, then path c' should not differ appreciably from zero. If the addition of this constraint is accompanied by a significant decrease in model fit (i.e., an increase in χ^2), then complete mediation is ruled out. If the researcher is interested in determining whether any mediation at all is occurring, then one could estimate a model without M to obtain c, then constrain the c' coefficient in the full model (containing M) to equal c. If mediation is occurring, then path c should be significant and c' should be smaller than c upon the addition of the mediator to the model. Such a situation would imply that the value estimated for the original path coefficient would be unreasonably large in the presence of the mediator. If the addition of this constraint is accompanied by a significant decrease in model fit, then support has been found for mediation.

A shortcoming of the nested model strategy is that it involves testing the hypothesis of *complete* mediation, or that the entire effect of X on Y is carried through M.[5] Whereas strong tests of hypotheses are generally to be encouraged, we reiterate Baron and Kenny's (1986) observation that complete mediation is probably rare in practice. Second, use of the difference in χ^2 has been criticized in the methodological literature on the basis that it is heavily dependent on sample size. Given a moderately large sample, the nested model strategy will virtually always result in rejection of the hypothesis of complete mediation.

PRODUCT OF COEFFICIENTS STRATEGIES

Most methodologists agree that the product of the coefficients a and b is a logical way to quantify an indirect effect.[6] The logic behind the product of coefficients strategy is simple. If M mediates the effect of X on Y, then X should affect M and M should affect Y while controlling for X. If either a or b is zero, then their product will be zero. If both a and b are nonzero, as is the case if M mediates the X→Y relationship, then the product will be nonzero. The product of a and b will be further from zero as the strength of the indirect effect increases. Furthermore, typically $ab = (c - c')$, which is one way mediation is operationalized using the causal steps strategy. Therefore, it seems sensible to use ab as a basis for statistical inference and confidence interval construction. Three broad strategies—the product of coefficients, distribution of the product, and bootstrapping—quantify the indirect effect in this way, and differ mainly in how they construct and use the sampling distribution of *ab*. We discuss each in turn.

Given that the indirect effect is quantified by the point estimate *ab*, the goal is to determine whether *ab* is significantly different from some specified value (usually zero) or to estimate its precision and report a confidence interval for the population value of *ab*. Assuming normality of the sampling distribution of *ab*, all that is required to construct a confidence interval for the population *ab* is the sample point estimate *ab* and its standard error (i.e., the mean and standard deviation of the sampling distribution of *ab*). A number of approaches can be used to derive the standard error under the assumption of normality. The multivariate delta method, for example, proceeds by first forming a Taylor series expansion of the function of interest (here *ab*) and applying the definition of a variance to that expansion. Preacher, Rucker, and Hayes (2007) provide detailed derivations of the variances[7] of several indirect effects, one of which is for the simple mediation model, using a matrix expression for the second-order delta method. Aroian (1947), Goodman (1960), Folmer (1981), MacKinnon et al. (1995), and Sobel (1982, 1986, 1988) provide alternative derivations that converge on the same result. In the case of simple mediation involving only one mediator, the second-order expression for the estimated standard error of *ab* is

$$SE_{ab} = \sqrt{b^2 s_a^2 + a^2 s_b^2 + s_a^2 s_b^2}$$

where s_a^2 and s_b^2 are the asymptotic variances of *a* and *b*. These quantities are readily available from standard regression or SEM software. The third term in the expression above, $s_a^2 s_b^2$, is sometimes omitted from the standard error expression not only because it does not appear in the first-order solution for the variance but also because it tends to be trivially small in practice (MacKinnon et al., 1995). Goodman (1960) provides an unbiased variance estimator that subtracts rather than adds $s_a^2 s_b^2$ in the equation above, but we do not recommend using Goodman's approach as it can sometimes result in a negative value for the standard error (MacKinnon et al., 2002).

Regardless of the standard error estimator used, hypothesis tests are conducted by dividing the point estimate *ab* by the standard error and comparing the resulting ratio to a standard normal distribution. This is known as the *Sobel test* for an indirect effect (Sobel, 1982). Alternatively, the standard error can be used in conjunction with critical values for the standard normal distribution (e.g., ±1.96) to form a confidence interval for the population indirect effect. The product of coefficients approach has been found to perform well in simulation studies with sample sizes greater than 50 or so, but the standard error tends to be overestimated in small samples (MacKinnon et al., 1995). The advantages of the product of coefficients approach are that it is easy and intuitive, and it is implemented in numerous software applications (see the Computer Software section below). One disadvantage is that it requires a large sample in order to be confident that the sampling distribution of *ab* divided by its standard error is normal, which one must assume to derive a *p*-value or compute a confidence interval using this approach. In addition, the Type I error rate and power tend to be lower than optimal (MacKinnon, Lockwood, & Williams, 2004; Pituch et al., 2005). Of greatest concern is the normality assumption. This is usually a safe assumption in extremely large samples, but in practice, *ab* tends to be positively skewed and highly leptokurtic (Bollen & Stine, 1990; MacKinnon et al., 2002; MacKinnon et al., 2004), compromising the validity of statistical inference. However, the performance of the product of coefficients approach improves with increased sample size.

Bobko and Rieck (1980) describe a related procedure that involves computing the significance of the product of regression coefficients *a* and *b* in Figure 2.1 when *X*, *M*, and *Y* have been standardized. Under these circumstances, $a = r_{MX}$ and *b* is the standardized partial regression weight for *M* when *Y* is regressed on *M* and *X*. Type I error rates are comparable to those for the Sobel test (MacKinnon et al., 2002). In theory, Bobko and Rieck's (1980) approach should provide identical results to the first-order version of the Sobel test because the scales of the variables involved should not influence whether or not the empirical evidence is consistent with an indirect effect. In support of this, MacKinnon et al. (2002) found that this method resembled the first-order Sobel test in terms of power and Type I error rates.

Again drawing on our running example, we used the Sobel test to assess the presence of an indirect effect of perceived customization on attitude toward the portal through perceived interactivity. From the regression analyses performed earlier, $a = 0.4013$ and $b = 0.3011$, so $ab = (0.4013)(0.3011) = 0.1208$. Using the second-order estimator of the standard error of *ab*,

$$SE_{ab} = \sqrt{(0.3011)^2(0.0778)^2 + (0.4013)^2(0.0917)^2 + (0.0778)^2(0.0917)^2}$$
$$= 0.0442$$

Dividing the estimated indirect effect by this standard error yields $Z = 0.1208/0.0442 = 2.7330$, which exceeds the critical value of ±1.96 for a hypothesis test at $\alpha = .05$, assuming that the sampling distribution of *ab* is normal. These results are consistent with the claim that perceived interactivity mediates the effect of perceived customization on attitudes. In addition to conducting a significance test, we could use this standard error to create confidence limits for the indirect effect in the usual way. For example, the lower and upper bounds of a 95% confidence interval are given by $ab \pm 1.96 SE_{ab}$. The 95% confidence interval computed on the basis of sample data is $0.1208 \pm 1.96(0.0442)$ or 0.0342 to 0.2074.

DISTRIBUTION OF THE PRODUCT STRATEGIES

The product of coefficients strategy is simple to apply but suffers from the limitation that it requires the assumption of normality of the sampling distribution of ab. In practice, this sampling distribution is rarely normal, although it may approach normality in large samples. The distribution of the product family of strategies (see MacKinnon, Lockwood, & Hoffman, 1998; MacKinnon et al., 2002; MacKinnon et al., 2004) circumvents the need to assume normality by making use of the known distribution of the product of two normally distributed variables (Aroian, 1947; Craig, 1936; MacKinnon et al., 2004; Springer, 1979). With this approach, the assumption of normality of the sampling distributions of a and b is still invoked, but this assumption is much more realistic than the assumption of normality of the distribution of their product, ab. The form of the distribution of the product is highly complex, but values of the function are tabulated in Springer and Thompson (1966) under the null condition that $a = b = 0$. Although there are tables that do not assume both a and b are zero (Meeker, Cornwell, & Aroian, 1981), for hypothesis testing their use still requires assumptions about the true value of either a or b, information that is not usually available. However, these tables can be used for generating confidence intervals, and confidence intervals can be used as an indirect means of testing a hypothesis by assessing whether the null hypothesized value of the indirect effect is inside of the confidence interval. Recently, MacKinnon, Fritz, Williams, and Lockwood (in press) have made SPSS, SAS, and R macros available that can be used for generating confidence intervals using the distribution of products method. These macros make implementation of this method easier than it has been in the past.

BOOTSTRAPPING

The Sobel test relies on distributional assumptions that are typically violated in practice. Through the use of the normal distribution for deriving p-values and confidence intervals, the Sobel test assumes that the sampling distribution of the indirect effect is normal. But there is strong reason to be suspicious of this assumption, especially in small to moderately sized samples. It is documented theoretically and through simulation that the sampling distribution of the indirect effect converges to normal as the sample size increases, but not quickly enough to justify the routine use of the Sobel test. More and more, statisticians are advocating a move away from statistical procedures that rely on assumptions, particularly when they are unrealistic, to computationally intensive methods such as *bootstrapping*, as these methods typically make fewer unwarranted assumptions and, as a result, can produce more accurate inference (see, e.g., Efron & Tibshirani, 1998; Good, 2001; Lunneborg, 2000; Mooney & Duval,

1993; Rodgers, 1999). Statistical methodologists who study mediation have taken this call seriously and are advocating bootstrapping as one of the better methods for estimating and testing hypotheses about mediation (e.g., Bollen & Stine, 1990; Lockwood & MacKinnon, 1998; MacKinnon et al., 2004; Preacher & Hayes, 2004, 2007; Shrout & Bolger, 2002).

To bootstrap an indirect effect, an empirical approximation of the sampling distribution of the product of the *a* and *b* paths is generated by taking a new sample of size *n with replacement* from the available sample and estimating *a* and *b* as usual. That is, each time a case is drawn from the original sample, that case is put back into the pool, potentially to be chosen again as the sample of size *n* is constructed. These estimates of *a* and *b* are used to calculate ab^*, the indirect effect in a single resample of size *n* from the original data. This process is repeated over and over for a total of *k* times, preferably at least 1,000. The distribution of the *k* values of ab^* serves as an empirical, nonparametric approximation of the sampling distribution of *ab*. The mean of the *k* estimates of ab^* can be used as a point estimate of the indirect effect, and the standard deviation functions as the standard error of the sampling distribution of *ab*. A *g*% confidence interval for *ab* is derived by sorting the *k* values of ab^* from low to high. The lower and upper bounds of the confidence interval are defined, respectively, as the $0.5(1 - g/100)k^{th}$ and $1 + 0.5(1 + g/100)k^{th}$ values of ab^* in the sorted distribution. For instance, when *k* = 1,000, the lower and upper bounds of a 95% confidence interval are the 25th and 976th values of ab^* in the sorted distribution of estimates. This procedure yields what is called a *percentile-based* confidence interval. More accurate confidence intervals can be derived through the process of *bias correction* or *bias correction and acceleration* (see Efron, 1987; Efron & Tibshirani, 1998; Lunneborg, 2000; Preacher & Hayes, 2007; MacKinnon et al., 2004; and Stine, 1989, for details on these corrections). The null hypothesis of no indirect effect is tested by determining whether zero is inside of the confidence interval. If not, the researcher can claim that the indirect effect is different from zero. Although still a relatively new approach to testing mediation hypotheses, research to date has shown that bootstrapping the indirect effect is superior to the causal steps, product of coefficients, and distribution of product methods, both in terms of power and Type I error rates (MacKinnon et al., 2004).

The primary advantage of bootstrapping is that no assumptions are made about the sampling distributions of *a*, *b*, or their product, because bootstrapping approximates the sampling distribution of *ab* empirically, with no recourse to mathematical derivations. The result is that bootstrapping provides confidence intervals that cannot be obtained with the product of coefficients method (Lockwood & MacKinnon, 1998). For instance, the Sobel test and product of coefficients method assume that the sampling distribution of *ab* is symmetrical. But this is not usually true. Bootstrapping can produce confidence intervals that are asymmetric, in that the lower bound of the confidence interval may be more or less distant from the point estimate than the upper bound. Furthermore, bootstrapping enables researchers to use smaller samples than would be necessary to satisfy the distributional assumptions of other methods (although samples should not be *too* small).

The disadvantages of bootstrapping are few and minor. First, the accuracy of confidence limits obtained through bootstrapping depends on the number of resamples, and resampling takes time. However, with today's fast desktop computers this is no longer a realistic limitation. Second, if the same sample is subjected to bootstrapping multiple times, the same confidence limits will never be obtained (MacKinnon et al., 2004). Third, bootstrapping is useful only to the extent that the distributions of the variables in the original sample closely approximate the population distribution. Large samples are likely to be more representative than small samples. Fourth, raw data must be available in order to use bootstrapping; if only correlations or covariances are available, some other method must be used to assess mediation. Finally, only a handful of software applications currently implement bootstrapping, but this situation is changing rapidly. Nevertheless, given its superior performance relative to alternatives combined with its few and weak assumptions, we believe bootstrapping is the preferred method and thus strongly advocate its routine use.

To illustrate, we bootstrapped the indirect effect of perceived customization on attitude toward the portal through perceived interactivity using the SPSS macro described by Preacher and Hayes (2004, 2007). With 5,000 bootstrap samples, the point estimate was 0.1222, with a 95% confidence interval from 0.0409 to 0.2618. As zero is not in the confidence interval, these results are consistent with the claim that perceived customization's effect on attitude is at least partially indirect through perceived interactivity. Unlike the Sobel test and other methods described earlier, we need not assume anything about the shape of the sampling distribution of ab to have confidence in this conclusion. Notice as well the asymmetry in the confidence interval, with the upper bound being much farther from the point estimate than the lower bound. This reflects the true asymmetry of the sampling distribution of the indirect effect.

Extensions to More Complex Mediator Models

In the previous section, we described many of the existing methods for estimating and testing indirect effects in simple mediation models. In this section, we extend some of these methods to models with more than a single mediator and to models in which the paths to or from the mediator are allowed to vary systematically as a function of one or more other variables.

MULTIPLE MEDIATOR MODELS

Variables often exert their effects through multiple mediators, and it behooves researchers to consider explanations beyond simple mediation, preferably before the data collection so that such explanations can be tested statistically. Shah, Cho, Eveland, and Kwak (2005), for instance, examined a model in which both interactive civic messaging and interpersonal discussion functioned as mediators of the effect of news exposure on civic participation. Beaudoin and Thorson (2004) examined the mediating role of reliance on the news media and elaboration of its contents in explaining the effect of learning motivations on political knowledge. Additional examples of multiple mediator models in the communication literature include Kiousis, McDevitt, and Wu (2005), Slater and Rasinski (2005), and Holbert et al. (2003).

A graphical depiction of a model involving multiple mediators can be found in Figure 2.2. We call this a *single-step multiple mediator* model, in that although it contains several mediators, no mediators affect each other. That is, it takes only a single step to get from X to Y, through one and only one of the mediators. Other models involving multiple mediators are possible (e.g., $X \rightarrow M_1 \rightarrow M_2 \rightarrow Y$; Cheung, 2007; Taylor, MacKinnon, & Tein, in press), but we restrict our discussion to single-step models such as in Figure 2.2. The top panel of the figure represents the total effect of X on Y, represented with the unstandardized path coefficient c, and the bottom panel represents both the *direct effect* of X on Y (path c') and the *direct effects* of M on Y (the b paths). The *specific indirect effect* of X on Y via mediator j is defined as the product of the two unstandardized paths linking X to Y via that mediator. For example, the specific indirect effect of X on Y through M_1 is quantified as $a_1 b_1$. The *total indirect effect* is the sum of the specific indirect effects, $\Sigma_i(a_i b_i)$, $i = 1$ to j, where j is the number of proposed mediators. The total effect of X on Y is the sum of its direct effect and the j specific indirect effects; that is, $c = c' + \Sigma_i(a_i b_i)$, $i = 1$ to j.

The dual challenge for the researcher in investigating models such as these is to assess the presence and strength of the total indirect effect through the set of mediators and to assess the presence and strength of the specific indirect effects through individual mediators. Although the researcher might be tempted to employ a set of simple mediation analyses, one for each proposed mediator, this approach is problematic for a number of reasons. One cannot simply add up the indirect effects calculated in several simple mediation analyses to derive the total indirect effect, as the mediators in a multiple mediator model typically will be intercorrelated. As a result, the specific indirect effects estimated using several simple mediation analyses will be biased and will not sum to the total indirect effect through the multiple mediators. Furthermore, hypothesis tests and confidence intervals calculated for specific indirect effects without controlling for the other mediators in the model will be

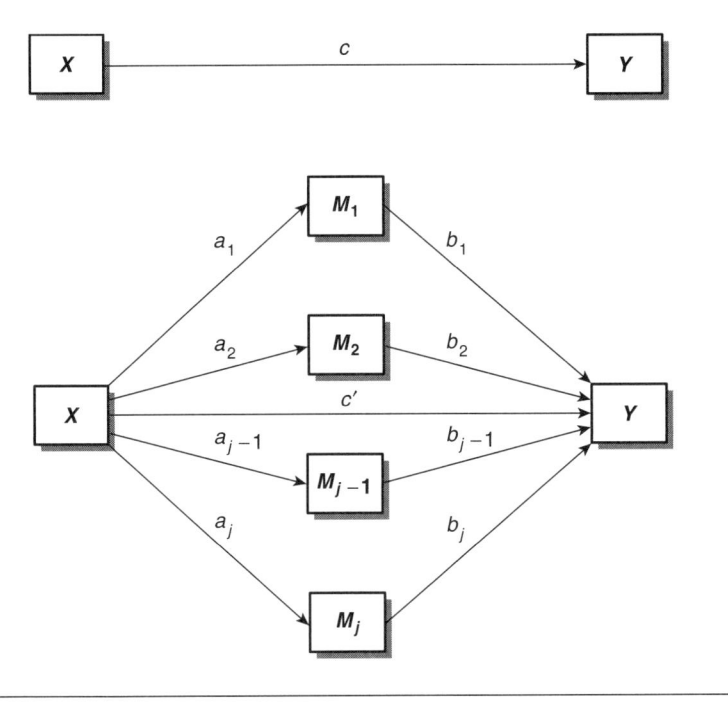

Figure 2.2 A Single-Step Multiple Mediator Model

invalid. Although the total indirect effect can be estimated easily as $c - c'$ using two regression analyses, this simple subtraction is purely descriptive. A multiple mediation analysis is more appropriate under such circumstances. For excellent overviews of methods to examine and interpret total and specific indirect effects, consult Alwin and Hauser (1975), Bollen (1987), Brown (1997), Sobel (1982, 1986, 1988), and sources cited therein. MacKinnon (2000) suggests an extension of the product of coefficients approach to assessing the significance of the total indirect effect and pairwise contrasts between specific indirect effects. Holbert and Stephenson (2003) describe the advantages of a distribution of the products method in a multiple mediator model. Preacher and Hayes (2007) elaborate on MacKinnon's methods, providing software to facilitate the use of the product of coefficients approach and to bootstrap confidence intervals for both total and specific indirect effects, as well as pairwise contrasts of specific indirect effects. Large-scale simulation studies have also been undertaken to examine and compare approaches to assessing multiple mediation (Azen, 2003; Briggs, 2006; Williams, 2004) and generally show bootstrapping to be the preferred method. We refer the reader to these sources for in-depth discussions and mathematical treatments.

As an example of a multiple mediation analysis, consider the hypothesis that the effect of perceived customization (X) on attitude (Y) is mediated by perceived interactivity, perceived novelty, and perceived community. Referring to Figure 2.2 and our running example, let X refer to perceived customization; let M_1, M_2, and M_3 refer to perceived interactivity, perceived novelty, and perceived community, respectively; and let Y refer to attitude toward the portal. We estimated the paths in this model using an SPSS macro described in Preacher and Hayes (2007) and available online at http://www.comm.ohio-state.edu/ahayes/. The output from this macro can be found in the Appendix.

Of course, the total effect of X on Y, path c, does not change as a function of the nature and number of mediators, so it remains 0.5119 and statistically different from zero. We find that the total indirect effect is $a_1 b_1 + a_2 b_2 + a_3 b_3 = 0.3104$. Using the multivariate delta method as discussed in Preacher and Hayes (2007), the estimated standard error is 0.0931. Dividing the total indirect effect by the standard error yields $Z = 0.3104/0.0931 = 3.3330$, which leads to a rejection of the null hypothesis of no total indirect effect at any reasonable α level. The specific indirect effects are $a_1 b_1 = (0.4013)(0.2535) = 0.1018$ (through perceived interactivity), $a_2 b_2 = (0.6446)(0.1700) = 0.1096$ (through perceived novelty), and $a_3 b_3 = (0.5829)(0.1699) = 0.0990$ (through perceived community). Dividing these by their estimated standard errors yields:

$$z_{a_1 b_1} = \frac{0.1018}{0.0408} = 2.4948, p = .0126$$

$$z_{a_2 b_2} = \frac{0.1096}{0.0645} = 1.6989, p = .0983$$

$$z_{a_3 b_3} = \frac{0.0990}{0.0657} = 1.5063, p = .1320$$

From these analyses, we can conclude that perceived interactivity mediates the effect of perceived customization on attitudes. It seems that more customized Web portals are perceived as more interactive, and this interactivity leads to a more positive attitude. However, perceived novelty and perceived community do not mediate the effect of customization on attitudes.

This approach of dividing a specific indirect effect by its standard error to test the hypothesis requires the same assumption as this test in a simple mediation context—that the sampling distribution of the indirect effect is normal. There is just as much reason to be skeptical of this assumption in the multiple mediator context as in the simple mediation context. Bootstrapping is a useful means of relaxing this assumption, and the logic of its implementation in the multiple mediator context is the same—each indirect effect is estimated multiple times by repeatedly sampling cases with replacement from the data and estimating the model in each resample. Bias-corrected and accelerated bootstrap confidence intervals for the total and specific indirect effects are provided in the Appendix (from the SPSS macro described in Preacher and Hayes, 2007). In the section in the Appendix labeled "BOOTSTRAP RESULTS FOR INDIRECT EFFECTS," notice that the bootstrap estimates yield a different conclusion. Because zero is not in the confidence interval for perceived community (variable name "commune") and perceived interactivity (variable name "inter"), we can argue a claim that perceived customization exerts its effect on attitudes in part through perceived community as well as perceived interactivity. These bootstrap results are more trustworthy than the Sobel test because they require fewer assumptions and simulation studies demonstrate their superiority. Notice as well that we can claim an indirect effect through community even though the path linking perceived community to attitudes is not statistically different from zero (from the section labeled "Direct Effects of Mediators on DV (b paths)")—an advantage of quantifying and testing the indirect effect explicitly rather than relying on the causal steps strategy.

Some caveats must be mentioned where multiple mediators are concerned. First, a specific indirect effect should be interpreted as the indirect effect of X on Y through a given mediator *controlling for all other included mediators*. If the mediators are mutually uncorrelated, then each specific indirect effect may be interpreted as if it were a simple indirect effect. The more general (and likely) case is that mediators will be correlated, in which case each specific indirect effect represents the unique ability of each intervening variable to mediate the $X{\rightarrow}Y$ effect, above and beyond the other mediators. As in any linear model with correlated predictors, high correlations between the mediators can produce instability in estimates of the b paths, meaning that although each might function as a mediator considered on its own, when combined, the specific indirect effects may wash each other out through multicollinearity. Second, when multiple intervening variables are included in a model, it is difficult to tell which ones act as mediators and which, if any, act as *suppressors* (MacKinnon, Krull, & Lockwood, 2000). Interpretation should be made with care. Finally, there are other ways in which multiple mediators may be included in a single model. For example, Hyman (1955) notes that whenever an intervening variable is included in a model, the researcher may be tempted to explore potential mediators of the $X{\rightarrow}M$ and $M{\rightarrow}Y$ links. Taylor, MacKinnon, and Tein (in press) address the situation in which multiple mediators operate serially rather than in parallel, for example, $X{\rightarrow}M_1{\rightarrow}M_2{\rightarrow}Y$, but little other work has been done on this topic. Theory should guide the decision of how and whether to include multiple mediators.

MODERATED MEDIATION AND MEDIATED MODERATION

Moderated mediation can be defined as occurring when the size of an indirect effect is contingent on the level or value of a moderator variable. A moderator variable can be defined as a variable that influences or is related to the size of the relationship between two other variables. So if the relationship between X and Y varies as a function of W, then it is said that W moderates the relationship between X and Y, or that W is a moderator of the relationship. Moderation is also known as *interaction*. A process can be described as moderated mediation if the size of the indirect effect of the putative cause on the outcome through the mediator varies as a function of the moderator variable(s).

Although communication researchers routinely employ regression and analysis of variance to test hypotheses about moderation, rarely are tests of whether indirect effects vary as a function of one or more moderator variables formally conducted, even though intuition suggests that such moderated mediation is probably a fairly common phenomenon in communication processes both empirically and theoretically. One example is the differential gains hypothesis. Scheufele (2002) provides evidence that newspaper hard news use and interpersonal discussion about politics interact in influencing political knowledge, and political knowledge in turn predicts political participation. Thus, the magnitude of the indirect effect of newspaper hard news use on participation through knowledge depends on how much a person discusses politics with others. Conversely, the magnitude of the indirect effect of interpersonal discussion on participation through knowledge depends on newspaper hard news use. Slater, Hayes, and Ford (2007) provide another example in which the effect of adolescent sensation seeking on perceptions of the risks of alcohol use are mediated by attention to news about alcohol-related accidents and crime, with the magnitude of the indirect effect being contingent on both prior bad experiences with alcohol and exposure to network news.

Early literature on the subject addressed moderated mediation using an extension of the causal steps strategy (Baron & Kenny, 1986; James & Brett, 1984). For example, James and Brett (1984) considered models involving regression equations requiring "the addition of a moderator for either the $\hat{m} = f(x)$ or $\hat{y} = f(m)$ relations, or both." Moderated mediation is also addressed by Edwards and Lambert (2007), Wegener and Fabrigar (2000), Morgan-Lopez and MacKinnon (2006), Rose, Holmbeck, Coakley, and Franks (2004), and Muller, Judd, and Yzerbyt (2005), but most employ inconsistent definitions of moderated mediation. Preacher et al. (2007) address the problem by considering *conditional indirect effects,* which they define as indirect effects conditional on the values of at least one moderator. Their general strategy can be used to address all previously offered definitions of moderated mediation. They consider several basic models in which it would be sensible to examine conditional indirect effects:

1. The independent variable (X) functions as a moderator of the b path.
2. Some fourth variable (W) affects the a path.
3. W affects the b path.
4. W affects a while yet another variable (Z) affects b.
5. W affects both a and b.

These five models are depicted graphically in Figure 2.3, allowing for the possibility that X may still have a direct effect on Y. For each of these basic model forms, Preacher et al. (2007) provide product of coefficients and bootstrapping strategies (and software) for investigating the significance of the $X \rightarrow M \rightarrow Y$ indirect effect at conditional values of the moderator(s). This strategy is a direct extension of strategies used to probe significant interaction effects (e.g., Aiken & West, 1991; Muller et al., 2005; Tein, Sandler, MacKinnon, & Wolchik, 2004), and a recent example of its use in the communication literature can be found in Slater et al. (in press). Alternatively, the researcher may obtain the values of the moderator for which the indirect effect is statistically significant, an extension of the Johnson-Neyman technique (Johnson & Neyman, 1936; Rogosa, 1980, 1981). This strategy does not require the researcher to select arbitrary conditional values of the moderator at which to investigate the significance of the indirect effect.

Moderated mediation is easily confused with *mediated moderation,* a related but different process. Whereas moderated mediation relates to the moderation of the size of an indirect effect, mediated moderation occurs when the interactive effect of two variables on the outcome variable is carried indirectly through a mediator. Revisiting the differential gains hypothesis, Scheufele (2002) did include a test of mediated moderation using the causal steps strategy. He showed that the interaction between newspaper hard news use and interpersonal discussion in predicting political participation, the outcome variable, was in part indirect through their interactive influence on political knowledge, the mediating variable.

As researchers elaborate on theories to include interaction effects, models incorporating both mediation and moderation are expected to increase in frequency. Much work remains to be done. Good conceptual and statistical overviews of both moderated mediation and mediated moderation can be found in Edwards and Lambert (2007), Muller et al. (2005), and Preacher et al. (2007).

MEDIATION IN MULTILEVEL MODELS

With the increasing popularity of multilevel models (see Chapter 8 in this volume, as well as the October 2006 issue of *Human Communication Research*), attention has turned to assessing mediation in contexts involving hierarchical data. When data are organized hierarchically, multilevel regression is a more appropriate strategy than OLS regression. In such data, cases (Level-1 units) are said to be nested within clusters (Level-2 units). Common examples of nested data include employees (Level 1) nested within organizations (Level 2) and repeated measures nested within individuals.

In multilevel models, the familiar regression coefficients relating Level-1 variables may themselves vary across Level-2 units. It might at first seem reasonable to apply the same methods used for assessing mediation in OLS regression in the case of multilevel regression. However, when the regression equations for mediation are framed as multilevel regressions,

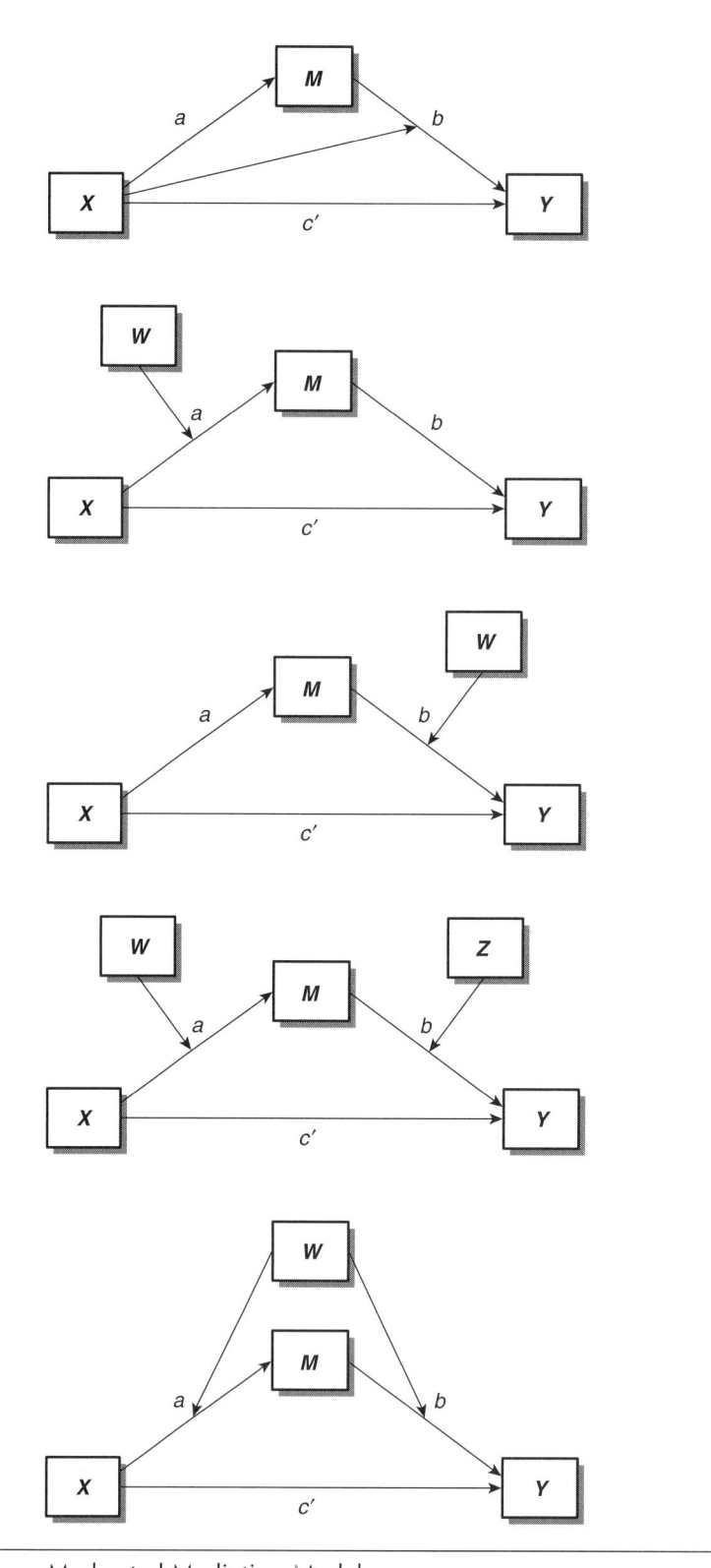

Figure 2.3 Some Moderated Mediation Models

some difficulties emerge. For example, ab no longer necessarily equals $c - c'$ in a given analysis, although on average, they tend to be the same and the discrepancy disappears as Level-1 and Level-2 sample sizes increase (Krull & MacKinnon, 1999). In addition, having random slope coefficients implies that mediation may be stronger for some Level-2 units than for others, so applying traditional methods in the multilevel case may misrepresent large portions of the sample.

Work investigating mediation processes in multilevel designs has only just begun and is an active area of research. Raudenbush and Sampson (1999) provide a method of examining mediation in multilevel models when X and M are Level-2 predictors and Y is a Level-1 outcome. Krull and MacKinnon (1999) examined the case in which X is a Level-2 predictor and both M and Y are Level-1 outcomes (a 2–1–1 model). They recommend that the first-order standard error of the indirect effect derived for use in single-level regression can still be used in the multilevel context. Krull and MacKinnon (2001) and Pituch, Stapleton, and Kang (2006) expanded on this work by investigating the use of single-level techniques in situations where X, both X and M, and neither X nor M are measured at Level 2 (2–1–1, 2–2–1, and 1–1–1 models, respectively), with random intercepts but no random slopes. Kenny, Korchmaros, and Bolger (2003) and Bauer, Preacher, and Gil (2006) investigated mediation in multilevel models where all variables are measured at Level 1 and all relevant slopes are random, whereas Pituch et al. (2005) investigated Level-1 mediation when slopes are fixed. An important point emerging from this literature is that it is desirable to assess not only the mean indirect effect characterizing a sample but also the variability in indirect effects across Level-2 units. Explaining variability in slopes across Level-2 units permits a new way to test moderated mediation hypotheses (Bauer et al., 2006; Kenny et al., 1998).

Controversies, Questions, and Miscellaneous Issues

This section includes brief discussions of concerns we commonly hear from researchers engaged in testing mediation hypotheses.

MEDIATION AND CAUSALITY

We have used the word "causal" with some regularity in this chapter. It cannot be stressed enough that mediation is a causal process, so any investigation of mediation should ensure that necessary preconditions for causality have been met. This is especially true given that hypotheses of mediation are usually tested with correlational data. Regardless of the strategy used to assess the strength and significance of mediation, no statistics can establish whether or not an effect is causal. Necessary preconditions for causal inference include temporal precedence (causes must occur before their presumed effects), concomitant variation (the variables covary in some expected pattern), and the elimination of spurious covariation (other potential causes of covariation have been eliminated).

Establishing the conditions necessary for making claims of causality is an issue of research design more than of statistical inference. For example, whereas measuring M before Y does not ensure that changes in M lead to changes in Y, it certainly makes the inference of causality more tenable (on the other hand, Cole and Maxwell [2003] point out that even when variables are *measured* in the proper order, that does not ensure that the constructs *occur* in the proper order). Similarly, causal inferences may be made with more confidence when X is experimentally manipulated than when X is merely observed. It is also frequently wise to include covariates to help eliminate likely sources of spurious correlation between M and Y, and to avoid situations in which shared method variance may spuriously inflate the regression weights used to assess mediation (Kenny et al., 1998). Often, however, mediation tests are based on correlational data, so frequently the best that can be claimed is that the data are consistent with (or do not contradict) the hypothesis of mediation. Hoyle and Robinson (2004) and Cole and Maxwell (2003) discuss means by which designs may be improved so that causality can be more confidently assumed. In addition, under some circumstances, the mediator may be experimentally manipulated in order to better establish the causal relationship between M and Y (Aron & Monin, 2005; Hoyle & Robinson, 2004; Spencer, Zanna, & Fong, 2005), but this strategy introduces complications. For example, the putative mediator must be amenable to both measurement and manipulation in order to use this *experimental-causal-chain* strategy (Spencer et al., 2005).

EFFECT SIZE

The methods presented so far address the statistical significance or precision of the estimate of the indirect effect. However, it is almost always the case that the researcher will also want to characterize an indirect effect in terms of both statistical and *practical* significance. A common way to express practical significance is in terms of *effect size* as a sort of objective gauge of the importance of an effect (Wilkinson et al., 1999). There are many measures of unstandardized and standardized effect size that can be employed in various analyses (e.g., R^2 or the squared semipartial correlation in regression, and η^2 or ω^2 in ANOVA; see, e.g., Hayes, 2005). Standardized effect-size measures have the advantage that they do not rely on the scales of the variables involved, and thus can be interpreted without knowledge of those scales. Unstandardized effect-size measures remain interpretable only in units of the variables' original scales, which may be an advantage in many circumstances.

A few methods exist for quantifying effect size in mediation analysis. MacKinnon and Dwyer (1993; see also Alwin & Hauser, 1975; MacKinnon, 1994) and Sobel (1982) propose the proportion of the total effect that is mediated, calculated as $ab/(ab + c')$ or ab/c, as a measure of the extent to which the $X \to Y$ effect is mediated.[8] MacKinnon and Dwyer (1993) and Sobel (1982) also propose the ratio of the indirect to the direct effect, or ab/c'. Sobel (1982) shows how asymptotic standard errors for these indices may be derived. Our stance is that these methods provide useful heuristics but suffer from some limitations. First, ab/c does not constitute a proper proportion, as it is not necessarily bounded by 0 and 1. Second, both measures can give misleading estimates of the magnitude and importance of an effect. For example, if the total effect c is very small, then even trivial indirect effects may appear to be very large or important. The reverse is also possible. Finally, point estimates of these measures have been found to be unstable unless the sample size is at least 500 (and in some cases more than 5,000; MacKinnon et al., 1995).

An alternative method of quantifying practical significance for indirect effects might be to simply interpret the point estimate in substantive terms. Products of slopes can be interpreted in much the same way as slopes themselves. Consider the equations for slopes a and b in a simple mediation model:

$$a = r_{XM} \frac{SD_M}{SD_X}$$

$$b = \frac{r_{MY} - r_{XY} r_{XM}}{1 - r_{XM}^2} \left(\frac{SD_Y}{SD_M} \right)$$

where SD is the standard deviation of the variable subscripted. When a and b are multiplied to form the indirect effect ab, the SD_M terms cancel, leaving:

$$ab = r_{XM} \frac{r_{MY} - r_{XY} r_{XM}}{1 - r_{XM}^2} \left(\frac{SD_Y}{SD_X} \right)$$

or more simply:

$$ab = \tilde{b}_{MX} \tilde{b}_{YM.X} \frac{SD_Y}{SD_X}$$

where $\tilde{b}_{MX}$ is the standardized regression weight estimating M from X and $\tilde{b}_{YM.X}$ is the standardized regression weight estimating Y from M controlling for X. Note that in this expression, the indirect effect is devoid of the metric of *M*. Thus, *ab* can be interpreted as the expected change in *Y* per unit change in *X* that occurs indirectly through *M*.

Because the practical significance of the indirect effect should not depend on the metrics of the variables involved, consider the special case in which *X* and *Y* (although not necessarily *M*) have been standardized, in which case the ratio of standard deviations drops out. We propose the following *index of mediation* as a rough measure of effect size:

$$ab' = \tilde{b}_{MX} \tilde{b}_{YM.X}$$

This index is identical to the standardized indirect effect proposed by Bobko and Rieck (1980). Note that *ab'* is standardized in the sense that *ab'* does not depend on the scales of the variables involved. Also note that whereas the proportion and ratio measures of effect size may indicate that an indirect effect is large even when the total effect is small, *ab'* would indicate a small effect, commensurate with intuition. A *very* rough rule of thumb for interpreting *ab'* is to compare it to the product of the correlation relating *X* to *M* and the semipartial correlation relating *M* to *Y* that would be considered meaningful. For example, if both $r_{MX} = 0.2$ and $r_{YM.X} = 0.3$ are considered "small" in a particular research area, then *ab'* values of about 0.06 might reflect a small effect. We urge caution, however, because there are many values that $\tilde{b}_{MX}$ and $\tilde{b}_{YM.X}$ might assume that would yield the same index of mediation. The *ab'* index would perhaps need to be modified in more elaborate models. Quantifying effect size for mediation effects would be a fruitful avenue for future research.

STATISTICAL POWER

As with most inferential statistical techniques, power (the probability of finding a given nonzero effect statistically significant) is of concern in mediation analysis. If an indirect effect exists, we would like to identify it. The causal steps strategy has been found consistently to suffer from low power relative to the alternatives discussed here. This criticism can also be leveled at the product of coefficients approach, partly as a consequence of violating the assumption of normality. However, the product of coefficients strategy tends to have higher power than the causal steps strategy (MacKinnon et al., 2002; Pituch et al., 2005). Distribution of the product strategies have been found to have superior power and Type I error rates when compared to virtually all other methods for assessing mediation (MacKinnon et al., 2002; Pituch et al., 2005), with the possible exception of bootstrapping, which also performs very well (MacKinnon et al., 2004). Most methods of assessing mediation, however, are characterized by Type I error rates that are below nominal levels when both *a* and *b* are zero in the population, but can be too small or too large when either *a* or *b* is nonzero (MacKinnon et al., 2004; Pituch et al., 2006).

Judd and Kenny (1981) note that a large a path is associated with mediation, yet a strong association between X and M also implies some degree of collinearity, which in turn may increase the standard error of b, compromising power for any test of mediation. Measurement error can also reduce power (Judd & Kenny, 1981). Hoyle and Kenny (1999) investigated the power of the product of coefficients strategy in simple mediation models as a function of the reliability of the mediator. They found that even modest unreliability can have drastic consequences for statistical power, especially in small samples (below 200 or so). They recommend that the sample size be at least 100 to achieve adequate power for detecting mediation with a highly reliable mediator, and that the sample size be at least 200 if the mediator has less than optimal reliability. Stone and Sobel (1990) found the product of coefficients strategy to work well with sample sizes as small as 200.

Regardless of the method used to assess mediation, steps often can be taken to increase statistical power. For example, representing X, M, and/or Y as latent variables with multiple indicators may improve power and reduce parameter bias (Kenny et al., 1998), as can judicious inclusion of covariates.

DISTAL VERSUS PROXIMAL MEDIATORS

Mediators that are causally "nearer" to the independent variable than to the dependent variable are called *proximal mediators*, whereas those that are measured very close to the dependent variable are termed *distal mediators*. Proximal and distal may, but will not necessarily, correspond closely to time of measurement. Common examples of the former are manipulation checks, which, if the manipulation is good, are essentially determinate functions of X. Mediators that are "too" proximal or distal may inflate a or b beyond realistic levels, compromising generalizability (Kenny et al., 1998; Kraemer, Wilson, Fairburn, & Agras, 2002). More generally, the time that elapses between measurement of X, M, and Y may have powerful effects on tests of mediation hypotheses. For example, if X is expected to cause immediate effects on M, then it may be important to measure X and M in close succession, whereas if M is expected to exert its effect on Y over time, a longer lag would be appropriate. Identifying the appropriate lag may itself be a considerable research undertaking. Investigators should keep in mind that the generalizability of conclusions drawn about mediation may be quite limited unless careful attention is paid to the time intervals separating measurements (see Cole & Maxwell, 2003; Shrout & Bolger, 2002).

SHOULD THE TOTAL EFFECT BE SIGNIFICANT BEFORE ASKING ABOUT MEDIATION?

Many researchers (e.g., Frazier, Tix, & Barron, 2004; Hyman, 1955; Judd & Kenny, 1981) state that the $X \rightarrow Y$ effect should be significant prior to testing an indirect effect; that is, there first ought to exist an effect for the mediator to explain or the question of whether or not M is a mediator becomes moot. This recommendation is implicit in the Baron and Kenny (1986) criteria. However, others (Kenny et al., 1998) argue that this requirement is not necessary. It is possible for an indirect effect to be statistically significant in the absence of a significant $X \rightarrow Y$ relationship (Sobel, 1986), leading many to consider mediation as a special case of an indirect effect that accompanies a significant $X \rightarrow Y$ relationship. The debate is largely semantic. We urge researchers to consider the predictions of theory and to frame hypotheses accordingly.

There are other situations in which it makes sense to investigate indirect effects in the presence of a nonsignificant $X \rightarrow Y$ effect. In models involving multiple mediators, for example, the indirect effects of two variables may have opposite signs and "cancel out," leading to situations in which there is a negligible direct effect both before and after adding mediators, yet an interesting pattern of large and significant indirect effects. In this situation, one of the intervening variables may act as a *suppressor* and the other as a mediator (Collins, Graham, & Flaherty, 1998; Frazier et al., 2004; MacKinnon, 2000; MacKinnon et al., 2000; Sheets & Braver, 1999; Shrout & Bolger, 2002).

SHOULD WE USE ORDINARY LEAST SQUARES REGRESSION OR STRUCTURAL EQUATION MODELING?

Throughout this chapter, we have assumed that the regression coefficients a and b have been estimated via ordinary least squares (OLS) regression analyses. But there are other ways to obtain these coefficients. In particular, multiple regression may be seen as a special case of path analysis, which in turn is a special application of structural equation modeling (SEM) with no latent variables. OLS regression is usually adequate for conducting a mediation analysis. However, there are some advantages to using SEM. For example, the $X \rightarrow M \rightarrow Y$ simple mediation model may comprise a small part of a larger network of relationships hypothesized to exist among variables. Mediation hypotheses can be assessed in the context of these larger models. Second, in SEM, models can contain a mix of measured and latent variables. Using latent variables with multiple measured indicators can improve the power and validity of a model by dealing effectively with measurement error. Third, as we mentioned earlier, parameter constraints may be added in SEM, permitting the comparison of nested models. Fourth, SEM software often permits the user to choose from among several estimation methods, including OLS, maximum likelihood (ML), generalized least squares (GLS), asymptotically distribution-free (ADF) methods, and others. Different assumptions must be satisfied for the various estimation methods, but mediation may be assessed using any of them. Furthermore, several SEM software applications conduct a product of coefficients test for total indirect effects upon request even for very complex indirect effects. On the other hand, it should be noted that SEM is a large-sample technique. Hoyle and Kenny (1999) found that using SEM to investigate simple mediation in cases where the mediator is specified as a latent variable can be problematic if the sample size is less than 100 or so. Finally, Cheung (2007) describes an elegant and very general method for using SEM to test a variety of mediation effects. We urge the reader to consult an introductory SEM text to learn more (Bollen, 1989; Loehlin, 1998; Maruyama, 1998).

PARTIAL VERSUS COMPLETE MEDIATION

If c' is smaller than c but c' is different from zero, it is sometimes said that the mediator *partially mediates* the effect of X on Y (Judd & Kenny, 1981), or that the evidence is consistent with *partial mediation*. If c' is statistically indistinguishable from zero, *complete* or *full mediation* is said to have occurred (Baron & Kenny, 1986; James & Brett, 1984; Kenny et al., 1998). We regard these coarse designations of effect size as having limited utility, depending as they do on the size of the total effect and on sample size. Using popular criteria, *complete* mediation should occur most often when the total effect is negligible (but statistically significant) and when the sample size is small. Much larger and potentially more important effects may be characterized as partial in larger samples even if they would ordinarily be considered large effects in an absolute sense. Furthermore, the conclusion of complete mediation may quell future research into other possible mediators (Pituch et al., 2005). The recognition that all indirect effects are partial may serve as a cue that other mediators can always be considered or may lead to the hypothesis that mediation is stronger for one group than for another (Shrout & Bolger, 2002). Because the terms *partial* and *complete* denote practical significance but are most often defined in terms of statistical significance, we urge researchers to abandon these terms altogether. Researchers are encouraged to focus instead on clearly distinguishing statistical and practical significance and to consider reporting effect size assessed by means discussed earlier.

THE ROLE OF THEORY

Mediation models are confirmatory models rather than exploratory ones. In other words, it is not appropriate to try all possible assignments of X, M, and Y to roles as independent, dependent, and mediator variables and see what turns out to be significant. The framework assumes that the causal ordering of the variables is known or at least strongly rooted in theory. Given that ordering, the methods described here are useful for helping the researcher decide whether and to what extent the data are *consistent* with mediation (mediation, and indeed any other scientific hypothesis, can never be definitively proved). When the appropriate ordering of variables is not known, theory should be used to determine the proper order (Hoyle & Robinson, 2004).

COMPUTER SOFTWARE

We are somewhat reluctant to address the issue of software for two reasons. First, software changes quickly, and many of our comments on existing software applications may no longer be relevant in the near future. Second, methods used to assess indirect effects are logically independent of the software designed to implement them, and some can be understood and applied without specialized software. Nevertheless, software applications greatly ease the burden of computation and lower the probability of committing errors of calculation. Following is a discussion of software applications that are, at the time of this writing, capable of addressing indirect effects.

Stone (1985) provided a Fortran program (CINDESE) for computing standard errors of indirect effects. MacKinnon and Wang (1989a, 1989b) and J. Scott Long (in Sobel, 1988) provide SAS/IML code for conducting tests of indirect effects using output from SEM software. Similar code is now incorporated in LISREL (Jöreskog & Sörbom, 1996), EQS (Bentler, 1997), AMOS (Arbuckle, 1999), and Mplus (Muthén & Muthén, 2004). Tests of indirect effects in these applications are limited to tests of total indirect effects, the exception being Mplus (which can also conduct tests of specific indirect effects), but all of them can handle models with multiple mediators in complicated configurations and allow for control variables. Preacher and Leonardelli (2001) authored a JavaScript Web page that provides tests of indirect effects in single-mediator models using first-order, second-order, and bias-corrected variances. Preacher and Hayes (2004) provide SPSS and SAS code for conducting the causal steps approach as well as the Sobel test. Similarly, Dudley, Benuzillo, and Carrico (2004) describe SPSS and SAS macros (Dudley & Benuzillo, 2002) that perform tests of the indirect effect in single-mediator models. Their macros also provide two measures of effect size, the percentage of the total effect that is mediated and the ratio of the indirect effect to the direct effect. MacKinnon, Fritz, Williams, and Lockwood (in press) provide SPSS, SAS, and R macros for generating confidence intervals using the distribution of products method.

Resampling approaches to assessing indirect effects are somewhat newer. Lockwood and MacKinnon (1998) provide an SAS macro (BOOTME) to bootstrap confidence intervals in single-mediator models. Their code also provides a confidence interval for the indirect effect using the first-order variance and has been recently updated (MacKinnon et al., 2004). Shrout and Bolger (2002) provide EQS and SPSS syntax for bootstrapping confidence intervals of indirect effects, as well as instructions for using AMOS (Arbuckle, 1999) for the same purpose. Preacher and Hayes (2004) provide SPSS and SAS macros that bootstrap confidence intervals and provide normal-theory results for the product of coefficients method. SAS code provided by Morgan-Lopez (2003) conducts a test of the indirect effect using the first-order variance and provides asymmetric confidence intervals using the bootstrap and bias-corrected bootstrap methods (and, assuming one has the Meeker et al. [1981], tables in the proper format, constructs intervals from the distribution of the product). Specialized SAS and SPSS macros also exist to bootstrap confidence intervals for total and specific indirect effects in multiple mediator models with and without statistical controls (Preacher & Hayes, 2007) and for conditional indirect effects in moderated mediation models (Preacher et al., 2007). SAS code for investigating mediation in multilevel models is provided by Bauer et al. (2006) and Kenny et al. (2003). Cheung (2007) provides LISREL, Mplus, and Mx code for testing a variety of mediation hypotheses in SEM using normal-theory methods, bootstrapping, and asymmetric likelihood-based confidence intervals.

Concluding Remarks

In this chapter, we have considered and evaluated strategies that can be used to address mediation hypotheses in communication research. We considered causal steps, correlational, difference in coefficients, nested model, product of coefficients, distribution of the product, and bootstrapping strategies for estimating and testing indirect effects. We have also discussed several topics relevant to indirect effects, including reporting effect size and considering statistical power. We covered several useful extensions of the basic mediation model that are receiving increasing attention in the methodological literature, including mediated moderation, moderated mediation, mediation in multilevel data structures, and models with multiple mediators. We briefly touched on issues concerning causality and several other points of contention and confusion. Finally, we discussed software implementation. Throughout, we occasionally illustrated key points with a running example.

No mediation model is ever correct, for the simple reason that no model is ever correct, period. Models serve as approximations to processes and should not be expected to precisely mirror the underlying processes giving rise to observed data (MacCallum, 2003). Models are merely parsimonious metaphors to reality created for the purpose of testing and comparing ideas, so it is arguably meaningless to ask whether a model is "correct." We do not intend to imply that investigating mediation is a pointless undertaking, merely that the researcher should keep in mind that models are simply tools to clarify our understanding of phenomena and that some models are better tools than others. Mediation models may be incorrect for a variety of reasons, including reasons of causal misspecification, confounds, and omitted variables that threaten any research enterprise (Judd & Kenny, 1981). In addition, mediation models carry with them a host of often untested assumptions. The inference procedures may involve assumptions of normality, heteroscedasticity, and independence of regression residuals. We assume that our samples are representative of the population toward which inference and generalization are desired. We usually assume that a linear model conveys all the information useful for making conclusions about mediation. Strictly speaking, none of these assumptions is ever exactly met in practice, but steps can be taken to minimize the impact of violating these assumptions in specific applications. By the same token, no mediation model is ever complete, in the sense that yet more mediators may always be introduced to explain any direct effect in a mediation model. Again, we say this not as a deterrent to investigating mediation but rather to suggest that introducing more proximal mediators may help the researcher better understand the process under scrutiny (see Hyman, 1955, pp. 325–327).

RECOMMENDED READING

We have attempted to provide an overview of many (but definitely not all) of the issues involved in assessing mediation effects in communication research. We did not go into depth on these topics, and we avoided the underlying mathematics. However, we provided a number of relevant citations under each heading; the interested reader is urged to consult them for more detail. For good overviews of mediation analysis we recommend Baron and Kenny (1986), Frazier et al. (2004), Judd and Kenny (1981), MacKinnon et al. (2002), MacKinnon, Fairchild, and Fritz (2007), Mallinckrodt, Abraham, Wei, and Russell (2006), and Shrout and Bolger (2002). For issues of design, we recommend Cole and Maxwell (2003) and Hoyle and Robinson (2004). An old and extensive literature exists on quantifying indirect effects, using the multivariate delta method, and computing the variances of products of random variables. For readers who wish to delve more into the quantitative aspects surrounding mediation analysis, we recommend consulting MacKinnon et al. (1995), Sobel (1982, 1986), Bollen (1987), Preacher and Hayes (2006), and Preacher et al. (2007), as well as sources cited therein.

Notes

1. We use the terms *mediation* and *indirect effect* interchangeably here. Holmbeck (1997, p. 603) points out, however, that the two should be disentangled. Cole and Maxwell (2003, p. 558) usefully define an *indirect effect* as "the

degree to which a change in an exogenous variable produces a change in an endogenous variable by means of an intervening variable."

2. In their article, Kalyanaraman and Sundar (2006) proposed two additional mediators—*perceived involvement* and *perceived relevance*. We excluded these mediators in this example because, in our judgment, these constructs overlap with the manipulation in such a way that it could be argued that their experimental manipulation of customization also manipulated involvement and relevance.

3. In rare cases, it is even possible to observe c (nonsignificant) > c' (significant) or c (significant) < c' (nonsignificant).

4. Model B is said to be nested in Model A if its free parameters are a subset of those in Model A. Any model in which parameters are constrained to zero will fit worse than a model with fewer or no zero-constraints on the same set of parameters.

5. Later, we argue that the distinction between complete and partial mediation is not a useful distinction to make.

6. To our knowledge, Hyman (1955, p. 284) was the first to suggest quantifying mediation by multiplying a and b paths: ". . . the original relationship is seen to be the result of the marginal terms—the product of the relationships between the test factor and each of the original variables. Symbolically, $[xy] = 0 + 0 + [xt][ty]$," where the 0s represent partial or conditional relationships (assumed constant in the simple mediation context) and xt and ty represent the a and b paths, respectively.

7. The standard error will be the square root of this asymptotic variance estimate.

8. MacKinnon and Dwyer (1993) present this measure as a percentage rather than as a proportion.

Appendix

Output from an SPSS macro for conducting a multiple mediation analysis (Preacher & Hayes, 2007). The macro, also available for SAS, can be downloaded from http://www.comm.ohio-state.edu/ahayes/.

```
indirect y = attitude/x = custom/m = inter novel commune/
   contrast = 1/normal = 1/boot = 5000.

Run MATRIX procedure:

Dependent, Independent, and Proposed Mediator Variables:
DV    = attitude
IV    = custom
MEDS  = inter
        novel
        commune

Sample size
        60
```

```
IV to Mediators (a paths)
              Coeff      se         t         p
  inter       .4013     .0778    5.1592    .0000
  novel       .6446     .0704    9.1555    .0000
  commune     .5829     .0604    9.6462    .0000
Direct Effects of Mediators on DV (b paths)
              Coeff      se         t         p
  inter       .2535     .0924    2.7447    .0082
  novel       .1700     .1019    1.6688    .1008
  commune     .1699     .1154    1.4721    .1467
Total Effect of IV on DV (c path)
              Coeff      se         t         p
  custom      .5119     .0588    8.7138    .0000
Direct Effect of IV on DV (c' path)
              Coeff      se         t         p
  custom      .2016     .1061    1.8993    .0628
Fit Statistics for DV Model
    R-sq    Adj R-sq      F        df1       df2       p
    .6666     .6424    27.4948   4.0000   55.0000   .0000
*********************************************************
        NORMAL THEORY TESTS FOR INDIRECT EFFECTS
Indirect Effects of IV on DV through Proposed Mediators
(ab paths)
              Effect     se         Z         p
  TOTAL       .3104     .0931    3.3330    .0009
  inter       .1018     .0408    2.4948    .0126
  novel       .1096     .0645    1.6989    .0893
  commune     .0990     .0657    1.5063    .1320
  C1         -.0078     .0830   -.0944     .9248
  C2          .0027     .0793    .0346     .9724
  C3          .0106     .0933    .1134     .9097
*********************************************************
          BOOTSTRAP RESULTS FOR INDIRECT EFFECTS
Indirect Effects of IV on DV through Proposed Mediators
(ab paths)
              Data      Boot      Bias       SE
  TOTAL       .3104     .3099   -.0005     .0996
  inter       .1018     .1012   -.0005     .0474
  novel       .1096     .1123    .0027     .0594
  commune     .0990     .0963   -.0027     .0571
  C1         -.0078    -.0111   -.0033     .0736
  C2          .0027     .0049    .0021     .0707
  C3          .0106     .0160    .0054     .0822
```

```
Bias Corrected and Accelerated Confidence Intervals
              Lower     Upper
    TOTAL     .1164     .5069
    inter     .0286     .2197
    novel    -.0050     .2303
    commune   .0015     .2311
    C1       -.1487     .1444
    C2       -.1348     .1479
    C3       -.1693     .1626

******************************************************

Level of Confidence for Confidence Intervals:
   95

Number of Bootstrap Resamples:
5000

******************************************************

  INDIRECT EFFECT CONTRAST DEFINITIONS: Ind_Eff1 MINUS
                    Ind_Eff2

    Contrast    IndEff_1    IndEff_2
    C1          inter       novel
    C2          inter       commune
    C3          novel       commune
 ---- END MATRIX ----
```

References

Aiken, L. S., & West, S. G. (1991). *Multiple regression: Testing and interpreting interactions.* Newbury Park, CA: Sage.

Alwin, D. F., & Hauser, R. M. (1975). The decomposition of effects in path analysis. *American Sociological Review, 40,* 37–47.

Arbuckle, J. L. (1999). *AMOS 4* [Computer software]. Chicago: Smallwaters Corp.

Aroian, L. A. (1947). The probability function of the product of two normally distributed variables. *Annals of Mathematical Statistics, 18,* 265–271.

Aron, A., & Monin, B. (2005, January). *Mediational analysis in social psychology experiments: Two limitations and strategies to address them.* Poster session presented at the annual meeting of the Society for Personality and Social Psychology, New Orleans, LA.

Azen, R. (2003, August). *Multiple mediator models: A comparison of testing approaches.* Poster presented at the 111th Annual Convention of the American Psychological Association, Toronto, Ontario.

Baron, R. M., & Kenny, D. A. (1986). The moderator-mediator distinction in social psychological research: Conceptual, strategic, and statistical considerations. *Journal of Personality and Social Psychology, 51,* 1173–1182.

Bauer, D. J., Preacher, K. J., & Gil, K. M. (2006). Conceptualizing and testing random indirect effects and moderated mediation in multilevel models: New procedures and recommendations. *Psychological Methods, 11,* 142–163.

Beaudoin, C. E., & Thorson, E. (2004). Testing the cognitive mediation model: The roles of news reliance and three gratifications sought. *Communication Research, 31,* 446–471.

Bentler, P. (1997). *EQS for Windows* (Version 5.6) [Computer software]. Los Angeles: Multivariate Software, Inc.

Bobko, P., & Rieck, A. (1980). Large sample estimators for standard errors of functions of correlation coefficients. *Applied Psychological Measurement, 4,* 385–398.

Bollen, K. A. (1987). Total direct and indirect effects in structural equation models. In C. C. Clogg (Ed.), *Sociological methodology* (pp. 37–69). Washington, DC: American Sociological Association.

Bollen, K. A. (1989). *Structural equations with latent variables.* New York: Wiley.

Bollen, K. A., & Stine, R. (1990). Direct and indirect effects: Classical and bootstrap estimates of variability. *Sociological Methodology, 20,* 115–140.

Briggs, N. E. (2006). *Estimation of the standard error and confidence interval of the indirect effect in multiple mediator models.* Unpublished doctoral dissertation, Ohio State University, Columbus, OH.

Brown, R. L. (1997). Assessing specific mediational effects in complex theoretical models. *Structural Equation Modeling, 4,* 142–156.

Chang, C. (2001). The impacts of emotion elicited by print political advertising on candidate evaluation. *Media Psychology, 3,* 91–118.

Cheung, M. W.-L. (2007). Comparison of approaches to constructing confidence intervals for mediating effects using structural equation models. *Structural Equation Modeling, 14,* 227–246.

Clogg, C. C., Petkova, E., & Shihadeh, E. S. (1992). Statistical methods for analyzing collapsibility in regression models. *Journal of Educational Statistics, 17,* 51–74.

Cole, D. A., & Maxwell, S. E. (2003). Testing mediational models with longitudinal data: Questions and tips in the use of structural equation modeling. *Journal of Abnormal Psychology, 112,* 558–577.

Collins, L. M., Graham, J. W., & Flaherty, B. P. (1998). An alternative framework for defining mediation. *Multivariate Behavioral Research, 33,* 295–312.

Craig, C. C. (1936). On the frequency of xy. *The Annals of Mathematical Statistics, 7,* 1–15.

Dudley, W., & Benuzillo, J. (2002, December). *Sobel test of mediated effects* [Computer software]. Available from http://www.ats.ucla.edu/stat/sas/code/sobel.htm and http://www.nurs.utah.edu/faculty/dudley/sas.html

Dudley, W. N., Benuzillo, J. G., & Carrico, M. S. (2004). SPSS and SAS programming for the testing of mediation models. *Nursing Research, 53,* 59–62.

Edwards, J. R., & Lambert, L. S. (2007). Methods for integrating moderation and mediation: A general analytical framework using moderated path analysis. *Psychological Methods, 12,* 1–22.

Efron, B. (1987). Better bootstrap confidence intervals. *Journal of the American Statistical Association, 82,* 171–185.

Efron, B., & Tibshirani, R. J. (1998). *An introduction to the bootstrap.* Boca Raton, FL: CRC Press.

Eveland, W. P. (2001). The cognitive mediation model of learning from the news. *Communication Research, 28,* 571–601.

Eveland, W. P., Shah, D. V., & Kwak, N. (2003). Assessing causality in the cognitive mediation model. *Communication Research, 30,* 359–386.

Folmer, H. (1981). Measurement of the effects of regional policy instruments by means of linear structural equation models and panel data. *Environment and Planning A, 13,* 1435–1448.

Frazier, P. A., Tix, A. P., & Barron, K. E. (2004). Testing moderator and mediator effects in counseling psychology research. *Journal of Counseling Psychology, 51,* 115–134.

Freedman, L. S., & Schatzkin, A. (1992). Sample size for studying intermediate endpoints within intervention trials of observational studies. *American Journal of Epidemiology, 136,* 1148–1159.

Good, P. I. (2001). *Resampling methods: A practical guide to data analysis.* Boston: Birkhäuser.

Goodman, L. A. (1960). On the exact variance of products. *Journal of the American Statistical Association, 55,* 708–713.

Hart, Z. P., & Miller, V. D. (2005). Context and message content during organizational socialization: A research note. *Human Communication Research, 31,* 295–309.

Hayes, A. F. (2005). *Statistical methods for communication science.* Mahwah, NJ: Erlbaum.

Holbert, R. L., Shah, D. V., & Kwak, N. (2003). Political implications of prime-time drama and sitcom use: Genres of representation and opinions concerning women's rights. *Journal of Communication, 53,* 45–60.

Holbert, R. L., & Stephenson, M. T. (2003). The importance of indirect effects in media effects research: Testing for mediation in structural equation modeling. *Journal of Broadcasting & Electronic Media, 47,* 556–572.

Holmbeck, G. N. (1997). Toward terminological, conceptual, and statistical clarity in the study of mediators and moderators: Examples from the child-clinical and pediatric psychology literatures. *Journal of Consulting & Clinical Psychology, 65,* 599–610.

Holmbeck, G. N. (2002). Post-hoc probing of significant moderational and mediational effects in studies of pediatric populations. *Journal of Pediatric Psychology, 27,* 87–96.

Hoyle, R. H., & Kenny, D. A. (1999). Sample size, reliability, and tests of statistical mediation. In R. Hoyle (Ed.), *Statistical strategies for small sample research.* Thousand Oaks, CA: Sage Publications.

Hoyle, R. H., & Robinson, J. C. (2004). Mediated and moderated effects in social psychological research: Measurement, design, and analysis issues. In C. Sansone, C. C. Morf, & A. T. Panter (Eds.), *The Sage handbook of methods in social psychology* (pp. 213–233). Thousand Oaks, CA: Sage.

Hyman, H. (1955). *Survey design and analysis: Principles, cases and procedures.* Glencoe, IL: The Free Press.

James, L. R., & Brett, J. M. (1984). Mediators, moderators, and tests for mediation. *Journal of Applied Psychology, 69,* 307–321.

Johnson, P. O., & Neyman, J. (1936). Tests of certain linear hypotheses and their applications to some educational problems. *Statistical Research Memoirs, 1,* 57–93.

Jöreskog, K. G., & Sörbom, D. (1996). *LISREL 8 user's reference guide.* Uppsala, Sweden: Scientific Software International.

Judd, C. M., & Kenny, D. A. (1981). Process analysis: Estimating mediation in treatment evaluations. *Evaluation Review, 5,* 602–619.

Judd, C. M., Kenny, D. A., & McClelland, G. H. (2001). Estimating and testing mediation and moderation in within-subject designs. *Psychological Methods, 6,* 115–134.

Kalyanaraman, S., & Sundar, S. S. (2006). The psychological appeal of personalized online content in Web portals: Does customization affect attitudes and behavior? *Journal of Communication, 56,* 1–23.

Kenny, D. A., Kashy, D. A., & Bolger, N. (1998). Data analysis in social psychology. In D. Gilbert, S. T. Fiske, & G. Lindzey (Eds.), *The handbook of social psychology* (4th ed., Vol. 1, pp. 223–265). New York: McGraw-Hill.

Kenny, D. A., Korchmaros, J. D., & Bolger, N. (2003). Lower level mediation in multilevel models. *Psychological Methods, 8,* 115–128.

Kiousis, S., McDevitt, M., & Wu, X. (2005). The genesis of civic awareness: Agenda setting in political socialization. *Journal of Communication, 55,* 756–774.

Knobloch, L. K., & Carpenter-Thune, K. E. (2004). Topic avoidance in developing romantic relationships. Associations with intimacy and relational uncertainty. *Communication Research, 31,* 173–205.

Kraemer, H. C., Wilson, T., Fairburn, C. G., & Agras, W. S. (2002). Mediators and moderators of treatment effects in randomized clinical trials. *Archives of General Psychiatry, 59,* 877–883.

Krull, J. L., & MacKinnon, D. P. (1999). Multilevel mediation modeling in group-based intervention studies. *Evaluation Review, 23,* 418–444.

Krull, J. L., & MacKinnon, D. P. (2001). Multilevel modeling of individual and group level mediated effects. *Multivariate Behavioral Research, 36,* 249–277.

Lee, K. M., & Nass, C. (2004). The multiple source effect and synthesized speech: Doubly-disembodied language as a conceptual framework. *Human Communication Research, 30,* 182–207.

Lockwood, C. M., & MacKinnon, D. P. (1998). Bootstrapping the standard error of the mediated effect. In *Proceedings of the 23rd Annual SAS Users Group International Conference 1992* (pp. 997–1002). Cary, NC: SAS Institute, Inc.

Lockwood, C. M., & MacKinnon, D. P. (2000). *A detailed description of the discrepancy in formulas for the standard error of the difference between a raw and partial correlation: A typographical error in Olkin and Finn* (1995). (Technical Report). Tempe: Arizona State University.

Loehlin, J. C. (1998). *Latent variable models: An introduction to factor, path, and structural analysis* (3rd ed.). Mahwah, NJ: Lawrence Erlbaum.

Lunneborg, C. A. (2000). *Data analysis by resampling: Concepts and applications.* Pacific Grove, CA: Duxbury.

MacCallum, R. C. (2003). Working with imperfect models. *Multivariate Behavioral Research, 38,* 113–139.

MacCorquodale, K., & Meehl, P. E. (1948). On a distinction between hypothetical constructs and intervening variables. *Psychological Review, 55,* 95–107.

MacKinnon, D. P. (1994). Analysis of mediating variables in prevention and intervention research. In A. Cazares & L. A. Beatty, *Scientific methods for prevention intervention research. NIDA Research Monograph 139,* pp. 127–153. Rockville, MD: Superintendent of Documents, U.S. Government Printing Office.

MacKinnon, D. P. (2000). Contrasts in multiple mediator models. In J. Rose, L. Chassin, C. C. Presson, & S. J. Sherman (Eds.), *Multivariate applications in substance use research: New methods for new questions* (pp. 141–160). Mahwah, NJ: Lawrence Erlbaum.

MacKinnon, D. P., & Dwyer, J. H. (1993). Estimating mediated effects in prevention studies. *Evaluation Review, 17,* 144–158.

MacKinnon, D. P., Fairchild, A. J., & Fritz, M. S. (2007). Mediation analysis. *Annual Review of Psychology, 58,* 593–614.

MacKinnon, D. P., Fritz, M. S., Williams, J., & Lockwood, C. M. (in press). Distribution of the product confidence limits for the indirect effect: Program PRODCLIN. *Behavior Research Methods.*

MacKinnon, D. P., Krull, J. L., & Lockwood, C. M. (2000). Equivalence of the mediation, confounding, and suppression effect. *Prevention Science, 1,* 173–181.

MacKinnon, D. P., Lockwood, C., & Hoffman, J. (1998, June). *A new method to test for mediation.* Presented at the Annual Meeting of the Society for Prevention Research, Park City, UT.

MacKinnon, D. P., Lockwood, C. M., Hoffman, J. M., West, S. G., & Sheets, V. (2002). A comparison of methods to test mediation and other intervening variable effects. *Psychological Methods, 7,* 83–104.

MacKinnon, D. P., Lockwood, C. M., & Williams, J. (2004). Confidence limits for the indirect effect: Distribution of the product and resampling methods. *Multivariate Behavioral Research, 39,* 99–128.

MacKinnon, D. P., & Wang, E. Y.-I. (1989a). *INDIRECT: A program to calculate indirect effects and their standard errors* [Computer program].

MacKinnon, D. P., & Wang, E. Y.-I. (1989b). A SAS/IML matrix program to estimate indirect effects and their standard errors. In *SUGI 14: Proceedings of the Statistical Analysis System Conference* (pp. 1151–1156). Cary, NC: SAS Institute, Inc.

MacKinnon, D. P., Warsi, G., & Dwyer, J. H. (1995). A simulation study of mediated effect measures. *Multivariate Behavioral Research, 30,* 41–62.

Mallinckrodt, B., Abraham, W. T., Wei, M., & Russell, D. W. (2006). Advances in testing the statistical significance of mediation effects. *Journal of Counseling Psychology, 53,* 372–378.

Maruyama, G. M. (1998). *Basics of structural equation modeling.* Thousand Oaks, CA: Sage.

McGuigan, K., & Langholtz, B. (1988). *A note on testing mediation paths using ordinary least-squares regression.* Unpublished note.

McLeod, J. M., Kosicki, J. M., & Pan, Z. (1996). On understanding and misunderstanding media effects. In J. Curran & M. Gurevitch (Eds.), *Mass media and society* (pp. 235–266). London: Edward Arnold.

McLeod, J. M., & Reeves, B. (1980). On the nature of mass media effects. In S. B. Withey & R. P. Abeles (Eds.), *Television and social behavior: Beyond violence and children* (pp. 17–54). Hillsdale, NJ: Lawrence Erlbaum.

Meeker, W. Q., Cornwell, L. W., & Aroian, L. A. (1981). *Selected tables in mathematical statistics, Vol. VII: The product of two normally distributed random variables.* Providence, RI: American Mathematical Society.

Millar, M. (2002). Effects of guilt induction and guilt reduction on door in the face. *Communication Research, 29,* 666–680.

Mooney, C. Z., & Duval, R. D. (1993). *Bootstrapping: A nonparametric approach to statistical inference.* Newbury Park, CA: Sage.

Morgan-Lopez, A. A. (2003). *A simulation study of the mediated baseline by treatment interaction effect in preventive intervention trials.* Unpublished doctoral dissertation, Arizona State University, Tempe.

Morgan-Lopez, A. A., & MacKinnon, D. P. (2006) Demonstration and evaluation of a method to assess mediated moderation. *Behavior Research Methods, 38,* 77–87.

Muller, D., Judd, C. M., & Yzerbyt, V. Y. (2005). When moderation is mediated and mediation is moderated. *Journal of Personality and Social Psychology, 89,* 852–863.

Muthén, L. K., & Muthén, B. O. (2004). *Mplus user's guide* (3rd ed.). Los Angeles: Authors.

Olkin, I., & Finn, J. D. (1995). Correlation redux. *Psychological Bulletin, 118,* 155–164.

Park, H., Eveland, Jr., W. P., & Cudeck, R. (2007). Multilevel modeling in communication research. In A. F. Hayes, M. D. Slater, & L. B. Snyder (Eds.), *The SAGE handbook of advanced data analysis methods for communication research* (pp. 219–246). Thousand Oaks, CA: Sage.

Pituch, K. A. (2004). Textbook presentations on supplemental hypothesis testing activities, nonnormality, and the concept of mediation. *Understanding Statistics, 3,* 135–150.

Pituch, K. A., Stapleton, L. M., & Kang, J. Y. (2006). A comparison of single sample and bootstrap methods to assess mediation in cluster randomized trials. *Multivariate Behavioral Research, 41,* 367–400.

Pituch, K. A., Whittaker, T. A., & Stapleton, L. M. (2005). A comparison of methods to test for mediation in multisite experiments. *Multivariate Behavioral Research, 40,* 1–23.

Preacher, K. J., & Hayes, A. F. (2004). SPSS and SAS procedures for estimating indirect effects in simple mediation models. *Behavior Research Methods, Instruments, & Computers, 36,* 717–731.

Preacher, K. J., & Hayes, A. F. (2007). *Asymptotic and resampling strategies for assessing and comparing indirect effects in multiple mediator models.* Manuscript submitted for publication.

Preacher, K. J., & Leonardelli, G. J. (2001, March). *Calculation for the Sobel test: An interactive calculation tool for mediation tests* [Computer software]. Available from http://www.quantpsy.org/

Preacher, K. J., Rucker, D. D., & Hayes, A. F. (2007). Assessing moderated mediation hypotheses: Theory, methods, and prescriptions. *Multivariate Behavioral Research, 42,* 185–227.

Raudenbush, S. W., & Sampson, R. (1999). Assessing direct and indirect effects in multilevel designs with latent variables. *Sociological Methods & Research, 28,* 123–153.

Rodgers, J. L. (1999). The bootstrap, the jackknife, and the randomization test: A sampling taxonomy. *Multivariate Behavioral Research, 34,* 441–456.

Rogosa, D. (1980). Comparing nonparallel regression lines. *Psychological Bulletin, 88,* 307–321.

Rogosa, D. (1981). On the relationship between the Johnson-Neyman region of significance and statistical tests of parallel within group regressions. *Educational and Psychological Measurement, 41,* 73–84.

Rose, B., Holmbeck, G. N., Coakley, R. M., & Franks, L. (2004). Mediator and moderator effects in developmental and behavioral pediatric research. *Journal of Developmental and Behavioral Pediatrics, 25*, 1–10.

Rozeboom, W. W. (1956). Mediation variables in scientific theory. *Psychological Review, 63*, 249–264.

Scheufele, D. A. (2002). Examining differential gains from mass media and their implications for participatory behavior. *Communication Research, 29*, 46–65.

Shah, D. V., Cho, J., Eveland, W. P., Jr., & Kwak, N. (2005). Information and expression in a digital age modeling Internet effects on civic participation. *Communication Research, 32*, 531–565.

Sheets, V. L., & Braver, S. L. (1999). Organizational status and perceived sexual harassment: Detecting the mediators of a null effect. *Personality and Social Psychology Bulletin, 25*, 1159–1171.

Shrout, P. E., & Bolger, N. (2002). Mediation in experimental and nonexperimental studies: New procedures and recommendations. *Psychological Methods, 7*, 422–445.

Slater, M. D., Hayes, A. F., & Ford, V. (2007). Examining the moderating and mediating roles of news exposure and attention on adolescent judgments of alcohol-related risks. *Communication Research, 34*, 355–381.

Slater, M. D., & Rasinski, K. A. (2005). Media exposure and attention as mediating variables influencing social risk judgments. *Journal of Communication, 55*, 810–827.

Sobel, M. E. (1982). Asymptotic confidence intervals for indirect effects in structural equation models. *Sociological Methodology, 13*, 290–313.

Sobel, M. E. (1986). Some new results on indirect effects and their standard errors in covariance structure models. In N. B. Tuma (Ed.), *Sociological methodology*. San Francisco: Jossey-Bass.

Sobel, M. E. (1988). Direct and indirect effects in linear structural equation models. In J. S. Long (Ed.), *Common problems / proper solutions: Avoiding error in quantitative research* (pp. 46–64). Newbury Park, CA: Sage.

Spencer, S. J., Zanna, M. P., & Fong, G. T. (2005). Establishing a causal chain: Why experiments are often more effective than mediational analyses in examining psychological processes. *Journal of Personality and Social Psychology, 89*, 845–851.

Springer, M. D. (1979). *The algebra of random variables.* New York: John Wiley & Sons.

Springer, M. D., & Thompson, W. E. (1966). The distribution of independent random variables. *SIAM Journal on Applied Mathematics, 14*, 511–526.

Stine, R. A. (1989). An introduction to bootstrap methods: Examples and ideas. *Sociological Methods and Research, 18*, 243–291.

Stone, C. A. (1985). CINDESE: Computing indirect effects and standard errors in the Jöreskog covariance structure model. *Educational and Psychological Measurement, 45*, 601–606.

Stone, C. A., & Sobel, M. E. (1990). The robustness of estimates of total indirect effects in covariance structure models estimated by maximum likelihood. *Psychometrika, 55*, 337–352.

Taylor, A. B., MacKinnon, D. P., & Tein, J. T. (in press). Tests of the three-path mediated effect. *Organizational Research Methods.*

Tein, J.-Y., Sandler, I. N., MacKinnon, D. P., & Wolchik, S. A. (2004). How did it work? Who did it work for? Mediation in the context of a moderated prevention effect for children of divorce. *Journal of Consulting and Clinical Psychology, 72,* 617–624.

Wegener, D. T., & Fabrigar, L. R. (2000). Analysis and design for nonexperimental data: Addressing causal and noncausal hypotheses. In H. T. Reis & C. M. Judd (Eds.), *Handbook of research methods in social and personality psychology* (pp. 412–450). New York: Cambridge University Press.

Wilkinson, L., & the APA Task Force on Statistical Inference (1999). Statistical methods in psychology journals: Guidelines and explanations. *American Psychologist, 54,* 594–604.

Williams, J. (2004). Resampling and distribution of the product methods for testing indirect effects in complex models. Unpublished doctoral dissertation, Arizona State University, Tempe, AZ.

Assessing Change and Intraindividual Variation

3

Longitudinal Multilevel and Structural Equation Modeling

Kimberly L. Henry

Michael D. Slater

Communication processes and their influence on people as individuals and on collectivities are dynamic and unfold with time. Within the field of communication research, studies of change assess a multitude of processes. These include, for example, (a) investigation of the development of communication skills during childhood, (b) the evolution of communication patterns over the course of personal relationships, (c) examination of attitudinal and behavioral change in response to a health communication or political campaign, or (d) exploration of the effect of exposure to violent media on change in aggressive behavior. These questions as well as many others in the field of communication require a longitudinal framework in order to properly study the mechanisms of communication influence on human behavior, as well as the influence of human dispositional, experiential, and environmental differences on choices regarding communication behavior.

Although at one time the quantitative study of change was problematic given the lack of appropriate techniques (Singer & Willett, 2003), the development of innovative and accessible longitudinal methodologies has

Authors' Note: This research was supported by grants K01 DA017810–01A1 (awarded to Kimberly L. Henry) and R01 DA12360 (awarded to Michael D. Slater) from the National Institute on Drug Abuse.

flourished over the past 25 years. One of the primary methodological developments is a class of models known as *latent growth models*. These models have allowed researchers to make great strides in modeling and understanding hypotheses that concern individual growth, development, and change. Researchers use these models to study change for a multitude of reasons. In its simplest form, a growth model captures the status of a variable at a particular point in time (referred to as the intercept) and the pattern of change over time (as described by, e.g., linear, quadratic, or even piecewise change parameters).

A researcher interested in adolescent drug prevention may want to understand how attitudes toward antidrug advertising on television changes from late childhood to adolescence. By measuring these attitudes over multiple occasions from age 10 to age 16, the researcher can capture the average patterns of change in the sample (i.e., describing an average curve of change in attitudes during this period of time). Perhaps, on average, children tend to express desirable or healthy attitudes toward the advertising messages (i.e., they believe the messages) during childhood, but as they make the transition into adolescence, these healthy attitudes begin to deteriorate. Understanding developmental change is a key benefit of growth modeling.

In addition to describing the average patterns of change in the population, growth models also capture the interindividual (or between-person) variation in change. This feature allows a researcher to understand how much individuals differ from the average pattern in the population. For example, in the present scenario, a growth model would allow the researcher to examine the extent to which young people differ in the way that their attitudes toward antidrug advertising changes from childhood to adolescence. This type of basic model is called an *unconditional growth model* because it doesn't consider any other predictors. An unconditional growth model that demonstrates significant variance around the average curve (i.e., individuals demonstrate different rates or patterns of change) should motivate a researcher to test hypotheses of *interindividual* differences in *intraindividual* (or within-person) change. For example, imagine that the researcher found that the largest decline in healthy attitudes about antidrug messages occurred between the ages of 12 and 14 and hypothesized that an intervention designed to expose adolescents of this age to more targeted antidrug messages (i.e., messages that appeal to adolescents in this age range) would help them to maintain healthy attitudes toward the messages and ultimately reduce drug use. After drawing a sample of 11-year-old students and randomly assigning students to a treatment condition (i.e., students exposed to the targeted advertising) or control condition (i.e., students exposed to the regularly broadcasted advertising), the researcher exposes the treatment students to the targeted messages over the course of the next 3 years. She also interviews the students in both conditions every 6 months from ages 11 through 14. At the end of the study, she analyzes the data using a growth model.

She begins her analysis by specifying an unconditional growth model of healthy attitudes toward antidrug advertising, paying particular attention to the amount of variance in the rate of decline of these healthy attitudes. Next, she assesses the extent to which the interindividual variation in the rate of change (e.g., the extent to which students' healthy attitudes deteriorate) can be predicted by exposure to the targeted messages. Her hypothesis is supported if the students exposed to the targeted messages demonstrate either maintained healthy attitudes toward the advertising (while the control students demonstrate deterioration) or deteriorate at a slower rate than the students in the control condition.

By extending this example, we may consider another valuable application of growth modeling. Imagine that after finding that the targeted prevention did help students to maintain healthy attitudes toward the antidrug advertisements, the researcher seeks to determine if this maintenance has a mitigating effect on increased drug use during adolescence. To test her hypothesis, she specifies two growth models, one for change in attitudes toward the advertising and one for change in drug use. By correlating the growth parameters (e.g., the rate of change), she may assess the extent to which maintenance of healthy attitudes is associated with a slower rate of increase in drug use. That is, if her hypothesis is correct, then a negative correlation between rate of deterioration of desirable attitudes and rate of change of drug use will exist. In other words, students whose healthy attitudes rapidly decline during adolescence are more likely to increase their use of drugs.

Although it is beyond the scope of this chapter, rate of change of healthy attitudes could also be tested as a mediator (i.e., an explanatory factor) of the effect of exposure to the targeted advertisements (i.e., the treatment) on change in drug use. That is, the researcher could determine if the effect of her intervention had a positive effect on drug use *because* adolescents exposed to the targeted advertisements maintained desirable attitudes toward the campaign. This technique is thoroughly described by Cheong, MacKinnon, and Khoo (2003).

Let us consider one final modeling strategy. Imagine that the researcher decided to conduct a follow-up study to examine varying levels of exposure to the targeted advertisements. She hypothesizes that students will demonstrate less drug use during the period(s) of heightened exposure to the ads. To test her hypothesis, she creates a study in which a sample of adolescents is exposed to varying amounts of advertising for a period of 6 months. The exposure is manipulated such that it varies on a semicontinuous scale ranging from no exposure to high exposure. She carefully keeps track of the total amount of exposure during each month of the study. In addition, at the end of each month the students record their drug use. After the 6 months of intervention, she assesses her hypothesis using a growth model of drug use. In this example, her predictor of interest is a *time-varying covariate* (amount of exposure at each month). She examines the effect of degree of exposure by regressing the time-varying measure of drug use on the time-varying measure of exposure. In this way, she can determine if students' use of drugs was attenuated during times when they were more heavily exposed to the advertisements.

This series of examples describes an applied research study. The implications for theory development and testing, however, should be apparent with a little thought. Theories of political socialization, of human relationship development and change, of parent-child communication, and certainly nearly any theory of media effects could be extended, reconceptualized if need be, and studied using such models, with substantial gains in insight regarding underlying processes and mechanisms of communicative influence. To do so requires increased specificity in theory building regarding the nature of dynamic processes, with attention to recursive or mutually reinforcing relationships, subgroup effects, and the appropriate lag times for measurement in longitudinal data collection (Slater, in press).

We hope that this introduction has piqued the reader's interest and perhaps provided some ideas about how hypotheses of change might contribute to their own work. In the next sections, we first provide a step-by-step introduction to growth modeling through the use of a hypothetical example. Next, we provide a descriptive and detailed example of two approaches to growth modeling (structural equation modeling and multilevel modeling). Finally, we demonstrate examples of each of the four types of analyses of change described above (an unconditional growth model, a conditional growth model with a time-independent covariate, a conditional growth model with a time-dependent covariate, and a parallel process growth model using real data sets.

An Introduction to Growth Modeling

Growth models allow users to parsimoniously capture change in a certain variable over time. Once specified, these models describe both the average change in a certain variable within a specific population and the degree to which individuals differ in the way that they change. In order to model change, a study must have three important features (Singer & Willett, 2003). First, a study needs at least three waves of data (although four or more is preferable so that one can better assess the functional form and fit of the growth model), a dependent variable (i.e., the outcome variable of interest) that changes systematically over time, and a reasonable metric for time (e.g., age, time since the start of an intervention). If these three criteria are met, then the assessment of development and change can offer a unique and valuable perspective for many research questions.

For example, let us consider parent-child communication, which is known to be affected by developmental change. The quality of communication between a parent and child is of great interest to child and adolescent researchers. The literature suggests that adolescents and their parents often experience significant communication problems (see Sillars, Koerner, & Fitzpatrick, 2005). Let's suppose that a researcher measured parent-child communication among a sample of individuals on a yearly basis from age 10 to age 14 and that he used a scale that ranged from 0 to 10 in which a higher score represented a more effective communication style. Figure 3.1 presents the individual data points for eight of the individuals in his sample. For now, disregard the lines and focus on just the data points. Examination of plots such as these are a useful starting point as they help the analyst to visualize the different types of change that have taken place in the sample (Singer & Willett, 2003). The plots also allow for the assessment of both within-person change (e.g., Has change occurred? Does change tend to follow a straight line? Does there appear to be curvilinear change?) and interindividual differences in patterns of change (e.g., Is there variability in where participants begin? Is there variability in the participants' shape or rate of change?)

Inspection of the plots in Figure 3.1 reveals that there is an obvious overall decline in parent-child communication as the children move further into adolescence. However, there is also interindividual variability in parent-child communication at each age (i.e., individuals vary in the quality of parent-child communication according to some hypothetical measure, which we will refer to as communication quality or COMM) and also in the rate of change over time (i.e., some individuals decline rapidly, some change very little, and one greatly improves). These plots provide the researcher with a good first glance at the data, and it is advisable for all studies of change to begin at this simple level. In cases where the data set is very large (and examination of every individual's plotted scores is not plausible), one may select a random sample of subjects to plot (Singer & Willett, 2003).

Once these individual plots have been examined, it is useful to next smooth the trajectories implied by the data points by fitting an ordinary least squares (OLS) regression line to each person's data (Singer & Willett, 2003). To accomplish this task, it is necessary to first choose a functional form for the model. Although there are many functional forms possible, we will discuss three commonly used functional forms (intercept only, linear, and quadratic forms).[1] An intercept only model hypothesizes no change (e.g., individuals differ on their quality of parent-child communications at each age but their scores do not change over time; i.e., people who start out high remain high and people who start out low remain low). A linear model hypothesizes linear change (e.g., change over time follows a straight line). Finally, a quadratic model hypothesizes curvilinear change (e.g., rate of change changes over time; i.e., it accelerates or decelerates over time). Given the observation of the raw data presented in Figure 3.1, a linear change model appears to be a good place to start.

Fitting an OLS regression line to each person's data can be performed in most statistical programs (e.g., SAS, SPSS, STATA). However, the data

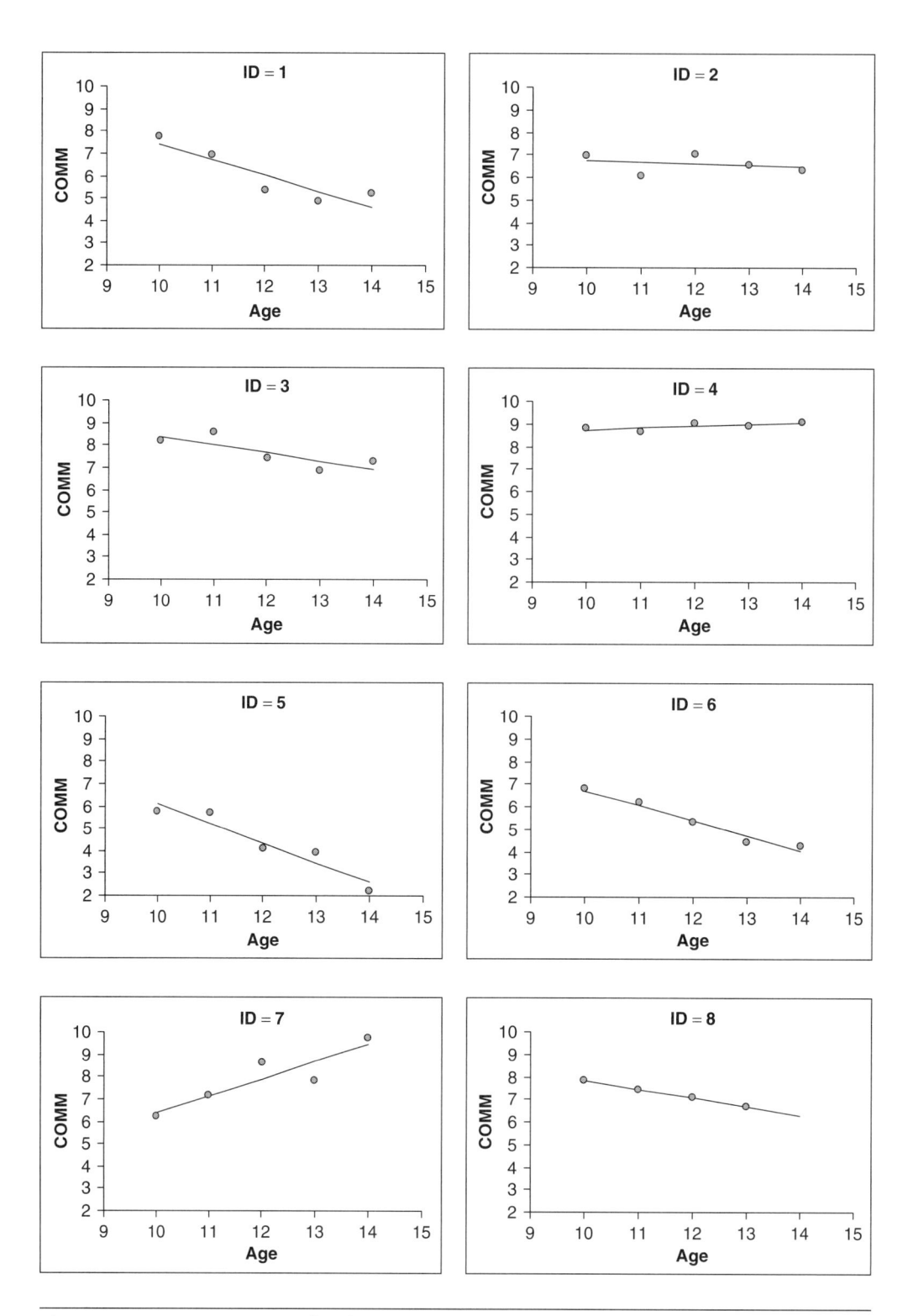

Figure 3.1 Raw Scores and Individual Fitted OLS Regression Lines of Parent-Child Communication

set typically needs to be put into a certain format (however, Carrig, Wirth, & Curran, 2003, offer a convenient SAS macro to plot individual trajectories that doesn't require this special format). The required format for most applications is commonly referred to as a person-period data format. An example of such a format is presented in Table 3.1 (see papers by Singer, 1998, 2002; and Peugh & Enders, 2005, for the syntax used to get the data into this format). The table presents the repeated measurements of parent-child communication quality for three subjects. Rather than having a separate variable for each measurement occasion (i.e., communication at age 10, communication at age 11, etc.), each individual has a separate row of data for each measurement occasion. The COMM variable identifies the communication score at each AGE from age 10 to age 14. AGECEN is a transformed form of AGE where a value of 10 is subtracted. As the reader will see shortly, this transformed variable allows the intercept of the model to take on a more meaningful value.

Table 3.1 Example of a Person-Period Data Set

ID	AGE	AGECEN	COMM
81	10	0	8.3
81	11	1	6.9
81	12	2	6.7
81	13	3	6.3
81	14	4	5.4
82	10	0	7.4
82	11	1	7.7
82	12	2	7.9
82	13	3	8.6
82	14	4	9.5
83	10	0	8.3
83	11	1	6.4
83	12	2	5.8
83	13	3	5.5
83	14	4	3.5

Once the data are in this format, one simply regresses the variable of interest (e.g., the communication variable, COMM) on an intercept (i.e., a vector of 1s) and the variable representing time (e.g., AGECEN) for each individual in the sample. The default in SAS (as well as most other statistical packages) is to include an intercept automatically. Estimation of a separate regression model for each person allows each individual's trajectory to be described by an intercept (e.g., the true level of communication when AGECEN = 0; i.e., when the student was 10 years old) and a slope (i.e., the regression coefficient for AGECEN, which represents the rate of change). In this example, one would obtain an estimate of the intercept and slope for every person in the sample (see the lines for each plot in Figure 3.1). For example, the participant with ID #1 in Figure 3.1 has an estimated intercept of 7.43 and an estimated slope of −.71. We can describe this person's data in equation form as COMM = 7.43 − 0.71AGECEN + r. At age 10, the participant's predicted COMM is 7.43 (i.e., 7.43 − 0.71 × 0), while at age 14, the predicted score is 4.59 (i.e., 7.43 − 0.71 × 4).

Note that the definition of the intercept becomes the true level of the dependent variable when the time variable is 0, because in any regression model, the intercept is the predicted value of the dependent variable when all independent variables are 0. In an unconditional growth model, the only predictor is time. Therefore, the intercept represents the predicted value of the dependent variable when time is 0. In our coding of time, 0 represents age 10. However, we could easily change the intercept by recentering time. For example, if we wanted the intercept to represent the predicted value of COMM at age 14, we would code AGECEN as follows: −4 at age 10, −3 at age 11, −2 at age 12, −1 at age 13, and 0 at age 14 (in other words, we would subtract 14 from the AGE variable rather than 10 as we did in the previous example). This specification of time would lead to an identical estimate for the slope coefficient (i.e., the regression coefficient for AGECEN) for each individual, but the intercept estimates would change accordingly, facilitating interpretation depending on the researcher's need.

Each individual's slope describes the rate of change in parent-child communication from age 10 to age 14. The difference between an individual's observed scores and his or her predicted scores are the residuals. The variance of these residuals captures the variance in communication not accounted for by linear change over time. By assessing each individual's R-squared statistic, we can get an estimate of the variance explained by linear change. For example, the individual with ID #1 has an R-squared estimate of 0.81, indicating that 81% of their variance in parent-child communication (COMM) over time is explained by linear change (AGECEN). These OLS regression parameters can be plotted against the observed values for each individual to visually assess the fit of the proposed functional form (e.g., a linear model). The plots in Figure 3.1 suggest that a linear model provides a reasonably good fit for each of these eight subjects.

In Figure 3.2, we display the OLS lines for each individual in a single plot. The figure makes obvious several interesting observations. First, we see that, on average, students tend to have reasonably positive communication with their parents at age 10 but that this communication tends to decline over time. Second, at age 10 (the intercept of the OLS regression lines) there is a good deal of variability across individuals in the quality of communication. Third, the rate of change over time varies substantially across individuals. Finally, it seems that students who start out with poorer scores at age 10 tend to decline at a faster rate. This information is precisely the kind of information that a growth model captures. That is, a growth model can tell us about the average change of a certain variable in a certain population, the extent to which individuals vary in the way that they change over time, and the relationship between initial status and rate of change.

Once the data have been thoroughly inspected using these types of methods, an analyst is ready to formally estimate a growth model. In the next section, we will compare two different methods for estimating a growth model.

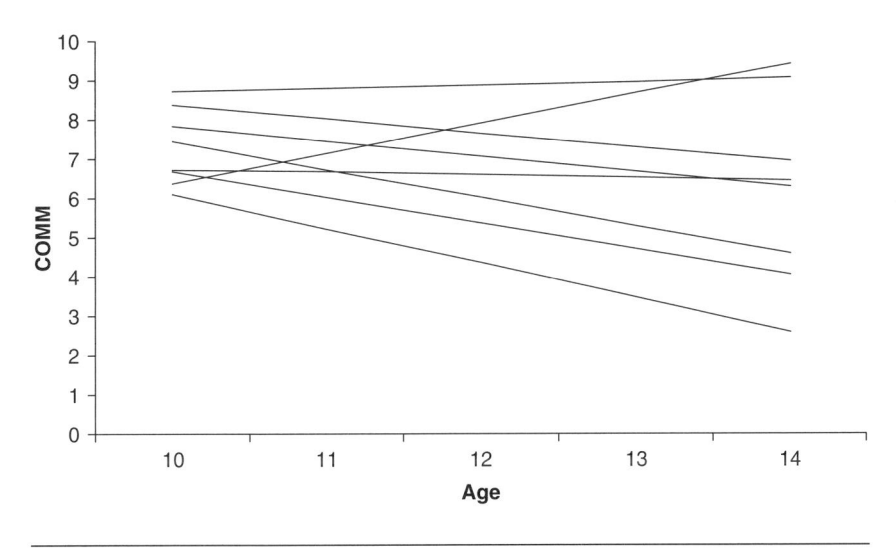

Figure 3.2 OLS Regression Lines for Eight Individuals

Comparing Two Approaches: Growth Modeling Within a Multilevel and Structural Equation Modeling Framework

There are two common techniques used to estimate the kinds of growth models described in the introduction of this chapter. One estimation method considers the growth process from the perspective of a nested data structure (i.e., repeated measurement occasions nested in persons) and utilizes multilevel modeling (MLM) software (e.g., The SAS Institute's Mixed Procedure, SPSS's multilevel commands, HLM, MLwin, MIXREG) to describe processes of change. A second estimation method utilizes structural equation modeling (SEM) software (e.g., Mplus, LISREL, AMOS, EQS) to specify latent variables that define the growth parameters (e.g., an intercept, linear slope, acceleration) of a change process.[2]

Under many conditions, the MLM and SEM approaches are empirically and analytically equivalent (Curran, 2003); however, in some circumstances MLM is more convenient, while in other circumstances SEM is preferred. The benefits of each type of model will be discussed below.

A MULTILEVEL APPROACH TO GROWTH MODELING

We will first consider the MLM approach to growth modeling. A growth model within this framework takes a hierarchical perspective, viewing repeated measurement occasions as nested within individuals. As such, the data structure presented in Table 3.1 is needed. Because of this structure, multilevel models can easily handle data sets where study participants vary on the number of measurement occasions available (in this case, the number of rows of data vary across participants) as well as the dates of measurement or the amount of elapsed time between measurement occasions (in this case, the scores on the time variable vary across participants).

For example, if desired, one could define age as the exact age of each participant at each measurement occasion rather than simply specifying age as a whole number as was utilized in the preceding example. Most SEM programs (with Mplus being the exception at the time of writing) define the growth model by putting constraints on the factor-loading matrix, and these constraints must be consistent across persons; therefore, individuals need to be measured at the same interval and for the same number of occasions (although there are some ways around these limitations, e.g., in the case of a cohort-sequential design or a multiple group model). This represents one important advantage of a multilevel framework over an SEM framework; however, the current version of Mplus allows for unequally spaced observations across subjects in an SEM (see the description of t-scores in the Mplus User's Manual, Muthén & Muthén, 2004).

Estimation of a growth model under a multilevel framework is carried out in a fashion that is conceptually similar to the method used to obtain the OLS estimates for each participant in the preceding example. However, when a multilevel growth model is specified, the result is not a separate regression equation for every participant in the sample. Rather, the result is a fixed-effect estimate of each growth parameter (e.g., the population average estimates of the intercept and slope) and an estimate of the variation around these average effects due to interindividual variation in the growth parameters (e.g., the extent to which people differ in where they begin and how fast they change).

A multilevel model for growth is commonly written as a set of two equations. The first is referred to as the within-person (or Level-1) model and describes within-person change (i.e., the individual growth model). The second is referred to as the between-persons (or Level-2) model and describes the average trajectory in the population and the extent to which growth (or within-person change) differs across individuals (Bryk & Raudenbush, 1987; Rogosa & Willett, 1985; Singer & Willett, 2003).

In the parent-child communication example, the Level-1 model captures the quality of communication for each child when the child is 10 (the intercept) and his or her rate of change over time (the slope). The Level-1 model for our example is written as follows (where i represents individuals and j represents measurement occasions):

$$COMM_{ij} = \pi_{0i} + \pi_{1i} AGECEN_{ij} + \varepsilon_{ij}$$

This model asserts that an adolescent's score on the parent-child communication variable can be described by an intercept (π_{0i}) and a slope (π_{1i}). The i subscript denotes that each individual in the sample has their own trajectory that is described by their own intercept (e.g., their estimated true value of communication at age 10) and slope (e.g., the rate at which their communication score changes from age 10 to age 14). The residual term in the Level-1 equation (ε_{ij}) captures the net scatter of child i's observed communication scores around her hypothesized growth trajectory (Singer & Willett, 2003).

The multilevel model for change is not complete until the Level-2 or between-persons model is considered. The Level-2 model tells us about the average trajectory in the population and how individuals differ on their growth parameters (e.g., communication at age 10 and rate of change during adolescence). For example, the Level-2 model in the proposed communication example is represented by two equations:

$$\pi_{0i} = \gamma_{00} + \zeta_{0i}$$
$$\pi_{1i} = \gamma_{10} + \zeta_{1i}$$

The first equation indicates that the Level-1 intercept (π_{0i}) is described by a fixed effect (γ_{00}—the average estimated value of communication at age 10 in the population) and a random effect ζ_{0i}—the extent to which individuals vary in their communication score at age 10). Similarly, the second equation indicates that the Level-1 slope (π_{1i}) is described by a fixed effect (γ_{10}—the average rate of change of communication in the population) and a random effect (ζ_{1i}—the extent to which individuals vary in their rate of change).

By substituting the Level-2 equations into the Level-1 equation, we obtain a single equation:

$$\text{COMM}_{ij} = \{\gamma_{00} + \gamma_{10}\text{AGECEN}_{ij}\} + \{\zeta_{0i} + \zeta_{1i}\text{AGECEN}_{ij} + \varepsilon_{ij}\}$$

We've rearranged the terms in order to allow the fixed-effect estimates to be presented in the first bracket and the random-effect estimates to be presented in the second bracket. We fit this model to our simulated data and obtain the estimates presented in Table 3.2. First, consider the fixed effects. The estimate of the intercept (γ_{00}) equals 7.207 and describes the average estimated value of communication at age 10 in the population. Its standard error is much smaller than the parameter estimate (*t*-values are interpreted in the usual way to determine if a "statistically significant" effect exists), indicating that the value of 7.207 is indeed statistically different from zero. The estimate of the slope (γ_{00}) equals -0.404 (95% C.I.: –0.358, –0.450) and describes the average estimated change in communication quality between ages 10 and 14. Its standard error is also quite small in comparison, indicating that there is a significant overall decline in communication between ages 10 and 14.

Of course, not everyone in the population is expected to follow this exact trajectory. Indeed, we would expect (and observed in the OLS plots) that adolescents vary in their scores at age 10 (some will have much better communication with their parents and some will have much worse) and

Table 3.2 A Multilevel Growth Model of Parent-Child Communication (estimated with SAS Proc Mixed)

	Estimate	S.E.	Est./S.E.
Fixed Effects			
Intercept, centered at age 10, γ_{00}	7.207	0.037	192.40
Rate of change, γ_{10}	−0.404	0.023	−17.29
Random Effects			
Intercept variance, $V(\zeta_{0i})$	0.469	0.045	10.37
Rate of change variance, $V(\zeta_{1i})$	0.234	0.017	13.51
Covariance between ζ_{0i} and ζ_{1i}	0.085	0.020	4.31
Residual variance, $V(\varepsilon_{ij})$	0.388	0.014	27.39

demonstrate different trajectories of change over time (some will deteriorate at different rates, some won't change, and some will improve). This between-persons variance in the age 10 scores and rate of change is captured by the random effects. In Table 3.2, the random effect for the intercept (the variance of ζ_{0i} describes the extent to which individuals vary in their communication score at age 10) is estimated to be 0.469, indicating that 10-year-olds' scores for communication vary significantly across children. Likewise, the random effect for the slope (the variance of ζ_{1i} describes the extent to which individuals vary in their rate of change) is estimated to be 0.234, indicating that the rate of change in communication during adolescence differs significantly across individuals. The covariation between the intercept and slope is estimated to be 0.085, indicating that 10-year-old students who demonstrate better parent-child communication deteriorate less as they grow older. That is, the better the communication at age 10, the more likely the student will maintain strong communication with his parents as he moves through adolescence. The final parameter estimate (ε_{ij}) captures the within-person residual variance. The large variance estimate (0.388) indicates that linear change does not explain all of the within-person variance in communication from age 10 to age 14. Although we report the Wald test for the random effects (i.e., the estimate divided by its standard error), it should be noted that the validity of these significance tests of the variances and covariances is of concern, particularly when the population variance is near zero and the sample size is small (Hedeker & Gibbons, 2006). Alternative methods that utilize likelihood ratio tests to compare nested models are recommended when one is interested in determining if a certain random effect is significantly larger than zero (see Singer & Willett, 2003, and Hedeker & Gibbons, 2006, for details on carrying out these tests). In this example, the Wald tests for the random effects concur with the more accurate likelihood ratio tests. For example, for testing two nested models, one that includes the fixed effect for rate of change and a random effect for both the intercept and rate of change, compared to another that includes the same fixed effects but only a random effect for the intercept, the log-likelihood ratio test (with 2 degrees of freedom—one for the random effect for rate of change and one for the covariance between the random effects for the intercept and rate of change) equals 1340.4. Of course, this greatly exceeds the 0.001 critical X^2 value of 13.82, indicating that these random effects are significantly greater than zero.

Figure 3.3 presents the trajectory described by the fixed-effect estimates of the intercept and slope (the dark, thick line) and the estimated trajectories of 50 randomly selected individuals. This figure illustrates each of the effects estimated in the multilevel model. We see great variability in both the level of communication at age 10 and the rate of change. In addition, we see that students who demonstrate better scores at age 10 decline less over time. If these were real data, we might develop hypotheses to explain

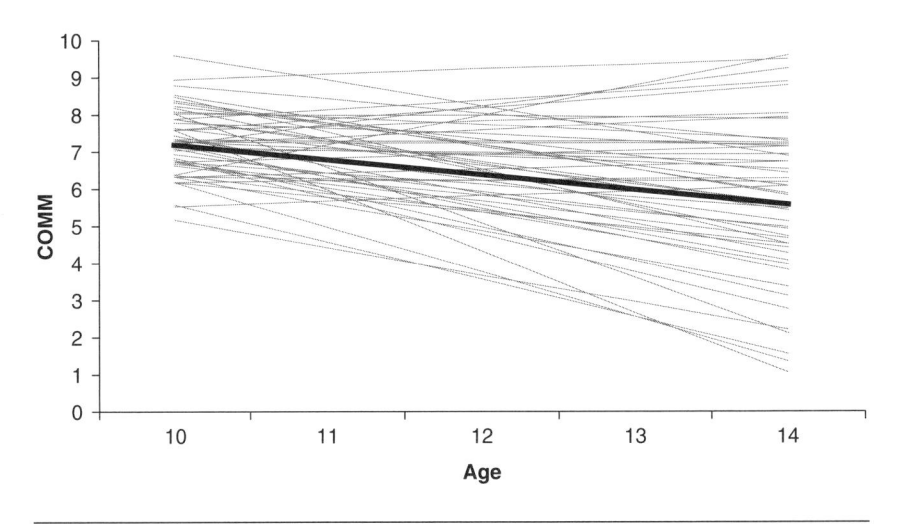

Figure 3.3 The Estimated Average Age Trajectory as Well as the Trajectories for 50 Randomly Selected Children

the between-persons variation in the intercept and slope. For example, perhaps variables such as the child's gender, level of parent education, or family structure would describe why students differ on their scores at age 10 and their rate of change during adolescence.

We might also postulate that certain time-varying covariates (i.e., variables that change within an individual over time) are salient predictors of within-person variability of communication scores. For example, the child's association with delinquent peers at each age or the incidence of a divorce at a particular age may predict the child's communication score beyond the effect of what is predicted by linear change. We will explore these types of research questions in the examples section of this chapter.

Before turning to the specification of a growth model within an SEM framework, we note one other important advantage of the multilevel approach. In addition to considering the nesting of measurement occasions within-person, a multilevel modeling approach also allows for other nested structures. For example, imagine that our example data were collected in schools or from multiple siblings nested in families. That is, the sample of children was drawn from 100 different schools or 100 families. This would constitute a third level (e.g., measurement occasions at Level 1, students at Level 2, and schools or families at Level 3; see Chapter 8 in this volume for details on studying context effects in multilevel models). This third level can easily be handled with multilevel modeling software; however, while Mplus now allows for one additional level of nesting within an SEM framework, other SEM packages do not allow for additional nesting.

A STRUCTURAL EQUATION MODELING APPROACH TO GROWTH MODELS

Next, we consider the SEM approach to growth modeling. In this framework, latent growth parameters capture the growth process. The growth parameters are considered latent because they are not directly observed but, rather, are inferred from the observed data. This approach uses information about the covariance structure and the mean structure of the repeated measures.

Curran (2003) explains that a latent growth model considers the observed repeated measures (e.g., communication at ages 10 to 14) to be "fallible indicators of an unobserved true growth trajectory" (p. 19). When estimated, the results describe the intra- and interindividual variability of the growth process in much the same way as a multilevel model. In fact, under certain estimators and with certain constraints, the results of the two modeling strategies are identical. Figure 3.4 displays a growth model for our example data, presenting both the conceptual structure of the model and the estimates for our example data.

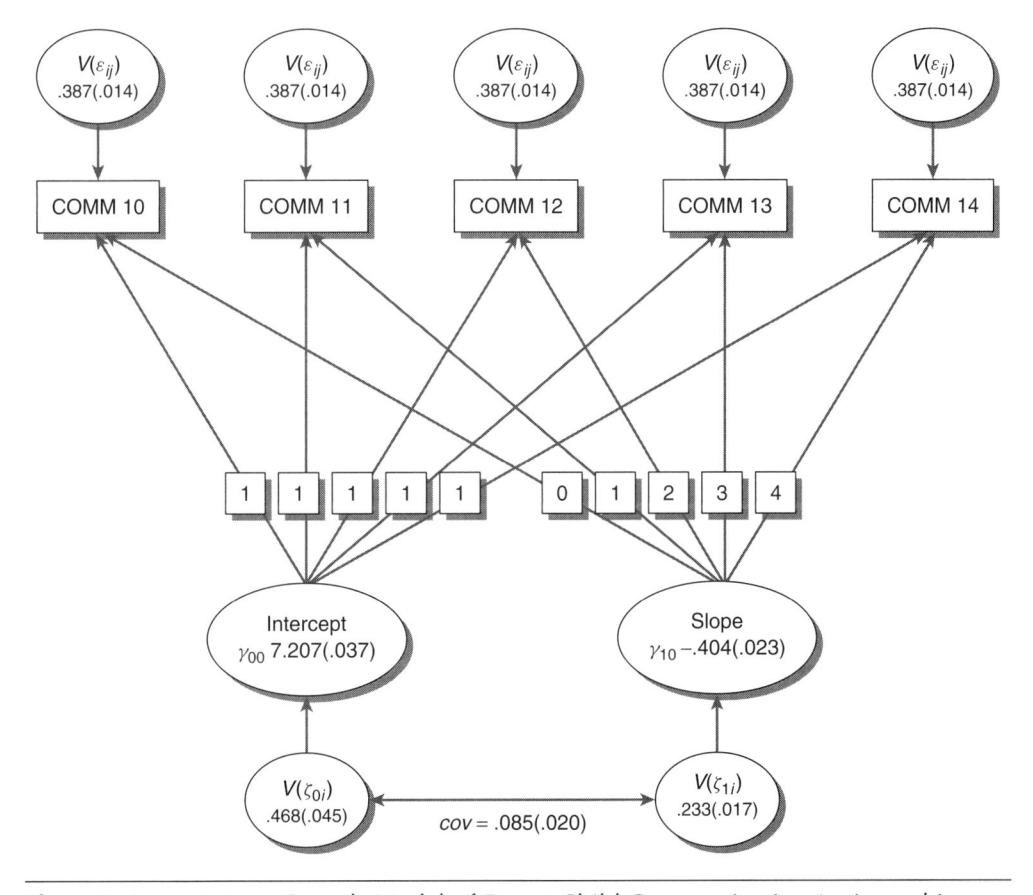

Figure 3.4 A Latent Growth Model of Parent-Child Communication (estimated in Mplus)

In specifying a growth model within an SEM framework, a person-period data set is not needed. Rather, the variable named COMM10 represents communication at age 10, COMM11 represents communication at age 11, and so forth. The other obvious difference between the SEM and multilevel approaches is the treatment of time. In the traditional SEM approach, time is introduced to the model by constraining the factor loadings for the observed variables on the latent slope variable to equal the appropriate metric for time (see the boxes on the factor loadings relating the COMM variables to the intercept and slope latent variables). In this model, we still allow the intercept latent variable to represent age 10. We do this by constraining the factor loadings relating the intercept to the repeated measures to be equal to 1 and by specifying the factor loading for COMM10 (communication at age 10) for the slope factor to be 0. The remaining repeated measures are related to the slope factor with a linear specification by setting the factor loading for COMM11 at 1, the factor loading for COMM12 at 2, the factor loading for COMM13 at 3, and the factor loading for COMM14 at 4. Just as we could change the centering point in a multilevel framework, we can also change the centering point in the SEM framework by simply changing the factor loadings for the slope latent variable.

In order to identify the model, the means and variances of the latent growth parameters (intercept and slope) and their covariance are freely estimated; however, while the variances of the residuals or disturbances (i.e., variance in the repeated measures not accounted for by the growth parameters) are estimated, the intercepts of the repeated measures are fixed at zero. We've used the same notation to represent the various estimates as presented in the multilevel model (Table 3.2). As observed in Figure 3.4, the estimates are very similar to those in the multilevel model.

The difference between the two types of strategies becomes apparent when one begins to exercise some of the added flexibility that is afforded by an SEM approach. While a thorough description of all the modeling possibilities is beyond the scope of this chapter, we highlight a few. First, one has more flexibility in specifying the error-covariance structure of a model (Bollen & Curran, 2006). In addition, many interesting hypotheses can be tested within an SEM framework that cannot (or cannot easily) be tested within a multilevel framework. For example, parallel process growth models (such as those discussed in the introduction and in the examples section of this chapter) can be tested. These models specify two growth processes (e.g., change in parent-child communication and change in delinquency) and assess the extent to which the growth parameters across processes are related. While predictors of the growth process (e.g., the effect of gender on the intercept and slope) can easily be incorporated in either framework, the effect of the growth parameters on a distal outcome (e.g., the effect of deteriorating parent-child communication on the probability of becoming a high school dropout) can be assessed only within an SEM framework. That is, within an SEM framework, one can use the growth parameters as predictors of another outcome.

Many theoretical and applied questions may also be assessed using the multiple group features available in SEM programs. That is, the growth process itself as well as predictors, distal outcomes, and other relationships can be assessed separately for different groups (e.g., boys compared to girls). Cross-group constraints may be used to determine if these effects differ significantly as a function of group membership. In addition, growth mixture models can be estimated with Mplus to examine the possibility that one single-population average growth trajectory does not adequately describe the population.

Finally, specification of growth models within an SEM framework allows the user to take advantage of Full Information Maximum Likelihood, which easily accounts for missing data in the longitudinal measures forming the growth model as well as other covariates in the model. These examples represent just a few of the ways that an SEM approach to growth modeling can extend the range of research questions that may be answered.

ASSESSING THE FIT OF THE GROWTH MODEL

The example models that we have just presented assume that a linear model adequately describes each individual's true change during the time period of interest. Singer and Willett (2003) indicate that the determination of the correct model for capturing change over time can be difficult, particularly when there are just three or four measurement occasions. Ideally, one's choice can be at least partially guided by theory (e.g., what kind of change over time might be expected given the nature of the dependent variable and the time frame considered?). The decision can also be explored analytically by testing alternative specifications for time and comparing the change in fit for various models. For example, perhaps change in communication isn't linear but, rather, is curvilinear (e.g., the change either accelerates or decelerates over time). This type of curvilinear change may be assessed by adding a quadratic time trend. In a multilevel framework, this would entail creating a new variable by squaring AGECEN. This new variable (AGECEN^2) may be added as an independent variable to the model. With both time variables in the model, AGECEN would represent the instantaneous change at age 10 (or wherever the intercept was centered), and AGECEN^2 would represent the extent to which change accelerates or decelerates as subjects grow older. The same task can be accomplished within an SEM framework by including a third latent variable. In our example, this third latent growth parameter, called acceleration, would have the following factor loadings: COMM10 at 0, COMM11 at 1, COMM12 at 4, COMM13 at 9, and COMM14 at 16 (i.e., the squared values of the linear time scores). One can determine analytically if a quadratic (or any other nested alternative specification) better describes the participants' data by comparing the −2 log likelihood (i.e., the deviance statistic; see Singer & Willett, 2003, pp. 116–126, for a thorough discussion) in either a multilevel or SEM framework, or the chi-square in a SEM framework for a model with and without the additional term. Curvilinear change is present if the fit of the model becomes significantly better (i.e., the log likelihood or the chi-square becomes significantly smaller) with the addition of the quadratic term. With a few exceptions (e.g., when robust standard errors are used) a traditional chi-square difference test can be used to determine if the fit significantly improves, comparing the difference in fit for the two models given the difference in the number of estimated parameters.

It should be noted that the estimation of polynomial trajectories requires more than three waves of data in order for the model to be identified. This is because model identification requires that a model have at least as many identified parameters as unknown parameters (e.g., parameters that need to be estimated by the model). If one were to attempt to estimate a quadratic model with just three measurement occasions, twelve parameters would need to be estimated (mean and variance of the intercept, slope, and quadratic latent variables; three residual variances; and three covariances of the latent growth parameters), but only nine identified parameters exist (three means, three variances, and three covariances). However, with four waves of data there are fourteen known parameters (four means, four variances, and six covariances), and this allows the model to be identified. As such, one needs to collect at least four waves of data to estimate a quadratic growth model. In general, estimating a polynomial of degree d requires $d + 2$ repeated measurement occasions. For example, $d = 1$ for a linear trajectory and it requires at least three repeated measurements, $d = 2$ for a quadratic trajectory and it requires at least four repeated measurements (Bollen & Curran, 2006).

Within the SEM framework, several measures of practical fit are also available. One of the most widely used indices is the root mean square error of approximation (RMSEA; Browne & Cudek, 1993). A perfect fitting model has an RMSEA value of 0. Although there are no specific rules for selecting an RMSEA value that denotes a good fit, Browne and Cudek (1993) suggest that a value of about .05 or less indicates a reasonably well-fitting growth model. Two other commonly used fit indices are the Tucker-Lewis index (TLI; Tucker & Lewis, 1973) and the comparative fit index (CFI; Bentler, 1990). The TLI generally ranges between 0 and 1, where a value of 1 represents perfect fit. Values much above 1 (e.g., 1.2) are possible and may indicate that the model is overfitting the data, and values much lower than 1 (e.g., < .90) indicate a poor-fitting model (Bollen & Curran, 2006). The CFI is capped at 1 (any values greater than 1 are reset to equal 1). As with the TLI, values much less than 1 (e.g., <.90) indicate poor model fit. The cutoff points for these indices are somewhat arbitrary and are probably best considered rules of thumb rather than stringent criteria. In addition, it is generally recommended to report multiple measures of fit. In the communication models just presented, $X^2(14) = 8.584$, $p = .8567$, CFI = 1.000, TLI = 1.002, and RMSEA = .000, all indicating excellent fit.

Model fit can also be assessed (and adjusted if necessary) by examining the error covariance structure. Assessing this structure, and ensuring that the model assumptions are correct, is essential. There are many different ways to assess the error covariance structure, including comparison of alternative models that specify different error covariance structures and examination of the resultant residuals. The details of carrying out this examination are beyond the scope of this introductory chapter, but we refer the reader to excellent applied discussions offered by Singer and Willett (2003) and Bollen and Curran (2006).

Illustrative Examples

In this final section, we demonstrate several of the growth models that have been discussed using two real data sets. We will alternate modeling strategies (i.e., MLM and SEM frameworks) in order to provide the reader with examples of both. One of the data sets includes 4,216 male and female students who participated in a drug prevention trial called Community Action for Drug Prevention (CADP). The students were in the sixth or seventh grade at the first measurement occasion and proceeded to provide data on three additional measurement occasions over a period of approximately 18 months. The data were collected using a written survey administered in 32 schools across the United States between the years 1999 and 2003. The data were not collected on a fixed schedule; that is, the students varied on the amount of time that elapsed between each measurement occasion.

The second data set[3] includes 532 male and female students from six rural schools in Pennsylvania who participated in a prevention trial called the ADAPT Project (Adoption of Drug Abuse Prevention Trial). All of the students considered in the example were exposed to a version of the Life Skills Training program (National Health Promotion Associates, 2002) from 1999 to 2002. To assess program effects, the students participated in a school-based written survey at the beginning of seventh grade, end of seventh grade, end of eighth grade, and end of ninth grade. All students across all schools took the survey within a period of two weeks of one another at each measurement occasion.

A GROWTH MODEL WITH TIME-INVARIANT PREDICTORS

In the first example, we utilize data from the CADP trial. The dependent variable of interest in this model is a measure of each student's use of violent media (in the form of movies, Internet sites, and video games that display violence). The scale ranges from 1 to 5, with a 5 indicating more exposure to violent media. The students varied in both age at the first measurement occasion and the spacing of time between measurement occasions. As such, it is not appropriate to introduce a constant representation of age across all subjects. Rather, we estimate the model using an MLM framework (although the model could have also been specified in Mplus Version 3.0 or higher within an SEM framework), introducing time as a predictor variable with a random effect and controlling for age at the first measurement occasion.

We start with a Level-1 model, in which use of violent media is regressed on time. Time is centered at the first survey assessment. For example, a student who completed the first survey in December of sixth grade, the second survey in March of sixth grade (3 months or .25 of a year after the initial survey), the third survey in September of seventh grade (9 months or .75 of a year after the initial survey), and the fourth survey in June of seventh grade (18 months or 1.5 years after the initial survey) would have the following time scores, respectively (0, .25, .75, 1.5). To adjust for the age heterogeneity at the initial survey, we control for age at the first survey (centered at age 13 to create a meaningful intercept—i.e., 13 was subtracted from each person's age before analysis) in predicting both the intercept (use of violent media at the first measurement occasion) and rate of change in use of violent media over time (e.g., an age by time interaction). Before including the predictor of interest (i.e., gender), we first examined the adequacy of the fit of the growth model. We specified four nested models: (1) a linear growth model with homoscedastic residual variances (i.e., the residuals were constrained to be equally variable at each survey), (2) a linear growth model with heteroscedastic residual variances (i.e., the residual variances were freely estimated at each survey), (3) a quadratic growth model with homoscedastic residual variances, and (4) a quadratic growth model with heteroscedastic residual variances. Across these four models, we compared the −2 log likelihood and the Bayesian Information Criteria (BIC). Assessment of these statistics indicated that a linear growth model with heteroscedastic errors best fit the data; therefore, this model was retained.

We then proceeded to assess the effect of gender on both the intercept (use of violent media at the first measurement occasion) and rate of change by including gender and its interaction with time in the model. The results are presented in Table 3.3. The interpretation of the fixed effects is similar to that of a regular regression model's. The intercept indicates the predicted average value of use of violent media when all independent variables are 0. In the present model, this refers to the average level of violent media use at the first measurement occasion among 13-year-old female students. Because all of the predictor variables (time, age, and gender) are included with their interaction with time, these coefficients must be interpreted in concert with one another. For example, the coefficients for age and gender describe their effects when time is equal to zero (i.e., at the first measurement occasion). Both gender and age are significant predictors, indicating that boys and older students tended to use more violent media at the first measurement occasion. The effect for time represents the

Table 3.3 A Growth Model of Violent Media Use Predicted by Gender and Age (CADP data, estimated with SAS PROC MIXED)

	Estimate	S.E.	Est./S.E.
Fixed Effects			
Intercept, centered at Time 1, γ_{00}	2.301	0.019	124.03
Rate of change, γ_{10}	0.152	0.016	9.27
Gender (male = 1, female = 0), γ_{01}	0.779	0.022	34.65
Age at Time 1, centered at age 13, γ_{02}	0.063	0.012	5.09
Gender × Rate of change, γ_{11}	0.030	0.019	1.59
Age at Time 1 × Rate of change, γ_{12}	0.007	0.010	0.64
Random Effects			
Intercept variance, $V(\zeta_{0i})$	0.358	0.012	29.43
Rate of change variance, $V(\zeta_{1i})$	0.090	0.010	9.04
Covariance between ζ_{0i} and ζ_{1i}	−0.029	0.009	−3.42
Residual variances			
Time 1 $V(\varepsilon_i)$	0.230	0.010	24.12
Time 2 $V(\varepsilon_i)$	0.256	0.008	31.09
Time 3 $V(\varepsilon_i)$	0.273	0.009	29.76
Time 4 $V(\varepsilon_i)$	0.360	0.015	23.83

predicted average rate of change for females who were age 13 at the first measurement occasion. For this group of students, time is a significant predictor of violent media use, indicating that use of violent media increases during this period of adolescence. The two interaction terms, age × time and gender × time, tell us the extent to which the rate of change of violent media use differs by age at the first measurement occasion and gender. Neither interaction effect is statistically significant, indicating that the average rate of increase in use of violent media is similar for students of different age at baseline and gender.

The random effects for the intercept and rate of change are statistically significant,[4] indicating that students differ significantly in their level of violent media use and in their rate of change during adolescence (controlling for gender and age at baseline). The negative covariance between the intercept and rate of change indicates that students who were using more violent media at baseline tended to increase at a slower rate. This is a common observation in growth models and may represent a ceiling effect. That is, adolescents who are using a lot to begin with have less room to increase over time. Finally, the variance of the within-person residuals (ε_{ij}) is large and significantly different from zero, indicating that there is still variance within persons that remains to be explained.

To demonstrate the effect of gender, we have used the equation presented in Table 3.3 to construct predicted trajectories for boys and girls (assuming both were age 13 at the first measurement occasion). Figure 3.5 demonstrates that boys on average always use more violent media than girls, but rate of change over time in use of violent media is similar for boys and girls.

It's important to note that this latent growth model could have been specified in a variety of other ways. For example, we could have recentered the model at a different point in time (e.g., the final measurement occasion) or at a certain age (e.g., age 13). This choice should be driven by one's research question(s).

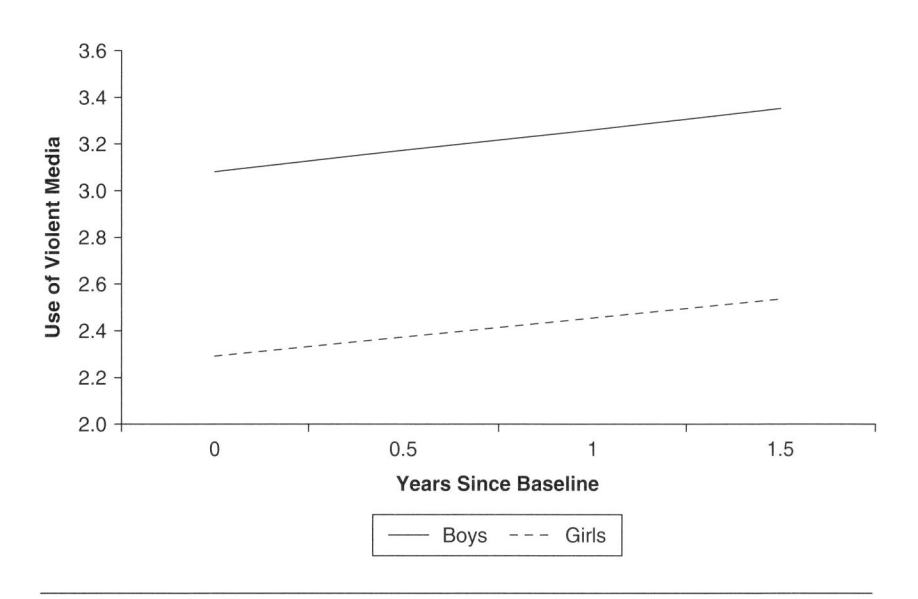

Figure 3.5   Estimated Trajectories of Violent Media Use by Gender

A GROWTH MODEL WITH A TIME-VARYING COVARIATE: ANALYZING EFFECTS OF INTRAINDIVIDUAL OR WITHIN-PERSON VARIABILITY, CONTROLLING FOR BETWEEN-PERSON DIFFERENCES

We need not only consider predictors that are time independent (e.g., gender). We may also consider predictors that change over time. In the violent media growth model presented in the previous section, we determined that there is a significant amount of within-person variance not accounted for by linear change. This within-person variance may be accounted for by salient time-varying covariates. For example, perhaps certain variables may be identified that can predict whether a student will use more or less violent media than what would be predicted given a linear growth model.

In this example, we consider the relationship between sensation seeking and use of violent media. In the CADP study, sensation seeking was measured at all four measurement occasions using a scale that included three items that assessed the frequency with which students engaged in risky activities without regard for the consequences. Each item was assessed on a 5-point scale ranging from 1 (not at all) to 5 (very often).

We assess two different models. In the first model, we include the effect of linear change, age at baseline, gender, and sensation seeking. In this model, the effect of sensation seeking captures the extent to which engagement in risky behaviors is associated with use of violent media after adjusting for linear change and the time-independent covariates. It should be noted that even though the sensation-seeking variable presented in Model 1 (Table 3.4) is a time-varying (within-persons) predictor, its association with use of violent media may capture both differences between individuals in their average or overall level of sensation seeking and within-person change in frequency of sensation-seeking activities over time.

Raudenbush and Bryk (2002) have shown that the "effect of a level 1 predictor can be biased if the aggregate of the level 1 predictor has a separate and distinct relationship with the intercept" (p. 183). Indeed, it is quite possible that the average level of sensation seeking across all measurement occasions may have a unique relationship with use of violent media. The within-person effect of sensation seeking on use of violent media estimated in Model 1 may be due to a characteristic of the adolescent (e.g., an adolescent who tends to consistently engage in risky activities views more violent media), rather than within-person changes (during times when a student's involvement in risky activities is elevated, he or she will also demonstrate elevated use of violent media). Raudenbush and Bryk (2002) recommend adding the mean of a time-varying covariate as a predictor in the equation in order to disentangle the true within-person effect from the between-persons effect. Others have also discussed this technique (Hedeker, 2004; Osgood, 2001; Schwartz & Stone, 1998).

Following Raudenbush and Bryk's (2002) recommendation, we specify a second model (Model 2 in Table 3.4) that includes the average level of sensation seeking across all measurement occasions. In Model 2, the within-person effect of sensation seeking assesses the extent to which within-person change in sensation seeking is related to use of violent media beyond that affected by a student's own linear trajectory of change. The between-persons effect of sensation seeking represents the extent to which a student's overall average sensation-seeking score across all four measurement occasions affects use of violent media after adjusting for the within-person effect of

Table 3.4 Sensation Seeking and the Use of Violent Media (CADP data, estimated with SAS PROC MIXED)

	Model 1			Model 2		
	Estimate	S.E.	Est./S.E.	Estimate	S.E.	Est./S.E.
Fixed Effects						
Intercept, centered at Time 1, γ_{00}	2.416	0.016	149.57	2.425	0.016	150.94
Rate of change, γ_{10}	0.070	0.014	4.90	0.077	0.014	5.38
Gender (male = 1, female = 0), γ_{01}	0.578	0.020	29.06	0.543	0.020	26.70
Age at Time 1, centered at age 13, γ_{02}	0.023	0.011	2.13	0.016	0.011	1.52
Gender × Rate of change, γ_{11}	0.038	0.016	2.40	0.038	0.016	2.37
Age at Time 1 × Rate of change, γ_{12}	−0.001	0.009	−0.07	0.000	0.009	−0.04
Sensation seeking (Time dependent), γ_{20}	0.380	0.008	50.60	0.341	0.009	36.39
Average sensation seeking (grand mean centered), γ_{03}	—	—	—	0.113	0.014	7.94
Random Effects						
Intercept variance, $V(\zeta_{0i})$	0.238	0.010	24.88	0.234	0.009	24.77
Rate of change variance, $V(\zeta_{1i})$	0.068	0.008	9.07	0.068	0.008	9.03
Sensation seeking variance, $V(\zeta_{2i})$	0.040	0.004	9.43	0.040	0.004	9.57
Covariance between ζ_{0i} and ζ_{1i}	−0.033	0.006	−5.07	−0.032	0.006	−5.02
Covariance between ζ_{0i} and ζ_{2i}	0.021	0.004	4.99	0.022	0.004	5.32
Covariance between ζ_{1i} and ζ_{2i}	−0.013	0.003	−3.71	−0.013	0.003	−3.79
Residual variances						
Time 1 $V(\varepsilon_t)$	0.206	0.009	24.20	0.204	0.008	24.25
Time 2 $V(\varepsilon_t)$	0.218	0.007	29.46	0.217	0.007	29.61
Time 3 $V(\varepsilon_t)$	0.227	0.008	26.75	0.225	0.008	26.74
Time 4 $V(\varepsilon_t)$	0.242	0.011	21.53	0.247	0.011	21.75

sensation seeking. This between-persons effect is described by Raudenbush and Bryk (2002) as the compositional or contextual effect. For example, some students consistently reported a high involvement in risky activities over the four measurement occasions, while others reported a consistently low involvement in risky activities. Consider two students who, at a certain point in time, have the same sensation-seeking score; the student with a higher average sensation-seeking score across all measurement occasions will view more violent media if a contextual effect exists.

Before considering the results of the model, it is important to consider one implication of interpreting the effect of the average of a time-varying covariate. When forming this type of average variable, it is easy to imagine that the value of such an average score depends greatly on the total number of measurement occasions for which a particular student provides data, particularly for variables that increase or decrease as students grow older. For example, imagine a student who provides data at only the first two measurement occasions and then drops out of the study. His average score represents something different from a student who is observed at all four measurement occasions (i.e., the average during the first year of the study rather than the average over the full study). In order to account for this, we chose to employ multiple imputation to account for missing measurement occasions. While the details of this procedure are beyond the scope of this chapter, we refer readers to Allison (2002) or Chapter 12 in this volume to learn more about multiple imputation and other missing data procedures.

The results of both models are presented in Table 3.4. In comparing the time-varying effect of sensation seeking in Models 1 and 2, we see that some of the relationship in the Level-1 model is accounted for by between-persons differences. This is evidenced by the fact that the true within-person effect (the effect presented in Model 2) is smaller than the effect presented in Model 1. By interpreting the coefficients in Model 2, we conclude that the relationship between sensation seeking and use of violent media has a within-person effect (i.e., during times when a student's involvement in risky activities has increased, he/she is predicted to view more violent media than would be otherwise expected) and a contextual effect (i.e., students who tend to consistently engage in risky activities view more violent media than students who tend to rarely engage in risky activities) after adjusting for linear change over time, age at baseline, and gender. The random effect associated with the within-person effect (ζ_{2i}) is statistically significant,[5] indicating that the relationship between change in sensation seeking and use of violent media differs across students. Likewise, the within-person residual variance (ε_{ij}) is also significantly larger than zero, indicating that there is still variance at the within-person level to explain. We might then hypothesize that the relationship between sensation seeking and use of violent media differs by situational characteristics (e.g., the effect of change in sensation seeking is more robust during times when a student has also demonstrated increased involvement with delinquent peers) and/or by personal characteristics (e.g., the effect of change in sensation seeking is more robust among children who are aggressive). For an example of this type of analysis, see Slater, Henry, Swaim, and Cardador (2004).

It's important to note that assessment of a contemporaneous time-varying predictor does not capture directionality. For example, the analyses just presented can point only to a significant relationship between sensation-seeking behavior and use of violent media. This analysis cannot indicate if sensation seeking leads to use of violent media or if use of violent media leads to sensation seeking. By including lagged predictors, one may be able to test temporal ordering hypotheses, provided that the time lag between assessments is appropriate. However, even in this case, the effect cannot be determined to be causal.

As a final note, it is important to recognize that the interpretation of the time-independent predictors (i.e., age at baseline and gender) is different now that the time-dependent predictor is included in the model. For example, the effect of gender on the rate of change of use of violent media represents the difference in linear change over time between boys and girls controlling for the effect of sensation seeking.

A GROWTH MODEL WITH A DISTAL OUTCOME

In addition to considering predictors of the growth parameters, we may also use an SEM framework to consider outcomes of the growth parameters. That is, we may assess the extent to which the growth parameters (e.g., intercept and slope) predict the value of a certain variable. To demonstrate this technique, we consider the change in media resistance skills among the students participating in Project ADAPT. The students responded to two items: "When I see or hear an alcohol advertisement, I tell myself that drinking alcohol won't make my life better," and "When I see or hear a cigarette advertisement, I tell myself that smoking cigarettes won't make my life better." Both items were measured on a 5-point Likert scale ranging from strongly disagree (1) to strongly agree (5). The average of the items was used as a scale score.

Figure 3.6 presents the model under consideration. The growth model considers linear change in media resistance skills from the beginning of seventh grade to the end of eighth grade. Notice the loadings for the slope factor (0, 0.75, and 1.75). These were chosen because we want the intercept to represent the predicted value of media resistance skills at the beginning of seventh grade. Furthermore, the second measurement occasion took place at the end of seventh grade (approximately 9 months after the first assessment), and the third measurement occasion took place at the end of eighth grade (one year and 9 months after the first measurement occasion). As such, the loadings of 0, .75, and 1.75 correctly specify the time lag, where each .25 increment equals a 3-month period of time.

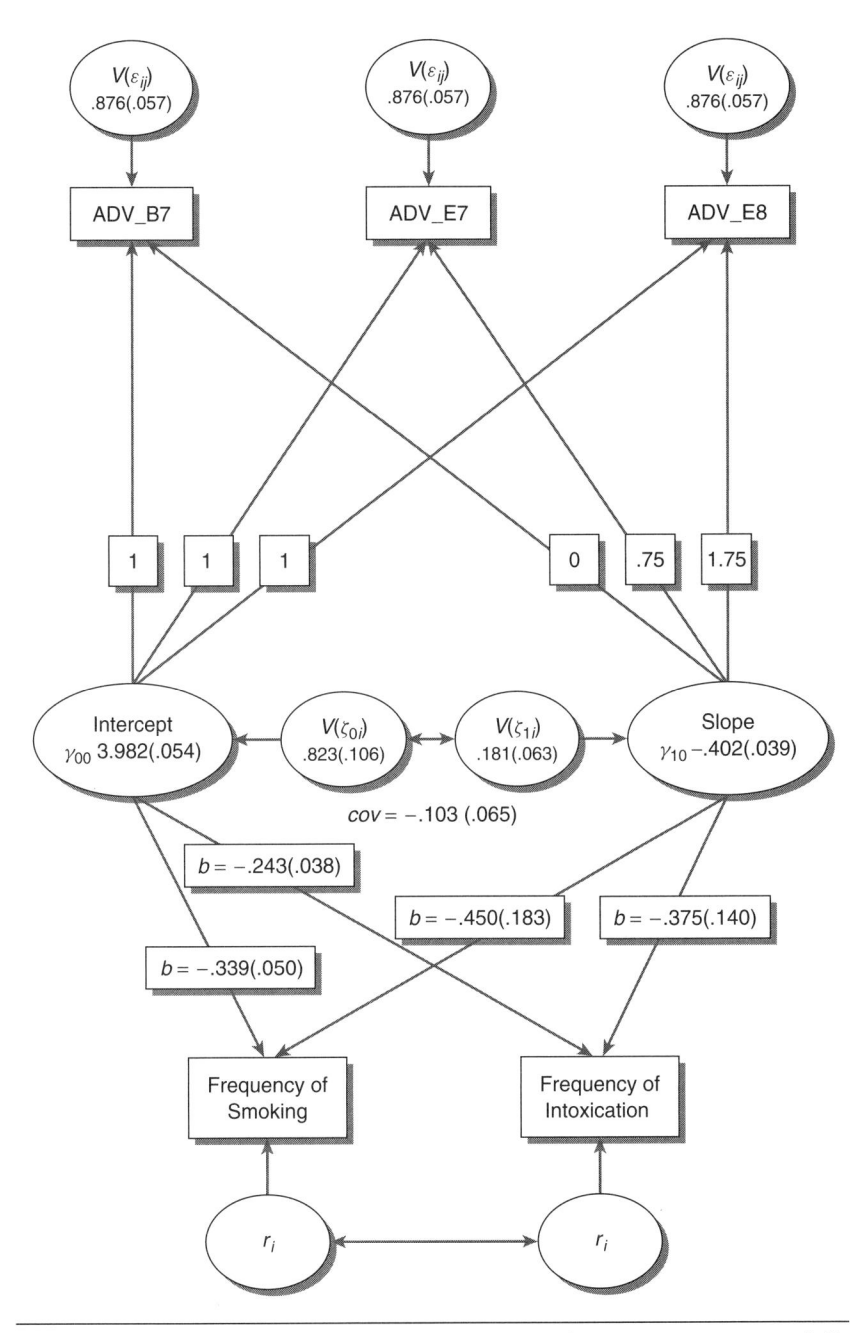

Assessing Change and Intraindividual Variation

Figure 3.6 A Latent Growth Model of Media Advertising Resistance Skills With Distal Outcomes (ADAPT data, estimated in Mplus)

Two drug use outcomes are considered, use of cigarettes and intoxication. Both variables were measured using an 8-point scale that ranged from 1 (never) to 8 (every day) and were logged because of high positive skew. In the model, both variables are regressed on the intercept and rate of change of media resistance skills.

The resultant model fits the data very well. The χ^2 equals 4.659 with 5 degrees of freedom, indicating excellent fit. The practical fit indices indicate perfect fit: TLI = 1.001, CFI = 1.000, RMSEA = 0.000.

Confident that the model fits the data well, we may now interpret the parameter estimates. The estimated values of the intercept and slope indicate that at the beginning of seventh grade, students tend to have high media resistance skills but that the skills on average decline over time. The variance around both the intercept and slope are statistically significant,[6] indicating that students vary significantly on their level of media resistance skills at the beginning of seventh grade and in their rate of decline from the beginning of seventh grade to the end of eighth grade. By regressing frequency of cigarette use and frequency of intoxication at the end of ninth grade on both the intercept of media resistance skills (i.e., media resistance skills at the beginning of seventh grade) and rate of change, we determine that students who demonstrate lower media resistance skills at the beginning of seventh grade and students whose skills deteriorate at a faster rate smoke and get drunk more often than students who demonstrate better skills and students who maintain their skills. As with any regression model, these effects represent the independent effect after adjusting for the other.

PARALLEL PROCESS GROWTH MODELS

For the final example, we extend the growth model of media resistance skills to consider a simultaneous growth process. As media resistance skills decline during adolescence, we might hypothesize that this process is accompanied by an increase in normative perceptions of peer use of drugs. That is, as students begin to perceive that more students use drugs, they may become less likely to resist media influences. In the ADAPT data, normative perceptions are measured by five items that assess the students' perceptions of the number (ranging from none [1] to all [5]) of peers their age who use various types of drugs (the average of the five items is used as the scale score). Although we could hypothesize directionality and regress the growth parameters of one process on the other (e.g., regress the growth parameters of media resistance skills on the growth parameters of normative beliefs), we instead simply covary the growth parameters for this example. Figure 3.7 presents the results of the parallel process growth model. As seen in the figure, two growth models are specified (one for media resistance skills and one for normative beliefs). The growth parameters of the two processes are allowed to covary.

The model fits the data well. The chi-square is not statistically significant (χ^2 = 15.718 with 11 degrees of freedom, $p > .10$). Evaluation of the TLI (TLI = .983), CFI (CFI = .988), and RMSEA (RMSEA = .028) also suggests that the model fits very well. Only one of the cross-process covariances, the covariance between the rate of change of media resistance

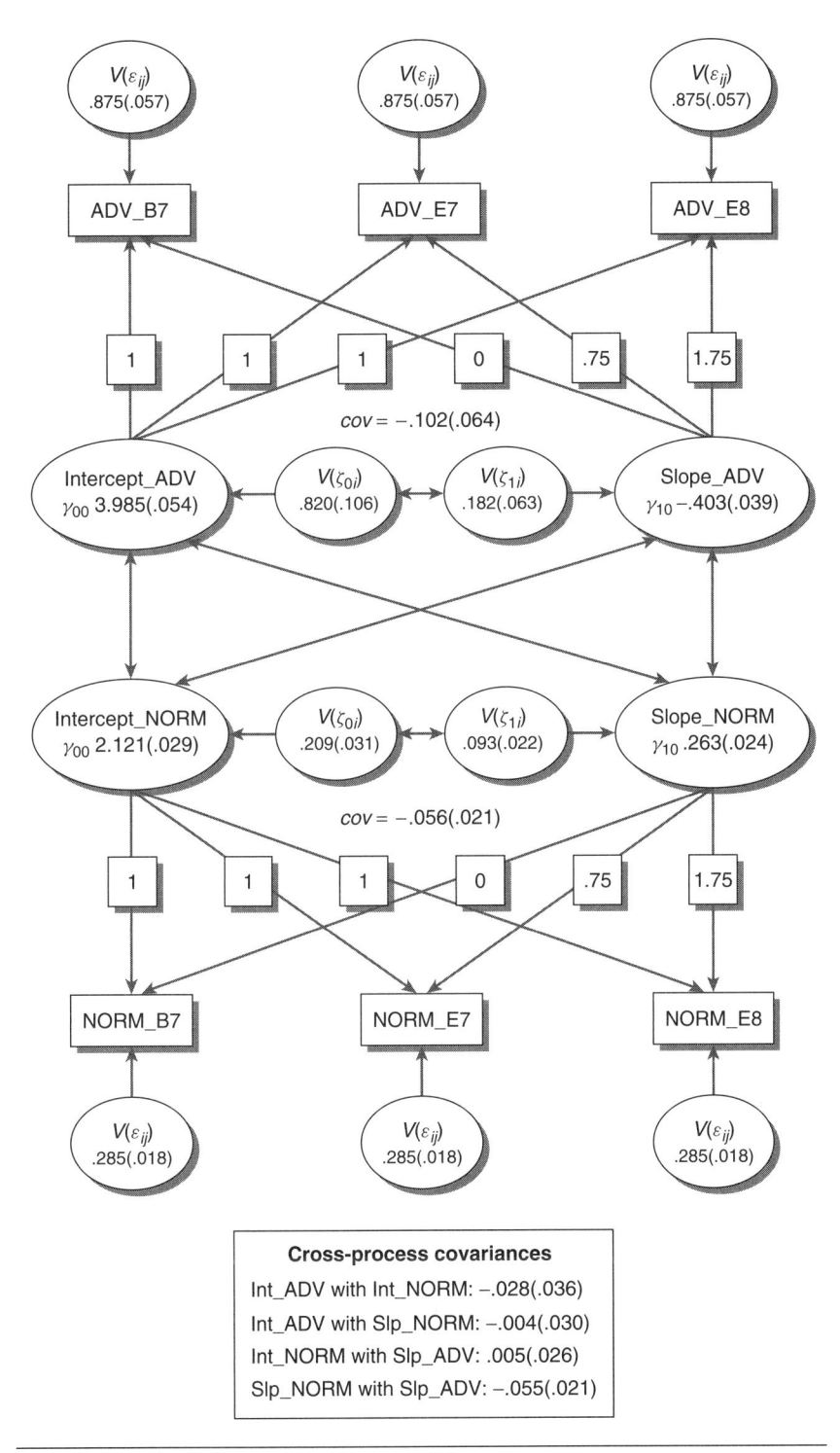

Figure 3.7 A Parallel Process Growth Model of Media Advertising Resistance Skills and Normative Beliefs (ADAPT data, estimated in Mplus)

skills and the rate of change of normative beliefs, is statistically significant.[7] This negative covariance indicates that students' increased normative perceptions over time (i.e., students begin to perceive that more of their peers use drugs) are accompanied by deterioration of media resistance skills.

Conclusion

In this chapter, we've discussed and demonstrated many different techniques for modeling growth and change in communication-related variables. Indeed, the systematic study of growth and change using contemporary longitudinal modeling techniques provides enormous potential for furthering communication theory development. Over the past decades, improvement in estimation methods and development of new programs have overcome some of the initial limitations (e.g., robust standard error estimators, estimations methods for noncontinuous outcomes) and recent simulation studies have demonstrated that latent growth models can in many cases be estimated with a relatively small sample size (Muthén & Muthén, 2004). The continual development of these techniques is important because many salient research questions can and should be answered through a better understanding of change. That is, latent growth models make it possible to theorize and test theories about the process of change, the impact of various types of change, the predictors of change, and the extent to which other time-varying variables affect change. Change may be in communication behavior or media use, change may be in other outcomes of interest as influenced by communication behavior or media use, or change may be in both, with one influencing the other or a process of reciprocal influence. Communication as a social science discipline will be considerably advanced if our theories are conceptualized and tested in terms of such processes of change over time.

Notes

1. Please note that other forms are useful for many types of change; however, they are beyond the scope of this introductory chapter. Please refer to the reference section at the end of this chapter for resources that consider other types of change.

2. Mplus and LISREL both originated as structural equation modeling programs, but now also include multilevel capabilities.

3. We thank Edward Smith, PhD, at The Pennsylvania State University for allowing us to use these data. The ADAPT study was funded by the National Institute on Drug Abuse, grant R01 DA011254–03 (P.I. Edward A. Smith).

4. As described on page 67, the Wald test of significance for the random effects can be dubious. To consider this problem, we also estimated the statistical significance of all random effects of interest using likelihood ratio tests. In all cases the results were the same.
5. Ibid.
6. Ibid.
7. Ibid.

Resources

Good books and articles describing latent growth modeling within a multilevel framework include Raudenbush and Bryk (2002), Hedeker (2004), Singer and Willett (2003), Singer (1998, 2002), and Snijders and Bosker (1999). Latent growth modeling within an SEM framework is described in Bollen and Curran (2006), Curran and Hussong (2002), Duncan et al. (1999), Singer and Willett (2004), and Willett and Sayer (1994, 1995). Carrig, Wirth, and Curran (2003) provide a useful SAS macro for automating the process of creating OLS lines for data inspection. Patrick Curran's Web site (http://www.unc.edu/~curran/example.htm at the time of publication) provides an example data set and example syntax for conducting growth models within a variety of statistical programs (both multilevel modeling and SEM frameworks).

Software for conducting growth models within a multilevel modeling framework include HLM (http://www.ssicentral.com), LISREL (http://ssicentral.com), MIXREG (http://tigger.uic.edu/~hedeker/mix.html), MLwin (http://www.mlwin.com), Mplus (http://statmodel.com), SAS (http://www.sas.com), SPSS (http://www.spss.com), and STATA (http://www.stata.com). Within an SEM framework, programs include AMOS (http://smallwaters.com), EQS (http://mvsoft.com), LISREL (http://ssicentral.com), and Mplus (http://statmodel.com).

References

Allison, P. D. (2002). *Missing data*. Thousand Oaks, CA: Sage.
Bentler, P. M. (1990). Comparative fit indexes in structural models. *Psychometrika, 107*(2), 238–246.
Bollen, K. A., & Curran, P. J. (2006). *Latent curve models: A structural equation perspective*. Hoboken, NJ: John Wiley & Sons.
Browne, M. W., & Cudek, R. (1993). Alternative ways of assessing model fit. In K. A. Bollen, & J. S. Long (Eds.). (1993). *Testing structural equation models* (pp. 136–162). Newbury Park, CA: Sage.

Bryk, A. S., & Raudenbush, S. W. (1987). Application of hierarchical linear models to assessing change. *Psychological Bulletin, 101,* 147–158.

Carrig, M., Wirth, R. J., & Curran, P. J. (2003). An SAS macro for estimating and visualizing individual growth curves. *Structural Equation Modeling: An Interdisciplinary Journal, 11,* 132–149.

Cheong, J., MacKinnon, D. P., & Khoo, S. T. (2003). Investigation of mediational processes using parallel process latent growth curve modeling. *Structural Equation Modeling, 10*(2), 238–262.

Curran, P. J. (2003). Have multilevel models been structural equation models all along? *Multivariate Behavioral Research, 38,* 529–569.

Curran, P. J., & Hussong, A. M. (2002). Structural equation modeling of repeated measures data: Latent curve analysis. In D. S. Moskowitz & S. L. Hershberger (Eds.), *Modeling intraindividual variability with repeated measures data: Methods and applications* (pp. 59–86). Mahwah, NJ: Lawrence Erlbaum Associates.

Duncan, T. E., Duncan, S. C., Strycker, L. A., Li, F., & Alpert, A. (1999). *An introduction to latent variable growth curve modeling: Concepts, issues, and applications.* Mahwah, NJ: Lawrence Erlbaum Associates.

Hedeker, D. (2004). An introduction to growth modeling. In D. Kaplan (Ed.), *Handbook of quantitative methodology for the social sciences* (pp. 215–234). Thousand Oaks, CA: Sage.

Hedeker, D., & Gibbons, R. D. (2006). *Longitudinal data analysis.* Hoboken, NJ: John Wiley & Sons.

Hu, L., & Bentler, P. M. (1999). Cutoff criteria for fit indexes in covariance structure analysis: Conventional criteria versus new alternatives. *Structural Equation Modeling, 6*(1), 1–55.

Muthén, L. K., & Muthén, B. O. (2004). *Mplus user's guide, Version 3.1.* Los Angeles: Muthén & Muthén.

National Health Promotion Associates. (2002). http://www.lifeskillstraining.com/program.cfm

Osgood, D. W. (2001). Advances in the application of multilevel models to the analysis of change (pp. 97–104). In L. M Collins & A. G. Sayer (Eds.), *New methods for the analysis of change.* Washington, DC: American Psychological Association.

Peugh, J. L., & Enders, C. K. (2005). Using the SPSS mixed procedure to fit hierarchical linear and growth trajectory models. *Educational and Psychological Measurement, 65*(5), 717–741.

Raudenbush, S. W., & Bryk, A. S. (2002). *Hierarchical linear models: Applications and data analysis methods* (2nd ed.). Thousand Oaks, CA: Sage.

Rogosa, D. R., & Willett, J. B. (1985). Understanding correlates of change by modeling individual differences in growth. *Psychometrika, 50,* 203–228.

Schwartz, S. E., & Stone, A. A. (1998). Strategies for analyzing ecological momentary assessment data. *Health Psychology, 17*(1), 6–16.

Sillars, A., Koerner, A., & Fitzpatrick, M. A. (2005). Communication and understanding in parent-adolescent relationships. *Human Communication Research, 31,* 102–128.

Singer, J. D. (1998). Using SAS PROC MIXED to fit multilevel models, hierarchical models, and individual growth curve models. *Journal of Educational and Behavioral Statistics, 24,* 323–355.

Singer, J. D. (2002). Fitting individual growth models using SAS PROC MIXED. In D. S. Moskowitz & S. L. Hershberger (Eds.), *Modeling intraindividual variability with repeated measures data: Methods and applications* (pp. 135–170). Mahwah, NJ: Lawrence Erlbaum Associates.

Singer, J. D., & Willett, J. B. (2003). *Applied longitudinal data analysis: Modeling change and event occurrence.* New York: Oxford University Press.

Slater, M. D. (in press). Spirals of influence: A system dynamics model of media use and effects. *Journal of Communication.*

Slater, M. D., Henry, K. L., Swaim, R. C., & Anderson, L. (2003). Violent media content and aggressiveness in adolescents: A downward spiral model. *Communication Research, 30*(6), 713–736.

Slater, M. D., Henry, K. L., Swaim, R. C., & Cardador, J. (2004). Vulnerable teens, vulnerable times: How sensation-seeking, alienation, and victimization moderate the violent media content-aggressiveness relation. *Communication Research, 31*(6), 642–668.

Snijders, T. A. B., & Bosker, R. J. (1999). *Multilevel analysis: An introduction to basic and advanced multilevel modeling.* London: Sage.

Tucker, L. R., & Lewis, C. (1973). A reliability coefficient for maximum likelihood factor analysis. *Psychometrika, 38,* 1–10.

Willett, J. B., & Sayer, A. G. (1994). Using covariance structure analysis to detect correlates and predictors of change. *Psychological Bulletin, 116,* 363–381.

Willett, J. B., & Sayer, A. G. (1995). Cross-domain analyses of change over time: Combining growth modeling and covariance structure analysis. In G. A. Marcoulides & R. E. Schumacker (Eds.), *Advanced structural equation modeling: Issues and techniques* (pp. 22–51). Hillsdale, NJ: Lawrence Erlbaum Associates.

Time Series Analysis

Traditional and Contemporary Approaches

Itzhak Yanovitzky
Arthur VanLear

One commonly hears that communication is a process, but most communication research fails to exploit or live up to that axiom. Whatever the full implications of viewing communication as a process might be, it is clear that it implies that communication is dynamically situated in a temporal context, such that time is a central dimension of communication (Berlo, 1977; VanLear, 1996). We believe that there are several reasons for the gap between our axiomatic ideal of communication as process and the realization of that ideal in actual communication research. Incorporating time into communication research is difficult because of the time, effort, resources, and knowledge necessary. Temporal data not only offers great opportunity and advantage, but it also comes with its own set of practical problems and issues (Menard, 2002; Taris, 2000). The paucity of process research exists not only because of the greater effort and difficulty in time series data collection but also because the exploitation and analysis of time series data call for knowledge and expertise beyond what is typically taught in our communication methods sequences in graduate school, and mastering these techniques by self-teaching is difficult for many. This chapter is designed as the first step in developing the knowledge and skills necessary to do communication process research.

Authors' Note: We wish to thank Stacy Renfro Powers and Christian Rauh for use of the interaction data used in the example of frequency domain time series, and we wish to thank Jeff Kotz and Mark Cistulli for unitizing and coding that data.

A time series is a set of observations obtained by measuring a single variable regularly over a period of time. The number of news stories about breast cancer appearing each month in the *New York Times* between 2000 and 2005 or the amount of time spent smiling in every 2-second interval over a 10-minute conversation are both examples of time series.[1] Time series data are different from cross-sectional data in that observations have a temporal order, and the analysis of such data leads to new and unique problems in statistical modeling and inference. Characteristic properties of a time series are that the data are not independently sampled, their dispersion varies in time, and they are often governed by a trend and cyclic components. In particular, the correlation introduced by the sampling of adjacent points in time can severely restrict the applicability of the many conventional statistical methods traditionally dependent on the assumption that observations are independent and that errors are therefore uncorrelated. Statistical procedures that suppose independent and identically distributed data are, therefore, excluded from the analysis of time series. The systematic approach for the statistical modeling of such data is commonly referred to as time series analysis.

The main objective of this chapter is to offer readers a reasonably broad and nontechnical exposition of traditional and contemporary time series analysis methods as they apply to communication research. We intentionally leave out any technical details related to the statistical application of these methods. Time series analysis is quite complex, and there are several excellent texts on this topic that we would recommend to readers who are interested in applying time series analysis methods to their data (see Chatfield, 1989; Cromwell, 1994; Cromwell, Labys, & Terraza, 1994; Gottman, 1981; McCleary & Hay, 1980; McDowall, 1980; Ostrom, 1990; Sayrs, 1989; Shumway & Stoffer, 2000; StatSoft, 2003; Watt & VanLear, 1996). Our goal here is to provide a conceptual introduction to time series analysis, one that (a) illustrates to readers the benefits of incorporating time series analysis into the existing repertoire of communication research methods, (b) describes the common application of time series analysis and the potential weaknesses of this approach, and (c) introduces a set of standards that communication scholars should use when reporting on or evaluating studies that employ time series analysis methods. Thus, we begin with an overview of the potential application of time series analysis methods in communication research and provide examples of how these methods have been used by communication scholars to date. Our discussion here focuses on the kinds of research questions that can be addressed through this family of methods and the proper use of time series analysis in communication research. Next, we review the basic terminology and critical assumptions of time series analysis, distinguish between the time domain approach and the frequency domain approach to time series analysis, and outline the traditional approach to the analysis of time series data. Here, our primary interest is to point out a number of problems in the application of these approaches to communication research and suggest some alternatives.

Time Series Analysis Methods in Communication Research

The impact of time series analysis on scientific applications within the field of communication can be partially documented by listing the kinds of communication research to which time series methods have been applied. In the area of mass communication research, time series analysis methods have been most commonly applied to the study of agenda-setting processes in a variety of contexts including AIDS policy (Rogers et al., 1991), breast cancer screening by women 40 years and older (Yanovitzky & Blitz, 2000), marijuana use among adolescents (Stryker, 2003), drunk driving policy and behavior (Yanovitzky & Bennett, 1999), global warming (Trumbo, 1995), consumer confidence (Blood & Phillips, 1995; Fan & Cook, 2003), and political judgments (Gonzenbach, 1996; Shah, Watts, Domke, & Fan, 2002; Shah, Watts, Domke, Fan, & Fibison, 1999), to name a few. For example, Yanovitzky and Blitz (2000) employed time series regression analysis to compare the contribution of news coverage of mammography screening and physician advice to the utilization of mammography by women 40 years and older in the United States between 1989 and 1991. Data on mammography-related national media attention between January 1989 and December 1991 were generated by analyzing the content of seven nationally and regionally prominent newspapers (the *New York Times, Washington Post, Los Angeles Times, Chicago Tribune, Boston Globe, St. Petersburg Times,* and *USA Today*). All relevant news stories appearing in these newspapers in a course of each month during the research period ($N = 36$ months) were aggregated to represent the volume of media attention to this issue in that particular month. Comparable national-level data on mammography utilization by women ages 40 and older and prevalence of physicians' advice to have a mammogram were compiled from the Behavioral Risk Factor Surveillance System (BRFSS) that is administered each month by the Centers for Disease Control and Prevention (CDC) to a representative cross-section of noninstitutionalized adults nationwide. The proportion of women 40 years and older in each month who had a mammogram in the year preceding the interview served as the dependent variable in the analysis. To estimate the prevalence of physician advice to have a mammogram in each month, the proportion of women 40 years and older indicating that having a mammogram in the past year was their physician's idea was used. Using time series analysis to examine the direction of influence between these three variables controlling for potential confounding variables, the researchers found that both channels of communication (news coverage and physician advice) accounted together for 51% of the variance over time in mammography-seeking behavior by women 40 years and older. Moreover, they found that physician advice was particularly influential for women who had regular access to a physician, while news coverage of mammography was more influential among women who did not have regular access to a physician (mainly due to lack of health insurance).

In this and other similar studies, the typical approach taken by the researchers was to correlate national news coverage of issues over time with outcomes related to public opinion or public policy on these issues during the same time period (Dearing & Rogers, 1996). In virtually all cases, some form of aggregated data was used and most studies were limited to the investigation of the relationship between two time series. However, the time series methods employed in these studies vary considerably, ranging from trend analysis (Brosius & Kepplinger, 1992; Funkhouser, 1973; Smith, 1980; Tedrow & Mahoney, 1979) and cross-correlation methods (Brosius & Kepplinger, 1992; Winter & Eyal, 1991), to time series regression and traditional ARIMA methods (Gonzenbach, 1996; Shoemaker, Wanta, & Leggett, 1989; Trumbo, 1995; Yanovitzky & Bennett, 1999), and to nonlinear methods (Fan, 1988; Fan & Cook, 2003; Yanovitzky, 2002a).

There is little doubt that time series analysis methodology has enriched agenda-setting research in a number of important ways, including the ability to describe and analyze the agenda-setting process and to correlate it with a host of hypothesized outcomes over time (for a complete review, see Gonzenbach & McGavin, 1997). For example, by applying these methods, researchers were able to estimate lagged effects of news coverage on individuals, groups, and institutions (Yanovitzky, 2002b) and calculate the rate in which these effects decay for different issues (Fan, 1988; Watt, Mazza, & Snyder, 1993). They were also able to compare media effects across issues and populations (e.g., McCombs & Zhu, 1995; Yanovitzky & Blitz, 2000) as well as to examine indirect (or mediated) effects between the news, the policy agenda, and personal behavior over time (Yanovitzky & Bennett, 1999). Perhaps more importantly, the use of these methods allows more rigorous tests of agenda-setting theory (Gonzenbach & McGavin, 1997) and facilitates multilevel theorizing and research (Pan & McLeod, 1991; Slater, Snyder, & Hayes, 2006).

In the interpersonal domain, time series analysis has greatly enhanced our understanding of the interaction patterns used by relational partners including reciprocity and compensation, conversational control and coordination among adult dyads and mother-infant dyads (Cappella, 1981, 1996; Street & Cappella, 1989; VanLear et al., 2005), relationship emergence and development (Huston & Vangelisti, 1991; VanLear, 1987, 1991), and decision emergence in small groups (Poole, 1981; Poole & Roth, 1989; VanLear & Mabry, 1999).

One of the best examples in the literature is the research program carried out by Joseph Cappella during the 1980s and 1990s on reciprocity and compensation as forms of mutual adaptation in dyadic conversations (Cappella, 1981, 1996; Street & Cappella, 1989). For example, Cappella (1996) and his colleagues coded conversational behaviors (e.g., vocalizing, smiles, body orientation, eye gaze, illustrators) at every 0.3 second along with an identification of which partner "held the floor" (as defined by Jaffe & Feldstein, 1970). Each data point was an individual's frequency of that behavior in a 3-second window over 30 minutes of conversation (Cappella, 1996). A cluster of behaviors (vocalizing, illustrator gestures, and averting gaze) were highly correlated and clearly associated with actually "holding the floor." Cappella fit each dyadic partner's time series for the composite variable ("turn index") using time domain time series analyses (ARIMA). The ARIMA diagnostics showed that most of the series displayed a first-order autoregressive process, with a few showing trends, first-order moving averages, or some combination (see our later discussion). He then ran individual time series analyses to correlate the time series of speaker A with that of speaker B covarying out the effects of actually "holding the floor." Finally, treating each dyad's analysis as a separate study, he used meta-analysis to aggregate the effects (mutual adaptation scores) across dyads (see later discussion of aggregating postanalysis). The fact that the turn index (along with actually holding the floor) exhibited strongly complementary alternations between dyadic partners is hardly surprising and almost trivial. However, by covarying out the effects of actually "holding the floor," Cappella (1996) was able to show that there is still some mutual adaptation in the form of compensation between the "turn-taking" complex of behaviors, especially among low-expressive dyads and especially between newly acquainted dyads. Cappella (1996) interprets this compensation as "exaggerated politeness" in which partners respond to these behaviors by their partner to avoid "stepping into each other's conversational space" (p. 384).

IMPORTANT ADVANTAGES AND LIMITATIONS OF TIME SERIES ANALYSIS

There are a number of obvious reasons to collect and analyze time series data when studying communication-related phenomena. Among these are the desire to describe variation in variables of interest over time, to gain a better understanding (or explanation) of the data-generating mechanism, to be able to predict future values of a time series, and to allow for the optimal monitoring and control of a system's performance over time (Chatfield, 1989). More importantly, however, time series analysis can greatly enhance our ability to study human communication as a set of dynamic phenomena and to devise more rigorous empirical tests of theoretical propositions about communication-related processes, their determinants, and their effects. Many communication-related phenomena are by definition time-bound processes, and many of the theories that guide research in the field, such as cultivation (Gerbner, Gross, Morgan, & Signorielli, 1986), diffusion of innovations (Rogers & Shoemaker, 1973), structuration (Poole, Seibold, & McPhee, 1996), and relational pragmatics (Fisher, 1978), treat communication, inherently, as a process. Yet, empirical investigations of communication-related phenomena are seldom process oriented, with most being limited to the investigation of simultaneous or short-term relationships between communication variables of interest (Poole, 2000; Watt, 1994).

Time series analysis methods can be a powerful instrument for studying communication processes (Watt & VanLear, 1996). For one, they allow researchers to avoid the pitfalls of studying a communication-related phenomenon in isolation from its past and future. Most communication variables, being realizations of underlying communication processes, are ever evolving (VanLear, 1996). For example, individuals often modify their verbal and nonverbal communication many times in the course of a single discussion (Cappella, 1996), and news coverage of a particular issue, such as the AIDS epidemic, can greatly change in volume and content over a period of a decade (Rogers, Dearing, & Chang, 1991). Some of the changes observed in these variables over time may be random, but many tend to be systematic or deterministic. For instance, certain variables, such as the use of the Internet to search for health information, may trend upward over time (Rice & Katz, 2001), others, such as ambiguity in group decision making, will follow a curvilinear pattern over the course of deliberations (VanLear & Mabry, 1999), while still others, such as television viewing, may follow regular seasonal patterns (Barnett, Chang, Fink, & Richards, 1991) or shorter cycles of attention (Meadowcroft, 1996). Such trends and cycles, in turn, may explain why communication-related phenomena vary across units of analysis at a given point in time or for the same unit of analysis at different points in time. Even stability over time (or inertia) can be quite consequential in this respect. For example, suppose we would like to explain, or even predict, the degree to which a certain person depends on newspapers alone to get the news. We could probably come up with several competing explanations, but our task would be less complicated if we find out that this person has been relying primarily on newspapers to get the news for the past 20 years. We could reasonably propose, then, that this person's current preference for newspapers as the source of news can be explained, to a great degree, by this old habit. Importantly, this habit can also help to explain why this person's current preference for newspapers is similar to or different from those of another person: If they share the same habit, we would predict similarity in current behavior; if they do not share this habit, we would predict a difference. The bottom line is that studying variables in relation to their past can greatly enhance researchers' ability to more fully understand and to predict communication-related phenomena.

Other than facilitating one's capacity to model and to predict communication-related processes, time series analysis methods also have some desirable properties in terms of enhancing causal inference about the relationships between phenomena of interest. One important advantage in this respect is the ability to establish the temporal ordering of variables as a way of delineating which of two variables may be the likely cause of the other. Establishing temporal order between variables may not be an issue when the researcher controls the timing of introducing the independent variable, as is the case when experimental or quasi-experimental methodology is used,[2] but is crucial (though rarely sufficient) for drawing causal inference in the context of cross-sectional or nonexperimental research where researchers cannot have such control. In these cases, the ability to establish temporal ordering can greatly enhance researchers' ability to draw causal inference from their data. For example, employing time series analysis to the relationship between news coverage of mammography and the observed increase in mammography utilization by women 40 years and older between 1989 and 1991, Yanovitzky and Blitz (2000) found convincing evidence that news coverage preceded the observed behavior change, thus supporting the argument that exposure to news coverage about mammography contributed positively to mammography utilization during this period. Similarly, VanLear, Brown, and Anderson (2003) found a series of complex relationships between social support and emotional quality of life among recovering alcoholics such that the supportiveness of an AA sponsor predicted long-term improvement in emotional quality of life, but the emotional quality of life predicted the perceived quality of the relationship with the alcoholic's significant other. In both cases, establishing the temporal order between variables of interest afforded the opportunity to gain better insight into the nature of the relationships that exist between these variables.

One other notable benefit of employing time series analysis when studying the relationships between two or more time-bound variables is the ability to model and test hypotheses about lagged effects. For example, a recent study using time series analysis showed an almost instantaneous effect of news coverage of drunk driving on policymakers' attention to the issue but a delayed effect (of about three months) on policymakers' legislative behavior (Yanovitzky, 2002b). Similarly, in online support groups, the level of self-presentation of a speaker affects not only the self-presentation and other-orientation of the next speaker but of speakers at subsequent lags as well (VanLear, Sheehan, Withers, & Walker, 2005). Standard methods, including those that are seemingly sensitive to the temporal ordering of variables such as repeated-measures ANOVA, are not well equipped to differentiate instantaneous from delayed effects either because measures of all variables are taken at one particular point in time (as is the case when cross-sectional or posttest-only experimental data are used) or because repeated measurements of variables are frequently limited (typically, 2–3 time points at most) and taken at time intervals that are either too close or too distant to capture lagged effects. In contrast, time series designs allow for the collection of time-sequenced data over multiple and equally sequenced time intervals and are better equipped to detect both instantaneous and delayed effects, providing that decisions about the frequency in which data are collected are grounded in strong theoretical or empirical rationale about the expected or hypothesized timing of effects.

Time series analysis may also be useful when comparing two or more communication processes or estimating the effect that these different processes have on a particular outcome. For example, Yanovitzky and Stryker (2001) used time series analysis to estimate the extent to which adolescents' exposure to information about other peers' use of alcohol occurred through the mass media or interpersonal channels. By comparing two different hypothesized processes of exposure (direct exposure to media content vs. diffusion of information within peer networks), they were able to determine that exposure to mass communication channels had an independent contribution to adolescents' perception of alcohol use by peers (see also Zhu, Watt, Snyder, Yan, & Jiang, 1993).

Finally, time series analysis has the advantage of modeling both linear and nonlinear relationships between variables over time. Most standard data analysis methods used in communication research such as ANOVA and OLS regression assume linear association between variables of interest. Frequently, however, nonlinear functions provide better approximation of the true relationship between communication-related variables (Brosius & Kepplinger, 1992; Poole, 2000). Thus, whereas this chapter focuses mainly on linear time series methods with the goal of helping novice users of time series analysis to acquire the methodological foundations of this approach, readers should be aware of recent developments regarding the application of nonlinear time series methods in communication and related disciplines (Fan, 1988; Heath, 2000; Poole, 2000).

On the other hand, many of the well-known problems of collecting and analyzing longitudinal data are relevant to time series analysis. For example, measuring participants repeatedly can influence their behavior and perceptions over time in addition to the impact that independent variables of interest may have on these changes. Similarly, when subject attrition is systematic, trends may reflect the changing nature of the sample rather than the dynamics of the phenomena under investigation. Other confounding influences may be created by historical events and changes in measures or recording practices of variables over time. It is also often difficult to disentangle cohort effects from true temporal trends (Menard, 2002; Taris, 2000). One of the most significant of the temporal problems is "regression toward the mean" where people with extreme scores in their first measurement tend to score closer to the mean on subsequent measures (Campbell & Kenny, 1999). One way of dealing with many of these problems is to use a revolving panel design in which measurements are repeated on a subgroup four times with different participants being rotated into the sample at different waves of the study (Menard, 2002). Subsamples can even be rotated in for several waves, rotated out for several waves, and rotated back into the sample (Mansur & Shoemaker, 1999). Generally, differences can be observed between groups rotated into the sample for the first time and those groups that have been in the sample for some time, and this has been referred to as "time-in-sample bias" (Mansur & Shoemaker, 1999). In some cases, these effects can be statistically controlled for or appropriate transformations may be used to debias the data if a rotating panel design is used.

SUMMARY

Given the importance of the potential contributions to achieving progress in communication research, it is surprising that only a handful of studies have applied this methodology to research problems relevant to communication. There may be several reasons for this, including the cost of collecting time series data (Tabachnick & Fidell, 2001), the inherent complexity of this data analysis method (Shumway, 1988), and the fact that communication-related variables are rarely included in longitudinal survey systems that collect time series data such as the Monitoring the Future Project and the General Social Survey (though such sources could be augmented with comparable communication time series data such as aggregated measures of news coverage of a particular issue). It is also worth noting that time series analysis is not always the best approach to analyzing longitudinal data. Time series approaches are generally appropriate for answering research questions regarding systematic and random patterns of change in a series over time, the association between two or more time series over time, and the effect of interventions (also known as interrupted time series analysis). When longitudinal designs feature large numbers of cases (say, hundreds) but small numbers of repeated observations (e.g., less than 30), then other methods are often utilized such as hierarchical linear modeling and latent growth models (see Chapter 3 of this volume). The strength of the time series models discussed here is in their ability to detect, analyze, and explain complex temporal processes. Their main weakness is in their lack of a model for generalizability across cases. We will discuss the issue of aggregating time series across multiple cases later in this chapter.

The Basics of Time Series Analysis

There are two separate but not necessarily mutually exclusive approaches to time series analysis: the time domain approach and the frequency domain approach. The *time domain* approach is motivated by the presumption that correlation between adjacent points in time is best explained in terms of the dependence of current values on past values of the same series. This approach focuses on modeling some future values of a time series as a linear function of current and past values. The most popular time series analysis techniques that follow this approach—autoregressive integrated moving average (ARIMA) models—receive special attention in this chapter. The *frequency domain* approach, on the other hand, assumes that the primary characteristics of interest in time series analysis involve the periodic or systematic sinusoidal variations found naturally in most data. These periodic variations are often caused by external or environmental factors of interest or may be an intrinsic feature of the phenomenon (e.g., biological rhythms). The partition of the various kinds of periodic variations is typically achieved through Fourier or spectral analysis, which we discuss in detail later on.

BASIC TERMINOLOGY

Before we move to discuss the underlying logic of these two approaches, it is useful to introduce the basic terminology of time series analysis. A time series' most basic unit of analysis is a *point in time* (i.e., a second, an hour, a day, a week, a month, a year, etc.). For each point in time we record the value of a certain variable (e.g., media salience, domestic violence incidents, eye gaze, etc.). The temporal distance between two time periods is a *lag* and is quantified by the number of time units that are included in this time interval. A *first-order series* is a series in which one lag is separating two correlated observations, while a *second-order series* is a series in which two lags are separating two correlated observations, and so on. A time series is said to be *continuous* when observations are made continuously without interruption in time (e.g., heart beats as recorded by EKG trace). A time series is said to be *discrete* when observations are taken only at specific time intervals (usually equally spaced). An *aggregated* time series is a discrete time series in which values are aggregated over equal intervals of time (e.g., the total number of news stories on the economy published each day in the *Washington Post* during the month of January). A *pooled* time series of cross sections contains measures of a particular variable taken from a relatively large number of units of observations (such as individuals, countries, or organizations) over a relatively large number of time points (also called "cross-sectional time series").

One major consideration in analyzing a process captured by a time series involves assumptions about the relationship between observations of the same variable at different time points. Many standard data analysis methods such as regression analysis assume that observations are independent of each other and, therefore, the errors are uncorrelated. Time series analysis, on the other hand, is based on the assumption that successive observations are usually dependent and that we must account for the time order of the observations in our analysis of the time series data.[3] This assumption is formalized in the notion of autocorrelation (also called serial correlation), namely, the correlation of a variable with itself over successive time intervals. Autocorrelation has one important consequence regarding time series data: When successive observations are dependent, we can predict future values from past observations of the same variable and not exclusively by exogenous variables. If a time series future value can be predicted from past values, the time series is said to be *deterministic*.

This characteristic of time series data forces us to identify the internal mechanism that is capable of having produced the set of observed values of a variable over time. With cross-sectional data, this mechanism is the covariance of two or more variables at the same point in time. In contrast, with time series data, this mechanism is assumed to be a *stochastic process*. In order to provide a statistical setting for describing the character of data that seemingly fluctuate in a random fashion over time, we assume that a time series can be defined as a collection of random variables indexed according to the order in which they are obtained in time. Put differently, a stochastic process is a random function that varies in time. For this reason, the future values of a time series (being a realization of a stochastic process) can be predicted with only a certain probability of being correct. This assumption does not mean that the process behaves in a completely unpredictable manner, only that its behavior is partially governed by a random mechanism. In fact, the Wold decomposition thereom holds that a time series can be thought of as a combination of a trend, a deterministic cycle, and a stochastic process (Gottman, 1981). VanLear (1996; VanLear & Li, 2005) has used this theorem to suggest that communication processes can be decomposed into scheduled or programmed processes (i.e., deterministic) and unscheduled stochastic adaptations as they evolve over time.

A second common assumption in many time series techniques (e.g., time domain time series) is that the data are *stationary*. A stationary process has the property that the mean, variance, and autocorrelation structure do not change over time. Stationarity can be defined in precise mathematical terms, but for our purpose we mean a series free of a trend and periodic fluctuations (seasonality). In reality, however, the behavior of most time series is determined by two basic classes of systematic components: trend and seasonality. *Trend* represents a general systematic linear or (most often) nonlinear component that changes over time and that does not repeat in our data (e.g., a monotonic increase or decrease in the level of the series over time). *Seasonality* may have a similar nature, but it tends to repeat itself in systematic intervals over time. Those two general classes of time series components may coexist in real-life data.

Figure 4.1 illustrates these phenomena through a hypothetical example: local news coverage of outdoor events held in a particular community between 1987 and 1995. Just by inspecting the time series visually, we can detect a slight upward trend in the number of outdoors events covered by the local news media from year to year. In addition, as one may expect, news

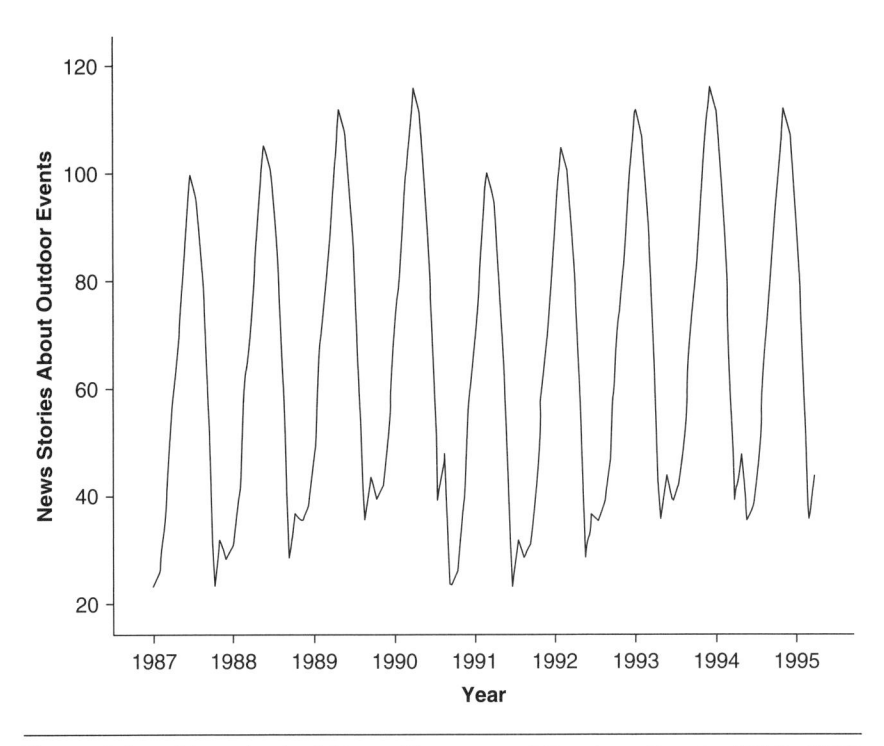

Figure 4.1 Hypothetical News Coverage of Outdoor Events, 1987–1995

coverage in each year peaks during the spring and summer months and declines during the winter months. These "cycles" are responsible for seasonal effects on the level of the series. The problem with using standard methods (e.g., regression analysis) to model the process underlying a time series is that such deterministic components can introduce large systematic errors into the estimation procedure that likely violate critical assumptions such as the assumption that models' residuals are uncorrelated or that they are equally distributed among the different categories of the independent variable (homoscedasticity). Thus, before we can use a time series as a "conventional" variable, we must make sure it is stationary or free from any systematic and deterministic effects over time. If it is not a stationary time series, it must be transformed into one (a procedure that is often referred to as *prewhitening*) before standard statistical procedures could be employed.

The Time Domain Approach to Modeling Time Series Data

This basic rationale of time series analysis guides the common approach to analyzing time series data. In this respect, traditional time domain approaches to time series analysis are best understood as techniques for adapting standard regression methods to the problematic nature of time series data. As noted above, the classical regression model was developed for the static case, namely, when a dependent variable is allowed to be influenced by current values of the independent variable. In the time series case, it is desirable to allow the dependent variable to be influenced by the past values of the independent variables and possibly by its own past values. The need to incorporate these lagged relationships into the explanation of a variable's variance over time led to the development of the *autoregressive integrated moving average* (ARIMA) model that was popularized by Box and Jenkins (1976) and that seeks to uncover persistent patterns in the behavior of time series, often so that unbiased estimates of standard deviations can be calculated and that accurate forecasts of future values can be generated.

It is worth noting that because of its power and flexibility, ARIMA is a rather complex technique—it is not easy to use, it requires a great deal of experience, and although it often produces satisfactory results, those results depend on the researcher's level of expertise. Readers who are interested in applying this approach could benefit from reading texts dedicated to these methods (e.g., McCleary & Hay, 1980) as well as books, monographs, and book chapters that discuss the application of ARIMA methods in agenda-setting research (e.g., Gonzenbach, 1996; Gonzenbach & McGavin, 1997; Trumbo, 1995). Our discussion below leaves out much of the technical details of fitting ARIMA models and focuses instead on the gist of this approach, which can be summarized in a few basic steps: (a) plotting the data against time, (b) possibly transforming the data, (c) identifying the dependence order of the model (identification), (d) estimating the ARIMA parameters (estimation), and (e) evaluating the estimated model's goodness of fit (diagnostics).

ARIMA METHODOLOGY: A PRIMER

The first step to take in any time series analysis is to plot the time series against time. In many cases, the researchers can detect the presence of possible deterministic components just by inspecting the behavior of the series of time, as is the case in Figure 4.1. Depending on the degree of fluctuations in a time series behavior over time, one may also find it useful to use some form of a *smoothing* procedure. Smoothing techniques are used to reduce irregularities (random fluctuations) in time series data and thus provide a clearer view of the true underlying behavior of the series. Two common smoothing procedures are moving average and natural log transformation, but other options exist (for more options, see Chatfield, 1989). However, the visual display may be misleading at times, particularly when no systematic change in the series' level can be detected. In these cases, researchers are strongly cautioned against concluding that the time series is stationary before more formal statistical tests are performed (e.g., the Box-Ljung Q statistic).

Two additional tools that most common statistical packages (e.g., SPSS, SAS, STATA) offer are the autocorrelation function (ACF) and the partial autocorrelation function (PACF) *correlograms.* Autocorrelation correlograms are a commonly used tool for checking randomness in a series' behavior over time. This randomness is ascertained by computing correlations for data values at varying time lags. If random, such autocorrelations should be near zero for any and all time-lag separations. If nonrandom, then one or more of the autocorrelations will be significantly nonzero. Partial autocorrelations are the autocorrelations between two time points separated by a certain lag controlling for any dependence on the intermediate time points within this lag. If a lag of 1 is specified (i.e., there are no intermediate elements within the lag), then the partial autocorrelation is equivalent to autocorrelation. In a sense, the partial autocorrelation provides a "cleaner" picture of serial dependencies for individual lags (not confounded by other serial dependencies). Data can be assumed to be stationary if no partial autocorrelation is found to be statistically significant. Autoregressive models are created with the idea that the present value of the series can be explained as a linear function of past values on this series.

Figure 4.2 shows the ACF correlogram for a hypothetical discrete series measuring exposure to media messages about domestic violence per 100,000 viewers in a finite population over a period of 145 weeks ($N = 145$ equally spaced time points). Figure 4.3 presents the corresponding PACF correlogram. The bars in each diagram represent the estimated autocorrelation coefficients and are bounded by 95% confidence intervals to detect statistically significant autocorrelations. It is apparent from Figure 4.2 that a significant degree of autocorrelation exists within the series (as indicated by the presence of a statistically significant correlation in each of the lags), which suggests a nonstationary series. The PACF plot in Figure 4.3 indicates that the autocorrelation in the series is of first order (namely, that the strongest autocorrelations exist between observations separated by a single time lag).

When a time series is determined to be nonstationary, the ACF and PACF correlograms have an important role in the identification of deterministic components using the ARIMA approach. ARIMA stands for the three types of mathematical processes that can be employed to generate a stationary process: (1) autoregression (AR), (2) trend or integrated series (I), and (3) moving average (MA). The *autoregressive* component in the ARIMA model accounts for the autocorrelation or the magnitude of the dependency between adjacent observations. These dependencies can be removed by regressing the present value of the series on the linear function of past values of the same series at *k* lags and replacing the original

Time Series Analysis

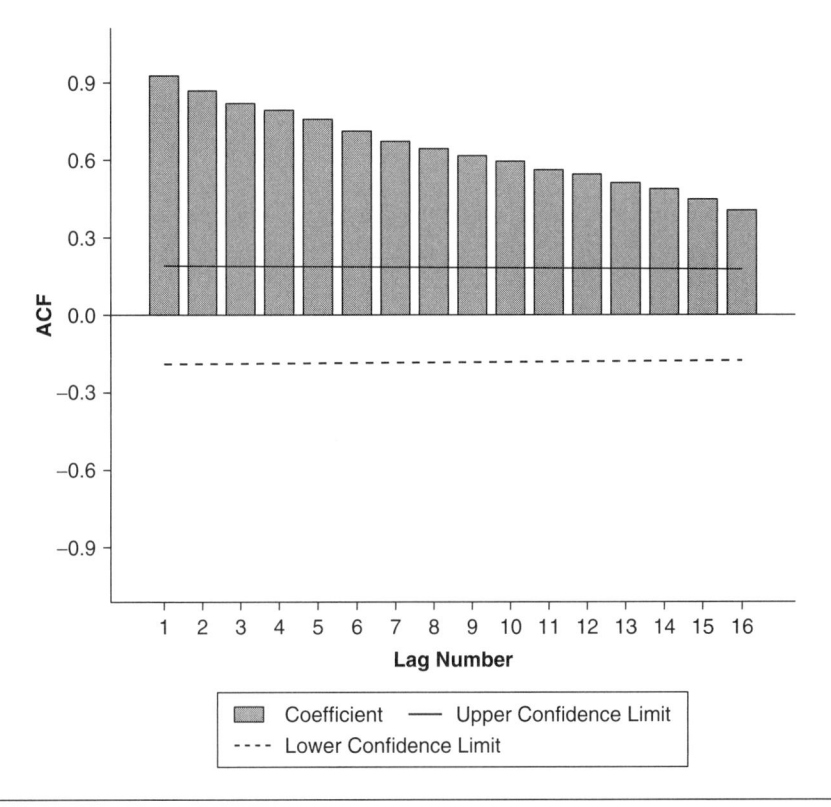

Figure 4.2 Autocorrelation Function (ACF) Correlogram

series with the newly created residual series. The *integrated* component in the ARIMA model addresses the issue of stationarity in the average level of the series over time (note, however, that it does not address the issue of stationarity in variance over time). Many, if not most, time series can be made stationary by *differencing*. The method of differencing replaces each time series observation with the difference of the current observation and its adjacent observation k steps backward in time. The moving average component is a bit less intuitive. It addresses the persistence of a random shock (or a past error that cannot be accounted for by an autoregressive process) from one observation to the next. A shock is an external event that takes place at a particular point in the series and whose impact is not contained to the point at which it occurs. The method of moving averages dampens fluctuations in a time series by first taking successive averages of groups of observations and then replacing each successive overlapping sequence of k observations in the series with the mean of that sequence.

ACF and PACF correlograms are typically used to identify the three ARIMA model's parameters that correspond to each of these three components. The autoregressive parameter (p) represents the number of time lags that separate two correlated observations. Thus, a first-order series,

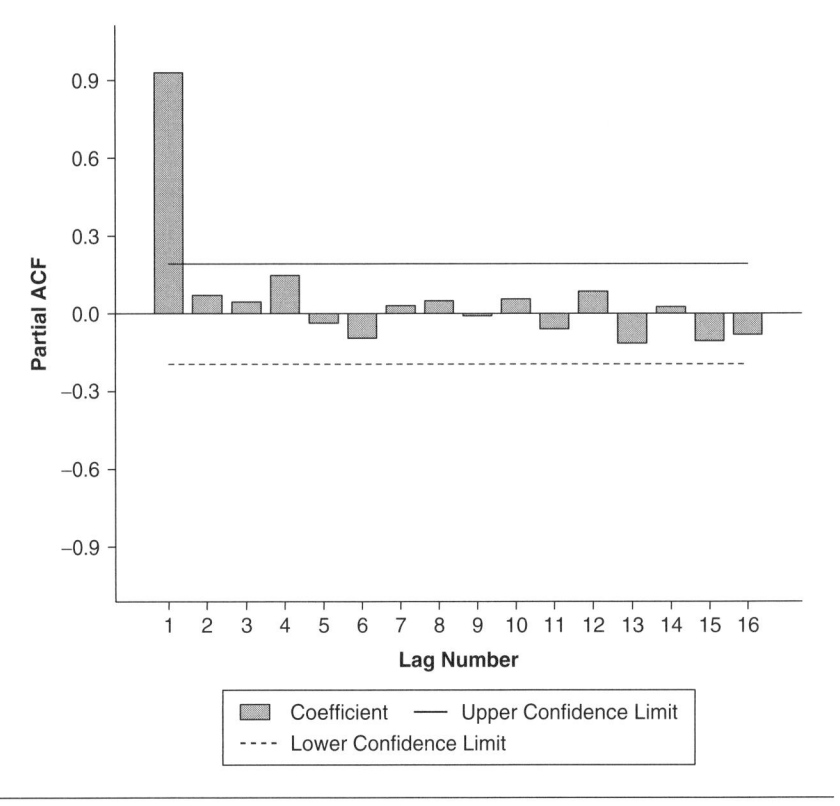

Figure 4.3 Partial Autocorrelation Function (PACF) Correlogram

abbreviated $AR_{(1)}$, is a series in which one lag is separating two correlated observations, while a second-order series, $AR_{(2)}$, is a series in which two lags are separating two correlated observations, and so on. The integrated parameter (d) represents the shape of the trend that exists within the time series: A first-order d parameter ($d = 1$) indicates a linear trend, a second-order d parameter indicates a quadratic trend, and a third-order d parameter indicates a cubic trend. The moving average parameter (q) represents the number of time lags (or window) over which the effect of a random shock persists in the series. A first-order moving average parameter ($q = 1$) means that current observations are correlated with shocks at lag 1, a second-order q parameter means they are correlated with shocks at lag 2, and so on. By convention, these parameters are represented as (p,d,q) and denote the ARIMA term. Thus, an ARIMA (1,0,0) indicates a series characterized by a first-order autoregressive component with no trend or moving average components. Particular ARIMA models tend to be associated with a particular output of the ACF and PACF correlograms. For example, an ACF output that demonstrates an exponential decay of serial correlations of the type shown in Figure 4.2 and a PACF output demonstrating a spike at lag 1 with no serial correlations for other lags, as is the case in

Figure 4.3, suggest the presence of a first-order autoregressive process (1,0,0). Note that the boundary lines around the functions in these figures are the 95% confidence bounds. If the bar representing an autocorrelation at some lag crosses the boundary lines, the interpretation is that this autocorrelation is significantly different from zero and that it should be included in the ARIMA model. ACF and PACF representations of other ARIMA processes are included in most basic texts about time series (e.g., Box & Jenkins, 1976; McCleary & Hay, 1980) as well as manuals of commonly used statistical packages (for example, the SPSS Trends manual). At times, a series may have seasonal components (seasonal autocorrelations) or structural dependency among observation separated by one period or cycle, such as an annual cycle or 6-month cycles. Seasonal components are evident in ACF and PACF plots that wear the shape of cycles with strong positive ACFs equal to the length of the cycle and negative ACFs equal to one half the period of the cycle. A seasonal ARIMA model takes the seasonal components into account while using the same components of a regular ARIMA (with seasonal parameters denoted by uppercase letters: P,D,Q).

Once the ARIMA model's parameters have been identified, they can be used to estimate the ARIMA model that best fits the data. ARIMA models use a maximum likelihood estimation procedure that is designed to maximize the likelihood of the observed series, given the estimated parameter values. This can be done using any standard statistical package that includes a time series module. The next step is the evaluation (diagnosis) of the estimated model's fit to the observed series. Here, a combination of three strategies is recommended. The first is to verify that each ARIMA parameter in the model is statistically significant using standard hypothesis testing procedures (e.g., effect/standard error). If not significant, the respective parameter can in most cases be dropped from the model without affecting substantially the overall fit of the model. A second straightforward test involves the accuracy of the estimated model's forecast of future values of the series. Typically, this procedure entails estimating the ARIMA model based on partial data (e.g., the first two thirds of the observations in a series) and using it to predict the remaining observations, which are then compared with the known (original) observations. However, a good model should not only provide sufficiently accurate forecasts, it should also produce small, random, and statistically independent residuals. The patterns of ARIMA model–generated residuals are typically inspected through the use of ACF and PACF correlograms. If no serial dependencies are detected (namely, no remaining autocorrelations or partial autocorrelations at various lags appear to cross the 95% boundary lines in the ACFs' and PACFs' plots), the series is said to be stationary. If serial dependencies are detected, the ARIMA model would need to be reestimated using a different combination of parameters until stationarity is achieved.

The procedure described thus far pertains to a time series that consists of single observations recorded sequentially over equal time increments (or a *univariate time series*). To conduct a *multivariate time series analysis*, several additional steps are necessary. An important requirement of the ARIMA approach is that all time series involved in the analysis of multivariate relationships will be made stationary (or prewhitened) before standard correlation or regression methods are used. However, there is a disagreement among researchers about the most appropriate prewhitening approach. Box and Jenkins recommended differencing (ARIMA 0,1,0) as the preferred method of removing deterministic components from each nonstationary series (Box & Jenkins, 1976). However, some (e.g., Cappella, 1996) proposed that a better approach is to use the same ARIMA model used to prewhiten the independent series to prewhiten the dependent series, while others (e.g., Granger, 1969) prescribe that using an autoregressive model (ARIMA 1,0,0) would suffice in most cases given that most time series studied in the social sciences seem to be governed by a first-order autoregressive process (McCleary & Hay, 1980). A reasonable approach has been proposed by Watt (1994), who expressed the concern that while first-order differencing may produce a stationary series, it also destroys all information about the absolute value and the trend in the original data that are theoretically important for explaining the variance in the series over time. Watt proposed instead that variables be made stationary by fitting a least squares regression line to the data and creating a transformed time series based on the regression residuals. This technique was used successfully in a number of studies (e.g., Yanovitzky & Bennett, 1999; Yanovitzky & Blitz, 2000), though the other approaches work as well. The disadvantage of this approach is that either linear or polynomial trends can lead to unrealistic forecasts of values far beyond the temporal horizon of the study. Therefore, this approach should be used with caution for forecasting.

Next, a combination of cross-correlation analysis and a Granger causality test typically allows researchers to sort out the causal direction between two or more variables. The *cross-correlation function* is a measure of the degree of the linear relationship between two time series as a function of the time lag between the two. Conceptually, it is similar to the autocorrelation function except that it compares values in two different time series instead of comparing different values within the same series. In cross-correlation analysis, the correlation of one time series with a time-lagged version of a second time series is examined, as illustrated in Figure 4.4, where the association between exposure to media messages about domestic violence and volume of calls received at a domestic violence hotline within a week's period is examined. A statistically significant correlation at a certain lag indicates the time lag required for the independent (or leading) series to affect the dependent series. A cross-correlation matrix is computed for each relationship of interest where in each case the independent series in Step 1 becomes the dependent series in Step 2. A time series will be considered as leading another time series if statistically significant correlations are observed only in the lags that represent its effect on the second time series. In this example, the only statistically significant cross-correlation appears to be at lag +1, indicating that exposure to domestic violence messages leads the behavior of calling a domestic violence hotline such that messages received influence behavior one week later. On the other hand, the nonsignificant effect at lag −1 indicates that we cannot say that the number of calls to the hotline necessarily influences media messages about domestic violence.

However, when working with a set of variables and a range of lags, a large set of correlations is produced and spuriousness becomes a concern. If a nonrandom distribution of positive or negative correlations is observed, the spuriousness hypothesis is rejected. If the only meaningful and significant correlation is to be found at unity (time t_0), the cross-correlation analysis indicates the existence of covariation between the two series. On the other hand, if no significant correlation is found in any of the lags, one may conclude that the two time series are independent. The information gathered from the cross-correlation analysis is used in the computation of *transfer function models*. These are essentially multiple

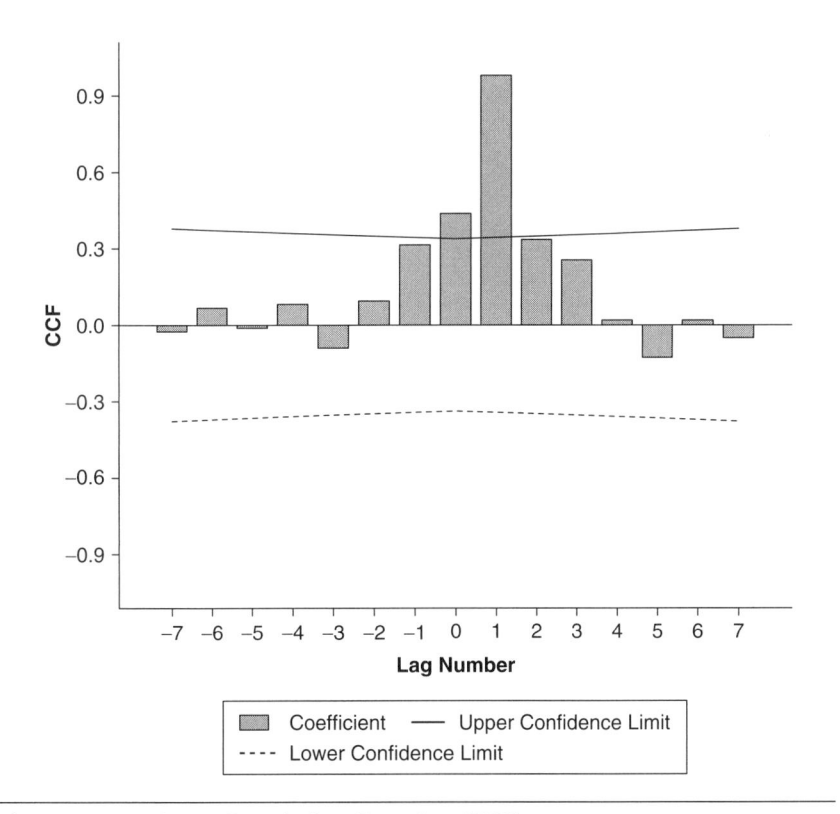

Figure 4.4 Cross-Correlation Function (CCF)

regression models in which the dependent variable is the given series' residuals and the independent variables are created based on all the cross-lagged correlations that were statistically significant.

The *Granger causality test* (Granger, 1969) compares the effect of one time series on another in order to verify the causal direction between the two time-bound variables. The basic logic of this test is that time series X may be considered a cause of time series Y when X predicts Y significantly better than Y predicts itself. To test this proposition, both series are prewhitened first, and then Y is regressed on its previous (lagged) values alone. In the next step, Y is regressed on both its lagged values and the lagged values of X. After being transformed to white noise (i.e., made stationary), Y should have a very limited ability to predict itself based on its previous value. The R^2 for the initial and second models are then compared with an F-test to determine if any predictive improvement due to the effect of X is actually significant. The procedure is then repeated for the effect of Y on X. In the final step, the regression coefficients representing the effect of each series on the other controlling for previous values of the dependent series are compared to determine which series (if any) leads the other.

LIMITATIONS OF THE ARIMA APPROACH AND SOME USEFUL ALTERNATIVES

The ARIMA approach, then, is an iterative model-building procedure through which any deterministic component of the time series is identified and removed in order to make the data stationary before standard data analysis methods could be used with time series data. Although powerful and flexible, this approach has some known limitations (Shumway, 1988). For instance, the ARIMA method performs best when the number of sequential observations available for analysis is 50 or greater, the unit of time is consistent among all variables measured, and each time series is uniform and unbroken. These may not be reasonable requirements for much of the data collected or used by communication researchers, particularly when researchers have no control over data collection such as when secondary time series data are used. The greatest difficulty involves the analysis of unequally spaced time series observations. In data analysis practice, such a characteristic of time series data is often ignored and standard analyses that treat data as equally spaced are used. This practice can clearly introduce a significant bias into estimates of ARIMA parameters leading to incorrect predictions. It is therefore necessary to use continuous time series models for serial correlations (see Jones & Ackerson, 1990), which can be quite complicated. In addition, ARIMA assumes that the values of the estimated parameters are constant throughout the life of a series (i.e., stationarity of process), which may be a false assumption in some cases. Furthermore, ARIMA can model only linear relationships between time series, whereas relationships between communication-related variables often take a nonlinear form. Finally, although much of time series analysis focuses on analyzing the mean behavior of a time series, there has been increasing attention to the study of volatility or variability of a time series. ARIMA models assume constant variance and, therefore, cannot be used in these cases. Autoregressive conditionally heteroscedastic (ARCH) models (Engle, 1982) should be used instead.

More importantly, though, ARIMA is appropriate only for a time series that is stationary (i.e., its mean, variance, and autocorrelation should be approximately constant through time). This may not be a problem if one is interested in forecasting future values of a series, a common objective of time series analysis in economic research. However, communication scholars are often more interested in studying theoretically meaningful communication processes than in forecasting. That is, they are far more interested in explaining systematic changes in the behavior of variables over time (such as trends and cycles in news coverage of issues) than removing them statistically so that they may produce more precise prediction of future values on these variables. In this sense, as suggested by Watt (1994), the powerful filters employed by ARIMA models remove much or all of the variance in a time series that communication scholars may seek to explain.

A number of statistical alternatives to the ARIMA approach have emerged in recent years (Brockwell & Davis, 2002), two of which are *distributed lag models* (Ostrom, 1990) and *differential equation models* (Fan, 1988; Zhu, 1992). Differential equation models can be used to model both linear and nonlinear relationships in time, but a discussion of this approach is beyond the scope of this chapter (for an overview, see Fan & Cook, 2003). However, distributed lag models are briefly discussed here.

Distributed lag analysis is a specialized technique for examining the relationships between variables that involve some delay. This technique relies on a simple structural equation model that can be estimated by an ordinary least squares (OLS) regression and is mathematically expressed as follows:

$$Y_t = b_0 + b_1 Y_{t-1} + b_2 X_{t-1} + e_t$$

where Y_t is the dependent series at time t, Y_{t-1} is the dependent series lagged by a single time point, X_{t-1} is the independent series that is also first-order lagged, and e_t is the error in estimation of Y_t. The model estimates three parameters: the constant or intercept (b_0) and two partial time series regression coefficients (b_1 and b_2). Similar to the logic of a Granger causality test, X is said to cause Y when lagged values of X are significantly related to Y after controlling for the previous history of Y (i.e., lagged values of Y). To ensure that the standard regression assumptions are not violated when estimating the model, three statistical tests are employed. The first, the Durbin-Watson test of correlated errors (serial correlation), is designed to detect first-order autocorrelations. When there is no serial correlation, the expected value of the Durbin-Watson statistic is approximately 2, whereas a value under 1.5 indicates a positive serial correlation and a value above 2.5 a negative serial correlation. The second, tolerance, estimates the amount of variation in a single predictor that is not explained by its association to other predictors in a multiple regression model. Tolerance values range from 0 (perfect collinearity) to 1 (no collinearity). Finally, the autoregressive conditional heteroscedasticity (ARCH) test (Engle, 1982) is used to test the null hypothesis of homoscedasticity in the errors. This statistic has a chi-square distribution with 1 degree of freedom, where a nonsignificant result (i.e., a value of 7.8 or lower) indicates that the errors are homoscedastic.

The Frequency Domain Approach to Modeling Time Series Data

The logic of frequency domain time series analysis is somewhat different from that of time domain time series analysis. Time domain time series generally treat temporal patterns (e.g., trends, seasonal or cyclical fluctuations) as potential confounds that can create "spurious" relationships between two time series and, thus, obscure the true influence of one series on another. For example, if the level of self-disclosure of one person is correlated with the level of self-disclosure of his/her relational partner over time, it could be because they are both following the same developmental norm of incremental increase rather than either person's disclosure level influencing the disclosure level of the other (i.e., reciprocity). Likewise, if TV advertising and TV programming follow the same seasonal pattern, they may be correlated because of that common pattern rather than because programming variation leads to advertising variation. Hence the prewhitening process seeks to eliminate these confounding effects from the data so that the effects of one variable on another can be observed. Frequency domain time series, on the other hand, begins by looking for hidden temporal patterns in the data (especially cyclical or periodic patterns) and models them. Bivariate spectral analysis then attempts to correlate two time series by identifying and correlating the common patterns. For example, Chapple (1970) argued that people's physiological rhythms entrain their behavioral rhythms, which in turn influence the rhythms of their social interaction. In a series of studies, Warner (1996) utilized frequency domain time series to demonstrate correlations between people's physiological rhythms and their communicative behavior as well as the behavioral rhythms of their relational partners. Altman, Vinsel, and Brown (1981) argued that as relationships evolve, relational partners experience a dialectic tension between openness and closeness, and this leads to a cyclical pattern of openness behaviors over the course of a relationship; in successful relationships, partners match and time their cycles of openness to create a synchronous pattern. Utilizing frequency domain time series, VanLear (1991) found that (a) relational partners did evidence cyclical patterns of openness using both behavioral and perceptual data, (b) relational partners generally matched and timed their behavioral cycles in a synchronous pattern, and (c) the nature of the cycles of openness were associated with communication and relationship satisfaction. Despite these differences in perspective, the Wiener-Khintchine theorem shows that mathematically, the time domain and frequency domain are just two sides of the same coin. They are mathematically the same (Gottman, 1981).

Frequency domain time series begins with the recognition that a*ny* time series, from an extremely patterned process to a random, white-noise process, can be represented by a series of weighted, orthogonal, sinusoidal (i.e., sine and cosine) functions. These functions involve several parameters. The height of the cycle from zenith to baseline is the *Amplitude R*. The *period* is the time it takes to complete a single cycle. Instead of the period, one could choose to use the frequency ω, the number of full repetitions the function makes in a single unit of time (usually measured in radians per unit of time). Finally, we identify the phase angle φ (in radians) with respect to the time of origin.

Given that any time series can be described by a set of weights representing the sinusoids' amplitudes and frequencies, that set of weights is given by the Discrete Fourier Transform (DFT). This set is chosen because they are orthogonal, and given the sum of these $N-1$ sine and cosine coefficients, they can completely represent the data. Of course, that number of functions offers no more parsimonious representation than the raw data, so the goal is to find a small number of functions that, when inverted, will adequately reconstruct the data with little error. Watt (1994; VanLear & Watt, 1996) suggests a stepwise procedure that will identify the major patterns in the data (Bloomfield, 1976). First, the amplitudes (or amplitudes squared) of the Fourier coefficients are plotted against the Fourier frequencies in what is called a *periodogram* (see Figure 4.6). The amplitude is an indication of the strength of a given pattern in the data. Peaks in the periodogram at various frequencies indicate that those frequencies are particularly strong patterns within the data. If the strongest pattern in the data is not at one of the Fourier frequencies, the frequencies closest to the one that actually represents the pattern will show a peak. When the strongest function is found, a sinusoidal function representing that frequency is fit to the data using least squares minimization, much as a linear trend is fit to the data in ordinary regression. The frequency can be adjusted to find the optimal frequency of the strongest component, even when it doesn't fall on one of the Fourier frequencies (Watt, 1996). If this model explains a substantial portion of the variance of the series, then the residuals around that function can be extracted, a DFT can be calculated for the residual series, a new periodogram can be plotted, and the next-strongest frequency can be identified and fitted to the data. This iterative process is continued until the series is adequately explained and no more major functions are identified (VanLear & Watt, 1996). Once all meaningful functions are identified, the series is a white-noise process. In a white-noise process, the periodogram values will display an "exponential distribution" (StatSoft, 2003). Watt (1998) has developed a program (FATS, Fourier Analysis of Time Series) that will perform the stepwise procedure and also can fit a priori cyclical models to a time series.

There are some cautions and limitations involved in the stepwise method. It can be shown that while this procedure is very sensitive to the identification of actual hidden patterns in the data, it can yield "false positives" (i.e., false evidence of a pattern that is only a random variation) when examining both significance and amount of variance explained by a function. This bias is most pronounced with short time series and diminishes as the length of the series increases (VanLear & Li, 2005). Therefore, we recommend that several precautions be used. First, statistical significance should not be used as the primary decision rule even though the program (FATS) generates such tests. Second, this procedure should ideally be used on very long time series data sets (hundreds of time points).[4] Third, the researcher should assess what size of effect could be obtained by a random process. This can be determined by running a number of random series of the same length as the actual data in the study and adjusting the decision rule to substantially exceed that baseline value. It can be shown that this problem is mainly due to fitting such a large number of potential functions in a stepwise procedure, such that this bias does not pose a major problem when fitting an a priori model to the data (VanLear & Li, 2005). Finally, it is wise to limit the extraction of sinusoidal components to a small number of very strong components and to be wary of patterns that do not have a clear theoretical interpretation. Nevertheless, because this procedure can be shown to detect real patterns in data obscured by random noise, it should not be completely shunned as an inductive method, especially for uncovering hidden periodicity. We like to use this procedure in conjunction with the examination of ACFs and PACFs for detecting hidden patterns in time series data (VanLear & Li, 2005).[5] Sometimes researchers will "smooth" their time series data and apply these methods to the smoothed series. This is typically referred to as spectral analysis (Gottman, 1981). When analyzed, a smoothed series will not tend to show the random spikes in the periodogram. One looks for the frequencies with the greatest "spectral densities," which are the frequency regions with many adjacent frequencies that account for most of the overall periodic behavior in the series.

Figure 4.5 provides a graphic view of this procedure on real data. A dyad interacted over a mediated channel for about 10 minutes regarding a controversial political issue. Each member was coded for smiling (smiles,

Time Series Analysis

doesn't smile) every half second, and the number of smiling units in every 2 seconds of interaction comprised the measure. Each member of the dyad in this analysis is represented by a time series of 248 repeated measures.

The data for person A is graphed in Figure 4.5 along with the first three sinusoidal components extracted using the stepwise procedure. The periodogram for this series is presented in Figure 4.6. The first component extracted has a period of 64.7 (32.3 seconds). This component explains 20.3% of the variance in the series, which well exceeds what would be expected if this were a random series. After the first component was analyzed, it was removed and the residual series was analyzed. The second sinusoidal component has a period of 49 units (24.5 seconds) and accounts for an additional 10% of the variance of the series (total R^2 = .305, ΔR^2 = .102), which also exceeds what would be expected in a random series of this length. The third component in the stepwise procedure has a

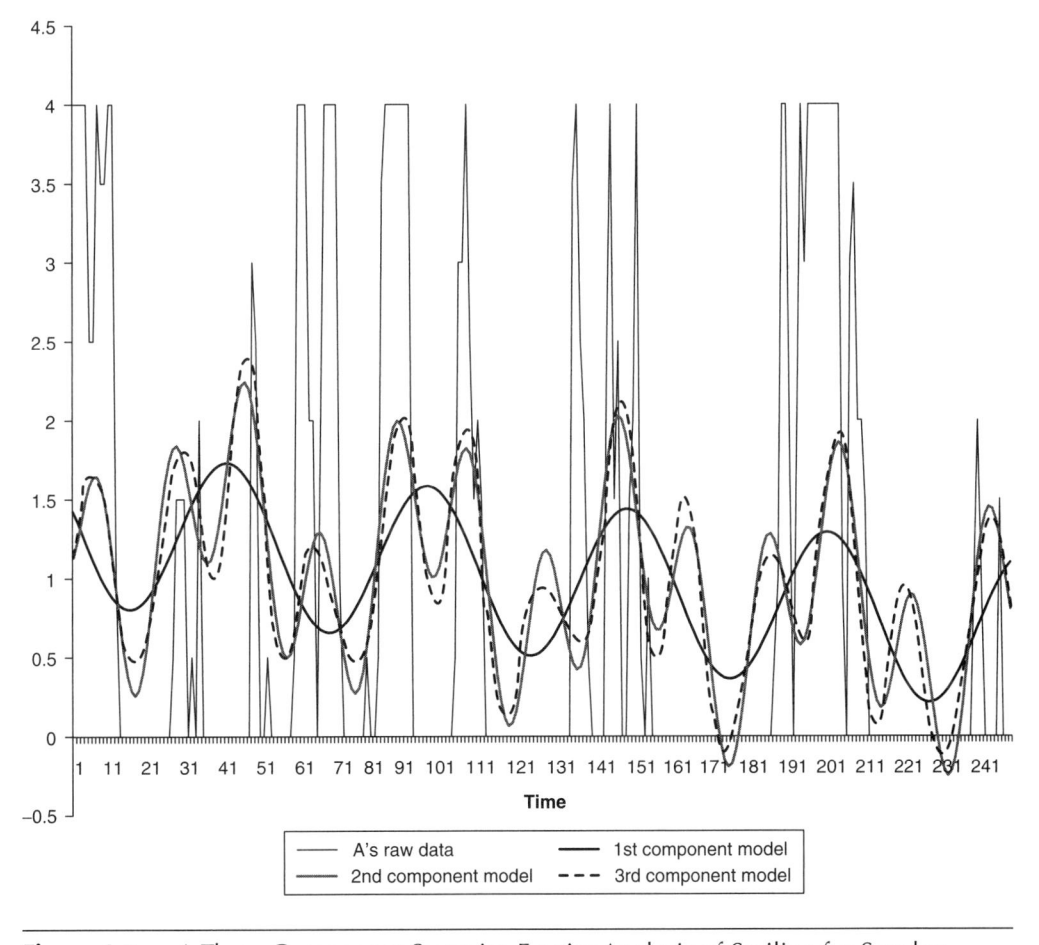

Figure 4.5 A Three-Component Stepwise Fourier Analysis of Smiling for Speaker

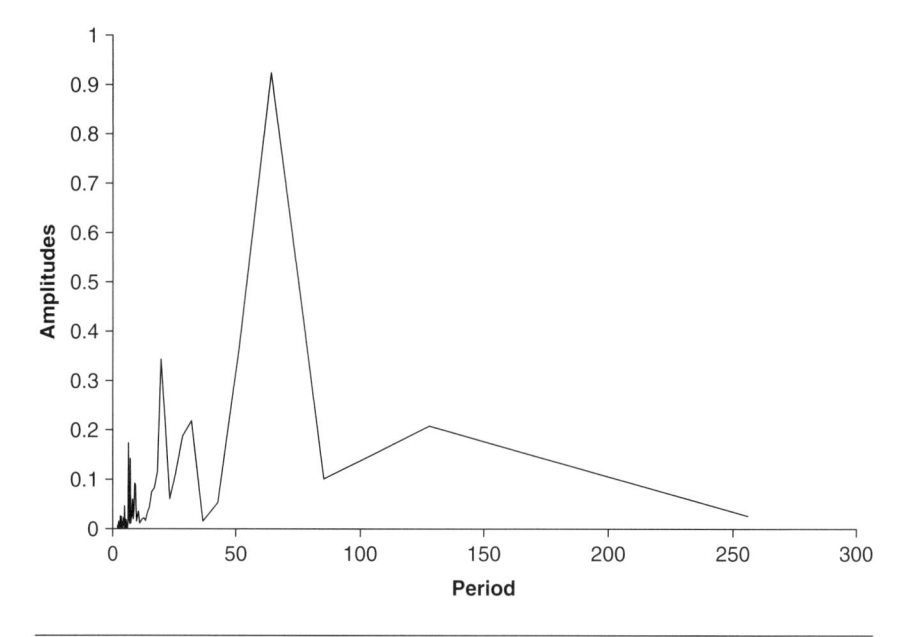

Figure 4.6 The Periodogram for Speaker A's Time Series of Smiling

period of 19.3 units (9.65 minutes) and explains an additional 6.7% of the variance of the series (total $R^2 = .371$, $\Delta R^2 = .066$). Although this exceeds the average amount of explained variance for random series of this length, it did so by a small amount. Therefore, the third component must be interpreted with more caution. Figure 4.6 shows what the periodic function formed from the summation of these three components looks like as plotted against the raw data. Figure 4.7 shows the ACFs for speaker A on the same series. The significant negative ACF (−.27) at lag 31 and the corresponding positive ACFs at lags 58, 59, and 60 ($r_s = .18$, .21, and .18, respectively) correspond closely to the first component revealed through the stepwise Fourier analysis. This evidence suggests that speaker A's smiling behavior follows a periodic cyclical pattern.

Suppose that we have a theoretical reason to expect a cycle of a given frequency/period. A sinusoidal function representing that frequency can be fit to the data and assessed for the amount of variance explained. Because we are fitting one function to the data, this procedure does not contain the same potential for false positives as the stepwise procedure (VanLear & Li, 2005). For example, one might predict that alcohol advertising will follow the same seasonal cycle as TV programming. Or if one has daily measures of mood or emotion, one might predict a weekly cycle with lows on Mondays and highs on Fridays and that the same cycle might be evidenced in certain spontaneous nonverbal behaviors known to communicate emotion. One could fit the cycle found in the emotion series to the contemporaneous behavioral series.

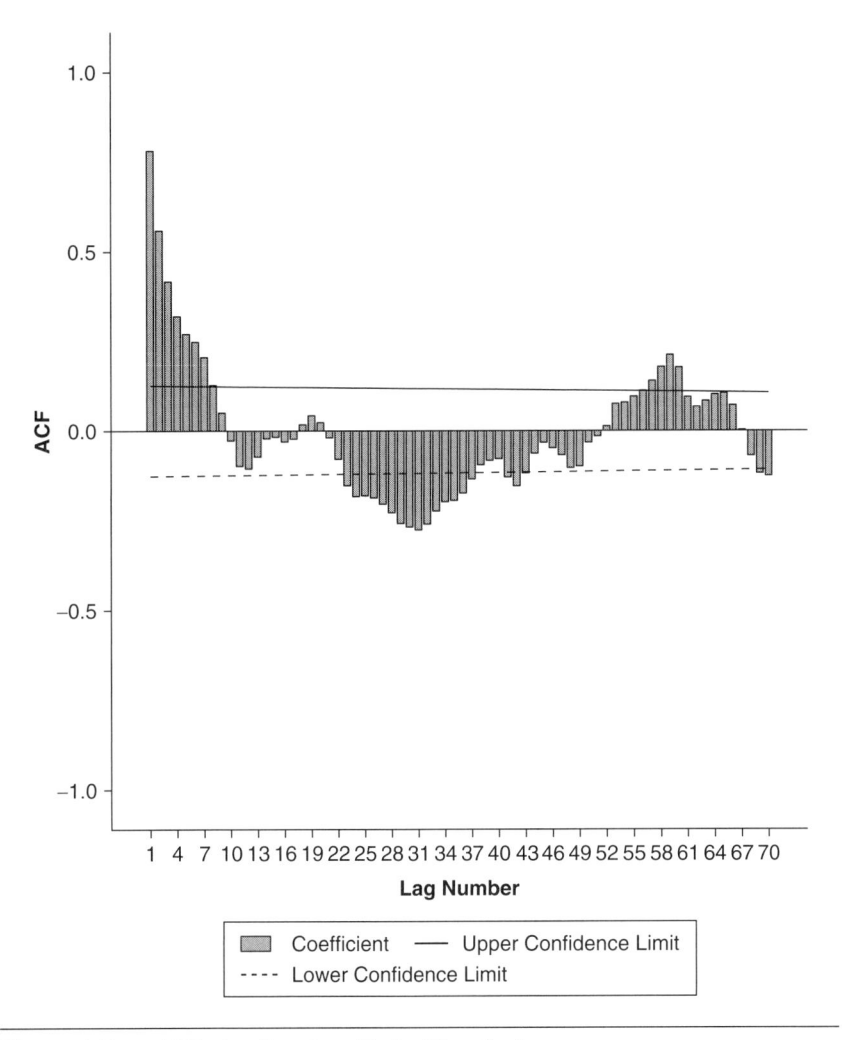

Figure 4.7 ACFs for Speaker A's Smiling Series

VanLear and Watt (1996) presents procedures in which these techniques can be used in an experimental design to detect how an experimental stimulus affects not just the level of a variable but also the nature of cycles that a whole time series displays (e.g., frequency, amplitude). Likewise, models built on one part of a time series can be used to forecast the future values of the series. In a related design (interrupted time series), the technique can be used to model changes in processes occurring after a significant event, whether the event was manipulated by the researcher or was a naturally occurring phenomenon.

Finally, one of the most common ways to use frequency domain time series is to examine the relationship between two concurrent time series. This can be accomplished through *cross-spectral analysis*. In this approach, the DFTs are calculated for each variable's series, and the values of the two periodograms can be multiplied to produce a "cross-periodogram" (or if the series are smoothed, a "cross-spectrum"). A cross-periodogram will show large peaks at the frequencies that the two series have in common. Cross-spectral analysis analyzes the cross-amplitude and the relative phase of the two series at each frequency. A standardized measure analogous to the square of the correlation at each frequency is given by the squared "coefficient of coherence" (Gottman, 1981; StatSoft, 2003).[6] Each series has a gain value for each frequency in a cross-spectral analysis. The gain values for each frequency are interpreted like the standardized betas in a regression for that series at that frequency. The "phase shift" estimates are measures of the extent that one series "leads" the other at each frequency. SPSS is capable of conducting cross-spectral analysis of time series data.

For example, we can take the sinusoidal function that best fit the data for person A in the above example and fit one-, two-, and three-component models to the time series representing person B's smiling. Figure 4.8 graphs the fit of these functions. The first sinusoidal component from speaker A's model (period = 64.67) explained 4.9% of the variation in speaker B's time series. The two-component model from A's series explained 13.8% (ΔR^2 = .09) of the variation in B's smiling over time. The three-component model from A's series explains 23.2% (ΔR^2 = .094) of the variance of B's series. The fit is both significant and meaningful. Speaker B's smiling appears to match

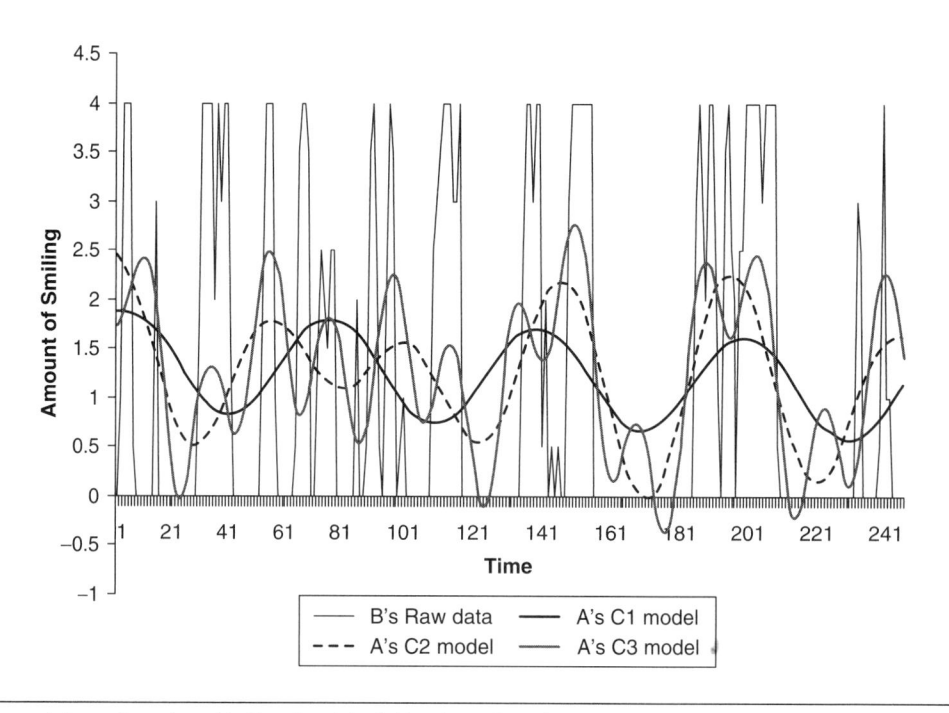

Figure 4.8 Speaker A's Fourier Model's Fit to Speaker B's Data

Time Series Analysis 117

the rhythm of speaker A's smiling. We also matched speaker B's model to speaker A's data as well. The first component of speaker B's model explained 5.4% of A's variance, the second component explained 12.8% of A's variance, and the third component explained 13.8% of A's variance. Speaker A seems to match speaker B's pattern, especially the second component (a cycle with a period of 19), although the fit is not quite as good as when matching speaker A's model to speaker B's data.

Figure 4.9 displays the cross-periodogram for speaker A's and speaker B's smiling from the above example. This figure shows the largest peaks (cross amp = .24) at the adjacent Fourier periods of 64 ($\omega = .098$) and 51.2 ($\omega = .123$) and a smaller peak at period 19.7 ($\omega = .319$, cross amp = .18). These generally correspond to the peaks at the frequencies identified in modeling the individual series. We can conclude that these two speakers tend to synchronize their smiling behavior by matching their periodic behaviors.

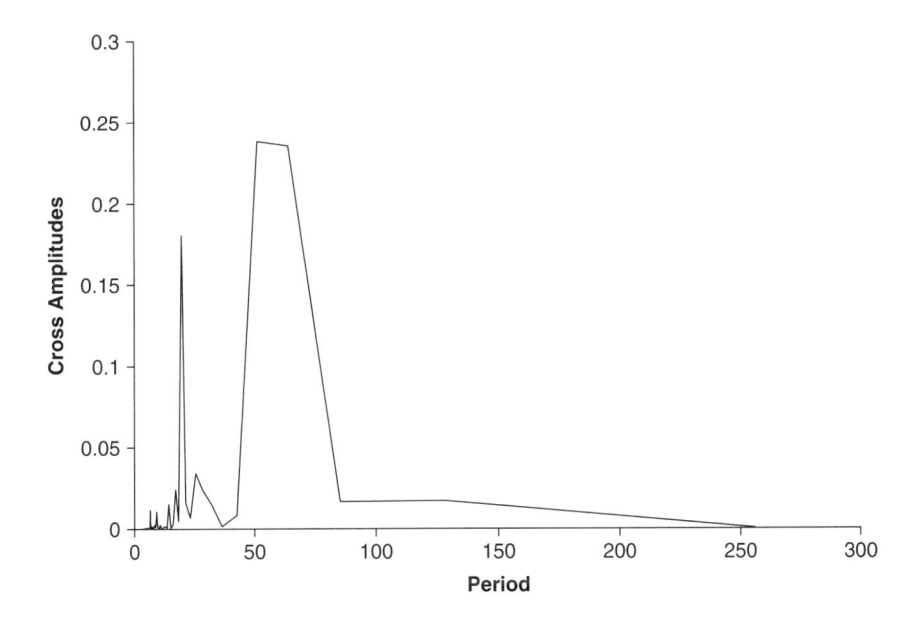

Figure 4.9 The Cross-Periodogram Between Speakers A's and B's Time Series of Smiling Behavior

Pooling and Aggregation of Time Series

The strength of time series analyses is assessing complex patterns and relationships over time and forecasting future values, not generalizing to a population of similar cases. If one has a large number of cases and a small number of replications, then one can use either structural equation modeling, where each time point is a different set of variables, or multi-level modeling (see Chapter 3, this volume). The sophisticated types of temporal patterns modeled by individual time series are not easily assessed with these methods. Time series analyses are often useful when one has a large number of repeated measures on a single or small number of cases. An organizational communication consultant may have measures on a single client company over an extended period of time. A marital therapist may have interaction data on a single client couple. A media consultant may have data on the client station or network over an extensive period of time. Or we may have a research question that we wish to explore on a small number of cases (e.g., the major networks) over an extensive number of time periods. Many time series are conducted on data that are already pooled or aggregated across cases (e.g., Nielsen ratings, public opinion poll results, economic indices, and crime statistics). However, often communication scholars wish to gather data over many time points across many cases and conduct sophisticated analyses of temporal processes. In such cases, the data must be aggregated or pooled.

There are two ways in which data can be pooled or aggregated: preanalysis or postanalysis. Pooling time series from different cases before the analysis has the great advantage that only one set of time series analyses needs to be conducted. If there are a large number of cases (e.g., hundreds), this is a tremendous advantage. Imagine conducting a whole set of analyses like those presented in the above examples hundreds of times. However, in order to pool the series before analysis, certain conditions should be met. First, the various series representing different cases must be exactly contemporaneous and in sync. For example, if hundreds of TV viewers are measured every 3 seconds as they watch the same half-hour program and each measure in time is synchronized to the exact same point in the program, then the data meet this first condition. However, if people do daily monitoring of their communication with their significant other over a 3-month period, each person's time series is unlikely to be synchronized with other participants if the relationships have been in existence for different periods of time and different participants begin their data recording on different days. The second condition is that the different time series must be homogeneous with regard to process across cases. If some series trend, some are first-order autoregressive processes, some are first-order moving average processes, and some show seasonal cycles that others do not, then aggregating before analysis will lose important between-case variance and may be inappropriate. If one can meet the first condition, but is unsure about the second, then a random subsample of the cases could be assessed using individual time series as explained here. If all or nearly all of the cases have the same kind of pattern of serial dependency, then the data could be pooled and the pooled data assessed for that pattern.

When the conditions for preanalysis aggregation cannot be met, then postanalysis aggregation can be employed. In this situation, each case is analyzed separately as if it were a study unto itself, and then the results are aggregated using meta-analysis if the results are homogeneous. If the results are not homogeneous, they can be input as scores for each case and their variation analyzed using traditional statistics to search for moderating variables. For example, Street and Cappella (1989) used this approach in the time domain to analyze the adaptation of children to adults' speech characteristics, and VanLear (1991) used this approach in the frequency domain to analyze dialectic cycles of openness in relationships.

Conclusion

Gathering and analyzing time series data presents communication researchers with a unique set of challenges. Meeting these challenges requires time, effort, training, and skill. Nevertheless, we believe that this extra training and effort are worth the payoff. Communication is a dynamic process, and to be true to this axiom, we must be willing to model communication over time. The present chapter is an introduction. Scholars interested in the dynamic modeling of communication processes are advised to study these techniques in depth.

Notes

1. Sometimes time series analyses are distinguished from repeated measures with time series analysis referring to methods used to analyze data consisting of large numbers of replications (at least 30 or so) and repeated measures referring to data with smaller numbers of replications across a large number of cases. We will use the term "time series" in the broader sense and use the term "pooled time series" or "cross-sectional time series" for the latter group of analyses. The analytical methods we focus on are individual time series.

2. However, even experimental designs are not well suited for identifying reciprocally or mutually causal processes involving feedback loops, which are usually held to be central to viewing communication as a process (Berlo, 1960, 1977; VanLear, 1996). Likewise, some variables cannot be easily or ethically manipulated experimentally while retaining ecological validity.

3. Observations in a time series are not independently sampled even if there is no autocorrelation or when the statistical dependency is removed. As a result, inferential tests do not provide evidence of generalizability to other cases, though they may be used to forecast values of future observations of the cases analyzed.

4. If significance tests are used, the problem actually gets worse with longer time series, whereas if effect size is used (R^2), the problem diminishes as the length of the series increases.

5. SPSS uses a default of 16 lags for ACFs and PACFs, which is usually adequate for detecting AR and MA processes but is often too short to detect long cycles. Because of the large number of ACFs possible in a series, ACFs can also

lead to the detection of false positives if significance of one lag is a sufficient criterion for the presence of a pattern.

6. One should be careful in interpreting these values by themselves, because one can obtain large values for coherency when the spectral density values of both series (the divisor when coherency is computed) are both small, indicating no strong periodic components in the data.

References

Altman, I., Vinsel, A., & Brown, B. (1981). Dialectic conceptions in social psychology: An application to social penetration and privacy regulation. In L. Berkowitz (Ed.), *Advances in experimental social psychology: Vol. 14* (pp. 76–100). New York: Academic Press.

Barnett, G. A., Chang, H. J., Fink, E. L., & Richards, W. D. (1991). Seasonality in television viewing: A mathematical model of cultural processes. *Communication Research, 18,* 755–772.

Berlo, D. K. (1960). *The process of communication.* New York: Holt, Rinehart & Winston.

Berlo, D. K. (1977). Communication as process: Review and commentary. In B. D. Ruben (Ed.), *Communication yearbook I* (pp. 11–27). New Brunswick, NJ: Transaction Books.

Blood, D. J., & Phillips, P. C. B. (1995). Recession headline news, consumer sentiment, the state of the economy and presidential popularity—a time-series analysis 1989–1993. *International Journal of Public Opinion Research, 7,* 1–22.

Bloomfield, P. (1976). *Fourier analysis of time series: An introduction.* New York: John Wiley.

Box, G. E., & Jenkins, G. M. (1976). *Time series analysis: Forecasting and control.* San Francisco: Holden-Day.

Brockwell, P. J., & Davis, R. A. (2002). *Introduction to time series and forecasting* (2nd ed.). New York: Springer.

Brosius, H. B., & Kepplinger, H. M. (1992). Linear and nonlinear models of agenda-setting in television. *Journal of Broadcasting & Electronic Media, 36,* 5–23.

Campbell, D. T., & Kenny, D. A. (1999). *A primer on regression artifacts.* New York: Guilford.

Cappella, J. N. (1981). Mutual influence in expressive behavior: Adult-adult and infant-adult dyadic interaction. *Psychological Bulletin, 89,* 101–132.

Cappella, J. N. (1996). Dynamic coordination of vocal and kinesic behavior in dyadic interaction: Methods, problems, and interpersonal outcomes. In J. H. Watt & C. A. VanLear (Eds.), *Dynamic patterns in communication processes* (pp. 353–386). Thousand Oaks, CA: Sage.

Chapple, E. D. (1970). *Culture and biological man: Explorations in behavioral anthropology.* New York: Holt, Rinehart & Winston.

Chatfield, C. (1989). *The analysis of time series: An introduction* (4th ed.). London; New York: Chapman and Hall.

Cromwell, J. B. (1994). *Multivariate tests for time series models.* Thousand Oaks, CA: Sage.

Cromwell, J. B., Labys, W. C., & Terraza, M. (1994). *Univariate tests for time series models.* Thousand Oaks, CA: Sage.

Dearing, J. W., & Rogers, E. M. (1996). *Agenda-setting.* Thousand Oaks, CA: Sage.

Engle, R. (1982). Autoregressive conditional heteroscedasticity with estimates of the variance of United Kingdom inflation. *Econometrica, 50,* 987–1007.

Fan, D. P. (1988). *Prediction of public opinion from the mass media: Computer content analysis and mathematical modeling.* New York: Greenwood Press.

Fan, D. P., & Cook, R. D. (2003). A differential equation model for predicting public opinions and behaviors from persuasive information: Application to the index of Consumer Sentiment. *Journal of Mathematical Sociology, 27,* 29–51.

Fisher, B. A. (1978). *Perspectives on human communication.* New York: Macmillan.

Funkhouser, G. R. (1973). The issues of the sixties: An exploratory study in the dynamics of public opinion. *Public Opinion Quarterly, 37,* 62–75.

Gerbner, G., Gross, L., Morgan, M., & Signorielli, N. (1986). Living with television: The dynamics of the cultivation process. In J. Bryant & D. Zillman (Eds.), *Perspectives on media effects* (pp. 17–40). Hillsdale, NJ: Lawrence Erlbaum Associates.

Gonzenbach, W. J. (1996). *The media, the president, and public opinion: A longitudinal analysis of the drug issue, 1984–1991.* Mahwah, NJ: Lawrence Erlbaum Associates.

Gonzenbach, W. J., & McGavin, L. (1997). A brief history of time: A methodological analysis of agenda setting. In M. McCombs, D. L. Shaw, & D. Weaver (Eds.), *Communication and democracy: Exploring the intellectual frontiers in agenda-setting theory* (pp. 115–136). Mahwah, NJ: Lawrence Erlbaum Associates.

Gottman, J. M. (1981). *Time-series analysis: A comprehensive introduction for social scientists.* Cambridge, UK: Cambridge University Press.

Granger, C. W. J. (1969). Investigating causal relations by econometric models and cross-spectral methods. *Econometrica, 37,* 424–438.

Heath, R. A. (2000). *Nonlinear dynamics: Techniques and applications in psychology.* Mahwah, NJ; London: Lawrence Erlbaum Associates.

Huston, T. L., & Vangelisti, A. L. (1991). Socioemotional behavior and satisfaction in marital relationships: A longitudinal study. *Journal of Personality and Social Psychology, 41,* 721–733.

Jaffe, J., & Feldstein, S. (1970). *Rhythms of dialogue.* New York: Academic Press.

Jones, R. H., & Ackerson, L. M. (1990). Serial correlation in unequally spaced longitudinal data. *Biometrika, 77,* 271–731.

Mansur, K. A., & Shoemaker, H. H. (1999). The impact of changes in the current population survey on time-in-sample bias and correlations between rotation groups. *Proceedings of the survey methods section of the American Statistical Association* (pp. 180–185). Retrieved January 23, 2006, from http://www.amstat.org/sections/srms/Proceedings/papers/1999_028.pdf

McCleary, R., & Hay, R. (1980). *Applied time series analysis for the social sciences.* Beverly Hills, CA: Sage.

McCombs, M., & Zhu, J. H. (1995). Capacity, diversity, and volatility of the public agenda: Trends from 1954 to 1994. *Public Opinion Quarterly, 59,* 495–525.

McDowall, D. (1980). *Interrupted time series analysis.* Beverly Hills, CA: Sage.

Meadowcroft, J. M. (1996). Attention span cycles. In J. H. Watt & C. A. VanLear (Eds.), *Dynamic patterns in communication processes* (pp. 255–276). Thousand Oaks, CA: Sage.

Menard, S. (2002). *Longitudinal research* (2nd ed.). Thousand Oaks, CA: Sage

Ostrom, C. W. (1990). *Time series analysis: Regression techniques* (2nd ed.). Newbury Park, CA: Sage.

Pan, Z., & McLeod, J. M. (1991). Multilevel analysis in mass communication research. *Communication Research, 18,* 140–173.

Poole, M. S. (1981). Decision development in small groups: A comparison of two models. *Communication Monographs, 50,* 206–232.

Poole, M. S. (2000). *Organizational change and innovation processes: Theory and methods for research.* Oxford, UK; New York: Oxford University Press.

Poole, M. S., & Roth, J. (1989). Decision development in small groups V: Test of a contingency model. *Human Communication Research, 15,* 549–589.

Poole, M. S., Seibold, D. R., & McPhee, R. D. (1996). A structurational approach to theory-building in group decision-making research. In R. Y. Hirokawa & M. S. Poole (Eds.), *Communication and group decision-making* (2nd ed., pp. 114–146). Thousand Oaks, CA: Sage.

Rice, R. E., & Katz, J. E. (2001). *The internet and health communication: Experiences and expectations.* Thousand Oaks, CA: Sage.

Rogers, E. M., Dearing, J. W., & Chang, S. (1991). AIDS in the 1980s: The agenda setting process for a public issue. *Journalism Monographs, 126.*

Rogers, E. M., & Shoemaker, F. (1973). *Communication of innovations.* Glencoe, IL: Free Press.

Sayrs, L. W. (1989). *Pooled time series analysis.* Newbury Park, CA: Sage.

Shah, D. V., Watts, M. D., Domke, D., & Fan, D. P. (2002). News framing and cueing of issue regimes—explaining Clinton's public approval in spite of scandal. *Public Opinion Quarterly, 66*(3), 339–370.

Shah, D. V., Watts, M. D., Domke, D., Fan, D. P., & Fibison, M. (1999). News coverage, economic cues, and the public's presidential preferences, 1984–1996. *Journal of Politics, 61,* 914–943.

Shoemaker, P. J., Wanta, W., & Leggett, D. (1989). Drug coverage and public opinion, 1972–1986. In P. J. Shoemaker (Ed.), *Communication campaigns about drugs: Government, media, and the public* (pp. 67–80). Hillsdale, NJ: Lawrence Erlbaum Associates.

Shumway, R. H. (1988). *Applied statistical time series analysis.* Englewood Cliffs, NJ: Prentice-Hall.

Shumway, R. H., & Stoffer, D. S. (2000). *Time series analysis and its applications.* New York: Springer.

Slater, M. D., Snyder, L. B., & Hayes, A. F. (2006). Thinking and modeling at multiple levels: The potential contribution of multilevel modeling to communication theory and research. *Human Communication Research, 32,* 375–384.

Smith, T. (1980). America's most important problems—a trend analysis, 1946–1976. *Public Opinion Quarterly, 44,* 164–180.

StatSoft, Inc. (2003). *Time series analysis.* Retrieved August 8, 2005, from www.statsoft.com.

Street, R. L., & Cappella, J. N. (1989). Social and linguistic factors influencing adaptation in children's speech. *Journal of Psycholinguistic Research, 18,* 497–519.

Stryker, J. E. (2003). Media and marijuana: A longitudinal analysis of news media effects on adolescents' marijuana use and related outcomes, 1977–1999. *Journal of Health Communication, 8,* 305–328.

Tabachnick, B. G., & Fidell, L. S. (2001). *Using multivariate statistics* (4th ed.). Needham Heights, MA: Allyn & Bacon.

Taris, T. W. (2000). *A primer in longitudinal data analysis.* London: Sage.

Tedrow, L. M., & Mahoney, E. R. (1979). Trends in attitudes toward abortion: 1972–1976. *Public Opinion Quarterly, 43,* 181–189.

Trumbo, C. (1995). Longitudinal modeling of public issues: An application of the agenda-setting process to the issue of global warming. *Journalism and Mass Communication Monographs, 152.*

VanLear, C. A. (1987). The formation of social relationships: A longitudinal study of social penetration. *Human Communication Research, 13,* 299–322.

VanLear, C. A. (1991). Testing a cyclical model of communicative openness in relationship development: Two longitudinal studies. *Communication Monographs, 58,* 337–361.

VanLear, C. A. (1996). Communication process approaches and models: Patterns, cycles, and dynamic coordination. In J. H. Watt & C. A. VanLear (Eds.), *Dynamic patterns in communication processes* (pp. 35–70). Thousand Oaks, CA: Sage.

VanLear, C. A., Brown, M., & Anderson, E. (2003, May). *Communication, social support, and emotional quality of life in the twelve-step sobriety maintenance process: Three studies.* A paper presented at the annual meeting of the International Communication Association, San Diego, CA.

VanLear, C. A., & Li, S. (2005, May). *Dynamic modeling of scheduled and nonscheduled communication processes.* A paper presented at the annual meeting of the International Communication Association, New York, NY.

VanLear, C. A., & Mabry, E. A. (1999). Testing contrasting interaction models for discriminating between consensual and dissentient decision-making groups. *Small Group Research, 30,* 29–58.

VanLear, C. A., Sheehan, M., Withers, L., & Walker, R. (2005). AA online: The enactment of supportive computer mediated communication. *Western Journal of Communication, 69,* 5–26.

VanLear, C. A., & Watt, J. H. (1996). A partial map to a wide territory. In J. H. Watt & C. A. VanLear (Eds.), *Dynamic patterns in communication processes* (pp. 3–34). Thousand Oaks, CA: Sage.

Warner, R. M. (1996). Coordinated cycles in behavior and physiology during face-to-face social interactions. In J. H. Watt & C. A. VanLear (Eds.), *Dynamic patterns in communication processes* (pp. 327–351). Thousand Oaks, CA: Sage.

Watt, J. H. (1994). Detection and modeling of time-sequenced processes. In A. Lang (Ed.), *Measuring psychological responses to media messages* (pp. 181–207). Hillsdale, NJ: Lawrence Erlbaum Associates.

Watt, J. H. (1998). *FATS: Fourier analysis of time series program user's guide.* Troy, NY: Rensselaer Polytechnic Institute.

Watt, J. H., Mazza, M., & Snyder, L. (1993). Agenda-setting effects of television news coverage and the effects decay curve. *Communication Research, 20,* 408–435.

Watt, J. H., & VanLear, C. A. (1996). *Dynamic patterns in communication processes.* Thousand Oaks, CA: Sage.

Winter, J. P., & Eyal, C. (1991). Agenda-setting for the civil rights issue. In D. L. Protess & M. E. McCombs (Eds.), *Agenda setting: Readings on media, public opinion, and policymaking. Communication textbook series* (pp. 101–107). Hillsdale, NJ: Lawrence Erlbaum Associates.

Yanovitzky, I. (2002a). Effect of news coverage on the prevalence of drunk-driving behavior: Evidence from a longitudinal study. *Journal of Studies on Alcohol, 63*(3), 342–351.

Yanovitzky, I. (2002b). Effects of news coverage on policy attention and actions—a closer look into the media-policy connection. *Communication Research, 29,* 422–451.

Yanovitzky, I., & Bennett, C. (1999). Media attention, institutional response, and health behavior change—the case of drunk driving, 1978–1996. *Communication Research, 26,* 429–453.

Yanovitzky, I., & Blitz, C. L. (2000). Effect of media coverage and physician advice on utilization of breast cancer screening by women 40 years and older. *Journal of Health Communication, 5,* 117–134.

Yanovitzky, I., & Stryker, J. (2001). Mass media, social norms, and health promotion efforts: A longitudinal study of media effects on youth binge drinking. *Communication Research, 28,* 208–239.

Zhu, J. (1992). Issue competition and attention distraction: A zero-sum theory of agenda-setting. *Journalism & Mass Communication Quarterly, 68,* 825–836.

Zhu, J., Watt, J. H., Snyder, L. B., Yan, J., & Jiang, Y. (1993). Public issue priority formation: Media agenda-setting and social interaction. *Journal of Communication, 43,* 8–29.

Event History Analysis for Communication Research

5

Leslie B. Snyder

Ann A. O'Connell

Many of the questions we ask in communication research involve how and why people change from one state to another. Examples of such questions include how a romantic relationship moves through the stages of escalation or de-escalation, which people change their behavior following a communication campaign, or which factors predict whether a person will change his or her opinion to move toward group consensus. States may involve a person or group making a transition from one category to another, such as stages of romantic relationships, levels in an organizational hierarchy, or stages of behavior change. Making a decision, beginning a behavior, or otherwise making an abrupt change can be thought of as making a transition to a new state. Phenomena that involve changes in states can be studied using a family of statistical techniques called *event history analysis*. The "event" in event history is the moment of change—the transition.

In medicine, actuarial science, and demography, the method is known as *survival analysis*. For example, it can be used to predict whether one cancer drug causes users to have a greater survival rate than another drug.

Authors' Note: The preparation of this chapter was supported by U.S. Centers for Disease Control and Prevention grant P01-CD000237, and the data used in the chapter were collected under a grant from the National Institute of Alcohol Abuse & Alcoholism, 1R01AA11551, both to Leslie B. Snyder.

Researchers can plot survival curves to show the number of patients still alive under each treatment option. What is of interest is the elapsed time from the start of treatment until the event—in this case, death. The field of engineering also uses the method, and they refer to it as *failure analysis.* If the research question asks how long it takes for a part or structure to fail, the event of interest is the failure to perform up to a standard. Researchers studying instructional settings could similarly examine time to teacher burnout or student failure.

What events have in common is that they mark the change from one discrete state to another. There needs to be a minimum of two possible states in order to have an event. States may be dichotomous (having only two outcomes), as in watching or not watching television, compliant or not compliant, present or absent, in agreement or not in agreement. States may also be polytomous, having multiple categories. For example, relational status may be operationalized as the states of being single, married, divorced, or widowed. In agenda-setting research, believing that a public issue is one of the most important at a given point in time may be thought of as a state, with the other top issues as alternative states.

Study outcomes in communication research that are defined in terms of categories can also be thought of as states. In particular, questions that focus on whether or not someone (or an organization or group) did or became something or when they did it would probably best be answered through event history analysis. In fact, these two questions—regarding "whether" and "when" events occur—lead to contexts that justify the use of survival analysis methods (Singer & Willett, 2003).

The phenomena of interest may deal overtly with the time until something happened, as in age of first cigarette or first kiss, when private companies' stocks are likely to go public, or when a person lapses from an exercise or diet regimen. Time may be implied, as in the question of whether couples have children or not, which can be studied by analyzing how long from first dating before a couple had their first child, if ever. Time until an event can be measured from a common starting point, such as the starting date of the study. Or the starting time may vary per person or group or organization under study, such as age (time since birth), or time from breakup to next relationship, or time from trial to adoption of an innovation. To study the factors related to adoption and cessation of a behavior promoted by a communication campaign (specifically, the use of oral rehydration therapy to prevent dehydration among children), Snyder (1990) treated time in both ways within the same study: Adoption was operationalized as the time since study baseline (which was before the campaign, when no one did the recommended behavior) to first use of the behavior, and cessation was operationalized as time from first adoption to cessation of the behavior.

Communication-Related Research Utilizing Event History Analysis

A range of communication issues has been examined using event history analysis. Studies of interpersonal discourse and conversations employing event history analysis have focused on classroom discourse (Nystrand, Wu, Gamoran, Zeiser, & Long, 2003), mother-infant communication (Hsu & Fogel, 2003), affective expression in parent-child and spousal interactions (Griffin, 1993; Griffin & Gardner, 1989), jury decision making (Snyder, 1991), and flight controller conversations (Kuk, Arnold, & Ritter, 1999). Language development has also been studied using event history analysis (Tamis-Lemonda, Bornstein, Kahana-Kalman, Baumwell, & Cyphers, 1998). In media studies, television viewing (Westerik, Renckstorf, Lammers, & Wester, 2006; Westerik, Renckstorf, Wester, & Lammers, 2005), newspaper subscription patterns (Gamst, 1985), and communication campaign effects (Snyder, 1990, 1991; Unson, 1999) studies have used event history analysis.

In other social sciences, event history analysis has been used to evaluate programs or interventions. The event of interest is achieving the goal, which can be assessed in the positive (starting the desired behavior) or negative (failing to maintain the desired behavior). Examples of evaluations that used event history analysis include physical activity promotion (Armitage, 2005), smoking cessation (Stevens & Hollis, 1989), breast-feeding promotion (Sunil & Pillai, 2001), welfare-to-work programs (Barton & Pillai, 1993), foster care programs (McMurtry & Lie, 1992), recidivism prevention (Walters, 2005), and methadone maintenance treatment for drug abuse (Hser, Anglin, & Liu, 1990–1991). Similarly, it was used to study the adoption of public smoking restriction policies by Canadian municipalities, comparing the effects of print media and health advocacy (Asbridge, 2004). Event history analysis can be used to test theory to inform campaign or intervention design. For instance, Armitage (2005) found that perceived behavioral control (from the theory of planned behavior) predicted exercising at a gym over time.

The technique can also be useful in program design when trying to understand risk. Researchers have used event history analysis to study risky events, such as homelessness (Caton, Dominguez, Schanzer, Hasin, Shrout, Felix, et al., 2005), depression (Kendler, Karkowski, & Prescott, 1999), adolescent arrests (Keiley & Martin, 2005), premarital sex (Djamba, 2003), and drug use (Brunswick & Messeri, 1986; Hoffmann & Cerbone, 2002). In marketing, event history analysis has been suggested to measure brand loyalty over time (DuWors & Haines, 1990).

Event history analysis has also been used to analyze stages and life transitions, as in marriage and divorce (Gager & Sanchez, 2003; Hannan, Tuma, & Groeneveld, 1977), welfare-to-work outcomes (Barton, Pillai, & Dietz, 1996), and fatherhood (Pears, Pierce, Kim, Capaldi, & Owen, 2005).

In organizational research, event history analysis has been used to study membership and organizational turnover, such as cadet attrition at a military academy (Morita, Lee, & Mowday, 1989), nurse staff turnover (Somers, 1996), and the effect of union participation on public school teachers (Iverson & Currivan, 2003). Similarly, event history analysis is useful for studying absence and attendance (Fichman, 1988). Other studies have used the organization as the unit of analysis, such as studies of factors relating to organizations' forming of strategic alliances (Oliver, 2001) and adopting a drug-testing policy (Spell & Blum, 2001).

Despite the range of phenomena that is appropriate for event history analysis, it remains seldomly used in communication journals. A search found only four articles in communication journals and one dissertation that use the keywords "event history," "survival analysis," or "failure analysis" (Snyder, 1990, 1991; Unson, 1999; Westerik et al., 2005, 2006). This limited use of event history methods is unfortunate, given the variety of contexts and event-based outcomes of interest that may be critical to furthering the field of communication research. Thus, in this chapter, we provide a basic coverage of event history analysis designed to aid communication researchers in understanding how to use and interpret event models in their own work.

ADVANTAGES OF EVENT HISTORY ANALYSIS AND LIMITATIONS

There are several methodological advantages to selecting event history analysis rather than alternative approaches to studying events situated in time. First, event history analysis is flexible in how time until an event is measured. Second, it is possible to include predictor variables in the analysis that are either stable (time invariant) or vary over time (time varying). Third, event history analysis uses all the available information about a person over time, even if those data are censored. Censoring occurs, for example, when a person drops out or withdraws from the study before the end of data collection. These advantages will be explained further when we detail more about how event history analysis is conducted.

Event history analysis has been extended to multilevel models, so that it may be used for complex samples and multiple-level predictors (Donner & Klar, 2000; Muthén & Masyn, 2005). It can also be applied to repetition of events and transitions in and out of event states (Goldstein, Pan, & Bynner, 2004; Willett & Singer, 1995). For example, Westerik et al. (2005) used television diary data from 225 couples in the Netherlands to examine multiple transitions to television viewing in an evening.

Despite the advantages of event history models, the approach is limited to situations in which time to event is recorded. Event history analysis is not appropriate for outcomes measured as counts or rates, such as studies involving the number of times a person communicates or the rate of group accomplishments, for there is no outcome measured as a discrete event or state into which people may transition. Other approaches for counts or rates should be used to analyze these kinds of continuous outcomes, such as Poisson regression, logistic regression with a binomial link, overdispersed Poisson, or negative binomial models (Gardner, Mulvey, & Shaw, 1995; Zhao, Chen, & Schaffner, 2001).

Measurement Involving Time in Event History Analysis

Event history analysis (EHA) involves the analysis of a time-related process. As with all longitudinal or time-related processes, the measurement of time becomes critically important when deciding on appropriate methods of analysis of the data. The critical distinction is between *continuous* measurement of the time to event, in which each person could have a unique time to event, or a *discrete* approach, in which many people undergo events during the same time period.

TIME MEASURED CONTINUOUSLY

Continuous measures of time mean that a person could experience the event at any time within the time period. There are a number of ways in which time may be measured in a continuous fashion. A continuous measure of time to event may be gleaned from records, such as duration of marital counseling, computer usage patterns, or media use diaries. For example, DuWors and Haines (1990) used both diaries and store scanner data to examine brand loyalty over time. For some phenomena, it may be possible to observe event occurrences prospectively, as in small-group decision making (Snyder, 1991), patient-care provider interactions, observational studies of media use, and laboratory experiments. It is also possible to measure time to event retrospectively from interviews, such as asking about an adolescent's first cigarette or the timing of relational escalation. Unfortunately, depending on how memorable the event is, retrospective data are often subject to validity problems.

TIME MEASURED DISCRETELY

Alternatively, time to event can be inferred from repeated observations or questioning of people at specific points in time. This is possible with multiwave panel data, in which the same people are repeatedly assessed over multiple waves of data collection about the state of interest. In the discrete measure of time, people answer questions about their state at the moment of questioning, and transitions from one state to another are inferred from changes in states between waves. For example, an evaluation of a campaign asking about adoption of a particular behavior could be used to determine the first wave by which the behavior was adopted. Because time is characterized in discrete, rather than continuous, units, the statistical approaches used to analyze event data within panels are referred to as discrete-time event history analyses.

Figure 5.1 poses several possible patterns for five people in a hypothetical event history study and illustrates the difference between time conceptualized as continuous and time that is discrete. In the top panel of Figure 5.1, we can imagine capturing the exact time at which the event of interest occurred for the first three people, perhaps in minutes, or hours, or more crudely, in days. Their event variable is coded as a "1" to indicate event occurrence (event = 1), and their data are complete—that is, not censored (censored = 0). According to the time chart, neither of the last two persons experienced the event during the period of observation. Their event variable is coded as "0," and since the event was not observed during the time frame of the study, their data are censored (censored = 1). In the discrete setting (bottom panel of Figure 5.1), time is split into blocks representing waves of data collection, and events are recorded as occurring or not by the end of each block. Multiwave panel studies yield data that correspond to this discrete time-to-event perspective.

An advantage of discrete time approaches is that depending on the type of event and the length of time between waves, using multiwave panel data may provide more valid data than retrospective accounts. For some phenomena, it may be prohibitively expensive to collect data continuously but more affordable to collect panel data. A disadvantage is that it is not known precisely when between-the-waves change occurred, and this may affect the ability of the model to reliably predict changes, depending on the span of time that elapses between waves of data collection.

Given that multiwave panel studies are becoming increasingly popular in the social and behavioral sciences, many event history analyses use discrete-time approaches studying onset, relapse, and occurrence or reoccurrence of events. For example, Hill, Hawkins, Catalano, Abbott, and Guo (2005) used a prospective longitudinal design to study smoking initiation patterns among youth and adolescents. They followed 808 fifth graders over several years, with beginning- and end-of-year surveys at Grade 5, annual surveys until Grade 10, and additional follow-ups at Grade 12 (or its age equivalent) plus 3 years beyond Grade 12. Results of their discrete-time EHA indicated, in part, that family factors such as the existence and use of rules, consistent family discipline, family bonding, and family smoking history were predictive of the onset of daily smoking among adolescents.

Person	Time	Event	Censored
a	45	1	0
b	59	1	0
c	26	1	0
d	..	0	1
e	..	0	1

Time (Continuous)

Discrete time

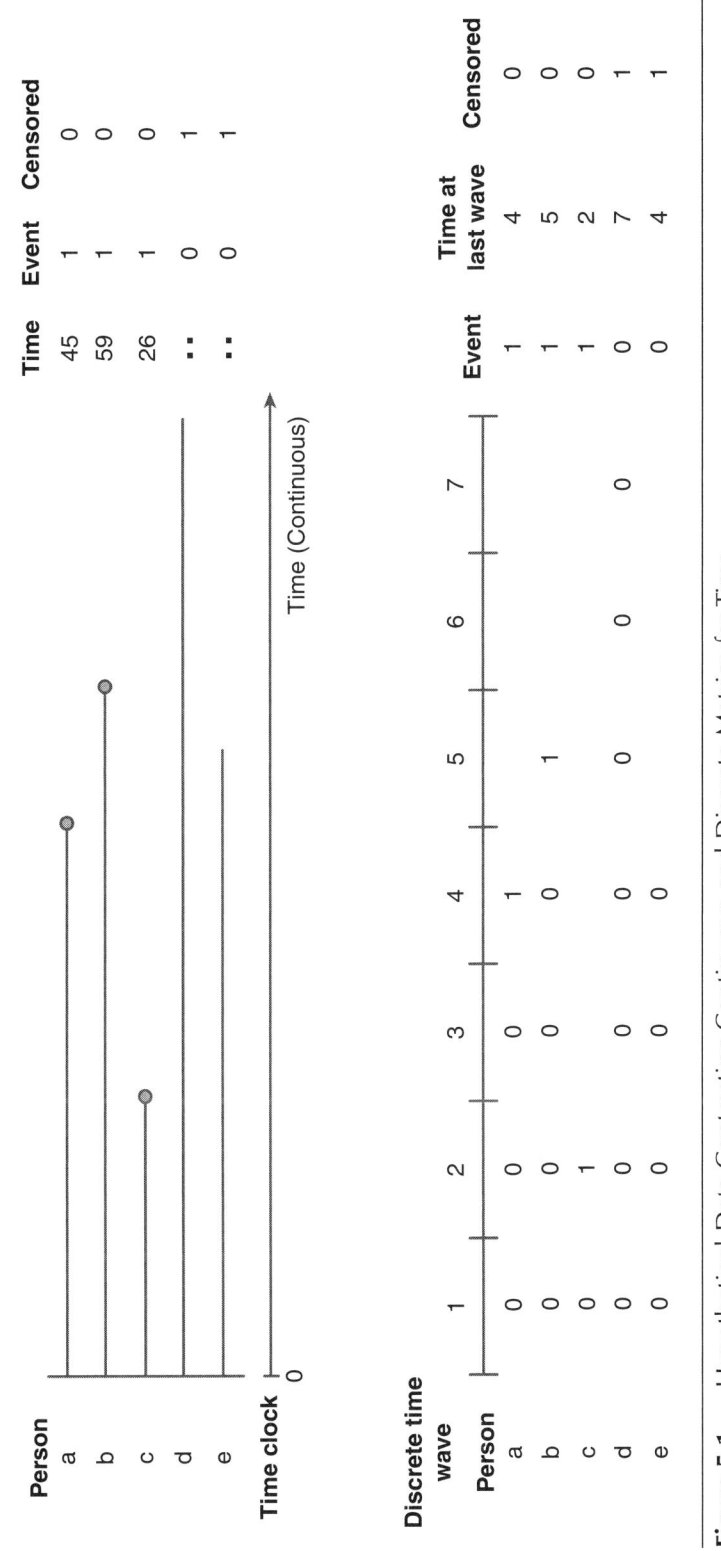

wave	1	2	3	4	5	6	7	Event	Time at last wave	Censored
Person										
a	0	0	0	1				1	4	0
b	0	0	0	0	1			1	5	0
c	0	1						1	2	0
d	0	0	0	0	0	0	0	0	7	1
e	0	0	0	0				0	4	1

Figure 5.1 Hypothetical Data Contrasting Continuous and Discrete Metrics for Time

Note: Circles represent event occurrence.

FLEXIBILITY IN TREATMENT OF TIME TO EVENT

Researchers are allowed a good deal of freedom in determining appropriate metrics for measuring time to event in event history analysis. Event history approaches tolerate uneven time intervals for individuals in the sample (varying schedules), as well as different numbers of people in the analysis at different points in time (unbalanced data). Singer and Willett (2003) point out that "time should be recorded in the smallest possible units relevant to the process under study" (p. 313), within practical limitations. Continuous-time data of information processing, for example, may measure an event in seconds, while diary data may cover larger blocks of time. For multiwave panel data, it is important to think about how long it takes for events to occur and time the waves of data collection appropriately in order to capture new events. Survey researchers should think about the event timing rather than automatically establish annual surveys, for example.

TIME-VARYING PREDICTORS

Event history analysis is able to incorporate time-varying explanatory variables in the models. Variables such as attitudes, amount of communication, degree of media exposure, number of sexual partners, and so on are expected to exhibit variability over time within persons. Gender and ethnic origin, on the other hand, or age at the beginning of a research study are time-invariant predictors that vary between persons but do not change within persons across the course of a research study. Both kinds of predictors can have salient effects on likelihood of event occurrence. For example, a study could examine how newspaper consumption patterns (time-varying) and gender (time invariant) affect participation in civic organizations. Incorporating time-varying predictors into the event history model allows researchers to examine how shifts or variability in the time-varying predictors contributes to occurrence of the event.

In order to include a time-varying predictor in a model, the predictor needs to be measured with at least the same periodicity as the events. Variables readily meet this requirement in discrete-time models because predictors and event occurrence outcomes are typically measured in the same waves of data collection (Singer & Willett, 2003). The discrete-time example we present below includes a time-varying predictor. However, it is often more difficult to collect a continuous version of a predictor variable for a continuous time-to-event model, such as retrospective accounts of media exposure and attitude change over time. When appropriate data are available, it is possible to conduct an event history analysis that includes the time-varying predictor using a procedure called Cox regression or proportional hazards model (Cox, 1972). In the example of continuous time-to-event analysis presented below, which is based on retrospective data, it was not feasible for the study to collect continuous retrospective information on the independent variables of interest; thus, our continuous-time example below includes only time-invariant predictors. However, examples of models with time-varying predictors can be found in Hosmer and Lemeshow (1999) and Willett and Singer (2003).

CENSORED CASES—MISSING CASES OR UNOBSERVED EVENTS OVER TIME

An important advantage of event history analysis is that it uses the available information about a person over time, even if the person drops out of the study before the end of data collection, is not observed to experience the event, or enters the study late. Any of these situations results in *censored data*. *Right-censoring* occurs when (a) a person does not experience the event during the study's time frame, such as the fourth person in the top panel of Figure 5.1, or (b) information about event occurrence is unknown (missing) for a person during a study's time frame because he or she dropped out of the study, such as the fifth person in the top panel of Figure 5.1. In either of these situations, the result is incomplete data on the time to event for these participants (Hosmer & Lemeshow, 1999). Right-censoring refers to the fact that time to event is measured on a time continuum from left (baseline or time 0) to right; what is censored is information on the right of the time line about when or if the person experiences the event. For example, if the event of interest is joining a civic organization, and the person had not joined an organization before the end of data collection, we do not know whether the person joined just after the end of the study, after a few years, or never. The event history analysis would include data that the person had not joined an organization before the end of the study and that his or her status after the end of the study is unknown. The study would also include data on people who had not experienced the event before they withdrew, dropped out, or otherwise ceased providing data from the study, noting that their data were censored as of the moment of withdrawal, if the timing of withdrawal is known. The partial data for the person who withdrew early rather than at the end of the study may still be used to understand patterns of event occurrence within the sample.

Withdrawal in longitudinal studies often arises due to persons moving out of the study area, death from a nonstudy-related event, or attrition for other reasons. A typical assumption made during event history analysis is that the pattern of censorship is random (or "noninformative"; Hosmer & Lemeshow, 1999; Singer & Willett, 2003). If attrition is not random (such as when people with certain characteristics have a greater tendency to drop out of a study) and steps are not taken to correct for known attrition problems, the estimates in the study will be biased. As with all longitudinal studies, care should be taken to limit attrition as much as possible in order to protect against bias (Singer & Willett, 2003).

Other forms of censoring include left-censoring (the event may already have occurred for some individuals in the sample prior to the start of the study), interval-censoring (missed wave of data collection), or delayed entry (also called truncation) into a research study. Hosmer and Lemeshow (1999) and Singer and Willett (2003) review methods for dealing with each of these partial data situations in event history models.

The ability to retain information in the analysis from censored cases is a strong advantage of event history analysis. As we shall see in our example, the event history analysis allows estimation of expected rates of event occurrence within specific time intervals based on only those cases that are "at risk" for experiencing the event. In the case of continuous time to event, these intervals could theoretically be very small. For the time intervals in which a case is present, the data are included; cases are not included in the risk set if they have been censored during any previous interval. Both noncensored and censored cases contribute to our understanding of risk for experiencing the event under study, and information from both kinds of cases is used to summarize and characterize the distribution of event occurrence (Allison, 1984, 1995; Hosmer & Lemeshow, 1999; Singer & Willett, 1993, 2003).

Alternative approaches and censoring. Although event history models handle censored data by incorporating as much information as is known about these cases, alternative analysis strategies typically eliminate cases that have censored data. One alternative approach is to conduct a logistic regression comparing whether or not people experienced an event. For example, a logistic regression may compare people who joined a civic organization at any time during the study to those who never joined. This approach treats the person with censored data the same as people who never joined during the study. It also collapses all the information about *when* a person experienced a transition into a single state of having had the transition. Thus, there is no differentiation between people who joined early and people who joined later. The consequent loss of information about timing when comparing joiners to nonjoiners affects the results and addresses a different kind of research question than the one permitted through event history analysis.

Still another approach to data analysis might involve examining *when* people joined a civic organization, making the dependent variable potentially suitable for a multiple regression of the amount of elapsed time until they joined a civic organization. While this approach preserves the information on the timing of events, it means throwing out data on people who never joined (since their event time is unknown). In a survival analysis of drug efficacy, this approach would mean excluding data on people who were still alive at the end of the study—clearly a group that one would want to include in the analysis, because they are providing data on the positive contribution of the drug. Exclusion of censored cases can result in large biases (Sørensen, 1977; Tuma & Hannan, 1978, 1984).

Suppose the researcher tries to use the multiple regression approach but wants to retain the censored cases by assigning them the value of the last possible date of the event. Unfortunately, the results are still biased because the "correction" underestimates the true value of the dependent variable (Allison, 1984, 1995). Chances are there is variance among the censored cases, such that some may transition close to the end of the study but others may transition at a much later date. Assigning a single transition date in the absence of information about the real date of transition is arbitrary and effectively misleading—not attractive options for a responsible researcher.

Finally, the fact that event history analysis can handle varying schedules and different numbers of people in the sample is an advantage over typical repeated-measures ANOVA approaches to analyzing longitudinal data. These approaches require balanced data across time points—the same number of people at each point in time—as well as a consistent data collection schedule for all persons in the study, and thus would be inappropriate for time-to-event outcomes. (See O'Connell and McCoach, 2004, for a summary of advantages and disadvantages of analysis of variance approaches to longitudinal data.)

Basic Concepts: Odds, Survivor, and Hazard Functions

Event history analysis examines *survivor* and *hazard* functions. In order to understand these, it is important to understand odds and odds ratios. A brief review is presented here, and a more extensive treatment of odds and hazards and their relationship to event history models can be found in Hosmer and Lemeshow (1999, 2000), Agresti (1996), and O'Connell (2006). Our examples will also emphasize the most important concepts.

Odds. The probability of event occurrence can be assessed as the number of persons in a given sample experiencing an event, such as joining a civic organization, divided by the total number of people in the sample who would be considered available or "at risk" for experiencing that event (also called "in the risk set"). For instance, if 20 out of 100 people join a civic organization, the probability of joining for a randomly selected individual from that sample is .20 or 20%. Odds are another way of representing probabilities and quantify the ratio probability that an event occurs, p, to the probability that it does not occur, $1 - p$. If the odds of an event are quite small, then the probability of failure (the nonevent occurrence) is larger than the probability of event occurrence. For example, given a 20% probability of joining a civic organization, the odds of joining a civic organization are .20/(1 − .20) = .20/.80 = .25. If the odds of an event are 1.0, then the likelihood of joining and not joining are the same (odds = .5/.5 = 1.0). Thus, values for the odds that are less than 1.0, such as the simple example above, characterize a less than 50% chance of experiencing the event; and odds that are greater than 1.0 characterize a more than 50% chance of experiencing the event. Odds are always nonnegative and range from 0 to infinity.

Odds ratios. Odds ratios (ORs) are used to examine the impact on the odds of an explanatory or independent variable, such as gender or ethnic origin, on a binary (two-category) outcome. For example, if we wanted to compare the odds of joining a civic organization between women and men, the OR is a quotient representing the odds for women divided by the odds for men. Odds ratios are also nonnegative; they are bounded below by 0 but have no upper bound. An OR of 1.0 indicates that an explanatory variable has no effect on the odds of success; that is, the odds of joining a civic organization for females are the same as the odds of joining for males.

Suppose, for example, that we use simple dummy coding (0 and 1 for males and females, respectively) to code a gender variable. Small values of the OR (< 1.0) indicate that the odds of experiencing the event of interest for the persons with the smaller value of the predictor used in the denominator (here, males) are greater than the odds of experiencing the event for the persons with the higher value of the predictor used in the numerator (here, females). Thus, the risk of experiencing the event or joining a civic organization is smaller for females than for males. The opposite is true for values of the OR that exceed 1.0. In that case, the odds for females of joining a civic organization is greater than the odds for males; or the risk for females is larger than the risk for males.

Although we used dummy coding to illustrate this example, other coding schemes are possible, and extensions to continuous predictors are straightforward. For OR > 1, the odds of experiencing the event becomes greater as the independent variable increases in value.

Survivor functions and hazard functions. In an event history analysis, we are not interested in just whether or not an event has occurred, but rather in whether or not the event has occurred given that the event has not yet occurred up to some specific point in time, t. The term "survival" is used to represent cases that do *not* experience the event; that is, that they have survived up to time t without experiencing the event. The *survival function*, $S(t)$, describes the pattern of survival probabilities or rates across time intervals in the sample. The survival function is used to estimate the survival probabilities by dividing the number of people surviving beyond time t by the number of people in the sample, after making adjustments for censoring (Morita, Lee, & Mowday, 1989; Singer & Willett, 2003).

In the presence of censoring, the survivor function cannot be estimated directly, but it can be estimated through the *hazard function, h(t)*. The hazard is a way of expressing risk of an event, and the hazard function describes the pattern of hazards across time intervals in the sample. If time is continuous, the hazard is a rate per unit of time that describes the conditional probability of the event occurring in any interval of time (which can be quite small), given that the event has not yet occurred. In the context of a discrete event-based outcome, the hazard is "algebraically equivalent to the probability that the event will occur in the current time period, given that it must occur now, or sometime in the future" (Singer & Willett, 2003, p. 330), and is a conditional probability. For details on how the hazard is calculated in either case, see Hosmer and Lemeshow (1999) and Singer and Willett (2003).

Similar to the odds ratio, the hazards ratio is used to examine the effect of an independent variable on the hazard. The hazard ratio compares the risk of event occurrence for two groups, such as males and females, or for levels of a continuous variable. Event history analysis provides hazard ratios to determine if there are differences in the hazard profiles attributable to levels of an explanatory variable.

An Example in Discrete Time: Alcohol Advertising Exposure and Initiating Drinking During a Panel Study

The logic of event history analysis is fairly straightforward. Since it can be difficult at first to feel comfortable thinking about phenomena as events, states, and transitions, it may be valuable to look at an example in more depth. We provide two examples below. In the first example, we illustrate the fundamental concepts of risk set, hazards, and survival probabilities using a discrete time-to-event approach. We describe data structures for the analysis of event history data under the discrete time-to-event approach, and we provide a series of nested models to demonstrate and interpret event history models containing both time-invariant and time-varying predictors. In our second example, we demonstrate a continuous time-to-event analysis through Cox regression using predictors similar to our first example, and we construct and interpret survival and hazard curves.

One research question that lends itself to event history analysis is whether or not alcohol advertising exposure influences when a teen begins to drink. Drinking at a younger age is associated with a host of problems later, including greater likelihood of adult addictions (Chassin & DeLucia, 1996), and the effect of alcohol advertising on alcohol consumption remains controversial (Snyder, Fleming-Milici, Slater, Sun, & Strizhakova, 2006). The event of interest is the transition from being a nondrinker to drinking. We are not concerned in this analysis with how much alcohol they consume when they use it, but rather the dichotomous state of no alcohol consumed compared to one or more drinks consumed. Analysis of the factors affecting how much they drink would need to use a method suitable for a quantitative outcome, such as a Poisson or multiple regression model.

We were able to examine the occurrence of onset of drinking among a sample of adolescents followed for up to 2 years. The data are from a multiwave panel national telephone study of alcohol advertising effects collected by the first author, and a subset of variables are used here for demonstration purposes. Interviews were conducted with a random sample of youth ages 14 to 19 at baseline. The first wave, $N = 2,069$, was conducted May through August 2002. The second wave, $N = 1,583$, took place about 2 months later, August to October 2002. The third wave took place May to July 2003, about a year after the baseline ($N = 1,131$), and the fourth wave was a year after the third wave, May to July 2004 ($N = 834$). The panel data enabled assessment of the onset of drinking prospectively—during the study period. Such a prospective measure is more reliable than retrospective accounts, which may be subject to greater recall biases. Only data from those who did not drink any alcoholic beverages in the past year at baseline are included in the analysis, for those are the people in the risk set (at risk of becoming a drinker). The sample sizes used in the analysis at waves 1 through 4 were 726, 598, 434, and 333, respectively. There was attrition between waves, and the waves were unevenly spaced in time.

The dependent variable is described in the next section. The independent variables included gender and age and a time-varying covariate assessing exposure to alcohol advertising. Among the nondrinkers, 52.8% were female, and the average age was 16.3 years at baseline. Alcohol advertising exposure was summed from a series of open-ended questions about the number of times in the prior month the person remembered exposure to advertising on each of four media (television, radio, billboards, and magazines) for each of five types of alcoholic beverages (beer, wine, liquor, premixed drinks/malternatives, and malt liquor). An example question was, "About how many times in the past four weeks have you noticed billboards for beer?" The mean advertising exposure level at baseline for nondrinkers was 63.7 ($SD = 64.8$). (For a detailed description of the measures, see Fleming-Milici, 2006.)

EVENT SERIES

Using discrete-time event history procedures, the timing of events is inferred from the multiwave panel data. In this example, we were interested in the first time a person becomes a drinker after being a nondrinker—an event that each individual can experience only once. The survey measured the amount of drinking since the last wave and was dichotomized into none (0) or any (1). Table 5.1 shows the possible event series (or sequences) of drinking, nondrinking, and missing across the four waves of data. The first sequence, 0000, indicates that those people ($n = 115$) reported no drinking during each wave. By design, all sequences begin with 0 at baseline (our sample consisted of only nondrinkers at the beginning of the study). Sequence 27, 0111, was for adolescents who responded affirmatively to all three follow-up waves ($n = 52$). In the event history analysis, the wave for the first affirmative response following baseline is taken as the event of interest: time to first drink. The table notes whether or not people in the sequence experienced the event, and if so, at which wave the event occurred. Sequences 3 and 7, for example, had their event wave recorded as Time 4 and Time 3 in column 4, respectively, and their event outcome recorded as 1 (column 6). For participants withdrawn from the study (e.g., sequences 2 or 5), the third column indicates the last wave during which data were obtained. These sequences are noted as censored (column 5) and not experiencing the event (column 6). Sequence 1 also provides censored cases, since the time to event of first drink was not observed during the duration of the study. Reentry into the study after a missing wave of data was not incorporated into the determination of event occurrence. For example, the two people who responded with sequence 18 were treated in the event history analysis as censored cases; they provided no additional information after wave 1, and it is not known whether or not they drank during the missing wave.

The event sequences are an interesting way of inspecting patterns in event occurrence over time. In the last two columns of Table 5.1, we present the mean age for each sequence, as well as the percent female. Visual inspection suggests that withdrawn cases seem to be older, which may violate the assumption of a random censoring mechanism and pose a limitation to the results of our analysis. In the event history analysis, we examined age and gender as predictors of the onset of drinking, which helped control statistically for the effect of age on drinking (although it will not correct for censoring biases). In addition to these two time-invariant predictors, we included a time-varying predictor, exposure to alcohol advertising, to assess whether increasing levels of exposure contribute to earlier risk in terms of experiencing the event of first drink.

RISK SETS, HAZARDS, AND SURVIVAL FUNCTIONS

Before turning to the analytic model, *life tables* were constructed for the entire sample in Table 5.2 and separately by gender in Table 5.3. We followed the format utilized by Singer and Willett (2003). The examination of life tables provides a descriptive and informative summary of the

Table 5.1 Event Patterns for the Alcohol Advertising Study, N = 726

Sq.[a]	Pattern	n	Last Wave Observed,[b] or Event Wave	Censored (yes [1] or no [0])	Event (yes [1] or no [0])	Mean Age	% Female
1	0 0 0 0	115	T4	1	0	15.75	47.8
2	0 0 0 *	68	T3	1	0	16.11	50.2
3	0 0 0 1	42	T4	0	1	16.30	50.0
4	0 0 * 0	9	T2	1	0	16.14	55.6
5	0 0 * *	100	T2	1	0	16.68	57.0
6	0 0 * 1	6	T2	1	0	16.34	50.0
7	0 0 1 0	18	T3	0	1	15.52	61.1
8	0 0 1 *	25	T3	0	1	16.71	44.0
9	0 0 1 1	35	T3	0	1	16.10	48.6
10	0 * 0 0	2	T1	1	0	15.94	50.0
11	0 * 0 *	2	T1	1	0	18.25	50.0
12	0 * 0 1	1	T1	1	0	19.53	100.0
13	0 * * 0	3	T1	1	0	16.68	0.00
14	0 * * *	107	T1	1	0	16.93	55.14
15	0 * * 1	7	T1	1	0	16.87	50.0
16	0 * 1 0	0	T1	1	0	—	—
17	0 * 1 *	4	T1	1	0	18.64	25.0
18	0 * 1 1	2	T1	1	0	16.39	100.0
19	0 1 0 0	13	T2	0	1	15.91	61.5
20	0 1 0 *	10	T2	0	1	15.66	70.0
21	0 1 0 1	10	T2	0	1	15.84	30.0
22	0 1 * 0	1	T2	0	1	17.12	0.0
23	0 1 * *	53	T2	0	1	16.36	60.4
24	0 1 * 1	5	T2	0	1	17.71	80.0
25	0 1 1 0	12	T2	0	1	15.05	50.0
26	0 1 1 *	24	T2	0	1	16.48	62.5
27	0 1 1 1	52	T2	0	1	16.02	42.3
Total		726		426	300	16.31	52.8

[a] Sq. is sequence number; for each pattern, 0 indicates the event was not reported, 1 indicates the event was reported, * indicates missing data for that wave.
[b] Reentry into study (as in pattern sequences 6 and 12) is not incorporated into determination of last wave observed.

hazard and survival functions for these data, which can be found in the last two columns of Tables 5.2 and 5.3. The rows include the cases in the risk set at each wave—the set of individuals who are at risk for experiencing the event at the beginning of any interval. The risk set excludes previously censored cases and cases that already experienced the event. For example, our data set was constructed around a baseline such that no individuals had experienced the event ($n = 726$). However, at wave 2, there were already 128 censored cases (teens not measured at wave 2); these censored cases are not included in the risk set at wave 2. The hazard (number of people experiencing the event divided by the number in the risk set) at wave 2 is $180/598 = .301$. Over the 24-month duration of the study, the hazards tended to decline over time (there was a slight increase in risk at wave 4), with the period of greatest risk occurring just after baseline. At wave 2, the sample survival probability is $(1)(1 - .301) = .699$—the prior wave's survival rate multiplied by 1 minus the current wave's hazard rate.[1]

Although hazard functions can increase or decrease over time, all survival functions share a common pattern; they are a "monotonically nonincreasing function of time" (Singer & Willett, 2003, p. 343). Indeed, this is what we observe in our own example. Based on our sample, only 38% of adolescents remained nondrinkers beyond the 24-month duration of the study. In fact, according to these data, the median lifetime occurs in wave 3; the average adolescent begins drinking after 12 months from baseline but not a full 24 months later.

Table 5.3 presents the hazard and survival data by gender. The profiles are similar based on a visual inspection, although the hazard for females at wave 2 may be slightly elevated relative to males. Based on these profiles,

Table 5.2 Life Tables for the Alcohol Advertising Example

Wave	Time Interval (months)	Number Nondrinking at Beginning of Interval (risk set)	Number Drinking During Interval	Number Censored at End of Interval	Proportion Drinking During Interval (h_t)	Proportion Still Nondrinking at End of Interval (S_t)
1	base	726	0	128	0.00	1.00
2	[0, 2)	598	180	115	.301	.699
3	[2, 12)	303	78	68	.257	.519
4	[12, 24)	157	42	115	.268	.380

Note: $S_t = S_{t-1}(1 - h_t)$

Table 5.3   Life Tables for the Alcohol Advertising Study by Gender

Wave	Time Interval (months)	Number Nondrinking at Beginning of Interval (risk set)	Number Drinking During Interval	Number Censored at End of Interval	Proportion Drinking During Interval (h_t)	Proportion Still Nondrinking at End of Interval (S_t)
Males						
1	base	343	0	61	0.00	1.00
2	(0, 2)	282	83	50	.294	.706
3	(2, 12)	149	39	29	.262	.521
4	(12, 24)	81	21	60	.259	.386
Females						
1	base	383	0	67	0.00	1.00
2	(0, 2)	316	97	65	.307	.693
3	(2, 12)	154	39	39	.253	.518
4	(12, 24)	76	21	55	.276	.375

however, it seems reasonable to expect that there would be no gender differences found in the hazard functions once the analytic event history model is applied to the data.

STRUCTURING THE DATA

Table 5.4 was constructed based on the event series and relevant data on censoring and event occurrence. The top portion of Table 5.4 provides a prototype illustration of the obtained multiwave panel data for five separate individuals in the data set. The data are set up as a traditional longitudinal spreadsheet, also called a *person-oriented* data file. The first individual (*id* = 1) in our sample was slightly older than 15 and female, she experienced successively higher levels of exposure to alcohol advertising over time, and her data were censored prior to report of experiencing the event due to withdrawal from the study (loss to follow-up). In this data setup, there are four possible waves of data collected on each individual, as evidenced by the time-varying predictor identified here as *expos1* to *expos4*. The variables *last wave*, *censored*, and *event* values describe the specific outcome for this young girl. No event was recorded, data were censored, and this participant was lost to follow-up after wave 3. Participant 5's data also were censored, but all four waves of data were collected. This young man did not experience the event by wave 4, and thus is also a censored case. Participant 8 contributed two waves of information to the study before being censored, participant 20 contributed one wave of data, and participant 25 experienced the event during wave 4, thus contributing four full waves of data to the event history analysis.

Discrete-time event history models can be fit using traditional software procedures for logistic regression once the data have been appropriately restructured (Allison, 1995; Hosmer & Lemeshow, 1999; Singer & Willett, 1993, 2003). The required data setup involves creating a person-period data set in which each wave of data collection for an individual is represented by a single line in the data file. The setup between the person-oriented data file and the person-period data file corresponds to the difference between a multivariate structure to repeated-measures data and a univariate structure to repeated-measures data. Thus, as shown in the bottom portion of Table 5.4, person 1 contributed three waves of data to the analysis and thus is represented by three lines in the person-period data file. Similarly, person 5 contributed four waves of data and thus has four lines of information in the restructured data file. For each row in the restructured data file, the time-varying *exposure* variable contains the corresponding value of *expos1* to *expos4*, and the outcome of interest remains whether or not the event has occurred. Whether the event occurs or not is the final column, with 0 = no event, and 1 = yes event. Continuing on, participant 8 contributes two rows, participant 20 contributes one row, and participant 25 contributes four rows. Participant 25 is the only person in this subset example who experienced the event, indicated by the value of 1 in the final column and during the last interval of data collection. All other event values for earlier intervals are coded as 0, for no event.

THE EVENT HISTORY MODEL

The person-period data set is ready for analysis using logistic regression (Fox, 1997; O'Connell, 2006; Zwick & Sklar, 2005). We used SPSS for our analyses. As the subset of data used in the analysis was based on nonevent at wave 1 (by definition, no one was yet a drinker), the initial interval has no variation in the outcome. The time intervals are indicated in the analytic models by the dummy variables, *T2, T3,* and *T4* (see Table 5.4). The model of interest is of the discrete-time hazard function. Because logistic regression is applied to the dichotomous event indicator variable, the outcome is transformed via the logistic transformation.

Table 5.4 Data Structures for Discrete Time-to-Event Analysis for the Alcohol Advertising Study

\multicolumn{9}{c	}{*Person-Oriented Data Set (original data setup)*}
ID	AGE	FEMALE	EXPOS1	EXPOS2	EXPOS3	EXPOS4	LASTWAVE	CENSORED	EVENT
1	15.31	1.00	335.0	330.0	575.0	–	7.00	1.00	0
5	14.68	.00	12.0	7.0	15.0	6.0	8.00	1.00	0
8	19.27	1.00	43.0	50.0	–	–	6.00	1.00	0
20	19.76	1.00	81.0	–	–	–	5.00	1.00	0
25	19.70	.00	14.0	6.0	9.0	3.0	8.00	.00	1

\multicolumn{9}{c	}{*Person-Period Data Set (restructured data setup)*}
ID	AGE	FEMALE	EXPOSURE	T1	T2	T3	T4	EVENT
1	15.31	1.00	335.0	1	0	0	0	.00
1	15.31	1.00	330.0	0	1	0	0	.00
1	15.31	1.00	575.0	0	0	1	0	.00
5	14.68	.00	12.0	1	0	0	0	.00
5	14.68	.00	7.0	0	1	0	0	.00
5	14.68	.00	15.0	0	0	1	0	.00
5	14.68	.00	6.0	0	0	0	1	.00
8	19.27	1.00	43.0	1	0	0	0	.00
8	19.27	1.00	50.0	0	1	0	0	.00
20	19.76	1.00	81.0	1	0	0	0	.00
25	19.70	.00	14.0	1	0	0	0	.00
25	19.70	.00	6.0	0	1	0	0	.00
25	19.70	.00	9.0	0	0	1	0	.00
25	19.70	.00	3.0	0	0	0	1	1.00

We fit three models (below) to illustrate the event history analysis for discrete time-to-event data. The first model, Model A, is the baseline hazard model, which results when time is the only predictor. This baseline hazard model can be used to reproduce the sample hazards previously calculated and presented in Table 5.2. Our second model, Model B, includes the time-invariant predictors of *age* at baseline and *female* (female = 1, male = 0). Finally, Model C is used to demonstrate the inclusion and interpretation of a time-varying predictor, alcohol advertising *exposure*. In these models, the i and j subscripts refer to the value for the ith person during the jth discrete-time interval. Results are provided in Table 5.5 and discussed below.

Model A: $\text{logit } h(t_{ij}) = \ln\left(\dfrac{h_{ij}}{1-h_{ij}}\right) = (a_1 T2_{ij} + a_2 T3_{ij} + a_3 T4_{ij})$

Model B: $\text{logit } h(t_{ij}) = \ln\left(\dfrac{h_{ij}}{1-h_{ij}}\right) = (a_1 T2_{ij} + a_2 T3_{ij} + a_3 T4_{ij})$
$+ \beta_1(age5)_{ij} + \beta_2(female)_{ij}$

Model C: $\text{logit } h(t_{ij}) = \ln\left(\dfrac{h_{ij}}{1-h_{ij}}\right) = (a_1 T2_{ij} + a_2 T3_{ij} + a_3 T4_{ij})$
$+ \beta_1(age5)_{ij} + \beta_2(female)_{ij}$
$+ \beta_3(exposure)_{ij}$

Results. Model A is the baseline hazards model. Notice that there is no error term, which is not unusual for a logistic model. The intentional omission of the error term corresponds to the assumption that there is no

Table 5.5 Discrete-Time Event History Analysis for the Alcohol Study Data: Model Comparison for Main Effect of Time (A), Inclusion of Time-Invariant Predictors (B), and Inclusion of Time-Varying Predictors (C)

	Model A			Model B			Model C		
	b	SE b	W^a (df)	b	SE b	W^a (df)	b	SE b	W^a (df)
T2	−.84	.09	89.31 (1) **	−1.81	.79	5.24 (1) *	−2.00	.80	6.26 (1) *
T3	−1.06	.13	65.01 (1) **	−2.01	.79	6.54 (1) *	−2.19	.80	7.58 (1) **
T4	−1.01	.18	31.21 (1) **	−1.95	.79	6.10 (1) *	−2.10	.80	6.94 (1) **
Age				.06	.05	1.47 (1)	.06	.05	1.61 (1)
Female				.04	.14	.09 (1)	.03	.14	.04 (1)
Ad exposure							.003	.001	6.08 (1) *
Model χ^2 (df)			207.10 (3) **			208.6 (5) **			214.56 (6) **
Block			207.10 (3) **			1.533 (2)			5.96 (1) *
Deviance			1259.60			1258.07			1252.11

[a] Wald test; * $p < .05$; ** $p < .01$

unobserved heterogeneity, which implies that all variability in hazard profiles is accounted for by the specified model (Singer & Willett, 1993). In Table 5.5, the coefficients for the time indicators form a set of intercepts, one for each time period. Singer and Willett (2003) describe these intercepts as "the value of logit hazard (the log odds of event occurrence) in that particular time period" (p. 371). These values, then, are the predictions for the logit hazards contained in Table 5.2. In a logistic model, exponentiating a predicted logit provides the estimated odds: e^{logit} = odds, and the odds are a quotient of two complementary probabilities: odds = $p/(1-p)$, where p is the probability of the event. Since the hazard is a conditional probability, this means that the odds from our model are:

$$odds = \frac{h(t)}{1 - h(t)}.$$

Rearranging terms and solving for the hazard yields:

$$h(t) = \frac{odds}{1 + odds}.$$

We can easily see the correspondence between Model A and Table 5.2 by calculating the estimated hazards based on our model. For the second time period, T2, the parameter estimate for the intercept is $\alpha_1 = -0.840$. Exponentiating to obtain the odds, odds = $e^{-.084}$ = 0.432. Solving for the hazard, $\hat{h}(t) = 0.432/(1 + 0.432) = 0.302$, within rounding error of our sample hazard calculated in Table 5.2. Following this same process for the remaining two entries, for T3, $\hat{h}(t) = 0.257$, and for T4, $\hat{h}(t) = 0.267$, which are also within rounding error of the sample hazards in Table 5.2.

The Wald test is used to inform about the contribution of specific predictors in the model. A Wald test (Table 5.5, columns 4, 7, and 10) for each of the intercepts indicates that each of the logit hazards across the time intervals is statistically different from zero, which is equivalent to saying that the odds are statistically different from 1.0.

The overall likelihood ratio chi-square can be used to examine model fit. For Model A, $\chi^2(3) = 207.10$, $p < .01$; thus we conclude that Model A fits the data better than a null, or empty, model. A null model would yield a flat hazards profile and the intercepts would all be assumed equal (Singer & Willett, 2003). The deviance for Model A, shown at the bottom of Table 5.5, can be used to compare the fit of Model A relative to models in which it is nested, such as B or C, given the number of parameters estimated in the two models being compared. In general, the smaller the deviance, the better the model fit. In addition, the Block test (also provided in Table 5.5) is another type of likelihood ratio test in which the contribution to reduction in deviance is assessed only for the collection of variables added. In Model A, all three intercepts were added to an empty model, so the Model χ^2 test is the same as the Block test.

The baseline hazard provides a starting point from which to view changes, or shifts, in the hazard function based on values of the explanatory variables. In Model B, baseline age and gender are included as predictors of the hazard. Although neither of these time-invariant predictors is statistically significant (see Table 5.5), we can use the values of the parameter estimates to determine predicted hazards. For example, let's predict the hazard in time period *T4* for females (*female* = 1) for someone of average age (from Table 5.1, we'll choose 16.31 years of age). We can follow a similar three-step process to that used in the baseline model example above to find (1) the estimated logit = (−1.95) + 0.06(16.31) + 0.04(1) = −.9314; (2) the estimated odds = e^{logit} = 0.394; and (3) the estimated hazard = odds/(1 + odds) = 0.283. Finally, although neither parameter estimate is statistically significant, both effects are positive. For example, exponentiating the gender effect yields a hazards ratio that indicates how much the hazard differs between boys and girls. Here, e^{004} = 1.04. (*Note:* This is close to 1.0 since the effect is not statistically significant.) The estimated odds of first drink in a given time interval are 1.04 times greater for females than for males. This can be compared with the actual hazards ratio for females to males using entries in Table 5.3. At time *T2*, the hazard for females relative to the hazard for males is 0.307/0.294 = 1.044; at *T3* this ratio becomes 0.97; and at *T4* the ratio becomes 1.070. On average across time intervals, the hazard ratio for females to males is about 1.040, as estimated from the model.

The model estimate of the hazard brings us to the definition of a second assumption regarding the application of the discrete-time event history analysis. The model imposes a proportionality constraint for each predictor. The assumption of proportional hazards means, for example, that the estimated hazards ratio for females to males remains constant across all time intervals. This is a restrictive but parsimonious assumption. Methods for investigating departures from proportionality and allowing nonproportionality for some or all of the predictors are discussed in Allison (1995), O'Connell (2006), and Singer and Willett (1993, 2003).

Supporting what the Wald tests have indicated, the contribution of *age* and *female* as a set is not statistically significant, and these two variables do not provide a statistically significant reduction in the deviance relative to Model A, Block $\chi^2(2)$ = 1.533, $p > .05$. Because Models B and A are nested, this value can also be found through the differences of deviances: Deviance$_{model\ A}$ − Deviance$_{model\ B}$ = 1259.60 − 1258.07 = 1.533, with a difference of 2 parameters between the two models (3 parameters estimated in Model A and 5 parameters estimated in Model B). As a set, the two predictors are not associated with shifts or differences in the baseline hazard rate for first drinking.

Model C adds a time-varying predictor, advertising *exposure*, to the set of sequential models. The advertising exposure effect is statistically significant at $p < .05$. Interpretation of a time-varying predictor is not too different from a time-invariant one, but conceptualizing a relationship back to sample hazards tables such as Table 5.2 tends to be more complex. First, we see that the effect of advertising exposure on the logit hazard is positive, and $e^{0.003} = 1.003$. This means that within any specific time interval and for any specific combination of time-invariant predictors, as exposure increases (by one unit), so does the logit hazard, which increases the odds, which then increases the hazards associated with first drinking. Since exposure is continuous, as is age, there is an infinite possibility of combinations of exposure and the predictors, so deciding on combinations to compare is critical. Singer and Willett (1993) suggest using extreme values at either end of the time-varying continuum to visually examine effects of the predictor. Despite the fact that advertising exposure changes over time, however, the proportionality assumption is still in place. That is, holding all else constant, the effect of advertising exposure on the logit hazard is assumed and constrained to be constant over time.

The addition of *exposure* to the model containing *age* and *female* is statistically significant, both by the Wald test, Wald(1) = 6.08, $p < .05$, and by the likelihood ratio test for the block, $\chi^2(1) = 5.96$, $p < .05$. We can use the deviances of nested Models A and C to assess improvement in fit for Model C relative to the baseline model: Deviance$_{model\ A}$ − Deviance$_{model\ C}$ = 1,259.60 − 1,253.41 = 6.19, with a difference of 3 parameters added, yields $\chi^2(3) = 6.19$, $p < .05$. Overall, advertising exposure does provide improvement in fit within Model C and also relative to the baseline hazards model, Model A. From Model C, participants who experience one unit more of exposure are $e^{0.003} = 1.003$ times as likely to initiate drinking alcoholic beverages. Given that the standard deviation for the exposure measure is approximately 65 ads recalled, it is appropriate for interpretive purposes to compute the effect of change for a larger number of units at a time. We can find the effect for a change of 30 units (almost one half of a standard deviation) using $e^{30(0.003)} = e^{0.09} = 1.09$; and this degree of change (30 units of exposure) increases the hazard by 9% across all time intervals [100(OR − 1)] (Hosmer & Lemeshow, 1999). Thus, we can conclude that alcohol advertising exposure does contribute to initiating alcohol consumption.

An Example in Continuous Time: Retrospective Accounts of Age at First Drink

The same study was used to examine retrospective accounts of the age at which a respondent initiated drinking, in order to provide an example of event history analysis using a continuous-time-dependent variable. Only the baseline data were analyzed, because that is when the retrospective data were taken. Age of drinking onset was measured using the following open-ended question: "How old were you when you first began drinking, other than just having tastes?" Refusals and don't knows were excluded from the analysis, yielding a total sample size of 2,045.

The research question for this analysis was whether alcohol promotions in the form of merchandising (e.g., clothing with brand logos) relate to age of onset of drinking. Because the accounts are entirely retrospective, it was not possible to establish time order and therefore causal inferences were inappropriate. Current *ownership* of promotional items was assessed by the question, "Do you own any merchandise from an alcohol company? Merchandise is stuff like caps or pens or T-shirts." The possible responses were yes (1) or no (0). As in the prior analysis, the models also included baseline age and gender as independent variables.

The data were analyzed using Cox regression in SPSS. Another name for Cox regression is the *cumulative* or *proportional hazards model*, which highlights the assumption made in a Cox analysis: The effects of explanatory variables on the hazards are assumed to be constant across time (Cox, 1972). As with the discrete-time approach, this can be a restrictive, but parsimonious and often reasonable, assumption. See Allison (1995), Hosmer and Lemeshow (1999), O'Connell (2006), and Singer and Willett (2003) for demonstrations of how to investigate and relax this assumption.

The setup for a Cox regression is similar to multiple regression with the addition of the specification of a "status" variable indicating whether or not the case was censored. (Since Cox regression is done using a traditional person-oriented data set structure, the data did not need to be transformed to a person-period data set, as was required for the discrete-time analysis above.) In this analysis, people who did not report any drinking in the prior year and those who said they never drank more than a few sips or tastes were considered censored ($n = 721$). Ties in event times, which can lead to estimation challenges for continuous-time-to-event data, were adjusted for using the default approach in SPSS based on Breslow (1974). The Cox regression model predicts continuous-time hazards, $h(t_{ij})$, and although the model shares a lot of parallels with the discrete-time approach, Cox regression uses a log rather than logit link. Thus, the final model fit to our data can be written as:

$$\ln(h(t_{ij})) = \ln(h_0(t_{ij})) + \beta_1 age + \beta_2 female + \beta_3 ownership$$

Here, h_0 represents the intercept or baseline hazard, but as with most regression models, we focus our attention on the interpretation of each variable's effect, quantified by the coefficients in the model.

Results. The first model presented in Table 5.6 shows the effects of baseline *age* and *female* on drinking initiation. *Age* was negatively related to drinking initiation, $b = -.35$, and the Wald test was significant, $Wald(1) = 221.7$,

$p < .001$. The exponentiation of b provides the estimated hazard ratio for age of 0.706 (95% confidence interval of 0.654 to 0.717). Because the hazard ratio is below 1.0, the hazards of initiating drinking are lower among older teens and higher among younger teens. *Female* was not a significant factor, as its coefficient was small and not statistically significant, with a hazard ratio close to 1.0 (0.971). The overall model fit the data well, with a deviance or −2 log likelihood of 17849.12, which differed from the deviance of the null model by 231.09 ($p < .001$; see the row for Model χ^2 in Table 5.6).

The next model added *ownership* of alcohol promotional items as a predictor. *Ownership of promotional items* was significantly related to drinking initiation, controlling for *age* and *female* ($b = .75$, Wald(1) = 157.0, $p < .001$). The hazard ratio was quite large at 2.125 (95% confidence interval = 1.888 to 2.390), which means that people who owned promotional items had more than twice the risk of initiating drinking relative to persons who did not own promotional material. Again, the model fit the data well, Model $\chi^2(3) = 387.41$, $p < .001$. The new block also contributed significantly to the model fit, block $\chi^2(1) = 142.57$, $p < .001$.

Figure 5.2 shows the survival (top panel) and hazard (bottom panel) functions for the dependent variable, age of first drink. It is clear from the graphs that fewer people remained in the risk set over time—survival (remaining a nondrinker) decreased, while the hazard (of becoming a drinker) increased. Figure 5.3 shows the survival function broken out by the main independent variable of interest, *ownership of promotional items*. The visual graphically shows that the survival rates were lower for teens who owned promotional items than for teens who did not own any promotional items.

Thus, the continuous time analysis of retrospective accounts of onset of drinking was complementary to the prospective data analyzed using discrete-time methods. Two different forms of marketing were assessed. Alcohol advertising exposure contributed to the onset of drinking during the course of the prospective study as shown through the discrete-time example. Advertising exposure would have been impossible to assess retrospectively in a continuous manner and with accuracy, so the prospective study was best to examine that facet of marketing. It was possible, however, to measure current ownership of alcohol merchandise at the beginning of the panel study, which was found to be related to the onset of drinking during the continuous-time-to-event analysis. It was not possible to know whether youths acquired the merchandise before or after the individual started drinking (among those who started drinking), so causality cannot be determined.

Using the retrospective data, the hazard of drinking initiation was greater among younger youth. The fact that age did not have an impact on onset of drinking prospectively in the discrete-time example may be because of a sample selection bias—the sample for the prospective study included only youth who were nondrinkers at the time of study enrollment, with a minimum age of 14. Youth who began drinking at an earlier

Table 5.6 Continuous-Time Event History Analysis for the Alcohol Study Data

	Model A				Model B				
	b	SE b	W^a (df)	e^b	95% CI(e^b)	b	SE b	W^a (df)	e^b	95% CI (e^b)
Age	−.35	.02	221.7 (1)***	.707	.675, .740	−.38	.02	258.9 (1)***	.685	.654, .717
Female	−.03	.06	.3 (1)	.971	.871, 1.083	.00	.02	.0 (1)	1.001	.901, 1.120
Ownership[1]						.75	.02	157.0 (1)***	2.125	1.888, 2.390
							.06			
Model χ^2 (df)			231.09 (2) ***					383.44 (3) ***		
Block			239.59 (2) ***					141.62 (1) ***		
Deviance(−2LL)			17849.12					17707.50		

Note: Deviance of −2 log likelihood for the model with no coefficients = 18088.71. ^{a} Wald test; * $p < .05$; ** $p < .01$; *** $p < .001$

[1] Ownership of promotional items

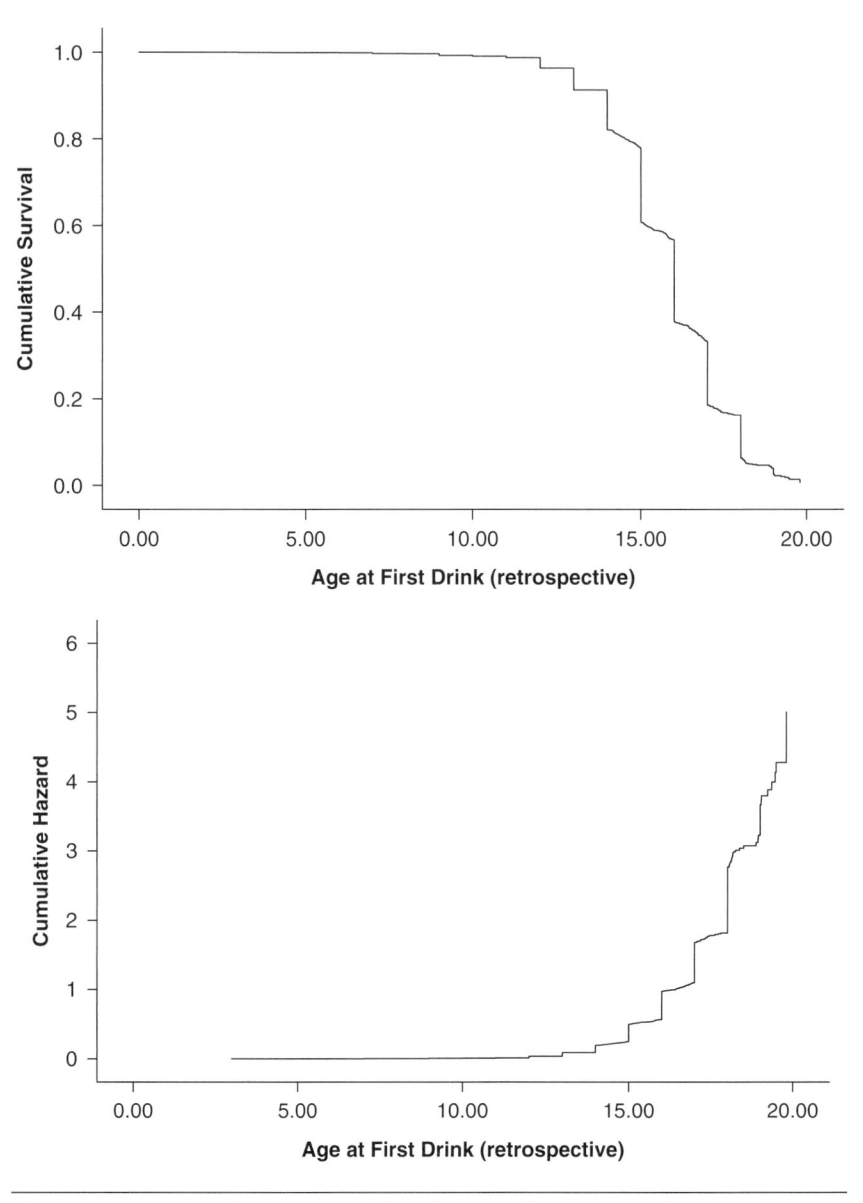

Figure 5.2 Cumulative Survival and Hazard Functions for Retrospective Age at First Drink at Mean of All Covariates

age were systematically excluded from the analysis, which is a form of left-censoring. (Tuma and Hannan, 1984, note the difficulties with left-censoring and suggest strategies for coping with some situations.)

In sum, there was a trade-off between the two approaches. With the retrospective (continuous) data, the entire sample was included in the analysis, but it was not feasible to measure exposure to advertising situated in time retrospectively; instead, a measure of "current" advertising was used (current ownership of promotional items). With the prospective (discrete)

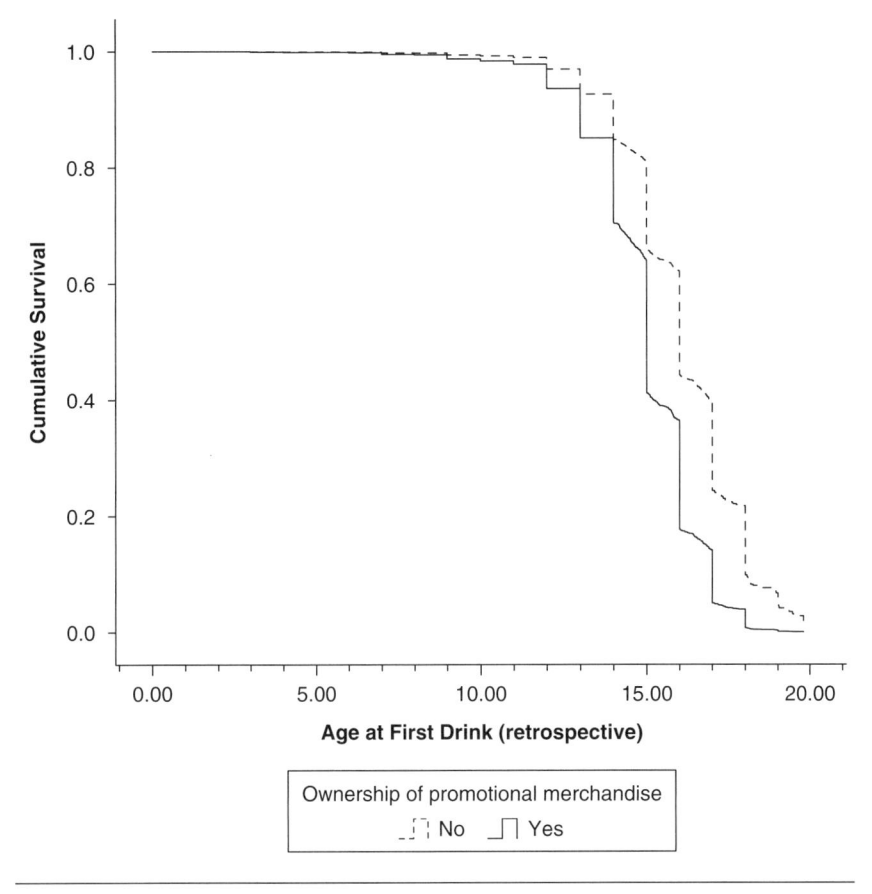

Figure 5.3 Cumulative Survival Functions for Retrospective Age at First Drink by Ownership of Promotional Materials

data, it was easy to measure exposure to advertising at the same time as measuring the dependent variable (first alcohol use), which makes for a stronger test of the relationship between exposure to alcohol advertising and drinking initiation than in the retrospective analysis. However, the sample used in the prospective analysis was limited to those who had not experienced the event of interest prior to the study, which may have biased the sample. Together, the two examples suggest that there is potentially an advantage of using both retrospective and prospective methods to triangulate the effect of alcohol advertising on drinking initiation.

Conclusion

Event history analysis provides a powerful set of tools for communication researchers interested in studying *whether* and *when* events or transitions occur. Using relatively simple examples, we have focused on basic terminology, data setup, model assumptions, model interpretations, and distinctions between the two fundamental approaches to understanding time to event: continuous and discrete metrics for measuring time.

As with all statistical methods, the field of survival and event history is rapidly evolving. Although we did not have the space here to incorporate detailed examples of current extensions to survival methods—such as multilevel event history analysis and multiple events—an understanding of the basics will certainly contribute to researchers' understanding of these extensions. The software used to analyze event history data is becoming more capable of handling the types of issues presented in other chapters in this book, including clustered or incomplete data structures. Researchers need to know how these advances affect their choices for analysis and design. Software capable of conducting these analyses includes SAS (http://www.sas.com), SPSS (http://www.spss.com), STATA (http://www.stata.com), and MIXOR or MIXGSUR (http://tigger.uic.edu/~hedeker/mix.html), among others.

We hope that communication researchers will consider applying event history analyses to their own relevant data. We also hope that by learning the possibilities that event history analysis affords us in understanding the timing of changes in states, researchers will ask new questions in order to better explain communication processes. For further detail, we recommend the reader consult Allison (1984, 1995), Blossfeld, Gotz, and Golsch (2007), and Willett and Singer (2003).

Note

1. In discrete time-to-event models, 1 minus the hazard rate provides an estimate of probability of survival through the end of this interval j for those who entered this interval (i.e., not previously experiencing the event or censored). The relationship between hazard and survival rates for a particular interval j is expressed by: $\hat{S}(t_j) = \hat{S}(t_{j-1}) [1-\hat{h}(t_j)]$. The values for the survival function in Tables 5.2 and 5.3 were found through the use of this formula.

References

Agresti, A. (1996). *An introduction to categorical data analysis.* New York: John Wiley & Sons.

Allison, P. D. (1984). *Event history analysis.* Beverly Hills, CA: Sage.

Allison, P. D. (1995). *Survival analysis using SAS: A practical guide.* Cary, NC: SAS.

Armitage, C. J. (2005, May). Can the theory of planned behavior predict the maintenance of physical activity? *Health Psychology, 24,* 235–245.

Asbridge, M. (2004). Public place restrictions on smoking in Canada: Assessing the role of the state, media, science and public health advocacy. *Social Science & Medicine, 58,* 13–24.

Barton, T. R., & Pilai, V. K. (1993). An evaluation of a prototype JOBS program using an event history analysis of AFCD cases. *Evaluation Review, 17,* 27–46.

Barton, T. R., Pillai, V. K., & Dietz, T. J. (1996). Program evaluation using event history analysis. *Evaluation Practice, 17,* 7–17.

Blossfeld, H. P., Gotz, R., & Golsch, K. (2007). *Event history analysis with Stata.* Mahwah, NJ: Lawrence Erlbaum Associates.

Breslow, N. E. (1974). Covariance analysis of censored survival data. *Biometrics, 30,* 88–99.

Brunswick, A. F., & Messeri, P. A. (1986). Pathways to heroin abstinence: A longitudinal study of urban black youth. *Advances in Alcohol and Substance Abuse, 5(3),* 111–135.

Caton, C. L., Dominguez, B., Schanzer, B., Hasin, D., Shrout, P. E., Felix, A., et al. (2005). Risk factors for long-term homelessness: Findings from a longitudinal study of first-time homeless single adults. *American Journal of Public Health, 95,* 1753–1759.

Chassin L., & DeLucia, C. (1996). Drinking during adolescence. *Alcohol Health and Research World, 20,* 175–180.

Cox, D. R. (1972). Regression models and life tales (with Discussion). *Journal to the Royal Statistical Society, Series B, 34,* 187–220.

Djamba, Y. K. (2003, August). Social capital and premarital sexual activity in Africa: The case of Kinshasa, Democratic Republic of Congo. *Archives of Sexual Behavior, 32,* 327–337.

Donner, A., & Klar, N. (2000). *Design and analysis of cluster randomized trials in health research.* New York: Oxford University Press.

DuWors, R. E., Jr., & Haines, G. H., Jr. (1990, November). Event history analysis measures of brand loyalty. *Journal of Marketing Research, 27,* 485–493.

Fichman, M. (1988). Motivational consequence of absence and attendance: Proportional hazard estimation of a dynamic motivational model. *Journal of Applied Psychology, 73,* 119–134.

Fleming-Milici, F. (2006). *Is this ad targeting me? The effects of perceiving oneself as a target of alcohol advertising for people under the legal drinking age.* Doctoral dissertation, University of Connecticut.

Fox, J. (1997). *Applied regression analysis, linear models, and related methods.* Thousand Oaks, CA: Sage.

Gager, C. T., & Sanchez, L. (2003). Two as one? Couples' perceptions of time spent together, marital quality, and the risk of divorce. *Journal of Family Issues, 24,* 21–50.

Gamst, G. (1985, Spring). Survival analysis: A new way to predict subscription order retention. *Newspaper Research Journal, 6,* 1–12.

Gardner, W., Mulvey, E. P., & Shaw, E. C. (1995). Regression analysis of counts and rates: Poisson, overdispersed Poisson, and negative binomial models. *Psychological Bulletin, 118,* 392–404.

Goldstein, H., Pan, H., & Bynner, J. (2004). A flexible procedure for analyzing longitudinal event histories using a multilevel model. *Understanding Statistics, 3,* 85–89.

Griffin, W. A. (1993). Transitions from negative affect during marital interaction: Husband and wife differences. *Journal of Family Psychology, 6,* 230–244.

Griffin, W. A., & Gardner, W. (1989). Analysis of behavioral durations in observational studies of social interaction. *Psychological Bulletin, 106,* 497–502.

Hannan, M. T., Tuma, N. B., & Groeneveld, L. P. (1977). Income and marital events: Evidence from an income maintenance experiment. *American Journal of Sociology, 82,* 1186–1211.

Hill, K. G., Hawkins, J. D., Catalano, R. F., Abbott, R. D., & Guo, J. (2005). Family influence on the risk of daily smoking initiation. *Journal of Adolescent Health, 37,* 202–210.

Hoffmann, J. P., & Cerbone, F. G. (2002, May). Parental substance use disorder and the risk of adolescent drug abuse: An event history analysis. *Drug and Alcohol Dependence, 63,* 255–264.

Hosmer, D. W., Jr., & Lemeshow, S. (1999). *Applied survival analysis: Regression modeling of time to event data.* New York: John Wiley & Sons.

Hosmer, D.W., Jr., & Lemeshow, S. (2000). *Applied logistic regression* (2nd ed.). New York: Wiley-Interscience Publications.

Hser, Y. I., Anglin, M. D., & Liu, Y. (1990–1991). A survival analysis of gender and ethnic differences in responsiveness to methadone maintenance treatment. *International Journal of Addictions, 25*(11A), 1295–1315.

Hsu, H. C., & Fogel, A. (2003). Stability and transitions in mother-infant face-to-face communication during the first 6 months: A microhistorical approach. *Developmental Psychology, 39,* 1061–1082.

Iverson, R. D., & Currivan, D. B. (2003, January). Union participation, job satisfaction and employee turnover: An event-history analysis of the exit-voice hypothesis. *Industrial Relations: A Journal of Economy & Society, 42,* 101–105.

Keiley, M. K., & Martin, N. C. (2005). Survival analysis in family research. *Journal of Family Psychology, 19,* 142–156.

Kendler, K. S., Karkowski, L. M., & Prescott, C. A. (1999). Causal relationship between stressful life events and the onset of major depression. *American Journal of Psychiatry, 156,* 837–841.

Kuk, G., Arnold, M., & Ritter, F. E. (1999). Effects of light and heavy workload on air traffic tactical operations: A hazard rate model. *Ergonomics, 42,* 1133–1148.

McMurtry, S. L., & Lie, G. Y. (1992). Differential exit rates of minority children in foster care. *Social Work Research and Abstracts, 28,* 42–48.

Morita, J. G., Lee, T. W., & Mowday, R. T. (1989). Introducing survival analysis to organizational researchers: A selected application to turnover research, *Journal of Applied Psychology, 74,* 280–292.

Muthén, B., & Masyn, K. (2005). Discrete-time survival mixture analysis. *Journal of Educational and Behavioral Statistics, 30,* 27–58.

Nystrand, M., Wu, L. L., Gamoran, A., Zeiser, S., & Long, D. A. (2003). Questions in time: Investigating structure and dynamics of unfolding classroom discourse. *Discourse Processes, 35,* 135–198.

O'Connell, A. A. (2006). *Logistic regression models for ordinal response variables: Quantitative applications in the social sciences.* Thousand Oaks, CA: Sage.

O'Connell, A. A., & McCoach, D. B. (2004). Applications of hierarchical linear modeling for evaluation of health interventions: Demystifying the methods

and interpretation of multilevel models. *Evaluation and the Health Professions, 27,* 119–151.
Oliver, A. L. (2001). Strategic alliances and the learning life-cycle of biotechnology firms. *Organization Studies, 22,* 467–489.
Pears, K. C., Pierce, S. L., Kim, H. K., Capaldi, D. M., & Owen, L. D. (2005, May). The timing of entry into fatherhood in young, at-risk men. *Journal of Marriage & the Family, 67,* 429–447.
Singer, J. D., & Willett, J.B. (1993). It's about time: Using discrete-time survival analysis to study duration and the timing of events. *Journal of Educational Statistics, 18,* 155–195.
Singer, J. D., & Willett, J. B. (2003). *Applied longitudinal data analysis: Modeling change and event occurrence.* New York: Oxford University Press.
Snyder, L. B. (1990). Channel effectiveness over time and knowledge and behavior gaps. *Journalism Quarterly, 67,* 875–886.
Snyder, L. B. (1991). Modeling dynamic communication processes with event history analysis. *Communication Research, 18,* 464–486.
Snyder, L. B., Fleming-Milici, F., Slater, M., Sun, H., & Strizhakova, Y. (2006, January). Effects of alcohol advertising exposure on youth drinking. *Archives of Pediatric and Adolescent Medicine, 160,* 18–24.
Somers, M. J. (1996). Modelling employee withdrawal behavior over time: A study of turnover using survival analysis. *Journal of Occupational and Organizational Psychology, 69,* 315–326.
Sørensen, A. B. (1977). Estimating rates from retrospective questions. In D. R. Heise (Ed.), *Sociological methodology 1977* (pp. 209–223). San Francisco: Jossey-Bass.
Spell, C. S., & Blum, T. C. (2001). Organizational adoption of preemployment drug testing. *Journal of Occupational Health Psychology, 6,* 114–126.
Stevens, V. J., & Hollis, J. F. (1989, June). Preventing smoking relapse, using an individually tailored skills-training technique. *Journal of Consulting and Clinical Psychology, 57,* 420–424.
Sunil, T. S., & Pillai, V. K. (2001). Breast-feeding programs and lactational amenorrhea: Evaluation using event history analysis. *The Social Science Journal, 38,* 409–419.
Tamis-Lemonda, C. S., Bornstein, M. H., Kahana-Kalman, R., Baumwell, L., & Cyphers, L. (1998, October). Predicting variation in the timing of language milestones in the second year: An events history approach. *Journal of Child Language, 25,* 675–300.
Tuma, N. B., & Hannan, M. T. (1978). Approaches to the censoring problem in analysis of event histories. In K. F. Schuessler (Ed.), *Sociological methodology 1979.* San Francisco: Jossey-Bass.
Tuma, N. B., & Hannan, M. T. (1984). *Social dynamics: Models and methods.* New York: Academic Press.
Unson, C. G. (1999, October). Non-use, disadoption, adoption and long-term use of family planning behaviors: The case of the 1993 Philippine National Communication Campaign on family planning (contraception). (Doctoral dissertation, University of Connecticut, 1999). *Dissertation Abstracts International, 60,* 4-B.
Walters, G. D. (2005, February). Recidivism in released Lifestyle Change Program participants. *Criminal Justice and Behavior, 32,* 50–68.

Westerik, H., Renckstorf, K., Lammers, J., & Wester, F. (2006, June). Transcending uses and gratifications: Media use as action and the use of event history analysis. *Communications, 31*(2), 139–153.

Westerik, H., Renckstorf, K., Wester, F., & Lammers, J. (2005). The situational and time-varying context of routines in television viewing: An event history analysis. *Communications, 30,* 155–182.

Willett, J. B., & Singer, J. D. (1995). It's déjà vu all over again: Using multiple-spell discrete-time survival analysis. *Journal of Educational and Behavioral Statistics, 20,* 41–67.

Willett, J. B., & Singer, J. D. (2003). *Applied longitudinal data analyis: Modeling change and event occurrence.* New York: Oxford University Press.

Zhao, L., Chen, Y., & Schaffner, D. W. (2001). Comparison of logistic regression and linear regression in modeling percentage data. *Applied and Environmental Microbiology, 67,* 2129–2135.

Zwick, R., & Sklar, J. (2005). A note on standard errors for survival curves in discrete-time survival analysis. *Journal of Educational and Behavioral Statistics, 30,* 75–92.

Estimating Causal Effects in Observational Studies

6

The Propensity Score Approach

Itzhak Yanovitzky

Robert Hornik

Elaine Zanutto

Communication scholars often want to estimate the effects of a treatment[1] on some outcomes of interest. For this purpose, randomized experiments or randomized controlled trials (RCTs) have known and highly desirable properties and are thus widely argued to be the gold standard in evaluation research (Rossi, Lipsey, & Freeman, 2004). The chief advantage of RCTs in this respect is the ability of the researcher to randomly assign units to receive a particular level of treatment or not to receive treatment at all. However, random assignment to treatment is not always feasible or ethical (Boruch, 1997), and social experimentation has some important drawbacks such as high cost, the potential to distort the operation of an ongoing program, the common problem of differential mortality between the experimental and control groups, and the problem of randomized-out controls seeking alternative forms of treatment (Smith & Todd, 2001). Moreover, observational (i.e., nonexperimental or quasi-experimental) studies permit greater generalizability of findings (high external validly) as they better simulate real-world settings (Rosenbaum, 2002). For these reasons, observational studies are quite common in the study of communication effects.

Observational studies, however, give researchers little or no control over the assignment of units to treatment. In these studies, discerning the effect of a treatment like health campaign exposure on an outcome of interest (e.g., attitude toward regular marijuana use) can be clouded by the fact that the person made the choice to be exposed to the campaign (the problem of selection bias). This person's score on this outcome is therefore a combined result of this person's propensity to choose the treatment (which is itself determined by a combination of external variables such as personality traits, demographic characteristics, and prior experience) and the effects of the treatment itself. As a result, estimates of treatment effects that are based on the comparison of the treated to the nontreated on the outcome of interest are likely to be biased, unless we find a way to screen out the effects of the person's propensity to choose that treatment.

To address this problem, a number of methods for reducing bias in estimates of treatment effects have been proposed including multiple regression and various matching methods (Dehejia & Wahaba, 2002). However, the most effective methods for reducing selection bias in estimates of treatment effects seem to be those that focus on modeling the selection process, such as the instrumental variable approach (Angrist, Imbens, & Rubin, 1996; Heckman, 1995) and propensity score methodology (Rosenbaum & Rubin, 1983). The use of propensity score methodology, in particular, has exploded in recent years within the health and behavioral sciences (Perkins, Tu, Underhill, Zhou, & Murray, 2000; Weitzen, Lapane, Toledano, Hume, & Mor, 2004) but was only recently introduced to the field of communication through the evaluation of the National Youth Anti-Drug Media Campaign (Hornik et al., 2002; Yanovitzky, Zanutto, & Hornik, 2005). This chapter aims to familiarize readers with the use of propensity score methodology to adjust estimates of treatment effects for selection bias. These comments are relevant both to the situation where there is some effort to assign or withhold treatment on a nonrandom basis and to situations where exposure to a treatment variable is only observed and not manipulated.

We begin by discussing the strength and weaknesses of available bias reduction methods and contrast them with those of propensity score methodology. We then go on to introduce the logic of propensity score methods and offer a nontechnical review of the steps involved in estimating and using the propensity score to adjust estimates of treatment effects for selection bias. We conclude with some recommendations and a cautionary tale.

Propensity Score and Other Methods for Bias Reduction

Researchers interested in adjusting estimates of treatment effects for potential selection bias may use a number of available techniques. The most commonly used technique is to employ a standard multiple regression analysis in which the effect of all observed potential confounders on a certain outcome is controlled by including these variables as predictors along with level of exposure to the treatment as an additional predictor. The rationale here is to control for a set of possible confounders in order to remove any part of the correlation between the treatment variable and the outcome that is not due to the effect of the treatment alone on the outcome (Winship & Morgan, 1999). However, there are three important limitations to this strategy (Perkins et al., 2000; Rubin, 1997). The first has to do with the assumption that the relationship between the outcome and the covariates within each exposure group follows a particular functional form such as a linear or a logistic function (Rubin, 1997). When there is insufficient overlap on covariates, regression models rely on such prespecified functional forms to extrapolate estimates of treatment effects, which may be biased. A second limitation is that the inclusion of many potential covariates in the regression model significantly reduces the number of degrees of freedom available for the analysis. If the overall sample size is not large, this will decrease statistical power and, regardless of sample size, may increase problems associated with multicollinearity (Allison, 1999). Third, there is no assurance that all potential confounders have been incorporated into the model, leaving the possibility that selection is still biasing estimates of treatment effects.

Two additional approaches used (albeit rarely) in communication campaigns studies are matching and the instrumental variable approach. Matching is an alternative technique that, in theory, avoids the pitfalls of using a standard regression analysis (Rubin & Thomas, 1996; Smith, 1997). Here the researcher selects a control group consisting of individuals with similar background scores on covariates to those in the treatment group. This technique makes no assumption about the functional form of the relationship between outcomes and covariates (Rubin & Thomas, 1996). In addition, it estimates treatment effects from only the portion of the covariates' distribution that overlaps between the treatment and control groups (Smith, 1997). This makes matching particularly appropriate in situations where the control group is much larger than the treated group and contains many individuals who are very dissimilar to members of the treatment group (e.g., Dehejia & Wahaba, 1999). Unfortunately, in practice, it is often difficult to find units that match on all important covariates, even when there are only a few background covariates of interest (D'Agostino, 1998). Similarly, as the number of covariates increases linearly, the sample size needed for efficient matching increases geometrically (Smith, 1997). These potential caveats are typical in studies where treatment and control constitute a dichotomy and are likely to intensify when treatment is measured as a categorical variable representing different dosages of treatment (Lu, Zanutto, Hornik, & Rosenbaum, 2001).

A third available technique for bias reduction is the instrumental variable (IV) approach (Angrist, Imbens, & Rubin, 1996; Heckman, 1995; Winship & Morgan, 1999). The basic logic of this approach is to define a variable or a set of variables (the IV or IVs) that have two properties: They affect or cause variation in assignment to treatment, but they can be assumed to have no direct effect on the outcome of interest except through influence on the treatment variable. These variables, if they can be found, can be used to adjust estimates of treatment effect on outcomes.

For example, one might want to know the effects of exposure to media smoking cessation campaigns. One surveys a population and finds that those who report higher exposure to the campaign are more likely to intend to stop smoking. However, an obvious concern in making a claim of campaign effects is that there is some confounder (e.g., interest in stopping smoking related to both recall of exposure to the campaign and intention to stop smoking) that is the true cause of the relationship. An instrumental variables analysis searches for a variable likely to be related to the exposure variable but not directly to the outcome (smoking cessation intention). One potential instrumental variable that might be considered would be state of residence if one can assume that the antismoking media campaign varied in its intensity across states, and that the cross-state variation is due to the effects of particular state legislatures' commitment of funds to smoking cessation. The independent variable of interest in this study is individual exposure, and the instrumental variable is state of residence (or funds committed by the state legislature to antismoking efforts).

The IV-adjusted estimate of treatment effect can be calculated in three steps (Winship & Morgan, 1999): (1) Regress the observed outcome on the potential IV to calculate a predicted outcome, (2) regress the treatment variable on the IV to calculate a predicted treatment, and (3) regress the predicted outcome variable on the predicted treatment assignment, which will be the estimate of treatment effect. Put differently, both the dependent (Y) and independent variable (X) are expressed as functions of the IV that is assumed to be uncorrelated with the error term for the effect of X on Y. Because of that, a consistent estimate of the treatment effect can be calculated by regressing the new predicted Y on the new predicted X. The IV approach is most appropriate in cases where compliance with assignment to treatment (and not assignment to treatment itself) is imperfect and when data are weak (namely, few observed covariates are measured). However, the IV approach has three important weaknesses. The first is that it is often difficult to identify an IV because the requirement that a variable be an important cause of treatment but not a potential cause of the outcome is rarely met (Perkins et al., 2000). In this example, if the state legislature's allocation of funds to smoking cessation efforts are a function the state's smoking rates, the assumption that the instrumental variable and the outcome variable have no direct relationship would be violated. Also, typically, most instrumental variables will have a weak relationship with the treatment variable. Then the standard errors produced by this procedure tend to be too large for generating precise estimates of effects unless the sample size is very large (Winship & Morgan, 1999). Finally, this bias reduction approach consistently estimates the true average treatment effect only when the treatment effect is constant for all individuals, an assumption that is often unreasonable (Newhouse & McClellan, 1998). The substantial advantage of the instrumental variables approach is that it does not require the assumption that all important potential confounders have been measured. If the assumption is met that the IV is a (nontrivial) direct cause of the treatment but not the outcome, there is no threat from unobserved confounders. Unfortunately, it is a rare thing that this assumption is credible in our experience in many areas of communication research.

PROPENSITY SCORE METHODOLOGY

In comparison to these alternatives, propensity score methods (Rosenbaum & Rubin, 1983, 1984) offer researchers a particularly desirable way of adjusting estimates of treatment effects for selection bias. A propensity score is the conditional probability that a person is assigned to get a certain treatment (or a certain level of treatment) given a set of observed covariates used to predict this person's treatment assignment (Rosenbaum & Rubin, 1983). For randomized experiments, and assuming two possible treatment assignments (i.e., treatment or control), this probability is .50 (or 50% chance), reflecting a person's equal probability of being assigned to treatment or control. With a quasi-experiment or an observational study, the true propensity score function is unknown and must be estimated as a function of covariates that are likely to affect the likelihood of receiving treatment or a certain level of treatment. Once this probability has been determined, propensity score methods create comparison groups that are similar on the covariates but different on their level of treatment, so that within each comparison group it is straightforward to estimate treatment effects by comparing average outcomes for units with different levels of treatment.

How can such equivalent comparison groups be created? The basic logic of the propensity score method draws on the experimental analogy. In the randomized experiment, randomization creates balance (at least on average) on the covariates, meaning that the distribution of the covariates is the same (on average) in the different treatment groups. Propensity scoring focuses on assuring that groups with different levels of the treatment are balanced on all observed covariates. In practice, this means that all of the observed covariates are used to predict actual assignment to treatment. This equation produces a predicted score representing the propensity to be treated. The analysis of the association of treatment and outcome is then controlled for the propensity to be exposed, which effectively controls for all of the observed covariates that went into the generation of the propensity score.

Perhaps the easiest way to illustrate this logic is the typical three-way cross-tabulation analysis done in trying to assess the actual association between a proposed independent and dependent variable. For example, perhaps one might be concerned that the observed association between self-reported exposure to an antidrug media campaign and intention to use marijuana in the next year was possibly spurious due to the effects of sensation-seeking tendencies (a personality trait) on both variables—that high-sensation-seeking youth were more likely to be exposed to antidrug advertising and they were more likely to intend to initiate drug use. This three-way association would very likely be examined in a three-way cross-tabulation like that presented in Table 6.1.

The proportion of nonusing youth (12–18-year-olds) who say they definitely do not intend to try marijuana in the next year is presented in all cells of Table 6.1. That intention measure is compared across three levels of reported exposure to the campaign and five levels of a personality trait called sensation seeking, which in this example is related both to exposure to the campaign and to intention to use marijuana. The original association between exposure and intention to use marijuana is displayed in the row labeled "true average" and indicates that the low-exposure group has

Table 6.1 Intentions to Use Marijuana in the Next 12 Months by Level of Campaign Exposure and Sensation-Seeking Tendencies Among 12–18-Year-Olds Who Have Never Tried Marijuana

Sensation Seeking (1–5-point scale)	Percent of Youth Reporting No Intention of Trying Marijuana in the Next 12 Months					
	Level of Campaign Exposure					
	Low	N	Medium	N	High	N
Very low	98.0	303	95.7	208	96.8	467
Low	95.0	180	96.0	173	94.4	391
Medium	90.9	164	89.0	236	88.2	405
High	86.3	160	84.1	182	84.1	446
Very high	73.9	130	75.9	199	71.3	453
True average[a]	90.8	937	88.1	998	86.7	2162
Average controlling for sensation seeking[b]	88.8		88.1		87.0	

[a] Average percent of all youth not intending to try marijuana in the next 12 months by campaign exposure level (without controlling for sensation seeking).
[b] Average percent of youth not intending to try marijuana in the next 12 months across all subgroups of sensation seeking by campaign exposure level.

the highest probability of not intending to use (90.8%), while the high-exposure group has the lowest probability (86.7%). However, we recognize that the observed association between exposure and intention to use marijuana may be confounded with the influence of background characteristics, like sensation seeking, on both exposure to the campaign and intentions to use marijuana. So Table 6.1 statistically controls for sensation seeking by dividing the continuous version of this variable into five categories and by looking to see whether the observed exposure-intention relation is maintained. A simple way to assess the residual relationship, once sensation seeking is controlled, is to take a new average across all the observed means but ignore the actual distribution of cases. Effectively, this averaging forces sensation seeking to be equally distributed across each of the exposure categories, thus essentially eliminating the association of sensation seeking and exposure. This new average, in the final row of Table 6.1, represents the effects of exposure controlled for sensation seeking. Whereas the original association showed a difference of 4.1% between the high- and low-exposure categories, this controlled association shows a smaller difference of 1.8%.

Clearly, sensation seeking is but one of many possible covariates that may confound the actual size of the exposure-intention association in the above example. There is a need to control for all potential covariates at once, and this would not be feasible if the only procedure was to add additional layers of cells representing all the possible combinations of values on the covariates. Propensity scores offer an effective alternative. The most attractive feature of this technique is the ability to replace a set of confounding covariates with a single function of these covariates, the propensity score, which is a scalar variable obtained by modeling the treatment assignment variable as a linear or nonlinear function of all observed covariates (D'Agostino, 1998). Individuals can then be matched or classified into subgroups based on their estimated propensity score rather than on multiple covariates. Next, assuming the propensity score model has been adequately estimated, the distribution of covariates across subgroups of participants with similar estimated treatment propensities should be similar and assignment to treatment may be deemed random (Rubin, 1997). Put differently, if two persons, one exposed to the treatment and the other not, share the same propensity score, we can treat them as two participants who were randomly assigned to each group. It follows that the propensity score, to the extent it is adequately estimated, is a balancing score or one that is expected to remove any initial bias from estimates of treatment effect that is due to selection bias (Joffe & Rosenbaum, 1999). In fact, the estimated propensity scores can be better than true propensity scores at removing bias because they also remove some chance imbalances on covariates (Joffe & Rosenbaum, 1999; Rosenbaum & Rubin, 1983). A reliable estimate of treatment effect can then be calculated based on the estimated propensity scores using various strategies such as matching (e.g., D'Agostino, 1998; Rubin & Thomas, 1996; Smith, 1997), stratification (D'Agostino, 1998; Perkins et al., 2000; Rubin, 1997), and regression adjustment (D'Agostino & Rubin, 2000).

The use of propensity score methodology has a number of additional advantages other than freeing researchers from complications associated with using a large number of covariates in a regression analysis or for matching. First, in many cases treatment effects can be estimated without the need to explicitly model the relationship between the outcomes and the covariates. Second, propensity score modeling is more robust to model misspecification than linear regression because it is less vulnerable to bias from variables that are included but in the wrong functional form (Drake, 1993; Rubin, 1997). Third, the diagnostics and fitting of a propensity score model are done independent of the outcome and, thus, approximate random assignment of participants to treatment. Fourth, a single propensity score can be used for adjusting treatment effects on multiple outcomes for selection bias simultaneously (whereas, for example, several different regression models would need to be fit to complete a similar task). Finally, if a more complex analysis is necessary, propensity scores can be used in conjunction with standard methods such as regression analysis and therefore allow for a simple and useful interpretation of results.

The following section provides readers a more detailed account of the actual steps involved in the implementation of propensity score methodology. The first and most critical step in the propensity score approach is the planning stage in which treatments, outcomes, and covariates are determined. From this point onward, propensity score adjustment is essentially composed of two stages: the balancing of covariates across treatment groups and the actual estimation of the propensity-score-adjusted treatment effect.

Building a Propensity Score Model

STEP 1: DETERMINE TREATMENTS, OUTCOMES, AND A CONFOUNDER POOL

The first and most critical step in employing a propensity score adjustment is to select a set of covariates (or potential confounders) from which to estimate the propensity score. In cases where observational studies are designed with a propensity score adjustment in mind (e.g., the evaluation of the National Anti-Drug Media Campaign; see Hornik et al., 2001), experimental control is replaced by a careful choice of treatment variables, outcomes, and covariates that is grounded in a solid theoretical framework and previous empirical evidence (Hornik & Yanovitzky, 2003). However, it is also possible to use propensity score methods with secondary data

Estimating Causal Effects in Observational Studies

that were not designed with a propensity score adjustment in mind, providing that key covariates related to treatment assignment are measured. Regardless of the design used to generate the data, the process of selecting covariates from which to estimate the propensity score should be made a priori on theoretical grounds and based on previous available empirical evidence about relationships between variables of interest. It should not be based on patterns of association between variables that are found in the actual data used for the evaluation of campaign effects. Figure 6.1 illustrates the logic of this process when measures of all variables are taken at the same time.

There are five types of variables in Figure 6.1: variables measuring treatment exposure, variables measuring outcomes, covariates (or confounders), mediators, and ambiguous variables. Only confounders should be included in the estimation of the propensity score. Confounders are those variables that can explain variations both in treatment assignment and in outcomes but are themselves not caused by treatment assignment or outcomes. Therefore, variables that can clearly cause both campaign exposure and campaign effects because they precede either in terms of temporal ordering (for example, a person's age, gender, and race) should be included in the confounder pool. On the other hand, variables that are associated with the outcomes but are themselves caused or hypothesized to be caused by campaign exposure (termed Mediators in Figure 6.1) should not be included in the confounder pool because including them would attenuate estimates of the true effects of the campaign. For example, if exposure to the messages of a campaign leads people to form the perception that tobacco use is hazardous to their health, and if this perception, in turn, is associated with lower intentions to use tobacco products, then it would be a mistake to include this perception in the confounder pool. Hence, all variables that are likely to be an outcome of campaign exposure should be excluded from the confounder pool.

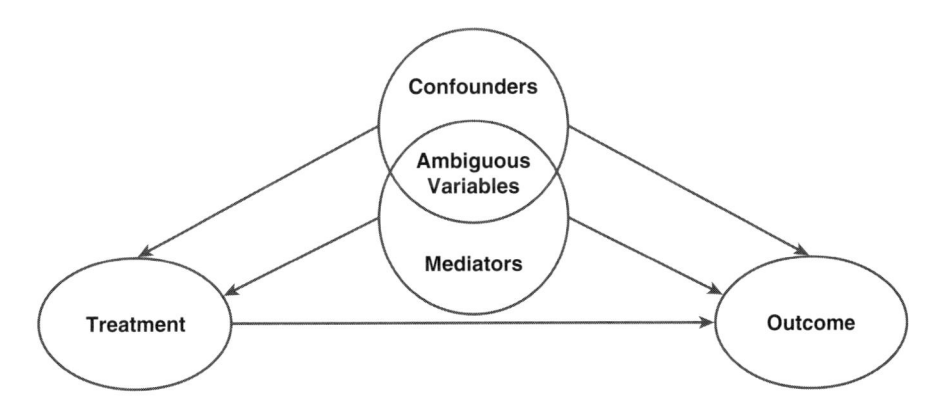

Figure 6.1 Types of Variables and the Selection of Potential Confounders

Decisions about which variables to include or exclude from the confounder pool become more complicated when one suspects that some variables (termed Ambiguous Variables in Figure 6.1) may play both confounding and mediating roles. As an example of an ambiguous variable, consider the potential role of an adolescent's frequency of association with alcohol-using peers. Adolescents that associate frequently with alcohol-using peers are likely to use alcohol themselves (that is, this variable is likely to impact the outcome). But it may also be the case that association with alcohol-using peers may impact an adolescent's likelihood of being exposed to an educational campaign about the risks of alcohol use in adolescence because exposure to alcohol in peer context sparks an interest in alcohol in general, in which case, this variable causes campaign exposure. Thus, frequency of association with alcohol-using peers may be a potential confounder. At the same time, there may be adolescents who reduced their frequency of interacting with alcohol-using peers as a result of exposure to the messages of the campaign, in which case, this variable serves as a mediator. Excluding ambiguous variables from the confounder pool may increase the risk of introducing bias (typically overestimation) into estimates of campaign effects because some of the observed association between campaign exposure and outcomes may be due to the excluded variable (Drake, 1993). On the other hand, if these variables are included in the confounder pool, there is some risk that the effect of campaign exposure on outcomes will be biased (typically underestimated) due to the inclusion of a mediator.

There are three strategies for dealing with ambiguous variables. The first is to be conservative and include them as covariates in the propensity modeling. The second is to exclude them and maximize the possibility of detecting an effect. The third is to make estimates with and without the ambiguous variables and see whether inferences about effects are sensitive to how they are treated. Confidence in claims of effects will be stronger if this decision about ambiguous variables does not affect the inferences. Similar decisions about ambiguous variables should be made following deliberations among investigators or experts, which can reduce the potential for mistakenly excluding potential confounders or including potential mediators.

STEP 2: DETERMINE THE INITIAL IMBALANCE ON CONFOUNDERS

Selection bias manifests itself in nonequivalent treatment and control groups. That is, treated participants are different from nontreated participants in terms of covariate values. One can estimate initial imbalance by examining whether the treatment variable is associated with each of the covariates. Imbalances on covariates with an interval level of measurement can be estimated through a two-sample *t*-test (for treatment with only two levels) or a one-way analysis of variance (for treatments with more than two levels) in which the treatment exposure is the independent variable. For dichotomous confounders, a two-sample test of differences in proportions (for treatments with only two levels) or a logistic regression with the confounder as the outcome and dummy variables for the treatment levels as the predictors (for treatment with more than two levels) can be used to assess initial imbalance.[2]

There are two straightforward reasons for beginning propensity score analysis with estimating the initial imbalance on confounders across treatment (or exposure) groups. If an imbalanced distribution of confounders exists, the information on imbalanced covariates may be used later as a benchmark against which to verify that the propensity score adjustment methodology has, in fact, increased the balance in the covariates. On the other hand, if it turns out that the distribution of covariates is adequately balanced, there is no need to employ the propensity score technique. Adequate balance can be defined as the amount of balance expected in a completely randomized experiment (i.e., approximately 5% of the significance tests for balance would be expected to be statistically significant at the .05 level purely by chance in a randomized experiment). However, before deciding that adequate balance exists, an additional criterion should be considered. If the sample is not large, this initial imbalance estimation process may fail to detect some covariates that are nontrivially related to the treatment but did not reach conventional statistical significance. Normand et al. (2001) have suggested employing an additional criterion. They argue that an absolute standardized difference between the treatment and control group on a covariate that is greater than 10% may indicate serious imbalance. The absolute standardized difference for binary covariates can be calculated using the equation below where P stands for the respective proportion of participants in each group who have a nonzero score on this particular covariate.

$$d = \frac{100(P_{treatment} - P_{control})}{\sqrt{\frac{P_{treatment}(1-P_{treatment})+P_{control}(1-P_{control})}{2}}}$$

The absolute standardized difference for continuous covariates can be calculated using the following equation:

$$d = \frac{100\left(\overline{X}_{treatment} - \overline{X}_{control}\right)}{\sqrt{\frac{S^2_{treatment}+S^2_{control}}{2}}}$$

If covariates are imbalanced on this criterion, even if fewer than 5% are statistically out of balance, it is appropriate to consider following the next steps.

STEP 3: ESTIMATE THE PROPENSITY SCORE

There are different statistical methods for estimating the propensity score for each participant including discriminant analysis, probit models (D'Agostino, 1998), and classification trees (Stone, Obrosky, Singer, Kapoor, & Fine, 1995), but the most common one is a logistic regression model predicting the likelihood of being exposed to the treatment from all candidate confounders. If the likelihood of treatment exposure is dichotomous (i.e., yes or no), the equation used to estimate the propensity score is as follows:

$$Log\left(\frac{P_i}{1-P_i}\right) = a + \sum_{j=1}^{m} b_j X_{ij}$$

where P_i is the probability of respondent i to be exposed to the treatment, X_{ij} is respondent i's score on potential confounder j, b_j is potential confounder j's logistic regression coefficient estimated from the data, and m is the number of potential confounders. The estimated propensity score is then calculated as the estimated probability of being exposed to treatment, conditional on the values of the m potential confounders. In cases where exposure is an ordinal variable, McCullagh's (1980) ordinal logistic regression model (also called the proportional odds model) can be used to generate an estimated propensity score per individual for each level of treatment (see O'Connell, 2005, for a less technical treatment of this topic). This ordinal logistic regression model for a treatment exposure variable with K levels has the following form:

$$Log\left(\frac{P(Y_i \leq k)}{1 - P(Y_i \leq K)}\right) = a_k + \sum_{j=1}^{m} b_j X_{ij}, \ k = 1 \text{ to } K - 1$$

where Y_i is the exposure level received by respondent i. In this case, the estimated linear predictor $\sum_{j=i}^{m} b_j X_{ij}$ (or the linear combination of all individual scores on confounders weighted by their estimated slope parameters) is a single scalar balancing score. This estimated linear predictor (that many available data analysis computer programs such as SPSS can save as a new variable in the data set) is a balancing score that can be used to construct matched pairs or strata that balance the covariates (Joffe & Rosenbaum, 1999; Lu, Zanutto, Hornik, & Rosenbaum, 2001; Zanutto, Lu, & Hornik, 2005).

Researchers who routinely use stepwise methods to delineate significant effects of independent variables on outcomes of interest may be tempted to estimate the propensity score only from imbalanced covariates. This may be a mistake. The absence of a statistically significant imbalance on a covariate does not necessarily imply that the existing difference on this covariate is small enough to be ignored. For one, this covariate may show a significant imbalance when other covariates are included, or in interaction with other covariates. For another, this covariate may be strongly associated with the outcome of interest, and omitting it from the estimation of the propensity score may diminish the model's ability to reduce bias in estimates of treatment effects. A better approach is to include all covariates listed in the confounder pool in the estimation of the propensity score. In addition, one may consider including two-way or higher-level interaction between covariates as well as nonlinear (e.g., quadratic and cubic) forms of covariates. One should include such complex terms at this stage if one has evidence that they add some predictive power to the simpler terms in accounting for treatment level. Otherwise they can be added in a subsequent stage, if balance has not been achieved. However, in general, analysts are encouraged to err on the side of inclusion. Propensity score models are more vulnerable to misspecification errors as the result of leaving out confounders than to overfitting as a result of including too many predictors (Rubin, 2004).

STEP 4: EVALUATE PERFORMANCE AND CHECK OVERLAP ON THE PROPENSITY SCORE

There are several approaches to evaluating the performance of a propensity score. We focus on one approach (stratification) and then briefly describe some alternatives. In the stratification or subclassification approach, participants are divided into (usually) five equally sized groups (strata) based on the distribution of the estimated propensity score. Studies have shown that creating five strata based on propensity scores can remove approximately 90% of the initial imbalance in each of the confounders between treatment groups (Cochran, 1968; Rosenbaum & Rubin, 1984). Using the subclassification method, one then checks for balance on each of the covariates using analogous procedures described above for assessing initial balance.

For example, for each continuous covariate, one would use two-way analysis of variance (ANOVA) analyses, where campaign exposure is one factor, the propensity score quintile to which the individual was assigned is a second factor (coded as a categorical variable with 4 degrees of freedom), and each one of the covariates (or confounders) is a dependent variable. An interaction between the exposure and propensity score would also be included. If balance is achieved, there should not be a statistically significant main effect of campaign exposure on the covariate. There should also not be a statistically significant interaction effect of exposure by quintile. For dichotomous covariates, logistic regression would be appropriate, with propensity quintile, exposure, and their interaction as predictors. In all cases, one would use the same interpretive logic as in the initial analysis of balance analyses, described above. One would not want more than 5% of the analyses to show a significant exposure main effect or interaction or an absolute standardized difference between the treatment and control group on a covariate that is greater than 10%.

If balance on the set of covariates is not achieved, the propensity score should be reestimated by adding interaction terms and/or nonlinear functions (e.g., quadratic or cubic) of covariates to the propensity score model. It would be sensible to focus on nonlinear terms and interaction terms that include variables that were out of balance. This process becomes iterative—(a) propensity score estimation, (b) test for balance, (c) if balance not achieved, reestimate propensity score, and (d) recheck for balance. The process ends when balance is achieved. As indicated above, the usual standard of "adequate balance" is the amount of balance that would be achieved on average in a completely randomized experiment.

There are several alternative approaches to achieving balance after the propensity score is estimated. In the multivariate matching approach (Dehejia & Wahaba, 2002; Rosenbaum & Rubin, 1985; Smith, 1997), a single member of the treatment group is randomly selected and matched to a participant in the control group with the closest propensity score. Both participants are subsequently eliminated from the pool of participants available for matching. This procedure is repeated until all participants are matched or no additional matches could be made. Matched pairs are then compared on all covariates using standard t-tests (for continuous covariates) or chi-square tests (for discrete covariates) to verify that no statistically significant differences exist or that absolute standardized differences on covariates are smaller than 10%.

In the propensity score weighting approach (Rosenbaum, 1987), treated and control observations are reweighed to make them representative of the population of interest. A treated participant's weight is the inverse of his or her propensity score. A control participant's weight is the inverse of 1 minus his or her propensity score. The weighting acts to bring the means of most covariates closer together and is, thus, expected to remove any initial imbalances on these covariates between the treatment and control groups. Lack of statistically significant differences among treatment group on covariates would indicate that the weighting adjustment worked as intended.

Researchers may also find themselves tempted to estimate the propensity model's goodness of fit using standard tests such as the Hosmer-Lemeshow goodness-of-fit statistics that accompany the results of a logistic regression in most standard statistical packages such as SPSS. Rubin (2004) notes confusion between two types of statistical diagnostics as it relates to propensity score models: (1) diagnostics for the successful prediction of treatment probabilities (and parameter estimates underlying these probabilities) and (2) diagnostics of the degree to which the propensity score was successful in removing imbalance on covariates. He argues that only the latter type is relevant in this case (Weitzen, Lapane, Toledano, Hume, & Mor, 2005).

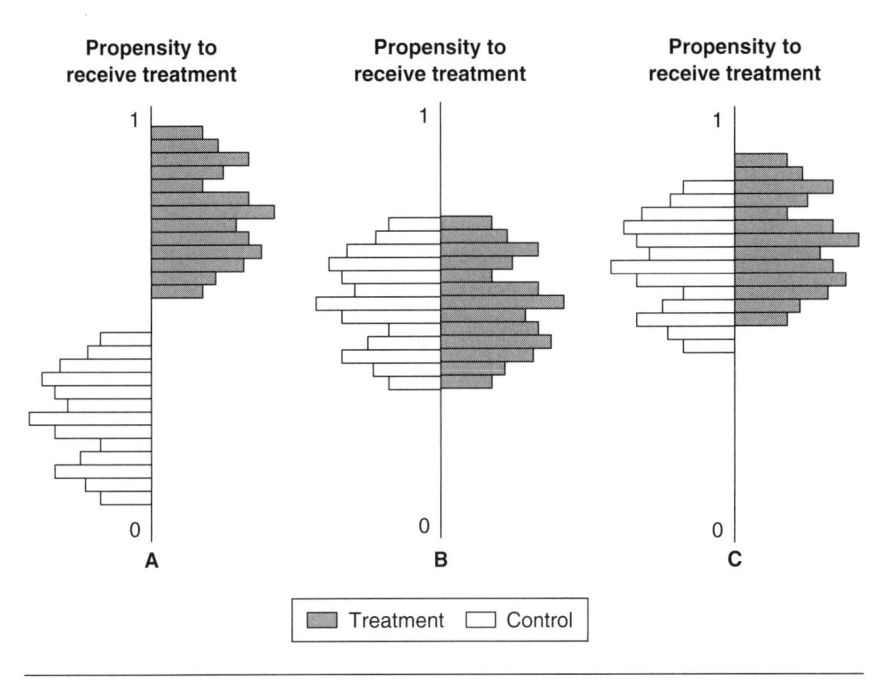

Estimating Causal Effects in Observational Studies

Figure 6.2 Histograms of Propensity Score Overlap Between Treatment and Control Groups

Before moving on to the next step, the distribution of the estimated propensity scores for the treatment and control groups should be checked for adequate overlap to verify that the data can support a comparison of treatment and control groups that are balanced on all covariates. This can be accomplished by creating overlapping histograms, or by comparing quintiles of the estimated propensity scores for the treatment and control groups. Examples of overlapping histograms are shown in Figure 6.2. If there is no overlap in the distribution of propensity scores between the treatment and control groups, as is the case in Example A, then no estimates of the treatment effect can be made without relying on unverifiable modeling assumptions. Example B represents an optimal case scenario where there is sufficient overlap in the distribution of the propensity score between the two groups (namely, it is possible to match all or most participants in both groups on all observed covariates). However, Example C is more typical, in a situation where the covariates are substantially associated with the treatment level. Even if the distribution of propensity scores across exposure groups does overlap considerably, treatment effects can be estimated only for the respondents who have propensity scores that overlap that of others. For example, if the estimated propensity scores for the control group range between 0.06 and 0.8 (assuming a dichotomous treatment) and the estimated propensity scores for the treatment group range between 0.5 and 0.95, then we can estimate treatment effects only for the portion of the population with propensity scores between 0.5 and 0.8. In the range 0.06 to 0.4, there are no treated units to compare to the observed control units, and in the range 0.8 to .95, there are no control units to compare to the observed treated units. This ability to highlight the ranges over which reliable treatment estimates can be made is an advantage of the propensity score methods. Further analysis should thus be restricted to those treatment and control units with overlapping propensity scores (for an illustration of this approach, see Dehejia & Wahaba, 1999; Zanutto et al., 2005). In some cases, there may be only a few treatment and control units in the nonoverlapping tail areas, and including them in the analysis may not adversely affect the balance of the covariates, in which case, there is no need to exclude these observations from the analysis.

STEP 5: CALCULATING CONFOUNDERS' ADJUSTED ESTIMATES OF TREATMENT EFFECTS

Once the propensity score has been estimated and adequate balance on covariates has been achieved for observations within the region of propensity score overlap, adjusted estimates of treatment effects may be calculated. There are several ways of using the propensity score to generate estimates of treatment effects (for more details, see D'Agostino, 1998; Perkins et al., 2000; Rosenbaum & Rubin, 1983; Rubin, 1997; Rubin & Thomas, 1996; Smith, 1997; Winship & Morgan, 1999). However, subclassification (or stratification) on the propensity score and on the calculation of the average treatment effect is the most advantageous because it does not rely on a particular functional form (e.g., linearity) and because it uses all the valuable data, especially when matching is incomplete (Rubin, 1997). First, average treatment effects are estimated separately within each propensity score quintile by subtracting the average outcome among treated individuals from that of untreated individuals. Next, an overall estimate of treatment effect is calculated by averaging the differences between treatment and control groups across all five quintiles. This procedure is summarized in the following expression:

$$\hat{\delta} = \sum_{k=1}^{5} \frac{n_k}{N} (\bar{Y}_{tk} - \bar{Y}_{ck})$$

where $\hat{\delta}$ is the estimated overall treatment effect, k indexes the propensity score quintile (quintiles 1 through 5), N is the total number of units, n_k is the number of units in the propensity score quintile k, and $\bar{Y}_{tk}$ and $\bar{Y}_{ck}$, respectively, are the average level of the outcome recorded for exposed (treatment) and unexposed (control) units within a specific propensity score quintile. It may be worth noting that in many cases (where there are treatment and control cases in every quintile), one fifth of the cases will be in each quintile, so this estimate reduces to the average difference between the treatment and control groups across the five quintiles. The estimated standard error of this estimated treatment effect is commonly calculated as follows:

$$\hat{s}(\hat{\delta}) = \sqrt{\sum_{k=1}^{5} \frac{n_k^2}{N^2}\left(\frac{S_{tk}^2}{n_{tk}} + \frac{S_{ck}^2}{n_{ck}}\right)}$$

where n_{tk} and n_{ck} are the number of treated and control units, respectively, in quintile k, and s^2_{tk} and s^2_{ck} are the sample variances of the treatment and control units, respectively, in quintile k. A similar strategy can be used to estimate the difference in treatment effect between two levels of a multi-level treatment variable (e.g., the difference between high and medium or medium and low exposure).

It is worth noting that this stratification approach will produce an estimate of the average treatment effect within the population (or subpopulation if the data are restricted to the region of propensity score overlap), similar to the regression coefficient for the effect of treatment assignment on outcomes controlling for other explanatory variables. If, for some reason, a researcher prefers to estimate effects for those people who are likely to get the treatment, if they are different from the population as a whole, one can define quintiles by the estimated propensity scores for the treatment units (rather than for all units). This approach will produce estimates of "treatment effect on the treated" that may be a useful estimate when only a select group of people tend to get the treatment and it is desired to estimate the treatment effect on those types of people who are likely to get the treatment, rather than the treatment effect on the population as a whole.

For those who feel more comfortable using standard regression methods, the propensity score, either in its continuous (raw) or categorical (propensity score quintile) form, can be used as a control variable in a regression analysis predicting a certain outcome of interest from level of treatment exposure. Important covariates or those not balanced by the propensity score could be included in this model as well. D'Agostino (1998) points out two advantages of employing a two-step procedure (namely, first estimating the propensity score and then including the estimated propensity score in a regression model as a covariate) over a one-step procedure that includes all possible covariates as predictors in a single regression model. The first is that the two-step procedure "saves" many degrees of freedom otherwise lost due to the inclusion of many predictors. The second is that the two-step procedure allows the researcher to focus on a simpler model for the treatment effect, containing only the most important variables that are related to outcomes and one additional variable, the propensity score. The regression approach, however, does not handle nonlinear associations properly (Rubin, 1997).

An Illustrative Example

To illustrate propensity score analysis, we compared treatment effects estimated from a randomized experiment to those estimated from a nonrandomized experiment following a propensity score adjustment. The experiment involved 445 undergraduate students enrolled in a large introductory class at a large public university in the Northeast of the United States. Participants first completed a baseline questionnaire that assessed demographic characteristics (e.g., sex, race, ethnicity, work status, etc.), religiosity, media exposure (e.g., television news), interest in politics, political activism, frequency of discussing politics with family and friends, party identification, and political efficacy using standard measures of these variables (see Cappella & Jamieson, 1997; Delli Carpini & Keeter, 1996). The treatment involved exposure to a scripted mock presidential debate (in a nonelection year, 2005) that provided information about the topics of jobs (employment) and stem-cell research. The outcome of interest was a participant's score on a brief test measuring knowledge of these two issues. Participants were then randomly assigned to participate in either a randomized experiment or a quasi-experiment. Those randomly assigned to participate in the randomized experiment ($n = 235$) were subsequently randomized to either treatment group ($n = 119$) or control group ($n = 116$). Participants assigned to the control group viewed a PBS documentary about the teenager's brain. On the other hand, those randomly assigned to participate in the quasi-experiment ($n = 210$) were allowed to choose either attending the mock presidential debate ($n = 79$) or view the documentary ($n = 131$). At the conclusion of the experiment, all participants completed a posttest that consisted of 20 questions measuring knowledge of the employment and stem-cell research issues. This design allowed us to compare the results of propensity score adjustments for quasi-experimental data relative to a randomized experiment that contained randomly equivalent participants.

Without propensity score analysis, the results of the quasi-experiment were somewhat biased compared to those of the randomized experiment. Specifically, those who participated in the randomized experiment and were randomly assigned to attend the mock presidential debate scored an average of four points higher on the political knowledge test than did those in the control group ($M = 10.61$ and $M = 6.69$, respectively; $F(1,233) = 85.41$, $p < .001$). In contrast, those who participated in the quasi-experiment and chose to attend the mock presidential debate scored an average of 4.65 points higher on the political knowledge test than did those who chose to view the documentary ($M = 11.61$ and $M = 6.96$, respectively; $F(1,208) = 79.65, p < .001$).

This difference between the results observed for the experimental procedure and those observed for the quasi-experimental procedure is due to selection bias. Specifically, those who chose to attend the mock presidential debate were, among other things, more likely to have an interest in politics, consume news in multiple media, and be politically active than their counterparts who chose not to attend the mock debate. In all, there were 25 variables in the data collected that were selected into the confounder pool based on theoretical consideration and prior empirical evidence. Of these, only six covariates were imbalanced between members of the treatment and control groups in the quasi-experimental procedure, as shown in Table 6.2. The propensity score was estimated using a logistic regression analysis predicting self-assignment to treatment from all covariates and all statistically significant two-way interactions. Twelve participants were dropped from the analysis because their estimated propensity score was outside the range of propensity scores estimated for individuals in the respective comparison group. The remaining participants were assigned to one of five quintiles based on their propensity score, and imbalances on covariates were examined again.

As Table 6.2 illustrates, following the propensity score adjustment, only two covariates had significant interaction F ratios, and none of the predictors had significant main effect F ratios. Thus, 2 of 48 tests (or 4.17%) of covariate balance were statistically significant, less than the 5% of the tests expected to be statistically significant by chance alone. Thus, we concluded that stratifying on the estimated propensity scores achieved reasonable balance across the treatment and control groups on these covariates.

Finally, to estimate the effects of treatment with a propensity score adjustment, treatment and control group means were computed as the unweighted average of the cell means over the five strata for each group. The results were that those who attended the mock presidential debates had an adjusted mean score on the political knowledge test that was 3.72 points higher than that of participants in the control group ($M = 11.25$ and $M = 7.53$, respectively; $F(1,201) = 36.61, p < .001$). We can evaluate this result against the data from the randomized experiment. For the political knowledge test, the initial difference between the randomized experiment and quasi-experiment was -0.73 points. That difference was reduced by 73% to 0.2 ($3.92 - 3.72$) after the stratification on propensity score quintiles.

It appears, then, that the propensity score approach was successful in approximating the estimates of treatment effects obtained from a randomized experiment. This is not surprising, given that the covariates used in the estimation of the propensity score explained about 65% of the variance in the outcome of interest (political knowledge) and 58% of self-selection into treatment. Including the strongest known covariates of political knowledge and exposure to presidential debates in the study's design and in the estimation of the propensity score greatly facilitated this outcome.

Table 6.2 Comparison of Differences Between Treatment and Control Groups on Significant Confounders Before and After Propensity Score Adjustment

Confounder	Treatment (N = 79) Mean	(SD)	Control (N = 131) Mean	(SD)	Preadjustment (N = 210) F-value[b]	Postadjustment (N = 198)[a] F-value[c] (main effect)	F-value (interaction effect)[d]
Interest in politics	4.50	(.50)	1.44	(.94)	712.9**	.80	7.2*
Political activism (weekly hours)	2.3	(.70)	0.84	(.30)	400**	.51	6.45*
News viewing hours on weekdays	2.86	(.75)	1.14	(.68)	291.3**	.43	2.78
News viewing hours on weekends	4.32	(1.6)	2.56	(1.8)	51.2**	.02	1.23
Newspaper reading on weekdays	3.75	(1.18)	2.50	(1.22)	53**	.03	1.04
Newspaper reading on weekends	2.56	(1.1)	1.24	(.57)	129**	.33	1.07

*$p < .05$ **$p < .001$

[a] 12 observations were dropped due to insufficient overlap in the propensity score.
[b] F-statistics was calculated by squaring two-sample t-statistics scores.
[c] F-statistics for main effect of general exposure after propensity score adjustment.
[d] F-statistics for the interaction effect of general exposure and propensity score quintile.

Elsewhere (Yanovitzky et al., 2005), we report a similar example of incorporating propensity score methods into a quasi-experimental evaluation design with similar success in the context of national campaign. Readers may benefit from consulting this work for an example of how to report and interpret a propensity score adjustment of treatment effects.

Advanced Issues in Propensity Score Analysis and a Cautionary Tale

PROPENSITY SCORE WITH MORE THAN TWO TREATMENT CONDITIONS

Nearly all work with propensity scores has been done comparing two groups, including the examples above. However, some researchers may be interested in adjusting for selection bias with more than two treatment conditions (for an example, see Yanovitzky et al., 2005). At least three different methods using propensity scores have been proposed in the literature. The first method, proposed by Rubin (1997), involves creating a separate propensity score model for each two-group comparison among the groups being compared. In the three-group case, three propensity score models would be required, one for comparing Groups 1 and 2, one for comparing Groups 1 and 3, and one for comparing Groups 2 and 3. The second method, proposed by Joffe and Rosenbaum (1999), involves the use of propensity scores with ordered doses. They showed that under certain conditions, ordinal logistic regression can be used to derive propensity scores that are subsequently used to match participants with different doses in a manner that tends to balance covariates. The technical details of this approach are discussed elsewhere (Lu et al., 2001; Yanovitzky et al., 2005; Zanutto et al., 2005). However, an ordinal logistic regression model does not always provide an adequate fit to the data. This is obviously true for nonordinal treatment levels. For example, a recent study (Ta-Seale, Croghan, & Obenchain, 2000) attempted to use propensity score methodology in a case where treatment consisted of a nominal variable with three categories (assignment of patients to three different drugs). In this sense, a third approach has an important advantage. Imbens (2000) proposed an extension of the propensity score methodology applicable to multilevel treatments, ordinal or nominal. He defined the generalized propensity score as the conditional probability of receiving a particular level of the treatment given the observed covariates. Thus, Imbens's method requires a propensity score model for each level of treatment and subclassification on each of these scores. It is also worth noting that the development of propensity score models for continuous treatments is currently under way (see, e.g., Hirano & Imbens, 2004).

THE PROBLEM OF HIDDEN BIAS AND SENSITIVITY ANALYSIS

The chief caveat of propensity score analysis in comparison to randomized experiments is the problem of hidden bias. In a randomized experiment, the treatment and control groups are equivalent on all covariates, observed and unobserved. In contrast, propensity score methods can adjust only for observed confounding covariates but not for unobserved ones. The propensity score methodology assumes that all variables related to both outcomes and treatment assignment are included in the vector of observed covariates used in the estimation of the propensity score. In other words, there is an assumption that the researcher knows and measures the selection model perfectly. This is the assumption of strongly ignorable treatment assignment (Rosenbaum & Rubin, 1983). If the propensity score model is incorrect or the covariates are measured imperfectly, then hidden bias may exist that can bias estimates of treatment effects. An omitted variable is most likely to affect conclusions about treatment effect when it is closely related to the outcome, seriously imbalanced by treatment exposure, or uncorrelated with the propensity score. Only when the strongly ignorable treatment assumption is met does propensity score methodology produce unbiased treatment effect estimates.

Given that researchers rarely, if ever, know the true selection model with full confidence, Rosenbaum (2002) has proposed to estimate the sensitivity of propensity scores to violation of the strongly ignorable treatment assumption. His sensitivity analysis approach essentially examines whether the qualitative conclusions of a study would change in response to hypothetical hidden biases of varying magnitudes. The method involves estimating how big the effect of an unmeasured variable would have to be in order to lead to a change in inference. It considers a range of hypothetical values for this effect and reports for each value the upper and lower bounds on the p-value for the test statistic. If a large bias is needed to alter the study findings, say, from a significant difference between groups to no significant difference or vice versa, then the study is said to be insensitive to hidden bias. Other ways of testing the strongly ignorable treatment assumption in the context of estimating the effects of communication campaigns were recently suggested by Do and Kincaid (2006). Conducting such tests may lead researchers to have more confidence in their inferences. Nonetheless, one can never be absolutely sure that one has eliminated all selection bias (Rosenbaum & Rubin, 1983; Rubin, 1997).

OTHER LIMITATIONS

Another problem may be the presence of a large number of missing values on covariates (D'Agostino & Rubin, 2000). A typical approach is to estimate the propensity score from both observed values of covariates and observed missing-data indicators such as dummy variables representing whether or not a participant was measured on a particular covariate (D'Agostino & Rubin, 2000). When the problem is more severe, researchers may want to consider a different strategy of handling missing values (e.g., deleting cases with a certain percent of missing values on all covariates) or consider multiple imputation for missing data (Allison, 2001; Rubin, 1987; Schafer, 1997).

The propensity score approach assumes that the investigator can distinguish between confounders (i.e., variables causally prior to treatment and outcome) and other variables that are potential consequences of treatment and outcomes. If variables that are not causally prior are included in the confounder pool, the effects of treatment may be biased.

In addition, most applied research using propensity scores has involved large samples. Propensity score analysis tends to work better in larger samples for the obvious reasons: Bigger samples produce smaller standard errors. However, this may be true particularly for propensity scoring because imbalances of some covariates after subclassification on the propensity score are likely to be minor in large samples but substantial enough to bias effect estimates in smaller samples (Rubin, 1997). Exactly how large of a sample is needed is not clear and needs further study.

Conclusion

As we have discussed, propensity score methodology is a useful tool for researchers who are interested in obtaining unbiased estimates of treatment effects when random assignment to treatment is not feasible or not appropriate (experimental and nonexperimental). This methodology is widely used in other fields, particularly in the area of applied medicine and biostatistics (D'Agostino, 1998; Weitzen et al., 2004). We therefore encourage researchers in the field of communication to go beyond this basic introduction and explore this methodology further. The work cited throughout this chapter provides an excellent source of information for those interested in applying this methodology for analyzing observational data.

Notes

1. In the language of experiments, a treatment is something done to a person that might have an effect. In observational studies, treatment variables are independent variables. In the context of communication campaigns, treatment is campaign exposure.

2. The approach described here is the traditional approach to assessing imbalance. Alternatively, one may use binary or ordinal logistic regression to predict level of treatment from confounders. This alternative approach seems to more appropriately conceptualize the confounders as influencing the probability of treatment assignment, but both approaches provide a broad sense for how units in different treatment groups vary on potential confounders.

References

Allison, P. D. (1999). *Multiple regression: A primer*. Thousand Oaks, CA: Pine Forge Press.

Allison, P. D. (2001). *Missing data*. Thousand Oaks, CA: Sage.

Angrist, J. D., Imbens, G. W., & Rubin, D. B. (1996). Identification of causal effects using instrumental variables. *Journal of the American Statistical Association, 91*, 444–472.

Boruch, R. F. (1997). *Randomized experiments for planning and evaluation: A practical guide*. Thousand Oaks, CA: Sage.

Cappella, J. N., & Jamieson, K. H. (1997). *Spiral of cynicism: The press and the public good*. New York: Oxford University Press.

Cochran, W. G. (1968). The effectiveness of adjustment by subclassification in removing bias in observational studies. *Biometrics, 24*, 205–213.

D'Agostino, R. B. (1998). Tutorial in biostatistics: Propensity score methods for bias reduction in the comparison of a treatment to a non-randomized control group. *Statistics in Medicine, 17*, 2265–2281.

D'Agostino, R. B., & Rubin, D. B. (2000). Estimating and using propensity scores with partially missing data. *Journal of the American Statistical Association, 95*, 749–759.

Dehejia, R. H., & Wahaba, S. (1999). Causal effects in nonexperimental studies: Reevaluating the evaluation of training programs. *Journal of the American Statistical Association, 94*, 1053–1062.

Dehejia, R. H., & Wahaba, S. (2002). Propensity score-matching methods for nonexperimental causal studies. *Review of Economics and Statistics, 84*(1), 151–161.

Delli Carpini, M. X., & Keeter, S. (1996). *What Americans know about politics and why it matters*. New Haven, CT: Yale University Press.

Do, M. P., & Kincaid, D. L. (2006). Impact of an entertainment education television drama on health knowledge and behavior in Bangladesh: An application of propensity score matching. *Journal of Health Communication, 11*, 301–325.

Drake, C. (1993). Effects of misspecification of the propensity score on estimators of treatment effect. *Biometrics, 49*, 1231–1236.

Heckman, J. J. (1995). *Instrumental variables: A cautionary tale* (Technical Working Paper No. 185). Cambridge, MA: National Bureau of Economic Research.

Hirano, K., & Imbens, G. (2004). The propensity score with continuous treatments. In A. Gelman & X.-L. Meng (Eds.), *Applied Bayesian modeling and causal inference from incomplete-data perspectives* (pp. 73–84). New York: Wiley.

Hornik, R., Maklan, D., Cadell, D., Barmada, C. H., Jacobson, L., Prado, A., et al. (2002). *Evaluation of the National Youth Anti-Drug Media Campaign: Fifth semi-annual report of findings.* Rockville, MD: Westat.

Hornik, R., Maklan, D., Judkins, D., Cadell, D., Yanovitzky, I., Zador, P., et al. (2001). *Evaluation of the National Youth Anti-Drug Media Campaign: Second semi-annual report of findings.* Rockville, MD: Westat.

Hornik, R., & Yanovitzky, I. (2003). Using theory to design evaluations of communication campaigns: The case of the National Youth Anti-Drug Media Campaign. *Communication Theory, 13*(2), 204–224.

Imbens, G. W. (2000). The role of the propensity score in estimating dose-response functions. *Biometrika, 87,* 706–710.

Joffe, M. M., & Rosenbaum, P. R. (1999). Invited commentary: Propensity scores. *American Journal of Epidemiology, 150*(4), 327–333.

Lu, B., Zanutto, E., Hornik, R., & Rosenbaum, P. R. (2001). Matching with doses in an observational study of a media campaign against drug abuse. *Journal of the American Statistical Association, 96,* 1245–1253.

McCullagh, P. (1980). Regression model for ordinal data. *Journal of the Royal Statistical Society. Series B, 42,* 109–142.

Newhouse, J. P., & McClellan, M. (1998). Econometrics in outcomes research: The use of instrumental variables. *Annual Review of Public Health, 19,* 17–34.

Normand, S. T., Landrum, M. B., Guadagnoli, E., Ayanian, J. Z., Ryan, T. J., Cleary, P. D., et al. (2001). Validating recommendations for coronary angiography following acute myocardial infarction in the elderly: A matched analysis using propensity scores. *Journal of Clinical Epidemiology, 54*(4), 387–398.

O'Connell, A. A. (2005). *Logistic regression models for ordinal response variables.* Thousand Oaks, CA: Sage.

Perkins, S. M., Tu, W., Underhill, M. G., Zhou, X.-H., & Murray, M. D. (2000). The use of propensity scores in pharmacoepidemiologic research. *Pharmacoepidemiology and Drug Safety, 9,* 93–101.

Rosenbaum, P. R. (1987). Model-based direct adjustment. *Journal of the American Statistical Association, 82,* 387–394.

Rosenbaum, P. R. (2002). *Observational studies* (2nd ed.). New York: Springer-Verlag.

Rosenbaum, P. R., & Rubin, D. B. (1983). The central role of the propensity score in observational studies for causal effects. *Biometrika, 70,* 41–55.

Rosenbaum, P. R., & Rubin, D. B. (1984). Reducing bias in observational studies using subclassification on the propensity score. *Journal of the American Statistical Association, 79,* 516–524.

Rosenbaum, P. R., & Rubin, D. B. (1985). Constructing a control group using multivariate matched sampling methods that incorporate the propensity score. *The American Statistician, 39,* 33–38.

Rossi, P. H., Lipsey, M. W., & Freeman, H. E. (2004). *Evaluation: A systematic approach* (7th ed.). Thousand Oaks, CA: Sage.

Rubin, D. B. (1987). *Multiple imputation for nonresponse in surveys.* New York: John Wiley & Sons.

Rubin, D. B. (1997). Estimating causal effects from large data sets using propensity scores. *Annals of Internal Medicine, 127*(Part 2), 757–763.

Rubin, D. B. (2004). On principles for modeling propensity scores in medical research. *Pharmacoepidemiology and Drug Safety, 13*(12), 855–857.

Rubin, D. B., & Thomas, N. (1996). Matching using estimated propensity scores: Relating theory to practice. *Biometrics, 52,* 249–264.

Schafer, J. L. (1997). *Analysis of incomplete multivariate data.* New York: Chapman & Hall.

Smith, H. L. (1997). Matching with multiple controls to estimate treatment effects in observational studies. *Sociological Methodology, 27,* 325–353.

Smith, J. A., & Todd, P. E. (2001). Reconciling conflicting evidence on the performance of propensity-score matching methods. *American Economic Review, 91*(2), 112–118.

Stone, R. A., Obrosky, D. S., Singer, D. E., Kapoor, W. N., & Fine, M. J. (1995). Propensity score adjustment for pretreatment differences between hospitalized and ambulatory patients with community-acquired pneumonia. *Medical Care, 33,* AS56–AS66.

Ta-Seale, M., Croghan, T. W., & Obenchain, R. (2000). Determinants of antidepressant treatment compliance: Implications for policy. *Medical Care Research and Review, 57,* 491–512.

Weitzen, S., Lapane, K. L., Toledano, A. Y., Hume, A. L., & Mor, V. (2004). Principles for modeling propensity scores in medical research: A systematic literature review. *Pharmacoepidemiology and Drug Safety, 13*(12), 841–853.

Weitzen, S., Lapane, K. L., Toledano, A. Y., Hume, A. L., & Mor, V. (2005). Weaknesses of goodness-of-fit tests for evaluating propensity score models: The case of the omitted confounder. *Pharmacoepidemiology and Drug Safety, 14*(4), 227–238.

Winship, C., & Morgan, S. L. (1999). The estimation of causal effects from observational data. *Annual Review of Sociology, 25,* 659–706.

Yanovitzky, I., Zanutto, E., & Hornik, R. (2005). Estimating causal effects of public health education campaigns using propensity score methodology. *Evaluation and Program Planning, 28*(2), 209–220.

Zanutto, E., Lu, B., & Hornik, R. (2005). Using propensity score subclassification for multiple treatment doses to evaluate a national antidrug media campaign. *Journal of Educational and Behavioral Statistics, 30*(1), 59–73.

Commentary on the Uses and Misuses of Structural Equation Modeling in Communication Research

R. Lance Holbert

Michael T. Stephenson

The study of process is central to theory building in communication science (Cappella, 1991), and structural equation modeling (SEM) allows researchers to analyze and assess a wide range of processes of influence (Holbert & Stephenson, 2003). Whether communication theories take on axiomatic or causal process forms (Reynolds, 1971), SEM is an analytical tool that has the potential to bring greater sophistication to the discipline's theoretical foundations (Boster, 2002). SEM is described by Kaplan (2000) as "a melding of factor analysis and path analysis into one comprehensive statistical methodology" (p. 3). This multivariate technique emerged from three separate lines of analytical research: path analysis, factor analysis, and simultaneous equation modeling. Karl Jöreskog, the modern-day founder of SEM, integrated his earliest contribution, confirmatory factor analysis (CFA), with simultaneous equation modeling to create the analytic framework we call SEM (e.g., Jöreskog, 1973). SEM has often been described as providing a window on causality (Ullman, 2001), but it is important to stress from the very beginning of this chapter that no one structural equation model can make up for a poor or inadequate theoretical foundation (Mueller, 1997).

Indeed, communication researchers should treat SEM as a double-edged sword that can be used either to the benefit or to the detriment of theory building. As Dunnette (1978) explained, too often researchers get caught in a game of "My model in nicer than your model!" which then leads to "a compulsion to forget the problem . . . because of the fun we may be enjoying with our apparatus" (p. 270). SEM is but one analytical tool within a communication researcher's analytical toolbox, albeit an extremely flexible tool. Inherent within SEM's flexibility are opportunities for misuse by communication researchers. This chapter is devoted to outlining some of the proper and improper uses of SEM for advancing communication theory building.

Communication was a relatively late adopter of SEM when compared to the nature and diversity of this analytical tool's use in other social scientific disciplines like sociology or psychology (see Alwin & Hauser, 1975; MacCallum & Austin, 2000). Although the field was introduced to causal modeling around 1975 (e.g., Cappella, 1975; Fink & Noell, 1975) and more formally to structural equation modeling by Cappella (1980), a critical mass of scholars did not begin to employ SEM as a standard technique until the 1990s. As a result, the discipline is not steeped in the history of SEM, and that history can be found most directly in the study of measurement (Hägglund, 2001; Sörbom, 2001).

Communication researchers immediately associate SEM with the study of associations between variables involved in some process of influence, and rightfully so given the nature of how this analytical tool has evolved. However, valid and reliable measurement is a necessary condition for the advancement of social science (Chaffee, 1991), and SEM is an extremely powerful instrument that can aid the cause of measurement. Sadly, SEM has been severely underutilized for this purpose in the field of communication.

Levine (2005) recently argued for the need to conduct CFAs in communication, and this chapter will begin by outlining the proper and improper uses of SEM as a tool for conducting CFAs. The chapter will then focus on the boundaries for assessing broader structural models that reflect processes of influence among variables. It is only by looking at the uses and misuses of SEM as an analytical tool for the study of measurement *and* structural relationships among variables that the discipline can best utilize this particular technique. The discipline suffers from not only the improper use of SEM but also an undervaluing of CFA. We wish to highlight what communication researchers are doing right and wrong with their present use of SEM, and we also want to note where there is the potential to expand the use of SEM for the purpose of theory building.

Measurement Models

SEM is grounded in the study of *latent variables* (Bollen, 1989). A latent variable cannot be directly measured but, rather, can be mathematically derived from variables that *can* be directly measured (Hayduk, 1996). Boorsboom, Mellenbergh, and van Heerden (2003) described a series of observable items linked to a single latent variable as being "proxy" measures of the latent variable. Most communication researchers are familiar with exploratory factor analysis (EFA), which entails isolating and assessing latent variables in the form of articulated factors. For example, Kaye and Johnson (2002) identified four articulated factors that reflect motivations for using the World Wide Web for political information: guidance, surveillance, entertainment, and social utility (see the Appendix). These four dimensions are derived from the traditional study of political media uses and gratifications (e.g., McLeod & Becker, 1981) and can be considered latent variables that are not directly observed. In other words, indices constructed from factors that emerge via EFA are really measuring latent variables, but doing so in ways that are theoretically crude relative to what can be done via SEM and CFA.

EFA is comparatively crude in that the analysis is driving the formation of the articulated factors (i.e., latent variables), whereas CFA is driven foremost by the theoretical claims of the researcher. The factor analysis literature commonly refers to EFA as the testing of an *unrestricted* model because no bounds are preestablished for the number of articulated factors, while CFA is commonly referred to as the testing of a *restricted* model (Kaplan, 2000). In an EFA, researchers simply enter all observable variables into a single analysis and wait to see how many articulated factors are produced to allow for an appropriate reducing of data. There are no restrictions placed on what the analysis will produce in terms of the number of articulated factors nor on which items will load together on a given factor. With CFA, a researcher posits a specific number of articulated factors in the form of latent variables, and a theory-driven set of associations between multiple observable variables and latent variables is outlined *prior* to any formal analyses. Thus, restrictions are being placed on the analysis of measurement in a CFA model. A researcher uses theory only after an EFA analysis to determine whether particular groupings of observable variables make conceptual sense and whether these variables align with the purposes of a given research agenda.[1]

Some of the greatest advancements made in the communication sciences occur when researchers have identified a latent variable. For example, Chaffee and Schleuder (1986) offered the following conclusion from their study of media exposure and attention: "Measurement of attention *in addition to* simple exposure more adequately reflects the person's use of television news [emphasis added]" (p. 104). These researchers are stating that media *use* is a latent variable that consists of two observable dimensions, *exposure* and *attention*. Media use as a theoretical construct is not something that can be directly measured. Instead, the best way to measure this latent variable is through the "proxy" observable variables of exposure and attention (Holbert, 2005a).[2]

The tactic of treating observable variables as "proxy" measures of more important latent constructs is symptomatic of an approach to measurement that requires a certain degree of humility that is appropriately articulated by Duncan (1975):

> All observation is fallible, no matter how refined the measuring instrument and no matter how careful the procedure of applying it. In a strict sense, therefore, we never measure exactly the true variables discussed in our theories. In this same strict sense, all (true) variables are "unobserved." (p. 113)

Communication researchers can never truly measure the variables of greatest interest to their theoretical arguments. This speaks to the importance of latent variables, which are never directly measured (Stephenson, Holbert, & Zimmerman, 2006). With this stated, the observable variables we do measure are by no means a pure representation of latent variables. Observable variables serve as proxy measures because they are ripe with error. Associated with each observable variable is an error term, and all error terms are "disturbances that disrupt the relation between the latent and observable variables" (Bollen, 1989, p. 18). An error term reflects that which we do *not* know about the observable variable, and what we do not know about the observable variable results in a lack of proper measurement of the latent variable. In addition, error associated with a single observable variable does not function in a vacuum relative to other observable variables in a model. Given that any one latent variable is most commonly associated with multiple observable variables, and there is an error term associated with each observable variable, the error terms *compound* to lead to an even less adequate measure of the latent variable. In short, greater error in the measurement of observable variables leads to less of an empirical understanding of the latent variable.

If communication research can begin to approach issues of measurement from a perspective that embraces not only the discipline's strengths but also its inherent limitations, then the field will truly begin to flourish in terms of building stronger measurement. With this perspective on latent variables, researchers can then begin to examine and improve measurement through the use of CFA.

Confirmatory Factor Analysis

CFA allows researchers to offer a theoretical model of associations between one or more latent variables and a set of observable variables. In the case of the politically based Web gratifications measures described earlier, we would use the Kaye and Johnson (2002) findings and existing uses and gratifications theory to hypothesize a 4-latent-variable, 13-observable-variable confirmatory measurement model (see Figure 7.1). This confirmatory measurement model reflects a *predetermined* number of latent variables and a set of associations between latent variables and observable variables that is grounded in theory and past empirical evidence. As a result, researchers need to be cognizant that these criteria result in CFA procedures representing the testing of theory (Jöreskog & Wold, 1982).

It is important to understand what Figure 7.1 is communicating theoretically. First, there is an error term (ε_1 to ε_{12}) associated with each observable variable (Y_1 to Y_{13}, which in practice would represent responses from a set of research participants to the 13 items listed in the Appendix) that reflects the error of measurement associated with the unreliability of the measure. The observable variable error terms represent that which is not accounted for in the observable variable by the set of associations constructed in the theoretical model. Second, there is a disturbance term (ζ_1 to ζ_4) associated with each latent variable. Once again, these terms are reflective of what cannot be explained in the latent variables by the model. Third, the latent variables, which are represented by ovals, are allowed to covary within a CFA measurement model. These curved covariance paths reflect the level of association between each of the latent variables. Fourth, there are paths leading from each latent variable to its respective observable variables. These paths reflect a theoretical understanding that the latent variable is the larger phenomenon that influences all observable variables associated with that specific latent variable. The CFA model is *not* stating that the observable variables are serving to create the latent variables. If this were the case, then the paths would be leading from the observable variables to the latent variables. Instead, the latent variable is a force at work that exists beyond direct human observation, but which influences a cluster of variables that the researcher has the ability to observe and measure.

FREE AND FIXED PATHS

All of the solid paths shown in Figure 7.1 are defined as "free" within the model. A free path is where a researcher asks an SEM software package to calculate a parameter estimate. Each calculated parameter estimate "costs" a single degree of freedom. The maximum degrees of freedom for any one model is the total number of estimates in the diagonal and subdiagonal of the variance-covariance matrix (see Hoyle, 1991). The variance-covariance matrix is simply an unstandardized matrix of associations and serves as the input to any SEM analysis. It reflects the variation in each observed variable as well as their relations to each other. In the case of Figure 7.1, there are 13 observable variables, so the number of elements in the diagonal and subdiagonal of the covariance matrix can be calculated as 13 + 12 + 11 + 10 + 9 + 8 + 7 + 6 + 5 + 4 + 3 + 2 + 1 = 91. Thus, the potential number of degrees of

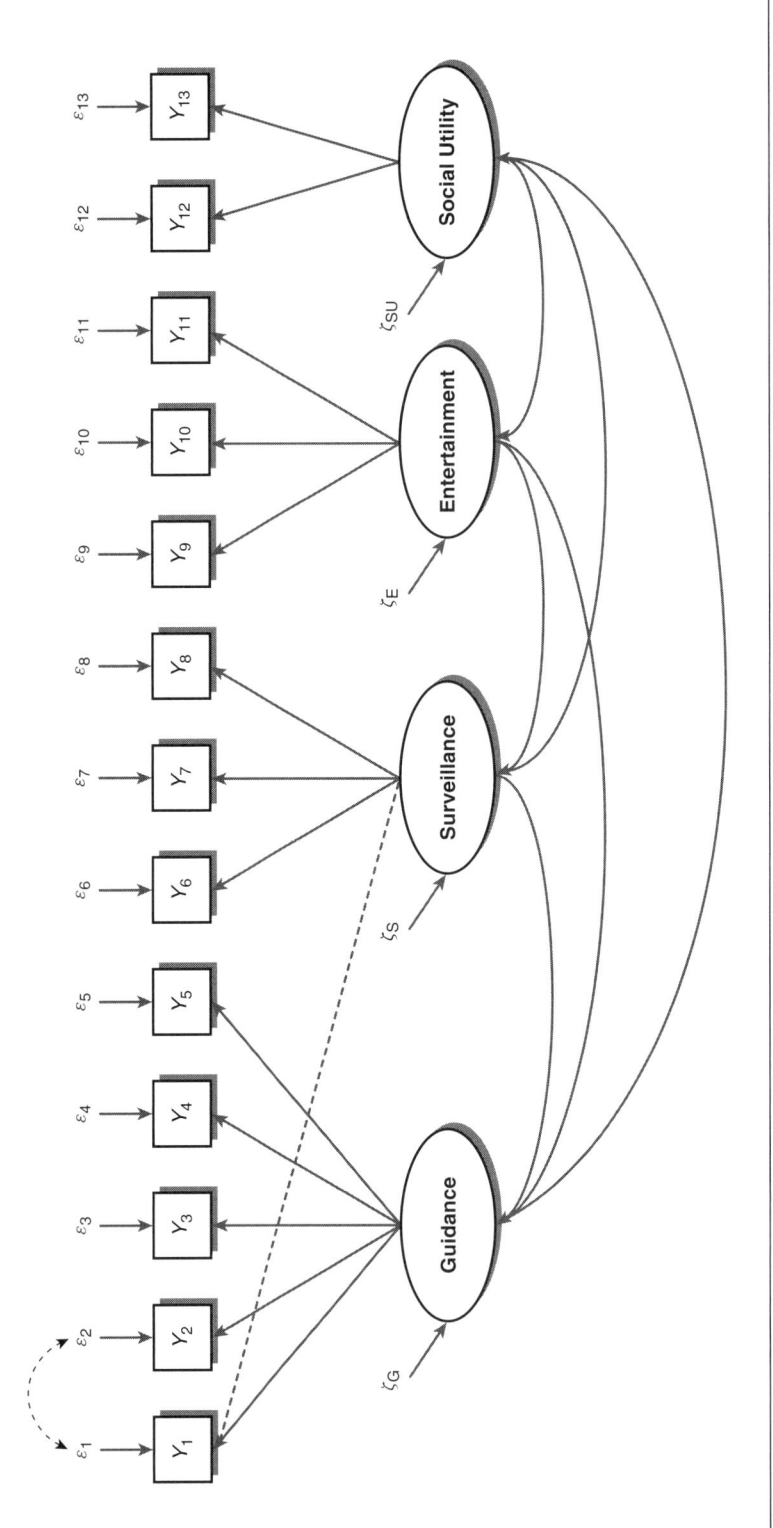

Figure 7.1 Hypothesized Kaye and Johnson (2002) CFA Measurement Model

freedom for any model of these 13 observable variables is 91. There are 13 error terms associated with the observable variables, so 13 degrees of freedom are lost with the estimation of these parameters. Four degrees of freedom are spent because each latent variable retains an error term. There are six covariance paths among the four latent variables, and each of these estimated relationships results in the loss of one degree of freedom. Finally, there are the individual factor score estimates leading from the latent variables to the observable variables. A single factor loading within each set of latent variable-to-observable variable loadings is set to 1 in order to properly scale the latent variable (Kline, 1998). Setting a single latent-to-observable path to 1 allows for the latent variable to be given a scale that is consistent with the same units used to measure the observable variable (Bollen, 1989). CFA models allow for infinite flexibility for the scaling of latent variables given that few measures used in the social sciences retain universal scaling. As a result, the researcher has to tell the SEM software package what constraints the latent variable should have in terms of its scaling. The researcher should allow a latent variable to work within the same scale constraints as the observable variables associated with that latent variable, and setting a single latent-to-observable path to 1 allows for this constraint to be created within the model. The setting of a specific value (in this case, 1) for a parameter does not result in the loss of a degree of freedom, so four of the latent-to-observable paths do not count against the model's overall degrees of freedom. As described below, these four paths are "fixed." Thus, 4 is subtracted from the 13 latent variable-to-observable variable path estimate total, resulting in the loss of 9 degrees of freedom. A total of $13 + 4 + 6 + 9 = 32$ degrees of freedom are consumed by the hypothesized measurement model, leaving 59 degrees of freedom to be reported for the tested model.[3]

The opposite of a "free" path is one that is defined as "fixed." A researcher defines a path as fixed if he or she does *not* want the given parameter estimated and instead chooses to constrain that path to a specific value. There are a number of fixed paths within the hypothesized model. Most obviously, not all latent variables are leading to each observable variable. For example, there is no path estimate being calculated for the relationship between the surveillance latent variable and the observable variable Y_1 (see straight dotted path from Surveillance to Y_1 in Figure 7.1). Researchers who are using SEM need to be aware that this multivariate technique works under the assumption that all variables and their respective error terms have the ability to be related to one another, and that any one hypothesized model is not judged against just the specific set of relationships outlined in that model but also all the potential relationships not outlined in the hypothesized model.

Another set of fixed relationships are the covaried error terms between the observable variables (e.g., see curved dotted relationship in Figure 7.1). It is often the case that error terms among observable variables are highly correlated, and this fact can be quite burdensome to the communication researcher (see Kline, 1998, for discussion of within-factor versus between-factor covaried observable-variable error terms). These are but two examples of various types of relationships that are deemed fixed within the hypothesized measurement model. Communication researchers need to have a firm understanding of which paths are free or fixed in their models and to also retain a grasp of the default free versus fixed settings for classifications of relationships preestablished by the various SEM software packages. Each software package makes certain assumptions for whether one class of relationships should be free or fixed, but it is up to the researcher to determine whether these default settings are appropriate for a given model being tested. Not understanding this information leads to the potential misuse of SEM in that the researcher might allow some paths to be estimated when in fact they should not be (or vice versa).

MODEL IDENTIFICATION

Inherent to a discussion of degrees of freedom is the issue of model identification. Communication researchers must be able to distinguish between overidentified, just identified, and underidentified models. "Identification is *not* a problem of too few cases [emphasis added]" (Bollen, 1989, p. 90). All structural equation models need to be overidentified in order to be properly estimated and evaluated (Hoyle, 1991; Raykov & Marcoulides, 2000). If a model retains one or more degrees of freedom, then the model is overidentified. Thus, the hypothesized Kaye and Johnson (2002) measurement model in Figure 7.1 is overidentified with 59 degrees of freedom. If the model has zero degrees of freedom, then a model is just identified. A model of this identification type is most commonly referred to as a "saturated" model (Kline, 1998). The fit of a just-identified model is always perfect and cannot be properly evaluated by standards of fit (MacCallum, 1995). Likewise, a model that is only slightly overidentified will have few degrees of freedom and a high probability of excellent model fit (i.e., low levels of falsifiability; see Raykov & Marcoulides, 1999). Claiming support for theory based on good fit statistics for a model that approaches saturation is not very credible but, unfortunately, is an all-too-common practice among some users of SEM. Conversely, if a model is underidentified, most programs will not perform the analysis. Communication scholars want to hypothesize, test, and interpret overidentified models. In addition, the more degrees of freedom, the better.

The proposed measurement model in Figure 7.1 is representative of a theoretical and analytical ideal. As Levine (2005) has stated, "The proposed model is treated as the null, and statistically significant results reflect a discrepancy between the predicted model and the data" (p. 337). When the data are inconsistent with the measurement structure outlined by theory, researchers generally engage a broad set of procedures that fall under the heading of model respecification.

MODEL RESPECIFICATION

Improperly fitted measurement models are as inevitable as death and taxes, so researchers should not feel inadequate when a given measurement model does not fit the data (MacCallum, Roznowski, & Necowitz, 1992). However, it is also very important to understand that some of the greatest misuses of SEM occur within the model respecification phase. This process cannot and should not be dominated by a blind adherence to the data. Too often researchers take the path of least resistance to achieving an adequate model fit by uncritically following *modification indices*. Modification indices report how the fixing or freeing of a given path within a model may aid in achieving a better model fit. Therefore, it is first necessary for communication researchers to understand the computer output in order to make judgments of where a model falls short in fitting the data. LISREL, EQS, and AMOS offer modification indices in the form of univariate Lagrange Multiplier (LM) estimates.[4] These estimates calculate the change in the χ^2-distributed test statistic as a result of the freeing of a given parameter estimate. In addition to the LM test, one can consult the Wald (W) statistic, which estimates the degree to which the χ^2-distributed test statistic will increase if a free parameter estimate were to be fixed (Bollen, 1989). Although these empirical estimates can provide important insights on where a model is particularly problematic relative to fit, we cannot overemphasize a key principle: Model modifications should not be undertaken as a purely data-driven endeavor. This is perhaps the most common misuse of SEM: claiming support for a theory based on good model fit after a data-driven process of respecifying models.[5] The primary appropriate use of model modifications is identifying possible problems in the way a model is set up, such as the need to modify the measurement portion of a model, or modifying variable relationships (e.g., dropping some correlations between control variables) that are trivial with respect to the theory tested but that may have an overly deleterious impact on model fit.

A two-pronged argument can be made for the necessity of theory driving model modification. The first issue is best articulated by Kline (1998). Kline points out that the number of potential culprits that could contribute to an improperly fitted model is so large that it is essential for a researcher to have some theoretical basis to separate the wheat from the chaff. Therefore, decisions should not be arbitrarily or by empirical output alone made. The second argument concerns the high likelihood of multiple models achieving a solid fit with the data (Cliff, 1983). As a result, the blind use of the modification indices associated with a single data set will often lead to the formation of a final model that would be exceedingly difficult to replicate (see Rosenthal, 1991, for discussion of replication). An alternate respecified model that also fits the data but is constructed around a strong theoretical foundation is much more likely to withstand the test of time. In both cases, the best insurance policy for engaging in model modification is to employ a combination of theoretical understanding and empirical insights offered by the various SEM software packages, with the theoretical horse always pulling the analytical cart.

HIGHER-ORDER FACTOR STRUCTURES

As unfortunate as the scant use of SEM-based CFAs and the number of unjustified model modifications in communication research is the dearth of testing of higher-order factor structures. More than 50 years of social scientific research has argued for the existence of higher-order factor structures (e.g., Thurstone, 1947). SEM allows for not only the direct assessment of a set of lower-order factors but also the existence of higher-order factors. Higher-order factor structures reflect the fact that "the latent variables directly influencing the observable variables may be influenced by other latent variables that need not have direct effects on the observable variables" (Bollen, 1989, pp. 313–314).

Building off the hypothesized lower-order Kaye and Johnson (2002) measurement model, we could look at Figure 7.1 with the added twist of introducing higher-order latent variables (see Figure 7.2, latent variables marked ξ_1 and ξ_2). The result is an alternative hypothesized model that can be tested and compared to the original model offered in Figure 7.1. It is imperative for the discipline to begin a more systematic assessment of higher-order factors in order to gain a broader understanding of underlying measurement structures. Otherwise, communication researchers may be getting lost in studying individual lower-order latent variables without seeing the broader measurement forces at work in their theoretical models.

There are a seemingly endless number of examples from other disciplines of the testing of higher-order factor structures (e.g., Cheung, 2000; Kaplan & Elliott, 1997; Russell & Cutrona, 1991). However, the movement toward the testing of higher-order factor structures reflects a subtle shift away from the testing of a pure measurement model. Inherent to the establishment of a higher-order factor is the testing of causal associations between latent variables. Thus, higher-order factor models can be viewed as a bridge between the testing of pure measurement models and hybrid models that test simultaneously measurement and structural associations within a single model (Kline, 1998).

A recent example of the construction of a higher-order latent variable in the communication literature can be found in Afifi et al.'s (2006) health communication study of interpersonal familial discussions of organ donation (see Figure 7.3). Two lower-order latent efficacy variables are included in the study, communication efficacy and coping efficacy. The communication efficacy latent variable is influencing two observable variables, while coping efficacy has direct relationships with three observable variables. The lower-order communication efficacy and coping efficacy latent variables

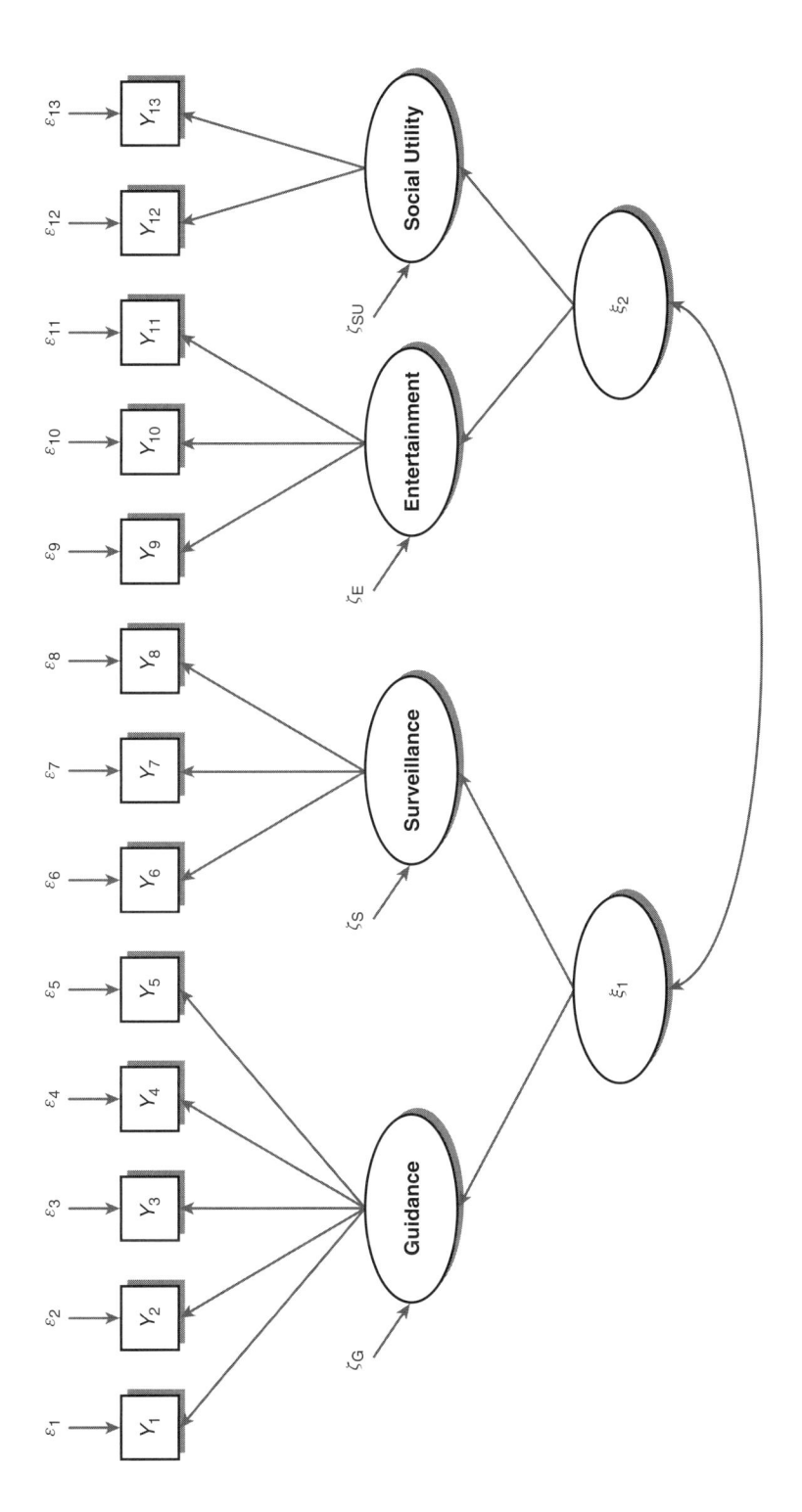

Figure 7.2 Alternative Higher-Order Kaye and Johnson (2002) CFA Measurement Model

Note: The higher-order latent variables are defined as exogenous, while all other variables are endogenous.

are then influenced by a more overarching higher-order latent variable, efficacy. Please take note of the fact that the only influence in the model on the lower-order efficacy latent variables comes from the higher-order efficacy latent variable. In other words, all that predicts efficacy in the model (i.e., anxiety and outcome expectancy) leads to only the higher-order efficacy latent variable, and the lower-order efficacy latent variables are no longer directly related to the final outcome variable, directness of talk. It is only the higher-order efficacy variable, not the lower-order efficacy variables, that serves as a predictor of the criterion variable in this model. Thus, with the introduction of higher-order latent variables come constraints on analyzing and discussing the direct effects of lower-order latent variables associated with the higher-order latent variable.

MODEL COMPARISONS

The comparison of the theoretical measurement models outlined earlier raises the broader issue of the testing of competing models. No one model is *the* model that reflects a given set of associations among variables (latent and/or observed). It is not uncommon to erroneously conclude that because a model fits the data well, it is the best or only model that reflects the true relationships among a given set of variables. However, there is always the possibility that alternative models exist that can fit the data just as well as or better than what has been originally theorized (Mueller, 1997).

Nested models. The ideal setting for testing competing models is the comparison of nested models. Two models are nested if "one is the subset of the other" (Kline, 1998, p. 131). When models are nested, communication researchers can conduct a direct comparison of these models using the χ^2-difference test. The test is self-explanatory in that a researcher compares the change in the χ^2-distributed test statistic across the tested models relative to the difference in degrees of freedom retained in the competing models. If the difference in χ^2 estimates is larger than the critical value associated with the difference in degrees of freedom, then the model with the lower χ^2 estimate is deemed to retain a statistically significant better fit with the data. The χ^2-difference test can be used only when a researcher is comparing nested models (in this sense, it is conceptually comparable to testing increment to *R*-squared for blocks of variables in hierarchical regression model testing).

Nonnested models. If the competing models are not nested, then the researcher must use descriptive measures of model fit (rather than inferential tests) to compare which model is a better fit with the data (see discussion of model fit below). The latter process does not offer a direct empirical test of which model is better and should be approached with

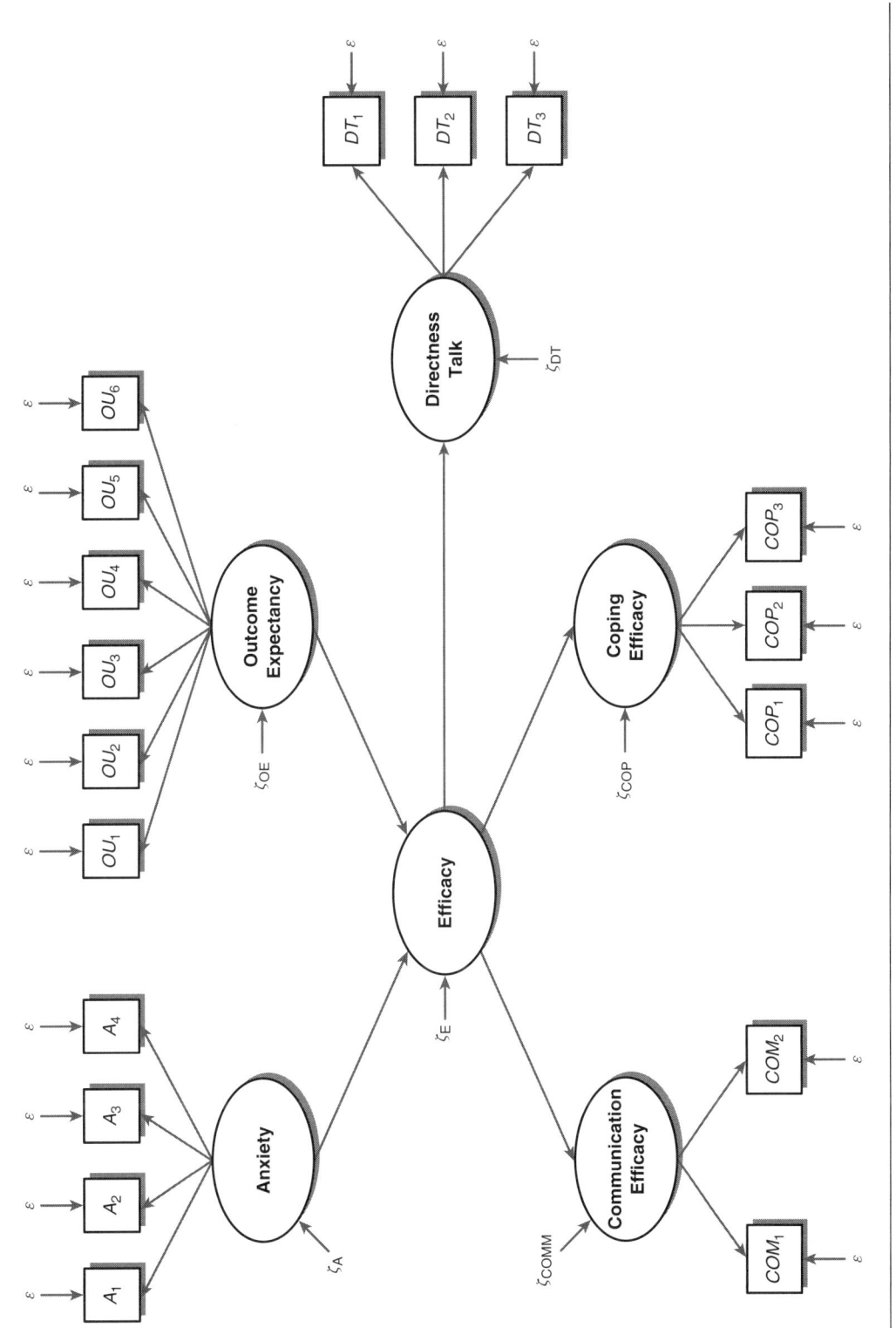

Figure 7.3 Portion of Afifi et al.'s (2006) Endogenous Decision to Talk Structural Equation Model

some caution. Typically, to claim better model fit within a given data set, fit would have to be consistently superior across a wide variety of fit statistics. Moreover, if a "rejected" model still has adequate fit, it in fact remains viable. Perhaps in another data set it would prove to be the better-fitting model. The tentative nature of such comparisons and the need for replication should at the least be acknowledged in interpretation and discussion of results. As Cohen, Cohen, West, and Aiken (2003) state, "There is no substitute for replication for increasing one's confidence in the findings" (p. 475).

Parsimony. The issue of competing models having an equal ability to achieve adequate fit with the same data raises some larger issues for social scientific theory building in general (MacCallum, Wegener, Uchino, & Fabrigar, 1993) and communication theory building in particular. Chaffee and Berger (1987) highlight the criterion of parsimony as being of value for the building of strong communication theory. William of Ockham (c. 1327) argued that "plurality should not be posited without necessity." Basically, when judging a host of different theoretical claims, the simplest statement will most likely be the best. The principle of parsimony has also been applied to the testing of SEM-based measurement models (Marsh & Hau, 1998), with an argument being made for simple models being more theoretically advanced than complex structures. Dillard (2002) has stressed the need for greater simplicity in the structural equation models being tested in the communication sciences, and we concur that more parsimonious models will best aid theory building.

RELIABILITY AND VALIDITY: A CAUTIONARY TALE

Communication researchers should recognize that the use of SEM for the construction and testing of measurement models raises a much broader set of questions about the assumptions we have come to take for granted of what makes for good measurement. Bollen and Lennox (1991) outline that our traditional conventions for the study of measurement (e.g., internal consistency of construct indicators, within-construct correlations need to be greater than between-construct correlations) should not be treated as unqualified conventions. These researchers conclude that "traditional measures of reliability and the examination of the correlation matrix of indicators are so ingrained" that we have forgotten that these traditional means of assessing reliability are not the solution for all measurement issues (p. 312). However, caution must be given to any discarding of our discipline's traditional assessments of reliability (e.g., Cronbach's α), and Bollen and Lennox (1991) echo this sentiment. With the use of SEM comes new perspectives on the study of measurement, but we argue for the need to report traditional reliability assessments of all indices. The reporting of a properly fitted CFA measurement model offers one type of empirical insight on the state of measurement reliability in a given study, but researchers should also report traditional estimates of index reliability. To some degree, SEM-based CFA offers communication researchers a brave new world for the study of measurement, but the discipline should proceed with caution as it navigates this new arena. One way in which to proceed with caution is to not throw the baby out with the bathwater in terms of traditional assessments of reliability that have served the communication sciences well for many years.

The introduction of latent variables in SEM-based CFA raises validity concerns as well. Cliff (1983) was one of the first to raise the issue of whether the latent variables described by various researchers are really measuring what they are supposed to be measuring. As Bollen (1989) has conceded, "Often the concept that the latent variable represents is not clearly defined and not enough attention is given to tests of measurement validity" (p. 79). If researchers do not have a strong conceptual foundation for their latent variables, then validity becomes a central concern. As a result, an SEM-based CFA should not be undertaken unless researchers have a solid theoretical understanding for their variables built from the process of meaning analysis (see Chaffee, 1991). In terms of assessing the content validity of a concept, "We need measures that fully represent its dimensions" (Bollen, 1989, p. 186). Each dimension of a concept should be represented by one or more indicators. Researchers should also engage in the testing of the construct validity of their concepts (Bollen, 1989). Construct validity deals with whether a given latent variable relates to other variables in a manner that is consistent with theory. Researchers can also empirically assess more specialty forms of validity like convergent and discriminant validity through the use of multitrait, multimethod (MTMM) matrix models (see Kenny & Kashy, 1992). The communication sciences need more direct testing and assessment of the validity of latent variables, and researchers should engage in such practice. If a given data set does not allow for a proper assessment of validity of latent variables, then researchers may not wish to engage in the use of SEM to conduct a CFA. At the very least, validity concerns should be raised as potential limitations of a given study.

WHEN TO CONDUCT A CFA

First, researchers must have a strong theoretical rationale in arguing for a specific number of latent variables and in outlining detailed associations between various observable and latent variables. Second, there is a need for researchers to have a firm conceptual grasp of their potential latent variables and for some degree of certainty to exist that each dimension of a given latent variable is represented within a list of observable measures. Third, a CFA ideal would be for researchers to retain at least three observable indictors for each latent variable (see Cliff, 1983), but this rule is only an ideal.[6] It may be the case that in some instances the best conceptualization of a latent variable consists of just two dimensions (e.g., dimensions of exposure and attention for latent variable of media use). Researchers should not allow the analytical ideal to trump theory, but CFA models at the very least need to be properly identified. Fourth, as with any other analytic tool, researchers should assess their data relative to a set of statistical assumptions associated with SEM (e.g., sample size, multivariate normality; see Ullman [2001] for brief discussion of statistical assumptions associated with SEM), and whether the breaking of these assumptions is warranted or allowable, whether any data transformations are necessary, or whether the analyses can be run at all.

Structural Models

Whereas measurement models establish the relations between measured variables and their unobserved latent constructs, structural models are designed to test theoretical relations between multiple constructs. A structural model is, in essence, a path model where variables are hypothesized to have influence on other variables in the model. An example of the use of SEM purely for the study of structural relationships among variables can be found in Scheufele and Shah's (2000) study of personality strength and social capital. The Scheufele and Shah model looks at multiple paths of influence originating with political interest and personality strength, respectively, and concluding with civic engagement. The list of mediators between the former independent variables and the latter dependent variable include television hard news use, newspaper hard news use, social trust, and life satisfaction. A portion of the Scheufele and Shah model is outlined in Figure 7.4. Interest in politics directly influences television hard news use, which then influences newspaper hard news use, and newspaper consumption has a direct effect on civic engagement. In addition to this three-step process of indirect influence, interest in politics has a direct effect on civic engagement. So, the overall influence of interest in politics on civic engagement consists of both a direct and an indirect effect. The Scheufele and Shah model represents a typical model used to study a set of associations among a series of variables that produces multiple processes of influence.

Most importantly, the structural relationships contained within any structural equation model are influenced in profound ways by the nature of the model constructed by the researcher. Specifically, structural relationships are most directly affected by how a researcher chooses to address measurement error. Communication scientists do this by using one of three model types: the observable-variable model, the latent-composite

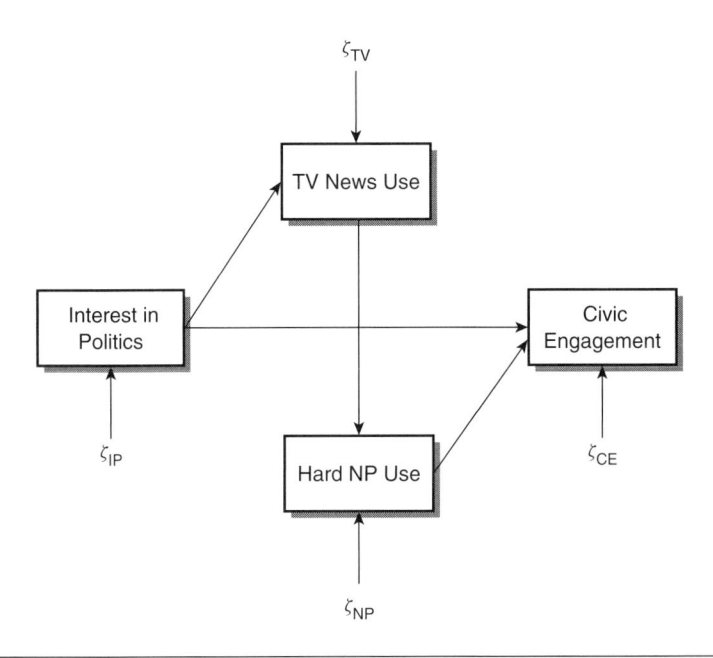

Figure 7.4 Portion of Scheufele and Shah's (2000) Civic Engagement Structural Equation Model

model, or the hybrid model (Holbert & Stephenson, 2002). Each model type reflects a different set of associations between observable variables, latent variables (potentially), and the measurement error that exists within each of these variable types. We offer below a summary of the three model types and examples of each from the communication literature in order to illustrate how these models are utilized in the discipline.

TYPES OF STRUCTURAL MODELS

Observable variable. The observable-variable model consists of additive indices (typically created in SPSS or SAS) or single-item measures. Scheufele and Shah's (2000) work is reflective of an observable-variable model. In this model type, the measurement error associated with each observable variable resides directly within the observable variable. Subsequently, this error has a direct effect on the structural relationships that exist between variables in the structural equation model.

It is important to recognize that the use of observable variables in SEM can attenuate path estimates considerably (Bollen, 1989). A good example of the potential for an attenuated path estimate in an observable-variable structural equation model is found in Nisbet, Scheufele, Shanahan, Moy, Brossard, and Lewenstein (2002). Nisbet et al. were studying mass media effects on individual-level perceptions of science. In particular, these scholars were focusing on the dependent variables of personal reservations about science and internal beliefs about the promise of science. One relationship analyzed in their observable-variable model leads from an eight-item additive index for procedural science knowledge to a four-item additive index representative of reservations about science. Both additive indices retain reliability estimates that are low, procedural science knowledge ($\alpha = .68$) and reservations about science ($\alpha = .54$). The path estimate for this relationship is found to be statistically significant. However, this significant path estimate is severely underestimating the true relationship between these two variables due to the high levels of measurement error directly impacting the association between them. Assessing this relationship while taking into account the measurement error that exists within these two variables can be achieved only through the use of one of two forms of latent-variable modeling, latent composite or hybrid.

Latent composite. A latent-composite model is very similar to the observed-variable model, but the primary difference is that the observed-composite variable (i.e., additive index) is allowed to load on a latent variable. A researcher wishing to construct a latent-composite model needs to set the values for two types of paths in the model: (1) All paths leading from the latent variables to single observable variables are set at 1. (2) The error terms for the observable variables are set to $1 - \alpha$ multiplied by the variance of the observed variables (Bollen, 1989). The combination of these fixed estimates, in essence, removes from the latent variable the variance attributable to measurement error in the observable variable. The researcher can then analyze the structural relationships between latent variables while the paths are corrected for measurement error (i.e., corrected for attenuation).[7] As is the case with the observable-variable model, the latent-composite model is all about the structural relationships. There is no measurement model component to either model type. The only difference between the two model types is that the latent-composite model accounts for measurement error while the observed-variable model does not.

Pfau et al.'s (1997) study of processes involved in inoculation and the resistance to unwanted persuasive influence is an example of communication research using latent-composite modeling. These researchers tested competing processes of influence across the moderator variable of topic involvement (high, moderate, and low). Communication researchers reviewing this work can take note of a relationship between involvement and threat in the moderate topic involvement condition (see Figure 3, p. 207, of Pfau et al.'s article). Involvement is found to lead directly to threat in this model, and the path estimate reported by Pfau et al. corrects for attenuation. However, there also needs to be recognition of the fact that the path estimate found for this relationship in the latent-composite model would not deviate greatly from what would be found if Pfau et al. constructed an observable-variable model. In this particular instance, involvement is a six-item additive index with an extremely high reliability ($\alpha = .94$), and the same can be said of the five-item threat index ($\alpha = .96$). These high reliabilities reflect very little error that has to be extracted from the respective latent variables; thus there would be very little attenuation in the path estimate if Pfau et al. were to use an observable-variable model. Communication researchers should recognize how measurement error is affecting various path estimates, but there is also a need to be cognizant of when a latent-variable model may do little in terms of altering path estimates from what would be generated through the use of observable-variable modeling techniques.

Hybrid. The hybrid model is the only model type that combines measurement and structure, making the hybrid model type reflective of the SEM ideal. Once a researcher has established that a measurement model is consistent with the data, there is very little additional work required to include a structural component to the measurement model. The covaried relationships between the latent variables are discarded once a measurement model is established. Then, communication researchers insert the paths of influence between various latent variables in their model that reflect a series of hypotheses derived from theory. This process of first addressing measurement and then turning to structure is defined as the two-step approach to SEM (Anderson & Gerbing, 1988).[8] The primary advantage of using the two-step approach is that if a final hybrid model is not found to fit, whereas the original measurement model did fit the data, then communication researchers can point directly to the structural component of the model being problematic. Steps can then be undertaken through model respecification to address this structural issue.[9]

Caplan (2005) employed a hybrid model for his recent study of problematic Internet use.[10] The study focused on four latent variables: social control skill, preference for online social interaction, compulsive Internet use, and negative outcomes. It was advantageous for Caplan to use a hybrid model in this instance given that two of the four latent variables retained a fairly substantial amount of measurement error, with both the social interaction and negative outcome variables having a Cronbach's α of .76. The other two variables retained stronger reliabilities, but there was still error in these measures ($\alpha = .87$ for both social skill and problematic Internet use). If Caplan were to have used an observable-variable model, then each of his standardized path estimates would be reduced by roughly 20%.[11] This is no small discrepancy in path estimates between the hybrid and observable-variable models (see Stephenson & Holbert, 2003). The comparison of the Caplan models is a solid example of why researchers should recognize that the path estimates generated by a structural equation model are determined in large part by the nature of the structural model. Different model types serve different purposes for the communication researcher and are appropriate at different times, and consumers of

SEM-based analyses should also be critical consumers of which structural model type may do the best service for a particular research effort. In addition, authors using SEM should make an argument in their method section for why they have chosen to employ one model type versus another (see Holbert, 2004, for example of argument for the use of observable-variable models).

The use of latent variables in the structural model is perhaps the biggest statistical advantage to utilizing SEM for data analytic procedures (see Jöreskog, 1973), and we have stressed repeatedly that the communication sciences are underutilizing this analytic technique by continuing to employ only observable variables (Holbert & Stephenson, 2002; Stephenson & Holbert, 2003; Stephenson, Holbert, & Zimmerman, 2006). Using latent-variable analysis provides researchers the opportunity to extract measurement error in order to assess the unattenuated relationships between variables in the structural model. And as we know, "Random error of measurement distorts virtually every statistic computed in modern studies" (Schmidt & Hunter, 1996, pp. 199–200). It is unfortunate, then, that SEM is frequently misused by researchers who do not utilize latent variables when analyzing structural relationships.

LIMITATIONS OF HYBRID MODELING

Although hybrid modeling is the SEM ideal, communication researchers must recognize that it is a technique not without its limits. Most importantly, the pure hybrid model requires the use of multiple indicators for all latent variables within a given model. There are many instances when researchers are unable to meet this criterion (e.g., when conducting secondary analyses of existing data; see Holbert, 2004). When a researcher is employing the use of a number of single-item measures within a given model, then the use of an observable-variable model is more appropriate. Another analytical avenue to be explored when single-item measures dominate a given study would be to discard the use of SEM entirely and employ a form of ordinary least squares (OLS) multiple regression analysis.

In addition, the complexity of one's model can also influence whether a hybrid approach to SEM is appropriate (Cohen et al., 2003). If a given model contains a large number of latent variables (e.g., more than six or seven), and each latent variable is associated with multiple indicators, then the ability to achieve an adequate model fit becomes increasingly difficult. The blind use of hybrid modeling for these complex models may lead to the discarding of analyses that could aid theory building. Once again, researchers who are studying fairly complex communicative processes of influence may wish to turn to the use of OLS regression or a form of SEM that puts aside the measurement component (latent-variable modeling or observable-variable modeling). Overall, communication researchers need to work within the bounds of what their data and theory allow in terms of building structural models. The best structural equation models are those that recognize the strengths and limitations of a given modeling approach relative to the theories being tested and the data used for the analyses. Finally, SEM need not be the do all end all in analyses. As with any statistical technique, the use of SEM needs to be weighted against the use of other analytical procedures that may do a better job in addressing a given set of hypotheses or research questions.

RECURSIVE VERSUS NONRECURSIVE STRUCTURE

Structural equation models may be recursive or nonrecursive. Recursive models are most easily explained as models with unidirectional influences (i.e., they move from left to right only). By contrast, "Nonrecursive models contain reciprocal causation, feedback loops, or they have correlated disturbances" (Bollen, 1989, p. 83). Communication scholarship using SEM is overwhelmingly recursive. Less than 10% of all models analyzed by Holbert and Stephenson (2002) in their critical review of the use of SEM in the communication sciences were nonrecursive models.

Covaried disturbances. The most common form of nonrecursive model found in the field contains covaried disturbances. Two variables are often allowed to freely covary in a model when a significant, nonzero relationship exists between the two constructs and the researcher cannot determine the causal nature of the relationship between the two variables (e.g., Holbert, 2004). This type of nonrecursive model is the least theoretically interesting because it is most often created based on what a researcher does *not* know (i.e., nature of causal direction) rather than on what can be properly hypothesized. If a structural equation model retains a fair number of free paths that reflect covaried observable or latent variables, then communication researchers need to recognize what this type of model is telling them. This model is saying that there are many unknowns, and when there are many unknowns in a structural model, the researcher needs to reevaluate whether SEM is the right analytical tool.[12] In cases where there are a number of free covariances within the structural component of a model, we would advise the use of OLS-based regression path analysis to test a process of influence.

Reciprocal relationships and feedback loops. Nonrecursive structural models that hypothesize reciprocal relationships or feedback loops reflect greater theoretical sophistication. As we have stated in the past (e.g., Holbert & Stephenson, 2002), communication scientists have often made theoretical arguments that point to reciprocal relationships between variables (e.g., DeFleur & Ball-Rokeach, 1989; Palmgreen, 1984). However, there has been little movement toward the specification, estimation, and evaluation of structural models that match some of the discipline's more refined theoretical arguments. Communication researchers need to be aware that they can step outside the relatively limited scope of testing purely recursive models; SEM allows for the testing of more sophisticated theoretical arguments (see Skumanich & Kintsfather [1998] for an example of a communication-based structural model that contains a feedback loop).

Nonrecursive issues. Nonetheless, the discipline needs to be aware of when a structural model inappropriately moves from a recursive to a nonrecursive format. A good example of this can be found in Jones (2004) and her study of emotional support and comforting (see Figure 2, p. 352, of Jones's article). Jones tested a model where two variables (nonverbal immediacy and person centeredness) influence two covaried variables, helper competence (a latent variable) and affective improvement (an observable variable). There are pairs of paths leading from each predictor variable to the respective dependent variables. However, Jones also allows nonverbal immediacy to freely covary with one of the observable indicators (i.e., expressiveness) of the latent variable, helper competence (see Figure 7.5, top dotted curved line). In addition, person centeredness is also allowed to covary with one of the helper-competence observable variables, conversation management (see Figure 7.5, bottom dotted curved line). The Jones model is no longer recursive with the freeing of these two covariances. In addition, the structure becomes questionable because a predictor variable like nonverbal dependency is directly influencing the latent variable, helper competence, while *also* being nondirectionally associated with one of the latent variable's indicators, expressiveness. The same argument applies for the relationship between person centeredness and communication management. Jones argues that nonverbal immediacy leads to helper competence, but this causal relationship is placed into question with the covariance established between the former variable and one of the indicators of the latter latent variable. In short, there are instances when the creation of a nonrecursive model out of what was originally theorized to be a recursive model should raise red flags with communication researchers consuming SEM-based analyses.

Issues of reciprocal influence and feedback processes are, of course, better addressed in longitudinal data, for which SEM techniques (notably, latent growth models) are very well suited. These are addressed in Chapter 3 of this volume.

DIRECT AND INDIRECT EFFECTS (DECOMPOSITION OF EFFECTS)

In many ways, researchers using SEM have not fully considered communication as a *process* (Stephenson et al., 2006). Cudeck and Henly

Commentary on the Uses and Misuses of Structural Equation Modeling

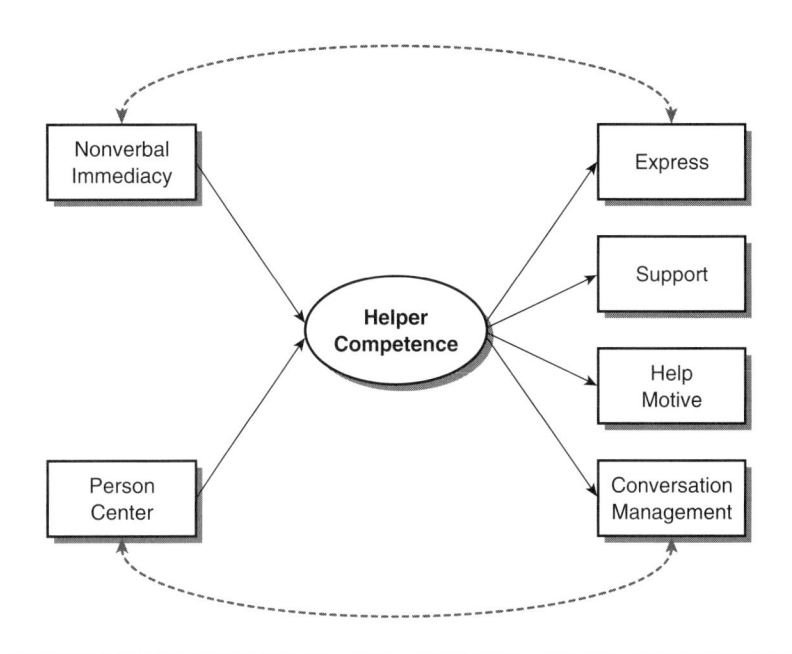

Figure 7.5 Portion of Jones's (2004) Helper Competence Structural Equation Model

(1988) stated that a model is a way to "operationalize a complex behavioral process that is intriguing but incompletely understood" (p. 517). As argued elsewhere, communication as a process can be more fully understood by considering both direct *and* indirect effects (Holbert & Stephenson, 2003). To date, however, most SEM-based communication research has focused on only direct effects, neglecting the important assumption that communication can work indirectly through other variables (McGuire, 1986). Our empirical assessment of communication research and the decomposition of effects revealed that only 14.4% of communication studies using SEM from 1995 through 2000 analyzed indirect effects. This focus on only direct effects is generally inconsistent with the theoretical foundations that drive much of our communication research. By overlooking the role of indirect effects, researchers miss the opportunity to fully estimate the overall influence of communication in a number of different contexts.

Therefore, we have encouraged scholars to decompose the effects (i.e., study the direct *and* indirect effects) in an SEM model in order to provide a deeper understanding of communication as a process. This helps move communication research beyond the study of direct effects only. For example, McLeod, Scheufele, and Moy (1999) studied the influence of newspaper public affairs use, television public affairs use, and interpersonal communication on institutional versus nontraditional forms of political participation. McLeod et al. (1999) determined that political interest in local politics directly influenced institutionalized political participation (Figure 1, p. 328). The direct effect was 0.21. Yet, political interest further influenced institutionalized participation indirectly through TV hard news consumption, interpersonal discussion, and newspaper hard news consumption. Hence, after examining the indirect effect of political interest through the various mass media and interpersonal channels, it was determined that the total effect on political participation increases to a total effect of 0.35. This total effect is almost double what an analysis of only the direct effect would produce. Moreover, the study sheds light on the relations among the mass media and interpersonal channels in a political context. A review of their model shows that TV hard news use influences newspaper hard news use both directly and indirectly through interpersonal discussion. Hence, various forms of communication can act as mediators of one another in a given model (Holbert, 2005b). McLeod et al.'s conclusions are far richer as a result of examining the direct *and* indirect effects of the media and interpersonal communication on political participation. For more on approaches to testing indirect effects, see Chapter 2 in this volume.

Model Fit

In addition to the uses and misuses of measurement and structural models that we have just outlined, inherently linked to the assessment of any type of model in SEM is the issue of model fit. Unfortunately, model fit is the Achilles' heel of SEM, largely because SEM experts have failed to reach consensus on a single index of fit (Hu & Bentler, 1995). This is particularly problematic for researchers in knowing *which* fit index or indices should be reported. It is not uncommon for SEM researchers to report a string of fit statistics without any reasoning behind their selection. While there remains some latitude in how to describe the fit of a model, there are also some fairly clear guidelines of what one should not report. Ultimately, our goal is to see greater consistency in the reporting of fit statistics in SEM-based analyses reported by communication researchers.

As it stands, the research on the adequacy of each fit index, in addition to a proposed cutoff value, remains dynamic. While "golden rules" or "rules of thumb" for fit indices and their cutoff values exist (Hu & Bentler, 1999; Marsh, Hau, & Wen, 2004), a number of other issues (e.g., sample size, model complexity, violations of nonnormality) influence fit indices in one fashion or another, making it difficult for scholars to put a finger on which index is a most accurate fit of their model (Browne & Cudeck, 1993; Hu & Bentler, 1995; Tanaka, 1993).

Until the late 1990s when Hu and Bentler (1998, 1999) published their extensive review of fit indices, there was little consistency in which fit indices were believed to "best" describe the adequacy of the model to capture patterns observed in the data. From their simulation studies, Hu and Bentler (1999) proposed a "two-index" strategy with which to report model fit. When sample size falls below 250, Hu and Bentler (1999) recommended that researchers report the standardized root mean squared residual (SRMR) plus one other incremental fit index that reflects misspecification in the structural model, with the options being the Tucker-Lewis index (TLI), the Bollen 1989 (BL89), the relative noncentrality index (RNI), the comparative fit index (CFI), or Gamma Hat. Specifically, Hu and Bentler (1999) "recommend that practitioners use a cutoff value close to .95 for TLI (BL89, RNI, CFI, or Gamma Hat) in combination with a cutoff value close to .09 for SRMR to evaluate model fit" (p. 27). However, when sample size exceeds 250, the SRMR should be paired with the RMSEA (root mean squared error of approximation; Brown & Cudeck, 1993). In this case, the SRMR should be close to .09 and the RMSEA close to .06 or less.

Showing a desire for some consistency and direction, Hu and Bentler's recommendations were adopted fairly quickly into the literature. The honeymoon, however, was short, as other scholars came forth with limitations to Hu and Bentler's approach. For instance, Marsh, Hau, and Wen (2004) argued that the Hu and Bentler two-index strategy with cutoff criteria should not be overgeneralized, noting that the level of misspecification in Hu and Bentler's simulation studies was actually very minor.

Despite researchers' inability to agree on (a) which fit indices perform best, (b) cutoff values for these indices, and (c) when such indices should be used, there remains some consistency in this literature. Following Hoyle and Panter's (1995) recommendations, which remain timely, we recommend that authors report three indices. First, although there exist problems (as we discuss in detail in the next section), researchers should indicate the χ^2-distributed test statistic accompanied by degrees of freedom, the sample size, and the p-value. In Holbert and Stephenson (2002), we argued that the primary value of the χ^2-distributed test statistic is that we can determine the number of degrees of freedom in the model as a way of assessing whether the author has properly specified and reported the model. Similarly, Hoyle and Panter (1995) note that "the value of the statistic itself holds the most promise for the development of an index of fit for which the sampling distribution is known" (p. 167). Second, in terms of an absolute index of fit, we recommend the RMSEA (Browne & Cudeck, 1993; MacCallum & Austin, 2000). RMSEA is desirable because (a) it contains a built-in parsimony index, (b) the average misfit per degree of freedom is standardized, and, perhaps most importantly, (c) it has a known noncentral χ^2 distribution that does not have restrictive distributional assumptions. RMSEA values of .05 or less indicate good fit, .08 or less indicates marginal fit, and .09 and up indicate unacceptable fit. Note that the RMSEA should *always* include its 90% confidence interval, which is calculated by all the major SEM software packages. Third, in terms of an incremental index of fit (in that the specified model is compared to a superior alternative model), we recommend NNFI, CFI, or the RNI. The NNFI is not recommended when sample size is small. The RNI is a nonnormed version of CFI, in that RNI is not truncated at 0 (lower bound) and 1.00 (upper bound), but CFI is. Values above .90 are desired.

THE χ^2-DISTRIBUTED TEST STATISTIC

The use of the "χ^2 test" in SEM was made popular by Jöreskog (1969). The χ^2-distributed test statistic provided clarity as a decisional rule for the adequacy of a CFA because it was "free of the many subjective decisions that were historically associated with exploratory factor analysis" (Hu & Bentler, 1995, p. 77). Its popularity, however, was short-lived when researchers argued that the χ^2-distributed test statistic was influenced by sample size and model misspecification (Bentler, 1990; Lei & Lomax, 2005; Steiger & Lind, 1980), thereby signifying the beginning of the alternative fit indices we described above.

The "χ^2 test," or more accurately the χ^2-distributed test statistic, T, is problematic for several reasons. First, as sample size increases, so does the value of the χ^2-distributed test statistic. In some ways, this is paradoxical since it is often reported that large samples are desirable for estimation structural models. Although this is true, the size of one's sample will adversely affect the χ^2-distributed test statistic. Second, violations of multivariate normality can also be problematic for the χ^2-distributed test statistic. Most recently, Lei and Lomax (2005) revealed that the "χ^2 test" is the least robust of all fit indices for nonnormality, even with large sample sizes.

Aside from these issues, it is also difficult to get a nonsignificant χ^2 when one employs the hybrid approach for SEM that we outlined above (see also Stephenson & Holbert, 2003). As the number of parameters increase, it is increasingly difficult to reject the null model (Kaplan, 2000). Despite this information, we continue to recommend that researchers report the χ^2-distributed test statistic along with the same size and degrees of freedom.

Whereas fit statistics assess the "global fit" of the model, researchers are equally interested in the "local fit" of the relationships between variables. In measurement models, researchers are interested in knowing which items load poorly on the latent construct of interest as a way of pursuing the best way to measure something. In structural models, researchers desire information about the hypothesized relations between variables, their significance, and the implications for theory. To assess the "local fit," the output generated by the statistical program provides the statistical significance of either an item in measurement models or a path in structural models. Much as with conventional statistical tests, a significant relationship exists if the ratio of the parameter estimate to its standard error is

1.96 or greater. When relationships are not significant, the researcher is faced with a decision whether to retain these paths or make changes. That debate, of course, brings us full circle to model modification, which we addressed early in the chapter.

Conclusion

SEM is a data analytical tool that provides researchers with a tremendous amount of flexibility. Under most circumstances, this flexibility is an advantage to communication researchers in the pursuit of a deeper understanding of the theories that are the foundation for a line of research. At the same time, the flexibility has great potential to be misused. Specifically, we appeal to researchers to (a) understand the role of latent variables in both measurement and structural models and the implications of latent variables for model fit, degrees of freedom, and structural path coefficients; (b) push the limits of our knowledge about second-order factors, nonrecursive models, and decomposition of effects; (c) understand how implications of model comparisons influence theory building; and (d) appropriately assess the fit of measurement and structural models with multiple fit indices.

Our intent was to identify some of the ways SEM is beneficial in advancing knowledge about communication theories as well as ways SEM can be misused by researchers who fail to see the intricate nuances of this tool. Most importantly, a consistent theme in this chapter has been the importance of theory in the specification, estimation, and evaluation of structural equation models. With the increased marketing of SEM as an analytical tool and the ease of use of the more advanced SEM software packages has come the potential for researchers who are not well versed in this particular analytical technique to create and test models that are far from theoretically and analytically ideal (Mueller, 1997). Although increased technical and analytical proficiency will aid in reducing the ability of researchers to inflict damage on both themselves and the discipline, an equally strong SEM insurance policy comes in the form of a strong theoretical foundation established prior to even thinking about the construction of a model. Finally, SEM needs to be judged by researchers against other analytical procedures in determining how best to test a given set of hypotheses and research questions. SEM is not made to address all that we posit as communication researchers, nor is it often the best tool for a given job. Communication researchers must remain steadfast in placing SEM in its proper context and resist the temptation to unnecessarily "structural equationize" their own research or the likelihood for misuse will begin to outweigh the proper use of this technique in our collective cause of theory building.

Notes

1. See Bollen (1989, p. 232) for a more advanced discussion of the relative limitations of EFA when compared to CFA.

2. The operationalization of media use as a latent variable consisting of two observable variables, exposure and attention, is reflective of a single conceptualization. This single conceptualization does not preclude the existence of alternative conceptualizations, and, as a result, alternative operationalizations of media use. For example, some researchers may argue for distinct exposure and attention observable measures, with no latent variable, while others may argue for a single exposure latent variable consisting of multiple exposure items to various media forms and a single latent attention variable with multiple observable attention items for various media forms. SEM allows for any of these manifestations of media use to be employed by a researcher, but it is up to the researcher to make strong theoretical claims for a particular set of associations between these variables, latent and/or observed.

3. It is important that all communication researchers have a firm understanding of the degrees of freedom associated with various structural equation models. Holbert and Stephenson (2002) brought attention to the fact that roughly 10% of the structural equation models offered in communication journals from 2000 to 2005 provided improperly reported degrees of freedom relative to what was being communicated in the journal articles. One of the first tasks for any consumer of an SEM-based analysis is to count the degrees of freedom of a model. If the reported degrees of freedom do not match that which can be calculated by the consumer of the article in question, then there are other parameters being estimated that have not been properly reported.

4. EQS also supplies multivariate LM estimates.

5. In addition, a solid fit for a model addresses only the question of whether a single theorized model appears to match a given data set. Model fit does not signal whether the model is representative of reality (i.e., the communicative act at play beyond the research study). As Mueller (1997) has stated, "An unfortunate truth, however, is that empirical fit indices cannot confirm the model-reality link, only address the data-model consistency question" (p. 361).

6. However, the retaining of three observable variables per latent construct in certain measurement models is necessary to ensure proper model identification (see Cliff, 1983).

7. Although the process of correcting for attenuation is promoted in this chapter, this particular procedure is not without its critics. Communication researchers can look to Boorsboom and Mellenbergh (2002), an article that outlines potential problems with the statistical assumptions associated with correcting for measurement error.

8. Communication researchers may also wish to review literature on a more recent approach to model building, the four-step approach (see Mulaik & Millsap, 2000).

9. All points raised with regard to model respecification of a measurement model apply to the respecification of the structural components of a model.

10. Caplan (2005) does use a series of three composite variables as observable variables associated with the latent variable, social control skill.

However, his final model functions in all intents and purposes as a hybrid model given that there are multiple indicators associated with each latent variable and no path estimate values are set in a manner that befits a latent-composite model.

11. The authors would like to thank Dr. Caplan for granting access to his data to allow for the testing of an observable-variable model of the proposed structural relationships outlined in his work.

12. There is no golden rule for when a model retains too many covaried relationships. The number of allowable covaried structural paths is proportionate to the total number of free structural paths in the model. If the number of free paths representing covariances makes up a disproportionate number of total free structural paths in a model, then the researcher may wish to rethink the use of SEM.

Appendix

Kaye and Johnson (2002) observable gratifications items and factors

Guidance

1. To help me decide how to vote
2. To help me decide about important issues
3. To see what a candidate will do if elected
4. To judge personal qualities of candidates
5. For unbiased viewpoints

Surveillance

6. Because information is easy to obtain
7. To find specific political information I'm looking for
8. To keep up with main issues of the day

Entertainment

9. Because it is entertaining
10. Because it helps me to relax
11. Because it is exciting

Social Utility

12. To give me something to talk about with others
13. To use as ammunition in arguments with others

References

Afifi, W., Morgan, S. E., Stephenson, M. T., Morse, C., Harrison, T., Reichert, T., & Long, S. (2006). Examining the decision to talk with family about organ donation: Applying the theory of motivated information management. *Communication Monographs, 73,* 188–215.

Alwin, D. F., & Hauser, R. M. (1975). The decomposition of effects in path analysis. *American Sociological Review, 40,* 37–47.

Anderson, J. C., & Gerbing, D. W. (1988). Structural equation modeling in practice: A review and recommended two-step approach. *Psychological Bulletin, 10,* 411–423.

Bentler, P. M. (1990). Comparative fit indices in structural models. *Psychological Bulletin, 107,* 238–246.

Bollen, K. A. (1989). *Structural equations with latent variables.* New York: John Wiley & Sons.

Bollen, K. A., & Lennox, R. (1991). Conventional wisdom on measurement: A structural equation perspective. *Psychological Bulletin, 110,* 305–314.

Boorsboom, D., & Mellenbergh, G. J. (2002). True scores, latent variables, and constructs: A comment on Schmidt and Hunter. *Intelligence, 30,* 505–514.

Boorsboom, D., Mellenbergh, G. J., & van Heerden, J. (2003). The theoretical status of latent variables. *Psychological Review, 110,* 203–219.

Boster, F. J. (2002). On making progress in communication science. *Human Communication Research, 28,* 473–490.

Browne, M. W., & Cudeck, R. (1993). Alternative ways of assessing model fit. In K. A. Bollen & J. S. Long (Eds.), *Testing structural equation models* (pp. 136–162). Newbury Park, CA: Sage.

Caplan, S. E. (2005). A social skill account of problematic internet use. *Journal of Communication, 55,* 721–736.

Cappella, J. N. (1975). An introduction to the literature of causal modeling. *Human Communication Research, 1,* 362–377.

Cappella, J. N. (1980). Structural equation modeling: An introduction. In P. M. Monge & J. N. Cappella (Eds.), *Multivariate techniques in human communication research* (pp. 57–110). New York: Academic Press.

Cappella, J. N. (1991). Review of *Theories of Human Communication* (3rd ed.) by S. W. Littlejohn. *Communication Theory, 1,* 165–171.

Chaffee, S. H. (1991). *Communication concepts 1: Explication.* Newbury Park, CA: Sage.

Chaffee, S. H., & Berger, C. R. (1987). What communication scientists do. In C. R. Berger & S. H. Chaffee (Eds.), *Handbook of communication science* (pp. 99–122). Newbury Park, CA: Sage.

Chaffee, S. H., & Schleuder, J. (1986). Measurement and effects of attention to media news. *Human Communication Research, 13,* 76–107.

Cheung, D. (2000). Evidence of a single second-order factor in student ratings of teaching effectiveness. *Structural Equation Modeling, 7,* 442–460.

Cliff, N. (1983). Some cautions concerning the application of causal modeling methods. *Multivariate Behavioral Research, 18,* 115–126.

Cohen, J., Cohen, P., West, S. G., & Aiken, L. S. (2003). *Applied multiple regression/correlation analysis for the behavioral sciences* (3rd ed.). Mahwah, NJ: Lawrence Erlbaum Associates.

Cudeck, R. (1989). Analysis of correlation matrices using covariance structure models. *Psychological Bulletin, 105,* 317–327.

Cudeck, R., & Henly, S. J. (1988). Multiplicative models and MTMM matrices. *Journal of Educational Statistics, 13,* 131–147.

DeFleur, M. L., & Ball-Rokeach, S. (1989). *Theories of mass communication* (5th ed.). New York: Longman.

Dillard, J. P. (2002). Structural equation modeling and the virtues of simplicity. In M. Pfau (Chair), *Structural equation modeling in mass communication.* Symposium conducted at the annual meeting of the National Communication Association, New Orleans, LA.

Duncan, O. D. (1975). *Introduction to structural equation models.* New York: Academic Press.

Dunnette, M. D. (1978). Fads, fashions, and folderol in psychology. In R. Dubin, *Theory building* (Rev. ed., pp. 268–280). New York: Free Press.

Fink, E. L., & Noell, J. J. (1975). Interpersonal communication following the Wallace shooting. *Human Communication Research, 1,* 159–167.

Hägglund, G. (2001). Milestones in the history of factor analysis. In R. Cudeck, S. Du Toit, & D. Sörbom (Eds.), *Structural equation modeling: Present and future: A festschrift in honor of Karl Jöreskog* (pp. 11–38). Chicago: Scientific Software International.

Hayduk, L. A. (1996). *LISREL: Issues, debates, and strategies.* Baltimore, MD: Johns Hopkins University Press.

Holbert, R. L. (2004). Political talk radio, perceived fairness, and the establishment of President George W. Bush's political legitimacy. *Harvard International Journal of Press/Politics, 9,* 12–27.

Holbert, R. L. (2005a). Back to basics: Revisiting, resolving, and expanding some of the fundamental issues of political communication research. *Political Communication, 22,* 511–514.

Holbert, R. L. (2005b). Intramedia mediation: The cumulative and complementary effects of news media use. *Political Communication, 22,* 447–462.

Holbert, R. L., & Stephenson, M. T. (2002). Structural equation modeling in the communication sciences, 1995–2000. *Human Communication Research, 28,* 531–551.

Holbert, R. L., & Stephenson, M. T. (2003). The importance of analyzing indirect effects in media effects research: Testing for mediation in structural equation modeling. *Journal of Broadcasting & Electronic Media, 47,* 553–569.

Hoyle, R. H. (1991). Evaluating measurement models in clinical research: Covariance structure analysis of latent variable models of self-conception. *Journal of Consulting and Clinical Psychology, 59,* 67–76.

Hoyle, R. H., & Panter, A. T. (1995). Writing about structural equation models. In R. H. Hoyle (Ed.), *Structural equation modeling: Comments, issues, and applications* (pp. 158–176). Thousand Oaks, CA: Sage.

Hu, L., & Bentler, P. M. (1995). Evaluating model fit. In R. H. Hoyle (Ed.), *Structural equation modeling: Concepts, issues, and applications* (pp. 76–99). Thousand Oaks, CA: Sage.

Hu, L., & Bentler, P. M. (1998). Fit indices in covariance structure modeling: Sensitivity under parameterized model misspecification. *Psychological Methods, 3,* 424–453.

Hu, L., & Bentler, P. M. (1999). Cutoff criteria for fit indices in covariance structure analysis: Conventional criteria versus new alternatives. *Structural Equation Modeling, 6,* 1–55.

Jones, S. (2004). Putting the person into person-centered and immediate emotional support: Emotional change and perceived helper competence as outcomes of comforting in helping situations. *Communication Research, 31,* 338–360.

Jöreskog, K. G. (1969). A general approach to confirmatory maximum likelihood factor analysis. *Psychometrika, 36,* 183–202.

Jöreskog, K. G. (1973). A general method for estimating a linear structural equation system. In S. Goldberger & O. D. Duncan (Eds.), *Structural equation models in the social sciences* (pp. 85–112). New York: Seminar Press.

Jöreskog, K. G., & Wold, H. (1982). *Systems under indirect observation, part I and part II.* Amsterdam: North-Holland.

Kaplan, D. (2000). *Structural equation modeling: Foundations and extensions.* Thousand Oaks, CA: Sage.

Kaplan, D., & Elliott, P. R. (1997). A model-based approach to validating education indicators using multilevel structural equation modeling. *Journal of Educational and Behavioral Statistics, 22,* 323–348.

Kaye, B. K., & Johnson, T. J. (2002). Online and in the know: Uses and gratifications of the Web for political information. *Journal of Broadcasting & Electronic Media, 46,* 54–71.

Kenny, D. A., & Kashy, D. A. (1992). Analysis of the multitrait-multimethod matrix by confirmatory factor analysis. *Psychological Bulletin, 112,* 165–172.

Kline, R. B. (1998). *Principles and practice and structural equation modeling.* New York: Guilford.

Lei, M., & Lomax, R. G. (2005). The effect of varying degrees of nonnormality in structural equation modeling. *Structural Equation Modeling, 12,* 1–27.

Levine, T. R. (2005). Confirmatory factor analysis and scale validation in communication research. *Communication Research Reports, 22,* 335–338.

MacCallum, R. C. (1995). Model specification: Procedures, strategies, and related issues. In R. H. Hoyle (Ed.), *Structural equation modeling: Concepts, issues, and applications* (pp. 16–36). Thousand Oaks, CA: Sage.

MacCallum, R. C., & Austin, J. T. (2000). Applications of structural equation modeling in psychological research. *Annual Review of Psychology, 51,* 201–226.

MacCallum, R. C., Roznowski, M., & Necowitz, L. B. (1992). Model modification in covariance structure analysis: The problem of capitalization on chance. *Psychological Bulletin, 111,* 490–504.

MacCallum, R. C., Wegener, D. T., Uchino, B. N., & Fabrigar, L. R. (1993). The problem of equivalent models in applications of covariance structure analysis. *Psychological Bulletin, 114,* 185–199.

Marsh, H. W., & Hau, K.-T. (1998). Is parsimony always desirable: Response to Hoyle, Sivo & Wilson, Markus, Mulaik, Tweedledee, Tweedledum, the Cheshire Cat, and others. *Journal of Experimental Education, 66,* 274–285.

Marsh, H. W., Hau, K. T., & Wen, Z. (2004). In search of golden rules: Comment on hypothesis testing approaches to setting cutoff values for fit indices and dangers in overgeneralising Hu & Bentler's (1999) findings. *Structural Equation Modeling, 11,* 320–341.

McGuire, W. J. (1986). The myth of massive media impact: Savagings and salvagings. In G. Comstock (Ed.), *Public communication and behavior* (pp. 173–257). New York: Academic Press.

McLeod, J. M., & Becker, L. B. (1981). The uses and gratifications approach. In D. D. Nimmo & K. R. Sanders (Eds.), *Handbook of political communication* (pp. 67–99). Beverly Hills, CA: Sage.

McLeod, J. M., Scheufele, D. A., & Moy, P. (1999). Community, communication, and participation: The role of mass media and interpersonal discussion in local political participation. *Political Communication, 16,* 315–336.

Mueller, R. O. (1997). Structural equation modeling: Back to basics. *Structural Equation Modeling, 4,* 353–369.

Mulaik, S. A., & Millsap, R. E. (2000). Doing the four-step right. *Structural Equation Modeling: A Multidisciplinary Journal, 7,* 36–73.

Nisbet, M. C., Scheufele, D. A., Shanahan, J., Moy, P., Brossard, D., & Lewenstein, B. V. (2002). Knowledge, reservations, and promise? A media effects model for public perceptions of science and technology. *Communication Research, 29,* 584–608.

Palmgreen, P. (1984). Uses and gratifications: A theoretical perspective. *Communication Yearbook, 8,* 20–55.

Pfau, M., Tusing, K. J., Koerner, A. F., Lee, W., Godbold, L. C., Penaloza, L. J., et al. (1997). Enriching the inoculation construct: The role of critical components in the process of resistance. *Human Communication Research, 24,* 187–215.

Raykov, T., & Marcoulides, G. A. (1999). On desirability of parsimony in structural equation model selection. *Structural Equation Modeling, 6,* 292–300.

Raykov, T., & Marcoulides, G. A. (2000). A method for comparing completely standardized solutions in multiple groups. *Structural Equation Modeling, 7,* 292–308.

Reynolds, P. D. (1971). *A primer in theory construction.* New York: Macmillan.

Rosenthal, R. (1991). Replication in behavioral research. In J. W. Neuliep (Ed.), *Replication in the social sciences* (pp. 1–30). Newbury Park, CA: Sage.

Russell, D., & Cutrona, C. E. (1991). Social support, stress, and depressive symptoms among the elderly: Test of a process model. *Psychology and Aging, 6,* 190–201.

Scheufele, D. A., & Shah, D. V. (2000). Personality strength and social capital: The role of dispositional and informational variables in the production of civic participation. *Communication Research, 27,* 107–131.

Schmidt, F. L., & Hunter, J. E. (1996). Measurement error in psychological research: Lessons from 26 research scenarios. *Psychological Methods, 1,* 199–223.

Skumanich, S. A., & Kintsfather, D. P. (1998). Individual media dependency relations within television shopping programming: A causal model reviewed and revised. *Communication Research, 25,* 200–219.

Sörbom, D. (2001). Karl Jöreskog and LISREL: A personal story. In R. Cudeck, S. Du Toit, & D. Sörbom (Eds.), *Structural equation modeling: Present and future: A festschrift in honor of Karl Jöreskog* (pp. 3–10). Chicago: Scientific Software International.

Steiger, J. H., & Lind, J. C. (1980, May). *Statistically-based tests for the number of common factors.* Paper presented at the annual meeting of the Psychometric Society, Iowa City, IA.

Stephenson, M. T., & Holbert, R. L. (2003). A Monte Carlo simulation of observable-versus latent-variable structural equation modeling techniques. *Communication Research, 30,* 332–354.

Stephenson, M. T., Holbert, R. L., & Zimmerman, R. S. (2006). Structural equation modeling in health communication. *Health Communication, 20,* 159–168.

Tanaka, J. S. (1993). Multifacted conceptions of fit in structural equation models. In K. A. Bollen & J. S. Long (Eds.), *Testing structural equation models* (pp. 10–39). Newbury Park, CA: Sage.

Thurstone, L. L. (1947). *Multiple-factor analysis.* Chicago: University of Chicago Press.

Ullman, J. B. (2001). Structural equation modeling. In B. G. Tabachnick & L. S. Fidell (Eds.), *Using Multivariate Statistics* (4th ed., pp. 653–771). Boston: Allyn & Bacon.

Multilevel Modeling

Studying People in Contexts

Hee Sun Park

William P. Eveland, Jr.

Robert Cudeck

Communication research often involves people interacting within contexts such as dyads or small groups, social networks, organizations, communities, media systems, or cultures, in which individuals' cognitions, attitudes, and behaviors are not independent of one another's. This interdependence, however, can pose difficulties for data analysis, because an assumption of many of the most commonly used statistics in communication research is that observations are statistically independent. Many of the methodologies for gathering the data to which statistics are applied—random-digit dial telephone survey research may be the best example—do in fact produce generally independent observations. But the assumption of independent observations is not always viable, and many of the most interesting questions that communication researchers would like to ask require the understanding of individuals operating within certain contexts in which independence cannot be assumed.

This chapter will discuss a group of techniques most generally referred to as "multilevel modeling" (MLM) designed not only to account for nonindependence of observations but actually to model the effect of various sources of nonindependence as an interesting and important component of the analysis. We begin by making the case for the need to think about and analyze data using models that account for variation across levels of analysis. This case is made specifically for the field of communication. We then discuss the central concepts in MLM and the capabilities of the technique. Next, we devote considerable effort to demonstrating the applicability of MLM across the various domains of communication research, including interpersonal, small-group, organizational, and mass communication. This section can be thought of as a call for the application of MLM as a more appropriate means of addressing old questions and as a heuristic device for leading us to new questions that have not been sufficiently addressed in prior research. We close with a discussion of software programs for MLM and an empirical example of an MLM analysis in the context of communication.

Why Multilevel Modeling Is Important in Communication

The field of communication is, in a sense, made for the use of multilevel modeling. Paisley (1984) argues that communication is a "variable" field rather than a "level" field. Level fields, such as biology, psychology, and sociology, tend to be oriented at a single level of analysis while focusing on all relevant variables at that level of analysis. By contrast, variable fields focus on a particular subset of variables across multiple levels. Paisley argues that communication research, systems research, and cybernetics are the fundamental (i.e., content-free) variable fields, and political science, economics, business, and education make up some of the higher-order (i.e., contextualized) variable fields.

It is the fundamental nature of a variable field to cut across levels. Indeed, this is part of the added value of variable fields compared to segregated research on a given variable within separate level fields. That is, the micro level processes pertaining to communication can be addressed within psychology, the interaction processes pertaining to communication can be addressed within social psychology, and the macro-level processes pertaining to communication can be addressed within sociology. One structural advantage of the field of communication is our ability to integrate theories and research across these levels of analysis, with a focus on communication processes specifically. By doing so, the field of communication can provide a unique perspective beyond those offered by more traditional fields.

Moreover, there is good reason for communication researchers to pursue theorizing and research across levels of analysis. Communication has been considered a fractured discipline due to the historical segregation of mass and interpersonal communication research (see Delia, 1987; Rogers, 1994). Efforts to truly integrate theories and data across the interpersonal–small-group–organizational–media divide are uncommon. However, clearly these contexts for communication each have implications for one another. For instance, *organizations* and their routines influence the content of mass *media* (Gans, 1979), individuals may select media content for *group* identity purposes (Abrams, Eveland, & Giles, 2003), and individuals discuss the content of the media with one another in *interpersonal* and small-group settings (Walsh, 2004).

The discussion regarding the need to consider variables and relationships that cross levels became prominent in communication decades ago (e.g., Chaffee & Berger, 1987; Dimmick & Coit, 1982; McLeod, Pan, & Rucinski, 1995; Pan & McLeod, 1991; Price, 1988) and continues to have considerable relevance today (Slater, Snyder, & Hayes, 2006). In order to conduct empirical research in communication that cuts across level fields, researchers must gather data at multiple levels of analysis. Once the data are in hand, more sophisticated statistical tools than are typically employed in communication today are necessary to account for the multiple levels of data. This is where the multilevel modeling approach comes into play.

Multilevel Modeling: A Statistical Tool for Analyzing Data Across Levels

MLM is a statistical technique that permits the modeling of variance not just at a single level but at two or more levels simultaneously. That is, it permits the apportioning of variance such that variance is identified as that which is *between* macro units such as dyads or neighborhoods and that which is *within* macro units (e.g., between individuals within the same macro-level unit). Then, variables measured at each different level may be employed to account for variance that exists in a given outcome variable. For instance, macro-level variables such as the length of a romantic relationship or the quality of a community's newspaper, as well as micro-level variables such as gender or frequency of newspaper reading, may be used to account for micro-level variation in some micro-level outcomes (e.g., relational satisfaction, community attachment). Macro-level predictors may also be used to account for variation in the strength or direction of relationships between micro-level predictors and micro-level outcomes (so-called cross-level interactions).[1]

The need for MLM is based on the notion of nonindependent observations.[2] Standard ordinary least squares (OLS) regression modeling requires the assumption that each observation is drawn randomly from some larger population and that each observation is statistically independent of the next. This latter assumption, in practice, is violated frequently. Often data employed in communication are in one way or another nonindependent due to some form or another of nesting within higher-level units. For instance, most national survey data gathered by face-to-face interviewing—the General Social Survey and the American National Election Study are two prominent examples—employ multistage cluster sampling approaches instead of the "cleaner" but also dramatically more expensive simple random sampling (SRS). The purpose of clustering is, at least in part, to reduce costs associated with enumerating the whole U.S. population (which would be necessary for SRS), plus travel and time costs involved in interviewing respondents in the absence of geographic clustering. So researchers first randomly sample, for instance, metropolitan areas, and then within metropolitan areas census tracts are randomly sampled, then households, and finally adults within the household.

Aside from this "nuisance" problem of nonindependence due to the pragmatic use of multistage cluster sampling designs, there are other sampling designs in which the actual theoretical goal is to observe data within a naturally nested structure. For instance, nested data are often inevitable, if not essential, for small-group and organizational communication, because research in these areas of communication often focuses on individuals interacting in a group and/or organization. For interpersonal communication research, nonindependence in individuals' communication behaviors is implied by the interactive nature of interpersonal communication settings.

Figure 8.1 represents four different data structures, three of which include some sort of meaningful nesting of individuals under some higher-order structure. Beginning in the upper-left quadrant, we see data gathered from individuals who are entirely independent. These data may reflect individuals interviewed as part of a national random-digit dial-telephone survey. That is, the data here are presumably unstructured at any higher level of consequence to the research, and thus represent data that are appropriately analyzed using a traditional statistical model such as OLS regression.

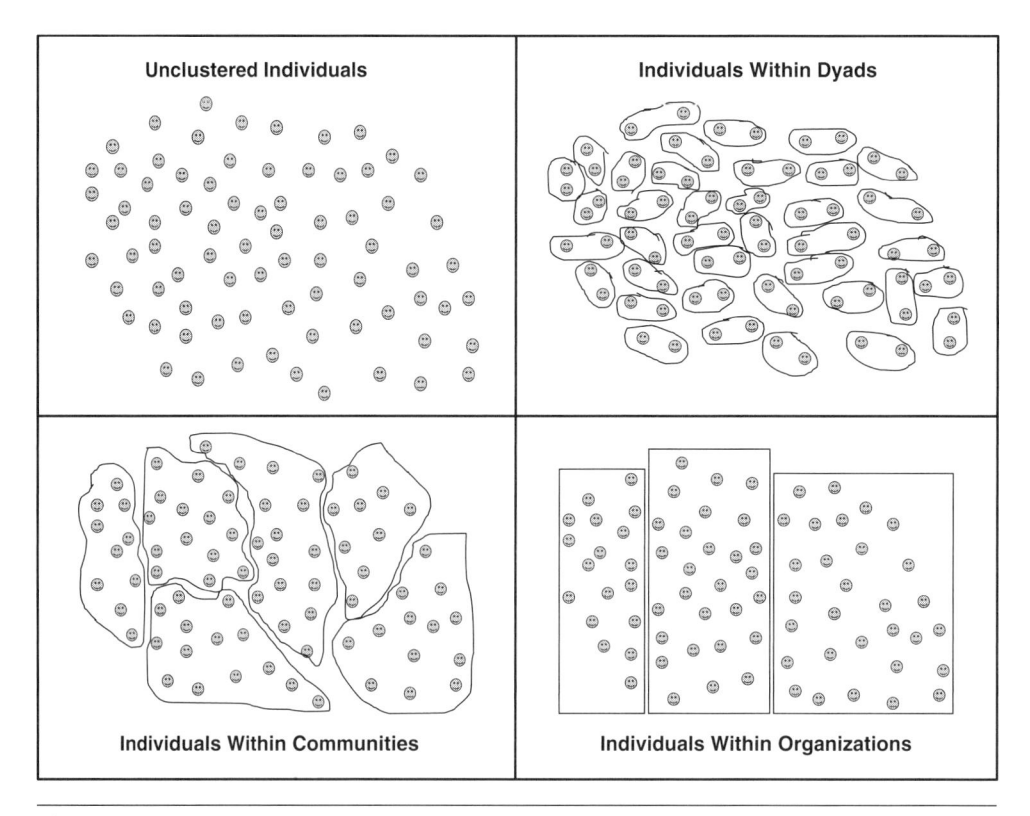

Figure 8.1 Data Structures

The upper-right quadrant shows the same data but under a sampling scheme in which there is a higher-level ordering of the individuals into pairs. One could imagine that these are, for instance, parent-child pairs in a study of family communication patterns, romantic partners in long-distance relationships, or political discussion partners. In any case, the data are structured such that individual observations within the dyad are likely no longer independent of one another on the variables of interest.

The lower-left quadrant shows the same data again but this time organized within higher-level units that describe communities. One example might be survey data gathered using a cluster sampling design, in which case, communities were the primary sampling unit. Another example could be individuals from different communities in a state who receive different local newspapers (i.e., media markets), or individuals in different voter precincts that have different candidates running for office. Again, individuals are likely not independent on theoretically relevant variables in this data scheme.

Finally, the lower-right quadrant shows the same data structured by organization. Imagine these data coming from a study of middle managers, and we have sampled middle managers from the three largest Japanese automobile companies. Ignoring the different employers and work contexts, and the nonindependence of middle managers within each of the organizations, would be inappropriate.

In all but the example in the upper-left quadrant, the assumption of independence of observations may be violated because the data have a hierarchical, nested structure; that is, individuals are nested within dyads or communities or organizations. This nesting, and the nonindependence that it can introduce, means that the application of traditional statistical techniques based on simple random sampling and independent observations are typically inappropriate. The result of inappropriate application of standard statistical techniques in these situations is, at best, error in the estimation of standard errors, leading to the possibility of flawed inferences about statistical significance. At worst, the coefficients of the model may be biased or otherwise incorrectly estimated.

DIFFERENTIATING ORDINARY LEAST SQUARES REGRESSION FROM MLM

Standard OLS regression usually is used for a single-level analysis.[3] Consider an example study for which researchers want to examine the effect of a predictor, x_i, on a criterion variable, y_i. The standard model is

$$y_i = b_0 + b_1 x_i + r_i$$

where b_0 is an intercept, b_1 is the regression coefficient (or "slope") for the effect of x_i on y_i, and r_i is a residual in the estimation of y from x. In this equation, x_i and y_i are individual-level variables if the measurements of x_i and y_i consist of values observed for each individual i ($i = 1, 2, \ldots, n$). If we can assume that the errors in estimation are statistically independent (with the errors manifested as the residuals, r_i), then this model and the inferential techniques widely used and implemented in statistical programs that conduct OLS regression are appropriate.

In another case, a researcher may want to examine the effect of a group-level predictor, g_j on a group-level criterion variable, z_j. Then, the equation becomes:

$$z_j = c_0 + c_1 g_j + e_j$$

where c_0 is an intercept, c_1 is a coefficient for the effect of g_j on z_j, and e_j is the residual. Group-level variables, z_j and g_j, are measured with values observed for each group j ($j = 1, 2, \ldots, J$). This model would be appropriate for group-level analysis, examining how variation in group features measured with g predicts group features measured as z. However, this model would be much less appropriate if z_j and g_j have corresponding individual-level measurements that show substantial variation across individual members of each group.

When researchers have an individual-level predictor and a group-level predictor for an individual-level criterion variable, it is informative to calculate the intraclass correlation to assess the extent to which observations within the group are nonindependent. The intraclass correlation measures the proportion of total variance in the individual-level dependent variable attributable to a grouping variable. When there is a significant and/or substantively meaningful intraclass correlation on the individual-level dependent variable, researchers constrained to using OLS regression will have to either employ regressions separately for each level or incorrectly include the predictors of different levels in one analysis.

Unfortunately, conducting OLS regressions separately for each level has multiple disadvantages, including statistical power reduction and the inability to examine individual-level and group-level predictors together. Moreover, including the predictors of different levels in one OLS regression analysis requires either aggregation or disaggregation, both of which present potential problems. Making inferences about individuals on the basis of results aggregated to the group level is known as the *ecological fallacy* (Galtung, 1967; Robinson, 1950). The ecological fallacy occurs when variables found to be correlated at the group level are assumed correlated at the individual level. On the contrary, the *individualistic fallacy* involves generalizing results obtained at the individual level to the group level (Alker, 1969). These fallacies often result from using a single-level analysis in conjunction with aggregation or disaggregation. MLM is one way of examining individual-level and group-level variables simultaneously at their proper levels rather than aggregating without theoretical justification (i.e., combining information about individual members to represent attributes of a group) and disaggregating (i.e., assigning group-level information to individuals).

Unlike the single-level analysis represented by standard OLS regression, most cases of MLM for a two-level model include two or more simultaneous equations—one equation for Level-1 (e.g., individual-level) variables and one or more for Level-2 (e.g., group-level) variables.[4] For example, a basic but highly versatile set of multilevel model equations is

Level-1 model: $y_{ij} = \beta_{0j} + \beta_{1j}x_{ij} + r_{ij}$, $r_{ij} \sim N(0, \sigma^2)$

Level-2: $\beta_{0j} = \gamma_{00} + \gamma_{01}g_j + u_{0j}$ $\begin{pmatrix} u_{0j} \\ u_{1j} \end{pmatrix} \sim N(0, \Phi)$ where $\Phi = \begin{pmatrix} \varphi_{00} & \\ \varphi_{10} & \varphi_{11} \end{pmatrix}$

$\beta_{1j} = \gamma_{10} + \gamma_{11}g_j + u_{1j}$

where y_{ij} indicates scores on the dependent variable for individual i ($i = 1, 2, \ldots, n_j$), who is a member of group j ($j = 1, 2, \ldots, J$), and r_{ij} is the individual-level residual. β_{0j} is a Level-1 intercept for group j and β_{1j} is the coefficient (a.k.a. "slope") for the effect of x on y for group j. Unlike standard OLS regression, in which b_0 and b_1 (or c_0 and c_1) are fixed effects (i.e., only one intercept and one slope for the entire sample), β_{0j} and β_{1j} can be estimated as random effects, thereby allowing the intercept and slope to vary across groups. In the model above, β_{0j} and β_{1j} are dependent variables in the Level-2 equations, and u_{0j} and u_{1j} are group-level residuals. These residuals quantify the discrepancy between the aggregate intercept and slope and the intercept and slope for group j. Level-2 predictors (e.g., g_j) can be included in the Level-2 equations to account for variance in the Level-1 intercept and slope, with φ_{00} and φ_{11} quantifying those variances, respectively, and φ_{10} quantifying their covariance. The coefficients in the Level-2 model link the group-level variables to the group-level intercept and coefficient(s) for the Level-1 predictors.

In the above sections, we have described the overall need for accounting for multiple levels of analysis in communication and discussed MLM as a statistical technique that is designed for addressing these issues. In the following section, we discuss specific contexts in communication—interpersonal and small-group, organizational, and mass mediated—for which MLM may be an appropriate technique. We then provide a data-based application of MLM using a communication context to provide details on the use and interpretation of MLM and end with a brief discussion of some of the software available that researchers can use to conduct MLM. Those interested in more detailed discussions of MLM should consult some or all of the sources listed at the end of this chapter.

Example Applications of MLM in Communication Research

INTERPERSONAL AND SMALL-GROUP COMMUNICATION

The nature of the interactions that characterize interpersonal and small-group communication provides a reason why multilevel modeling has considerable potential in interpersonal and small-group communication research. By definition, interpersonal and small-group communication involves two or more people interacting with each other, communicating verbally and/or nonverbally. Often, the phenomena that are interesting and relevant to researchers of interpersonal and small-group communication are the processes developed in the interaction and the outcomes resulting from the processes. As such, inherent in the interaction between and among people are reciprocity and mutual influence, which often result in interdependence in attitudes and communication behaviors within dyads and groups. The examination of individuals' attitudes, preferences, styles, and behaviors without considering the influence of their interaction partners or surrounding relational contexts or situations can be limiting, and the application of standard statistical techniques are inappropriate.

In interpersonal communication, one popular area of research is the personal and social relationships that people form, develop, maintain, and dissolve. Several recent studies of dyadic communication—including Caughlin's (2002) study of the relationship between communication patterns and marital satisfaction and Caughlin and Afifi's (2004) investigation of the relationship between topic avoidance and relational dissatisfaction among parent-child dyads and dating couples—have employed MLM. Reid and Ng (2006) provide a recent example of the application of MLM to small-group research. However, many more studies of interpersonal communication could benefit from the application of MLM

One usage of MLM is dyadic analysis. MLM enables researchers to separate within-dyad effects, between-dyad effects, and interactions between within-dyad factors and between-dyad factors (i.e., cross-level interaction). For example, when examining an individual's self-disclosure as the outcome variable, MLM allows researchers to examine how much variation in self-disclosure is due to within-dyad variables such as each partner's individual characteristics (e.g., personalities, traits, age, previous relational history) as well as dyad characteristics such as relationship length and relationship types (i.e., between-dyad variables). Additionally, MLM helps examine whether the effect of within-dyad variables (e.g., empathic concern) on self-disclosure varies as a function of between-dyad variables (e.g., relationship types such as marriage, dating, friendship).

Another context in which MLM would be appropriate is when multiple raters evaluate a single individual. For example, various groups of peers may provide ratings of communication satisfaction with each individual in their network. In this case, the outcome variable would be the ratings of communication satisfaction. Each rater's own individual characteristics (e.g., age and gender) and each rater's relational characteristics (e.g., interaction length and the number of conflicts with the target) could serve as within-individual variables/predictors. The individual characteristics of the people being rated could serve as between-individual-level variables/predictors for their direct or moderating effect on peer communication satisfaction.

Another benefit of the application of MLM in group communication research is the ability to examine context effects. For group-level constructs, Kozlowski and Klein (2000) offer three types: global, shared, and configural constructs. With no relation to individual member attributes, global constructs are based on the objective characteristics of a group as a whole. One example might be group types, such as face-to-face versus virtual groups. Global constructs can serve only as between-group variables in MLM. Shared constructs stem from individual member attitudes and perceptions that are held in common within a group. For example, to the extent that there is a substantial amount of similarity among group members in their attraction to the group, the aggregated scores of all the members' attraction to the group can represent group-level cohesion. Configural constructs represent the pattern or variability of member attributes; for example, age, gender, or ethnicity can be the basis for categorizing each group as a homogeneous or heterogeneous one, or for creating a diversity index for each group.

For shared and configural constructs, MLM enables researchers to test context effects, which refer to the effect of shared or configural variables on an outcome of interest after controlling for the effects of the individual-level variables (see Raudenbush & Bryk, 2002). That is, if a shared or configural variable has a significant effect on an outcome variable even after removing the effect of the relevant individual-level variable, there exists a group-level context effect that is above and beyond the effect of the relevant individual-level variable. Because individuals' characteristics or attributes provide the basis for shared or configural variables, if the effect of the relevant individual-level variable is not controlled, then the effect of a shared or configural variable on an outcome can contain both individual-level and group-level effects.

For example, when examining the effect of group cohesiveness on individuals' participation in group discussion, each individual member's attraction to his or her group can be used as a Level-1 predictor in MLM, and a group cohesiveness score obtained by aggregating individual members' attraction scores can be used as a Level-2 predictor. If group cohesiveness is found to be related to individual participation in group discussion after controlling the effect of individual attraction to the group, the result shows that being part of a cohesive group (regardless of individuals' own attraction level) does have an impact on individuals' participation.

ORGANIZATIONAL COMMUNICATION

The application of MLM in organizational behavior research has been increasing in popularity. For example, the *Journal of Management* fielded a special issue on MLM in 1997, and *Leadership Quarterly* produced a special issue on MLM in 2002. On the other hand, it is relatively rare for organizational communication studies to employ MLM (but see Myers & McPhee, 2006, for a recent example). The utility of MLM in organizational communication research is obvious for many reasons, one of which is the hierarchical structure of organizations where individuals are nested in workgroups or divisions, which themselves are nested in higher-level units both within and across organizations. Multiple levels within the nested structure of an organization pose one of the major challenges to researchers when designing a study of organizational communication phenomena, because a single level of analysis may not be sufficient to examine the complexities of the hierarchical nature of organizational dynamics (see Miller, 2001). Miller (2001) proposed quantitative analysis techniques such as meta-analysis, confirmatory factor analysis, structural equation modeling, and the use of computer technologies (e.g., simulations) in theory development for aiding research endeavors and overcoming challenges. MLM techniques need to be added to this list.

Although the difficulty in dealing with levels of analysis may be reflected in the separation of micro and macro perspectives in organizational communication research, examining more than one level can yield to a "meso" paradigm. This is a term used by House, Rousseau, and Thomas-Hunt (1995) and refers to an approach that aims to simultaneously cover micro (e.g., individuals) and macro (e.g., organizations) elements (Miller, 2001). The benefit of the meso paradigm is that it produces a better understanding of the complexities inherent in organizational communication. MLM can be one of many useful tools for addressing the combination of micro and macro approaches to organizational communication. Although theories and models commonly used in organizational communication tend to focus more heavily on either micro- or macro-level constructs and variables, many of them implicitly contain the elements of the meso paradigm and can be refined and clarified with empirical results obtained from the application of MLM.

One theory useful for understanding organizational communication is Giddens's (1984) structuration theory. The key feature of structuration theory is its recognition of dualities of structures; that is, structure is not only a medium but also an outcome of action. Structures give rise to group members' interaction, and, simultaneously, rules and resources are produced in and by group members' interaction. The concept of structuration captures the nature of structure and its relation with a system. Structuration refers to "the process by which systems are produced and reproduced through members' use of rules and resources" (Poole, Seibold, & McPhee, 1996, p. 117). By focusing on the process of structuration, structuration theory emphasizes the dynamic interrelationship between structure and systems, rather than static systems or structures alone. Structuration theory has provided the basis for examining organizational communication both qualitatively and quantitatively. In an attempt to avoid "a polarization of micro and macro approaches" (p. 114), Poole et al. argue that structuration theory addresses "interdependence of individuals and systems" (p. 114) because "an adequate theory must provide an integrative account of the interplay of member behavior and structural properties" (p. 115). Despite its potential as a multi-level theory, however, the quantitative testing and application of structuration theory or its modified versions (e.g., adaptive structuration theory; DeSanctis & Poole, 1994) have yet to fully utilize MLM.

Basically, structuration theory can specify two levels. Level 1 (i.e., individual level) consists of individual actors situated in an organization. Level 2 (i.e., organizational level) is composed of structures and systems. The process of members producing rules and resources and members drawing upon rules and resources illustrates interaction between Level 1 and Level 2. For example, of the major constructs in structuration theory, "appropriation," can be reconceptualized as a multilevel construct. Appropriation refers to the process of "adopting structural features from the institution and developing a situated version of them" (Poole et al., 1996, p. 126). Individual differences in bringing in new rules and resources to his or her organization or drawing upon his or her own organization's rules and resources can be studied at the individual level. In addition, the way organizations adopt and develop rules and resources can be studied at the organizational level. On the other hand, the individual level and organizational level can be examined simultaneously, rather than separately, by conceptualizing appropriation as an interactive process between individuals and organizations.

MLM can also be applied to organizational communication by examining the interdependence in outcome variables of interest, such as individual employees' attitudes and behaviors. MLM can be applied to examining organizational and coworkers' influences on individual employees' attitudes and behaviors regarding, for example, communication technologies. In an attempt to theorize technology use, Fulk, Schmitz, and Steinfield (1990) proposed the social influence model that recognizes the importance of social influence on media-related attitudes and behaviors in organizations. The social influence model considers communication media perceptions as "subjective and socially constructed" (p. 121) and determined by coworkers' attitudes and behaviors. In addition, Fulk et al. reject previous theories' and models' assumptions of individuals as independent choice makers.

Thus, the social influence model appears to assume that individuals are nested in their groups or organizations as implied by the emphasis on coworkers' influence. In addition, the model allows between-individual analysis to compare individuals' media use, which is proposed to be a function of media experience and skills as indicated in the third proposition of the social influence model. On the other hand, the same proposition also suggests that media use is subject to social influence. This implies the possibility of between-group analysis because various groups of coworkers can be taken as the units for analysis and an investigation can be done on how different the social influence process is between different work groups or organizations. In sum, as long as nonindependence exists in individual workers' uses and perceptions of communication technologies in the organization, individual as well as group characteristics can be examined for their effects on individual workers' uses and perceptions of these technologies.

The study of leadership, which can include dyadic, group, and organizational aspects of communication research, can also benefit from MLM. In fact, diverse approaches to theorizing and analyzing leadership at multiple levels were discussed in detail in Dansereau and Yammarino (1998). Gavin and Hofmann (2002) provided an example of applying MLM to leadership studies by testing the effects of task significance (individual-level predictor) and the direct and moderating (i.e., cross-level interaction) effects of leadership climate (group-level predictor) on hostility. One of the popular research topics in organizational communication has been the supervisor-subordinate dyadic relationship. Commonly, a supervisor has multiple subordinates, who may form a group. Subsequently, work groups are embedded in an organization. When researchers are interested in examining factors affecting employees' participation in decision-making processes or subordinates' effectiveness in upward influence, data from each employee form Level-1 outcome variables and independent variables. Data from each of the employees' supervisors comprise Level-2 independent variables. Data pertaining to the characteristics of organizations (e.g., organizational policy and procedure, organization types such as profit-oriented or nonprofit-oriented) are Level-3 independent variables. This way, researchers can examine how much variation in employees' upward influence behaviors are due to each employee's own characteristics, the employees' supervisors' characteristics, organizational characteristics, and the interaction between any of the variables across these three levels.

MASS COMMUNICATION

MLM has not been used widely in the study of mass communication. In part, this could be due to the focus of empirical mass communication research at the individual level (see McLeod, Kosicki, & Pan, 1991). The few exceptions have applied MLM in the context of large-population cross-sectional sample surveys to test cross-level interactions between individual and community characteristics in predicting individual outcomes (Eveland & Dylko, 2006; Hindman, 2004; Kim & Ball-Rokeach, 2006; Paek, Yoon, & Shah, 2005) and to test the influence of over-time variations in media content on individual-level relationships between media use and political knowledge and participation in repeated cross-sectional survey data (Eveland & Liu, 2005). Henry and Slater's chapter in this volume addresses the other prominent potential application of MLM in the study of mass communication—its use to conduct multiwave panel data analysis (Linebarger & Walker, 2005; Slater, Henry, Swaim, & Anderson, 2003) and other forms of repeated measurement analyses (Southwell, 2005).

One key value of MLM in the study of mass communication is the ability to take community context into account. For example, research on the knowledge gap hypothesis has clearly identified community characteristics, including levels of community pluralism and conflict, that could lead to closing or opening of gaps in knowledge between high and low socioeconomic status groups (Donohue, Tichenor, & Olien, 1975; Gaziano, 1988). However, most studies of the knowledge gap have been based on single communities (Kwak, 1999) or national samples analyzed as single communities (Liu & Eveland, 2005). Researchers could make use of the clustered design of many face-to-face national sample surveys (e.g., General Social Survey, American National Election Study) to test the implied cross-level interaction between community characteristics such as community conflict or community pluralism or even newspaper ownership structure (locally owned vs. corporate vs. chain) and the availability of competition and the relationship between socioeconomic status and knowledge. The same approach could be applied to data gathered at the state level (see Eveland & Dylko, 2006).

Although not directly related to work on the knowledge gap, the hierarchical design of many national cluster samples provides the opportunity to better specify tests of the hypothesis that reading newspapers increases political knowledge. Given the variability of newspaper content across communities of various sizes, it seems unwise to predict identical effects of newspaper reading from community to community. Instead, researchers could hypothesize effects of various content characteristics—from as simple as the amount of coverage to as complex as a coding scheme for quality coverage—and then content analyze the major newspapers in each cluster. These content variables would serve to describe the macro-level units, and the MLM could be specified to test the cross-level interaction hypothesis that clusters with better newspaper-content quality would produce stronger relationships between exposure and knowledge. And, of course, there would likely also be a direct effect of the newspaper-content variables on knowledge, such that overall knowledge would be greater in those clusters with higher-quality news content. This suggestion is a variation on the study by Eveland and Liu (2005) that examined temporal changes in national newspaper-content quality (where the macro variable was "year") instead of variations across communities at a single time point. It is also a variation on the study by Jerit, Barabas, and Bolsen (2006), who examined the amount of media coverage across political issues as the macro-level variable moderating the individual-level relationship between education and knowledge about those issues. Others have also estimated multilevel models to test the effects of media or campaign contexts on individual-level behaviors such as political participation (Jackson & Sides, 2006).

Neighborhood variations within a larger community such as a metropolitan area could also be important predictors of individual-level communication behaviors or moderators of individual-level communication effects (e.g., Kim & Ball-Rokeach, 2006). For instance, the extent of violence in local schools might exacerbate the relationship between child television viewing and aggression by providing more opportunities for students to choose a violent response to provocation, or possibly a supportive normative environment for aggression. High levels of residential mobility and high neighborhood crime rates—both macro-level variables— might encourage television viewing as an entertainment activity relative to socializing with neighbors. Highly competitive campaigns in a state or a congressional district, or large ad buys in particular media markets, might increase attention to political news during a campaign. Each of these examples suggests how some aspect of a geographical community may influence individual behavior or modify the impact of one individual-level variable on another.

Another potentially useful application of MLM techniques would be to advance the value of content analysis studies. Researchers who sampled content by first sampling organizations that produced the content (e.g., newspapers, movie studios, television networks) and then sampled content could employ MLM analyses to determine the organizational characteristics that lead to various types of media content. For instance, measuring organizational routines, salary scales, ownership, or organizational structure, then incorporating them as macro-level variables in predicting the quality of newspaper coverage or the likelihood of Academy Award nominations or ratings shares could provide valuable information about the content production side of the mass communication equation.

Public opinion research methodologists could also make use of MLM when studying the effects of interviewer characteristics on data quality (e.g., Pickery & Loosveldt, 2002). In this case, respondents are nested within interviewers (because each interviewer interviews multiple respondents), and thus interviewer-level variables like age, experience, gender, and ethnicity serve as macro-level variables predicting respondent values for variables such as thoroughness of open-ended responses, consistency of responses across similar questions, partially completed interviews, and item nonresponse on sensitive items such as personal income. The logic here is that if some trait of an interviewer influences responses to the interview, then respondent answers to survey questions may be nonindependent. Although this may be of most pragmatic relevance to public opinion researchers and methodologists, it is also an interesting communication question since the structured interview is, in fact, an example of strategic dyadic communication.

Experimentalists can also make good use of the MLM approach. For instance, in research with children conducted in schools and daycare agencies in which a stimulus is delivered in a group setting, researchers are sometimes forced to settle for randomly assigning classes (instead of students) to condition. Since students within a class share a teacher and a social environment that could make them nonindependent on any number of relevant variables, this experimental design approach calls for MLM to separate the effects of macro-level variables produced by classroom membership (teacher disciplinary style, teacher quality, student social interaction, and so on) from the effect of the stimulus. Quasi-experimental and field-experimental data, in which a stimulus is delivered through mass-mediated channels to communities that are randomly assigned (or that simply vary by community naturally), can also make use of MLM using the same logic.

The application of this approach can also be made to more general experimental media effects research in which participants are exposed to the stimulus in a group setting, even when the assignment to conditions has been made randomly at the individual level. In research on the effects of exposure to presidential debates, for instance, some studies randomly assign undergraduate students to watch one or another version of the debate in a classroom setting. Unfortunately, the stimulus then includes not only the debates but also the verbal and nonverbal behavior of other students in the room. In one room students might be rowdy, making hearing the debate more difficult for all members of that viewing room, or some students might laugh or scowl at a candidate's statement, producing an effect separate from the debate itself. This suggests that the large-group viewing context—atypical in most cases other than movies watched in theaters and thus a threat to external validity—could be at least partially assessed by modeling the viewing group and its characteristics (e.g., coded observational data including discussion, laughing, muttering, heckling, or characteristics such as the size of the viewing group) as macro-level variables in addition to the randomly assigned condition in the experiment.

The same logic might also be applied to natural television or movie viewing. For instance, how might the emotional effects of viewing the Superbowl at a Superbowl party vary depending on whether the favored team of an individual matched or contradicted the team favored by the majority present—or whether the individual viewed the game alone? How might responses to a horror film vary depending on whether it is viewed with a group of friends versus a romantic partner? Does viewing a newscast in the presence of others increase or decrease learning, and could either result be the product of the extent and/or nature of conversation that takes place during the newscast? All of these questions suggest important implications of the social context in which television is viewed, and that context is a macro-level variable.

An Example Multilevel Analysis

To illustrate how MLM can be applied to a communication problem and to demonstrate how to analyze and interpret some MLM output from a popular statistical package, HLM6, below we present a multilevel analysis of data from a study on individual- and group-level variable influences on individual-level satisfaction with group processes. It is expected that an individual's job satisfaction is positively related to his or her satisfaction with group processes. That is, an individual who likes his or her job may be able to interact with his or her group members more constructively toward accomplishing a group goal. On the other hand, group-level job satisfaction (quantified as an aggregation of individual members' job satisfaction) may moderate the effect of individual job satisfaction on satisfaction with group processes. Theories suggest that individuals prefer interacting with similar others and find similarity as validation for their perceptions and beliefs (Byrne, 1971; Festinger, 1954; Heider, 1958; Newcomb, 1956). Similarity is not only rewarding but also enables people to readily anticipate others' actions and act accordingly. Categorically speaking, when individuals work with group members (coworkers) who like their jobs, they are more satisfied with group processes than when they work with those who do not like their jobs. Thus, individuals working in a group with higher average job satisfaction should be more satisfied with group processes.

Group type is also expected to affect individuals' satisfaction with group processes. The two types of group investigated in the current study are cross-functional groups and permanent work groups. Cross-functional groups get formed by including members from various departments of an organization for a special project for a given duration and get dissolved once the project is concluded. On the other hand, permanent work groups have regular and long-term interactions. Considering that it takes time and effort for people with diverse backgrounds, interests, and expertise to find common ground and develop ways to be efficient and cooperative, it is expected that, in general, members of permanent work groups will be more satisfied with their group processes than members of cross-functional groups.

To empirically examine these questions, we discuss a study based on 200 employees working as civil engineers. These individuals were drawn from 37 work groups of companies in the construction industry. Three to nine individuals from each group (most frequently, groups consisted of five or six individuals) returned their completed questionnaire. Participants were almost exclusively male (92%). The average age was 33 years with a range from 20 to 50 ($SD = 5.08$). The outcome variable was individual workers' satisfaction with group processes (variable SAT), which was measured with Keyton's (1991) scale ($\alpha = .93$, $M = 3.54$, $SD = 0.58$). The Level-1 predictor was individuals' job satisfaction (i.e., JS), which was measured with four items (e.g., "I enjoy my job.") ($\alpha = .77$, $M = 3.10$, $SD = 0.70$). The measures used a 5-point response format (1 = *strongly disagree*, 5 = *strongly agree*). Individual scores were group-mean centered prior to analysis. In addition, the individual job satisfaction scores were aggregated to a group-level mean (i.e., group-level job satisfaction, or GJS: $M = 3.11$, $SD = 0.39$). GJS was used as a group-level (i.e., Level-2) predictor.[5] As another Level-2 predictor, group type (i.e., GT) was dummy-coded with cross-functional teams = 0 and permanent work groups = 1.

In this example, MLM analysis is explained as occurring in three steps. However, MLM is not necessarily done in this order or with this number of steps. Depending on the type of data available and the goal of their research projects, individual researchers should determine the order in which predictors are introduced into a multilevel model and the number of steps taken in building the model.

FIRST STEP

The first analytical step is typically to calculate the proportions of variance in the outcome variable that exist within and between groups. That is, the total variation in the outcome variable is divided into individual-level variance (i.e., variations attributable to individual differences net of group differences) and group-level variance (i.e., variations attributable to group differences). With no predictors included, an analysis is run on the outcome variable. This first step of the analysis reduces to a multilevel model with two simple equations:

$$\text{Level-1 model: SAT}_{ij} = \beta_{0j} + r_{ij}$$
$$\text{Level-2 model: } \beta_{0j} = \gamma_{00} + u_{0j}$$

where i indicates individuals 1, 2, ..., n_j in each group j for groups 1, 2, ..., J. Table 8.1 presents the results. The proportion of variance in SAT (i.e., individual-level satisfaction with group processes) *between* work groups is estimated by dividing the group-level variance (.049) by the total variance (.049 + .293), producing the intraclass correlation coefficient (ICC), which is .143. This ICC indicates that about 14.3% of the variance in SAT is between work groups. In other words, 85.7% of the variance in satisfaction with group processes is between individuals. A χ^2 statistic testing a null hypothesis that all work groups have the same mean ($\chi^2 = 68.634$,

Table 8.1 Results From Step 1

Fixed Effect	Coefficient	SE		
Average group mean, γ_{00}	3.540	.053		
Random Effects	Variance Component	df	χ^2	p-value
Group mean, u_{0j}	.049	36	68.634	.001
Level-1 residual, r_{ij}	.293			

$p = .001$) indicates that there is significant variation among the work groups in SAT.

SECOND STEP

The second step is to examine the relationship between the individual-level predictor (Job Satisfaction, or JS) and SAT within the 37 work groups. By treating each group as having "its own" regression equation with an intercept and a slope, we examine the average of the 37 regression equations (i.e., What are the average intercept and slope?) and the variation of the regression equations from work group to work group (i.e., How much do the intercepts vary and how much do the slopes vary?). The multilevel model is as follows:

$$\text{Level-1 model: SAT}_{ij} = \beta_{0j} + \beta_{1j}\text{JS}_{ij} + r_{ij}$$
$$\text{Level-2 model: } \beta_{0j} = \gamma_{00} + u_{0j}$$
$$\beta_{1j} = \gamma_{10} + u_{1j}$$

Table 8.2 provides the results of the analysis. The average of the group means is estimated to be 3.540. More importantly, the average of effect of JS on SAT is significantly different from zero, $t(36) = 2.15, p = .038$. This indicates that, on average, JS was significantly related to satisfaction within groups.

Table 8.2 also shows that the estimated variance around the mean (i.e., variance of Level-1 intercept) is .054, with a χ^2 statistic of 74.444, $p < .001$. This finding indicates that significant differences exist among the 37 group means; group means on satisfaction with group processes ranged from 2.90 to 4.44. The estimated variance of the JS slopes is .027 with a χ^2 statistic of 43.147, $p = .19$, indicating that there was no significant variation across work groups for the relationship between JS and SAT. Although the slope varied from –1.04 to 2.09 across groups, the variance in slopes was not

Table 8.2 Results From Step 2

Fixed Effect	Coefficient	SE	t-ratio	p-value
Overall satisfaction, γ_{00}	3.540	0.053	66.482	<.001
JS, γ_{10}	0.150	0.070	2.153	.038
Random Effects	Variance Component	df	χ^2	p-value
Group mean, u_{0j}	.054	36	74.444	<.001
JS, u_{1j}	.027	36	43.147	.192
Level-1 residual, r_{ij}	.269			
JS: Job Satisfaction (i.e., individual-level job satisfaction)				

significantly different from zero (see Figure 8.2). Thus, group-level predictors can be introduced to the model to explain the variations for the group mean of satisfaction with group processes. It may not be necessary, however, to include group-level predictors to explain the variations across groups in the slope of the relationship between JS and SAT.

In Table 8.2, the estimate of the individual-level variance in SAT is now .269. The estimated variance in the first step, which did not include JS as the Level-1 predictor, was .293. Thus, the inclusion of the individual-level predictors accounted for 8.2% of the individual-level variance in SAT [(.293 − .269)/.293 = .082].

THIRD STEP

Finally, group-level variables (group-level mean job satisfaction, GJS, and group type, GT) were introduced as predictors of the Level-1 intercept. Because the slope of the Level-1 predictor (JS) did not significantly vary across groups, it is not necessary to include group-level variables to predict variation in the slope. For the purpose of illustrating how a cross-level interaction could have been modeled, however, the group-level variables were nevertheless included as predictors in the model.[6]

$$\text{Level-1 model: SAT}_{ij} = \beta_{0j} + \beta_{1j}\text{JS}_{ij} + r_{ij}$$
$$\text{Level-2 model: } \beta_{0j} = \gamma_{00} + \gamma_{01}\text{GT}_j + \gamma_{02}\text{GJS}_j + u_{0j}$$
$$\beta_{1j} = \gamma_{10} + \gamma_{11}\text{GT}_j + \gamma_{12}\text{GJS}_j + u_{1j}$$

As shown in Table 8.3, GJS was a significant positive predictor of satisfaction with group processes, $t(34) = 2.419$, $p = .021$. That is, individuals

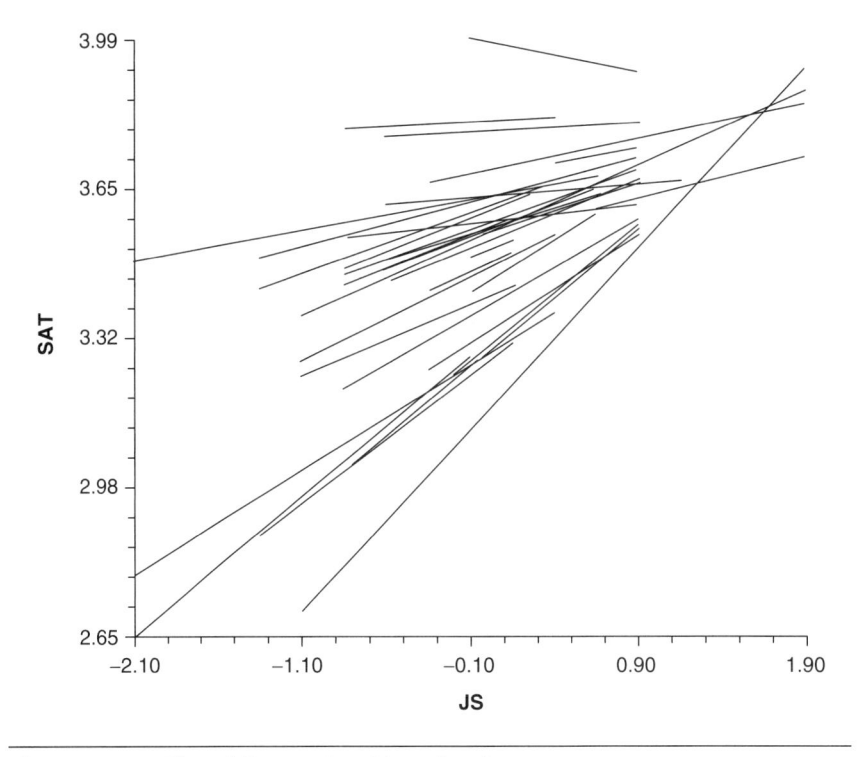

Figure 8.2 Plot of Regression Lines for Groups

working in a group with higher group average individual job satisfaction were more satisfied with group processes. GT, however, was not a significant predictor, $t(34) = -0.653$, $p = .518$. Comparing the variance of the intercept from the second-step analysis (Table 8.2) with the variance of intercept from the current analysis that included these Level-2 predictors (Table 8.3) revealed that the Level-2 predictors accounted for 22.2% of the between-group variance in SAT [$(.054 - .042)/.054 = .222$]. As cross-level predictors, the Level-2 predictors of the slope were not significant. Group type was not significantly related to the relationship between JS and SAT, $t(34) = -0.125$, $p = .902$. GJS was also not significant related to the relationship between JS and SAT, $t(34) = -1.364$, $p = .182$.

SUMMARY

The intraclass correlation coefficient demonstrated that among the total variance in satisfaction with group processes, 14.3% of the variance was between groups, while 85.7% existed between individuals. This suggested that group-level variables were potentially relevant in understanding such satisfaction. Analyses indicated that at the individual-level, individuals' job satisfaction was related positively to satisfaction with group processes. This

Table 8.3 Results From Step 3

Fixed Effect	Coefficient	SE	t-ratio	p-value
Model for group means				
Intercept, γ_{00}	3.632	0.150	24.222	<.001
GT, γ_{01}	−0.104	0.160	−0.653	.518
GJS, γ_{02}	0.325	0.134	2.419	.021
JS slopes				
Intercept, γ_{10}	0.156	0.179	0.873	.389
GT, γ_{11}	−0.026	0.204	−0.125	.902
GJS, γ_{12}	−0.273	0.200	−1.364	.182
Random Effects	Variance Component	df	χ^2	p-value
Group mean, u_{0j}	.042	34	63.272	.002
JS slope, u_{1j}	.040	34	42.021	.162
Level-1 residual, r_{ij}	.265			

Note: GT: Group Type (cross-functional groups *vs.* permanent work groups); GJS: Group Job Satisfaction (i.e., group-level mean job satisfaction); JS: Job Satisfaction (i.e., individual-level job satisfaction).

Level-1 predictor accounted for 8.2% of the individual-level variance. At Level 2, group average job satisfaction and group type accounted for about 22.2% of the group-level variance in satisfaction with group processes, although average group job satisfaction was the only significant predictor. On the other hand, the cross-level interaction was not significant, such that the Level-2 predictors did not significantly affect the relationship between individual-level job satisfaction and satisfaction with group processes.

Software for MLM

MLM is a general statistical methodology that can be applied in a variety of different contexts. Consequently, the computer software that has been developed to carry out multilevel analyses is very general and somewhat challenging to use initially. A further complication is that computing MLM is an area of active statistical research, so that computer programs are improved on a regular basis. For the typical kind of multilevel model such as has been reviewed in this chapter, several different computer programs are available. These include MIXED in the SAS system (Littell et al., 2006), HLM6 (Raudenbush & Bryk, 2002), LISREL (du Toit et al., 2005), MLwiN (Rasbash et al., 2005), and SPSS (Hayes, 2006; Peugh & Enders, 2005) among others. Programs differ in terms of the number and type of advanced models that can be accommodated; however, many interesting and sophisticated analyses are well within the capabilities of each, and there are no consistent practical advantages in any program over the others for most typical problems. In learning any new statistical method, a good way to start is by working through the initial chapters of a survey textbook and working sample problems with a computer running. Good introductions with several interesting examples have been presented by Kreft and de Leeuw (1998), Snijders and Bosker (1999), and Gelman and Hill (2007).

Conclusion

Multilevel modeling is a statistical technique that allows data for many communication questions to be analyzed more appropriately than traditional statistics have allowed. Moreover, it offers a logic that could actually spur theoretical development in new directions, encourage consideration of a wider range of variables, and allow communication to fulfill its function as a variable field that addresses communication processes across multiple levels of analysis (see Slater et al., 2006).

However, MLM is not a technique to be applied to every problem; no single statistical technique is. In this chapter, we hope to have provided a basic introduction to MLM and a case for why it is an important technique to consider for communication scholars. Moreover, we have reviewed some research relevant to communication that has already applied this technique, and we have proposed additional areas where its application is warranted. We encourage those readers who are persuaded of the value of MLM to consult additional, more detailed readings below for a fuller treatment of this technique.

Goldstein, H. (2003). *Mulilevel statistical models* (3rd ed.). New York: Oxford University Press.
Kreft, I., & De Leeuw, J. (1998). *Introducing multilevel modeling.* Thousand Oaks, CA: Sage.
Luke, D. A. (2004). *Multilevel modeling.* Thousand Oaks, CA: Sage.
Raudenbush, S. W., & Bryk, A. S. (2002). *Hierarchical linear models: Applications and data analysis methods* (2nd ed.). Thousand Oaks, CA: Sage.
Snijders, T., & Bosker, R. (1999). *Multilevel analysis: An introduction to basic and advanced multilevel modeling.* Thousand Oaks, CA: Sage.
Special issue of *Human Communication Research* (2006, October).

Notes

1. Beyond handling data structured as we have described here, MLM has a number of other more specialized applications, including meta-analysis and the analysis of repeated-measures data. Chapter 3 of this volume addresses the latter application of MLM.

2. Nonindependence of observations can be characterized by similarity in scores among those belonging to some higher-level unit (e.g., a community or a group) in such a way that after the effects of independent variables on a dependent variable are controlled, the residuals are no longer independent of each other but can be related to each other by unit membership. For more discussions of nonindependence (e.g., various sources contributing to nonindependence, measures of nonindependence), see Kenny & Judd (1986, 1996), Kenny, Mannetti, Pierro, Livi, & Kashy (2002), and Bliese (2000), for example, among others.

3. The symbols b and c are used here to represent OLS regression coefficients, to avoid confusion with their counterparts in MLM introduced soon.

4. The Greek symbols β and γ are used for MLM equations to be consistent with most MLM nomenclature.

5. For Level-1 predictors, three centering options exist: use of raw-metric (i.e., noncentering), group-mean centering, and grand-mean centering. Although it is beyond the scope of this chapter, various discussions of the implications of the different centering methods exist (e.g., Hofmann & Gavin, 1998; Hofmann, Griffin, & Gavin, 2000; Kreft, 1995; Kreft & de Leeuw, 1998; Kreft, de Leeuw, & Aiken, 1995; Longford, 1989; Paccagnella, 2006; Plewis, 1989; Raudenbush, 1989a, 1989b; Raudenbsh & Bryk, 2002). In the current analysis, JS was group-mean centered. Group-mean centering involves subtracting out the mean predictor value for the individuals in each group. Let JS^*_{ij} be the measure of job satisfaction for individual i in work group j. Then, the group-mean-centered job satisfaction is expressed as $JS_{ij} = JS^*_{ij} - \overline{JS}_j$.

6. In the current analysis, GT and GJS were grand-mean centered for easier interpretation of the coefficients. Grand-mean centering involves subtracting out the mean predictor value for the each group. Let GT^*_j be the measure of group type for group j. Then, the grand-mean centered group type is expressed as $GT_j = GT^*_j - \overline{GT}$. Let GLS^*_j be the measure of group-level mean job satisfaction for group j. Then, the grand-mean-centered group-level mean job satisfaction is expressed as $GLS_j = GLS^*_j - \overline{G}\,\overline{L}\,\overline{S}$

References

Abrams, J. R., Eveland, W. P., Jr., & Giles, H. (2003). The effects of television on group vitality: Can television empower nondominant groups? In P. Kalbfleisch (Ed.), *Communication yearbook 27* (pp. 193–219). Mahwah, NJ: Lawrence Erlbaum.

Alker, H. R. (1969). A typology of ecological fallacies. In M. Dogan & S. Rokkan (Eds.), *Quantitative ecological analysis in the social sciences* (pp. 69–86). Cambridge: MIT Press.

Bliese, P. D. (2000). Within-group agreement, non-independence, and reliability: Implications for data aggregation and analysis. In K. J. Klein & S. W. J. Kozlowski (Eds.), *Multilevel theory, research, and methods in organizations: Foundations, extensions, and new directions* (pp. 349–381). San Francisco: Jossey-Bass.

Byrne, D. (1971). *The attraction paradigm.* New York: Academic Press.

Caughlin, J. P. (2002). The demand/withdraw pattern of communication as a predictor of marital satisfaction over time: Unresolved issues and future directions. *Human Communication Research, 28,* 49–85.

Caughlin, J. P., & Afifi, T. D. (2004). When is topic avoidance unsatisfying? Examining moderators of the association between avoidance and dissatisfaction. *Human Communication Research, 30,* 479–513.

Chaffee, S. H., & Berger, C. R. (1987). What communication scientists do. In C. R. Berger & S. H. Chaffee (Eds.), *Handbook of communication science* (pp. 99–122). Newbury Park, CA: Sage.

Dansereau, F., & Yammarino, F. J. (1998). *Leadership: The multiple-level approaches.* Stamford, CT: JAI.

Delia, J. G. (1987). Communication research: A history. In C. R. Berger & S. H. Chaffee (Eds.), *Handbook of communication science* (pp. 20–98). Newbury Park, CA: Sage.

DeSanctis, G., & Poole, M. S. (1994). Capturing the complexity in advanced technology use: Adaptive structuration theory. *Organization Science, 5,* 121–147.

Dimmick, J., & Coit, P. (1982). Levels of analysis in mass-media decision-making: A taxonomy, research strategy, and illustrative data-analysis. *Communication Research, 9,* 3–32.

Donohue, G. A., Tichenor, P. J., & Olien, C. N. (1975). Mass media and the knowledge gap: A hypothesis reconsidered. *Communication Research, 2,* 3–23.

du Toit, S., du Toit, M., Mels, G., & Cheng, Y. (2005). LISREL for windows: SURVEYGLIM user's guide. Chicago: Scientific Software International.

Eveland, W. P., Jr., & Dylko, I. (2006, November). *Questioning the assumption of uniform effects of the news media: The moderating role of community and newspaper characteristics.* Paper presented at the annual meeting of the Midwest Association for Public Opinion Research, Chicago, IL.

Eveland, W. P., Jr., & Liu, Y. I. (2005, August). *Multilevel models of the impact of news use and news content characteristics on political knowledge and participation.* Paper presented at the annual meeting of the Association for Education in Journalism & Mass Communication, San Antonio, TX.

Festinger, L. (1954). A theory of social comparison processes. *Human Relations, 7,* 117–140.

Fulk, J., Schmitz, J., & Steinfeld, C. W. (1990). A social influence model of technology use. In J. Fulk & C. Steinfeld (Eds.), *Organizations and communication technology* (pp. 117–140). Newbury Park, CA: Sage.

Galtung, J. (1967). *Theory and methods of social research.* New York: Columbia University Press.

Gans, H. J. (1979). *Deciding what's news: A study of* CBS Evening News, NBC Nightly News, Newsweek *and* Time. New York: Vintage Books.

Gavin, M. B., & Hofmann, D. A. (2002). Using hierarchical linear modeling to investigate the moderating influence of leadership climate. *Leadership Quarterly, 23,* 15–33.

Gaziano, C. (1988). Community knowledge gaps. *Critical Studies in Mass Communication, 5,* 351–357.

Gelman, A., & Hill, J. (2007). *Data analysis using regression and multilevel/hierarchical models.* New York: Cambridge University Press.

Giddens, A. (1984). *The constitution of society: Outline of the theory of structuration.* Berkeley: University of California Press.

Hayes, A. F. (2006). A primer on multilevel modeling. *Human Communication Research, 32,* 385–410.

Heider, F. (1958). *The psychology of interpersonal relations.* New York: John Wiley & Sons.

Hindman, D. B. (2004, August). *Social capital in a community context: Community structural pluralism, media use, and conflict versus non-conflict forms of social participation.* Paper presented at the annual meeting of the Association for Education in Journalism & Mass Communication, Toronto.

Hofmann, D. A., & Gavin, M. B. (1998). Centering decisions in hierarchical linear models: Implications for research in organizations. *Journal of Management, 24,* 623–641.

Hofmann, D. A., Griffin, M. A., & Gavin, M. B. (2000). The application of hierarchical linear modeling to organizational research. In K. J. Klein & S. W. J. Kozlowski (Eds.), *Multilevel theory, research, and methods in organizations: Foundations, extensions, and new directions* (Ch. 11, pp. 467–511). San Francisco: Jossey-Bass.

House, R., Rousseau, D. M., & Thomas-Hunt, M. (1995). The meso paradigm: A framework for the integration of micro and macro organizational behavior. *Research in Organizational Behavior, 17,* 71–114.

Jackson, R. A., & Sides, J. C. (2006). Revisiting the influence of campaign tone on turnout in senate elections. *Political Analysis, 14,* 206–218.

Jerit, J., Barabas, J., & Bolsen, T. (2006). Citizens, knowledge, and the information environment. *American Journal of Political Science, 50,* 266–282.

Kenny, D. A., & Judd, C. M. (1986). Consequences of violating the independence assumption in analysis of variance. *Psychological Bulletin, 99,* 422–431.

Kenny, D. A., & Judd, C. M. (1996). a general procedure for the estimation of interdependence. *Psychological Bulletin, 119,* 138–148.

Kenny, D. A., Mannetti, L., Pierro, A., Livi, S., & Kashy, D. A. (2002). The statistical analysis of data from small groups. *Journal of Personality and Social Psychology, 83,* 126–137.

Keyton, J. (1991). Evaluating individual group member satisfaction as a situational variable. *Small Group Research, 22,* 200–219.

Kim, Y.-C., & Ball-Rokeach, S. J. (2006). Community storytelling network, neighborhood context, and civic engagement: A multilevel approach. *Human Communication Research, 32,* 411–439.

Kozlowski, W. J., & Klein, K. J. (2000). A multilevel approach to theory and research in organizations: Contextual, temporal, and emergent processes. In K. J. Klein & S. W. Kozlowski (Eds.), *Multilevel theory, research, and methods in organizations: Foundations, extensions, and new directions* (pp. 3–90). San Francisco: Jossey-Bass.

Kreft, I. (1995). The effects of centering in multilevel analysis: Is the public school the lower or the winner? A new analysis of an old question. *Multilevel Modeling Newsletter, 7*(3), 5–8.

Kreft, I., & de Leeuw, J. (1998). *Introducing multilevel modeling.* Thousand Oaks, CA: Sage.

Kreft, I. G. G., de Leeuw, J., & Aiken, L. S. (1995). The effect of different forms of centering in hierarchical linear models. *Multivariate Behavioral Research, 30,* 1–21.

Kwak, N. (1999). Revisiting the knowledge gap hypothesis: Education, motivation, and media use. *Communication Research, 26,* 385–413.

Linebarger, D. L., & Walker, D. (2005). Infants' and toddlers' television viewing and language outcomes. *American Behavioral Scientist, 48,* 624–645.

Littell, R. C., Milliken, G. A., Stroup, W. W., Wolfinger, R. D., & Schabenberger, O. (2006). SAS for mixed models (2nd ed.). Cary, NC: SAS Institute, Inc.

Liu, Y. I., & Eveland, W. P., Jr. (2005). Education, need for cognition, and campaign interest as moderators of news effects on political knowledge: An analysis of the knowledge gap. *Journalism & Mass Communication Quarterly, 82,* 910–929.

Longford, N. T. (1989). To center or not to center. *Multilevel Modeling Newsletter, 1*(3), 7, 8, 11.

McLeod, J. M., Kosicki, G. M., & Pan, Z. (1991). On understanding and misunderstanding media effects. In J. Curran & M. Gurevitch (Eds.), *Mass media and society* (pp. 235–266). London: Edward Arnold.

McLeod, J. M., Pan, Z., & Rucinski, D. (1995). Levels of analysis in public opinion research. In T. L. Glasser & C. T. Salmon (Eds.), *Public opinion and the communication of consent* (pp. 55–85). New York: Guilford.

Miller, K. (2001). Quantitative research methods. In F. M. Jablin & L. L. Putnam (Eds.), *The new handbook of organizational communication: Advances in theory, research, and methods* (pp. 137–160). Thousand Oaks, CA: Sage.

Myers, K. M., & McPhee, R. D. (2006). Influences of member assimilation in workgroups in high-reliability organizations: A multilevel analysis. *Human Communication Research, 32,* 440–468.

Newcomb, T. M. (1956). The prediction of interpersonal attraction. *American Psychologist, 11,* 575–586.

Paccagnella, O. (2006). Centering or not centering in multilevel models? The role of the group mean and the assessment of group effects. *Evaluation Review, 30,* 66–85.

Paek, H. J., Yoon, S. H., & Shah, D. V. (2005). Local news, social integration, and community participation: Hierarchical linear modeling of contextual and cross-level effects. *Journalism & Mass Communication Quarterly, 82,* 587–606.

Paisley, W. (1984). Communication in the communication sciences. In B. Dervin & M. J. Voigt (Eds.), *Progress in communication sciences* (Vol. 5, pp. 1–43). Norwood, NJ: Ablex.

Pan, Z., & McLeod, J. M. (1991). Multilevel analysis in mass communication research. *Communication Research, 18,* 140–173.

Peugh, J. L., & Enders, C. K. (2005). Using the SPSS MIXED procedure to fit cross-sectional and longitudinal multilevel models. *Educational and Psychological Measurement, 65,* 717–741.

Pickery, J., & Loosveldt, G. (2002). A multilevel multinomial analysis of interviewer effects on various components of unit response. *Quality and Quantity, 36,* 427–437.

Plewis, I. (1989). Comment on "centering" predictors. *Multilevel Modeling Newsletter, 1*(3), 6 & 11.

Poole, M. S., Seibold, D. R., & McPhee, R. D. (1996). The structuration of group decisions. In R. Y. Hirokawa & M. S. Poole (Eds.), *Communication and group decision making* (2nd ed., pp. 114–146). Thousand Oaks, CA: Sage.

Price, V. (1988). On the public aspects of opinion: Linking levels of analysis in public opinion research. *Communication Research, 15,* 659–679.

Rasbash, J., Steele, F., Browne, W., & Prosser, B. (2005). A user's guide to MLwiN version 2.0. Centre for Multilevel Modelling, University of Bristol.

Raudenbush, S. W. (1989a). "Centering" predictors in multilevel analysis: Choices and consequences. *Multilevel Modeling Newsletter, 1*(2), 10–12.

Raudenbush, S. W. (1989b). A response to Longford and Plewis. *Multilevel Modeling Newsletter, 1*(3), 8–11.

Raudenbush, S. W., & Bryk, A. S. (2002). *Hierarchical linear models: Applications and data analysis methods* (2nd ed.). Thousand Oaks, CA: Sage.

Raudenbush, S. W., Bryk, A. S., Cheong, Y. F., & Congdon, R. (2004). HLM 6: Hierarchical linear and nonlinear modeling. Chicago: Scientific Software International.

Reid, S. A., & Ng, S. H. (2006). The dynamics of intragroup differentiation in an intergroup social context. *Human Communication Research, 32,* 504–525.

Robinson, W. S. (1950). Ecological correlations and the behavior of individuals. *American Sociological Review, 15,* 351–357.

Rogers, E. M. (1994). *A history of communication study: A biographical approach.* New York: Free Press.

Slater, M. D., Henry, K. L., Swaim, R. C., & Anderson, L. L. (2003). Violent media content and aggressiveness in adolescents: A downward spiral model. *Communication Research, 30,* 713–736.

Slater, M. D., Snyder, L., & Hayes, A. F. (2006). Thinking and modeling at multiple levels: the potential contribution of multilevel modeling to communication theory and research. *Human Communication Research, 32,* 375–384.

Snijders, T., & Bosker, R. (1999). An introduction to basic and advanced multilevel modeling. Thousand Oaks, CA: Sage.

Southwell, B. G. (2005). Between messages and people: A multilevel model of memory for television content. *Communication Research, 32,* 112–140.

Walsh, K. C. (2004). *Talking about politics: Informal groups and social identity in American life.* Chicago: University of Chicago Press.

Communication Network Analysis 9

Thomas W. Valente

Network analysis is a theory and set of techniques used to describe the relations among individuals or other units such as organizations, states, or nations. Networks are most often used to represent who knows whom or who talks to whom within a community or organization and in some cases how these relations influence human behavior. Increasingly, network analysis is used to study the Internet and other electronic communications. There are numerous introductions and reviews of network methods and theory (Boissevain, 1974; Burt, 1980; Burt & Minor, 1983; Carrington, Scott, & Wasserman, 2005; Harary, 1965; Knoke & Kuklinski, 1982; Marsden, 1990; Marsden & Lin, 1982; Rogers & Kincaid, 1981; Scott, 2000; Wasserman & Faust, 1994; Wellman & Berkowitz, 1988). There are also texts that address social network application to specific domains such as collective action (Diani & McAdam, 2003), organizational behavior (Cross & Parker, 2003; Monge & Contractor, 2003; Nohria & Eccles, 2000), epidemiology (Morris, 2004), and substance abuse (Friedman et al., 1999), among other areas. This chapter provides a general introduction to the methods of network analysis, focusing on the mechanics and practical applications of networks in communication and behavioral science.

Social Networks

The central insight provided by network analysis is that individuals are connected to others in a nonrandom manner and these connections have

Auhor's Note: Time to work on this chapter has been supported by NIDA grant DA16094.

profound influences on people, groups, and systems. The connections between individuals constitute relations most often measured by interpersonal communication but also may be derived from any type of interaction. These relations can be studied along with the attributes of the individuals involved in the relations (such as the educational level, occupation, and income of the communicants). By focusing on relations, researchers can uncover relational and structural properties that explain variation in individual attitudes and behaviors and provide insight into how groups form and function. For example, understanding who goes to whom for advice within an organization can indicate individual levels of advice seeking within the organization and whether advice-seeking structure is centralized or decentralized. The individual and organizational levels of analysis may both be used as predictors of individual and organizational performance.

Figure 9.1 shows a graph of the friendships among 37 students in one class of sixth graders in one southern California middle school (Valente et al., 2003). This diagram was drawn using *Netdraw* (Borgatti, 2006), one of

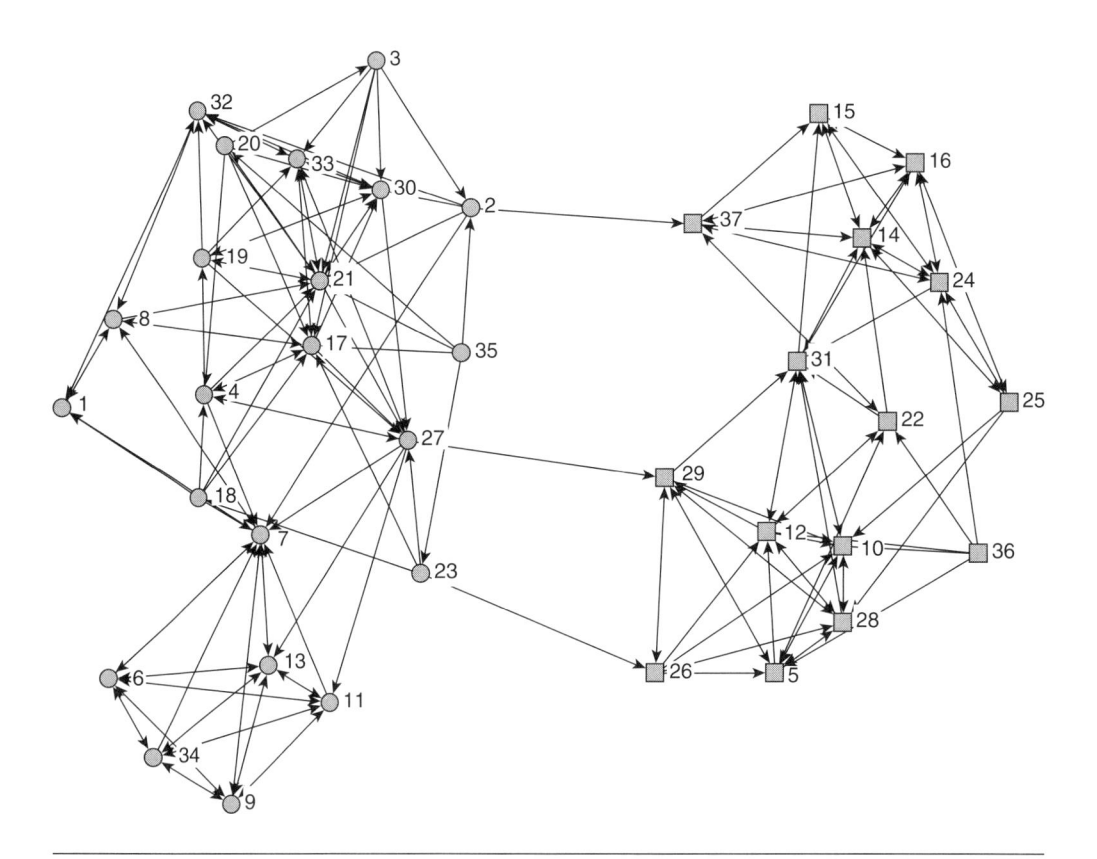

Figure 9.1 Friendship Network for Students in One Sixth-Grade Class in Southern California (circles represent girls; squares represent boys) (Valente et al., 2003)

several network graphing programs available (Freeman, 2000; Huisman & van Dujin, 2005). Each circle or square represents a student, and the lines connecting them indicate who chooses whom as a friend. Students receiving many choices are placed near the center, and those receiving few are placed on the periphery. Inspection of the diagram often provides insight into the network structure. For example, this network diagram shows that boys are more likely to choose boys as friends and girls are more likely to choose girls. The network has two large groups connected by a few bridges that are easy to locate. It is also easy to identify popular students in this graph, such as Person 21 among the girls and Person 14 among the boys. An implicit assumption in most network research is that communication (information, persuasion, affect, etc.) is or can be transmitted along the friendship paths in this network. The properties of networks therefore are important because they indicate what type of information a person is likely to be exposed to and how the network structure constrains or facilitates information flow.

Network Variables

To investigate research questions related to how network analysis can be used to understand individuals and groups, scholars typically calculate two types of variables: relational and structural.[1] Table 9.2 provides a description of the distinction between relational and positional measures (see Burt, 1980, for further discussion). *Relational* variables are those that are constructed from the respondent's set of direct ties. Examples of relational variables include connectedness, reach, the number of nominations received or sent, personal network density, reciprocity, group membership, and network density. Connectedness and reach measure the degree to which any member of a network can reach other members of the network. Number of nominations sent and number received measure how many others an individual nominates and the frequency an individual is nominated, respectively. Personal network density measures the degree to which an individual's set of ties knows and nominates one another. Reciprocity measures whether a person's nominations are reciprocated, and group membership refers to network analysis procedures that determine who belongs to which groups in a network. Network density measures the proportion of ties in a network relative to the total number possible. Group membership and network density variables use the entire network for their computations and hence are more structural measures and lead to a more complex analysis of the structure of a network.

Structural variables are those constructed from the entire network of connections and everyone's reports of whom they are connected to for their calculation. Examples of structural variables include *centrality* and *position*. Centrality can be measured in a variety of ways (Freeman, 1979).

For example, number of nominations sent and number received are measures of *centrality out-degree* and *in-degree,* respectively. *Centrality betweenness* measures the degree to which an individual lies between other individuals in the network. This measure provides a good indication of the strategic location of nodes based on how frequently communications pass through a node when others in the network communicate with one another. High centrality betweenness has been associated with earlier adoption of innovations (Valente, 1995). *Centrality closeness* measures the degree to which an individual is near all other individuals in the network (Freeman, 1979) and is useful if one wants to know which nodes can broadcast messages to others most rapidly. *Centrality power* measures the degree to which an individual can exert control over the network (Bonacich, 1987), and *centrality flow* (Freeman, Borgatti, & White, 1991) and *information* (Stephenson & Zelen, 1989) measure the capacity of individuals to carry information within the network.

Centrality is probably the most intuitive and certainly the most used measure in communication network analysis. Centrality measures provide an indication of a node's position in the network, which can be expected on both intuitive and theoretical grounds to be associated with a person's behavior. People at the center of a network are likely different from those on the periphery both because of the type of people who are likely to be central nodes and because being in the center can be a strategically advantaged position.

Structural analyses can also be conducted to define groups in a network based on similar patterns of communications (these groups are usually referred to as *positions*). For example, one structural measure is the degree to which two people are connected to the same others in the network. Every pair in the network can have a score that is the percentage of their nominations to the exact same other people. Two people who nominate the same others will score 100%. For example, in the network in Figure 9.1, Students 6 and 13 nominated the exact same others and so are perfectly equivalent or *structurally equivalent.* The pattern of equivalences between all pairs in the network can then be analyzed and the network partitioned into groups based on who is equivalent to whom. In this example, Students 6, 13, 34, 9, 11, and 7 form a group since they have very similar network links.

Many of these relational and structural variables exist at both the individual and system levels. For example, personal network density may be measured for each respondent and may also be measured for the whole network. Personal network density for Person 29 is 45.2%. The overall network density in Figure 9.1 is 13.4%. The various centrality measures can also be computed for both individuals and the whole network. System centrality, referred to as *centralization,* measures the degree to which links in a network are concentrated on one or a few individuals. Network influences on behavior can be a function of individual network scores, system or complete network scores, or an interaction between the two. Being a central person in a centralized network is different from being a central person in a decentralized network.

One can construct variables that combine network data and attributes. For example, *network exposure* is the number or proportion of others in one's personal network who hold a specific opinion or practice a behavior (see Figure 9.2). Network exposure is a fundamental organizing construct for studying network effects. Researchers wishing to know whether smoking is influenced by a friend's smoking can calculate the proportion of friends who smoke via network exposure and then correlate this with smoking. Alexander and others (2001) discovered that adolescents with a majority (50% or greater) of friends who smoke are twice as likely to smoke themselves. It may be, however, that network exposure is not associated with smoking and that there are thresholds to smoking initiation such that some smokers begin smoking with no or few peers who smoke while others wait until most or all of their friends smoke. Identifying smoking thresholds would be important for future prevention efforts to identify the influences on smoking for low-threshold smokers.

Network exposure is calculated by multiplying the matrix of social network connections by the vector of attributes for which one wants to calculate exposure. Matrix-level program languages (examples include R, Gauss, S-plus, SAS-IML, MATA) are required to calculate network exposure since one has to multiply the matrix of network links by the attribute on which one is calculating exposure. The network exposure model is very flexible since one can use many different types of network contact matrices (Burt, 1987; Marsden & Friedkin, 1993; Valente, 1995) such as links represented by the strength of the ties (frequency of communication, for example) or any of the relational and structural measures discussed above. To test whether network exposure varied by strength of tie,

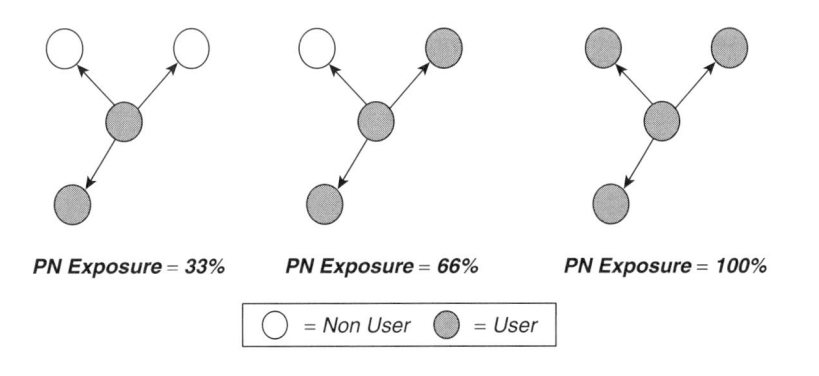

Figure 9.2 Network Exposure: The Percent (or Number) of Users in a Person's Network

one could compare exposure calculated using simple ties with one calculated with ties weighted by closeness or frequency of contact.

The network in Figure 9.1 was derived from data collected in a sixth-grade class in a southern California school. Schools and classes have well-defined boundaries. It is not always possible to study intact groups, so numerous methods have been developed to study networks in different settings. The variety of network data collection techniques creates different data management and analysis requirements. The variety of data collection techniques, their aspects, and their limitations can cause confusion in how to apply network analysis to various substantive areas and how to understand the network paradigm. Hence the next section describes network data collection and management procedures.

Network Data Collection

Table 9.1 displays the five major network data collection techniques: (1) survey, (2) egocentric, (3) snowball, (4) census, and (5) two-mode or joint. These five techniques most often represent increasing levels in their

Table 9.1 Network Analysis Data Types

	General	*Specific*
1. Survey	Standard survey questions	Standard survey questions
2. Egocentric	Measure a person's connections to certain social roles such as mother, father, brother, sister (Sarason et al., 1983)	Measure a person's closest friends by asking for first names (Burt, 1984; Marsden, 1987, 1993)
3. Snowball	Interview a random selection of indexes' alters (Klovdahl, 1989)	Interview all of the indexes' alters (Goodman, 1961; Heckathorn, 2002; Palmore, 1967)
4. Census	Ask for nominations within a bounded community (Valente, 1995, 1996; Valente et al., 2003)	Ask respondents to select from a roster of all members (Valente, 1996)
5. Two-mode or Joint	Nominations of events attended or organizational membership (Breiger, 1974; Davis et al., 1941)	Enumeration of membership lists (Mizruchi, 1992)

ability to measure social structure and decreasing levels in their generalizability. Each of these five measurement techniques has a general and a specific version in terms of the level of specificity required by the respondent. The remainder of this section describes each of these 10 data collection techniques.

SURVEY DATA

Survey data consist of data collected by asking individuals whether they talked to or consulted anyone about some topic. For example, general survey questions may be asked such as "Have you spoken to anyone about prenatal care?" For such questions, usually a list of social roles is presented as the response categories such as mother, father, teacher, doctor, and so on. More specific questions such as "Have you spoken to your spouse about prenatal care?" or "Have you consulted a doctor about prenatal care?" may also be asked. Although not typically referred to as network data, these types of survey questions represent the most rudimentary indicators of network concepts.

EGOCENTRIC DATA

Egocentric data (also referred to as local) consist of data collected by asking individuals to name others with whom they talk about important matters or with whom they talk most frequently about a topic. The specific question asked is called a name generator, because it is the question used to generate names. An example of an egocentric questionnaire is presented in Appendix 1. These data provide relational information in terms of the kinds of people individuals interact with most frequently. General egocentric questions ask that the respondent provide information on social roles, such as "How often do you talk to your father?" With general egocentric questions, a list of social roles is usually presented as the response categories, for example, mother, father, brother, sister, and so on, and the respondent provides information on each.

Specific egocentric questions ask for specific names, nicknames, first names, or initials and then ask the respondent to provide further information on that specific person. Demographic information such as sex, age, occupation, religion, and type of relation is collected for each tie. It is also advisable, when possible, to ask the respondent whether the persons named know one another in order to measure interpersonal network density.

The difference between egocentric data and simple survey questions is that egocentric questionnaires collect data from the respondent (ego) on the characteristics of the persons named. In addition to their characteristics (age, gender, location, type of relation, etc.), one can also ask the respondent to indicate whether the network members know one another or are otherwise connected. These data provide a measure of the respondent's personal or local network. The most well-known study of this type is the set of egocentric questions included in the 1985 version of the annual General Social Survey questionnaire administered by NORC (Burt, 1984; Marsden, 1987, 1993). These data were then used to describe American discussion networks in the sense that the average age and the variation in religion could be specified (Marsden, 1987). Marsden (1987) showed that Americans' discussion networks were homophilous, in that people nominated discussion partners who were similar in ethnicity, age, gender, and rural versus urban residence. In a follow-up analysis, McPherson and others (2005) showed that core discussion networks of Americans decreased over the past decade (McPherson et al., 2006).

Communication researchers can use egocentric survey techniques for any study. For example, in the evaluation of a Bolivian mass-media campaign to promote the use of contraceptives, we used egocentric survey questions to determine if campaign influences were contingent on respondents' personal networks (Valente & Saba, 1998). We found that the campaign was more effective for those who had a minority of contraceptive users in the personal network (so-called low-threshold adopters). This methodology provided a more explicit test and support for the classic two-step flow hypothesis.

Egocentric data provide measures of an individual's personal network in terms of the kind of people each respondent interacts with or is related to. These data, however, do not provide connected groups of respondents that can be mapped. Since the respondents are chosen randomly and no full names are elicited, there is no way to link specific individuals named with others that may be interviewed in the same study. It is conceivable that "virtual" networks could be constructed from egocentric data by creating imaginary nodes that are the composites of the sociodemographic characteristics. The next three types of data collection techniques return data in which respondents are linked to one another

SNOWBALL DATA

Snowball data consist of data collected by interviewing all or some portion of the people nominated by a respondent (Klovdahl, 1989). The general version of snowball sampling occurs when a sample of the index person's nominations are interviewed, whereas the specific version occurs when all the people the index person nominated are interviewed. Some researchers have used snowball sampling to develop respondent-driven sampling (RDS) methodologies useful for recruiting subjects into health promotion programs (Heckathorn, 1997). Research has shown that the respondent-driven approach provides a more diverse and more cost-effective means of reaching "hard to reach" populations than traditional outreach methods (Salganik & Heckathorn, 2004).

The advantages of general over specific snowball sampling are that general snowballs (Klovdahl, 1989) are less likely to end in a social cul-de-sac, provide more points of entry into the community or society, and provide better population parameter estimates of social structure. Snowball sampling is a method of cluster sampling in which the researcher samples social clusters rather than geographic ones (Klovdahl, 1989). A study using general snowball data could be conducted to measure, for example, how quickly and to whom a rumor was spread.

These first three types of data collection techniques (survey, egocentric, and snowball) are amenable to random sample-selection procedures. The researcher starts with a random sample of respondents selected from a given population and the results are then generalizable to that population. One shortcoming with sequenced data, however, is that network indices are highly dependent on the persons initially selected to generate the names. The two final techniques are used less frequently with random sample data, but instead are often used to provide more in-depth understanding of network and community structure.

CENSUS DATA

Census data are the type most people refer to when they discuss network analysis methods, and census data collection was the method used to collect the data that produced the diagram in Figure 9.1. *Census* or *saturation sampling* consists of interviews conducted with all (or almost all) members of a community. Organizations, schools, and rural communities represent the most common sampling frames used in this type of data collection (Rogers & Kincaid, 1981; Valente, 1995, 1996). Census sampling is preferred when the researcher can enumerate all members of the community such as all nations in the world, all organizations in an industry, or all employees of an organization. General census data collection consists of survey questions that ask for the names of those people with whom the respondent talks in his or her community. These names are then recorded by their study ID numbers since they represent other individuals included in the census sample. A classic study using census data was Rogers's (1979) investigation of the communication networks of Korean women from 25 rural villages in the 1970s. Rogers asked all of the married women to indicate to whom they went for advice about family planning. He mapped these networks and showed how the network of communication influenced the spread of contraceptives in these villages (Rogers & Kincaid, 1981).

Specific census data collection entails obtaining a roster of all the members of the community and asking the respondent to check those he or she knows (and/or how frequently the respondent communicates with each).

There is little difference in the specificity level between census nominations and that collected with the use of a roster. Roster census data collection usually produces many more nominations (limited only by the number of people on the roster), whereas nominations are usually limited to five or seven choices. The main challenge to census sample studies is defining the boundary of the community (Laumann, Marsden, & Prensky, 1983). The roster method is quite commonly used in schools. For example, we distributed class rosters to sixth graders in 16 southern California schools (84 classes) and asked students to write down the ID numbers of their five closest friends. We found that popular students (those receiving the most nominations) were more likely to become smokers than their less popular counterparts (Valente et al., 2005).

Census data provide a complete list of the people in the communication network so that researchers can study how information spreads through the network and how the network might affect the distribution of that information. This can be critical for organizational behavior studies in which knowing who communicates with whom is fundamental to organizational performance. Network data also provide a mechanism to change organizations either by realigning the communication network (Borgatti, 2006; Cross & Parker, 2003) or by identifying change agents within the organization (Lomas et al., 1991).

TWO-MODE DATA

Two-mode data (also referred to as *jointness* or *duality*) consist of data collected by recording instances in which individuals participate in or attend the same events. The most common two-mode network data are those collected on intercorporate interlocks by recording the names of individuals who are on the board of directors for each organization in an industry. Since many individuals sit on numerous boards, they function as a network connecting these various organizations (Pennings, 1980).

Two-mode data are often collected from archival sources, such as annual reports, and then converted to a network using matrix algebra. The original data consist of a table in which the rows are individuals and the columns are the organizations or events. This table is a matrix that can then be transposed and postmultiplied to yield a person-by-person matrix representing the number of joint memberships. The transposed matrix can be premultiplied to yield an event-by-event (or organization-by-organization) matrix. Thus, one data set provides two different networks: a person-by-person network indicating joint participation in activities or organizational membership and an organization-by-organization network indicating the number of members in common (Breiger, 1974).

The classic two-mode data set is the Southern Women study originally conducted by Davis, Gardner, and Gardner (1941). Davis and others extracted from newspaper reports social event attendance of 16 women at 12 events. These data constituted a 16-row, 12-column table. Breiger showed how this table, treated as a matrix, could be pre- and postmultiplied with its transpose as above to return the woman-by-woman and event-by-event networks. Breiger's analysis showed that there were two cliques of women based on who attended which events together. The two-mode methodology has been used to construct an interlocking directorates database of the *Fortune* 500 companies (e.g., Mizruchi & Stearns, 1988).

These five network data collection techniques are shown in Table 9.1 in order of increasing levels of relational information and decreasing levels of generalizability. That is, egocentric data provide more relational information than simple survey questions, and sequenced data provide more relational information than egocentric, census data still more, and two-mode data provide the most relational information, since they provide not only a person-by-person matrix of connections but also an event-by-event matrix.[2]

While more relational information is provided at each level, there is usually some loss of generalizability when one uses the census and two-mode techniques. The first three techniques are often used with random sample-selection procedures and thus can provide population parameter estimates. Snowball sampling, however, provides parameter estimates dependent on the starting nodes and dependent on the ability of follow-up with those named. Census and two-mode approaches retain some generalizability when communities (and organizations/events) are selected randomly. In addition, the characteristics of the communities sampled can be compared to known population estimates to determine the representativeness of studied communities. Increasingly, scholars are using the Internet and electronic forms of communication to gather communication network data. These data may come from tracking e-mail communications and provide a large repository of interpersonal communication.

While the data collection techniques mentioned so far rely primarily on asking respondents to report their network, network data are often

Table 9.2 Relational and Positional Measures of Network Structure at Three Levels of Analysis (adapted from Burt, 1980)

	Relational	*Structural*
Individual	Personal network density	Central or peripheral individuals
Group	Clique formation based on direct ties	Hierarchical partition based on tie similarity
Network	Dense versus sparse networks	Set of positions; centralization

collected from archival sources such as computer logs, diaries, and telephone logs. Diaries have been used to report size and composition of networks (Bernard, Killworth, & Sailer, 1982). Archival sources are frequently used to collect two-mode data in which intercorporate network data are collected by examining published reports of the board of directors (Pennings, 1980). A classic study of women attending social events was used to develop the two-mode methodology (Breiger, 1976). E-mail networks have also provided a direct tally of interpersonal communication behavior (Rice, 1982). Bibliometric network analysis consists of examining reference lists from publications to see who references whom. A network is then constructed to determine the structure of a scientific specialty (Hummon & Carley, 1993; Rice, Borgman, & Reeves, 1988).

Data Management

Network analysis is often conducted by asking respondents to name other individuals with whom they discuss important matters. This name-generating technique elicits the names of the respondents' personal network. Data collected with survey and egocentric methods are analyzed using standard statistical packages such as SPSS, SAS, or STATA. The statistical analyses consist of the creation of various network measures such as the average, heterogeneity, and range of the personal network characteristics.

Egocentric data can also be converted into a dyadic data set such that the unit of analysis is not the individual respondent but the respondent and each one of the persons he or she named in response to the network question. Each case is the respondent-friend pair or dyad. In a dyadic data set, a person who nominated two others contributes two cases to the data set, and one who nominated four contributes four. Once converted, the data are referred to as dyadic, and analysis proceeds by studying the dyads. Caution, of course, must be exercised when interpreting statistical tests since the usual assumption of independence is violated. Analysis is much easier, however, and standard statistical techniques such as multilevel modeling and generalized estimating equations exist to deal with the nonindependence. For example, dyadic analysis permitted a test of the hypothesis that showed that participants in a needle exchange program were more likely to engage in risky behavior (sharing syringes) with friends they named first or second rather than those named third, fourth, or fifth (Valente & Vlahov, 2001).

To analyze sequenced, census, and two-mode data, the ID numbers of the nominees are entered into the database. The persons nominated are often referred to as *alters,* and so the respondent and alter represent a dyadic link. The respondents' ID numbers and the alters' ID numbers are then output separately into a "node-list" or "link-list" format file consisting of respondent and alter ID numbers. For example, the network shown in Figure 9.2 can be stored in a data file as two columns, one for the ID number of the sender of the link and the other for the receiver. So in the example, the first three rows of the Excel file will read 1 7, 1 8, and 1 32 indicating links from person 1 to persons 7, 8, and 32. These data are then read into specialty network computer programs such as UCINET, PAJEK, R, GAUSS/SNAPS, VISUALIZER, or NEGOPY for analysis (Huisman & van Duijn, 2005).

These network computer programs convert the link-list or node-list data into a matrix in which the rows and columns represent the respondents in the study. UCINET is perhaps the most widely used computer program for network analysis. A companion program, NETDRAW, comes with UCINET for visualization of networks.[3] PAJEK is a network analysis and visualization program designed for large networks and freely available on the Web. The INSNA Web site (http://www.insna.org) has links to almost all of the programs available for network analysis, and a recent chapter by Huisman and van Duijn (2005) provides a review and comparison of network analysis programs.

The link-list or node-list input into the network analysis programs is converted into a matrix where each cell represents the presence or absence of a link between the two people who correspond to the row and column of the cell. For example, a 1 in row 1 column 7 indicates that person 1 nominated person 7. The rows represent the individuals sending the nominations, and the columns represent the individuals receiving the nominations. The attribute information (sex, education, age, and so on of the respondents) is stored in a separate file.

Matrix representation of networks enables quick computation of network properties. For example, a common measure of centrality is the number of nominations received. Summing the columns of a matrix provides a score of how many nominations each person received. These network scores are often output from the network package and are merged with the original data set to compare network scores with other variables. For SAS users, James Moody at The Ohio State University and Chih-Ping Chou at the University of Southern California have written SAS macros to calculate certain network scores that can be merged with the main data set.

Network diagrams, also called *sociograms,* often reveal the structure of a network, and there are a variety of techniques and computer programs available for graphing networks (McGrath et al., 2002). Drawing network diagrams is one of the most attractive features of social network analysis, as it provides a visual depiction of the overall structure of communication. Organizations, coalitions, and communities enjoy seeing their data reported back to them and viewing network diagrams because most people know their own personal networks, but no one can see the overall network structure unless the data are aggregated into a picture.

Data Characteristics

Networks have been measured on kinship, marriage, advice, love, friendship, and so on. The type of network is usually assessed by the content of the network questions. The most common type of network measure is collected with a question such as "Name up to five people that you talk to about important matters." Network data can be collected on a wide variety of substantive issues. In behavioral studies, it is advised to ask network questions such as "Name five other people who you talk to about X where X is any topic of interest." General questions can be further *funneled* to ask the respondent to name those whom he or she talks to about family health matters, then funneled to ask whether they've discussed cancer, and funneled still further to ask who he or she would talk to about breast cancer.

Network data are also directional in that ties may be *symmetric* (John talks to Mary and Mary talks to John) or *asymmetric* (John talks to Mary but Mary does *not* talk to John). Symmetric ties are reciprocal, whereas asymmetric ties are unreciprocated directly but may be reciprocated indirectly through intermediaries. Indirect reciprocation occurs when John talks to Mary, and while Mary does not talk to John, she does talk to Maria, who talks to John.

Network data may be *binary* or *valued*. That is, network nominations can be used to record the presence or absence of ties but also may record how frequently individuals communicate with one another. For example, a researcher might be interested in determining how often members of a community talk to one another by asking if the respondent talks to her nominees (1) never, (2) less than once per month, (3) monthly, (4) weekly, or (5) daily. In this manner, values can be attached to the ties corresponding to the frequency of interaction.

Although many network variables are calculated using binary network data, most may also be calculated with valued data. It is typical to convert valued data to binary data by calculating the mean strength of each tie and then dichotomizing the network on that average. Valued data can be used to weight network exposure by tie strength. A network exposure of 2 indicating that 2 of a person's friends smoke could be weighted by the interaction frequency for each of those 2 ties by multiplying the behavior by the frequency of interaction. No studies have demonstrated that weighting by interaction frequency increases the correspondence between an individual's behavior and that of his or her network. However, some evidence exists that closer, stronger ties are stronger influences on individual behavior than weaker, less close ones (Valente & Vlahov, 2001).

LEVELS OF ANALYSIS: SYSTEM, GROUP, AND INDIVIDUAL

A distinguishing characteristic of network analysis is that it simultaneously measures network properties at the individual, group, and overall system levels (Monge & Contractor, 2002). That is, network data are recorded on individuals, and these data are indicative of individual properties yet simultaneously contribute to group and system measures. For example, an individual's set of direct contacts constitute his or her personal network and provide individual relational measures such as the size of his or her network and its density.

The determination of whether this person is a member of a group and the characteristics of any groups to which he or she belongs are group-level measures that can also affect behavior. At the system level, it may be important to know whether this same person can reach many or a few others in the network and how many intermediaries exist between this specific person and other individuals in the network. Finally, the overall network density and centrality measures indicate whether this person is a member of a dense or sparse network and the degree of centralization of this network.

Researchers interested in creating a promotional campaign for adolescent students, for example, might be interested in finding popular students to help deliver the messages. However, the importance of these popular students may depend in part on whether the cliques that exist within the school are rigid or fluid and whether they are centralized or decentralized. All other things being equal, popular students (as measured by the number of friendship choices received) are likely to be more influential in settings with rigid and centralized clique structures than in those with fluid and decentralized structures (Valente, 1995).

Recent Developments

Social network analysis was originally applied mainly to the study of communication and interaction within small groups. Researchers investigated how the structure and patterns of their interactions reflected and affected individual outcomes such as depression, satisfaction, success, and so on. Researchers were also interested in how network structural indicators might affect the overall success and performance of the group, community, or organization. The predominance of inferential statistical approaches in the social sciences meant that the more contextual approach and methods of social networks were eclipsed in favor of random independent sampling studies.

However, by the mid-1990s, the growth in multilevel modeling (see Chapter 8 of this volume) and the Internet brought increased attention to connectedness and explicit data on interpersonal connections via computer communications. Social networks of online communities and patterns of communication via e-mail could be studied, and more powerful computer programs were developed to handle the analysis of large social networks. Thus, social network analysis has emerged as a strong intellectual tradition interfacing with many different disciplines across the social, physical, and natural sciences (Monge & Contractor, 2002).

There are many broad areas of emphasis currently being pursued in the network analysis field. There is continued development of better and faster algorithms for calculating network indices at the individual and network levels (Newman et al., 2006). There is also continued improvement in computer programs for the management, analysis, and display of social network data. Many researchers have also been investigating how social network data can be used to accelerate the diffusion of new ideas and practices. Researchers have also studied how networks may be used for disease control or to reduce security threats.

One of the central challenges facing social network research has been the difficulty of applying inferential statistics and methodology to the analysis of social network data. Network data violate the independence assumption of inferential statistics and therefore need to be analyzed and interpreted with caution. Scholars have now begun to develop programs that can analyze network dynamics and behavior and study their coevolution (Snijders, 2005). The P* framework was developed to statistically evaluate whether a network had certain structural characteristics. For example, researchers wanted to know whether links in a network were reciprocated, and the P* program provided a statistical test to show whether tie reciprocation occurred by chance in the network.

Higher-order structural models could also be tested. Transitivity occurs when A → B and B → C implies A → C. The P* framework provided a means to test for transitivity while controlling for reciprocity and the density of the network. Still higher-order structural properties could be analyzed by including attribute data in calculations. For example, researchers might theorize that gender influenced tie selection and test whether people of the same gender were more likely to be connected. The P* approach shifted network analysis from treating network measures as independent variables used to explain behaviors to a dependent variable to be predicted.

P* has been extended into a more general model called Exponential Random Graph Models (ERGM) that can be used to make statistical tests on network properties (Koehly et al., 2005; Robins et al., 2007). These developments are attempting to integrate individual attributes, behaviors, and network connections into one overall modeling and testing environment.

Computer programs such as MULTINET and SIENNA are platforms used to test network evolution and behavioral dynamics. Although it is in its infancy, the ability to understand the factors that affect the formation and dissolution of network ties at the same time one studies how attributes of nodes affect and are affected by network dynamics promises to have a profound influence on science.

Summary and Conclusion

The network analysis field is represented by a professional association (the International Network for Social Network Analysis, INSNA), a bulletin/journal (*Connections*), an electronic journal (*Journal of Social Structure*), and flagship print journal *Social Networks*. There is a Web site with many useful links at http://www.insna.com and a listserv available at that Web site that is active and helpful. This chapter has provided a general introduction to network analysis methods and examples from research on its application in the field of communication.

The network paradigm is made up of these five components: (1) network data collection and management (the 5 types), (2) network data characteristics (the type of question asked and whether the links are binary or valued), (3) individual network variables such as centrality or group membership, (4) network-level variables such as density or centralization, and (5) network exposure and other combinations of attributes with network data. Complexities and mathematical manipulations aside, the network data reflect who communicates with whom. Unfortunately, in most instances, what is said during these communications and the emotions and information exchanged are not measured. Network researchers have done a poor job at exploring what gets said by people in the network. We tend to look for structural patterns and extract indicators that reflect people's position in the network but do not measure what people say and how what is said is distributed in the network. For example, do people talk about different things with central members than with those on the periphery?

The network field has been enhanced by recent research conducted by physicists measuring the small-world phenomenon and scale-free networks. These have been important advances for the field with implications for how small-world networks (characterized by shorter distances connecting nodes) and scale-free networks (characterized by having a skewed distribution of connectedness) have structure communication and information transmission. What is left out of these studies is whether networks affect communication and actual behavior traces within the networks. It is hoped that recent advances in network methodology will create the opportunities for such analysis and that communication researchers will measure the content of communications.

Media effects and communication campaigns depend in large part on the social and interpersonal context within which the program or message is digested. The social context of media consumption and the interpersonal discussion that accompanies the use of news and entertainment programming amplifies their effects. Yet there has been little marriage of mass and interpersonal, particularly network, research. Again an opportunity exists for researchers to study how social networks mediate mass-media uses and their effects.

Finally, more effective communication campaigns are possible by incorporating sociometric segmentation. The marketing field has progressed from geographic, to demographic, to psychographic segmentation. Social network methodology will enable marketers to craft messages and strategy that appeal to different network typologies. Further, more targeted community-based interventions, such as those in schools, organizations, and communities, can use network data to locate the right messengers and change agents (Valente & Fosados, 2006). The messenger is the message, not the medium.

The possible hypotheses and extension of communication applications of network analysis are limitless and depend, naturally, on the substantive issue at hand. Networks define the social environment of individuals, and hence define the filter through which individuals are influenced by external sources such as media campaigns, collective actions, technology change, and outreach programs, to name a few. This chapter has provided an introduction to the science of network analysis and emerging paradigm that treats connections as the focal unit of analysis.

Notes

1. In a sense, the division between relational and structural variables is not rigid since relational and structural measures are often highly correlated.

2. We omit here any comment on the actual reliability or validity of the data collected and any direct comparison between methods (see Marsden, 1993, for an assessment of the reliability of egocentric data).

3. As of the date of this writing, a free evaluation version can be downloaded from http://www.analytictech.com.

Appendix A: Sample Egocentric and Sociometric Questionnaires

Please provide the first names or initials of up to five people you talk to about important matters.

	Name 1	Name 2	Name 3	Name 4	Name 5
a. How do you know _____?	1. Family member 2. Friend 3. Neighbor 4. Schoolmate 5. Other _____	1. Family member 2. Friend 3. Neighbor 4. Schoolmate 5. Other _____	1. Family member 2. Friend 3. Neighbor 4. Schoolmate 5. Other _____	1. Family member 2. Friend 3. Neighbor 4. Schoolmate 5. Other _____	1. Family member 2. Friend 3. Neighbor 4. Schoolmate 5. Other _____
b. Does he/she live within 5 miles of your home?	No Yes	No Yes	No Yes	No Yes	No Yes
c. Is _____ male or female?	Male Female	Male Female	Male Female	Male Female	Male Female
d. How long have you known him/her?	____ mos. ____ yrs.	____ mos. ____ yrs.	____ mos. ____ yrs.	____ mos. ____ yrs	____ mos. ____ yrs.
e. How often do you see him/her?	1. Daily 2. Once a week 3. Once a month 4. One time	1. Daily 2. Once a week 3. Once a month 4. One time	1. Daily 2. Once a week 3. Once a month 4. One time	1. Daily 2. Once a week 3. Once a month 4. One time	1. Daily 2. Once a week 3. Once a month 4. One time
f. Does he/she smoke?	No Yes	No Yes	No Yes	No Yes	No Yes
g. What do you usually discuss with this person?	1. Family 2. Politics 3. Neighborhood 4. Work 5. Other _____	1. Family 2. Politics 3. Neighborhood 4. Work 5. Other _____	1. Family 2. Politics 3. Neighborhood 4. Work 5. Other _____	1. Family 2. Politics 3. Neighborhood 4. Work 5. Other _____	1. Family 2. Politics 3. Neighborhood 4. Work 5. Other _____

Who are your five BEST FRIENDS in this class?

Write their names on the lines below starting with your best friend in this class. After you write their name, look at the list of names on the roster that has been provided. Match the name to the number and write the number in the boxes. If you can't think of five people in this class, then leave the extra lines blank.

For example, your best friend's name may be John Angeles. Then you would write his name and then look up his number, which is 1 2 3, and then write that in the boxes. It is written in as an example below.

	First Name	Last Name	Roster Number
	John	Angeles	1 2 3
1			
2			
3			
4			
5			

Now write your name.

	First Name	Last Name	Roster Number

Appendix B: Glossary

Bridge	The ability of an individual to connect otherwise unconnected individuals or groups (Granovetter, 1973, 1982).
Centrality Betweenness	The degree to which an individual lies on the shortest path connecting others in the network (Freeman, 1979).
Centrality Closeness	The degree to which an individual is near others in the network (Freeman, 1979).
Centrality Degree	The number of ties an individual sends (out-degree) or receives (in-degree) (Freeman, 1979).
Centrality Power	The degree to which an individual can exert control over other members of the network (Bonacich, 1987).
Clique	A set of individuals who communicate more frequently with one another than with others in the community.
Component	A set of individuals who are connected with another individual but not with others in the community (Scott, 1991).
Connectedness	The ability of two individuals to reach one another directly or through intermediaries (Scott, 1991).
Density-Personal Network	The proportion of ties among an individual's nominees (Scott, 1991).
Density-System	The proportion of ties in the network (Scott, 1991).
Egocentric	Network data collected from respondents about their contacts without interviewing those contacts (Burt, 1984; Marsden, 1987) (Appendix A).
ERGM	Exponential Random Graph Models used to test for structural properties of networks such as whether a network has a tendency for transitivity.
Flow	Measures the capacity of two individuals to transmit information to one another through all paths in the network (Freeman, Borgatti, & White, 1991).
Geodesic	The shortest path between two people (Harary, Norman, & Cartwright, 1965).
INSNA	International Network for Social Network Analysis: the professional association for network analysts (see www.insna.org).

Matrix	Array of rows and columns used to store network nominations. Usually a matrix is referred to as a letter and the number of rows and columns are subscripted. Each element in the matrix is given by its row and column number (Namboodori, 1983).
Multinet	Computer program for testing coevolution of networks and attributes.
NetworkExposure	The percentage of users of a health innovation in an individual's personal network (Valente, 1995).
Network	Set of relations between members of a community.
NetworkThreshold	The proportion of adopters in an individual's personal network necessary for an individual to adopt (Valente, 1995, 1996).
P*	A methodology for testing structural properties of a network such as whether there is a tendency for transitivity in the network (Wasserman & Faust, 1994).
Snowball Sampling	Snowball sampling consists of generating an initial sample of individuals and acquiring from this group a list of names of individuals who are then in turn interviewed, and the ties of these second-step individuals may also be interviewed, and so on.
Sociometric	Network data collected from the entire community (Wasserman & Faust, 1994).
Structural Equivalence	The degree to which individuals have similar patterns of network ties in the community (status similarity) (Burt, 1987). Sometimes referred to as positional equivalence.
R	Computer language used to program network measures that is an open source and freely available on the Web.
Reach	The ability of one node to contact another node through any number of intermediaries (Wasserman & Faust, 1994).
UCINET	University of California at Irvine (UCI) Network Analysis software: a comprehensive network analysis package so named because the authors were at UCI when they created it.

References

Albrecht, T. L., & Adelman, M. B. (Eds.). (1991). *Communicating social support.* Newbury Park, CA: Sage.

Alexander, C., Piazza, M., Mekos, D., & Valente, T. W. (2001). Peers, schools, and adolescent cigarette smoking: An analysis of the national longitudinal study of adolescent health. *Journal of Adolescent Health, 29,* 22–30.

Anderson, J. G., & Jay, S. J. (1985). The diffusion of medical technology: Social network analysis and policy research. *The Sociological Quarterly, 26,* 49–64.

Backer, T., & Rogers, E. (Eds.). (1993). *Organizational aspects of health communication campaigns: What works?* Newbury Park, CA: Sage.

Bernard, H. R., Killworth, P., & Sailer, L. (1982). Informant accuracy in social network data. *Social Science Research, 11,* 30–66.

Bogue, D. J. (Ed.). (1967). *Sociological contributions to family planning research.* Chicago: University of Chicago Press.

Boissevain, J. (1974). *Friends of friends: Networks, manipulators, and coalitions.* Oxford, UK: Basil Blackwell.

Bonacich, P. (1987). Power and centrality: A family of measures. *American Journal of Sociology, 92,* 1170–1182.

Borgatti, S. P. (2006). Identifying key players in a social network. *Computational and Mathematical Organization Theory, 12,* 21–34.

Borgatti, S. P., Everett, M. G., & Freeman, L. C. (2002). *UCINET for Windows: Software for social network analysis.* Cambridge, MA: Analytic Technologies.

Breiger, R. (1974). The duality of persons and groups. *Social Forces, 53,* 181–190.

Burt, R. (1984). Network items and the general social survey. *Social Networks, 6,* 293–339.

Burt, R. (1987). Social contagion and innovation: Cohesion versus structural equivalence. *American Journal of Sociology, 92,* 1287–1335.

Burt, R., & Minor, M. (1983). (Eds.). *Applied network analysis.* Beverly Hills, CA: Sage.

Burt, R. S. (1980). Models of network structure. *Annual Review of Sociology, 6,* 79–141.

Coleman, J. S., Katz, E., & Menzel, H. (1966). *Medical innovation: A diffusion study.* New York: Bobbs Merrill.

Cross, R., & Parker, A. (2003). *The hidden power of social networks: Understanding how work really gets done in organizations.* Cambridge MA: Harvard Business School Press.

Davis, A., Gardner, B. B., & Gardner, M. R. (1941). *Deep South: A social anthropological study of caste and class.* Chicago: University of Chicago Press.

Diani, M. & McAdam, D. (Eds.). (2003). *Social movements and networks: Relational approaches to collective action.* New York: Oxford University Press.

Freeman, L. (1979). Centrality in social networks: Conceptual clarification. *Social Networks, 1,* 215–239.

Freeman, L. (2000). Visualizing social networks. *Journal of Social Structure,* 1(1), February 4, 2000. www.cmu.edu/joss.

Freeman, L. C., Borgatti, S. P., & White, D. R. (1991). Centrality in valued graphs: A measure of betweens based on network flow. *Social Networks, 13,* 141–154.

Friedman, S. R., Curtis, R., Neaigus, A., Jose, B., & Des Jarlais, D. C. (1999). *Social networks, drug injectors' lives, and HIV/AIDS.* New York: Kluwer.

Galaskiewicz, J. (1985). Interorganizational relations. *Annual Review of Sociology, 11,* 281–304.

Goodman, L. A. (1961). Snowball sampling. *Annals of Mathematical Statistics, 32,* 148–170.

Gottleib, B. H. (1985). Social support and the study of personal relationships. *Journal of Social Personality Relationships, 2,* 351–375.

Granovetter, M. (1973). The strength of weak ties. *American Journal of Sociology, 78,* 1360–1380.

Granovetter, M. (1978). Threshold models of collective behavior. *American Journal of Sociology, 83,* 1420–1443.

Granovetter, M. (1982). The strength of weak ties: A network theory revisited. In P. V. Marsden & N. Lin (Eds.), *Social structure and network analysis.* Beverly Hills, CA: Sage.

Harary, F., Norman, R. Z., & Cartwright, D. (1965). *Structural models.* New York: John Wiley & Sons.

Heckathorn, D. D. (1997). Respondent-driven sampling: A new approach to the study of hidden populations. *Social Problems, 44,* 174–199.

Heckathorn, D. (2002). Respondent-driven sampling II: Deriving valid population estimates from chain-referral samples of hidden populations. *Social Problems, 49,* 11–34.

Huisman, M., & van Duijn, M. A. J. (2005). Software for social network analysis. In P. J. Carrington, J. Scott, & S. Wasserman (Eds.), *Models and methods in social network analysis.* Cambridge, UK: Cambridge University Press.

Hummon, N. B., & Carley, K. (1993). Social networks as normal science. *Social Networks, 15,* 71–106.

Kelly, J. A., St. Lawrence, J. S., Diaz, Y. E., Stevenson, L. Y., Hauth, A. C., Brasfield, T. L., et al. (1991). HIV risk reduction behavior following intervention with key opinion leaders of population: An experimental analysis. *American Journal of Public Health, 81,* 168–171.

Klovdahl, A. S. (1985). Social networks and the spread of infectious diseases: The AIDS example. *Social Science Medicine, 21,* 1203–1216.

Klovdahl, A. S. (1989). Urban social networks: Some methodological problems and possibilities. In M. Kochen (Eds.), *The small world.* Norwood, NJ: Ablex.

Klovdahl, A. S., Potterat, J. J., Woodhouse, D. E., Muth, J. B., Muth, S. Q., & Darrow, W. W. (1994). Social networks and infectious disease: The Colorado Springs study. *Social Science Medicine, 38,* 79–88.

Knoke, D., & Burt, R. S. (1983). Prominence. In R. S. Burt & A. Minor (Eds.), *Applied network analysis.* Beverly Hills, CA: Sage.

Knoke, D., & Kuklinski, J. H. (1982). *Network analysis.* Beverly Hills, CA: Sage.

Koehly, L., Goodreau, S., & Morris, N. (2005). Exponential family models for sampled and census network data. *Sociological Methodology, 34,* 241–270.

Laumann, E., Marsden, P., & Prensky, D. (1983). The boundary specification problem in network analysis. In R. Burt & M. Minor (Eds.), *Applied network analysis.* Beverly Hills, CA: Sage.

Lomas, J., Enkin, M., Anderson, G. M., Hanna, W. J., Vayda, E., & Singer, J. (1991). Opinion leaders vs. audit feedback to implement practice guidelines: Delivery after previous cesarean section. *Journal of American Medical Association, 265,* 2202–2207.

Lorrain, F., & White, H. C. (1971). Structural equivalence of individuals in social networks. *Journal of Mathematical Sociology, 1,* 49–80.

Marsden, P. V. (1987). Core discussion networks of Americans. *American Sociological Review, 16,* 435–463.

Marsden, P. V. (1990). Network data and measurement. *Annual Review of Sociology, 16,* 435–463.

Marsden, P. V. (1993). Reliability measurement. *Social Networks, 16,* 435–463.

Marsden, P. V., & Friedkin, N. E. (1993). Network studies of social influence. *Sociological Methods & Research, 22,* 127–151.

Marsden, P. V., & Lin, N. (Eds.). (1982). *Social structure and network analysis.* Beverly Hills, CA: Sage.

McGrath, C., Krackhardt D., & Blythe, J. (2002). Visualizing complexity in networks: Seeing both the forest and the trees. *Connections, 25*(1), 30–34.

McPherson, M., Smith-Lovin, L. & Brashears. M. (2006). Social isolation in America: Changes in core discussion networks over two decades. *American Sociological Review, 71,* 353–375.

Mizruchi, M. (1992). *The structure of corporate political action: Interfirm relations and their consequences.* Cambridge: Harvard University Press.

Mizruchi, M. S., & Stearns, L. B. (1988). A longitudinal study of the formation of interlocking directorates. *Administrative Science Quarterly, 33,* 194–210.

Monge, P. R., & Contractor, N. S. (2002). Theories of communication network. New York: Oxford University Press.

Morris, M. (Ed.). (2004). *Network epidemiology: A handbook for survey design and data collection.* Oxford University Press.

Namboodori, K. (1983). *Matrix algebra.* Beverly Hills, CA: Sage.

Neaigus, A., Friedman, S. R., Curtis, R., Des Jarlais, D. C., Furst, R. T., Jose, B., et al. (1994). The relevance of drug injectors' social and risk networks for understanding and preventing HIV infection. *Social Science & Medicine, 38,* 67–78.

Needle, R. H., Coyle, S. L., Genser, S. G., & Trotter, R. T. (1995). *Social networks, drug abuse, and HIV transmission.* NIDA research monograph #151, Rockville, MD.

Newman, M. E. J. Barabási, A. L., & Watts, D. J. (2006). *The structure and dynamics of networks.* Princeton, NJ: Princeton University Press.

Nohria, N. & Eccles, R. (Eds.). (1992). *Networks and organizations: Structure, form and action.* Cambridge, MA: Harvard University Press.

Palmore, J. A. (1967). The Chicago snowball: A study of the flow and diffusion of family planning information. In D. J. Bogue (Ed.), *Sociological contributions to family planning research* (pp. 272–263). Chicago: University of Chicago Press.

Pennings, J. M. (1980). *Interlocking directorates: Origins and consequences of connections among organizations' boards of directors.* San Francisco: Jossey-Bass.

Rice, R. E. (1982). Communication networking in computer-conferencing systems: A longitudinal study of group roles and system structure. In M. Burgoon (Ed.), *Communication yearbook,* Vol. 6 (pp. 925–944). Beverly Hills, CA: Sage.

Rice, R. E. (1988). Collection and analysis of data from communication system networks. In R. Allen (Ed.), *Proceedings of the ACM conference on office information systems* (pp. 134–141), Palo Alto, CA.

Rice, R. E. (1993). Using network concepts to clarify sources and mechanisms of social influence. In W. D. Richards & G. A, Barnett (Eds.), *Progress in communication sciences* (Vol. XII). Norwood, NJ: Ablex.

Rice, R. E., Borgman, C., & Reeves, B. (1988). Citation networks of communication journals, 1977–1985: Cliques and positions, citations made and citations received. *Human Communication Research, 15,* 256–283.

Robins, G., Pattison, P., Kalish, Y., & Lusher, D. (2007). An introduction to exponential random graph (P*) models for social networks. *Social Networks, 29,* 173–191.

Rogers, E. M. (1979) Network analysis of the diffusion of innovations. In P. W. Holland & S. Leinhardt (Eds.) *Perspectives on social network tesearch* (p. 137–164). New York: Academic Press.

Rogers, E. M. (2003). *Diffusion of innovations* (5th ed.). New York: Free Press.

Rogers, E. M., & Kincaid, D. L. (1981). *Communication networks: A new paradigm for research.* New York: Free Press.

Rosenfield, A. G., Asavasena, W., & Mikhanorn, J. (1973). Person-to-person communication in Thailand. *Studies in Family Planning, 14,* 145–149.

Salganik, M. J., & Heckathorn, D. D. (2004). Sampling and estimation in hidden populations using respondent-driven sampling. *Sociological Methodology, 34,* 193–239.

Sarason, I. G., Levine, H. M., Basham, R. B., & Sarason, B. R. (1983). Assessing social support: The social support questionnaire. *Journal of Personality and Social Psychology, 44,* 127–139.

Scott, J. (1991). *Network analysis: A handbook.* Newbury Park, CA: Sage.

Scott, J. (2000). *Network analysis: A handbook* (2nd ed.). Newbury Park, CA: Sage.

SNAPS (Social Network Analysis Procedures for Gauss, Version 1.0). (1989). Noah E. Friedkin, University of California at Santa Barbara.

Snijders, T. (2005). Models for longitudinal network data. In P. J. Carrington, J. Scott, & S. Wasserman (Eds.), *Models and methods in social network analysis* (p. 215–247). Cambridge, UK: Cambridge University Press.

Stephenson, K., & Zelen, M. (1989). Rethinking centrality: Methods and applications. *Social Networks, 11,* 1–37.

Valente, T. W. (1995). *Network models of the diffusion of innovations.* Cresskill, NJ: Hampton Press.

Valente, T. W. (1996). Social network thresholds in the diffusion of innovations. *Social Networks, 18,* 69–89.
Valente, T. W. (2005). Models and methods for innovation diffusion. In P. J. Carrington, J. Scott, & S. Wasserman (Eds.), *Models and methods in social network analysis.* Cambridge, UK: Cambridge University Press.
Valente, T. W., & Davis, R. L. (1999). Accelerating the diffusion of innovations using opinion leaders. *The Annals of the American Academy of the Political and Social Sciences, 566,* 55–67.
Valente, T.W., & Fosados, R. (2006). Diffusion of innovations and network segmentation: The part played by people in the promotion of health. *Journal of Sexually Transmitted Diseases, 33,* S23-S31.
Valente, T. W., Hoffman, B. R., Ritt-Olson, A., Lichtman, K., & Johnson, C. A. (2003). The effects of a social network method for group assignment strategies on peer led tobacco prevention programs in schools. *American Journal of Public Health, 93,* 1837–1843.
Valente, T. W., Jato, M. N., Van der Straten, A., & Tsitol, L. M. (1997). Social network influences on contraceptive use among Cameroonian women in voluntary associations. *Social Science and Medicine, 45,* 677–687.
Valente, T. W., Kim, Y. M., Lettenmaier, C., Glass, W., & Dibba, Y. (1994). Radio and the promotion of family planning in Gambia. *International Family Planning Perspectives, 20,* 96–100.
Valente, T. W., Poppe, P. R., & Merritt, A. P. (1996). Mass media generated interpersonal communication as sources of information about family planning. *Journal of Health Communication, 1,* 247–265.
Valente, T. W., & Saba, W. (1998). Mass media and interpersonal influence in a reproductive health communication campaign in Bolivia. *Communication Research, 25,* 96–124.
Valente, T. W., Unger, J., & Johnson, A. C. (2005). Do popular students smoke? The association between popularity and smoking among middle school students. *Journal of Adolescent Health, 37,* 323–329.
Valente, T. W., & Vlahov, D. (2001). Selective risk taking among needle exchange participants in Baltimore: Implications for supplemental interventions. *American Journal of Public Health, 91,* 406–411.
Vaux, A. (1988). *Social support: Theory, research, and intervention.* New York: Praeger.
Wasserman, S., & Faust, K. (1994). *Social networks analysis: Methods and applications.* Cambridge, UK: Cambridge University Press.
Watkins, S. C. (1994). *Social interaction and fertility change.* Paper prepared FOR the "Situating Fertility" workshop sponsored by the Social Sciences Research Council, Johns Hopkins University, Baltimore, MD.
Wellman, B., & Berkowitz, S. D. (1988). *Social structure: A network approach.* Cambridge, UK: Cambridge University Press.
Wickizer, T. M., Korff, M. V., Cheadle, A., Maeser, J., Wagner, E. H., Pearson, D., et al. (1993). Activating communities for health promotion: A process evaluation method. *American Journal of Public Health, 83,* 561–567.

Scaling and Cluster Analysis 10

David R. Roskos-Ewoldsen

Beverly Roskos-Ewoldsen

One of the most basic and central processes that humans engage in is the classification of objects into categories (Bailey, 1994). To classify an object as a member of a category, we must have an explicit or implicit understanding about how the objects can be similar or different. For example, some persuasive strategies use references to authority (e.g., experts, parental figures), whereas others may reference friends. Are these similar kinds of strategies? How would a researcher know how a person classifies persuasive strategies? As one might imagine, knowing *how* we classify is more complex than knowing *that* we classify. This chapter covers how to use scaling and clustering statistical methods to address questions of interest to communication researchers.

Borg and Groenen (1997) identified several goals of scaling and clustering procedures (see also Aldenderfer & Blashfield, 1986; Bailey, 1994; Kruskal & Wish, 1978). One goal is to simplify and describe data. All scaling and clustering methods help researchers reduce the complexity of a data set by identifying the underlying structure within a set of data. As an example, Wish (1976) wanted to know how people perceive different kinds of interpersonal situations. Using multidimensional scaling, he discovered four dimensions along which interpersonal situations varied: (1) cooperative and friendly versus competitive and hostile, (2) equal versus unequal, (3) socio-emotional and informal versus task-oriented and formal, and (4) intense versus superficial. Another example is a study by Hamilton and Nowak (2005) tracing the development of scholarship within the Information Systems Division (Division 1) of the International Communication

Association. In this study, they used cluster analysis to identify research trends from 1984 to 2004. Their analysis suggests a shift in focus from classic information and systems theory to a more cognitive orientation.

A second goal of scaling and clustering procedures is to test a hypothesis about the structure of a certain domain. For example, cultural analysis of soap operas has often focused on the role of gender and gender stereotypes within this genre of TV shows. Livingstone (1987, 1989, 1990) conducted several studies using multidimensional analysis to investigate how people understood characters in two nighttime dramas (i.e., soap operas), *Dallas* and *Coronation Street* (a British soap opera). Livingstone confirmed that gender played an important role in how viewers represented characters in soap operas. However, she also found that viewers' readings of gender roles within soaps appeared to be more complex than earlier nonempirical analysis had suggested. In particular, she demonstrated that it was not gender stereotypes per se that were driving the representation of the stories, but rather how the characters were depicted within the story (i.e., traditionally vs. nontraditionally). Importantly, multidimensional scaling offered a technique for testing an earlier structural hypothesis that had been proposed for how people interpreted and represented soaps operas.

A third goal of scaling and clustering techniques is to identify the underlying psychological representation of a set of stimuli. For example, Roskos-Ewoldsen (1997) used multidimensional scaling and cluster analysis to test whether people differentiated persuasive strategies dimensionally or categorically. He found that people perceived differences in persuasive strategies along continuous dimensions rather than as discrete categories of strategies. The dimensions were social desirability (using statistics vs. using fear appeals) and tactical (making references to friends vs. using high-quality arguments).

Though these statistical tools may be used for different goals, they share their reliance on proximity data, also called similarity data, to identify the underlying structure of a set of objects. In other words, scaling and cluster analyses are different statistical analyses in that both use proximity data. Though they have different assumptions, they can be used in complementary ways to aid in interpreting a data set (e.g., Deaux, Reid, Mizrahi, & Ethier, 1995). Our intent in this chapter is to describe how to gather proximity data, discuss the assumptions each statistical procedure makes about how information is represented, and illustrate how to use the procedures for communication research. Regarding representations, in brief, multidimensional scaling and individual differences scaling both assume a dimensional representation in which there are gradual differences among the objects along a continuous dimension (Carroll & Wish, 1974; Kruskal & Wish, 1978). A classic example of a dimensional representation is color. Cluster analysis assumes a categorical representation in which objects differ in terms of the discrete categories they comprise

(Tverksy, 1977). An example of categorical representation is type of bird (e.g., robin, penguin, etc.).

In the remainder of the chapter, we discuss several methods for gathering proximity data. Then we introduce multidimensional scaling, individual differences scaling, and cluster analysis. To highlight the use of the different techniques, we will use hypothetical similarity data for a subset of the strategies that Roskos-Ewoldsen used in his study of people's implicit theories of persuasion (see Table 10.1).

Table 10.1 List of the 20 Persuasive Strategies

1. Make reference to a trustworthy individual.
2. Make reference to an expert.
3. Use emotional and/or intense language.
4. Provide reasons.
5. Provide your own opinion.
6. Promise a reward.
7. Make references to negative consequences that could occur if the person does not change his or her mind.
8. Use sarcasm to point out limitations of the other person's position.
9. Use positive altercasting ("People with good qualities believe X.").
10. Try to redefine what is being discussed ("No, it's not a matter of X, the real issue is Y.").
11. Use emotional appeals.
12. Try to arouse the other person's fear.
13. Make reference to similarity ("I'm like you, and I believe X.").
14. Make reference to things that are important to the individual.
15. Use only high-quality, strong arguments.
16. Refer to empirical studies.
17. Make the argument that what is familiar, close, or is one's own is by its nature better or correct (appeal to familiarity).
18. Argue that X must be wrong because of who believes/advocates X (ad hominem).
19. Try to obscure the real issue by making a large number of irrelevant arguments.
20. Present arguments that the person is unlikely to have thought of or heard before (unique arguments).

Proximity Data

Multidimensional scaling, individual differences scaling, and cluster analysis all use proximity data. Proximity data involve measurements of how similar or dissimilar objects are to one another. Proximity data are typically discussed in terms of similarity because, in part, participants are usually asked to provide ratings of similarity. Ratings of similarity are used because rating the similarity of objects is psychologically easier than rating the dissimilarity of objects. There are a number of ways to obtain proximity data; we will describe the two most common (for others, see Borg & Groenen, 1997; Gordan, 1999).

ISSUES TO CONSIDER BEFORE GATHERING DATA

Before proximity data can be gathered, two issues must be addressed. The first issue involves setting boundaries for the objects to be chosen for inclusion. Researchers must clearly delineate what the focus of the study is and include only those objects that are within this boundary. For example, Roskos-Ewoldsen's (1997) study focused on *persuasive* strategies and not *compliance* strategies. Thus, the decision was made to exclude those strategies that were explicitly compliance-gaining strategies, such as threatening punishment.

Once the boundaries of the domain have been identified, the second issue is to identify objects representing that domain. This stage is of critical importance because if the domain of objects is incomplete, the ultimate solutions that are identified will be distorted and a partial picture will be created (Weller & Romney, 1988). There are at least three sources for finding relevant objects within a domain. The first is existing scholarship. One should conduct an extensive literature review of the research within the domain. For example, Roskos-Ewoldsen consulted public-speaking textbooks, empirical research on persuasion that had been conducted by both communication scholars and psychologists, and treatises on rhetoric. A second source is focus groups and interviews. Weller and Romney (1988) suggested a number of techniques for identifying a representative sample of objects from focus groups and intensive interviews. The third source is experts. A set of objects that has been generated through literature reviews or interviews preferably should be checked by experts in the field for completeness.

GATHERING AND PREPARING PROXIMITY DATA

After identifying items in the domain of study, the next step is to gather and prepare proximity data. Proximity data are collected by having participants rate the items on similarity scales or by having them sort the items into groups. Preparing proximity data involves transforming the data into a dissimilarity matrix.

Similarity ratings. The most common way to determine the similarity between two objects is to use a direct rating of their similarity using a standard 7- or 11-point scale. For example, a similarity rating between two persuasive strategies, "use logic" and "use emotional appeals," might be measured with the instructions below.

> For each pair of strategies, please judge how similar the strategies are to each other. In other words, rate how alike the two strategies are. Use your own interpretation of "similar" or "alike." There are no right or wrong answers. Circle the **number** that best describes your judgment of how similar the two strategies are.

Use Logic and Use Emotional Appeals										
0	1	2	3	4	5	6	7	8	9	10
Not at All Similar										Extremely Similar

In this way, the participants' judgments of the similarity of each pair of objects can be directly measured.

One decision to be made when using this technique is whether the particular ordering of the two items in a pair matters (e.g., use logic and use emotional appeals vs. use emotional appeals and use logic). A basic assumption underlying multidimensional scaling is that there is symmetry in ratings. That is, the similarity of A to B is equal to the similarity of B to A. If order matters, similarity judgments for both orders would be necessary. This assumption is usually but not always met. As a result, researchers typically assume that the order of the similarity judgments does not matter and obtain similarity ratings for only one order. In this case, the order of the objects to be compared is determined randomly. We will return to the assumption of symmetry later.

A disadvantage of this approach to collecting proximity data is that the number of judgments required to obtain a full or half matrix of similarity values grows rapidly with the number of objects in the set. For a full matrix, the number of ratings is $n \times (n - 1)$. For a half matrix, the number is $n \times (n - 1)/2$. For example, if there are 10 objects, the number of judgments for a half matrix is 45 ($10 \times 9/2$). With 20 objects, the number is 190 ($20 \times 19/2$). Roskos-Ewoldsen's (1997) study of persuasive strategies involved 89 strategies, which would have translated into 3,916 judgments for a half matrix or 7,832 for a full matrix.

To create an $n \times n$ half matrix of similarity data for n objects, the mean similarity rating is calculated across participants for each pair of objects. This matrix is used as the input to a clustering or scaling analysis.

Often the similarity matrix is converted to a dissimilarity matrix through a simple linear transformation (Corter, 1996). The value of the pair of items with the highest similarity score is subtracted from all of the similarity scores, and the absolute value of this difference becomes the dissimilarity score. Consequently, the pair of objects that was maximally similar now becomes minimally dissimilar. For example, the pair "Use emotional appeals" and "Use emotional or intense language" is the most similar pair in our data set, with a mean similarity rating of 8.36. The pair "Make reference to a trustworthy authority" and "Try to arouse the other person's fear" is the most dissimilar, with a mean rating of 0.25. If the similarity value for the former pair is subtracted from all pairs, it would have a dissimilarity value of 0 and the latter pair would have a dissimilarity value of 8.11 (Table 10.2).

Table 10.2 Matrix of Dissimilarities for 20 Persuasive Strategies

	TRUST	EXPERT	INTENSE	REASON	OPINIONS	REWARD	NEGCON	SARCA	POSALT
Trust	0	0.63	6.71	4.60	3.14	4.31	7.55	7.49	3.95
Expert	0.63	0	6.22	3.53	2.85	4.49	7.39	7.27	4.71
Intense	6.71	6.22	0	4.61	4.33	3.44	5.34	2.65	5.33
Reasons	4.60	3.53	4.61	0	3.10	4.47	7.28	6.56	6.19
Opinions	3.14	2.85	4.33	3.10	0	3.17	6.85	5.52	3.82
Reward	4.31	4.49	3.44	4.47	3.17	0	4.39	4.01	2.66
Negative Con	7.55	7.39	5.34	7.28	6.85	4.39	0	4.15	5.16
Sarcasm	7.49	7.27	2.65	6.56	5.52	4.01	4.15	0	5.62
Positive Alt	3.95	4.71	5.33	6.19	3.82	2.66	5.16	5.62	0
Redefine	5.56	5.33	5.13	5.42	4.65	3.88	4.58	4.35	3.24
Emotional	6.46	5.98	0.25	4.46	3.99	3.07	5.50	3.11	4.84
Fear	8.36	8.20	5.19	7.75	6.99	4.43	0.30	3.54	5.42
Similarity	3.17	3.95	5.85	5.82	2.79	2.93	6.08	6.20	0.87
Important	1.36	2.28	6.27	5.14	3.51	3.59	6.63	7.07	2.43
Strong	5.63	4.46	3.84	0.96	3.88	4.77	6.56	5.69	6.29
Empirical	4.66	3.57	3.65	1.64	3.65	4.16	6.28	5.70	5.61
Familiar	3.49	3.51	4.60	4.32	2.92	3.01	5.45	5.16	2.83
Ad Hominem	5.68	5.65	5.20	6.14	5.35	3.65	2.92	4.26	2.92
Obscure	7.87	7.53	4.39	6.27	6.24	4.78	5.31	2.70	6.32
Unique	6.12	5.69	4.44	3.52	4.47	4.33	5.64	3.60	5.93

Scaling and Cluster Analysis 281

Card sorting. A card-sorting task is probably the most utilized method for measuring similarity with larger sets of objects. In a sorting task, the name or a picture of each object is placed on a card. A randomly ordered (i.e., shuffled) set of cards is given to the research participants, and they are instructed to place similar items into piles with other similar items so that the items in the pile are more similar to each other than they are to items in other piles. What constitutes similar items is left to the participant to determine. Typically, the number of piles used by participants is unconstrained so that different participants may use different numbers of piles in their card sorts. Sometimes the number of piles that participants are allowed to use is established a priori by the researcher to control for individual differences in people's tendencies to create either a very few large piles or many small piles. However, even when the number of piles is unconstrained, the instructions may provide guidelines for the participants. For example, Roskos-Ewoldsen (1997) instructed participants to use as many or as few piles as they wanted, but also indicated that most

REDEFI	EMOTA	FEAR	SIMILA	IMPORTA	STRONG	EMPIR	FAMIL	ADHOM	OBSCURE	UNIQUE
5.56	6.46	8.36	3.17	1.36	5.63	4.66	3.49	5.68	7.87	6.12
5.33	5.98	8.20	3.95	2.28	4.46	3.57	3.51	5.65	7.53	5.69
5.13	0.25	5.19	5.85	6.27	3.84	3.65	4.60	5.20	4.39	4.44
5.42	4.46	7.75	5.82	5.14	0.96	1.64	4.32	6.14	6.27	3.52
4.65	3.99	6.99	2.79	3.51	3.88	3.65	2.92	5.35	6.24	4.47
3.88	3.07	4.43	2.93	3.59	4.77	4.16	3.01	3.65	4.78	4.33
4.58	5.50	0.30	6.08	6.63	6.56	6.28	5.45	2.92	5.31	5.64
4.35	3.11	3.54	6.20	7.07	5.69	5.70	5.16	4.26	2.70	3.60
3.24	4.84	5.42	0.87	2.43	6.29	5.61	2.83	2.92	6.32	5.93
0	4.91	4.70	3.63	5.26	5.07	4.84	3.36	1.97	2.11	2.66
4.91	0	5.40	5.49	5.85	3.59	3.37	4.10	4.94	4.70	4.46
4.70	5.40	0	6.39	7.54	6.88	6.80	5.86	3.01	5.01	5.70
3.63	5.49	6.39	0	2.23	6.40	5.49	2.61	3.66	6.85	6.12
5.26	5.85	7.54	2.23	0	5.82	4.90	2.05	5.20	7.67	6.03
5.07	3.59	6.88	6.40	5.82	0	1.42	4.02	5.67	5.47	3.18
4.84	3.37	6.80	5.49	4.90	1.42	0	3.86	4.87	5.71	3.81
3.36	4.10	5.86	2.61	2.05	4.02	3.86	0	3.59	5.28	3.92
1.97	4.94	3.01	3.66	5.20	5.67	4.87	3.59	0	4.25	4.39
2.11	4.70	5.01	6.85	7.67	5.47	5.71	5.28	4.25	0	1.62
2.66	4.46	5.70	6.12	6.03	3.18	3.81	3.92	4.39	1.62	0

participants used between 10 and 12 piles. In any case, there tends to be little difference in the multidimensional outcomes between constrained and unconstrained pile sorts (Weller & Romney, 1988).

There are several different variations on the card-sorting task (Weller & Romney, 1988). For example, people may be asked to complete two or more sorts of the same set of objects. Participants are informed prior to the initial sort that they will be completing multiple sorts and that they should use a different criterion for sorting the cards for each sort. When multiple sorts are used, additional dimensions of the data are often identified (Cantor, Brown, & Groat, 1985; Rosenberg & Kim, 1975). These data are analyzed using INDSCAL, which is a technique for combining multiple matrices of similarity data. INDSCAL will be discussed later.

Another technique for card sorting is to allow participants to place a card in more than one pile if they desire. Participants are asked to identify objects that may belong in more than one pile, and if they identify such objects, the name of the object is written on a second card and participants can place the object in an additional pile. Another technique is to present research participants with one card at a time and ask participants to identify all of the other cards in the pile that are similar to the identified card. Rosenberg and Kim (1975) and Wish (1976) discuss these alternative card-sorting tasks in more detail.

The data from the card-sorting task are organized by tabulating the co-occurrences of the items. To tabulate the co-occurrences, a matrix is set up in which all possible pairs of objects are represented. For example, a sort with 10 objects would produce a 10 × 10 half matrix with a row and column corresponding to each object. For this example, assume that a participant creates three piles, with the first pile containing 1, 2, 4, and 8; the second pile containing 3, 7, 9, and 10; and the third pile containing 5 and 6. Then a point of similarity would be given to 1 and 2, 1 and 4, 1 and 8, 2 and 4, 2 and 8, and 4 and 8. If a full 10 × 10 matrix were desired, a point would also be given to the opposite orders (i.e., 2 and 1, 4 and 1, 8 and 1, etc.), as well as to identity pairs (i.e., 1 and 1). Next, a point of similarity would be given to pairs within the second group and then the third group. This tabulation is done for each participant completing the pile sort. Finally, the matrices are added across participants. These raw frequencies are a simple measure of the similarity between each pair of objects, with higher numbers indicating greater similarity.

Often the co-occurrences are converted into dissimilarity scores in which higher numbers indicate greater dissimilarity. This relation affords a spatial metaphor in which the distance between two objects in a hypothetical space is a reflection of their similarity: Smaller distances indicate similarity, whereas greater distances indicate dissimilarity. When an item can be placed in only one pile, a simple way to transform co-occurrences into dissimilarity scores is to subtract the number of participants grouping each pair of objects from the total number of participants. Another way to calculate dissimilarity scores is to calculate them from the co-occurrence matrix using the following formula:

$$\delta_{ij} = \sqrt{\sum_{k=1}^{k}(s_{ik} - s_{jk})^2}$$

where δ_{ij} is the proximity of i and j, s_{ik} is the number of times objects i and k co-occur (i.e., the similarity between i and k), s_{jk} is the number of times objects j and k co-occur, and K is the set of objects in the sorting task. This transformation basically measures the extent to which objects i and j are placed in different piles. Higher scores indicate that the objects are often placed in different piles—they are dissimilar—and lower scores indicate that the objects are often placed in the same pile—they are similar. This transformation is typically referred to as the Δ (delta) transformation (van der Kloot & van Herk, 1991), and the matrix of proximity scores is called the Δ matrix (Kruskal & Wish, 1978). Rosenberg and Sedlak (1972) provide an analogy that aids in the understanding of this formula. A measure of social closeness between two individuals would be the number of times they interact with the same other people, regardless of whether they interact with the same other people simultaneously. Conversely, a measure of social distance would be the number of times they interact with different people.

The Δ transformation is typically used more often than the simple frequencies for several reasons (van der Kloot & van Herk, 1991). First, it provides more specific information about co-occurrences than frequencies. Second, the distribution of dissimilarity scores from the Δ transformation is typically smoother and less skewed than that for frequencies. Third, data that have been transformed typically result in configurations with lower stress values than data that have not been transformed. Stress is a measure of goodness of fit, with lower numbers indicating better fit, and will be discussed shortly. One consequence of lower stress is that the solution usually has fewer dimensions, which aids in interpretation.

Nevertheless, the two approaches overlap to a large extent. Van der Kloot and van Herk (1991) found very high correlations between the proximity data from the two approaches (all $rs > .90$), and the distances in the scaling configurations were also highly correlated (all $rs > .80$). However, they found a very slight advantage for the simple count matrix in the stress values in their analyses. Researchers should probably try both types of proximity data to determine which works best for understanding their data set.

Profiles. Proximity data can also be created out of a p (properties/subjects) × n (objects) rectangular matrix of data (Corter, 1996). For example, the matrix could contain participants' ratings of how likely they are to use different types of persuasive strategies. In this matrix, the columns would represent each strategy and the rows would represent the participants. Another example would be a matrix with columns representing different reality-TV programs with the rows of the matrix representing characteristics of the different programs (context vs. makeover; people appearing on a single episode vs. across season; etc.). Yet another example is when individuals complete multiple scales. An analysis of such matrices could be used to create a typology of different types of TV programs, persuasive strategies, or scales.

To create a half $n \times n$ matrix, the correlations between every pair of objects is calculated. This correlation matrix is used as the input for further analysis. Note that a matrix of correlations between different scales (e.g., need for cognition, self-monitoring, need for affiliation, and so forth) could be used to see how the different scores relate to each other. On another note, some have argued that correlations are not an appropriate measure of similarity because correlations are sensitive to the shape of a distribution of scores but not to the magnitude of the scores in distribution (Aldenderfer & Blashfield, 1984). Nonetheless, sometimes correlations are the best measures of similarity we can gather.

Final considerations. There are three final issues to consider before gathering and preparing proximity data. First, unlike inferential statistics, where the number of participants necessary to detect relations can be determined through a power analysis, there are no set procedures for determining the number of participants necessary for obtaining stable proximity data. Often, the data from 20–40 participants are used, but the exact number of participants probably depends on the nature of the rating task used to collect proximity data. In most cases, data are collapsed across participants and some measure of variability can be calculated. Ideally, the variability for each pair of objects should be relatively small, and the variability across pairs of objects should be roughly equivalent. As an example, for 20 persuasion strategies, participants' similarity ratings were averaged for each pair of strategies.

Second, although the scaling and clustering analyses we describe require proximity data in the form of dissimilarities, the data gathered are usually in the form of similarities. For this reason, we describe ways to transform similarity data to dissimilarity data. From a practical standpoint, however, most statistical packages will transform similarity values into dissimilarity values. It is critical to check which type of data the analysis uses and convert the data to that type. Alternatively, use the proper commands in your statistical program to indicate the type of input proximity data (similarities, dissimilarities, or correlations). If the program default assumes that the data are dissimilarities and if the data are similarity scores, the program will produce an inappropriate representation of the data.

Third, the default for some scaling and cluster analyses software is that there is a half matrix of data. That is, it is assumed that both halves of the matrix are identical. For example, the proximity data for 10 objects would be the bottom (or top) triangle of a 10 × 10 matrix and would comprise 45 (10 × 9/2) proximity values. However, most statistical packages will accept a half matrix or a full matrix of data, the latter either with or without the identity diagonal. As with the type of proximity data, use the proper commands to indicate whether a full or half matrix is used as input.

Multidimensional Scaling

The goal of multidimensional scaling (MDS) is to identify the dimensional representation of objects as represented in a spatial array of those objects.

ASSUMPTIONS OF MDS

There are three metric assumptions that underlie MDS. The first metric assumption is *minimality*, which is that any point must be at least as close to itself as it is to any other point. In terms of similarity data, an object must be most similar to itself. This assumption is taken for granted, and most statistical packages assign maximum similarity between an object and itself.

The second assumption is *symmetry*. Any point j must be just as close to point k as point k is to point j. For example, the similarity rating for "Use emotional appeals" and "Use logic" should be equal to the similarity rating for "Use logic" and "Use emotional appeals." As we discussed earlier, this assumption is rarely tested. However, to test this assumption using rating scales, researchers would ask participants to rate the similarity of the two objects using both orders (similarity of X to Y and similarity of Y to X) and then compare the ratings for each order. If the difference is not meaningful, then the two values can be averaged. In addition, many statistical packages can handle matrices in which the halves are not identical. If the difference is meaningful, it may be the case that MDS is not the optimal way to analyze the data. In particular, when the assumption of symmetry is violated, the data may be represented better categorically rather than dimensionally. When objects are best represented categorically, cluster techniques would be more appropriate than MDS.

The third assumption is *triangle inequality*. The metric assumption of triangle inequality is that any two points, j and k, that are both close to a third point, i, must be at least moderately close to each other. This assumption is based on the Pythagorean theorem, $c^2 = a^2 + b^2$, which describes the distances between points of a triangle. If a^2 represents the distance from j to i, and b^2 represents the distance from k to i, then the distance between *j* and *k*, represented by c^2, must be smaller than the combined distances between *j* and *i* (a^2) and *k* and *i* (b^2). In terms of similarity ratings, if "Use sarcasm" is close to "Use emotional or intense language" and "Use emotional appeals" is close to "Use emotional or intense language," then "Use sarcasm" should be relatively close to "Use emotional appeals," which it is. This assumption is the strictest assumption and must be met for the data to be considered metric (Carroll & Wish, 1974). However, pragmatically, most data sets will contain some violations of the triangle inequality, and MDS is robust to these minor violations. If there are a large number of violations or the violations are severe, then MDS is probably not appropriate (Carroll & Wish, 1974).

Although these three assumptions are typically taken for granted, they are important to consider. When the assumptions are met, then the objects are probably best represented dimensionally, and MDS would be the best technique to use for data analysis. When the assumptions are not met, however, then the objects are probably best represented categorically, and cluster analysis would be the appropriate tool to use.

THE NATURE OF DISTANCES IN MDS

MDS takes proximity data in the form of dissimilarities and converts them into distances within a dimensional space. The mathematics of how the proximity data are converted into distances is beyond the scope of this chapter. However, once the data are converted, there are several metrics that can be used to measure the distances in the space, including *Euclidean, city-block,* and *supremum* metrics. A critical question is which spatial metric should be used because most statistical packages include several metrics as options. Although the discussion of metrics may seem esoteric, and in fact is not necessary for conducting MDS, the different metrics represent how the dimensions are theoretically combined to make similarity judgments. Specifically, the choice between Euclidean and city-block metrics concerns whether the dimensions interact with one another. With the city-block metric, the dimensions are independent. Consequently, they are treated as separate dimensions when judgments of similarity are made and are additive when determining proximities. For example, when objects differ in terms of height and width, people can judge similarity based on the two dimensions separately. With the Euclidean metric, the dimensions are dependent on each other. Judgments of color provide a case in which the dimensions are integral. When making judgments of the similarity of two different colors, people do not consider brightness, saturation, and hue independently; instead, they are used holistically to make an overall judgment. Finally, in the unusual case when the supremum metric is operating, the objects are represented in a multidimensional space, but people are focusing on only the dimension along which the objects are most dissimilar when making similarity judgments (Carroll & Wish, 1974). To summarize, the Euclidean metric is most appropriate when dimensions in a space are integral, the city-block metric is best when the dimensions along which objects differ are separable, and the supremum metric is appropriate when only one dimension among several is used to make judgments.

The only case in which the choice of metric matters little is when there is a one-dimensional space. In a one-dimensional space, the distance d_{jk} between objects x_j and x_k is simply

$$d_{jk} = |x_j - x_k|$$

In an m-dimensional space, however, a choice between the Euclidean and city-block metrics must be made. The Euclidean distance is based on the Pythagorean theorem and is the straight-line distance between x_j and x_k:

$$d_{jk} = \sqrt{\sum_{m=1}^{M} |x_{mj} - x_{mk}|^2} = \left(\sum_{m=1}^{m} |x_{mj} - x_{mk}|^2\right)^{1/2}$$

where M is the number of dimensions. The city-block (or Manhattan) metric measures the distance between two objects as if they were located on city blocks. The city-block metric assumes that the distance between two objects is measured in one dimension and then in the other dimension, and then these distances are summed. More specifically, using a city-block metric, the distance between objects j and k is equal to the distance along the dimensions upon which the two objects differ. In an m-dimensional space, the distance between the objects is the sum of the distances between them on each dimension:

$$d_{jk} = \sum_{m=1}^{M} |x_{mj} - x_{mk}|$$

The three metrics are actually special instances of the Minkowski r-metric:

$$d_{jk} = \left(\sum_{m=1}^{M} |x_{mj} - x_{mk}|^r\right)^{1/r}$$

With the Minkowski r-metric, r can be any value between 1 and infinity (∞). The Euclidean metric is indicated when $r = 2$, and the city-block metric is indicated when $r = 1$. When $r = \infty$, the supremum metric is indicated.

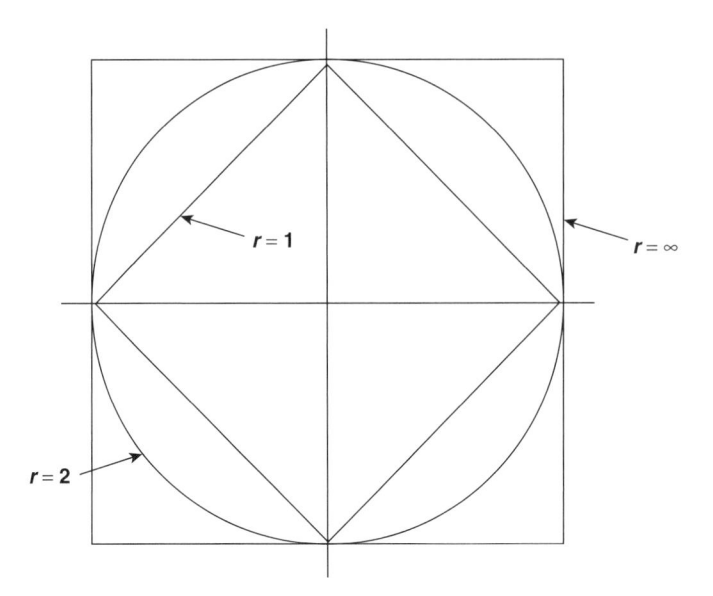

Figure 10.1 Distances Based on City-Block (small square), Euclidean (circle), and Supremum (large square) Metrics

If we had a point x at the origin in a two-dimensional space, the set of distances d from x would look different depending on the metric used. In Figure 10.1, the diamond shows all of the points that are a distance d from x if $r = 1$. The circle shows all of the points that are a distance d from x if $r = 2$. Finally, the large square shows all of the points that are a distance d from x if $r = \infty$.

TENSIONS BETWEEN DISTANCES AND PROXIMITIES

The goal of MDS is to construct a spatial representation of proximity data. A classic example of this is when the distances between major cities are treated as proximities and used as input into an MDS. The resulting two-dimensional configuration should perfectly fit the data, as demonstrated by a *Shepard diagram*. A Shepard diagram is a scatterplot of the proximities from the data set and the distances in the multidimensional space. When the fit between the spatial data and the distances matches perfectly, there is a perfect monotonic relation between the two: As proximity increases, so does distance, and distance can be predicted perfectly from proximity.

Of course, a perfect monotonic relation is the ideal case. Typically, there is error in the proximity data so that the relation is not perfect. Although the goal of MDS is to create the best fit possible between proximity data and distances in a dimensional space, the fit can differ in strength.

Scaling and Cluster Analysis

A strong monotonic relation occurs when larger dissimilarities always result in larger distances in the space. That is, when objects x and y are more proximal to each other than objects a and b ($\delta_{xy} < \delta_{ab}$), then the distance in the dimensional space between objects x and y cannot be larger than the distance between objects a and b ($d_{xy} < d_{ab}$). A weak monotonic relationship occurs when the distances are allowed to be equal ($d_{xy} \leq d_{ab}$). Figure 10.2 shows the Shepard diagram for a two-dimensional solution of the 20 persuasive strategies introduced earlier. Clearly, there is not a perfect monotonic relation between distance and proximity; rather, the relation would be considered moderate.

The measure of how poorly the distances in the space match the proximity data is called *stress* (Borg & Groenen, 1997). In other words, stress is a measure of nonmonotonicity in the data. The preferred formula for calculating stress (S) is:

$$S = \sqrt{\frac{\sum (d_{xy} - \delta_{xy})^2}{\sum d_{xy}^2}}$$

where d_{xy} is the distance between objects x and y in the MDS solution and δ_{xy} is the proximity estimated by the similarity judgments. Stress is invariant to (a) rigid transformations of the configuration, such as rotating or

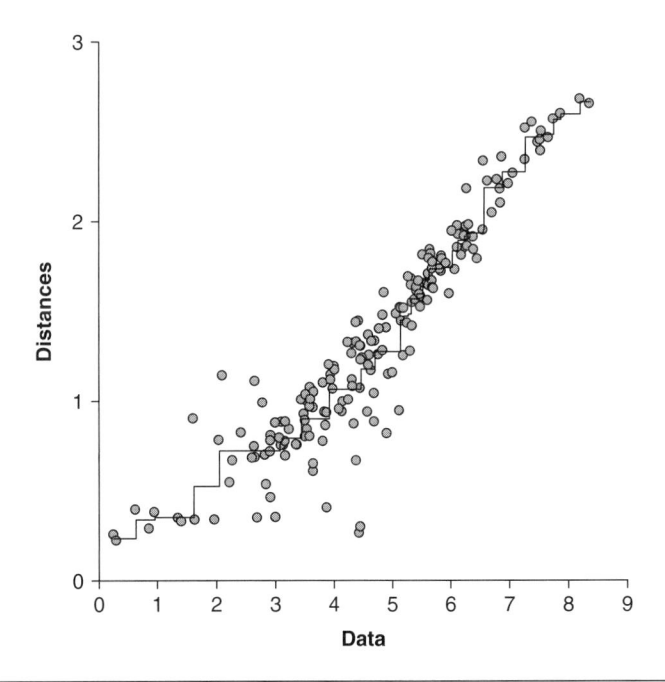

Figure 10.2 Shepard Diagram for the 20 Persuasive Strategies in a Two-Dimensional Space

reflecting the space, and (b) stretching or shrinking of the space that is uniform in nature. Stress ranges from 0 to 1. The closer S is to 1, the worse the fit, so values of S closer to 0 are desirable. There is no set value for an acceptable stress level, but a general rule of thumb is that an S less than .15 is satisfactory, but an S less than .10 is desirable.

METRIC VERSUS NONMETRIC MDS

A final distinction important to MDS is whether the data are interval or ordinal. Most statistical packages require the specification of whether the data are metric (ratio or interval) or nonmetric (ordinal). If the data are ratio or interval, than a metric (or linear) analysis should be used. If the data are ordinal, then a nonmetric (or ordinal) analysis should be used. Although ordinal data are not metric, the output of an ordinal analysis produces what is in essence a metric representation of the data (Carroll & Wish, 1974). One important advantage of an ordinal MDS analysis is that the stress value is always lower because of the looser requirements for the analysis, compared to a metric analysis.

DETERMINING THE NUMBER OF DIMENSIONS IN A SPACE

A set of n objects can be represented in a multidimensional space ranging from 1 to $n-1$ dimensions. There are no set rules for determining the appropriate number of dimensions for a set of objects. However, one rule of thumb is that the number of dimensions should be no greater than $n/4$ because a solution with more dimensions than this typically is lacking in parsimony and is difficult to interpret (Kruskal & Wish, 1978). For example, with our data set of 20 strategies, we would not want a solution greater than $20/4 = 5$ dimensions because the interpretation of the configuration would be extremely difficult with so few items relative to the number of dimensions.

Beyond determining the upper limit for the number of dimensions, there are several factors to consider in determining the number of dimensions that best captures the data set. The first factor is the stress level for each dimension. To obtain the stress levels, an MDS must be conducted for each possible number of dimensions. In our case, five analyses were conducted. Next, a scree plot of the stress values for each dimension is constructed, with the number of dimensions plotted on the x axis and stress plotted on the y axis. Figure 10.3 shows the scree plot for the 20 persuasive strategies. To determine the appropriate number of dimensions, look for an elbow in the scree plot in conjunction with the .10 rule. For example, in Figure 10.3, there is an elbow at two dimensions (stress = .11)

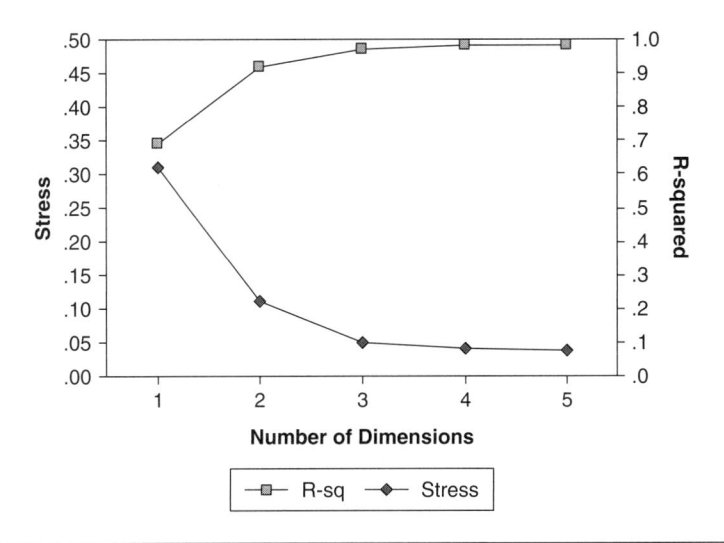

Figure 10.3 Scree Plot for the 20 Persuasive Strategies

and another at three dimensions (stress = .05). Because the stress level at three dimensions is in the desirable range whereas the one at two dimensions is not, a three-dimensional solution appears to be most appropriate for the 20 strategies.

The second factor is the amount of variance (R^2) in the proximity data that is accounted for by the distances in the MDS space. Most statistical packages will report an R^2 value for each dimension of an MDS solution. A scree plot of the R^2 values is then used to identify the appropriate number of dimensions. Although there are no set rules for an optimal R^2, the rule of thumb is that an R^2 greater than .90 is satisfactory but an R^2 greater than .95 is desirable. As with stress, to determine the appropriate number of dimensions, one would look for an elbow in the R^2 plot, in conjunction with the desired value. For our data (Figure 10.3), an elbow appears at two dimensions (R^2 = .92), but the R^2 at three dimensions is at the desirable level (R^2 = .97). Typically, the elbow for stress and R^2 will point to the same number of dimensions—in this case, three dimensions.

The final factor is the interpretability of the solutions. As the number of dimensions increases, the interpretability of the space becomes correspondingly more difficult. Trying to interpret a four- or five-dimensional space is extremely difficult, but not impossible. For example, Wish (1976) found a four-dimensional solution for interpersonal situations and was able to provide a clear interpretation of this four-dimensional space. However, this is an exception. Most researchers keep the number of dimensions to two or three for ease of interpretation.

For our data, a two-dimensional space rather than a three-dimensional space was chosen (Figure 10.4). There were several reasons for this choice. First, Roskos-Ewoldsen (1997) found clear support for a two-dimensional solution in his original study of 89 strategies; when in doubt, parsimony is preferred over complexity. Second, the two-dimensional solution was easier to interpret than the three-dimensional solution. Third, as we shall see in the section on AdTree, comparing a cluster analysis to an MDS analysis is easier when the MDS solution is two-dimensional.

WHAT DO THE DIMENSIONS MEAN? INTERPRETING THE SPACE

After the appropriate number of dimensions for the MDS space has been determined, the next step for the researcher is to provide an interpretation of the dimensions. It is important for researchers to know that the dimensions depicted in the visual representation, produced by the statistical software, are arbitrary (Borg & Groenen, 1997). By this, we mean that the space can be rotated, transposed (e.g., by multiplying the coordinates for each object in the space by −1), and in other ways manipulated *as long as the distances between the objects within the space remain constant*. Again, the dimensions provided by the software are completely arbitrary, and they should play no role in how the space is interpreted.

The first step in interpreting an MDS space is to inspect the space visually and identify possible dimensions that run through the space, regardless of the dimensions provided by the software. Although some researchers base their interpretation on a visual inspection, many researchers are uncomfortable doing so because it is an entirely subjective task. Instead, once a researcher identifies the possible dimensions, new participants rate each of the objects along each of the possible dimensions. For example, one possible dimension in Figure 10.4 is the perceived effectiveness of the strategy. Another is the social acceptability of the strategy. A third is the objective versus subjective nature of the strategy. Participants would rate each strategy along one dimension, and then rate each strategy along the second dimension, and so on. The ratings were made on 11-point scales. In some instances, the scales ranged from 0 (e.g., *not at all effective*) to 10 (*extremely effective*), and in others they ranged from −5 (e.g., *not at all socially acceptable*) to +5 (*extremely socially acceptable*). However, any continuous scale that is deemed appropriate for a dimension can be used.

To determine how well the possible dimensions capture the actual dimensions in the data, a multiple regression is conducted for each of the possible dimensions. The R^2 from the regression analysis is used as an estimate of the fit between the rated dimension and either of the dimensions in the MDS configuration. To conduct the analysis, the mean ratings of each object along the dimension serve as the predicted variable. The objects' coordinates for each dimension in the MDS space, located in the MDS output, are the predictor variables (Kruskal & Wish, 1978;

Scaling and Cluster Analysis

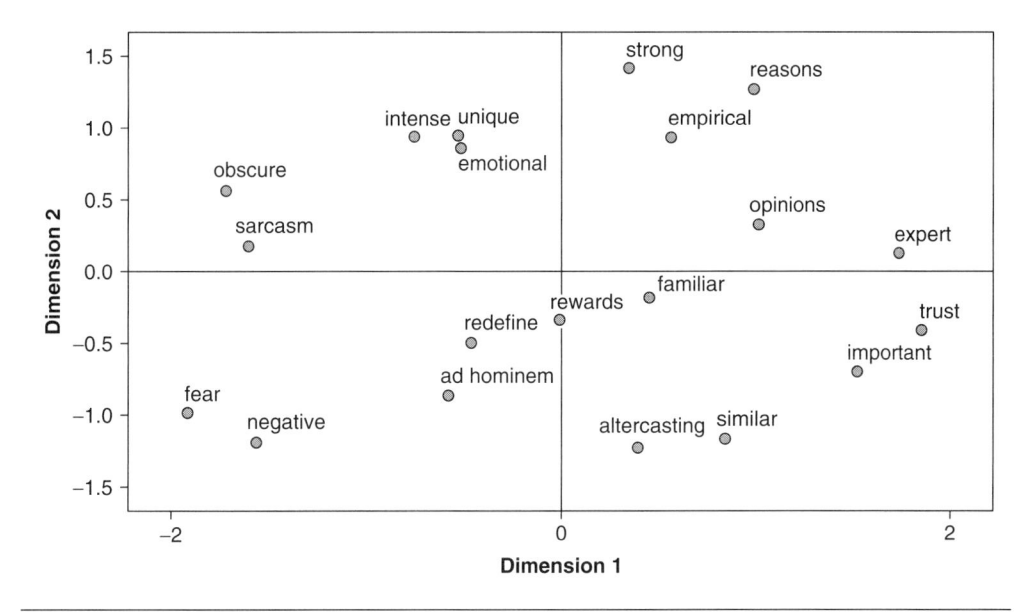

Figure 10.4 Two-Dimensional Solution for the 20 Persuasive Strategies

Rosenberg et al., 1968). Kruskal and Wish (1978) argue that, ideally, the R^2 should be greater than .90 for a rating dimension to be considered to have captured a dimension in the MDS space. Pragmatically, however, researchers may have to settle for lower R^2 values, particularly as the number of objects in the space increases. Table 10.3 presents the R^2 results from the regression analyses for the 20 persuasive strategies.

The next steps are to plot the possible dimensions that have the best fit with the data and choose the dimensions that are orthogonal. The regression weights from the regression analysis provide x and y coordinates for one point along the relevant dimension. This point and (0,0) are used to plot the dimension in the MDS space. Figure 10.5 shows two dimensions mapped onto the two-dimensional space for the 20 strategies. In most cases, many dimensions are plotted because they all appear to capture the true dimensions. Once plotted, try to choose dimensions that are relatively orthogonal. However, with social stimuli, it is rare to find dimensions that are perfectly orthogonal, so the question becomes, how orthogonal should the dimensions be? To measure the extent to which two dimensions are orthogonal, the mean ratings for the objects along one dimension are correlated with the mean ratings of the objects along a second dimension. Although there are no set rules, clearly if two dimensions are highly correlated ($r > .6$), they may be measuring the same thing. We have adopted a rule that correlations up to $r = .50$ are acceptable, but whether dimensions are too correlated depends on the research area and how much sense the dimensions make in terms of interpreting the space. For our example, the correlation between the two dimensions in Figure 10.5 was .45, which we considered acceptable.

Table 10.3 Regression Results for Possible Interpretations of the Two-Dimensional MDS Solution for 20 Persuasive Strategies

Dimensional Interpretation	R^2
Tactic (associative vs. message oriented)	.81***
Social Desirability	.71***
Provides Information	.45**
Verbally Aggressive	.34*
Obviously Trying to Persuade	.14

Note: R^2 is based on a multiple regression in which the mean ratings of each object along the possible dimension serve as the predicted variable, and the objects' coordinates for each dimension in the MDS space are the predictor variables.
* $p < .05$
** $p < .01$
*** $p < .001$

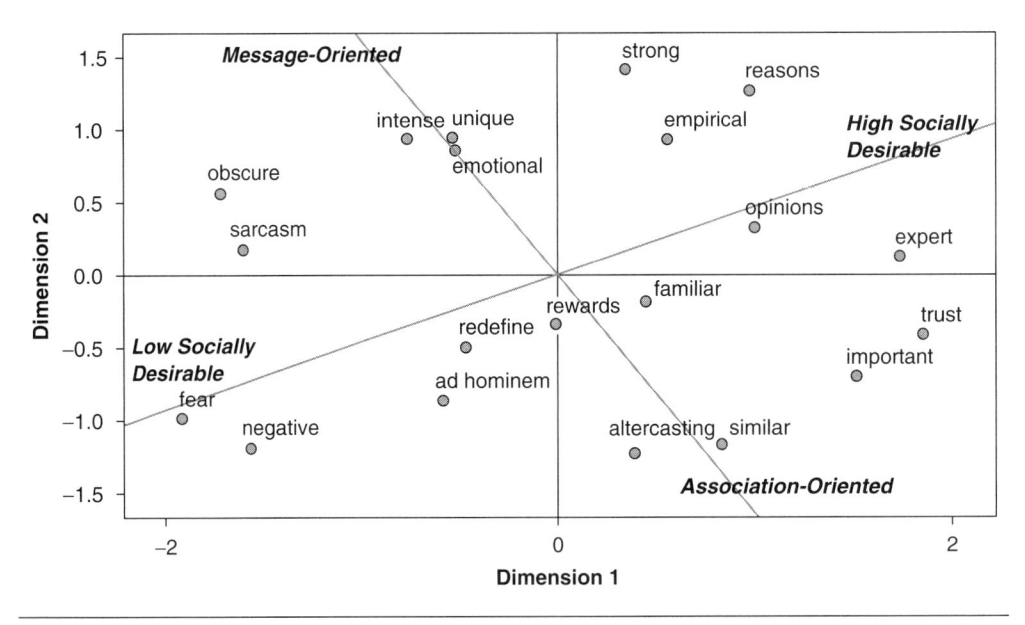

Figure 10.5 Two Possible Dimensions Mapped Onto the Two-Dimensional Solution for the 20 Persuasive Strategies

RELIABILITY OF THE SOLUTION

As a final step, to ensure that the MDS solution captures the true dimensionality and locations of the objects, one should check the reliability of the solution. There are several ways to do this (Kruskal & Wish, 1978). The most obvious way is to replicate the study to determine if the same solution occurs in the replication. A second way is to take a subset of the original objects and replicate the study on this subset of objects. As an example, Roskos-Ewoldsen's (1997) study of 89 persuasive strategies was replicated with a subset of 40 strategies. Yet another way to determine the reliability of the solution is to split the original data set in half and see if both halves of the data set replicate the original solution.

Individual Differences Scaling

So far in this chapter, we have acted on the assumption that all of the participants judge the similarities between the different objects in fundamentally the same way. In fact, this is an assumption of MDS analyses. But is it always a valid assumption? Although it seems to be a safe assumption for the perception of something physical, like colors, even for colors it may not be met. For example, the small percentage of people who are color blind would not rate colors the same as those who are not. Fortunately, there are two approaches designed to capture these differences in judgments.

One approach is to assume that there are fundamental differences in the spatial representations for different groups of people. In this case, a researcher would gather similarity data from the two groups and separately analyze their similarity matrices using MDS. The dimensionality of the spaces, the locations of the objects within the spaces, and the interpretations of the spaces may differ between the two groups.

A second approach is to assume that the underlying space is the same for both samples—that is, the dimensionality and locations of the objects are similar—but the two samples differentially weight the dimensions in making their judgments (Carroll & Wish, 1974). In our study of persuasive strategies, we might hypothesize that people who are high in need for cognition will perceive greater differences between tactics on the two extremes of the tactic dimension, compared with people who are low in need for cognition. In other words, high-need-for-cognition individuals stretch the tactic dimension because it is particularly important to them. This latter approach is used in *individual differences scaling* (INDSCAL).

With INDSCAL, there is a matrix for each type of group being considered. For example, if we were interested in how different groups of people perceived different video game genres, we might compare proximity data from nonplayers of video games, heavy players of first-person shooters, and heavy players of sports games. In this case, we would have three matrices of proximities. Because the groups add another dimension to the $n \times n$ proximity matrix, INDSCAL is often referred to as a three-way MDS.

INDSCAL makes four basic assumptions. First, it assumes that there is a set of common dimensions that underlie all of the different groups' judgments of the objects. Second, it assumes that these dimensions are shared by all of the individuals across the different groups. Third, it assumes that the similarity judgments for all of the participants across the different groups are linearly related to the distances in the space, and that all of the judgments within a group of participants are weighted in the same manner. Fourth, INDSCAL assumes that the distances in the space are represented by a modified Euclidean function:

$$d_{jk} = \left(\sum_{m=1}^{M} w_m \left| x_{mj} - x_{mk} \right|^2 \right)^{1/2}$$

where w_m is the weight that the participants apply to dimension m, corresponding to the importance of that dimension for participants' similarity judgments. If a dimension has a large weight for one group of participants, it means that participants in that group are placing a heavy emphasis on that dimension, with objects along this dimension being perceived as having greater dissimilarity, compared to another group whose weight is smaller on that dimension. Because the distances are weighted, INDSCAL is sometimes called a weighted Euclidean model. It is Euclidean because although distances in INDSCAL can mathematically come from other metrics, pragmatically, INDSCAL assumes a Euclidean space.

The output for INDSCAL contains two different spaces. The *group stimulus space* is the configuration of objects within an MDS space, collapsing across the groups. The *weight space* indicates how much each group weights a dimension or how salient that dimension is for each group. Figure 10.6 shows the group stimulus space for an INDSCAL analysis of our hypothetical strategy data (top) and the weight space for the low (Group 1) and high (Group 2) need for cognition groups (bottom). The two dimensions appear to be Social Desirability (Dimension 1) and Tactical Technique (Dimension 2). These are similar to the dimensions identified through MDS. The weight space indicates that the social desirability dimension was more salient for the low-need-for-cognition group, whereas the tactical technique dimension was more salient for the high-need-for-cognition group.

The weights are a critical part of the INDSCAL analysis and should be considered alongside the stimulus space when interpreting the solution. The weights should be greater than zero even though sometimes small negative weights are found. A weight of zero indicates that the group is not using that dimension to make judgments. A large negative weight is not interpretable and indicates a serious problem in the analysis, such as misspecified data. According to Arabie et al. (1987), if the weights are not

Scaling and Cluster Analysis

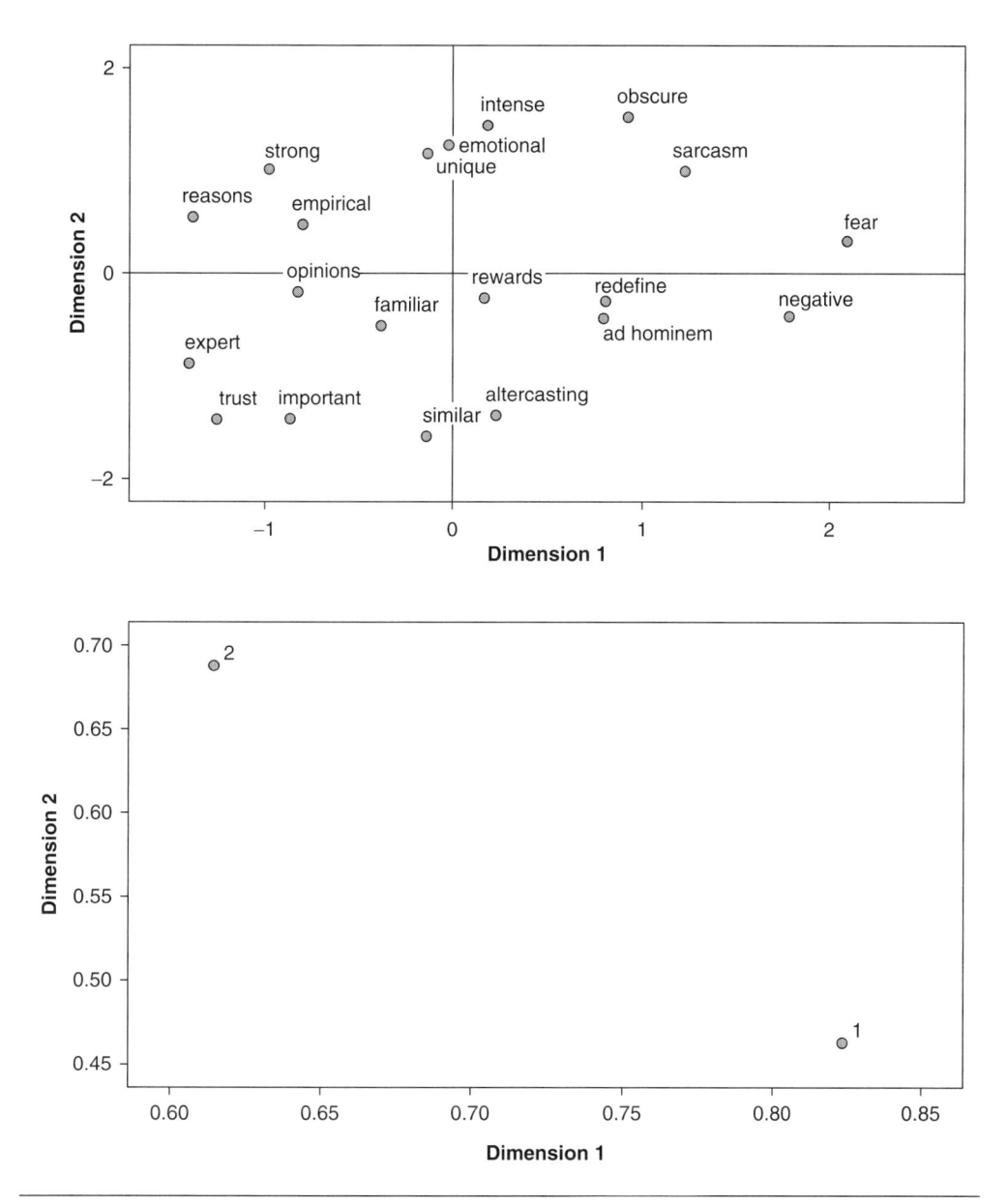

Figure 10.6 Top: The INDSCAL Group Stimulus Space for the 20 Persuasive Strategies

Bottom: The INDSCAL Weight Space for the Groups With Low Need for Cognition (Group 1) and High Need for Cognition (Group 2)

Dimension 1 is social desirability. Dimension 2 is tactical technique.

interpretable, then a two-way MDS should be used instead of the three-way MDS because nothing is being learned from the INDSCAL analysis. If a group has zero weights for all of the dimensions, this suggests possible problems with the data set, including a misspecified data set. Carroll and Wish (1974) discuss an interesting situation where there are two different groups and a four-dimensional solution is indicated. Group 1 has zero weights on Dimensions 1 and 2, which indicates that the group is not using these dimensions when making similarity judgments. In addition, Group 2 has zero weights on Dimensions 3 and 4, suggesting that Group 2 is ignoring Dimensions 3 and 4. In this case, Groups 1 and 2 are using completely different sets of dimensions to make their similarity judgments.

INDSCAL differs from a two-way MDS in three major ways. One is that the dimensions that are provided in an INDSCAL output are meaningful. It is these particular, interpretable dimensions that are stretched according to the weights. As a result, the dimensional space cannot be transformed as freely as it is in a two-way MDS. Critically, the space cannot be arbitrarily rotated as it can in a two-way MDS (Carroll & Wish, 1974). Nevertheless, there are four possible transformations that can be made in INDSCAL (Arabie et al., 1987). First, all of the objects' coordinates along a dimension could be multiplied by a constant. This simply rescales the weights by a multiplicative constant, so there would be no pragmatic effect of the transformation. Second, the space could be reflected (i.e., all of the weights for the dimension are multiplied by –1). This results in a mirror image of the original space. Again, unless this is done to align the space with an earlier MDS, there is no pragmatic effect of the transformation. Third, a matrix can be permutated, which simply means that one axis is switched with the other. In other words, the order of the coordinates for all of the objects is systematically switched. Fourth, the space can be translated by adding a constant to the coordinates for one of the dimensions. This will switch the origin of the axis, which may be useful, but it has no other effect on the space. These last three transformations—reflection, permutation, and translation—have no effects on the weights for the transformed dimension.

Another way in which INDSCAL differs from a two-way MDS is that the appropriate number of dimensions to be used in INDSCAL is determined solely by the improvement in the percent variance accounted for (R^2), because stress is not calculated in an INDSCAL analysis. However, when there are a large number of groups being compared with INDSCAL, there is a risk that the elbow in the R^2 scree plot is misleading. In particular, the case may arise where the next dimension beyond the elbow may not improve the percent of variance accounted for, but some of the groups are weighting that next dimension heavily. If they are, then the added dimension is interpretable in light of these groups, even though R^2 does not increase dramatically (Kruskal & Wish, 1978).

A third difference between INDSCAL and MDS is that INDSCAL can track changes across time. To do this, the initial configuration is specified a priori. This initial specification affords a comparison with previous studies. If the specification adapted from the old data fits the new data well, then the previous study is replicated. More importantly, specifying the configuration a priori in a longitudinal study can tell the researcher whether the passage of time has influenced the dimensional weights. For example, if a researcher had been studying the perception of realism in TV shows across time, the question could be asked how the introduction of so many reality programs during the past decade has influenced the weights regarding realism.

Cluster Analysis

The last type of analysis we discuss in this chapter is *cluster analysis*. Cluster analysis differs qualitatively from MDS and INDSCAL. A basic distinction between cluster analysis and MDS/INDSCAL involves the assumptions that each approach makes about the underlying representation of the objects (Tversky, 1977). As we have already discussed, MDS assumes that objects are represented along dimensions. The closer two items are on a dimension, the more similar they will be perceived. On the other hand, cluster analysis assumes that objects are differentiated *categorically*. The more features that two objects share in common, the more similar they will be perceived and the higher the likelihood that they are in the same category, but it is the unique features of an object that defines it as distinct from other members of other categories within the domain. Cluster analysis incorporates both the shared and unique features of objects to place similar items into their appropriate category (i.e., cluster).

There are many different kinds of cluster analysis. One characteristic along which cluster analyses differ is whether the clusters are unique. Some analyses create unique clusters, whereas others allow overlapping clusters. A second characteristic is whether they are hierarchical (Corter, 1996). Hierarchical analyses permit nested clusters, whereas nonhierarchical analyses do not. A third characteristic is whether the analysis is agglomerative or divisive. An agglomerative analysis begins with all of the objects forming a separate cluster, and then it creates structure by combining smaller clusters into larger clusters. Conversely, a divisive analysis begins with all of the objects in one large cluster and then creates structure by dividing the larger clusters into smaller clusters (Bailey, 1994). In this section, we will focus on hierarchical models with unique clusters, for two reasons. First, it is most appropriate for identifying the unique features of the objects as well as the relative importance of the features for categorizing (i.e., clustering) the objects. Second, it is the type of cluster analyses used most frequently by communication scholars.

ULTRAMETRIC TREES

Ultrametric trees are what come to mind when communication researchers think about cluster analysis. Ultrametric trees are often represented by *dendrograms,* or tree models, of the data. At a very basic level, the data analysis proceeds by putting the two most similar objects together into a cluster. Then the next two similar items are put together into a cluster. If the next two similar items are not part of the original cluster, a new cluster is created, but if one of the items is from the original cluster, the new item is added to that original cluster so that the first cluster is nested within the new cluster. The result is that each object is assigned to a nonoverlapping cluster and the clusters are organized hierarchically (Aldenderfer & Blashfield, 1984; Corter, 1996). This process of constructing and nesting clusters over time, when represented graphically, produces an ultrametric tree.

The basic assumption of ultrametric trees is that of *ultrametric inequality* (Corter, 1996). Basically, the ultrametric inequality assumption is that for any three objects in a tree, two of the objects must form a lower level, or subcluster, in relation to the third object. For example, if *x* and *y* form a cluster that is then linked with *z*, *x* and *y* would be a subcluster within the larger cluster involving *z*. Mathematically, the ultrametric inequality is:

$$\delta_{x,y} \leq MAX\ [\delta_{x,z}, \delta_{y,z}]$$

Of course, an actual matrix of similarity data rarely satisfies the ultrametric inequality for all triplets of objects in the matrix, which means that the ultrametric tree will not fit the data perfectly.

One important issue for cluster analysis is how the data are linked together into clusters. There are a number of different techniques for creating linkages (Aldenderfer & Blashfield, 1984). Unfortunately, the different models for creating linkages can result in very different clusters. We will briefly discuss three of the more common and well-established methods: single linkage, average linkage, and the Ward method (Aldenderfer & Blashfield, 1984).

Single linkage. The single linkage method creates the lowest-level cluster by combining the two most similar (i.e., least dissimilar) items. The critical element of the single linkage model is how additional objects are added to existing clusters. A new object is added to the cluster based on the object in the cluster to which it is most similar. If *x* and *y* are joined into the first cluster, and if the next highest similarity is between *z* and *x*, then *z* will be added to that cluster regardless of how similar *z* is to *y*. An example of a single linkage cluster analysis for our set of 20 persuasive strategies is found in Figure 10.7 (top). One of the advantages of the single linkage model is that the solution is invariant to transformations of the dissimilarity data. Many of the other linkage models are sensitive to transformations of the data. However, a disadvantage with the single linkage method is that it has a tendency to create chains of clusters, which means that one large cluster is often formed by adding object after object to it. The result is an impoverished representation of the clusters in the original data set (Aldenderfer & Blashfield, 1984; Bailey, 1994). For example, with our data, it appears that there are only two clusters: a large one that contains 17 of

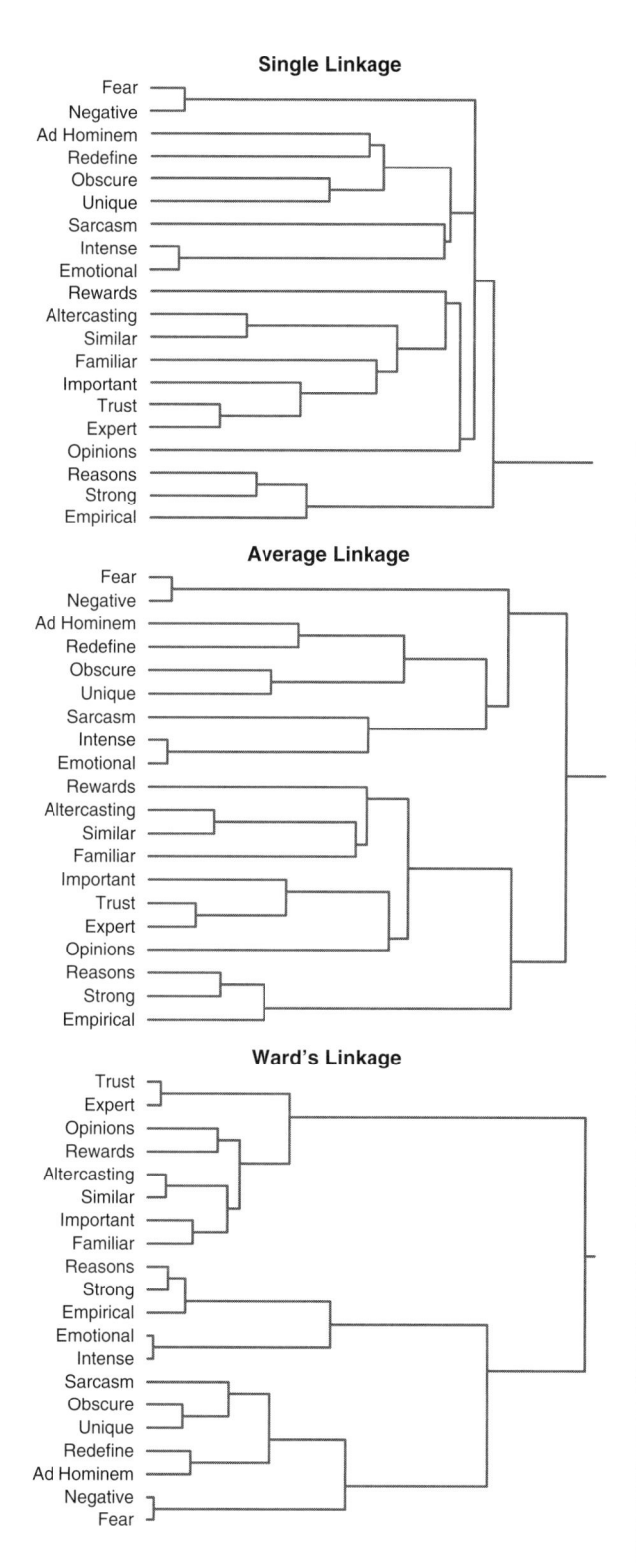

Figure 10.7 Examples of Three Methods for Creating Hierarchical Clusters: Single Linkage (top), Average Linkage (middle), and the Ward Method (bottom)

the 20 strategies and a small one that contains only 3 ("Use reasons," "Use strong arguments," and "Refer to empirical studies").

Average linkage. The second method for creating linkages is the average linkage method. The basic distinction between the average linkage method and the single linkage method is how the similarity of a new object to an existing cluster is calculated to determine whether it should be added to the cluster. In the average linkage method, a new object is added to a cluster based on the average similarity of the object to the objects already in the cluster. The object with the highest similarity (i.e., lowest dissimilarity) to the averaged object's similarity within the cluster is added to the cluster. The middle panel in Figure 10.7 shows the results of using the average linkage method for our 20 persuasive strategies. There appear to be two major clusters. One cluster is composed of nine socially undesirable strategies such as "Using sarcasm" and "Obscure the issue." The other cluster contains 11 more socially desirable strategies. As is clear, the clusters that are formed through this technique are more compact than the clusters created through the single linkage method.

Ward method. The final method is the Ward method. This method takes a unique approach to adding objects to clusters. The goal of the method is to minimize the variability of the dissimilarity scores across the clusters. The first two objects that are joined together are those that result in the lowest variability, in particular, the lowest sum of the squared differences between the objects. This calculation translates into the two most similar objects. Additional objects are joined into clusters based on which object results in the smallest increase in the variability of the dissimilarity scores across the clusters. The Ward method tends to result in clusters having approximately equal numbers of objects within them (Aldenderfer & Blashfield, 1984). The bottom panel in Figure 10.7 shows the results of using this method for our 20 persuasive strategies. There are three clusters in this tree. One cluster contains eight objects, including "Appeal to an expert" and "Appeal to similarity." The strategies in this cluster appear to be the association strategies found at one end of the tactic dimension in the MDS space. The second cluster contains five strategies, including "Provide reasons" and "Use intense language." At first glance, it is unclear which features the five strategies in this cluster share, but it may be that these are arguments used by someone who feels intensively about an issue or otherwise thinks the issue is important. The final cluster contains seven strategies, including "Use sarcasm" and "Refer to negative consequences." These strategies clearly involve negative appeals.

ADDITIVE TREES

Ultrametric trees are actually a special case of additive trees (Corter, 1996, 1998). Whereas ultrametric trees assume ultrametric inequality,

Scaling and Cluster Analysis

additive trees have a less restrictive assumption, called the *tree inequality*. Mathematically, the tree inequality is

$$\delta_{x,y} + \delta_{z,w} \leq MAX[\delta_{x,z} + \delta_{y,w}, \delta_{y,z} + \delta_{x,w}]$$

This assumption allows the length of the arcs within a tree to vary, which means that the objects in an additive tree can be different distances from the root of the tree. In contrast, the ultrametric inequality required that each object in the tree be the same distance from the root of the tree (Figure 10.8) (Corter, 1996). In fact, additive trees do not have to have a root. An example additive tree for the persuasive appeals data can be found in Figure 10.8.

When an additive tree has no root, the distances between the objects are typically interpreted as measuring the distinctiveness of the features for

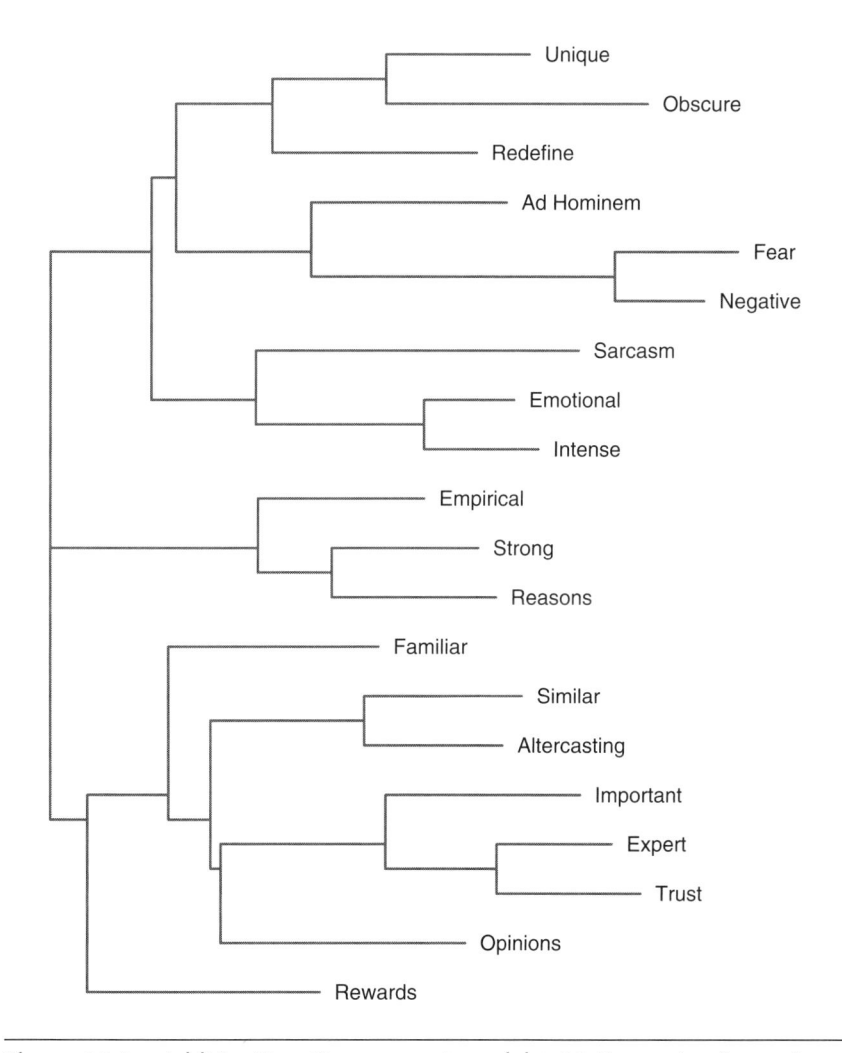

Figure 10.8 Additive Tree Representation of the 20 Persuasive Strategies

the objects in the tree. However, distances must have a starting point, and when there is no root from the analysis, the location of a root must be chosen. According to Tversky (1977), a rooted additive tree provides information about both the common features (the same as an ultrametric tree) and the unique features of each of the objects in the space. Unfortunately, there are no guidelines for where a root should be placed. Still, where the root is placed can have important implications for how the tree is interpreted (Corter, 1996). One factor that should be used to place the root is the interpretability of the tree. Researchers will need to consider this carefully in placing the root. Most computer programs will place the root in an additive tree based on the placement that will minimize the variability of the distances of the objects in the tree from the root of the tree. This placement results in a balanced tree (Sattath & Tversky, 1977) and should probably be the starting point in any consideration of root placement.

A final point we want to discuss concerning both hierarchical and tree cluster models involves the interpretation of the clusters. Typically, researchers simply provide their own interpretation of the clusters and that is an acceptable method. However, validity of the interpretation can be enhanced by obtaining ratings of the objects that were used in the study to test the interpretation of the cluster in much the same manner as was discussed with MDS. Where there are significant differences in the clusters based on these ratings can serve as a validity check on the proposed interpretations (Carroll & Wish, 1974; Kruskal & Wish, 1978).

INTERPRETING THE CLUSTERS

After the cluster analysis has been completed, the optimal number of clusters needs to be determined. As with MDS, there are no set rules for determining the appropriate number of clusters. Again, interpretability is one factor that influences how many clusters are chosen. Another factor is the amount of variance accounted for (R^2) by the solution. In this way, scree plots can be used to determine the appropriate number of clusters. Specifically, the number of clusters is plotted against the distance at which the clusters were joined. This information is typically part of the printout for the cluster analysis. In MDS, the elbow indicates that additional dimensions will not appreciably improve the fit of the solution. In cluster analysis, an elbow indicates that there are substantial dissimilarities between the next two clusters that would be merged. In other words, the elbow indicates that no more information is gained by further joining the clusters (Aldenderfer & Blashfield, 1984). Figure 10.9 is a scree plot for our 20 persuasive strategies, using the Ward method. The elbow suggests that the optimal number of clusters is three.

Most researchers focus primarily on the resulting clusters as the only information gained from the cluster analysis: Those objects that are in the same cluster are similar to each other, and those objects that appear in different clusters are distinct. However, the length of the arcs in the cluster

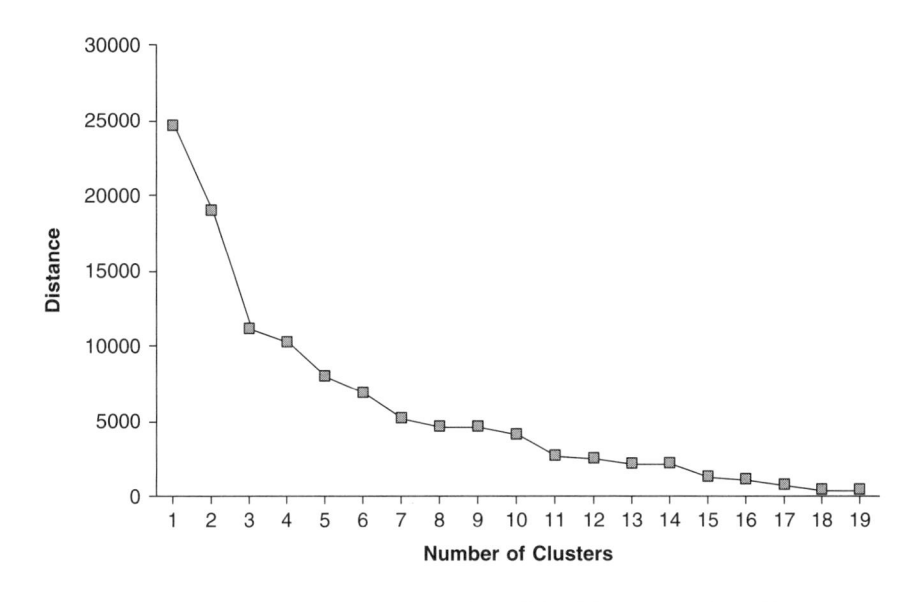

Figure 10.9 Scree Plot for Identifying the Number of Clusters Using the Ward Method

analysis is also informative (Corter, 1996). An arc is a line that connects two items or two clusters (i.e., branches) in the output. The length of the arc is a measure of how important the features shared by the objects in that branch of the tree are for judgments of similarity. If the arc is long, the shared features are very important for judging similarities within the cluster, and, conversely, if the arc is short, the shared features are relatively unimportant. For example, in the bottom panel of Figure 10.7 (Ward's Linkage), there is a long arc between the top cluster comprising association-oriented strategies and the other two clusters. This suggests that the feature or features that distinguish the top cluster from the other clusters are very important. Likewise, within that top cluster, there is a very short arc between "Refer to a trustworthy source" and "Refer to an expert" but a long arc between these two strategies and the other six strategies, which again indicates that the feature that distinguishes these two strategies from the other six strategies in this cluster is very important. We might speculate that the feature involves referring to some type of authoritative source. This is corroborated by the short arc between these two strategies, indicating that it does not distinguish between them.

Choosing a Method for Analysis

If one's research involves objects that are theoretically best represented categorically, the choice of analysis is between an ultrametric and an additive tree clustering method. Otherwise, MDS would be most appropriate. Assuming a categorical representation, which is the best clustering technique to use? Once again, there are no set rules for choosing which is more appropriate for a given data set. One way to judge would be to look at how well the two models fit the data by comparing the R^2 for the two trees. However, the additive tree has more free parameters, so it should always provide a better fit of the similarity data. The decision as to which is best usually comes down to the interpretability of the clusters.

From our experience, additive trees generally provide a more interesting cluster solution. Allowing the arcs more freedom to vary provides more information about how the participants were weighing different features or sets of features in making their judgments. Another useful component of the additive tree is that it can be directly compared with an MDS solution to determine whether a dimensional or categorical representation is more appropriate for the data set (see below). The ultrametric tree should be compared to MDS only when the MDS solution is one-dimensional because this is the only case in which the ultrametric tree and the MDS solution have the same number of free parameters. Typically, when people use MDS, they are not interested in a one-dimensional solution. The drawback to using an additive tree model is that most statistical packages do not include additive tree models as an option. As far as we are aware, SYSTAT is the only one of the major statistical packages that includes additive trees (i.e., the ADTREE option; Corter, 1998). However, MDS, INDSCALE, and the ultrametric tree analyses can be conducted using SPSS, a program popular among communication researchers.

If the choice is between MDS and additive tree, there are several useful criteria for making the choice. First, a two-dimensional MDS solution and an additive tree solution have the same number of free parameters, which allows for a fair comparison of the models in terms of fit (R^2) (Pruzansky, Tverksy, & Carroll, 1982; Sattath & Tversky, 1977). For our data set, R^2 for the two-dimensional MDS solution was .92, and R^2 for the additive tree model was .76. Both provide good fit to the data, but the MDS model provides a better fit, just as it did in the original study (Roskos-Ewoldsen, 1997).

Two additional criteria for judging the appropriateness of a dimensional solution or an additive tree are called *centrality* and *reciprocity*. Both measure the number of nearest neighbors that an object has (Tversky & Hutchinson, 1986; Tversky, Rinott, & Newman, 1983). The nearest neighbor of an object o_i is defined as the object o_j that is more similar to o_i than any other object in set k. It is assumed that within set k there will be only one nearest neighbor (o_j) to object o_i. Theoretically, there are no limits on the number of objects to which o_j can be the nearest neighbor. However, categorical and dimensional models constrain the number of nearest neighbors allowed, but in two different ways. In an additive tree, o_j can be a nearest neighbor to an unlimited number of objects in the set simply by being a higher node in the tree. If o_j is a higher node, it is closer to the lower nodes than to any of the other branches to which o_j is connected. However, in a two-dimensional space, o_j can be the nearest neighbor to only five objects (Tversky & Hutchinson, 1986). If five points are arranged as the corners of a pentagon, a central point can be closer to the five points than the five points will be to each other. However, it is impossible to construct a hexagon where all six points in the hexagon are closer to a central point than at least one pair of the six points are to each other. As a result, the number of nearest neighbors revealed by the centrality and reciprocity analysis allows a test of the appropriateness of a dimensional solution for a set of similarity data.

Centrality (C) is a general measure of whether a small set of objects within a set of data tends to be the nearest neighbor to a disproportionate number of objects in the set. Mathematically, centrality is

$$C = \frac{1}{(n+1)} \sum_{i=1}^{n} N_i$$

where n is the number of objects in the set and N_i is the number of objects for which object i is the nearest neighbor (Tversky & Hutchinson, 1986). In a dimensional space, C should be less than 2 (Tversky & Hutchinson, 1986; Tversky et al., 1983). Otherwise, MDS is inappropriate. *Reciprocity* (R) is a measure of the extent to which each of two objects is the nearest neighbor to the other. Mathematically, reciprocity is

$$R = \frac{1}{(n+1)} \sum_{i=1}^{n} R_i$$

where n is the number of objects in the set and R_i is the rank that i is in order of proximity to i's nearest neighbor (Tversky & Hutchinson, 1986). Again, R should be less than 2 if the space is dimensional (Tversky & Hutchinson, 1986). Otherwise, MDS is inappropriate. For our dissimilarity data (Table 10.2), $C = 1.43$, and $R = 1.33$. These results indicate that a dimensional interpretation is appropriate.

Two final points need to be made. The first is that MDS and cluster analysis are not mutually exclusive (Carroll & Wish, 1974). Rather, the two approaches can complement each other. For example, using the results of a cluster analysis to look for patterns within a multidimensional space can provide a great aid in interpreting the MDS configuration. As Figure 10.10 shows, a cluster analysis drawn in an MDS space provides a contour map of the space that can highlight clearly how to interpret the space. In the top part of Figure 10.10, there is a swirl involving two clusters of items. Consistent with the scree plot for the MDS solution, a swirl indicates that a higher-dimensional solution may be appropriate. Importantly, using cluster analysis and MDS together can help establish the validity of the results, if the two approaches converge on the same interpretation of the data.

The second point is the importance of replication. The overwhelming tendency for communication scholars is to conduct a single study and assume that the identified representation of the data is valid and reliable. However, humans have a profound ability to see structure where there is none (Breckenridge, 2000; Gordan, 1999). Fortunately, there are several ways to establish the reliability and validity of the results. First, simple visual inspection of the original and replication results is appropriate for establishing reliability. There are more technical approaches available for this but they are beyond the scope of this chapter (Borg & Groenen, 1997; Breckenridge, 2000; Gordan, 1999). Second, as we discussed earlier, using more than one type of technique with the same data set can aid in establishing the reliability of the results. If the proximity data are reliable, then the different techniques should converge on the same interpretation. Finally, using external data, such as ratings of the objects along a hypothesized dimension or judging their similarity to a particular cluster, can help establish the validity of the results.

In this chapter, we have discussed the scaling and clustering techniques used most often in the behavioral sciences, including communication studies. It is extremely important that one understands the assumptions of each type of analysis as well as the options that are available for each type. Only by attending to these issues will we produce results that can contribute to a greater understanding of human communication.

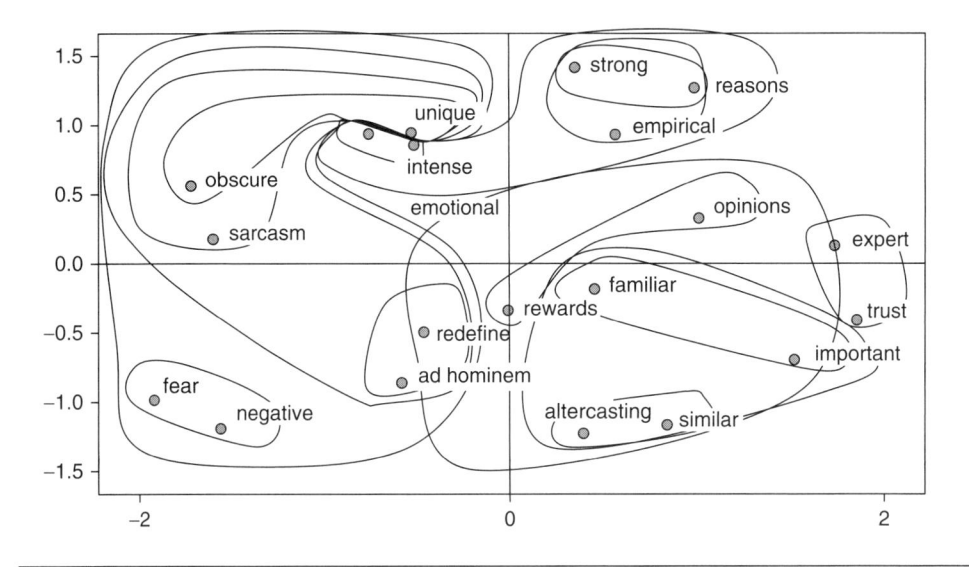

Figure 10.10 A Contour Map Using the Results From the Ward Method to Aid in the Interpretation of the Two-Dimensional Representation of the 20 Persuasive Strategies

References

Aldenderfer, M. S., & Blashfield, R. K. (1984). *Cluster analysis.* Beverly Hills, CA: Sage.

Arabie, P., Carroll, J. D., & DeSarbo, W. S. (1987). *Three-way scaling and clustering.* Newbury Park, CA: Sage.

Bailey, K. D. (1994). *Typologies and taxonomies: An introduction to classification techniques.* Thousand Oaks, CA: Sage.

Borg, I., & Groenen, P. (1997). *Modern multidimensional scaling: Theory and applications.* New York: Springer-Verlag.

Breckenridge, J. N. (2000). Validating cluster analysis: Consistent replication and symmetry. *Multivariate Behavioral Research, 35,* 261–285.

Cantor, D., Brown, J., & Groat, L. (1985). A multiple sorting procedure for studying conceptual systems. In M. Brenner, J. Brown, & D. Cantor (Eds.), *The research interview: Users and approaches* (pp. 79–114). London: Academic Press.

Carroll, J. D., & Wish, M. (1974). Multidimensional perceptual models and measurement methods. In C. Carterette & M. P. Friedman (Eds.), *Handbook of perception: Volume 3—Psychophysical judgment and measurement* (pp. 391–447). New York: Academic Press.

Corter, J. E. (1996). *Tree models of similarity and association.* Thousand Oaks, CA: Sage.

Corter, J. E. (1998). An efficient metric combinatorial algorithm for fitting additive trees. *Multivariate Behavioral Research, 33,* 249–271.

Deaux, K., Reid, A., Mizrahi, K., & Ethier, K. A. (1995). Parameters of social identity. *Journal of Personality and Social Psychology, 68,* 280–291.

Gordan, A. D. (1999). *Classification* (2nd ed.) Boca Raton. FL: Chapman & Hall/CRC.

Hamilton, M. A., & Nowak, K. L. (2005). Information systems concepts across two decades: An empirical analysis of trends in theory, methods, process, and research domains. *Journal of Communication, 55,* 529–553.

Kruskal, J. P., & Wish, M. (1978). *Multidimensional scaling.* Beverly Hills, CA: Sage.

Livingstone, S. M. (1987). The implicit representation of characters in Dallas: A multidimensional scaling approach. *Human Communication Research, 13,* 399–420.

Livingstone, S. M. (1989). Interpretive viewers and structured programs: The implicit representations of soap opera characters. *Communication Research, 16,* 25–57.

Livingstone, S. M. (1990). *Making sense of television: The psychology of audience interpretation.* Oxford, UK: Pergamon Press.

Nabi, R. L., Biely, E. N., Morgan, S. J., & Stitt, C. R. (2003). Reality-based television programming and the psychology of its appeal. *Media Psychology, 5,* 303–330.

Pruzansky, S., Tversky, A., & Carroll, J. D. (1982). Spatial versus tree representations of proximity data. *Psychometrika, 47,* 3–24.

Rosenberg, S., & Kim, M. P. (1975). The method of sorting as a data-gathering procedure in multivariate research. *Multivariate Behavioral Research, 10,* 489–502.

Rosenberg, S., Nelson, C., & Vivekananthan, P. S. (1968). A multidimensional approach to the structure of personality impressions. *Journal of Personality and Social Psychology, 9,* 283–294.

Rosenberg, S., & Sedlak, A. (1972). Structural representations of implicit personality theory. In L. Berkowitz (Ed.), *Advances in experimental social psychology* (Vol. 6, pp. 235–297). New York: Academic Press.

Roskos-Ewoldsen, D. R. (1997). Implicit theories of persuasion. *Human Communication Research, 24,* 31–63.

Sattath, S., & Tversky, A. (1977). Additive similarity trees. *Psychometrika, 42,* 319–345.

Schvaneveldt, R. W. (Ed.). (1990). *Pathfinder associative networks: Studies in knowledge organization.* Norwood, NJ: Ablex.

Tversky, A. (1977). Features of similarity. *Psychological Review, 84,* 327–352.

Tversky, A., & Hutchinson, J. W. (1986). Nearest neighbor analysis of psychological spaces. *Psychological Review, 93,* 3–22.

Tversky, A., Rinott, Y., & Newman, C. M. (1983). Nearest neighbor analysis of point processes: Applications to multidimensional scaling. *Journal of Mathematical Psychology, 27,* 235–250.

van der Kloot, W. A., & van Herk, H. (1991). Multidimensional scaling of sorting data: A comparison of three procedures. *Multivariate Behavioral Research, 26,* 563–581.

Weller, S. C., & Romney, A. K. (1988). *Systematic data collection.* Newbury Park, CA: Sage.

Wish, M. (1976). Comparisons among multidimensional structures of interpersonal relations. *Multivariate Behavioral Research, 11,* 297–324.

Contemporary Approaches to Meta-Analysis in Communication Research

11

Blair T. Johnson

Lori A. J. Scott-Sheldon

Leslie B. Snyder

Seth M. Noar

Tania B. Huedo-Medina

As in any modern science, progress in the field of communication hinges on having trustworthy generalizations from past research on a particular topic. The ever-growing mountain of evidence available about communication research on one hand is an amazing resource but on the other hand represents a considerable challenge to any scholar reviewing

Authors' Note: We express our gratitude for the comments on a previous draft of this chapter provided by Jessa LaCroix, Jennifer Ortiz, Karin Weis, and two anonymous reviewers. The preparation of this chapter was supported by U.S. Public Health Service grants R01-MH58563 to Blair T. Johnson and 1P01CD000237 to Leslie B. Snyder.

this evidence. Consequently, meta-analysis has become a nearly indispensable tool in order to statistically summarize empirical findings from different studies. Meta-analysis is also known as *research synthesis* or *quantitative reviewing*, slightly broader terms that incorporate not only statistical aspects but also the surrounding steps that constitute a review.

The first quantitative reviews of empirical data from independent studies appeared in the early 1800s (Stigler, 1986), but as Olkin (1990) summarized, relatively sophisticated techniques to synthesize study findings began to emerge around 1900, following the development of standardized effect-size indices such as *r*-, *d*-, and *p*-values. Two high-profile reviews on education and psychotherapy (Smith & Glass, 1977; Smith, Glass, & Miller, 1980) helped to popularize the technique and its new name, "meta-analysis," and scholars in communication sciences as well as other disciplines were quick to realize its potential. Simultaneously, increasingly sophisticated statistical techniques emerged to support such efforts (e.g., Hedges & Olkin, 1985; Rosenthal & Rubin, 1978; Schmidt & Hunter, 1977). Standards for meta-analysis have grown increasingly rigorous in the past 20 years, and more "how to" books have appeared (e.g., Lipsey & Wilson, 2001).

Despite early controversy regarding the methods used by meta-analysts (for a review, see Hunt, 1997), meta-analysis has become quite common and well accepted because scholars realize that careful application of these techniques often will yield the clearest conclusions about a research literature (Cooper & Hedges, 1994a; Hunt, 1997). Even the most casual reader of scientific journals can easily witness the widespread acceptance of meta-analysis. For example, a title keyword search for "meta-analysis," ignoring its synonyms, retrieved 5,942 hits in *PsycINFO* and 24,829 in *PubMed*; more broadly, a search for "meta-analysis" in Google retrieved more than 1,600,000 Web hits (January 7, 2007). The story is the same in the field of communication research. Notably, two early proponents of meta-analysis, Alice H. Eagly and John E. Hunter, trained numerous doctoral students who focused on communication research. Several volumes compile meta-analyses on broad areas of communication research, including persuasion (Allen & Preiss, 1998), interpersonal communication (Allen, Preiss, Gayle, & Burrell, 2002), and mass media (Priess, Gayle, Burrell, Allen, & Bryant, 2006). Noar's (2006) recent review documented the growing application of meta-analysis to one of the communication discipline's fast-growing subdisciplines—health communication. Along with numerous other outlets, *Communication Yearbook* specifically welcomes meta-analytic reviews. The International Communication Association annually presents the John E. Hunter Memorial Award for the best meta-analysis in communication. In addition, a recent keyword search of "meta-analysis" within *Communication Abstracts*, which catalogs approximately 50 communication journals, revealed that the number of published meta-analyses among communication journals has increased steadily since 1984 (Noar, 2006).

Those interested in synthesizing communication research have asked and answered many questions through the use of meta-analysis, and in a variety of domains. Noar's (2006) *Communication Abstracts* review noted above found some of the earliest communication meta-analyses to be focused on persuasion and social influence, such as Dillard, Hunter, and Burgoon's (1984) meta-analysis of foot-in-the-door and door-in-the-face techniques and Buller's (1986) meta-analysis of distraction during persuasive communication. In the 1980s and 1990s, communication scholars applied meta-analysis to a variety of communication literatures within mass and interpersonal communication. More recent applications of the technique have included areas as diverse as organizational (Rains, 2005), instructional (Allen et al., 2004), political (Benoit, Hansen, & Verser, 2003), and health communication (Noar, Carlyle, & Cole, 2006; Snyder et al., 2004). Communication scholars have also contributed to discussion of issues surrounding the technique of meta-analysis itself. For instance, a special section of the December 1991 issue of *Communication Monographs* was dedicated to "Issues in Meta-Analysis" (i.e., Hale & Dillard, 1991; Hall & Rosenthal, 1991), and other work on meta-analysis has appeared in the literature both before (Morley, 1988) and after (Hullett & Levine, 2003) this special issue was published.

Historically, scholars used informal methods known as *narrative reviewing*—a summary of the results of individual primary studies sometimes guided by a count of the number of studies that had either produced or failed to produce statistically significant findings in the hypothesized direction. Narrative reviews have appeared in many different contexts and still serve a useful purpose in writing that does not have a comprehensive literature review as its goal (e.g., textbook summaries, introductions to journal articles reporting primary research). Nonetheless, narrative reviews can also prove inadequate for reaching definitive conclusions about the degree of empirical support for a phenomenon or for a theory about the phenomenon.

One indication of this inadequacy is that independent narrative reviews of the same literature often have reached different conclusions. For example, conclusions from the narrative reviews in the Surgeon General's 1972 report on the effects of violent television viewing on aggressive behavior and subsequent major narrative reviews (e.g., Comstock, Chaffee, Katzman, McCombs, & Roberts, 1978; Comstock & Strasburger, 1990; Huston et al., 1992; National Institute of Mental Health, 1982) were contradicted by other reviews (e.g., Friedman, 1988), enabling the controversy over violent television to continue. With the growing popularity of meta-analysis, some of the controversy diminished, at least among scholars; a meta-analysis of 200-plus studies found that after they viewed violent television, children acted more aggressively (Paik & Comstock, 1994). Comparisons between narrative and meta-analytic reviews in other domains (e.g., delinquency prevention and job training) have found similar results with narrative reviews underestimating treatment effects

(Mann, 1994). The reasons for such inaccurate conclusions hinge on at least four problems that have received much past attention (e.g., Glass, McGaw, & Smith, 1981; Rosenthal, 1991; Rosenthal & DiMatteo, 2001):

1. Narrative reviews generally gather only a convenience sample of studies, perhaps consisting only of those studies that the reviewer happens to know. Because the review typically does not state how the studies were gathered or selected for inclusion, it is difficult to evaluate whether the correct literature was gathered or whether the search for studies was thorough. If the sample of studies was biased, the conclusions reached may also be biased.

2. Narrative reviews generally lack statements about which study characteristics were considered or about how the quality of the studies' methods was evaluated, with the result that the accuracy of the reviewers' claims about the characteristics of the studies and the quality of their methods is difficult to judge.

3. When study findings in a literature vary widely, narrative reviews generally have difficulty reaching clear conclusions about what differences in study methods best explain disparate findings. Because narrative reviewers usually do not systematically code studies' methods, these reviewing procedures are not well suited to accounting for inconsistencies in findings.

4. Narrative reviews typically rely much more heavily on statistical significance than on effect-size magnitude to judge study findings. Statistical significance is a poor basis for comparing studies that differ in sample size because effects of identical magnitude can differ widely in statistical significance. As a result, narrative reviewers often reach erroneous conclusions about a pattern in a series of studies, even in literatures as small as 10 studies (Cooper & Rosenthal, 1980).

These problems are compounded by the increasing number of studies available to review—and large literatures are more and more the norm. For example, meta-analyses obtained 138 studies on attitude-behavior relations (Kim & Hunter, 1993), 114 on the persuasive impact of various message sources on attitudes and behaviors (Wilson & Sherrell, 1993), 94 examining disclosure and liking (Dindia, 2002), and 67 on disclosure and reciprocity (Dindia, 2002). Beyond a certain number of studies, note taking quickly becomes an ineffective means of gathering information. In contrast, meta-analytic procedures used to gather, code, and analyze study outcomes provide an improved alternative method for synthesizing information gathered from a large number of studies. Indeed, meta-analysis is the best available tool to conduct these empirical histories of a phenomenon, to show how researchers have addressed the phenomenon, and to show how results may have changed over time. Meta-analysis has become critical in our understanding and contextualizing of new research findings. Acknowledging scholars' scientific, ethical, and financial responsibility to demonstrate how new research is related to existing knowledge, the British medical journal *The Lancet* now requires authors to reference an existing meta-analysis, conduct their own meta-analysis, or describe the quantitative findings that have appeared since a prior meta-analysis (Young & Horton, 2005).

Because of the importance of comparing study findings accurately, scholars have dedicated considerable effort to making the review process as reliable and valid as possible in an effort to circumvent the criticisms listed above. These efforts highlight the fact that research synthesis is a scientific endeavor with identifiable and replicable methods that are necessary in order to produce reliable and valid reviews (Cooper & Hedges, 1994a).

In spite of the advance it presents, meta-analysis is not without criticism (e.g., Sharpe, 1997). Six common criticisms (see Bangert-Drowns, 1997; Rosenthal & DiMatteo, 2001) are (1) bias in sampling the findings, (2) papers included may vary in quality, (3) nonindependence of effect sizes, (4) overemphasis on differences between individual effects (e.g., differences between means), (5) unpublished studies are underrepresented and published studies are overrepresented, and (6) the "apples and oranges" problem (i.e., summarizing studies with varying methodologies). Although these criticisms bear some resemblance to the criticisms of narrative reviews that we listed above, most of them have arisen out of a misunderstanding of meta-analytic methodology. We will address these criticisms throughout the remainder of this chapter, which provides a general introduction to the methodology of meta-analysis and emphasizes current advances in the technique. We (a) introduce and detail the basic steps involved in conducting a meta-analysis, (b) consider some options that meta-analysts should consider as they conduct such a review, (c) discuss appropriate standards for conducting and evaluating reviews, and (d) conclude with recent developments in meta-analytic methodology.

Meta-Analytic Procedures

Conducting a meta-analysis generally involves seven steps: (1) determining the theoretical domain of the literature under consideration—defining the question, (2) setting boundaries for the sample of studies, (3) locating relevant studies, (4) coding studies for their distinctive characteristics, (5) estimating the size of each study's effect on a standardized metric, (6) analyzing the database, and (7) interpreting and presenting the results. The details and success of each step heavily depend on those preceding steps. For example, it is easier to set boundaries for studies (Step 2) and to find them (Step 3) if the analyst has first done a good job of defining the meta-analytic question and reviewing relevant theoretical domains (Step 1). In symmetric fashion, even the earlier steps should be accomplished with an eye to the steps that follow. For example, defining a problem too broadly (Step 1) may result in ambiguities in the following methods (Steps 2 through 6) as well as interpretation (Step 7). Some of the steps are similar to conducting a content analysis, a procedure that is familiar to many in communication research (Berelson, 1952; Holsti, 1969; Krippendorf, 1980). In this section, we discuss each step in turn.

DEFINING THE QUESTION

The first conceptual step is to specify with great clarity the phenomenon under review. Ordinarily, a synthesis evaluates evidence relevant to a single hypothesis, defined in terms of the variables that underlie the phenomenon. To select the variables on which to focus, the analyst studies the history of the research problem and of typical studies in the literature. Typically, the research problem will be defined as a relation between two variables, such as the influence of an independent variable on a dependent variable as in Casey et al.'s (2003) investigation of the impact of the public announcement about Earvin "Magic" Johnson's positive HIV status on HIV testing (Casey et al., 2003). Another example is the impact that communication with a sexual partner has on subsequent condom use (Noar et al., 2006).

A synthesis must take study quality into account at an early point to determine the kinds of operations that constitute acceptable operationalizations of the conceptual variables. Because the measures in the studies testing a particular hypothesis often differ, it is no surprise that different operationalizations are often linked with variability in studies' findings. If the differences in studies' measures and other operations can be appropriately judged or categorized, it is likely that an analyst can explain some of this variability in effect-size magnitude.

Essential to this conceptual analysis is a careful examination of the history of the research problem and of typical studies in the literature. Theoretical articles, earlier reviews, and empirical articles should be examined for the interpretations they provide of the phenomenon under investigation. Theories or even scholars' more informal and less-developed insights may suggest moderators of the effect that could potentially be coded in the studies and examined for their explanatory power. When scholars have debated different explanations for the relation, the synthesis should be designed to address these competing explanations.

The most common way to test competing explanations is to examine how the findings pattern across studies. Specifically, a theory might imply that a third variable should influence the relation between the independent and dependent variables: The relation should be larger or smaller with a higher level of this third variable. Treating this third variable as a potential moderator of the effect, the analyst would code all of the studies for their status on the moderator. This meta-analytic strategy, known as the *moderator variable approach* (or *effect modification approach*), tests whether the moderator affects the examined relation across the studies included in the sample. This approach, advancing beyond the simple question of *whether* the independent variable is related to the dependent variable, addresses the question of *when*, or under what circumstances, the magnitude or sign of the association varies. This strategy aligns well with efforts to build communication theory by focusing on contingent conditions for communication effects (McLeod & Reeves, 1980).

In addition to this moderator variable approach to synthesizing studies' findings, other strategies have proven to be useful. In particular, a theory might suggest that a third variable serves as a mediator of the critical relation because it conveys the causal impact of the independent variable on the dependent variable (Baron & Kenny, 1986; McLeod & Reeves, 1980; also see Chapter 2 in this volume). If at least some of the primary studies within a literature have evaluated this mediating process, mediator relations can be tested within a meta-analytic framework by performing correlational analyses that are an extension of path analysis with primary-level data (Shadish, 1996). We discuss these options further in the sixth step, below; for now, note that there must be sufficient numbers of studies in order for the more sophisticated styles of meta-analysis to proceed.

It is also important to define a priori what constitutes "one study" for inclusion in the meta-analysis. Multiple publications may report on the same study. For example, a meta-analysis of mediated health campaigns chose the campaign as the unit of analysis, often drawing descriptive information about the campaign from one publication and information about campaign effects from another (Snyder et al., 2004). Alternatively, in the experimental literature, one publication often reports on several studies and each may be entered into the meta-analysis. Similarly, each study may be divided into substudies that, for the purpose of the review, are treated as independent studies: As an example, Johnson and Eagly's (2000) meta-analysis examining the role of participant involvement on persuasion treated as separate studies the strong and weak argument conditions of studies that manipulated this variable. In part, their results showed that outcome-relevant involvement increased persuasion for strong arguments and reduced it for weak arguments.

SETTING BOUNDARIES FOR THE SAMPLE OF STUDIES

Clearly, only some studies will be relevant to the conceptual relation that is the focus of the meta-analysis, so analysts must define boundaries for the sample of studies. This step is similar conceptually to defining the universe of content to be included in a content analysis. Decisions about the inclusion of studies are important because the inferential power of any meta-analysis is limited by the number of studies that are reviewed. Boundary setting is often a time-consuming process that forces reviewers to weigh conceptual and practical issues. The sample of studies is routinely defined by such criteria as the presence of the key variables and acceptable measures, the study quality, and the type of methodology used.

Presence of key variables. The starting point for establishing boundaries is typically conceptualization of the phenomenon that is to be the focus of the synthesis, including identification of key variables. The key variables need to be present and adequately measured for a study to be included in the meta-analysis. The study must report key effects in quantitative terms.

Study quality. As a general rule, research syntheses profit by including those studies that used stronger methods. To the extent that all (or most) of the reviewed studies share a particular methodological limitation, any synthesis of these studies would share the same limitation. It is important to note a key trade-off: Studies that have some strengths (e.g., independent variables with random assignment, laboratory controls) may have other weaknesses (e.g., deficiencies in ecological validity, lack of random sampling).

In deciding whether some studies may lack sufficient rigor to include in the meta-analysis, it is important to adhere to methodological standards within the area reviewed, and these vary widely from discipline to discipline as well as within subdomains. For instance, whereas a meta-analysis conducted within medicine might include only those studies that used a double-blind, random-assignment experimental design, a meta-analytic study in the communication discipline would likely *not* apply such a standard. Rather, a meta-analysis in communication would likely focus more on other methodological aspects such as research design and measurement of variables. For example, Witte and Allen's (2000) meta-analysis of the effects of fear appeals on attitude and behavior change included only those studies that manipulated fear or threat within an experimental or quasi-experimental research design. Studies were excluded if they (a) were cross-sectional, correlating fear or threat with attitude/behavior change but not manipulating them; (b) did not measure the key dependent outcomes under examination; and (c) had a failed fear/threat manipulation check, because the project focused on reactions to various fear-based conditions, such as high and low fear/threat. This meta-analysis provided the most comprehensive synthesis of the fear appeal literature to date, answering a sometimes controversial question regarding whether fear appeals are effective. Witte and Allen (2000) found that fear appeals did, in fact, elicit small but consistent positive effects on attitudes ($r = .14$), behavioral intentions ($r = .11$), and behavior change ($r = .15$). They also found, however, that fear appeals tended to elicit defensive responses such as reactance among participants ($r = .20$). Further analysis suggested that those fear appeals that included high-response and self-efficacy messages might have the greatest opportunity of being effective while minimizing the chances of defensive responses.

Although a large number of potential threats to methodological rigor have been identified (Campbell & Stanley, 1963; Cook & Campbell, 1979; Shadish, Cook, & Campbell, 2002), there are few absolute standards of study quality that can be applied uniformly in every meta-analysis. As a case in point, we have observed that scholars typically think that published studies have higher quality than unpublished studies. Yet many unpublished studies (e.g., dissertations) have high quality and many studies published in reputable sources do not. Obviously, unpublished studies may be unpublished for many reasons, only one of which is low quality. Similarly, many studies may have passed peer review to be published despite the presence of what some may call serious flaws in their methodology. Scholars conducting their first meta-analyses often express amazement that there are so many published studies of low quality. These considerations make it incumbent on the analyst to define the features of a high-quality study and to apply this definition to all obtained studies, regardless of such considerations as the reputation of the journal or whether the study had survived peer review.

Research design. The boundaries of a research literature to be synthesized often include research design specifications. Sometimes analysts set boundaries so that the studies included are relatively homogeneous methodologically. For example, a study of the effects of family planning interventions wanted to control for self-selection into condition as an alternative hypothesis for the effects of the interventions, so the selection criteria included random assignment to conditions (Bauman, 1997).

Sometimes boundaries encompass a variety of methodologies. A meta-analysis of the effect of violent video games selected studies with different methodologies—experimental, correlational, and longitudinal—and then treated methodology as a potential moderator (Anderson, 2004). The results revealed that results in experimental studies paralleled those in correlational studies, providing a better demonstration of causality. In addition, the meta-analysis found larger effect sizes in more methodologically rigorous studies (i.e., those with better sampling), suggesting that earlier pooled estimates of the effects of playing video games on affect, cognition, and behavior were likely underestimates, as they included many methodologically weaker studies. In the past, critics have argued that the synthesizers have combined, in a single analysis, studies that use noncomparable methods, a practice that came to be known as the "apples and oranges" critique (Glass et al., 1981). Nonetheless, methodologists have been generally unsympathetic to this line of argument because they regard it as the task of the meta-analyst to show empirically that differences in methods produce consequential differences in study outcomes (e.g., Hall, Tickle-Degnen, Rosenthal, & Mosteller, 1994; Rosenthal & DiMatteo, 2001). By treating the methodological differences as moderator variables—as in the video game meta-analysis—the model is fitted for type of fruit, to continue the metaphor. In short, do the results of "apple" studies differ from the results of "orange" studies? Of course, if the effects of methodological differences are known but ignored, analysts may be criticized appropriately as having given insufficient attention to the effects that diverse methods may have had on study outcomes.

Practical considerations sometimes impinge on reviewers' boundary conditions. In many domains, including a wide range of methods would make the project too large and complex to carry out in a reasonable time frame. In such instances, reviewers may divide a literature into two or more research syntheses, each addressing a different aspect of a broad research question. Keeping in mind the phenomena under study, the boundaries should be wide enough that interesting hypotheses about moderator variables can be tested within the synthesis. Yet if very diverse methods are included, the reviewer may need to define some moderator variables that can be implemented only within particular methodologies (e.g., participants' organizational status exists only within studies conducted in organizations).

Critical moderators. Analysts often set the boundaries of the synthesis so that the methods of included studies differ widely only on critical moderator dimensions. The moderators are intended to delineate the literature or expand upon the theory of interest. If other extraneous dimensions are held relatively constant across the reviewed studies by carefully defining the selection criteria, the moderator variable results ought to be more clearly and easily interpreted. An example of a situation suggesting the need for a moderator analysis was in a meta-analysis of studies evaluating HIV prevention interventions for adolescents. These programs varied in the degree to which they increased condom use for adolescents in the intervention compared to the control condition (Johnson et al., 2003). In such circumstances, the odds grow that different mean effects exist within different groups of studies. Indeed, subsequent moderator analyses showed, in part, that interventions were more successful the more condom-skills training was provided.

Cultural factors. For some questions, it may be appropriate to use geographic setting, culture, or study population as a limiting factor, such as when examining the effects of a culturally determined form of nonverbal communication. If the phenomenon under investigation is group specific, then including the studies covering other groups may only obscure the phenomenon. Alternatively, an analyst may choose to treat the setting, culture, or population as a moderating variable and test for differences when the literature includes enough studies for each group. Including reports from diverse settings, cultures, and populations also increases the degree to which the results can be generalized. In addition, to the extent that including such studies increases the ranges that moderator variables take, including studies from diverse settings, cultures, and populations increases the ability of the meta-analysis to detect moderator variable effects.

Developing selection criteria is often a process that continues as meta-analysts examine more studies and thereby uncover the full range of research designs that have been used to investigate a particular hypothesis. If some studies meeting preliminary criteria established conditions that are judged to be extremely atypical or flawed, the selection criteria may need to be modified to exclude them. The dimensions above highlight the intricate nature of the process. Errors in selection, coding, effect-size calculation, and analyses are more serious than is the case with primary-level research. In primary-level research, such errors typically apply to the unit of analysis, individual observations; in meta-analysis, the errors apply to the entire study. In meta-analysis, errors ought to be envisioned as multiplied by the number of observations in the report for which the error occurred. A mistake in coding for a study of 400 participants is 10 times worse than a study of 40 participants. In the case of communication literatures that bear on public policy issues, one can imagine that meta-analytic errors could alter the conclusions of a review, making the translation of the research results into public policy more prone to error. Even if lives are not at stake, scientific reliability and validity are. For these reasons, we strongly encourage the team concept to meta-analysis, which at least permits ongoing checks and balances against errors. Even the most expert of analysts is subject to human error.

LOCATING THE LITERATURE OF RELEVANT STUDIES

Because including a large number of studies generally increases the value of a quantitative synthesis, it is important to locate as many studies as possible that might be suitable for inclusion, the third step of a meta-analysis. It is conventionally the tacit goal of meta-analyses to obtain *all* of the relevant studies. The very best sample is a complete census of the relevant studies. Indeed, when meta-analyses omit significant numbers of studies, they are often roundly criticized. Because the ideal in meta-analysis is a census of all the relevant studies, meta-analysis is different from the typical content analysis, for which content is systematically *sampled* from the population of relevant content.

To ensure that most if not all studies are located, reviewers are well advised to err in the direction of being overly inclusive in their search procedures. As described elsewhere (e.g., Cooper, 1998; Lipsey & Wilson, 2001; White, 1994), there are many ways to find relevant studies, and analysts are almost always well advised to use them all. Because computer searches of publication databases seldom locate all of the available studies, it is important to supplement them by (a) examining the reference lists of existing reviews (or consulting systematic reviews in specific databases, such as the Cochrane Library Plus and the Campbell Library, which regularly do updates of existing reviews) and of studies in the targeted literature, (b) obtaining published sources that have cited seminal articles within the literature (using *Social Sciences Citation Index*), (c) contacting the extant network of researchers who work on a given topic to ask for new studies or unpublished studies, and (d) manually searching important journals to find some reports that might have been overlooked by other techniques. The last strategy is especially important for more recent papers that might not yet be included in the electronic databases. Although such a comprehensive search may seem overwhelming, it is imperative if the goal is to retrieve all studies relevant to the topic of interest. Indeed, researchers who have compared searches retrieved from several databases have found that database searching is an insufficient means of literature retrieval and even find differences among electronic reference databases (e.g., Glass et al., 1981; Lemeshow, Blum, Berlin, Stoto, & Colditz, 2005). The review team should carefully record their methods of locating studies, including the names and databases that were searched, and for each database the time period covered and the keywords used. The details of the search procedure should be included in the methods section of the meta-analysis report, to enable readers to make adequate judgments about the adequacy of the procedures used and to permit other analysts to replicate the search.

An important consideration at this stage is whether to include non-English reports, which typically have international samples as well. Decisions about how to deal with the language of the report, on the one hand, and setting, culture, and study populations, on the other hand, should be made separately. Assuming that the decision about whether to include studies from diverse settings, cultures, and populations was made in Step 2, there may be studies reported in foreign languages that otherwise meet the sample selection criteria. To include non-English reports at minimum has the advantage of increasing the sample size in the meta-analysis and thereby systematically increasing the statistical power available in all analyses. If non-English reports in fact comprise the majority of studies, then excluding them would bias the results as well as be an injustice to the excluded reports. Note that a decision to limit the search by setting, culture, or study population may seem to imply the exclusion of non-English-language reports, but it is still possible that studies published in another language sampled the target population. Decisions to exclude on the basis of the language of the publication need to be carefully justified based on the phenomena under study and the nature of the literature in that domain. Note that in meta-analysis, multilanguage ability often is a plus, and even when the analyst team cannot interpret a report on their own, there are software products available to assist in the process, and colleagues with the needed language can perform favors.

CODING STUDIES FOR THEIR DISTINCTIVE CHARACTERISTICS

Once the sample of studies is retrieved, the fourth step in the process is to code them. Coding a meta-analysis is very similar to coding a content analysis. A coding sheet or an electronic database worksheet needs to be created, pretested, and revised. The variables to be coded and the possible values need to be operationalized precisely. Study characteristics may be either quantitative variables with values existing along ratio, interval, or ordinal scales or categorical variables having discrete numbers of values that reflect qualitative differences between those values. There may be a master codebook that explains the details for each category, or the information can be included in the database worksheet.

To the extent that the analyst team codes many features of the study, they should distinguish between study features that they expect on an a priori basis to account for variation among the studies' effect sizes, on the one hand, and those that provide merely descriptive information about the usual context of studies in the literature, on the other hand. A meta-analysis may be criticized for "fishing" for significant findings if it appears that too many study dimensions were tested as moderators of the magnitude of effects. Separating the study dimensions has the advantage of keeping the review as theory driven as possible (testing a few moderator variables), while at the same time being appropriately descriptive of the literature in question (including many descriptive variables).

To increase the reliability and accuracy of the coding, (a) coding should be carried out by two or more coders, (b) coders should be carefully trained, (c) the coding instructions should contain sufficient detail so that a new coder could apply the scheme and get similar results, and (d) disagreements between coders should be resolved through discussion or with a third coder. Good supervision is critical, including spot checks, trial runs, and easy access by coders for inevitable problems and questions. An appropriate index of intercoder reliability (e.g., Krippendorff's α, Cohen's k, etc.; see Hayes & Krippendorff, in press; Krippendorff, 1980, 2004) should be calculated and reported in the report of the meta-analysis.

Some variables may necessitate additional coders. For example, meta-analysts may consider recruiting outside judges to provide qualitative ratings of methods used in studies. Meta-analyses often use either groups of experts or novices similar to those participating in the studies in order to judge stimuli from study reports. The mean judgments are then put into the database as potential moderator variables.

ESTIMATING THE MAGNITUDE OF EFFECT IN EACH STUDY

The fifth step in a meta-analysis is to estimate the standardized effect size for each study, which quantitatively captures the phenomenon under scrutiny. The problem is that the studies almost always vary widely in terms of choice of statistic as well as sample size, rendering a comparison across the studies complicated. The solution is to impose an effect-size metric on all of the studies. Fortunately, nearly all inferential statistics (e.g., t-tests,

F tests) and many descriptive statistics (e.g., means and standard deviations) can be converted into an effect size (for specifics, see Cooper & Hedges, 1994b; Glass et al., 1981; Johnson & Eagly, 2000; Lipsey & Wilson, 2001; Rosenthal, 1991). In consulting and using such guides, it is important to make sure that the best formulas are employed. Failing to do so could result in effect-size estimates that are biased in liberal or conservative directions. As an example, *t*-values and *F* values can derive from both within- and between-subjects designs and formulas exist for both types of designs (see Johnson & Eagly, 2000; Morris & DeShon, 2002). Applying the formulas for the between-subjects cases to the within-subjects cases overestimates their effect size considerably (Dunlap, Cortina, Vaslow, & Burke, 1996; see Morris & DeShon, 2002, for discussion, and Seignourel & Albarracín, 2002, for relevant calculations). Clearly, analysts must carefully consider how the designs of the studies may affect the calculated effect size. If there are enough studies, it may be fruitful to consider conducting parallel, separate meta-analyses for studies with differing designs. Nonetheless, the goal is to convert summary statistics into effect sizes that can be statistically integrated.

*Effect sizes of association (*r, d, *and* OR*).* Effect-size indices usually gauge the association between two variables; an exception to this rule is the arithmetic mean, to which we will turn at the end of this section. Among indices of association, the most commonly used are the standardized mean difference and the correlation coefficient, although odds ratios are popular in some fields, such as medicine and public health (Lipsey & Wilson, 2001). The standardized mean difference, which expresses the difference between two means in standard deviation units, was first proposed by Cohen (1969; Table 11.1, Equation 1). Hedges (1981) showed that Cohen's *d*, which is now often labeled *g*, overestimates population effect sizes to the extent that sample sizes are small and provided a correction for this bias (Equations 2 and 3); with the bias corrected, this effect estimate is conventionally known as *d* (McGrath & Meyer, 2006). Another common effect size is the correlation coefficient, *r*, which gauges the association between two variables (Equation 4). Table 11.2 provides other conventional equations to convert some commonly encountered inferential statistics into *g* (for others, see Lipsey & Wilson, 2001).

Like *d*-values, *r*-values have a bias, in this case, underestimating the population effect sizes, especially for studies with small samples and for *r*-values near .60 (Table 11.1, Equation 5); yet because this bias correction is very small for sample sizes larger than 20, it is often omitted. Because the sampling distribution of a sample correlation coefficient tends to be skewed to the extent that the population correlation is large, many analysts use Fisher's (1921) *r*-to-*Z* logarithmic transform (Equation 6) when conducting analyses (see also Hays, 1988), and then use Fisher's *Z*-to-*r* transform (Equation 7) to return the output to the *r* metric. Although all agree that the distribution of *r* is skewed, Hunter and Schmidt (1990, 2004) have

Table 11.1 Conventional Equations for the Standardized Mean Difference and the Correlation Coefficient, Which Are Effect Sizes of Association Between Two Variables

Equation	Description	Formula	Notes and Definitions of Terms
		The Standardized Mean Difference	
1	Cohen's d (now usually labeled g)	$g = \dfrac{M_A - M_B}{SD}$	M_A and M_B are the sample means of two compared groups, and SD is the standard deviation, pooled from the two observations. Cohen's d, or g, is a raw, uncorrected index of association.
2	Hedges's d	$d = c(m) \times g$	d is the unbiased approximation of the population effect size; $c(m)$ appears as Equation 3.
3	Correction factor	$c(m) \approx 1 - \dfrac{3}{4m - 1}$	m is $n_A + n_B - 2$, the degrees of freedom, where the ns are the sample sizes associated with the two compared groups.
		The Correlation Coefficient	
4	Pearson's r	$r = \dfrac{\sum_{i=1}^{N} z_{Xi} z_{Yi}}{N}$	z_{Xi} and z_{Yi} are the standardized forms of X and Y being related for each case i, and N is the number of observations. Pearson's r is a raw, uncorrected index of association.
5	Correction to r	$\widetilde{G}_{(r)} \cong r + \dfrac{r(1-r^2)}{2(N-3)}$	$\widetilde{G}_{(r)}$ is the unbiased estimate of the population effect size.
6	Fisher's r-to-Z transform	$Z_r = \dfrac{1}{2} \log_e \dfrac{1+r}{1-r}$	$\log_e$ is a natural logarithm operation and r is corrected via Equation 5.
7	Fisher's Z-to-r transform	$r = \dfrac{e^{(2Z_r)} - 1}{e^{(2Z_r)} + 1}$	e is the base of the natural logarithm, approximately 2.718.

argued against the use of the Z transformations; Law (1995) provided an excellent review of this issue.

Because r can be transformed into d (in its g form), and vice versa, the choice of an effect-size metric for meta-analysis may seem somewhat arbitrary. Nonetheless, d was designed and is quantitatively appropriate for group comparisons of quantitative variables. Other advantages of using the standardized mean effect size are that d is well known with formulas for a

Table 11.2 A Selection of Conventional Equations to Translate Inferential Statistics Into the Standardized Mean Difference Effect Size (g)

Equation	Source Statistic	Formula	Notes and Definitions of Terms
8	Between-groups, Student's *t*-test	$g = t\sqrt{\dfrac{n_A + n_B}{n_A n_B}}$	n_A and n_B refer to the sample sizes of the compared groups.
9	Within-participants, Student's *t*-test	$g = \dfrac{t}{\sqrt{n}}$	This equation gauges change between two observations; n is the within-cell n, not the total number of observations.
10	Between-groups, *F* test	$g = \sqrt{F\dfrac{n_A + n_B}{n_A n_B}}$	n_A and n_B refer to the sample sizes of the two compared groups compared by the *F* test. (This equation is not for use with *F* tests comparing more than 2 groups.)
11	Within-participants, *F* test	$g = \sqrt{\dfrac{F}{n}}$	This equation gauges change between two observations; *F* compares only two groups; n is the within-cell n, not the total number of observations. (This equation is not for use with *F* tests comparing more than 2 groups.)
12	Correlation coefficient	$g = \dfrac{2r_{pb}}{\sqrt{1 - r_{pb}^2}}$	r_{pb} is the point-biserial correlation (comparing two groups).

wide array of statistical outcomes available for conversions into *d*, there are forms of *d* that take into account baseline differences (see Becker, 1988), and *d* is easily interpreted (see Van Den Noortgata & Onghena, 2003, for a discussion). Similarly, in its Pearson form, *r* was designed for associations between two quantitative variables. A variant of the family of *r* values, the point-biserial correlation, r_{pb}, is also appropriate for group comparisons on quantitative variables. If two groups are compared on a dichotomous outcome, then the effect size of choice is the odds ratio. Again, a variant of the *r* family can be used, in this case the φ (phi) coefficient. If *r* is used with any categorical variable, then the analyst should use the appropriate version (r_{pb} or r_φ) and interpret the results accordingly (McGrath & Meyer, 2006). Finally, just as primary researchers are extolled not to "dumb down" continuous variables into categorical variables, meta-analysts should also avoid this practice (Sánchez-Meca, Marín-Martínez, & Chacón-Moscoso, 2003).

In sum, the convention is to use *r* as the effect size if most of the studies that are integrated report correlations between two quantitative variables. If most of the studies report ANOVAs, *t*-tests, and chi-squares for comparisons between two groups (e.g., experimental vs. control), analysts typically select *d*. If both variables are dichotomous, then they typically select the *OR* (Haddock, Rindskopf, & Shadish, 1998). The positive or negative sign of *r* or *d* is defined so that studies with opposite outcomes have opposing signs; instances with exactly 0 have exactly no association or no difference, respectively. Further, those with values less than 0 have results opposite to those with values more than 0. In the case of the *OR*, instances with exactly 1 show exactly no difference; values less than 1 are opposed from those more than 1. Analyses of the *OR* use the logged form and transform output values for interpretation in the raw *OR* form.

If a report provides only an inexact statistic, or if the report merely states "the difference was nonsignificant," a meta-analytic team might contact the authors of the study for more precise information. If the only information available is imprecise and there is no feasible way to make it more precise, meta-analytic convention is to maintain the imprecise information so that the study is not lost to the review (Rosenthal, 1991). For example, a nonsignificant difference might be represented as $d = 0.00$, $r = .00$, or $OR = 1.00$. An effect described as "$p < .05$" can be converted as an exact *p*-value ($p = .05$) to an effect size. These estimates are conservatively biased (i.e., closer to zero than they are likely to be in reality) but have the advantage of keeping the report in the sample.

When one or both of the variables that are related in the meta-analysis were operationalized in more than one way in a given report or in two or more reports of the same study, the analyst must decide whether to average the effect sizes in order to represent the study with a single effect-size estimate. It is desirable to pool the estimates, rather than treat them as separate studies, in order to ensure that the participants' data contribute to only one effect size and preserve the independence of each effect size in the meta-analysis. Pooling is also a more systematic way to treat the data than arbitrarily choosing to include one effect size from a study rather than another. When pooling data, there are more accurate averaging procedures than using the mean or median of the effect sizes (see Gleser & Olkin, 1994; Rosenthal, 1991). Several scholars have described procedures to combine effect sizes within studies, taking into account the magnitude of their observed associations (Rosenthal & Rubin, 1986) or independent groups and repeated measures (Morris & DeShon, 2002).

Reports may also contain more than one form of statistical information that could be used to calculate a given effect size. For example, a report might contain an *F* test as well as means and standard deviations. The analyst should compute the effect size from both such sources, which, in the end, are all fundamentally interrelated forms of information, and, as long as the effect sizes are similar, take a simple average of them. Yet keep in mind that more accurate statistics typically have more decimal places and that rounding errors can produce discrepancies in calculated effect sizes. If the effect-size estimates are highly dissimilar, there may be errors in the information reported or the analyst's calculations. In the absence of obvious errors, the analyst must judge which value to enter into the data set, if any. Sometimes an inspection of the report's quantitative information for its internal consistency suggests that one form of the information is more accurate. If the discrepancy is serious and not readily resolved, one possibility is to contact the authors of the report. Only as a final resort should the study be discarded as too ambiguous.

Finally, studies sometimes examine the relation of interest within levels of another independent variable. In such instances, effect sizes may be calculated within the levels of this variable as well as for the study as a whole. This procedure was followed in the example cited earlier for Johnson and Eagly's (1989) meta-analysis of involvement and persuasion. Overall, the effects of involvement on persuasion were uninteresting. By separating the effects of involvement separately for experimentally induced levels of argument strength, the results revealed that different forms of involvement had distinctively different effects on persuasion.

Artifact corrections of indices of association. No matter how reliable or valid, scientific measures are always subject to error. Consequently, any estimate of effect size is just that—an estimate. Corrections for measurement unreliability and other forms of error or bias can be implemented in a meta-analysis in order to estimate what the magnitude of a relation would be in the absence of such artifacts. Hunter and Schmidt (1990, 1994, 2004; Schmidt & Hunter, 1996) explained how to implement corrections in the independent and dependent variables for measurement error, artificial dichotomization of a continuous variable, imperfect construct validity, and range restriction. In theory, correcting for such errors permits a more accurate estimation of the true effect size—that is, what its value would take had studies not been affected by these biases. Even when it is possible to implement fully the corrections within a literature, problems may emerge. Rosenthal (1991) noted that corrected effect sizes can take on irrational values (e.g., correlations larger than 1.00); Schmidt and Hunter (1996) concluded that such observations are due to sampling error and thus more likely to occur with small samples.[1] In considering whether to use such corrections, we recommend that analysts consider their goals. If the goal is to estimate the effect size that would exist if there were no contamination by any artifacts of measurement, then the corrections would be desirable. In contrast, if the goal is to show how large a relation is in practice, then the corrections would be less useful.

Regardless of whether these corrections are implemented, it is wise for analysts to be aware of potential biases that might enter into their studies' effect sizes. In particular, the effect-size indices that we have considered are ratios of signal to noise, like all inferential statistics. For example, in a between-groups design, the signal is the difference in means, and the noise is the pooled standard deviation (see Tables 11.1 and 11.2). Methodological factors can influence the effect size through their impact on signal, noise, or both factors. If two identical studies are conducted and one controls for noise and the other study does not (e.g., by statistically controlling for an individual difference characteristic), the first study will have a smaller error term than the second and its effect size will be larger. We recommend equating as much as possible how the comparisons are made across studies, so that the effect sizes are not impacted by differing statistical operations. Once again, analysts are wise to keep in mind that their effect-size indices as well as other measured features are estimates.

The arithmetic mean as an effect size. The strategies we have presented above pertain to effect sizes that relate one variable to another, whether in *r, d,* or *OR* forms. In the past decade, reviewers have begun to conceptualize arithmetic means as effect sizes, which gauge the magnitude of a dimension present in a sample rather than how much two variables are associated (Lipsey & Wilson, 2001). For example, Twenge (2000) used meta-analytic techniques to show that levels of anxiety steadily increased from the early 1940s to the 1980s among children and college students in the United States and that the increases were associated with cultural trends. To use such a meta-analytic strategy, the studies must express the phenomenon of interest on the same scale or else the analyst team must convert the scales to a common metric, along with their variability estimates (e.g., standard deviation, variance, or standard error).

Meta-analyses using means are rare in communication research, at least as of this date, but the potential may be enormous. Analyst teams might well examine changes in attitudes, beliefs, knowledge, or behavior defined as change against a baseline, as a mean rather than as a standardized mean effect size. In such a fashion, the team could examine, for example, whether resistance to political persuasion or apathy is becoming more the norm across time. Or research teams might examine change in a key mass communication variable such as average hours of television watched, or a health communication variable such as average amount of time a doctor spends with a patient, or measures of relational or work satisfaction in order to see if these variables are increasing, decreasing, or stable over time. Or the concern may be how the mean changes in response to other factors of interest. Researchers who currently use archival data in time series analyses—an approach commonly used in political communication, for example—may benefit from applying lessons from meta-analysis to better combine studies that have varying sample sizes and operationalizations of key variables (see Chapter 4 in this volume for a discussion of time series analysis in communication).

The disadvantage of invoking means as effect sizes is that their observed levels are likely to be more inconsistent than one typically observes with indices of association. The increased variability reflects the impact of practically every conceivable factor (e.g., personality and cultural changes, biological factors, and temporal news events). When the effect size is instead, for example, a comparison of two groups in response to the same stimulus, then all these alternative causes are controlled (at least in experimental designs, less so in nonexperimental designs). The remaining difference presumably reflects factors related directly to group membership. Consequently, analysts who conduct reviews using the mean as an effect size should expect to find considerable unexplained variability.

Regression slopes as effect sizes. Similar to means, regression slopes defined as unstandardized regression coefficients also have been used as effect sizes in meta-analysis. The advantage to this strategy is in maintaining the units of the original scales so that inferences can maintain a clear application to some phenomenon. For example, an analyst may wish to see how increases in advertising relate to use of self-help Web sites. Keeping the effect size in real terms would permit a generalization about how much Web site usage increases as advertising increases. Such techniques have been used with different applications and in different contexts including validity generalization (economics, tourism, policy, psychology), dose-response models (epidemiology), and descriptive analysis (education, psychology, economics). Their use has been relatively rare in meta-analysis because their values depend on the scales used to measure the relevant variables (Hunter & Schmidt, 2004). Nonetheless, there are meta-analytic approximations for combining the slopes in meta-analysis (Raudenbush, Becker, & Kalaian 1988; Wu, 2006). When the same scale is used across studies, meta-analysis can be used to synthesize them.

ANALYZING THE META-ANALYTIC DATABASES

Once the effect sizes are calculated, the sixth phase in the process is to analyze the data. In this section, we will assume that the goal is to use quantitative techniques to gauge differences between or across clusters of studies; those who wish to use artifact corrections of effect sizes or to avoid significance testing may be wise to pursue other techniques (see Hall & Brannick, 2002; Schmidt & Hunter, 1996). An exhaustive survey of general analytic approaches to meta-analysis is beyond the scope of the current chapter, but further discussions and comparisons are available elsewhere (e.g., Field, 2001, 2005; Hall & Brannick, 2002; Hunter & Schmidt, 2004; Sánchez-Meca & Marín-Martínez, 1997). The general steps involved in the analysis of effect sizes usually are (a) to aggregate effect sizes across the studies to determine the overall strength of the relation between the examined variables, (b) to analyze the consistency of the effect sizes across the studies, (c) to diagnose outliers among the effect sizes, and (d) to perform tests of whether study attributes moderate the magnitude of the effect sizes.

Averaging effect sizes. As a first step in a quantitative synthesis, the study outcomes are combined by averaging the effect sizes with the effect for study i weighted by the inverse of its variance (v_i), which typically rests heavily on sample size (Hedges & Olkin, 1985); some approaches advocate weighting each effect size by N (e.g., Hunter & Schmidt, 2004). Such procedures give greater weight to the more reliably estimated study outcomes, which are in general those with the larger samples (e.g., Hedges, Cooper, & Bushman, 1992). An indirect test for significance of this weighted mean effect size (T_+) is typically conducted using a confidence interval based on its standard deviation in the data, $T_+ \pm 1.96\sqrt{v}$, where 1.96 is the unit-normal value for a 95% CI (assuming a nondirectional hypothesis) and v is the variance of the estimates across all studies. If the confidence interval (CI) includes zero (0.00), the value indicating exactly no difference, it may be concluded that aggregated across all studies there is no association between the independent and dependent variable (X and Y). For example, Benoit et al. (2003) found that, across 13 studies, debate viewing increased issue knowledge. In a different literature, Sherry (2001) found that, across 25 studies, children's and adolescents' violent–video game playing had a small effect on aggression.

Calculating the heterogeneity of the effect sizes. The next concern is whether the studies can be adequately described by a single effect size, which is assessed by calculating the heterogeneity of the effect sizes across studies, which gauges the amount of variability in the effect sizes around the mean (Cochran, 1954; Hedges, 1981; Hunter & Schmidt, 2004; Rosenthal, 1991). If the effect sizes share a common, underlying population effect size, then they would differ only by unsystematic sampling error. The test statistic Q evaluates the hypothesis that the effect sizes are consistent and has an approximate χ^2 distribution with $k - 1$ degrees of freedom, where k is the number of studies. If Q is significant, the null hypothesis of the homogeneity (or consistency) of the effect sizes is rejected. In this event, the weighted mean effect size may not adequately describe the outcomes of the set of studies because it is likely that quite different mean effects exist in different groups of studies. Further analysis is warranted to test potential moderating variables responsible for different mean effects. Q deserves careful interpretation, in conjunction with inspecting the values of the effect sizes. Even if the homogeneity test is nonsignificant, significant moderators could be present, especially when Q is relatively large (Johnson & Turco, 1992, and Rosenthal, 1995, provide further discussion). Also, Q could be significant even though the effect sizes are very close in value, especially if the sample sizes are very large. Finally, if the number of studies is small, tests of homogeneity are known to have low power to detect the null hypothesis of homogeneity (Hardy & Thompson, 1998; Harwell, 1997). Higgins and Thompson (2002) introduced a homogeneity index, I^2, whose values range from 0 to 100, where high values indicate more variability among the effect sizes. The I^2 index is subject to the same conditions and qualifications as is Q (Huedo-Medina, Sánchez-Meca, Marín-Martínez, & Botella, 2006). The primary benefit of I^2 is that its use would allow for standardized comparisons between meta-analyses while providing the same information as Q.

As an example, imagine a meta-analysis that attempts to determine X's impact on Y. Deciding not to accept the hypothesis of homogeneity implies that the association between these two variables likely is complicated by the presence of interacting conditions. In some studies, X might have had a large positive effect on Y, and in other studies, it might have had a smaller positive effect or even a negative effect on Y. The next task is to uncover the source of the variation in effect sizes. Because analysts usually anticipate the presence of one or more moderators of effect-size magnitude, establishing that effect sizes are not homogeneous is ordinarily neither surprising nor troublesome.

Finally, analysts often present other measures of central tendency in addition to the weighted mean effect size. For example, the unweighted mean effect size shows the typical effect without weighting studies with larger sample sizes more heavily. A substantial difference in the values of the unweighted and weighted mean effect sizes suggests that one or more studies with large sample sizes may deviate from the rest of the sample. Also, the median effect size describes a typical effect size but would be less affected than a mean effect size by outliers and other anomalies in the distribution of effect sizes.

Analysis of outliers. An analyst can attain homogeneity by identifying outlying values among the effect sizes and sequentially removing those effect sizes that reduce the homogeneity statistic by the largest amount (e.g., Hedges, 1987). Studies yielding effect sizes identified as outliers can then be examined to determine if they appear to differ methodologically from the other studies. Also, inspection of the percentage of effect sizes removed to attain homogeneity allows one to determine whether the effect sizes are homogeneous aside from the presence of relatively few aberrant values. Under such circumstances, the mean attained after removal of such outliers may better represent the distribution of effect sizes than the mean based on all of the effect sizes. In general, the diagnosis of outliers should occur prior to calculating moderator analyses; this diagnosis may locate a value or two that are so discrepant from the other effect sizes that they would dramatically alter any models fitted to effect sizes. Under such circumstances, these outliers should be removed from subsequent phases of the data analysis. More normally, outliers can be examined by analyzing potential moderators of effect sizes, as discussed in the next section. That is, effect sizes that are apparently outliers may in fact be associated with the coded features of the studies.

Analysis of potential moderators of effect sizes. Ordinarily, analyst teams want to test a priori hypotheses about what explains variations in effect sizes across studies. To determine the relation between study characteristics and the magnitude of the effect sizes, both categorical factors and quantitative factors can be tested. Instead of using such familiar primary-level statistics as t, F, or r to evaluate whether study dimensions relate to the magnitude of effect sizes, it is best to use statistics that take full advantage of the information in each study's effect size (for discussion, see Hedges & Olkin, 1985; Johnson & Turco, 1992). In *categorical models,* which are analogous to the analysis of variance, analyses may show that weighted mean effect sizes differ in magnitude between the subgroups established by dividing studies into classes based on study characteristics. In such cases, it is as though the meta-analysis is broken into sub-meta-analyses based on their methodological features. For example, Albarracín et al.'s (2003) meta-analysis found that face-to-face or video communications promoted condom use better than those presented in print format (i.e., brochures, posters, or other print). If effect sizes that were found to be heterogeneous become homogeneous within the classes of a categorical model, the relevant study characteristic has accounted for systematic variability between the effect sizes.

Similarly, *continuous models,* which are analogous to regression models, examine whether study characteristics that are assessed on a quantitative scale are related to the effect sizes. As with categorical models, some continuous models may be completely specified in the sense that the systematic variability in the effect sizes is explained by the study characteristic that is used as a predictor. For example, Albarracín et al. (2003) found that exposure to condom-related persuasive communications resulted in greater condom use to the extent that the sample contained more male participants. Goodness-of-fit statistics enable analysts to determine the extent to which categorical, continuous, or mixtures of these models provide correct depictions of study outcomes. Finally, multiple moderators may appear in these models, provided sufficient numbers of studies exist.

Fixed-effects models. The preceding subsection assumed the most basic form of meta-analytic statistic, models based on fixed-effects assumptions, which are the most popular and generally match the assumptions of primary-level research. Fixed-effects models assume that the underlying effect sizes are fixed either as a single group or else along the range of a set of moderator values. In the case of a fixed-effects model specifying a simple weighted mean effect size, the assumption made is that there is one underlying but unknown effect size and that study estimates of this effect size vary only in sampling error. In this case, the test of model specification is the Q or I^2 statistic; a large or significant test implies that the model is more complex than the model that the analyst assessed and that this simple model is inadequate as a description of the effect sizes.

In the case of a fixed-effects model assessing categorical, quantitative, or multiple predictors, large or significant Q_W or $Q_{Residual}$ values imply that the model is not correctly specified. To say that the effect sizes are fixed is to say that the differences are invariant save for sampling error either as a mean or along a range of moderator dimension(s). In other words, fixing effect sizes to the levels of the moderators has not explained enough of their variation in order for it to be plausible that only variation due to sampling error remains.

To the extent that they have sufficient numbers of studies and available moderators, analysts often add moderators in an effort to achieve a correctly specified model. They may very well do exploratory analyses using the descriptive features of the studies. An alternative is to pursue models with different assumptions, which we address next.

Random-effects models assume that each effect size is unique and that the study is drawn at random from a universe of related but separate effects (for discussions, see Hedges & Vevea, 1998; Hunter & Schmidt, 2000; Lipsey & Wilson, 2001). In addition to sampling error, such models assume that the variation due to the characteristics of studies estimates the between-studies variance present in the universe of effects. In essence, the random-effects model provides an estimate of the population effect size ignoring moderator dimensions, so it should be understood as such. Fitting a random-effects model to extremely heterogeneous sets of effect sizes may erroneously disguise distinct subpopulations of effect sizes. In contrast, when homogeneity tests are nonsignificant and therefore there is no population variance, random-effects models reduce to fixed-effects models: They produce exactly the same mean and confidence interval.

Reviewers of meta-analyses commonly demand random-effects models instead of fixed-effects models when the overall homogeneity statistic is significant. Yet such a criticism is unfounded when the goal of the review is to assess models with moderator dimensions; many reviewers do not realize that random-effects meta-analytic models provide only an estimate of mean effect size without moderators. Random-effects models do not provide estimates of moderators because the presence of moderators implies a dimension along which the effects are fixed.

Mixed-effects models. Models that attempt to maintain the overall random-effects assumption but also fix the effect sizes along certain moderator dimensions are called *mixed-effects models*. Such models assume that the variability in the effect-size distribution is attributed to some systematic between-study differences and an additional unmeasured random component. Strictly speaking, what is fixed is the coefficient of the moderator dimension, or coefficients in the case of multiple-predictor models, and what is random is the constant of the underlying general linear model. If the constant is of no interest to the analyst team and if the only interest is fixing the effect sizes according to levels of a moderator, then there would seem to be little reason to pursue such models. As in simple regression, the constant in either fixed-effects or mixed-effects models is defined as the point at which the line crosses the *y*-axis. The constant can be of great interest when it reflects meaningful levels at one end of the moderator dimension. Thus, the constant assesses the value of the effect size at level zero of the moderator or moderators. A last consideration is model fit in the mixed-effects case: Because variation in the effect sizes is effectively used to estimate the random constant, there is correspondingly less available to explain when fixing the effect sizes to any moderators. The consequence is that mixed-effects models tend to appear far better fitting than their fixed-effects counterparts, particularly when the distribution of effect sizes is heterogeneous (see Overton, 1998). The risk, as with random-effects models, is that an apparently well-fitting mixed-effects model erroneously disguises subpopulations of effect sizes.

Statistical power. Statistical power assumptions underlie all of the analyses that we have discussed, and power will vary according to the studies' sample sizes, the numbers of studies, and other features. Even tests of model specification are subject to these considerations: If there are few studies, then there is likely to be low power to assess the assumption that the effect sizes are consistent (Hedges & Pigott, 2001). Conducting power analyses is particularly important for interpreting moderator tests, and the failure to do so may result in misleading information (Hedges & Pigott, 2004). If power is found to be low, Hedges and Pigott suggest not conducting moderator analyses or including the power analysis so that readers may be able to correctly interpret the outcomes of the study.

Publication bias. Our discussion of published versus unpublished studies raises the issue of *publication bias*, defined as a bias by authors, reviewers, and editors against null reports or, worse, bias against reports whose data actually oppose a popular hypothesis. Although scholars commonly consider it a bias by the "establishment" against publishing null or reversed effects, in fact, even study authors may exhibit a bias about reporting data that fail to support a pet theory, leaving these findings in the proverbial file drawer, probably not even written up for publication (e.g., Greenwald, 1975). Of course, to the extent that a meta-analysis team has located and retrieved unpublished studies, it is possible to test for publication bias directly by using publication status as a moderator of effect sizes; in such cases, analyst teams should be alert to the possibility that the "unpublished" studies they have obtained are in fact those likely in the passage of time to become published. Yet even when only published studies are included, it is still possible to test for publication bias through the use of a growing number of techniques (for a review, see Thornton & Lee, 2000). The simplest way is to inspect a *funnel plot* of the distribution of effect sizes; these plots graph effect sizes and their sample sizes (or the inverse of their variance) and ought to reveal a normal distribution if publication bias is not present. Gaps or asymmetries in the graph therefore reveal potential publication bias. More sophisticated techniques attempt to quantify these gaps, as in the trim-and-fill method (Duval & Tweedie, 2000), or to estimate what the mean effect size would be if theoretically missing effect sizes were included (Hedges & Vevea, 1996; Vevea & Hedges, 1995). Another popular technique is to calculate the fail-safe *N*, which is the number of null-result studies necessary to reduce the mean effect size to nonsignificance (Rosenthal, 1991); an implausibly high number would suggest that publication bias is trivial. Despite the popularity of the technique, critics have noted that the index lacks a distribution theory, and therefore it is not known how likely a particular fail-safe *N* value would be to occur based on chance (Begg, 1994).

Even when publication bias seems obvious, analysts are wise to consider alternative reasons why the pattern may have occurred: It may be that the methods of larger studies differed systematically from those of smaller studies. In particular, publication bias is less of an issue when effect sizes lack homogeneity and when moderators can be identified. Publication bias should be considered in light of both the degree of homogeneity and of how effect sizes pattern according to features of the studies. Indeed, under such circumstances, publication bias often becomes a trivial or nonexistent concern.

Vote-counting techniques. In our introduction to this chapter, we mentioned that narrative reviewing has often relied on intuitive counts of the number of studies that had either produced or failed to produce statistically significant findings in the hypothesized direction. Although precision may be enhanced by relying on effect-size indices, statistical models actually exist for doing "vote counting" in a rather sophisticated manner (Darlington & Hayes, 2000). First, note that by sampling error and a conventional alpha level of .05, 1 in 20 studies should produce a significant result. Thus, one method for summarizing a literature would be to note the proportion of studies that obtained the predicted finding and to assess whether this outcome differs from that expected merely on sampling error (Wilkinson, 1951). Darlington and Hayes (2000) showed that such binomial analyses (and several extensions of them) can reduce or eliminate the criticisms that simple vote-counting techniques usually engender. Indeed, these techniques may prove an important adjunct to analyses of effect sizes in that they can provide refined estimates of the likely numbers of omitted reports (see also Bushman & Wang, 1996). Finally, such techniques may prove especially valuable for use in literatures for which many vague statistical reports appear.

INTERPRETING AND PRESENTING THE META-ANALYTIC RESULTS

Science offers no gauges of the truth, only tools with which to divine it. Meta-analysis is thus a tool whose "gauges," or output, must be interpreted in order to present them, which is the seventh step of the process. If the mean effect is nonsignificant and the homogeneity statistic is small and nonsignificant, an analyst might conclude that there is no relation between the variables under consideration. However, in such cases, it is wise to consider the amount of statistical power that was available; if the total number of research participants in the studies integrated was small, it is possible that additional data would support the existence of the effect. Even if the mean effect is significant and the homogeneity statistic is small and nonsignificant, concerns about the mean effect's magnitude arise.

To address this issue, Cohen (1969, 1988) proposed some guidelines for judging effect magnitude, based on his informal analysis of the magnitude of effects commonly yielded by psychological research. In doing so, he intended that a medium effect size would be "of a size likely to be visible to the naked eye of a careful observer" (Cohen, 1992, p. 156), that small effect sizes be "noticeably smaller yet not trivial" (p. 156), and that large effect sizes "be the same distance above medium as small is below it" (p. 156). As Table 11.3 shows, a "medium" effect turned out to be about $d = 0.50$ and $r = .30$, equivalent to the difference in intelligence scores between clerical and semiskilled workers. A "small" effect size was about $d = 0.20$ and $r = .10$, equivalent to the difference in height between 15- and 16-year-old girls. Finally, a large effect was about $d = 0.80$ and $r = .50$, equivalent to the difference in intelligence scores between college professors and college freshmen.[2]

In the field of mass communication, for example, meta-analyses have found small average effect sizes for the effect of health communication

Table 11.3 Cohen's (1969) Guidelines for Magnitude of d and r

	Effect Size Metric		
Size	d	r	R^2
Small	0.20	.100	.010
Medium	0.50	.243	.059
Large	0.80	.371	.138

Note: r appears in its biserial form.

campaigns on behavior (Snyder & Hamilton, 2002), the cultivation effect of television on beliefs (Shanahan & Morgan, 1999), and the association between television and video game use and body fat (Marshall, Biddle, Gorely, Cameron, & Murdey, 2004). The effect size for the impact of playing violent video games on violent behavior is slightly larger (roughly $r = .20$). It is valuable to be able to compare the magnitude of effects across phenomena, which over time will reveal new patterns across literatures of media effect studies.

Another popular way to interpret mean effect sizes is to derive the equivalent r and square it. This procedure shows how much variability would be explained by an effect of the magnitude of the mean effect size. Thus, under ideal circumstances (McGrath & Meyer, 2006), a mean of $d = 0.50$ and $r = .25$ produces an $R^2 = .09$. However, this value must be interpreted carefully because R^2, or variance explained, is a directionless effect size. If the individual effect sizes that produced the mean effect size varied in their signs (i.e., the effect sizes were not all negative or all positive), the variance in Y explained by the predictor X, calculated for each study and averaged, would be larger than this simple transform of the mean effect size. Thus, another possible procedure consists of computing R^2 for each individual study and averaging these values.

Trends in the Practice of Meta-Analysis

Although the quality of meta-analyses has been quite variable, it is possible to state the features that comprise a high-quality meta-analysis, including success in locating studies, explicitness of criteria for selecting studies, thoroughness and accuracy in coding moderator variables and other study characteristics, accuracy in effect-size computations, and adherence to the assumptions of meta-analytic statistics. When meta-analyses satisfy such standards, it is difficult to disagree with Rosenthal's (1994) conclusion that it is "hardly justified to review a quantitative literature in the pre-meta-analytic, prequantitative manner" (p. 131). Yet merely meeting these high standards does not necessarily make a meta-analysis an important scientific contribution.

One factor affecting scientific contribution is that the conclusions that a research synthesis is able to reach are limited by the quality of the data that are synthesized. Serious methodological faults that are endemic in a research literature may very well handicap a synthesis, unless it is designed to shed light on the influence of these faults. Also, to be regarded as important, the review must address an interesting question.

Moreover, unless the paper reporting a meta-analysis "tells a good story," its full value may go unappreciated by readers. Although there are many paths to a good story, Sternberg's (1991) recommendations to authors of reviews are instructive: Pick interesting questions, challenge conventional understandings if at all possible, take a unified perspective on the phenomenon, offer a clear take-home message, and write well. Thus, the practice of meta-analysis should not preclude incorporating aspects of narrative reviewing, but instead should strive to incorporate and document the richness of the literature.

One reason that the quality of published syntheses has been quite variable is that it is a relatively new tool among scholars who practice it. Yet as the methods of quantitative synthesis have become more sophisticated and widely disseminated, typical published meta-analyses have improved. At their best, meta-analyses advance knowledge about a phenomenon by explicating its typical patterns and showing when it is larger or smaller, negative or positive, and test theories about the phenomenon (see Miller & Pollock, 1994). Meta-analysis should foster a healthy interaction between primary research and research synthesis, at once summarizing old research and suggesting promising directions for new research. It is valuable if the meta-analytic team includes scholars who are intimately familiar with the literature, to help frame the most interesting research questions and assist in study design.

Another reason that published syntheses have varied widely in quality is the simple reason that meta-analysis can be difficult. The nuances that we have covered in this chapter bear witness to the many nuances and cautions that analyst teams should bear in mind in accomplishing a good research synthesis. Research synthesis is simultaneously a teleological as well as a historical process, qualitative as well as quantitative. Because of the clear advantages of meta-analysis, communication scholars may be more and more expected to conduct meta-analyses rather than narrative reviews. Editors and reviewers are well advised to consider that meta-analysis may usually be preferable to narrative reviewing, but that it is also much more taxing.

One misperception that scholars sometimes express is that a meta-analysis represents a dead end for a literature, a point beyond which nothing more needs to be known. In contrast, carefully conducted meta-analyses can often be the best medicine for a literature, by documenting the robustness with which certain associations are attained, resulting in a sturdier foundation on which future theories may rest. In addition, meta-analyses can show where knowledge is at its thinnest, thus helping plan additional, primary-level research (Eagly & Wood, 1994). For example, the meta-analysis of violent video games by Anderson (2004) found a dearth of studies examining the longitudinal effects of violent video games and called for more primary research to address the gap. As a consequence of a carefully conducted meta-analysis, primary-level studies can be designed with the complete literature in mind and therefore have a better chance of contributing new knowledge. In this fashion, scientific resources can be directed most efficiently toward gains in knowledge.

As time passes and new studies continue to accrue rapidly, it is likely that social scientists will rely more on quantitative syntheses to inform them about the knowledge that has accumulated in their research. Although it is possible that meta-analysis will become the purview of an elite class of researchers who specialize in research integration, as Schmidt (1992) argued, it seems more likely that meta-analysis is becoming a routine part of graduate training in many fields, developing the skills necessary for plying the art and science of meta-analysis to integrate findings across studies as a normal and routine part of their research activities.

Resources

Some general resources on meta-analysis:

1. http://www.psychwiki.com/wiki/Meta-analysis lists many resources on meta-analysis.

2. Dr. William R. Shadish's Web site offers extensive lists related to meta-analysis (see http://faculty.ucmerced.edu/wshadish/Meta-Analysis%20Software.htm).

Some resources for calculating effect sizes:

1. Lipsey and Wilson's (2001) *Practical Meta-Analysis* offers a wide range of equations and an associated Web site with a spreadsheet calculator (at time of publication, posted on Dr. David B. Wilson's Web site http://mason.gmu.edu/~dwilsonb/ma.html).

2. Biostat, Incorporated's, Comprehensive Meta-Analysis software offers many routines to calculate effect sizes (see http://www.meta-analysis.com/).

3. Glass et al. (1981) provided many routines that still do not appear elsewhere.

Some resources for modeling effect sizes:

1. Comprehensive Meta-Analysis will perform nearly all of the analyses that have been described in this chapter.

2. SAS (http://www.sas.com), SPSS (http://www.spss.com), and STATA (http://www.stata.com) will perform the analyses described in this chapter, but users are well advised to invoke the macros provided on Dr. Wilson's Web site, listed above. Wang and Bushman (1999) also provided extensive techniques for meta-analysis using SAS.

3. Analysts who wish to apply the Hunter and Schmidt (2004) artifact corrections can use software available with this book, or another from Dr. Ralf Schwarzer (http://web.fu-berlin.de/gesund/gesu_engl/meta_e.htm).

Notes

1. Charles's (2005) fine review lists historical examples of correlations larger than |1.0| and provides other possible explanations of such instances.
2. McGrath and Meyer (2006) discuss the assumptions involved in these effect-size benchmarks. For example, they point out that Cohen's (1969, 1988) r_{pb} standards assume that the compared groups are equivalent in size. To the extent that the sizes differ, the r_{pb} benchmarks for size will drop. For example, if one group has 99% and the other 1% of the observations, a "large" r_{pb} drops by 78%, from .37 to .08! This change of benchmark does not occur for d, which is insensitive to base rates.

References

Albarracín, D., McNatt, P. S., Klein, C. T. F., Ho, R. M., Mitchell, A. L., & Kumkale, G. T. (2003). Persuasive communications to change actions: An analysis of behavioral and cognitive impact in HIV prevention. *Health Psychology, 22,* 166–177.

Allen, M., Mabry, E., Mattrey, M., Bourhis, J., Titsworth, S., & Burrell, N. (2004). Evaluating the effectiveness of distance learning: A comparison using meta-analysis. *Journal of Communication, 54,* 402–420.

Allen, M., & Preiss, R. W. (1998). *Persuasion: Advances through meta-analysis.* Cresskill, NJ: Hampton Press.

Allen, M., Preiss, R. W., Gayle, B. M., & Burrell, N. A. (2002). *Interpersonal communication research: Advances through meta-analysis.* Mahwah, NJ: Lawrence Erlbaum Associates.

Anderson, C. A. (2004). An update on the effects of playing violent video games. *Journal of Adolescence, 27,* 113–122.

Bangert-Drowns, R. L. (1997). Some limiting factors in meta-analysis. In W. J. Bukoski (Ed.), *Meta-analysis of drug abuse prevention programs.* National Institute on Drug Abuse Research Monograph 170, pp. 234–252. Rockville, MD: U.S. Department of Health and Human Services.

Baron, R. M., & Kenny, D. A. (1986). The moderator-mediator variable distinction in social psychological research: Conceptual, strategic, and statistical considerations. *Journal of Personality and Social Psychology, 51,* 1173–1182.

Bauman, K. E. (1997). The effectiveness of family planning programs evaluated with true experimental designs. *Public Health Briefs, 87,* 666–669.

Becker, B. J. (1988). Synthesizing standardized mean-change measures. *British Journal of Mathematical and Statistical Psychology, 41,* 257–278.

Begg, C. B. 1994. Publication bias. In H. Cooper & L. V. Hedges (Eds.), *The handbook of research synthesis* (pp. 400–408). New York: Russell Sage Foundation.

Bem, D. J., & Honorton, C. (1994). Does psi exist? Replicable evidence for an anomalous process of information transfer. *Psychological Bulletin, 115,* 4–18.

Benoit, W., Hansen, G. J., & Verser, R. M. (2003). A meta-analysis of the effects of viewing U.S. presidential debates. *Communication Monographs, 70,* 335–350.

Berelson, B. (1952). *Content analysis in communication research.* New York: Free Press.

Buller, D. B. (1986). Distraction during persuasive communication. A meta-analytic review. *Communication Monographs, 53,* 91–114.

Bushman, B. J., & Wang, M. C. (1996). A procedure for combining sample standardized mean differences and vote counts to obtain an estimate and a confidence interval for the population standardized mean difference. *Psychological Methods, 1,* 66–80.

Campbell, D. T., & Stanley, J. T. (1963). *Experimental and quasi-experimental designs for research.* Chicago: Rand-McNally.

Casey, M. K., Allen, M., Emmers-Sommer, T., Sahlstein, E., Degooyer, D., Winters, A. M., et al. (2003). When a celebrity contracts a disease: The example of Earvin "Magic" Johnson's announcement that he was HIV positive. *Journal of Health Communication, 8,* 249–265.

Charles, E. P. (2005). The correction for attenuation due to measurement error: Clarifying concepts and creating confidence sets. *Psychological Methods, 10,* 206–226.

Cochran, W. G. (1954). The combination of estimates from different experiments. *Biometrics, 10,* 101–129.

Cohen, J. (1969). *Statistical power analysis for the behavioral sciences.* New York: Academic Press.

Cohen, J. (1988). *Statistical power analysis for the behavioral sciences* (2nd ed.). Hillsdale, NJ: Lawrence Erlbaum Associates.

Cohen, J. (1992). A power primer. *Psychological Bulletin, 112,* 155–159.

Comstock, G., Chaffee, S., Katzman, N., McCombs, M., & Roberts, D. (1978). *Television and human behavior.* New York: Columbia University Press.

Comstock, G., & Strasburger, V. C. (1990). Deceptive appearances: Television violence and aggressive behavior. *Journal of Adolescent Health Care, 11,* 31–44.

Cook, T. D., & Campbell, D. T. (1979). Quasi-experimentation: Design & analysis issues for field settings. Boston: Houghton Mifflin.

Cooper, H. (1998). *Integrative research: A guide for literature reviews* (3rd ed.). Thousand Oaks, CA: Sage.

Cooper, H., & Hedges, L. V. (1994a). Research synthesis as a scientific enterprise. In H. Cooper & L. V. Hedges (Eds.), *The handbook of research synthesis* (pp. 3–14). New York: Russell Sage Foundation.

Cooper, H., & Hedges, L. V. (Eds.). (1994b). *The handbook of research synthesis.* New York: Russell Sage Foundation.

Cooper, H., & Rosenthal, R. (1980). Statistical versus traditional procedures for summarizing research findings. *Psychological Bulletin, 87,* 442–449.

Darlington, R. B., & Hayes, A. F. (2000). Combining independent *p* values: Extensions of the Stouffer and binomial methods. *Psychological Methods, 5,* 496–515.

Dillard, J. P., Hunter, J. E., & Burgoon, M. (1984). Sequential-request persuasive strategies: Meta-analysis of foot-in-the-door and door-in-the-face. *Human Communication Research, 10,* 461–488.

Dindia, K. (2002). Self-disclosure research: Knowledge through meta-analysis. In M. Allen, R. W. Preiss, B. M. Gayle, & N. A. Burrell (Eds.), *Interpersonal communication research: Advances through meta-analysis* (pp. 169–185). Mahwah, NJ: Lawrence Erlbaum Associates.

Dunlap, W. P., Cortina, J. M., Vaslow, J. B., & Burke, M. J. (1996). Meta-analysis of experiments with matched groups or repeated measures designs. *Psychological Methods, 1,* 170–177.

Duval, S., & Tweedie, R. (2000). Nonparametric "trim and fill" method for accounting for publication bias in meta-analysis. *Journal of the American Statistical Association, 95,* 89–98.

Eagly, A. H., & Wood, W. (1994). Using research syntheses to plan future research. In H. Cooper & L. V. Hedges (Eds.), *The handbook of research synthesis* (pp. 485–500). New York: Russell Sage Foundation.

Field, A. P. (2001). Meta-analysis of correlation coefficients: A Monte Carlo comparison of fixed- and random-effects methods. *Psychological Methods, 6,* 161–180.

Field, A. P. (2005). Is the meta-analysis of correlation coefficients accurate when population correlations vary? *Psychological Methods, 10,* 444–467.

Fisher, R. A. (1921). On the "probable error" of a coefficient of correlation deduced from a small sample. *Metron, 1,* 1–32.

Friedman, J. L. (1988). Television violence and aggression: What the evidence shows. *Applied Social Psychology Annual, 8,* 144–162.

Glass, G. V., McGaw, B., & Smith, M. L. (1981). *Meta-analysis in social research.* Beverly Hills, CA: Sage.

Gleser, L. J., & Olkin, I. (1994). Stochastically dependent effect sizes. In H. Cooper & L. V. Hedges (Eds.), *The handbook of research synthesis* (pp. 339–355). New York: Russell Sage Foundation.

Greenwald, A. G. (1975). Consequences of prejudice against the null hypothesis. *Psychological Bulletin, 82,* 1–20.

Haddock, C. K., Rindskopf, D., & Shadish, W. R. (1998). Using odds ratios as effect sizes for meta-analysis of dichotomous data: A primer on methods and issues. *Psychological Methods, 3,* 339–353.

Hale, J. L., & Dillard, J. P. (1991). The uses of meta-analysis: Making knowledge claims and setting research agendas. *Communication Monographs, 58,* 464–471.

Hall, J. A., & Rosenthal, R. (1991). Testing for moderator variables in meta-analysis: Issues and methods. *Communication Monographs, 58,* 437–448.

Hall, J. A., Tickle-Degnen, L., Rosenthal, R., & Mosteller, F. (1994). Hypotheses and problems in research synthesis. In H. Cooper & L. V. Hedges (Eds.), *The handbook of research synthesis* (pp. 17–28). New York: Russell Sage Foundation.

Hall, S. M., & Brannick, M. T. (2002). Comparison of two random-effects methods of meta-analysis. *Journal of Applied Psychology, 87,* 377–389.

Hardy, R. J., & Thompson, S. G. (1998). Detecting and describing heterogeneity in meta-analysis. *Statistics in Medicine, 17,* 841–856.

Harwell, M. (1997). An empirical study of Hedge's homogeneity test. *Psychological Methods, 2,* 219–231.

Hayes, A. F., & Krippendorff, K. (in press). Answering the call for a standard reliability measure for coding data. *Communication Methods and Measures.*

Hays, W. L. (1988). *Statistics* (4th ed.). Fort Worth, TX: Holt, Rinehart & Winston Inc.

Hedges, L. V. (1981). Distribution theory for Glass's estimator of effect size and related estimators. *Journal of Educational Statistics, 6,* 107–128.

Hedges, L. V. (1987). How hard is hard science, how soft is soft science? The empirical cumulativeness of research. *American Psychologist, 42,* 443–455.

Hedges, L. V., Cooper, H., & Bushman, B. J. (1992). Testing the null hypothesis in meta-analysis: A comparison of combined probability and confidence interval procedures. *Psychological Bulletin, 111,* 188–194.

Hedges, L. V., & Olkin, I. (1985). *Statistical methods for meta-analysis.* Orlando, FL: Academic Press.

Hedges, L. V., & Pigott, T. D. (2001). The power of statistical tests in meta-analysis. *Psychological Methods, 6,* 203–217.

Hedges, L. V., & Pigott, T. D. (2004). The power of statistical tests for moderators in meta-analysis. *Psychological Methods, 9,* 426–445.

Hedges, L. V., & Vevea, J. L. (1996). Estimating effect size under publication bias: Small sample properties and robustness of a random effects selection model. *Journal of Educational and Behavioral Statistics, 21,* 299–333.

Hedges, L. V., & Vevea, J. L. (1998). Fixed- and random-effects models in meta-analysis. *Psychological Methods, 3,* 486–504.

Higgins, J. P. T., & Thompson, S. G. (2002). Quantifying heterogeneity in a meta-analysis. *Statistics in Medicine, 21,* 1539–1558.

Holsti, O. (1969). *Content analysis.* Reading, MA: Addison-Wesley.

Huedo-Medina, T. B., Sánchez-Meca, J., Marín-Martínez, F., & Botella, J. (2006). Assessing heterogeneity in meta-analysis: Q statistic or I^2 index? *Psychological Methods, 11,* 193–206.

Hullett, C. R., & Levine, T. R. (2003). The overestimation of effect sizes from F values in meta-analysis: The cause and a solution. *Communication Monographs, 70,* 52–67.

Hunt, M. (1997). *How science takes stock: The story of meta-analysis.* New York: Russell Sage Foundation.

Hunter, J. E., & Schmidt, F. L. (1990). *Methods of meta-analysis: Correcting error and bias in research findings.* Newbury Park, CA: Sage.

Hunter, J. E., & Schmidt, F. L. (1994). Correcting for sources of artificial variation across studies. In H. Cooper & L. V. Hedges (Eds.), *The handbook of research synthesis* (pp. 323–336). New York: Russell Sage Foundation.

Hunter, J. E., & Schmidt, F. L. (2000). Fixed effects vs. random effects meta-analysis models: Implications for cumulative research knowledge. *International Journal of Selection and Assessment, 8,* 275–292.

Hunter, J. E., & Schmidt, F. L. (2004). *Methods of meta-analysis: Correcting error and bias in research findings* (2nd ed.). Thousand Oaks, CA: Sage.

Huston, A. C., Donnerstein, E., Fairchild, H., Feshbach, N. D., Katz, P. A., Murray, J. P., et al. (1992). *Big world, small screen: The role of television in American society.* Lincoln: University of Nebraska Press.

Johnson, B. T., Carey, M. P., Marsh, K. L., Levin, K. D., & Scott-Sheldon, L. A. J. (2003). Interventions to reduce sexual risk for the Human Immunodeficiency Virus in adolescents, 1985–2000: A research synthesis. *Archives of Pediatrics & Adolescent Medicine, 157,* 381–388.

Johnson, B. T., & Eagly, A. H. (2000). Quantitative synthesis of social psychological research. In H. T. Reis & C. M. Judd (Eds.), *Handbook of research methods in social and personality psychology* (pp. 496–528). London: Cambridge University Press.

Johnson, B. T., & Turco, R. (1992). The value of goodness-of-fit indices in meta-analysis: A comment on Hall and Rosenthal. *Communication Monographs, 59,* 388–396.

Kim, M., & Hunter, J. E. (1993). Attitude-behavior relations: A meta-analysis of attitudinal relevance and topic. *Journal of Communication, 43,* 101–142.

Krippendorff, K. (1980). *Content analysis.* Beverly Hills, CA: Sage.

Krippendorff, K. (2004). Reliability in content analysis: Some common misconceptions and recommendations. *Human Communication Research, 30,* 411–433.

Law, K. S. (1995). The use of Fisher's Z in Schmidt-Hunter-type meta-analyses. *Journal of Educational and Behavioral Statistics, 20,* 287–306.

Lemeshow, A. R., Blum, R. E., Berlin, J. A., Stoto, M. A., & Colditz, G. A. (2005). Searching one or two databases was insufficient for meta-analysis of observational studies. *Journal of Clinical Epidemiology, 58,* 867–873.

Lipsey, M. W., & Wilson, D. B. (2001). *Practical meta-analysis.* Thousand Oaks, CA: Sage.

Mann, C. (1994). Can meta-analysis make policy? *Science, 266,* 960–962.

Marshall, S. J., Biddle, S. J. H., Gorely, T., Cameron, N., & Murdey, I. (2004). Relationships between media use, body fatness and physical activity in children and youth: A meta-analysis. *International Journal of Obesity, 28,* 1238–1246.

McGrath, R. E., & Meyer, G. J. (2006). When effect sizes disagree: The case of *r* and *d*. *Psychological Methods, 11,* 386–401.

McLeod, J. M., & Reeves, B. (1980). On the nature of mass media effects. In S. Withey & R. Abeles (Eds.), *Television and social behavior: Beyond violence and children* (pp. 17–54). Hillsdale, NJ: Lawrence Erlbaum Associates.

Miller, N., & Pollock, V. E. (1994). Meta-analysis and some science-compromising problems of social psychology. In W. R. Shadish & S. Fuller (Eds.), *The social psychology of science* (pp. 230–261). New York: Guilford.

Morley, D. D. (1988). Meta-analytic techniques: When generalizing to message populations is not possible. *Human Communication Research, 15,* 112–126.

Morris, S. B., & DeShon, R. P. (2002). Combining effect size estimates in meta-analysis with repeated measures and independent-groups designs. *Psychological Methods, 7,* 105–125.

National Institute of Mental Health. (1982). *Television and behavior: Ten years of scientific progress and implications for the eighties.* Washington, DC: U.S. Government Printing Office.

Noar, S. M. (2006). In pursuit of cumulative knowledge in health communication: The role of meta-analysis. *Health Communication, 20,* 169–175.

Noar, S. M., Carlyle, K., & Cole, C. (2006). Why communication is crucial: Meta-analysis of the relationship between safer sexual communication and condom use. *Journal of Health Communication, 11,* 365–390.

Olkin, I. (1990). History and goals. In K. W. Wachter & M. L. Straf (Eds.), *The future of meta-analysis* (pp. 3–10). New York: Russell Sage Foundation.

Overton, R. C. (1998). A comparison of fixed-effects and mixed (random-effects) models for meta-analysis tests of moderator variable effects. *Psychological Methods, 3,* 354–379.

Paik, H., & Comstock, G. (1994). The effects of television violence on antisocial behavior: A meta-analysis. *Communication Research, 21,* 516–546.

Preiss, R. W. Gayle, B. M., Burrell, N. A., Allen, M., & Bryant, J. (2006) *Mass media effects research: Advances through meta-analysis.* Hillsdale, NJ: Lawrence Erlbaum Associates.

Rains, S. A. (2005). Leveling the organizational playing field—virtually: A meta-analysis of experimental research assessing the impact of group support system use on member influence behaviors. *Communication Research, 32,* 193–234.

Raudenbush, S. W., Becker, B. J., & Kalaian, K. (1988). Modeling multivariate effect sizes. *Psychological Bulletin, 103,* 111–120.

Rosenthal, R. (1991). *Meta-analytic procedures for social research* (rev. ed.) Newbury Park, CA: Sage.

Rosenthal, R. (1994). Parametric measures of effect size. In H. Cooper & L. V. Hedges (Eds.), *The handbook of research synthesis* (pp. 231–244). New York: Russell Sage Foundation.

Rosenthal, R. (1995). Writing meta-analytic reviews. *Psychological Bulletin, 118,* 183–192.

Rosenthal, R., & DiMatteo, M. R. (2001). Meta-analysis: Recent developments in quantitative methods for literature reviews. *Annual Review of Psychology, 52,* 59–82.

Rosenthal, R., & Rubin, D. (1978). Interpersonal expectancy effects: The first 345 studies. *Behavioral and Brain Sciences, 3,* 377–415.

Rosenthal, R., & Rubin, D. (1986). Meta-analytic procedures for combining studies with multiple effect sizes. *Psychological Bulletin, 99,* 400–406.

Sánchez-Meca, J., & Marín-Martínez, F. (1997). Homogeneity tests in meta-analysis: A Monte-Carlo comparison of statistical power and Type I error. *Quality & Quantity, 31,* 385–399.

Sánchez-Meca, J., Marín-Martínez, F., & Chacón-Moscoso, S. (2003). Effect-size indices for dichotomized outcomes in meta-analysis. *Psychological Methods, 8,* 448–467.

Schmidt, F. L. (1992). What do data really mean? Research findings, meta-analysis, and cumulative knowledge in psychology. *American Psychologist, 47,* 1173–1181.

Schmidt, F. L., & Hunter, J. E. (1977). Development of a general solution to the problem of validity generalization. *Journal of Applied Psychology, 62,* 529–540.

Seignourel, P., & Albarracín, D. (2002). Calculating effect sizes for designs with between-subjects and within-subjects factors: Methods for partially reported statistics in meta-analysis. *Metodologia de las Ciencias del Comportamiento, 4,* 273–289.

Shadish, W. R. (1996). Meta-analysis and the exploration of causal mediating processes: A primer of examples, methods, and issues. *Psychological Methods, 1,* 47–65.

Shadish, W. R., Cook, T. D., & Campbell, D. T. (2002). *Experimental and quasi-experimental designs for generalized causal inference.* Boston: Houghton Mifflin.

Shanahan, J., & Morgan, M. (1999). *Television and its viewers.* Cambridge, UK: Cambridge University Press.

Sharpe, D. (1997). Of apples and oranges, file drawers and garbage: Why validity issues in meta-analysis will not go away. *Clinical Psychology Review, 17,* 881–901.

Sherry, J. L. (2001). The effect of violent video games on aggression: A meta-analysis. *Human Communication Research, 27,* 409–431.

Smith, M. L., & Glass, G. V. (1977). Meta-analysis of psychotherapy outcome studies. *American Psychologist, 32,* 752–760.

Smith, M. L., Glass, G. V., & Miller, T. I. (1980). *The benefits of psychotherapy.* Baltimore, MD: Johns Hopkins University Press.

Snyder, L. B., & Hamilton, M. A. (2002). A meta-analysis of U.S. health campaign effects on behavior: Emphasize enforcement, exposure, and new information, and beware the secular trend. In R. C. Hornik (Ed.), *Public health communications: Evidence for behavior change* (pp. 357–384). Mahwah, NJ: Lawrence Erlbaum Associates.

Snyder, L. B., Hamilton, M. A., Mitchell, E. W., Kiwanuka-Tondo, J., Fleming-Milici, F., & Proctor, D. (2004). A meta-analysis of the effect of mediated health communication campaigns on behavior change in the United States. *Journal of Health Communication, 9,* 71–96.

Sternberg, R. J. (1991). Editorial. *Psychological Bulletin, 109,* 3–4.

Stigler, S. M. (1986). *History of statistics: The measurement of uncertainty before 1900.* Cambridge, MA: Harvard University Press.

Surgeon General's Scientific Advisory Committee on Television and Social Behavior. (1972). *Television and growing up: The impact of televised violence.* Report to the Surgeon General, United States Public Health Service. Washington, DC: U.S. Government Printing Office.

Thornton, A., & Lee, P. (2000). Publication bias in meta-analysis: Its causes and consequences. *Journal of Clinical Epidemiology, 53,* 207–216.

Twenge, J. M. (2000). The age of anxiety? The birth cohort change in anxiety and neuroticism, 1952–1993. *Journal of Personality and Social Psychology, 79,* 1007–1021.

Van Den Noortgata, W., & Onghena, P. (2003). Estimating the mean effect size in meta-analysis: Bias, precision, and mean squared error of different weighting methods. *Behavior Research Methods, Instruments, & Computers, 35,* 504–511.

Vevea, J. L., & Hedges, L. V. (1995). A general linear model for estimating effect size in the presence of publication bias. *Psychometrika, 60,* 419–435.

Wang, M. C., & Bushman, B. J. (1999). *Integrating results through meta-analytic review using SAS® software.* Cary, NC: SAS Institute Inc.

White, H. D. (1994). Scientific communication and literature retrieval. In H. Cooper & L. V. Hedges (Eds.), *The handbook of research synthesis* (pp. 41–55). New York: Russell Sage Foundation.

Wilkinson, B. (1951). A statistical consideration in psychological research. *Psychological Bulletin, 48,* 156–158.

Wilson, E. J., & Sherrell, D. L. (1993). Source effects in communication and persuasion research: A meta-analysis of effect size. *Journal of the Academy of Marketing Science, 21*(2), 101–112.

Witte, K., & Allen, M. (2000). A meta-analysis of fear appeals: Implications for effective public health campaigns. *Health Education & Behavior, 27,* 591–615.

Wu, M. J. (2006, April). *Applications of generalized least squares and factored likelihood in synthesizing regression studies.* Paper presented at the annual meeting of the American Educational Research Association, San Francisco, CA.

Young, C., & Horton, R. (2005). Putting clinical trials into context. *The Lancet, 366,* 107–108.

Approaches to the Handling of Missing Data in Communication Research

12

Ofer Harel

Rick Zimmerman

Olga Dekhtyar

Communication researchers devote considerable thought, time, and energy to designing studies with applied or theoretical value to the discipline and the world at large. Careful consideration of how best to do such things as recruit participants, operationalize constructs, and (for experiments) manipulate focal independent variables facilitates our ability to empirically explore and understand the complexities of communication processes. However, try as hard as we do, there are many things that are not entirely under our control that can have dramatic effects on the quality of the data and the inferences that can be drawn from them. One of them is the ubiquitous problem of missing data. In spite of assurances of confidentiality and anonymity, not everyone is interested in answering or willing and able to answer every question we pose to them in surveys, and ethical rules tell us we cannot force people to answer questions they don't want to answer. Such rules also allow participants to drop out of studies at any time they desire, meaning that any variables collected after the time of withdrawal will be missing for some people. In longitudinal studies, data are often incomplete because people move, change their minds about participating, or even die in the middle of the data collection. As a result, variables may be measured incompletely for some of the participants who participated during the first wave of data collection but were unavailable later.

This chapter is about missing data in communication research—how it happens, what its effects are, and what can be done about it. This is a topic that, while tremendously important, is also something that we guess most communication researchers know little about. At the same time, it is also a tremendously difficult topic to cover thoroughly in a single chapter. Our intention here is not to be comprehensive but instead to give communication researchers a broad overview of some of the issues they need to think about when they encounter missing data. The books and papers we cite are good sources to turn to for further detail on those topics that we, by necessity, can only gloss over. We start by first examining what communication researchers typically do when they encounter missing data and use our findings as a springboard for making the case that we should all care about missing data and that the choice of how to manage the problem is not inconsequential.

Missing Data Reporting and Current Practice in Communication

Just how do communication researchers deal with missing data when they encounter it? Probably the best way of answering that question is to take a look at what they actually say they do in the places where they would be most likely to talk about it—in their published research. So we conducted a quick review of empirical articles published in 2005 and 2006 in five popular communication journals with a quantitative research focus: *Communication Monographs, Health Communication, Human Communication Research, Journal of Broadcasting and Electronic Media,* and *Media Psychology*. We scanned the articles looking for any discussion of missing data, how frequently it occurred, and what was done about it. Results for the analysis of 196 quantitative articles are presented in Table 12.1. As can be seen, only 22% of the articles mentioned *anything at all* about missing data, including the extent of missing data or how the missing data were handled. When anything about the handling of missing data was mentioned, the method most often used (75% of articles) was case deletion (also referred to as listwise deletion). With this approach, when a case in the database was missing data on any of the variables in the analysis, the case was deleted for the analysis. Indeed, we speculate that this is probably the method used most often as well when there was no mention about missing data in the article, but there is no way to know for sure when nothing whatsoever about missing data is discussed in the paper. The procedures used next most often (in 9% of the articles each) were *full information maximum likelihood* and *multiple imputation*. These methods will be briefly described later in the chapter. Other methods used were *mean imputation* (4% of the articles), where the average value for all of the individuals in the sample with a known value is used to estimate the values of those individuals with missing data on that variable, and *pairwise deletion* (2% of the articles), where for a given bivariate analysis, only those individuals were deleted that were missing one or both of those variables, meaning different analyses could be based on different subsets of the data.

Are communication researchers using the best methods for handling missing data? Based on the results of our review, it appears not. It seems that researchers, when they even report how they handled missing data, primarily relied on listwise deletion—a method that is known to be one of the worst available with respect to two important properties of statistical methods: statistical power and estimation bias. Depending on the missing data assumptions (a topic to be discussed in greater detail in the next section), if an entire case is deleted from the data set when even only one of the multiple variables in the analysis is missing, the sample size is reduced by 1 and statistical power at detecting effects has been slightly reduced. Depending on the topic of the investigation, the research design and the reasons for missing data (e.g., respondent carelessness, respondent desire to provide data in as little time as possible, respondent desire not to report some sensitive information, participant attrition), levels of missing data

Table 12.1 Treatment of Missing Data in Communication Journals, 2005–2006

Journal	Total Number of Articles	Number of Quantitative Articles	Number of Quantitative Articles Mentioning Missing Data	Percent of Quantitative Articles Mentioning Missing Data
Communication Monographs	45	40	5	13%
Health Communication	77	63	18	29%
Human Communication Research	42	36	10	28%
Journal of Broadcast and Electronic Media	44	39	9	23%
Media Psychology	19	18	2	11%
TOTALS	227	196	44	22%

may reach higher than 20%. In such cases, loss of statistical power as a result of listwise deletion can be considerable.

Poor estimation accuracy may result from deletion of cases that are not representative of the entire sample. As will be described in the next section, the impact of methods for handling missing data on statistical bias depends on the missingness—the extent to which individuals who are missing data differ from those individuals who are not missing data. Before reading that extended discussion, suffice it to say here that listwise deletion generally yields greater estimation bias than some of the other methods based more heavily on statistical theory, such as the EM algorithm (Dempster, Laird, & Rubin, 1977) or multiple imputation (Rubin, 1987) procedures.

So communication researchers should care about missing data because, depending on how missing data are handled, there may be significant loss of statistical power in detecting effects or there may be statistical bias in the analysis. Such problems are potentially greater the more missing data there are. When information is sensitive (and respondents may not want to report some information), when the study is longitudinal (and participant attrition occurs), or when respondents have difficulty in providing answers (e.g., when questions are ambiguous or language or reading barriers may be involved), data are more likely to be missing, and the proper handling of missing data becomes even more critical.

In the second and third sections of this chapter, we explain statistical issues related to missing data, such as missingness assumptions and the various methods of handling missing data. We then present a few concrete, empirical examples illustrating the impact of choices about handling missing data on results. The two examples come from two of our research group's studies. The first example involves a sample of rural ninth-grade students followed until the end of tenth grade to assess the impact of school- and computer-based interventions on initiation of sexual activity (Roberto et al., 2007; Zimmerman et al., in press). The second example is taken from a data set including adolescent female residents of inner-city housing developments involved in a study to assess the impact of an intervention to reduce sexual risk taking (Feist-Price, Cupp, Zimmerman, Abell, & Dekhtyar, 2007). In the fourth and concluding section of the chapter, we present recommendations for avoiding and handling missing data in communication research.

Statistical Issues: Missing Data Assumptions and Methods

Most estimation procedures were not designed with missing data in mind. Statistical software and methods assume in most cases complete *rectangular* data, where each case in the data file (such as a person in the study) is represented in a single row and each variable measured is located in columns. With complete data, one has a rectangular data set completely filled with data points. If data are missing, not every cell in the rectangular matrix contains data.

Methods to deal with missing data can be either *unprincipled* or *principled*. Unprincipled methods, in most cases, edit the data matrix in some fashion in order to produce a matrix of data that is complete. We call these methods unprincipled because typically there is no statistical theory supporting them, and they frequently do more harm than good. Unprincipled methods, such as case deletion (Little & Rubin, 2002) and single imputation (Little & Rubin, 2002) tend to yield statistics that are inaccurate or have a large sampling variance (i.e., are relatively *inefficient*). Principled methods, by contrast, have been developed based on some statistical theory that allows incomplete data. The principled methods are based, in most cases, on estimators that are relatively efficient and unbiased. Some examples of these methods are maximum likelihood (ML) (Little & Rubin, 2002), multiple imputation (MI) (Little & Rubin, 2002), and generalized estimating equations (GEE) (Little & Rubin, 2002). The shortcoming of principled methods is that in most cases they are computationally messy, difficult to understand, and not widely implemented in popular and commonly used statistical packages.

One of our goals as researchers is to make correct inferences about some population parameters. Given cost and other resource considerations, we usually collect data from a sample of a population and use information from the sample to make inferences about the population from which the sample was derived. With incomplete data, we are still interested in making valid inferences about population parameter, but we are forced to do it from an incomplete data set. The missing data in and of itself is not of interest, and we are not particularly concerned about correctly estimating, predicting, or recovering the missing values. We do not care about their values as long as we can reach the correct inference about the population from the data we do have. In that sense, approaches to handling missing data fundamentally focus on this very practical concern—making inferences and conclusions from our data that are accurate.

When dealing with incomplete data sets, it is beneficial if the researcher has some insight or understanding about the reasons some data are missing. Using this information will help the researcher pose some reasonable assumptions to help deal with the missing values. These assumptions will, in most cases, not be testable, but it is better to know what assumptions are being made and make them explicit. One recommended way to deal with this issue is the use of a *sensitivity analysis*. Using a sensitivity analysis, one would run the model using several different assumptions about the missing data or use different approaches to dealing with them and see what effects this has on the results and conclusions drawn from the analysis. If the results are similar, it means that there is limited importance to the assumptions. But if there are large differences in results depending on the assumptions made or approach to handling missing data, it means that the assumptions or approaches affect the final model, and therefore the interpretation of results needs to be done with great caution and a healthy dose of skepticism.

MISSING DATA ASSUMPTIONS

Missing data can occur in many different ways and for many different reasons. Often we do not know why some data are missing, so we must make some assumptions about this process producing the data we have. These assumptions may or may not be testable. Define **R** as a random vector or matrix containing n rows, where n is the sample size, and v columns, where v is the number of variables. For each cell in the vector of matrix, r_{ij}, set r_{ij} to 1 if the data point is observed, or $r_{ij} = 0$ if the data point is missing. **R** is a random matrix because a different sample of a given size will produce a different **R** matrix, depending on the process producing the missing data. Call **R** *missingness*. Using **R**, one can separate the data into two parts, observed and missing. The data matrix with "1"s in the corresponding elements in **R** is the observed data, and the data matrix with "0"s in the corresponding elements of **R** is the missing data.

Rubin (1976) introduced the missingness concept and explored the different assumptions it contains. Rubin (1976) stressed the importance of the missingness distribution, not in order to claim that it needs to be modeled, but rather in order to specifically define when it can be ignored. In general, when dealing with incomplete data, one needs to model the joint distribution of the data (Y) and missingness (**R**); some assumptions might relax this modeling need. The three most common assumptions are missing completely at random (MCAR), missing at random (MAR), and missing not at random (MNAR). Under MCAR and MAR, one need not model the distribution of the missingness but only the data. That is, one can ignore the missingness. When neither of these assumptions holds (i.e., the data are MNAR), one needs to model the joint distribution of the data and missingness. We now turn to some of these assumptions.

Missing completely at random. Missing completely at random (MCAR) occurs when the outcomes are independent of R, meaning that missingness is uncorrelated with variables to be used in the analysis. The process that causes the missing data (i.e., the set of reasons for missing data) is independent of any variables in the data. Missing by design is a case in which some records are being measured with some known probability (p), and is not measured with probability ($1 - p$). Consider a long survey in which the researcher knows that if all the questions are sent on one survey, there will be a high level of nonresponse. So instead of sending all questions to all potential respondents, different parts of the survey are sent to different respondents, with the part any given participant is sent being determined randomly. In such a situation, the researcher has caused missingness "by design," but we know this is MCAR, as people have been randomly chosen to have missing values on certain variables. Of course, it is possible for data to be missing and completely at random not by design. However, in practice, missing data often do not occur completely at random. Instead, some data are missing for systematic reasons, but the process producing the missingness may not produce problems with estimation and inference. But it may.

Missing at random. Missing at random (MAR) is one of the most common assumptions in applied statistics and the analysis of incomplete data sets. MAR occurs when there is dependence between the data and missingness, but the missingness depends on the observed part of the data but not on the unobserved data. That is, missingness can be related to other variables in the data set, but people are no more or less likely to have a missing value on a given variable depending on their true value on the variable. For example, in order for a self-report of substance use to be missing at random, people can't be more likely to leave the question about substance use blank depending on what the true response would be to the question. Missing outcomes that depend on fully observed covariates would be considered MAR, although some call this covariate dependent missingness, a form of MAR. For example, consider that we are interested in estimating the coefficients from a regression model predicting outcome Y from predictor variable X. If X is all observed and Y is partly missing, it would be necessary for us to understand or at least be willing to make some kind of assumption about the reason why the values are missing before we can interpret the analysis. If the probability of being missing on Y is unrelated to what the measurement would have been had it not been missing, even if that probability is related to X, then the data are MAR on Y. But if some values of Y are missing depending on what Y would have been had it not been missing, it would be considered missing *not* at random, discussed next.

Missing not at random. Missing not at random (MNAR) is an assumption similar to MAR, except that the dependence includes both the observed and unobserved components of the data. In the example just provided, if people who drink more than average tend to refuse to answer questions about how much they drink, then the data are missing not at random. It may or may not be the case that whether a person is missing on a question about alcohol use depends on other variables in the analysis. There is no statistical methodology to test between MAR and MNAR, and the decision between them should come according to scientific reasons or established using sensitivity analysis. One can run analyses based on both assumptions and see if there are differences; if there are differences, it follows that the assumption is important and more scientific reasoning should be put into the decision between the assumptions.

UNPRINCIPLED METHODS

Unprincipled methods are the ones most commonly used in communication. These methods are easy to implement and are available in many statistical packages that communication researchers use. Unfortunately, their use often produces results that are difficult to interpret.

Case deletion. Case deletion is the most widely used missing data procedure. Using complete case analysis, one either omits incomplete cases from the analysis entirely and treats the rest of the data as if they represent the actual sample or it omits cases only for specific analysis, depending on whether the case is missing data on one or more of the variables in the analysis.

Case deletion is the simplest method to implement because in most cases, it is the statistical package's default. Case deletion is practical when the existence of missing data does not affect the results (this can be checked using sensitivity analysis). On the other hand, case deletion may produce estimation bias and is nearly always less efficient (i.e., produces statistics with greater sampling variance) as it frequently discards a large amount of data. For example, consider a large study with multiple variables. Table 12.2 presents the amount of data left according to the number of variables in the data set and how much missing data there is for each variable (assumed to be randomly missing). Notice, for instance, that if each variable is missing for 10% of the cases and we have 10 variables in the analysis, using listwise deletion we can expect to be able to have only about 35% of the sample in the analysis (because roughly 65% will be missing on *at least one* variable). This assumes independence between variables with respect to missingness. If those respondents missing one variable are also more likely to be missing on others, the amount of missing data will of course be less than what is suggested here. Regardless, clearly one can lose a lot of data when using case deletion. There are many studies with 20 variables and more, and even with 5% missing values (on each variable), we can reduce our sample size by more than 60% using this method.

Reweighting. Reweighting (Little & Rubin, 2002) is the natural extension of case deletion. Using this method, after discarding the incomplete cases one reweights the remaining cases such that they resemble the full sample or population. There are several different ways to design the weighting scheme, some more complex than others. One can group the cases into classes in which the response probability is relatively homogeneous. One can decide on weighting the groups or the cases themselves. Another method is the use of a propensity score (Do & Kincaid, 2006; Rosenbaum & Rubin 1983). Each participant is assigned this score according to some model, and the weight for each participant is the inverse of this score.

The use of weighting is very common in the survey research (Bethelehem, 2002; Gelman & Carlin, 2002). It can correct for some of the biases in

Table 12.2 Percent of Data Remaining, Based on Percent of Missing Data and Number of Variables

Number of Variables	Percent Missing Data				
	1	5	10	15	25
1	99%	95%	90%	85%	75%
2	98%	90%	81%	72%	56%
5	95%	77%	59%	44%	24%
10	90%	60%	35%	20%	0.6%
20	82%	36%	12%	04%	0.3%

estimation but can also be inefficient. This method can correct for biases due to nonresponse related to the independent variables (the variables being used in the propensity scores or classification), but it does not correct for biases due to missing values related to the dependent variable(s). Using this method requires a model of the missingness.

Single imputation. Single imputation is the next most commonly used missing data procedure after case deletion. Using simple imputation, the analyst replaces the missing values with plausible values. The main advantage of single imputation is that the data matrix is restored to its original size and rectangular shape. There are numerous ways to impute the missing values and produce these plausible values (see Little & Rubin, 2002, for detailed descriptions of what follows). *Within-participant mean imputation* replaces each missing value with a case's mean. That is, the mean of a case's values on all variables for which observed data are available is substituted for the value of the missing variable. With *between-participant mean imputation,* missing values are replaced with its occasion (column) mean. That is, the mean across all cases who have observed data for this variable is used as a substitute for cases missing on that variable. *Last observation carried forward* is mostly used in longitudinal studies prone to dropout. Here all values after the time of participant dropout are replaced with the case's last observed value. Using *regression imputation,* missing values are estimated using other variables that are available using a regression model. With this method, a set of correlated variables is used to estimate the value of a missing variable based on multiple regression coefficients derived from cases not missing on the variable. Finally, *hot-deck imputation* fills in missing values on incomplete records using values from complete records for similar people in the same data set.

The problem with using single imputation methods is that it ignores the fact that there were missing values in the first place. This can seriously distort the uncertainty measures (variance, covariance, and correlations) that are often important in an analysis and can affect the estimates and quality of the inferences drawn.

PRINCIPLED METHODS

Principled methods rely on some form of statistical theory and are implemented in several readily available statistical packages. Using these methods will (in most cases) produce results that are likely to be more accurate than results produced using unprincipled methods. These methods will work under MAR or MCAR assumptions, but there are some methodological situations for MNAR scenarios as well.

Likelihood methods. The likelihood of a set of data is the probability of obtaining that particular set of data given the chosen probability distribution model. This likelihood expression contains the unknown model parameters that are of interest for the researcher. The values of these parameters that maximize the sample likelihood are known as the *maximum likelihood estimators* (MLEs).

Maximum likelihood estimation is an analytic maximization procedure (Dempster, et al. 1977). It applies to every form of complete, incomplete, or censored data. MLEs and likelihood functions generally have three very desirable, large-sample properties: (1) They become unbiased minimum variance estimators as the sample size increases, (2) they have approximate normal distributions and approximate sample variances that can be calculated and used to generate confidence intervals, and (3) likelihood functions can be used to test hypotheses about models and parameters. On the other hand, the drawbacks of MLEs are (a) with a small sample, MLEs may not be very precise and (b) calculating MLEs often requires specialized software for solving complex nonlinear equations. The latter becomes less of a drawback with each passing year, as more and more statistical packages are offering MLE capabilities.

Bayesian methods. Bayesian methods work in a similar way to the ML methods. In addition to the likelihood function, Bayesian methods use a priori information that, together with the likelihood, can be used to construct the posterior distribution of a variable. If one has additional information about the data, these methods can be very powerful as well (Gilks, Richardson, & Spiegelhalter, 1998).

Semiparametric methods. Semiparametric regression models are methods that assume linear or nonlinear regression models but relax assumptions about the distribution of the response; that is, they allow ordinal or dichotomous distributions of the dependent variable, as well as continuous distributions. The missing-data semiparametric procedures are an extension of generalized estimating equations (GEE) (Zeger et al., 1988). Robins et al. (1994) suggested weights in addition to the GEE to allow incomplete covariates. See Robins and Rotnitzky (1995) and Rotnitzky, Robins, and Scharfstein (1998) for more detail.

Multiple imputation. Multiple imputation (MI) (Rubin, 1987) is a simulation-based approach to dealing with missing values. MI is a general method that incorporates uncertainty into the imputation process. From an inferential point of view, one of the main reasons to use MI is because data collection information, both observed and unobserved, can be incorporated into the imputation using Bayesian methodology. There is an extensive literature on multiple imputation, including such influential books as Rubin (1987), Schafer (1997a), Little and Rubin (2002), and Allison (2002). In addition, there are many manuscripts on specific issues and examples using MI (see, for example, http://www.multiple-imputation.com). Reviews have been published by Rubin (1996), Schafer (1999a), Horton and Lipsitz (2001), and Harel and Zhou (2007).

Multiple imputation is composed of three stages: (1) the imputation stage, in which the missing data are imputed multiple ($m > 2$) times, (2) the analysis stage, in which each complete data set is analyzed using a complete-data technique, and (3) the final stage, in which the results from the analysis are combined in order to yield a final result that combines the uncertainty in the data and the uncertainty due to missing values.

In the imputation stage, a joint model for the complete data and the missingness indicator needs to be found. In most cases, the *ignorablility* assumption (meaning missing at random or missing completely at random) means no model of missingness is required and plausible values for the missing data can be generated using the observed data. This procedure is generally conducted using a Bayesian methodology called Markov Chain Monte Carlo (MCMC) (Gilks et al., 1998). This is the most complex stage of MI and requires knowledge of the data and statistical methodology. Although there are several statistical software packages that perform these imputations, we recommend consulting with an expert about the subject first. The imputation model and analysis model do not have to be the same. This is one of the advantages of MI, but it can cause difficulties as well (Collins, Schafer, & Kam, 2001; Meng, 1994). If the models for the imputation and the analysis differ, it is recommended that the imputation model have more variables such that it will be more general.

After the imputations, we now have m sets of complete data. Each data set is different from the others in the locations in which there were missing values. Each complete, imputed data set is then analyzed using complete-data methodology (regression, ANOVA, etc.) saving the estimates and their variances. For example, if we choose to run a regression with an intercept and a slope and impute $m = 10$ times, we would get 10 estimates for the slopes (and their variances) and 10 estimates for the intercept (and their variances) in any statistical software. These estimates are then combined using some simple rules (Rubin, 1987). The rules are programmed into several statistical software packages, but because of their simplicity, it is very easy to calculate the new estimates even by hand. Suppose that $\hat{Q}_j$ is an estimate of interest (e.g., a regression coefficient) obtained from data set j ($j = 1, 2, \ldots, m$) and U_j is its variance. The overall estimate is the average of the individual estimates:

$$\bar{Q} = \frac{1}{m} \sum_{j=1}^{m} \hat{Q}_j$$

For the overall standard error, one calculates the average within-imputation variance:

$$\bar{U} = \frac{1}{m} \sum_{j=1}^{m} U_j$$

and the between-imputation variance

$$B = \frac{1}{m-1} \sum_{j=1}^{m} \left(\hat{Q}_j - \bar{Q} \right)^2$$

The total variance of the estimator is

$$T = \bar{U} + \left(1 + \frac{1}{m}\right) B,$$

meaning the standard error is the square root of T. Confidence intervals are obtained by taking the overall estimate plus or minus a number of standard errors, where that number is a quantile of the student's t distribution with degrees of freedom:

$$df = (m-1)\left(1 + \frac{m\bar{U}}{(m+1)B}\right)^2$$

In most cases, it is enough to use a limited number of imputations (Harel & Zhou, 2007; Rubin, 1987; Schafer, 1997), but in cases where there is a large amount of missing information, more imputations will be needed. With today's high-powered desktop and laptop computers, this does not cause much difficulty.

Empirical Examples of the Effect of Method on Inference

In order to emphasize the risk of single imputation, we first present a very simple example. The data are simulated based on actual results for data we have collected from 5,500 ninth-grade students in rural high schools followed up with three waves of data collected through the end of tenth grade (Roberto et al., 2007; Zimmerman et al., 2007). For this analysis, we selected the approximately 3,800 students who had not yet had sex and assessed the relationship between intentions to have sex in the next 4 months (Y_1), where a high value indicates greater intentions to have sex, and attitudes about waiting to have sex (Y_2), where a higher value indicates a more negative attitude toward waiting to have sex. In order to assess the impact of different kinds of data imputation on our results, we designed a simulation based on cases for whom we had complete data, so we would know the "true" values that were being estimated. We simulated data for the two variables for 100 participants with two normal variables representing the variables mentioned above. The two normal variables had mean 2 and variance 1 (very close to the true values in the data), and the correlation between the variables was 0.6 (also the true value in the data). A plot of the complete data is shown in Figure 12.1. We deliberately caused 30% of the data to be missing at random (MAR) in Y_2. Our interest for the sake of

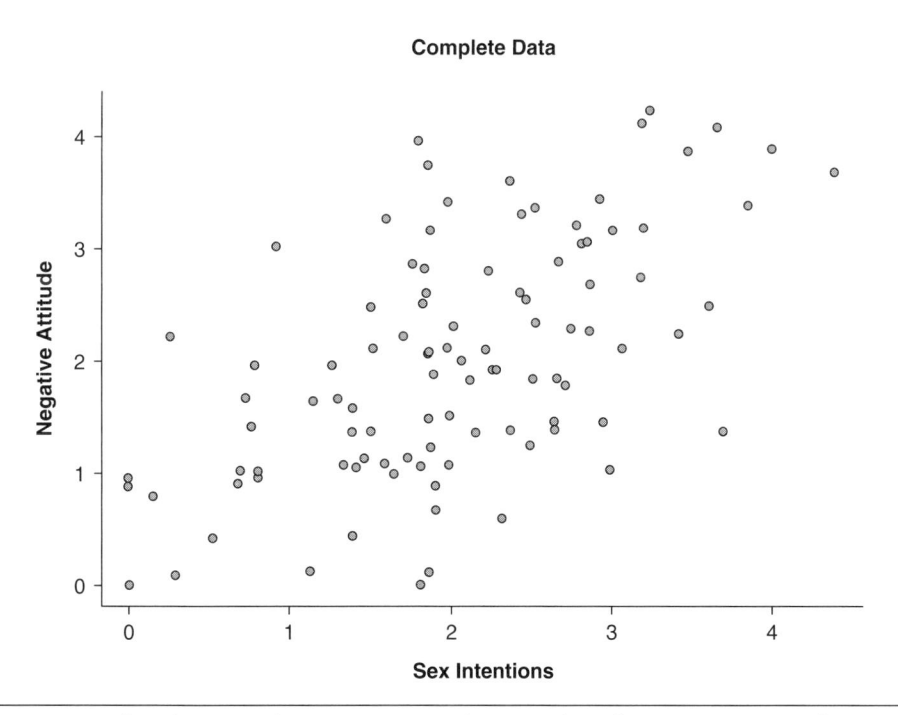

Figure 12.1 Plots for Complete Data Set and Imputed Within-Participant and Between-Participant Means *(Continued)*

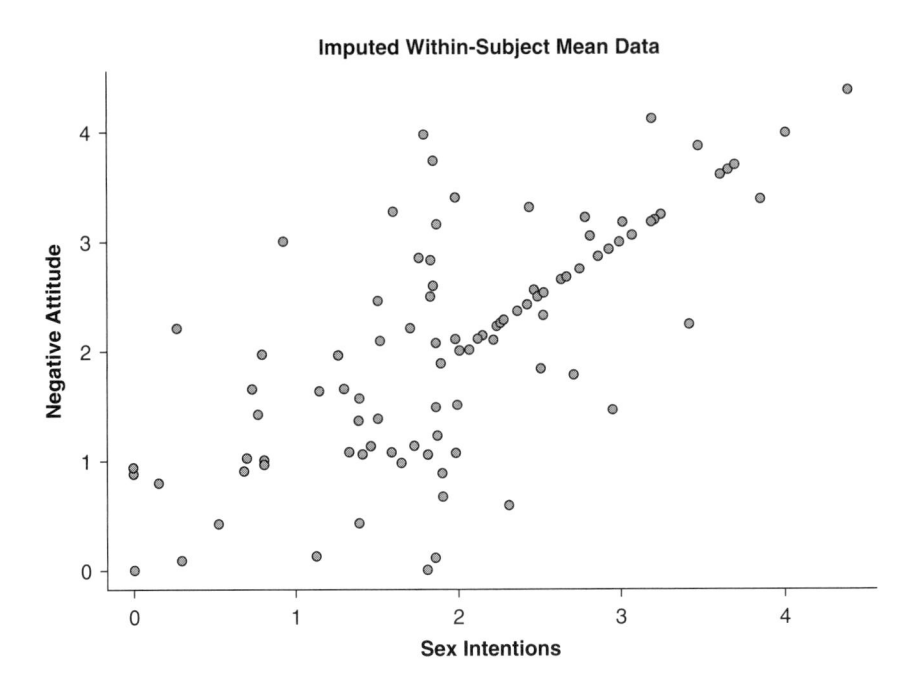

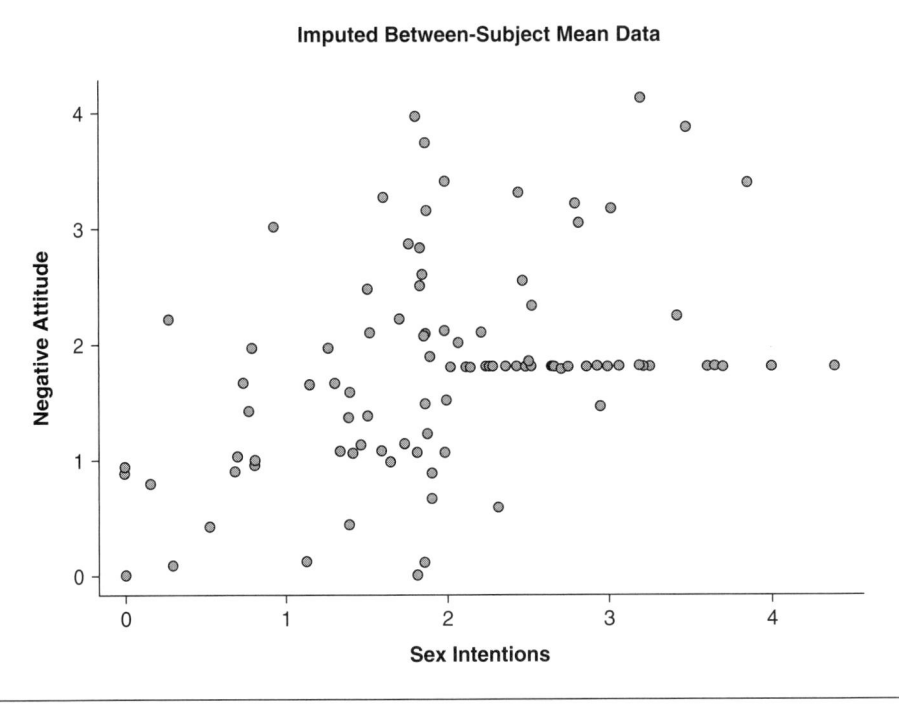

Figure 12.1 (Continued)   Plots for Complete Data Set and Imputed Within-Participant and Between-Participant Means

Table 12.3 Results From Simulated Data and Various Imputation Procedures

VALUE	Simulated Data (with no missing data)	Single Imputation — Between-Participant Mean	Single Imputation — Within-Participant Mean	Multiple Imputation
Y_2	2.01	1.804	2.114	2.057
$SD(Y_2)$	0.969	0.872	1.043	1.099
$Corr(Y_1, Y_2)$	0.571	0.413	0.709	0.598
b_1	0.520	0.445	0.636	0.509
b_2	0.648	0.385	0.790	0.702

this example is accurately estimating the mean and variance of Y_2 and the regression coefficients in a model of Y_1 from Y_2 as well as from Y_2 on Y_1.

In Table 12.3, we summarize the results from the simulations. The estimates of interest are represented in the rows such that we follow the mean of Y_2, its standard deviation, the correlation between Y_1 and Y_2, the regression coefficient in a model of the form $Y_1 = a_1 + b_1 Y_2$ (i.e., we present b_1), and the regression coefficient in a model of the form $Y_2 = a_2 + b_2 Y_1$. The columns represent the four different analyses: (1) the complete simulated data (considered as "the truth"), (2) single imputation using the between-participant mean (i.e., the mean for all cases with a valid value on this variable), (3) single imputation using the within-participant mean (i.e., the mean for each case on other variables with valid values for that participant), and (4) multiple imputation with 10 imputations.

The most compelling differences we can see are in the correlations and the regression coefficients. The single imputation either underestimates the correlation (between-participant or "occasion" mean) or overestimates it (within-participant mean). The reasons become very clear when looking at Figure 12.1. We can see the horizontal imputed values in the imputed occasion plot, which shows a decrease in the correlation; we can also see a nearly straight line at a 45-degree angle on the imputed subject plot, which shows an increased slope or correlation. Similar to the correlations we can see the risks of using single imputation in regression settings as well. On the other hand, the MI results are quite close to the original simulated data. The variances using MI will in most cases be larger in order to take into consideration the fact that we do not actually know the missing values.

Our second example is taken from a data set involving 547 female adolescents in five inner-city housing developments that were randomized to receive either an experimental intervention involving 6 hours of a skills-based, interactive psychosocial small-group intervention and peer-led community-wide activities related to HIV prevention (3 housing developments with $n = 303$ total in our study) or a brief HIV knowledge session combined with community-wide activities focused on career development (comparison intervention delivered in 2 housing developments with $n = 244$ in total; Feist-Price et al., 2007). All participants were interviewed using ACASI (audio computer-assisted self-interviewing on laptop computers) at three time points: (1) before the intervention was delivered, (2) 6 months later after the psychosocial or knowledge components of the intervention were delivered, and (3) 6 months later still after the entire intervention had been delivered. Here we assess the impact of the experimental versus comparison intervention on three variables: (1) attitudes about waiting to have sex, (2) refusal self-efficacy—participants' perceived ability to successfully refuse being pressured to have sex, and (3) "condom self-efficacy"—their perceived ability to successfully negotiate for condom use. Impact of the experimental as compared to the comparison intervention is assessed here from Time 1 to Time 2, 6 months later, controlling for participants' grades in school and perceived neighborhood belonging. The analysis was first conducted based on complete cases only, with significant proportions of missing data due to a variety of reasons, including some procedural difficulties with the ACASI hardware and attrition. Then the same analyses were performed using EM and MI procedures. The results of all three methods are discussed below.

The first step in doing an analysis with missing data involves deciding whether the missingness is completely at random (MCAR), missing at random (MAR), or not missing at random (MNAR). As described earlier in this chapter, the data are missing completely at random (MCAR) if the missingness does not depend on any values in the data set. The data are instead missing at random (MAR) if the missing response may depend on the independent variables but not on the dependent variables. "Not missing at random" means that missingness depends on the dependent variable as well. The MCAR condition can be checked empirically. However, the last two conditions (missing at random vs. not missing at random) are very difficult to check without knowing the distribution of missingness. If the data can be assumed to be MCAR, then listwise deletion of cases can be used with the valid estimates. However, when the data are not MCAR, the estimates and standard errors of the estimates based on the completed cases will be biased and so an imputation procedure should be used.

To check whether our data are MCAR, the MVA (missing value analysis) procedure in SPSS 15 was used. Within the "EM Estimation" option, a table of EM means is produced along with Little's MCAR test. The results among these three variables, when other variables in the data set are included, are significant for the chi-square assessing Little's MCAR test, meaning that the data for these variables are not missing completely at random. Thus, an analysis using methods based on listwise deletion of cases will be inaccurate. To deal with MAR assumptions instead, methods like maximum likelihood estimation, Bayesian estimation, or multiple imputation should be used. For our analysis, we performed two procedures: the EM estimation based on maximum likelihood estimation using SPSS and multiple imputation using NORM software.

The EM estimation was performed again using the missing values analysis procedures, and the option was chosen to "save completed data" with the name of the new data set being input, creating a new data set with EM estimates for all missing values. The desired analysis (repeated measures) was then conducted using this new data set to arrive at results using EM-imputed data.

Next, the steps needed to perform multiple imputation using the NORM software (Schafer, 1999b) are outlined. The first step involved saving SPSS data in ASCII format and assigning a missing value code to all variables that are missing. After opening the data set, the program allows variable transformations and a method of rounding the imputed values. For our analysis, none of the variables needed to be transformed, and the imputed variables were rounded up to the nearest observed variables for the ordinal variables and to the nearest hundredth for the composite variables. The EM algorithm menu in the NORM main window provided the starting values for the imputation. The maximum likelihood estimates of the starting values are computed using the EM algorithm. Using these starting values, the imputed data sets are generated. The program allows one to chose how many data sets need to be imputed by specifying the total number of the iterations in the Computing option (in our analysis, we chose 1,000), and to ensure the independence of the imputed data sets, every new data set is imputed after a certain number of iterations by selecting the Imputation option (after 1,000 iterations, in our case). The program imputed 10 data sets, with a total of 1,000 iterations, with an imputed data set generated after every 100 iterations. The imputed data sets were saved in the format that can be transformed back into SPSS and analyzed as separate data sets. The 10 imputed data sets from the NORM program were read back into SPSS, and each of them was analyzed using the repeated measures procedure saving the estimates for each imputed data set in a file. At the end of these analyses, 10 estimates and 10 standard errors were computed.

The next step was to calculate pooled estimates from the imputed data sets. NORM has an option of combining the estimates together to produce the average parameter estimates. In our case, one parameter and its standard error were estimated across the 10 data sets. The tables produced by NORM contain the average parameter estimate, the standard error, t-ratio, degrees of freedom, p-value, and the 95% confidence interval around the estimate.

Table 12.4 shows the results of the repeated measures analysis (contrast value for the difference on the three variables between the two groups over time) using the original data set with missing data, the imputed data set using the EM maximum likelihood procedure, and the imputed data set

Table 12.4 Repeated Measures Results for Original Data Set and EM and MI Imputations

Variable	% Missing Data	Original Data Set			EM Imputed Data			MI Data Sets		
		Contrast Value	Standard Error	p-value	Contrast Value	Standard Error	p-value	Contrast Value	Standard Error	p-value
Attitude about waiting for sex	33%	.062	.136	.647	.124	.107	.248	0.106	0.122	0.386
Refusal self-efficacy	56%	.207	.103	.046	.220	.080	.006	0.240	0.092	0.011
Condom self-efficacy	33%	.234	.118	.049	.184	.062	.003	0.234	0.084	0.007

using multiple imputation. For attitude about waiting to have sex, none of the three methods resulted in a significant result, with p-values ranging from .248 to .647. For refusal self-efficacy, which had more than half of the data missing over time, use of the original data set resulted in a just-significant result (p-value = .046), while the EM-imputed data resulted in a p-value for the difference in effect of group over time of .006, with a p-value for the contrast using the MI data set of .011, both much more significant results than with the original data set. Similarly, for condom self-efficacy, using the original data set, the results were just-significant (p = .049), but using EM-imputed and MI-imputed data sets, results were quite significant (p = .003 and .007).

Recommendations

In this final section, we outline some recommendations to communication researchers about how to minimize missing data and, when missing data occur, how to best handle them empirically.

KEEP MISSING DATA TO A MINIMUM

The best way to handle missing data is to design the research so that there will be no missing data, or at least so that missing data are kept to an absolute minimum. While we cannot provide here a complete discussion of methods for reducing missing data, we briefly summarize suggestions for reducing missing data within a survey study or experiment and for reducing attrition in a longitudinal study.

There are two basic strategies for reducing the amount of missing data on surveys: (1) improving the survey instrument by reducing ambiguity in questions or shortening the survey (Dillman, Eltinge, Groves, & Little, 2002; Fowler, 1995) and (2) using computerized self-administered interviews or surveys (CASI) procedures, which make leaving responses blank a bit more difficult (Trapl et al., 2005; Turner et al., 1998). When respondents are clear about what the question means or when surveys are shorter, respondents are less likely to leave specific questions or large numbers of questions, respectively, blank. Pilot-testing or using existing measures designed for the targeted sample are important components of this process. When researchers can use automated/digital data entry by respondents such as audio computer-assisted self-interviewing, computer-assisted self-interviewing, or audio-enhanced personal digital assistant technology, which require respondents to explicitly choose "no response" or "I choose not to answer" before moving on to the next question, missing data are also significantly reduced.

As a result of greater awareness that longitudinal research can yield stronger conclusions about developmental and causal processes, longitudinal research has increased over the past two decades. Along with this increase in longitudinal research has been increased knowledge about how to reduce attrition and increase retention in studies requiring following large groups of individuals over time (Tavis, 2000). Some of the strategies that have been found to be helpful in retaining participants in longitudinal research include (a) establishing strong partnerships with communities participating in the research; (b) selecting, training, and supporting motivated field staff; (c) collecting extensive locator information; (d) establishing an extensive computerized tracking database; (e) implementing a variety of procedures to maintain contact with respondents between data collection points, including sending birthday and holiday cards, reminder flyers and postcards, timely payment of stipends, certificates of participation at milestones during the project, project identity with a recognizable logo, and return receipt requested mailings; (f) flexibility in scheduling; (g) continuity of data collectors and establishing a relationship and rapport with respondents over a period of time; and (h) intensive focus on difficult cases (Boys, Marsden, Stillwell, Hatchings, Griffiths, & Farrell, 2003; Given, Keilman, Collins, & Given, 1990; Hill, 2004; Leonard, Lester, Rotheram-Borus, Mattes, Gwadz, & Ferns, 2003; Woolard et al., 2004).

DETERMINE IF DATA ARE MISSING COMPLETELY AT RANDOM (MCAR)

We have described how Little's MCAR test can be conducted using SPSS. When the data are missing completely at random, case deletion is an acceptable method for handling missing data, although the cost is a reduction in statistical power or estimation precision. If the number of cases to be dropped would be too large a cost to bear, EM or IM procedures would also be acceptable. If the data are not MCAR, then EM or IM imputation procedures are necessary.

CONDUCT A SENSITIVITY ANALYSIS

As described in this chapter, a sensitivity analysis involves conducting the planned analyses using different missing data methodologies (e.g., complete data only, EM-based missing data imputation, MI imputation procedures), and under different missing data assumptions, comparing the results, and then making a decision about the best missing data strategy for the analysis. In general, if results are essentially equivalent among methods, then most journals and readers prefer the use of complete data only, since no imputation is required. On the other hand, if results are different between the use of complete data analysis and principled methods, principled methods (e.g., EM or MI) are currently the most preferred methods. Under MCAR, we will expect all results to be the same. Under the other assumptions, we would expect different results.

USE EM OR MI METHODS IF NECESSARY

Based on the results of the sensitivity analysis and test for MCAR, if imputation is appropriate, one of the principled methods such EM or MI should be used. EM is available within AMOS, SPSS, SAS Proc MI, Missing data library of S-Plus, and STATA, to name a few programs currently available. Multiple imputation is available within SAS Proc MI, Missing data library of S-Plus, Stata, IVEWARE, NORM, and MICE.

Conclusion

In this chapter, we have shown that information about missing data is rarely described in journal articles in communication, leaving the reader guessing about both the extent of missing data and about whether the appropriate methods of handling those missing data were used. When missing data was discussed, we stated that the method used most is one that often produces estimates with poor statistical qualities. We discussed the important topic of missingness and explained missingness completely at random, missingness at random, and missingness not completely at random. Which missingness assumptions are reasonable to make for a given data set partly determines the appropriate methods to be used for handling missing data. When the data are missing completely at random, the researcher has flexibility in how missing data are handled. But when data are not missing completely at random, maximum likelihood methods (like the EM algorithm) or multiple imputation methods should be used. More discussion about missing data in publications as well as the use of the appropriate methods for handling missing data will improve the quality of the results of quantitative research in communication.

References

Allison, P. D. (2002). *Missing data.* Thousand Oaks, CA: Sage.
Bethelehm, J. G. (2002). Weighting nonresponse adjustments based on auxiliary information. In R. M. Groves, D. A. Dillman, J. L. Eltinge, & R. J. A. Little (Eds.), *Survey nonresponse* (pp. 275–288). New York: John Wiley & Sons, Inc.

Boys, A., Marsden, J., Stillwell, G., Hatchings, K., Griffiths, P., & Farrell, M. (2003). Minimizing respondent attrition in longitudinal research: Practical implications from a cohort study of adolescent drinking. *Journal of Adolescence, 26,* 363–373.

Collins, L. M., Schafer, J. L., & Kam, C.-M. (2001). A comparison of inclusive and restrictive strategies in modern missing data procedures. *Psychological Methods, 6,* 330–351.

Dempster, A. P., Laird, N. M., & Rubin, D. B. (1977). Maximum likelihood from incomplete data via the EM algorithm. *Journal of the Royal Statistical Society (Series B), 39,* 1–22.

Dillman, D. A., Eltinge, J. L., Groves, R., & Little, R. J. A. (2002). Survey nonresponse in design, data collection, and analysis. In R. M. Groves, D. A. Dillman, J. L. Eltinge, & R. J. A. Little (Eds.), *Survey nonresponse* (pp. 3–26). New York: John Wiley & Sons.

Do, M. P., & Kincaid, D. L. (2006). Impact of an entertainment-education television drama on health knowledge and behavior in Bangladesh: An application of propensity score matching. *Journal of Health Communication, 11,* 301–325.

Feist-Price, S., Cupp, P. K., Zimmerman, R. S., Abell, R., & Dekhtyar, O. (2007). *Effects of a skills-based HIV preventive intervention for inner city African-American adolescent females in housing developments.* Manuscript under review.

Fowler, F. J. (1995). *Improving survey questions: Design and evaluation.* Newbury Park, CA: Sage Publications.

Gelman, A., & Carlin, J. B. (2002). Post-stratification and weighting adjustments. In R. M. Groves, D. A. Dillman, J. L. Eltinge, & R. J. A. Little (Eds.), *Survey nonresponse* (pp. 289–302). New York: John Wiley & Sons, Inc.

Gelman, A., Carlin, J. B., Stern, H. S., & Rubin, D. B. (2003). *Bayesian data analysis.* Boca Raton, FL: Chapman & Hall/CRC.

Gilks, W. R., Richardson, S., & Spiegelhalter, D. J. (Eds.). (1998). *Markov chain Monte Carlo in practice.* London: Chapman & Hall Ltd.

Given, B. A., Keilman, L. J., Collins, C., & Given, C. W. (1990). Strategies to minimize attrition in longitudinal studies. *Nursing Research, 39,* 184–186.

Groves, R. M., Dillman, D. A., Eltinge, J. L., & Little, R. J. A. (2002). *Survey nonresponse.* New York: John Wiley & Sons.

Harel, O., & Zhou, X. H. (2007). Multiple imputation: Review of theory, implementation and software. *Statistics in Medicine, 26*(16), 3057–3077.

Hill, Z. (2004). Reducing attrition in panel studies in developing countries. *International Journal of Epidemiology, 33,* 493–498.

Horton, N. J., & Lipsitz, S. R. (2001). Multiple imputation in practice: Comparison of software packages for regression models with missing variables. *The American Statistician, 55,* 244–254.

Leonard, N. R., Lester, P., Rotheram-Borus, M. J., Mattes, K., Gwadz, M., & Ferns, B. (2003). Successful recruitment and retention of participants in longitudinal behavioral research. *AIDS Education and Prevention, 15,* 269–281.

Little, R. J. A. (1988). A test of missing completely at random for multivariate data with missing values. *Journal of the American Statistical Association, 83,* 1198–1202.

Little, R. J. A., & Rubin, D. B. (2002). *Statistical analysis with missing data.* New York: John Wiley & Sons.

Meng, X.-L. (1994). Multiple-imputation inferences with uncongenial sources of input. *Statistical Science, 9,* 558–573.

Raghunathan, T. E., Solenberger, P. W., & Van Hoewyk, J. (2000). *IVEware: Imputation and variance estimation software installation instruction and user guide* [Computer software]. Ann Arbor: University of Michigan.

Roberto, A. J., Zimmerman, R. S., Carlyle, K., Abner, E. L., Cupp, P. K., & Hansen, G. L. (2007). The effects of a computer-based pregnancy, STD, and HIV prevention intervention: A nine-school trial. *Health Communication, 21,* 115–124.

Robins, J. M., & Rotnitzky, A. (1995). Semiparametric efficiency in multivariate regression models with missing data. *Journal of the American Statistical Association, 90,* 122–129.

Robins, J. M., Rotnitzky, A., & Zhao, L. P. (1994). Estimation of regression coefficients when some regressors are not always observed. *Journal of the American Statistical Association, 89,* 846–866.

Rosenbaum, P. R., & Rubin, D. B. (1983). The central role of the propensity score in observational studies for causal effects. *Biometrika, 70,* 41–55.

Rotnitzky, A., Robins, J. M., & Scharfstein, D. O. (1998). Semiparametric regression for repeated outcomes with nonignorable nonresponse. *Journal of the American Statistical Association, 93,* 1321–1339.

Rubin, D. B. (1976). Inference and missing data. *Biometrika, 63,* 581–590.

Rubin, D. B. (1987). *Multiple imputation for nonresponse data in surveys.* New York: John Wiley & Sons.

Rubin, D. B. (1996). Multiple imputation after 18+ years. *Journal of the American Statistical Association, 91,* 473–489.

Schimert, J., Schafer, J. L., Hesterberg, T., Fraley, C., & Clarkson, D. B. (2001). *Analyzing data with missing values in S-PLUS* [Computer software]. Seattle, WA: Insightful Corp.

Schafer, J. L. (1997). *Analysis of incomplete multivariate data.* New York: Chapman & Hall.

Schafer, J. L. (1999a). Multiple imputation: A primer. *Statistical Methods in Medical Research, 8,* 3–15.

Schafer, J. L. (1999b). NORM (Version 2.03 for Windows) [Computer software]. Retrieved February 10, 2006, from http://www.stat.psu.edu/~jls/misoftwa.html

Tavis, T. W. (2000). *A primer in longitudinal analysis.* Thousand Oaks, CA: Sage.

Trapl, E. S., Borawski, E. A., Stork, P. P., Lovegreen, L. D., Colabianchi, N., Cole, M. L., & Charvat, J. M. (2005). Use of audio-enhanced personal digital assistants for school-based data collection. *Journal of Adolescent Health, 37,* 296–305.

Turner, C. F., Ku, L., Rogers, S. M., Lindberg, L. D., Pleck, J. H., & Sonenstein, F. L. (1998). Adolescent sexual behavior, drug use, and violence: Increased reporting with computer survey technology. *Science, 280*(5365), 867–873.

van Buuren, S., & Oudshoorn, C. G. M. (1999). *Flexible multivariate imputation by MICE.* Leiden: TNO Preventie en Gezondheid.

Woolard, R. H., Carty, K., Wirtz, P., Longabaugh, R., Nirenberg, T. D., Minugh, P. A., et al. (2004). Research fundamentals: Follow-up of subjects in clinical trials: Addressing subject attrition. *Academic Emergency Medicine Official Journal of the Society for Academic Emergency Medicine, 11,* 859–866.

Zeger, S. L., Liang, K.-Y., & Albert, P. S. (1988). Models for longitudinal data: A generalized estimating equation approach. *Biometrics, 44,* 1049–1060.

Zimmerman, R. S., Cupp, P. K., Hansen, G., Donohew, R. L., Roberto, A. J., Abner, E., & Dekhtyar, O. (in press). The effects of a school-based HIV and pregnancy prevention program in rural Kentucky. *Journal of School Health.*

Index

Additive trees, 302–304, 303 (figure)
Adoption of Drug Abuse Prevention Trial (ADAPT Project), 73, 80–84, 81 (figure), 83 (figure)
Agglomerative clusters, 299
Agenda-setting research, 126
Alcohol advertising/initiating drinking panel study, 137–148
  event history model, 143–148
  risk sets, hazards, and survival functions, 139–142
  structuring data, 142–143
American National Election Study, 221, 231
AMOS, 42–43, 64, 193
Analysis of variance (ANOVA), 135, 171, 333
Arithmetic mean as effect size, 329–330
Artifact corrections, of indices of association, 328–329
Asymmetric data, 260
Asymptotic standard errors, 37
Asymptotically distribution free (ADF) methods, 40
Attenuation, 202–203, 212n7
Autocorrelation function, in time series analyses, 92, 99, 102–103, 105, 112, 115 (figure)
Autoregressive integrated moving average (ARIMA)
  autoregressive component, 102–103
  autoregressive parameter (p), 103–104
  cross-correlation function, 106–107
  first-order (d) parameter, 104
  integrated component, 102–103
  limitations and alternatives, 108–110
  moving average parameter, 103–104
  multivariate time series, 106
  overview of, 92–93, 101–108
  second-order (d) parameter, 104
  univariate time series, 106
Average-linkage method, 301 (figure), 302

Bayesian methods, for missing data, 358, 365
Bayesian Information Criteria (BIC), 74
Behavioral Risk Factor Surveillance (BRFSS), 91
Between-participant mean imputation, 357
Between-wave panel studies, 130, 138
Bias correction, and acceleration, 26
Bias reduction. *See* Propensity scoring
Bibliometric, 258
Binary data, 260
Bollen 1989 (B89), 209
Bootstrapping, 22, 25–26, 30–31, 33, 42–43
Boundary-setting, in meta-analysis, 317–321
  critical moderators, 320
  cultural factors, 320–321
  presence of key variables, 318
  research design, 319–320
  study quality, 318–319

Card sorting, 281
Case deletion, 356
Categorical models, in meta-analysis, 333
Causal modeling, 186
Causal steps strategy, 17–20
Censored cases, 133–135
Census data, 255–259
Census sampling, 255–256
Centers for Disease Control and Prevention (CDC), 91
Centrality betweenness, 250, 267
Centrality closeness, 250, 267
Centrality degree, 267
Centrality flow, 250
Centrality in-degree, 250
Centrality of variables, 249–250
Centrality out-degree, 250
Centrality power, 250, 267
Centralized network, 250–251

Change studies, 55
  applied research study, 58
  growth modeling, 58–63
  interindividual differences, 56
  latent growth models, 5–6, 56
  problems with, 55–56
  time-varying covariate, 57–58
  unconditional growth models, 56–57
Chi-square, 72, 83, 110, 146, 172, 327, 364
Chi-square model fit index, 21
CINDESE, 42
City-block metric, 286–287, 288 (figure)
Clique, 267
Cluster analysis, 299–306
  additive trees, 302–304, 303 (figure)
  agglomerative clusters, 299
  average-linkage method, 301 (figure), 302
  choosing method for analysis, 305–308
  difference from MDS/INDSCAL, 299
  divisive clusters, 299
  hierarchical clusters, 299
  interpreting clusters, 304–305
  multidimensional scaling and, 10
  single-linkage method, 300–302, 301 (figure)
  ultrametric inequality, 300
  ultrametric trees, 299–302
  unique clusters, 299
  Ward method, 301 (figure), 302, 308 (figure)
  See also Scaling and cluster analysis
Co-occurrence matrix, 283
Cohen's effect size magnitude guidelines, 337 (figure)
Communication Abstracts, 312–313
Communication Monographs, 313, 350
Communication Yearbook, 312
Community Action for Drug Prevention (CAPD) study, 73, 75 (table), 77–80, 78 (table)
Comparative fit index (CFI), 72, 82, 209, 210
Compliance strategies, 278
Computerized self-administered interviews or surveys (CASI), 367
Conditional indirect effects, 32–33, 43
Confirmatory factor analysis (CFA), 8, 184–186, 188–200, 228
  fixed paths, 191–192
  free paths, 189–191, 190 (figure)
  higher-order factor structures, 194–196, 195 (figure), 197 (figure)
  hybrid model, 203–204
  hybrid model, limitations of, 204–205
  latent-composite model, 202–203
  model comparisons, 196–198
  model identification, 192
  model respecification, 193–194
  nested models, 196
  nonnested models, 196, 198
  nonrecursive issues, 206, 207 (figure)
  observable-variable model, 201–202
  parsimony, 198
  reciprocal relationships and feedback loops, 205–206
  recursive *vs.* nonrecursive structure, 205–206
  reliability, 198–199
  types of structural models, 201–204
  validity, 199
  when to conduct, 199–201
Confirmatory *vs.* exploratory models, 41
Confounder variables, 167 (figure), 167–169, 174–176
Connectedness, 267
Content analysis, 15, 231–233, 316, 318, 321
Continuous models, in meta-analysis, 333
Continuous time series, 98, 148–149
Continuous time-to-event management, 129, 131 (figure), 132–133, 148–153 (figure), 151 (figure), 152 (figure)
Conventional variable, 100
Correlograms, 102
Cox regression, 132, 137, 149
Cross-correlation, 106–107
Cross-group constraints, 71
Cross-periodogram, 116–117 (figure)
Cross-sectional time series, 98
Cross-spectral analysis, 115–117 (figure)
Curvilinear change, 59, 71–72

Data characteristics, 260–261
Data management, in network analysis, 258–260
Data type summary, 252 (table)
Degrees of freedom *(df)*, 21–22, 212n3
Delta transformation (Δ), 283
Dendograms, 299
Density-personal network, 267
Density-system, 267
Deterministic time series, 99
Differential equation models, 109
Differential gains hypothesis, 32
Direct effect, 16, 22, 28, 206
Discrete Fourier Transform (DFT), 111, 115–117 (figure), 116 (figure)
Discrete measurement, 129–131 (figure)
Discrete time series, 98
Dissimilarities, 284
Distributed lag models, 109
Divisive clusters, 299
Duality. *See* Two-mode data

Index

Dummy coding, 136, 235
Dummy variables, 143, 169, 181
Durbin-Watson test, 109–110

Ecological fallacy, 224–225
Effect modification approach, 317
Effect size, 36–38
   index of mediation measure of, 38
   of association (r, d, and OR), 324–328
   practical significance and, 36–37
   standardized effect-size measures, 36
   unstandardized effect-size measures, 36–37
Egocentric and sociometric questionnaires, in network analysis, 264–266
Egocentric data, 253–254, 257–258
EQS, 42–43, 64, 193
Euclidean metric, 286–287, 288 (figure)
Event history analysis (EHA), 7
   advantages and limitations of, 128–129
   alcohol advertising exposure/initiating drinking during panel study, 137–148
   censored cases, 133–135
   communication-related research using, 127–129
   continuous time-to-event management, 129, 131 (figure), 132–133, 148–153 (figure), 151 (figure), 152 (figure)
   Cox regression in, 132, 137, 149
   dichotomous state, 126
   discrete measurement, 129–131 (figure)
   flexibility in treatment of time to event, 132
   hazard function, 137, 141–142
   hazards ratio, 137
   left-censoring, 134
   life tables, 139–142, 140 (figure), 142 (figure)
   logistic regression, 133, 143
   measurement involving time, 129–137
   multiple regression, 135
   multiwave panel studies, 130
   odds, 135–136
   odds ratio, 136
   outcomes, 126
   polytomous state, 126
   retrospective accounts of age at first drink, example, 148–153
   right-censoring, 133–134
   survivor function, 136, 141
   time invariant predictor variables, 128
   time measured continuously, 129–131
   time varying predictor variables, 128
   time-varying predictors, 132–133
Experimental Random Graph Models (ERGM), 262

Failure analysis, 126
First-order standard error of indirect effect, 35
First-order time series, 98
Flow, in network analysis, 267
Fournier Analysis of Time Series (FAT), 112
Frequency domain time series, 100–110
Funnel-plot, 336

Gamma Hat, 209
General Social Survey, 97, 221, 231, 254
Generalized estimating equations (GEE), 353, 359
Generalized least squares (GLS), 40
Geodesic, in network analysis, 267
Goals of, 275–276
Golden rules, 208, 213n12
Goodness-of-fit, 101, 172, 283, 333
Granger causality test, 108
Growth model, 73–76 (figure), 80–82, 81 (figure)
   assessing fit of, 71–72
   latent, 69 (figure)
   with distal outcome, 80–82
   with time-invariant predictors, 73–76
   with time-varying covariate, 76–80, 78 (table)
Growth modeling, 69–71
   change studies, 58–63
   multilevel approach to, 64–68 (figure), 66 (figure)
   overview, 58–63
   parallel process in, 82–84, 83 (figure)
   unconditional, 56–57

Half matrix of data, 284–285
Hierarchical clusters, 299
Hierarchical linear modeling. *See* Multilevel modeling
HLM6, 234, 240
Hot-deck imputation, 357
Hypothetical constructs, 14

Imputation:
   between-participant mean, 357
   hot-deck, 357
   multiple, 359–360, 368–369
   regression, 357
   single, 357–358
Indirect effects:
   practical significance for, 37–38
   specific, 28
   statistical significance for, 14, 16–17, 23–24, 29
   standard errors for, 23, 26
   total, 28
Individual Differences Scaling (INDSCAL), 282, 295–299, 297 (figure)
Individualistic fallacy, 224–225

Inferential statistics, 8, 38, 261–262, 284, 323–324, 326 (table), 329
Instrumental variable (IV) approach, 161–163
International Network for Social Network Analysis (INSNA), 259, 263, 267
Interpretation. *See* Mediation
Interrupted time series, 115 (figure)
Intervening variables, in mediation, 14, 31
Iteration, 172

JavaScript Web, 42
Jointness. *See* Two-mode data
Journals:
    communication, 15, 350–352, 351 (figure)
    network analysis, 263

Kaye and Johnson measurement model, 190 (figure), 194, 195 (figure)

Lagged effects, 95–96
Lagrange Multiplier (LM), 193
Last observation carried forward, 357
Latent growth models, 5–6, 56, 69 (figure)
Latent variables, in structural equation modeling, 187–188, 212n2
Latent-composite model, 202–203
Left-censoring, 134
Life Skills Training Program, 73
Life tables, 139–142, 140 (figure), 142 (figure)
Linear growth model, 74
Linear modeling, 96
    linear growth model, 74
    nonlinear modeling, 96
    See also Multilevel modeling
Link-list format, 259
Link-list format, in network analysis, 259
LISREL, 42–43, 64, 193, 240
Local fit, 210–211
Longitudinal data
    latent growth models and, 5
    missing data, 11

Manhattan metric. *See* City-block metric
Marginal effect, 17–18
Markov Change Monte Carlo (MCMC), 359
Matrices, in network analysis, 259, 268
Maximum likelihood (MI), 40
Maximum likelihood methods (MLEs), 358
Mechanism, 14
Media effects research, 14–15
Mediation, 5
    bootstrapping, 22, 25–26, 30–31, 33, 42–43
    causal steps strategy, 17–20

causal steps strategy, limitations to, 20
causality and, 35–36
computer software, 42–43
differences in coefficients strategies, 21
direct and indirect effects, 206-208
distal *vs.* proximal mediators, 39
distribution of product strategies, 25
effect size, 36–38
extensions to more complex models, 27–35
mediated moderation, 33
moderated mediation, 31–32, 34 (figure)
multilevel models and, 33–35
multiple mediator models, 28–31
nested model strategy, 21–22
ordinary least squares regression *vs.* structural equation modeling, 40–41
partial correlation strategies, 20–21
partial mediation, 20
partial *vs.* complete mediation, 40–41
product of coefficients strategies, 22–24
recommended reading, 44
simple mediation model, 16–17 (figure)
single-step multiple mediator model, 28, 29 (figure)
SPSS macro output for multiple analysis, 45–47
statistical approaches to assessment, 16–27
statistical power, 38–39
theory and, 41–42
total effect, significance of, 39–40
Meta-analysis, 11, 228
    analyzing meta-analytic databases, 330–338
    arithmetic mean as effect size, 329–330
    artifact corrections of indices of association, 328–329
    averaging effect sizes, 331
    between groups, F test, 326 (table)
    between-groups, Students t-test, 326 (table)
    boundary-setting, 317–321
    calculating heterogeneity of effect sizes, 331–332
    categorical models, 333
    coding studies for distinctive characteristics, 322–323
    Cohen's d, 325 (table)
    continuous models, 333
    correction factor, 325 (table)
    Correction to r, 325 (table)
    correlation coefficient, 326 (table)
    criticisms of, 315
    data quality in published syntheses, 338–339
    defining, 316–317
    effect sizes of association, 324–328
    Fisher's r-to-Z transform, 325 (table)

Fisher's Z-to-r transform, 325 (table)
fixed-effects models, 333–334
funnel-plot, 336
health communication and, 312
Hedge's d, 325 (table)
interpreting and presenting results, 337–338
interpreting/presenting results, 337–338
literature review, 321–322
magnitude of effect, estimating, 323–327
mixed-effects models, 334–335
moderator variable approach, 317
multiple-predictor models, 334
narrative reviewing and, 313–315
outlier analysis, 332–333
Pearson's r, 325 (table)
potential moderators of effect sizes analysis, 333
procedures, 315–338
publication bias, 335–336
random-effects models, 334
regression slopes as effect sizes, 330
resources on, 340–341
statistical power assumptions, 335
trends in practice of, 338–340
trim-and-fill methods, 336
vote-counting techniques, 336
within-participants, F test, 326 (table)
within-participants, Students t-test, 326 (table)
Minkowski r-metric, 287–288
Missing at random (MAR), 355, 364
Missing completely at random (MCAR), 354–355, 364, 368
Missing data, 11–12, 349–350
  assumptions, 354–355
  Bayesian methods, 358, 365
  between-participant mean imputation, 357
  case deletion, 356
  current practice, 350–352
  EM or MI methods, 369
  generalized estimating equations, 353, 359
  hot-deck imputation, 357
  inference, method effect on, 361–367, 361–362 (figure), 363 (table)
  last observation carried forward, 357
  maximum likelihood methods, 358
  minimizing, 367–368
  missing at random, 355, 364
  missing completely at random, 354–355, 364
  missing completely at random, determining, 368
  missing not at random, 355, 364
  missing valley analysis, 364
  multiple imputation, 359–360, 368–369
  principled methods, 353, 358–360
  regression imputation, 357
  reweighting, 356–357
  semiparametric regression models, 358–359
  sensitivity analysis and, 353–354, 368–369
  single imputation, 357–358
  statistical issues, assumptions and methods, 352–360
  unprincipled methods, 353, 356–358
  within-participant mean imputation, 357
Missing not at random (MNAR), 355, 364
Missing value analysis (MVA), 364
MIXED, 240
Mixed-effects models, 334–335
MIXGSUR, 154
MIXOR, 154
Moderator variable approach, 317
Modification indices, 193
Monitoring the Future Project, 97
Moving average (MA), 103–104
Mplus, 42–43, 64
Multidimensional scaling (MDS), 285–295
  calculating stress (S), 289–290
  city-block metric, 286–287, 288 (figure)
  determining number of dimensions, 290–292
  distance/proximity tensions, 288–290
  Euclidean metric, 286–287, 288 (figure)
  interpreting space, 292–294
  metric vs. nonmetric, 290
  minimality assumption, 285
  Minkowski r-metric, 287–288
  nature of distances, 286–288 (figure)
  reliability of solution, 294–295
  Shephard diagram, 288
  supremum metric, 286–287, 288 (figure)
  symmetry assumption, 285
  triangle inequality assumption, 285
  two-dimensional solution for persuasive strategies, 290–291, 293 (figure), 294 (figure)
Multilevel modeling (MLM), 9–10, 219–220
  analyzing data across levels, 221–225
  example multilevel analysis, 234–239
  group-level variables, 237–238 (figure)
  importance of, 220–221
  individual level predictor relationships, 236–237 (table)
  interpersonal and small-group communication, example, 226–228
  mass communication example, 230–234
  ordinary least squares regression vs., 223–225
  organizational communication, example, 228–230

proportions of variance, 235–236, 236 (figure)
  software for, 64, 239–240, 262
Multilevel regression, 33
MULTINET, 263, 268
Multiple imputation (MI), 359–360, 368–369
Multiple-predictor models, 334
Multistage cluster sampling, 221–222
Multitrait, multimethod (MTMM)
  matrix models, 199
Multivariate delta method, 23
Multivariate time series, 106
Multiwave panel studies, 130, 231
Mx, 43

Narrative reviews, 313–315
Nearest neighbor clustering, 307
Nested model, 21–22, 196
Netdraw, 248–249
NETWORK, 259
Network analysis:
  asymmetric data, 260
  bibliometric, 258
  binary data, 260
  bridge, 267
  census data, 255–259
  centrality betweenness, 250, 267
  centrality closeness, 250, 267
  centrality degree, 267
  centrality flow, 250
  centrality in-degree, 250
  centrality of variables, 249–250
  centrality out-degree, 250
  centrality power, 250, 267
  centralized network, 250–251
  clique, 267
  component, 267
  connectedness, 267
  data characteristics, 260–261
  data collection, 252–258
  data management, 258–260
  data type summary, 252 (table)
  density-personal network, 267
  density-system, 267
  egocentric, 267
  egocentric data, 253–254, 257–258
  exponential random graph models
    (ERGM), 267
  flow, 267
  geodesic, 267
  International Network for Social Network
    Analysis, 259, 263, 267
  journals, 263
  link-list format, 259
  matrices, 259, 268
  multinet, 268
  network diagrams, 259–260
  network exposure, 251–252, 251 (figure), 268
  network in, 268
  network threshold, 268
  network variables, 249–252
  node-list format, 259
  p*, 268
  position of variables, 250
  professional associations, 263
  R, 268
  reach, 268
  recent developments, 261–263
  relational variables, 249
  sample egocentric and sociometric
    questionnaires, 264–266
  scale-free networks, 263
  sequenced data, 258–259
  small-world networks, 263
  snowball data, 254–255
  snowball sampling, 257, 268
  social context of, 264
  social networks, 247–249, 261–262
  sociometric, 268
  sociometric segmentation, 264
  structural equivalence, 268
  structural variables, 249–250
  survey data, 253
  symmetric data, 260
  two-mode data, 256–259
  UCINET software for, 268
  valued data, 260–261
Network data collection, 252–258
Network diagrams, 259–260
Network exposure, 251–252, 251 (figure), 268
Network threshold, 268
Network variables, 249–252
Network, in network analysis, 268
NNFI, 210
Node-list format, in network analysis, 259
Nonlinear modeling, 96
Nonnested models, 196, 198
NORM, 365, 369
Normality assumption, 24

Observational studies. See Propensity scoring
Odds ratio (OR), 136
Ordinary least squares (OLS) regression, 19, 33, 40
  for growth modeling, 64–65
  for lag analysis, 109
  hybrid modeling and, 204
  multilevel modeling vs., 223–225

Index

P*, 262–263, 268
PAJEK, 259
Panel-studies
   alcohol advertising and initiating
      drinking, 137–148
   between-wave, 130, 138
   multiwave, 130, 231
Parent-child communication, 58–62
Parsimony, 198
Partial autocorrelation function (PACF),
      102, 103–105, 104 (figure), 112
Perceived community, 19, 29–31
Perceived customization, 18–20, 29–31
Perceived interactivity, 19, 31
Perceived involvement, 45n2
Perceived novelty, 19, 29–30
Perceived received relevance, 45n2
Percentile-based confidence interval, 26
Periodogram, 111, 114 (figure)
   cross-periodogram, 116, 117 (figure)
Persuasive strategies, 276–278
Point estimate, 37–38
Position of variables, in network analysis, 250
Product of coefficients method, 26, 29, 33, 38
Product of coefficients strategies, 22–24
Professional associations, in network
      analysis, 263
Project ADAPT, 73–76 (figure),
      80–82, 81 (figure)
Propensity scoring, 7–8
   dummy variables, 181
   goodness-of-fit and, 172
   hidden bias, 180
   histogram of overlapping scores, 173 (figure)
   instrumental variable (IV) approach, 161–163
   limitations, 161
   logistic regression model, 170
   matching variable approach, 161
   methodology, 163–166, 164 (table)
   missing data, 180–181
   multivariate matching approach, 172
   other limitations, 180–181
   other methods for bias reduction, 160–166
   randomized/nonrandomized experiment
      of treatment effects, example,
      176–179, 178 (table)
   sample size, 181
   sensitivity analysis problems, 180
   standard regression analysis, 161
   weighting approach, 172
   with more than two treatment conditions,
      179–180
   See also Propensity scoring, building model for

Proximity data, 278–285
   card-sorting, 281–283
   final considerations, 284–285
   gathering and preparing proximity
      data, 278–279
   issues to consider before gathering data, 278
   profiles, 283–284
   similarity ratings, 279
Pythagorean theorem, 285, 287

Quadratic growth model, 74
Quantitative reviewing. *See* Meta-analysis
Quasi-experiment, 163, 176–177

R, 42
R, in network analysis, 268
Random coefficients regression.
      See Multilevel modeling
Random intercept, 36
Random sampling, 257
Random-effects models, 334
Randomized experiment, 163
Reach, in network analysis, 268
Rectangular data, 352–353
Regression imputation, 357
Regression models, semiparametric, 358–359
Regression toward mean, 96–97
Relational variables, in network analysis, 249
Relative noncentrality index (RNI), 209, 210
Replication and, 281
Research synthesis. *See* Meta-analysis
Respondent-driven sampling (RDS), 254
Restricted model, 187
Reweighting, for missing data, 356–357
Right-censoring, 133–134
Root mean squared error of approximation
      (RMSEA), 72, 209

SAS software, 42–43, 61–62, 259
Saturation sampling, 64, 154, 240, 255–256, 258
Scale-free networks, 263
Scaling and cluster analysis, 275
   card sorting, 281
   choosing method analysis, 305–308
   cluster analysis (*See* Cluster analysis)
Scatterplot, 288, 289 (figure)
Scree plot, 291 (figure), 305 (figure)
Second-order delta method, 23
SEM software, 21, 40, 41, 64, 68
Semiparametric regression models, 358–359
Sensitivity analysis:
   missing data and, 353–354, 368–369
   propensity scoring problems, 180

Sequenced data, in network analysis, 258–259
Serial approach. *See* Causal steps strategy
Serial correlation, 109–110
Shephard diagram, 288
SIENNA, 263
Similarity ratings, 279–280, 280–281 (table)
Simple mediation model, 16–17 (figure)
Simple random sampling (SRS), 221–222
Simulation studies, 23, 25, 29, 31, 84, 209, 288
Single imputation, 357–358
Single-linkage method, 300–302, 301 (figure)
Single-step multiple mediator model, 28, 29 (figure)
Sinusoidal function, in time series analyses, 98, 111–114, 116
Slope variability, 36
Small-world networks, 263
Smoothing, in time series analyses, 101, 112, 116
Snowball sampling, 254–255, 257, 268
Sobel test, 23–26, 31
Social influence model, 229–230
Social network analysis, 10
Social networks, 247–249, 261–262
Sociograms, 259–260
Sociometric, 268
Sociometric segmentation, 264
Southern Women Study, 256–257
Specific indirect effect, 28
SPSS software:
    mediation analysis and, 42–43, 45–47
    missing data and, 364
    network analysis and, 258
    time series analysis and, 119n5–120n5
Standard regression analysis, 161
Standardized effect-size measures, 36
Standardized root mean squared residual (SRMR) index, 209
STATA, 154, 258
Stationary data, in time series analyses, 99
Stepwise procedure, 111
    for Fournier Analysis of Time Series, 112–114, 113 (figure)
    propensity score and, 170–171
Stochastic process, 99
Stress (S), calculating, 289–290
Structural equation modeling (SEM), 8–9, 185–186, 228
    growth model, 73–76 (figure), 80–82, 81 (figure)
    growth model, assessing fit of, 71–72
    growth model, latent, 69 (figure)
    growth model, with distal outcome, 80–82

growth model, with time-invariant predictors, 73–76
growth model, with time-varying covariate, 76–80, 78 (table)
growth modeling, 69–71
growth modeling, multilevel approach to, 64–68 (figure), 66 (figure)
growth modeling, overview, 58–63
growth modeling, parallel process, 82–84, 83 (figure)
Project ADAPT, 73–76 (figure), 80–82, 81 (figure)
resources, 85
See also Structural equation modeling (SEM), uses and misuses of
Structural equation modeling (SEM), uses and misuses of
confirmatory factor analysis, 188–200
exploratory factor analysis, 187
latent variables in, 187–188
media as latent variable, 212n2
model fit, 208–211
observable gratifications items and factors, 213
proxy observable variables in, 188
Structural equivalence, in network analysis, 268
Structural variables, in network analysis, 249–250
Structuration theory, 228–229
Suppressors, 31
Supremum metric, 286–287, 288 (figure)
Survey data, in network analysis, 253
Survival analysis, 125–126
Symmetric data, in network analysis, 260

t test, two-sample, 168–169
Taylor series expansion, 23
Temporal order, 95
Test factors, 14
Time invariant predictor variables, 128
Time series analyses, 6–7
    ARIMA methodology, limitations and alternatives, 108–110
    ARIMA methodology, overview, 92–93, 97–98, 101–108
    autocorrelation function, 92, 99, 102–103, 105, 112, 115 (figure)
    basic terminology, 98–100
    basics of, 97–100
    benifits/limitations of, 93–97
    continuous time series, 98, 148–149
    cross-correlation function, 106–107
    cross-periodogram, 116, 117 (figure)
    cross-sectional time series, 98
    cross-spectral analysis, 115–117 (figure)

Index 381

deterministic time series, 99
differencing in, 103
differential equation models, 109
Discrete Fournier Transform, 111–112, 115–117 (figure), 116 (figure)
discrete time series, 98
distributed lag models, 109
false positives, 112
first-order time series, 98
Fournier Analysis of Time Series, 112–114, 113 (figure)
frequency domain approach to modeling data, 98, 110–117
frequency domain series, functions of, 100–110
Granger causality test, 108
interrupted time series, 115 (figure)
lag, 98, 102
modeling data, 100–110
multivariate time series, 106
partial autocorrelation function, 102, 103–105, 104 (figure), 112
periodogram, 111, 114 (figure)
point in time, 98
pooling and aggregation, 117–119
repeated measures *vs.*, 119n1
seasonal data and, 99–100
sinusoidal function, 98, 111–114, 116
smoothing techniques, 101, 112, 116
stationary data and, 99
stochastic process and, 99
transfer function models, 107–108, 107 (figure)
trend data and, 99
univariate time series, 106
uses of, 91–93
white noise process in, 112
Time varying predictor variables, 128
Total effect, 16
Total indirect effect, 28
Transfer function, in time series analyses, 107–108, 107 (figure)

Trend data, in time series analyses, 99
Triangle inequality assumption, 285
Trim-and-fill methods, 336
Tucker-Lewis index (TLI), 72, 209
Turn index, 93
Two-index strategy, 209
Two-mode data, in network analysis, 256–259
Two-sample *t* test, 168–169
Type I error, 20, 24, 26, 38
Type II error, 20

Ultrametric inequality, 300
Ultrametric trees, 299–302
Unbiased variance estimator, 23
Unconditional growth models, 56–57
UNICET, 259
Univariate time series, 106
University of California at Irvine (UCI) network analysis software (UCINET), 268
Unrestricted model, 187
Unstandardized effect-size measures, 36–37

Valued data, in network analysis, 260–261
Variables:
    confounder, 167–169, 167 (figure), 174–176
    conventional, 100
    dummy, 143, 169, 181
    intervening, 14, 31

Wald test of significance, 67, 85n4, 146
Ward method, 301 (figure), 302, 308 (figure)
Weighting approach, for propensity score, 172
White noise, 112
Withdrawal, in longitudinal studies, 133–134
Within-participant mean imputation, 357
Within-subject designs, 20
Wold decomposition theorem, 99

About the Editors

Andrew F. Hayes (PhD, Cornell University, 1996) is an Associate Professor in the School of Communication, The Ohio State University. He is the author of *Statistical Methods for Communication Science* (2005) and over 30 articles in the areas of public opinion, political communication, social psychology, and statistical methods, and he serves as associate editor of *Communication Methods and Measures*.

Michael D. Slater (PhD, Stanford University, 1988) is a Social and Behavioral Science Distinguished Professor at the School of Communication, The Ohio State University. He has served as principal investigator of NIH-funded studies of substance abuse prevention efforts and the impact of alcohol-related news coverage, alcohol advertisements, and alcohol warnings as well as conducting investigations of persuasion and media effects.

Leslie B. Snyder (PhD, Stanford University, 1986) is a Professor of Communication Sciences and Director of the Center for Health Communication and Marketing, a Centers for Disease Control Center of Excellence, at the University of Connecticut. In addition to overseeing the CDC Center grant, she has received research funding from the National Institutes of Health and has served as a consultant on a number of national campaigns. She conducts research on media effects, communication campaigns, health, and international communication. Current projects include creating a safe-sex video game for urban 18–25-year-olds, studying the effects of advertising exposure on youth alcohol consumption and nutrition behaviors, designing a community-based drug and alcohol prevention program using trained local musical artists, and meta-analyses of the effectiveness of health campaigns and interventions.

About the Contributors

Robert Cudeck (PhD, University of Southern California, 1980) is a Professor of Psychology with specialization in psychometric methods at The Ohio State University. His interests are in applications of mathematical models to data in the social and behavioral sciences, especially in structural equation models and random coefficient models. He is a past president of the Psychometric Society and the Society for Multivariate Experimental Psychology.

Olga Dekhtyar (MA, University of Maryland–College Park, 2000) is a Data Analyst at the Institute for HIV Prevention at the University of Kentucky. Her research interests include latent growth modeling and structural equation modeling.

William P. Eveland, Jr. (PhD, University of Wisconsin–Madison, 1997) is an Associate Professor of Communication and Political Science at The Ohio State University. He teaches courses in political communication, public opinion, mass-media effects, and research methods. His research interests center on the role of mass-mediated and interpersonal communication in producing informed and active citizens, with a particular interest in the mediating role of information processing. Some of his recent projects have employed multilevel modeling to identify how differences in media environments—either over time or across communities—moderate the influence of individual media use behaviors on political knowledge, participation, or community attachment.

Ofer Harel (PhD, Pennsylvania State University, 2003) is an Assistant Professor in the Department of Statistics and the Institute of Public Health Research at the Center for Public Health and Health Policy at the University of Connecticut. His expertise is in the areas of missing data techniques, diagnostic tests, longitudinal studies, Bayesian methods, sampling techniques, mixture models, latent class analysis, and statistical consulting. Dr. Harel received postdoctoral training at the University of Washington, Department of Biostatistics, where he worked for the HSR&D Center of Excellence VA Puget Sound Healthcare System and the National Alzheimer's Coordinating Center. Dr. Harel has served as a biostatistical consultant nationally and internationally since 1997. Through his consulting, Dr. Harel has been involved with a variety of research fields including, but not limited to, Alzheimer's, diabetes, and alcohol and drug abuse prevention.

Kimberly L. Henry (PhD, Pennsylvania State University, 2002) is an Assistant Professor of Psychology at Colorado State University. After completing a postdoctoral fellowship at the Tri Ethnic Center for Prevention Research at Colorado State University (one of the National Institute on Drug Abuse's [NIDA] Prevention Centers), she furthered her training as a research associate at the Institute of Behavioral Science (Program on Problem Behavior) at the University of Colorado. Dr. Henry's research examines the development of health-compromising and antisocial behaviors among adolescents and young adults (including substance abuse, violent behavior, and delinquency). Currently, she is studying the role of the school context in adolescent development. This work is funded by a grant from the National Institute on Drug Abuse.

R. Lance Holbert (PhD, University of Wisconsin–Madison, 2000) is an Associate Professor in the School of Communication, The Ohio State University. His content research interests include traditional political communication, entertainment media and politics, public opinion, and persuasion. In addition, he has written several articles on the topic of structural equation modeling in the communication sciences. He has published numerous empirical articles in such places as *Human Communication Research, Journal of Broadcasting & Electronic Media, Media Psychology,* and *Political Communication.* Professor Holbert is a member of several editorial boards for some of the leading academic journals in the field of communication, including *Communication Methods & Measures, Communication Monographs, Journal of Broadcasting & Electronic Media,* and *Journal of Communication.*

Robert Hornik (PhD, Stanford University, 1973) is the Wilbur Schramm Professor of Communication and Health Policy at the Annenberg School for Communication, University of Pennsylvania. Dr. Hornik directs the National Cancer Institute–Funded Center of Excellence in Cancer Communication Research at Penn State. He has led efforts to design or evaluate more than 25 large-scale public health communication and education programs in developing countries and in the United States, including the evaluation of the National Youth Anti-Drug Media Campaign. He is the author of the book *Development Communication,* coauthor of *Toward Reform of Program Evaluation* and *Educational Reform with Television: The El Salvador Experience,* and is the editor of *Public Health Communication: Evidence for Behavior Change.*

Tania B. Huedo-Medina (PhD, University of National Long Distance Studies, Madrid, Spain, 2006) is a Postdoctoral Fellow in the Center for Health, Intervention, and Prevention at the University of Connecticut. She has collaborated on research syntheses concerning different topics in clinical psychology and criminology. Much of her work has been focused on the quantitative techniques for meta-analysis, studying and developing relations among the effect-size indices, and the assessment of heterogeneity among effect sizes using Monte Carlo simulations.

Blair T. Johnson (PhD, Purdue University, 1988) is a Professor of Psychology at the University of Connecticut. He has received research funding from the National Institutes of Health and has served as a consultant on many research projects. Known for his research on various aspects of social influence, he has focused in recent years on a series of meta-analyses examining the factors that help to make health-promotion interventions work best, including interventions to prevent the spread of HIV. Another important focus of his research concerns enhancing the repertoire of techniques that reviewers use in conducting meta-analytic reviews of scientific studies. Dr. Johnson continues his research on social influence, psychological and structural predictors of behavior, and advances in the science of research synthesis, also known as meta-analysis.

Seth M. Noar (PhD, University of Rhode Island, 2001) is an Assistant Professor in the Department of Communication at the University of Kentucky. His research interests focus on health promotion and disease prevention from a health communication perspective. His research articles address behavioral theory, sexual communication and HIV prevention, health message design, mass and interactive media, and methodological topics and have appeared in journals in the social, behavioral, and health sciences. Dr. Noar is also coeditor of *Communication Perspectives on HIV/AIDS for the 21st Century*, an edited volume that will be published in 2008.

Ann A. O'Connell (EdD, Teachers College, Columbia University, 1993) is an Associate Professor in the School of Educational Policy and Leadership at The Ohio State University. She teaches graduate-level statistical methods including multilevel modeling, logistic and ordinal regression, sampling and survey research methods, and multivariate analysis. Her collection of published work focuses, in general, on research applications using these and other advanced statistical/research techniques, primarily in the fields of HIV prevention and health-promotion program evaluation; she has also published on methods of teaching to improve learning in applied statistics courses. Dr. O'Connell's work has appeared in journals including *Women and Health, Evaluation and the Health Professions, Measurement and Research in Counseling and Development, MMWR*, and *Journal of Modern Applied Statistical Methods*. Her published books include a treatment of ordinal response data and an edited volume on multilevel modeling. She was the 2005–2006 president of the Educational Statisticians' Special Interest Group of the American Educational Research Association.

Hee Sun Park (PhD, University of California at Santa Barbara, 2003) is an Assistant Professor in the Department of Communication, Michigan State University. She teaches courses in organizational communication, cross-cultural and intercultural communication, and research methods and statistics. She is interested in examining the processes of how people build shared understanding through communication. Her research projects involve multilevel effects of group and organizational communication, cross-cultural differences in workplace norms and interaction patterns, and social influence processes and outcomes in these contexts.

Kristopher J. Preacher (PhD, The Ohio State University, 2003) is an Assistant Professor at the University of Kansas. Much of his work involves finding ways to improve upon and refine the application of common multivariate techniques. His research focuses primarily on the use of factor analysis, structural equation modeling, and multilevel modeling to analyze longitudinal and correlational data. Other interests include developing strategies to test mediation and moderation hypotheses, bridging the gap between theory and practice, and studying model evaluation and model selection in the application of multivariate methods to social science questions.

Beverly Roskos-Ewoldsen (PhD, Indiana University, 1989) is an Associate Professor of Psychology at the University of Alabama. She teaches courses in perception, visual-spatial cognition, and statistics. Her research interests involve visual-spatial cognition, especially individual and group differences in the comprehension, representation, and use of visual and spatial information. Some of her recent projects have used scaling and clustering analyses to understand how people's mental models of a movie change over time, and how people understand and use different strategies to (a) find their way in real and virtual environments and (b) search for information on the Internet.

David R. Roskos-Ewoldsen (PhD, Indiana University, 1990) is a Professor in the Department of Psychology at the University of Alabama and coordinator of the social psychology Ph.D. program in that department. He teaches courses in media psychology, research methods, and multicultural issues in psychology. His research focuses on attitude accessibility, persuasion, decision making, and health-related behaviors in adolescents. A second line of research involves the comprehension of media messages. Recent projects that have employed multidimensional scaling and cluster analysis include whether audiences with different interpretations of a film have different mental representations of the film, and differences in White and African-American adolescents' mental representations regarding smoking.

Lori A. J. Scott-Sheldon (PhD, University of Connecticut, 2006) is a Postdoctoral Research Associate at the Center for Health and Behavior, Syracuse University. Dr. Scott-Sheldon's research focuses on understanding the psychological underpinnings of risky behavior and applying those findings to facilitate behavioral change. Her research explores the highly interrelated themes of (a) social cognitive processes related to health behaviors, (b) health-related literatures to discover the conditions under which people adopt or continue risky behavior, and (c) communication tools necessary to facilitate attitudes and behavioral change. Dr. Scott-Sheldon also has interests in quantitative methods, specifically meta-analytic techniques and practices.

Michael T. Stephenson (PhD, University of Kentucky, 1999) is an Associate Professor in the Department of Communication at Texas A&M University. His research interests include health communication campaigns, media effects, and structural equation modeling. Dr. Stephenson's research is published in the *American Journal of Public Health, Human Communication Research, Communication Research, Communication Monographs, Drug and Alcohol Dependence and Addiction,* among others. He is the senior editor for *Health Communication* and serves on six other editorial boards.

Thomas W. Valente (PhD, University of Pennsylvania, 1991) is an Associate Professor in the Department of Preventive Medicine, Keck School of Medicine, the University of Southern California. After completing his Ph.D., he spent nine years at the Johns Hopkins University Bloomberg School of Public Health. He is the author of *Evaluating Health Promotion Programs* (2002), *Network Models of the Diffusion of Innovations* (1995), and over 80 articles and chapters on social networks, behavior change, and program evaluation. Dr. Valente uses network analysis, health communication, and mathematical models to implement and evaluate health-promotion programs, primarily aimed at preventing tobacco and other substance abuse, unintended fertility, and STD/HIV infections.

Arthur VanLear (PhD, University of Utah, 1985) is an Associate Professor in the Department of Communication Science at the University of Connecticut at Storrs. His primary areas of research are in interpersonal communication including communication and relationships in alcoholism and addiction recovery, relationship development, and marital and family communication. His primary methodological interests are in dynamic modeling of communication processes, including longitudinal and time series studies. He is coeditor of *Dynamic Patterns in Communication Processes* with James Watt and has published in *Human Communication Research, Communication Monographs, Journal of Communication, Journal of Social and Personal Relationships, Journal of Marriage and the Family, Small Group Research, Communication Yearbook,* and *The Cambridge Handbook of Personal Relationships,* among other sources.

Itzhak Yanovitzky (PhD, University of Pennsylvania, 2000) is an Associate Professor of Communication at Rutgers University. Dr. Yanovitzky's areas of expertise include health communication, persuasion and normative influence, communication and social change, and program evaluation. His work in these areas was published in journals such as *Communication Research*, *Communication Theory*, *Health Communication*, *Journal of Health Communication*, and *Evaluation and Program Planning*.

Elaine Zanutto (PhD, Harvard University, 1998) is currently Senior Director of Methodology at National Analysts Worldwide Research and Consulting after serving as an Assistant Professor in the Statistics Department of The Wharton School of the University of Pennsylvania. Dr. Zanutto's areas of expertise include sample design, weighting and variance estimation for complex sample surveys, imputation methods for missing data, analysis of conjoint and preference data, causal analysis of nonexperimental data, and Bayesian modeling. Her research into new statistical methods has been applied in the areas of marketing, public health, communication, program evaluation, management, and education and has been funded by the National Science Foundation, the National Cancer Institute, the National Institute on Drug Abuse, and the National Institute of Child Health and Human Development.

Rick Zimmerman (PhD, University of Wisconsin–Madison, 1983) is a Professor in the Department of Communication at the University of Kentucky. He specializes in the study of theories of health behavior change, adolescent and young adult risk behavior prevention, and methodology and statistics.